ROUTLEDGE HANDBOOK OF SPORT POLICY

It is difficult to fully understand the role that sport plays in contemporary global society without understanding how and why governments, NGOs and other organizations formulate and implement policy relating to sport. The *Routledge Handbook of Sport Policy* is the only book to offer a comprehensive overview of current perspectives, techniques and approaches to the analysis of sport policy around the world.

The book introduces a diverse range of approaches to policy analysis across the full range of political and societal contexts, including developed and developing economies, state-centric, mixed economy and market-led systems, and both liberal democracies and political systems characterized by a dominant elite. It is arranged into five sections addressing the key topics and themes in the analysis of contemporary sport policy, including:

- theory and its implications for methodology
- globalization, governance, partnerships and networks
- elite sport policy
- development, sport and joint policy agendas
- sport policy and social theory.

With contributions from leading policy analysts around the world, including Europe, North America, the Middle East and Asia, this book is important reading for any student, researcher or professional working in sport management, sport development, sport and society, or mainstream public policy, policy analysis or social policy.

Ian Henry is Professor and Director of the Centre for Olympic Studies and Research at Loughborough University, UK. His research has incorporated a wide range of work in the field of sport policy analysis and in Olympic research commissioned by transnational bodies such as the IOC, UNESCO and the EU, as well as by a range of governmental and sporting bodies in the UK.

Ling-Mei Ko is Assistant Professor of the Department of Leisure, Recreation and Tourism Management in the College of Business at Southern Taiwan University of Science and Technology. Her current research interests lie in issues relating to sport and leisure policies and sport management, particularly in the area of human capital.

ROUTLEDGE HANDBOOK OF SPORT POLICY

Edited by Ian Henry and Ling-Mei Ko

Routledge
Taylor & Francis Group

LONDON AND NEW YORK

First published 2014
by Routledge
2 Park Square, Milton Park, Abingdon, Oxon OX14 4RN

First published in paperback 2016
by Routledge
2 Park Square, Milton Park, Abingdon, Oxon OX14 4RN

Simultaneously published in the USA and Canada
by Routledge
711 Third Avenue, New York, NY 10017

Routledge is an imprint of the Taylor & Francis Group, an informa business

British Library Cataloguing in Publication Data
A catalogue record for this book is available from the British Library

Library of Congress Cataloging in Publication Data
Routledge handbook of sport policy / edited by Ian Henry and Ling-Mei
Ko.
pages cm
Includes bibliographical references.
1. Sports and state--Handbooks, manuals, etc. 2. Sports and society--
Handbooks, manuals, etc. I. Henry, Ian.
GV706.35.R68 2013
306.4'83--dc23

2012050845

ISBN: 978-0-415-66661-9 (hbk)
ISBN: 978-1-138-12170-6 (pbk)
ISBN: 978-0-203-80721-7 (ebk)

Typeset in Bembo
by GreenGate Publishing Services, Tonbridge, Kent

MIX
Paper from
responsible sources
FSC   FSC® C013056
www.fsc.org

Printed and bound in Great Britain by
TJ International Ltd, Padstow, Cornwall

CONTENTS

Contents

Contents

FIGURES

TABLES

CONTRIBUTORS

Andrew Adams is a Senior Lecturer at the Centre for Event and Sport Research at Bournemouth University. Andrew teaches across a range of sport and social policy modules and has published in the same area. Recent publications have focused on the examination of sport, policy and the social impacts for grass-roots sport organizations. His most recent work focuses on sport, Big Society and social capital, human rights in sport, and grass-roots sport and community development.

Mahfoud Amara is Lecturer in Sport Policy and Management, and Deputy Director of the Centre for Olympic Studies and Research at Loughborough University. Dr Amara's principal research area is comparative sports policy, and he has a specific interest in sport in Arab and Muslim contexts (society, history, culture, religion, economy, political and philosophical thoughts), having published material on the politics, policy and business of sport in the Arab world. His other research interests are sport, multiculturalism and intercultural dialogue. He has recently published a book titled *Sport, Politics and Society in the Arab World* (Palgrave Macmillan).

Dawn Aquilina is a Research Fellow at the Swiss Graduate School of Public Administration (IDHEAP) based at the University of Lausanne in Switzerland. She gained her PhD from Loughborough University (UK) in 2009 having obtained a BEd from the University of Malta, and an MSc from Loughborough in Sport and Leisure Management. She also worked in the Institute of Sport and Leisure Policy at Loughborough University as a Research Associate on a number of European Community commissioned sports policy projects relating to athletes and education, sport and inter-cultural dialogue, and sport and social inclusion of refugees and asylum seekers. In 2009–2010 she worked at UEFA primarily on the evaluation of research proposals and the development of a Master's degree programme in cooperation with a number of European universities.

Christoph Breuer is Full Professor at German Sport University Cologne and Director of the Institute of Sport Economics and Sport Management. Dr Breuer publishes widely in journals such as *Applied Economics, Journal of Sport Economics, Journal of Sport Management, International Journal of Sport Finance, Sport Management Review* and *European Sport Management Quarterly*. He is a member of the editorial board of the *International Journal of Sport Finance*, *Sport Management Review* and the *International Journal of Sport Management and Marketing*, as well as a member of the World Anti-Doping Agency (WADA) Finance and Administration Committee. Moreover, he is a founding member and Secretary General of the European Sports Economics Association.

Laurence Chalip is the Brightbill-Sapora Professor at the University of Illinois, where he serves as Head of the Department of Recreation, Sport and Tourism. He has authored over 100 articles and chapters, as well as several books and monographs. He serves on the editorial board of nine scholarly journals. For his contributions to sport policy, he has received the Earle F. Zeigler Award from the North American Society for Sport Management and the Distinguished Service Award from the Sport Management Association of Australia and New Zealand. He was also named to the International Chair of Olympism by the International Olympic Committee and the Centre for Olympic Studies.

Jean-Loup Chappelet is Professor of Public Management at the Swiss Graduate School of Public Administration of the University of Lausanne, Switzerland. He has studied and been involved in the management and governance of international sport for more than 40 years. He has done research work in this area for organizations such as the European Union, the Council of Europe, the International Olympic Committee and the Union of European Football Associations. He has also helped design Swiss sport policies at the municipal, cantonal and federal levels. His current research interests focus on the governance and autonomy of sport organizations, and on sport event public hosting policies.

Shushu Chen graduated from Beijing Technology and Business University with a BSc in Bioengineering in 2007. In her four years of undergraduate study, she went to Finland as an exchange student, during which she developed an interest in management and marketing. It was mainly Beijing hosting the 2008 Olympic Games that inspired her to study in this field. In 2008, she came to the UK and gained an MSc in Sport Management from Loughborough University. Shushu is now undertaking a funded PhD studentship in the Centre for Olympic Studies and Research, Loughborough University. Her PhD project, to be completed in 2013, is in relation to the London 2012 Olympic Games legacy evaluation in a non-hosting region, using Leicester and Leicestershire as a case study. Her research interests include Olympic legacy, Olympic values and Olympism, meta-evaluation, and gender, sport and nationalism.

Kathryn Cureton works at Collingwood Neighbourhood House, a not-for-profit community service organization in Vancouver, Canada. She specializes in community development work with seniors, newcomers and low-income groups. She completed her Master's degree in May 2010 with Dr Wendy Frisby and has published previously with the *International Journal of Sport Policy and Politics*.

Veerle de Bosscher is Professor at the Department of Sports Policy and Management (Faculty of Physical Education) in the Vrije Universiteit Brussels (VUB), Belgium. Her research expertise is in the area of elite sport, sport development, sport policy and management, effectiveness, benchmarking and competitiveness. She has published her work in diverse refereed journals, written book chapters and edited several English and Dutch books, including *The Global Sporting Arms Race* and *Managing High Performance Sport*. She leads a worldwide international network on research in high performance sport, called SPLISS (Sports Policy factors Leading to International Sporting Success), which was also the subject of her PhD in 2007. Veerle is a member of the board of the European Association of Sport Management (EASM) and of the Steering Committee of elite sport in Belgium (Flanders), and counselled to elite sport development of several organizations and countries over the past years.

Paul Dimeo is Senior Lecturer in the School of Sport, University of Stirling (Scotland's University for Sporting Excellence). He has been a Visiting Fulbright Commission Scholar at the University of Texas, Austin. His research on doping in sport led to an award-winning monograph examining the historical development of drug use and anti-doping policy. He has been involved with three projects for the World Anti-Doping Agency on the following topics: the comparison of attitudes between team and individual sports contexts; education, attitudes and behaviours among Kenyan runners; and the role of coaches in disseminating anti-doping information. His collaboration with Thomas Hunt has focused on the IOC's role in anti-doping and on doping in the Cold War period.

Wendy Frisby is a Professor and Associate Director of Community and Student Development in the School of Kinesiology at the University of British Columbia in Canada. She has received numerous research grants and awards for her participatory action research with recent immigrants, women living on low incomes, and various community partners, with the aim of co-creating more inclusive local sport and recreation organizations. Her most recent teaching and research involves university–community partnerships in the areas of interculturalism, health and physical activity.

Borja García is Lecturer in Sport Policy and Management at Loughborough University. His main research interests are the governance of professional sport and the European Union sport policy. He is the founder of the Association for the Study of Sport and the European Union and a member of the European Commission's expert group on sport policy and physical activity. Dr García has published in international journals such as the *Journal of European Public Policy* and the *International Journal of Sport Policy and Politics*. As a result of his expertise, Dr García has advised members of the European Parliament, UEFA, and the English and Norwegian FAs.

Kirstin Hallmann is a Senior Lecturer at the German Sport University Cologne, Institute of Sport Economics and Sport Management. Her key research areas are sport consumer behaviour in sport tourism and sport management, sport event research, policy analysis and volunteer management. Her work is published widely in sport management and tourism journals. She has undertaken research projects for various bodies such as the European Olympic Committee and the German Sport Aid Foundation, and public authorities such as the city of Munich.

Bob Heere is a Faculty Member of the Sport Management Program at the University of Texas at Austin. His research is focused on the social impact of sport events on societies around the world, and he has published on topics such as social identity, social capital and community development. He has worked with events and other clients around the world, including in nations such as China, Japan, Korea, New Zealand, the Netherlands, Great Britain, South Africa and the United States. In 2012, he published his first book in the Netherlands, *Het Olympisch Speeltje*, a critical account of the current Dutch ambition to host the 2028 Summer Olympics. The chapter in this book served as an inspiration for that book.

Ian Henry is Professor of Leisure Policy and Management and Director of the Centre for Olympic Studies and Research at Loughborough University. He has published extensively in the field of policy analysis and evaluation, and has undertaken research projects for a wide range of bodies including the International Olympic Committee, UNICEF, UNESCO, the European Union, the Council of Europe, UK Sport, Sport England and UK government departments. His most recent work has been focused in four areas: Olympic policy, Olympism and management; sport and interculturalism; athlete management, education and lifestyle; and policy innovation.

Barrie Houlihan is Professor of Sport Policy in the School of Sport, Exercise and Health Sciences at Loughborough University, UK, and Visiting Professor at the Norwegian School of Sport Sciences. His research interests include the domestic and international policy processes for sport. He has a particular interest in sports development, the diplomatic use of sport, and drug abuse by athletes. He has authored or edited 19 books and over 50 journal articles. His most recent books are the *Routledge Handbook of Sports Development* (edited with Mick Green, Routledge, 2011) and *Sport Policy in Britain* (with Iain Lindsey, Routledge, 2012). In addition to his work as a teacher and researcher, Barrie Houlihan has undertaken consultancy projects for various UK government departments, UK Sport, Sport England, the Council of Europe, UNESCO, the World Anti-Doping Agency and the European Union. He is the Editor in Chief of the *International Journal of Sport Policy and Politics*.

Russell Hoye is the Associate Dean (Research) and Director of the Research Centre for Sport and Social Impact in the Faculty of Business, Economics and Law at La Trobe University, Australia. His areas of expertise include corporate governance, volunteer management, sport policy and the role of social capital in sport organizations. Russell is the editor of the Sport Management Series produced by Routledge and a member of the editorial boards for *Sport Management Review* and the *International Journal of Sport Policy and Politics*, and a graduate of the Australian Institute of Company Directors.

Thomas M. Hunt, JD, PhD, is Assistant Professor in the Department of Kinesiology and Health Education at the University of Texas at Austin, where he also holds an appointment as Assistant Director for Academic Affairs at the H. J. Lutcher Stark Center for Physical Culture and Sports. Dr Hunt has published articles in, among others, the *Journal of Sport History*, the *International Journal of the History of Sport* and *Olympika: The Journal of Olympic Studies*. His book *Drug Games: The International Olympic Committee and the Politics of Doping, 1960–2008* was published in January 2011 by the University of Texas Press.

Ren-Shiang Jiang is a PhD student in the Institute of Sport and Leisure Policy and the Centre for Olympic Studies and Research at Loughborough University. His research concentrates on the governance of sport from the perspective of theories of the state and strategic relations.

Chris Kennett obtained his PhD from Loughborough University in the field of sports management. He has worked on a series of research projects at the national, European and international level with organizations such as the European Commission and the International Olympic Committee. As head of research at the Olympic Studies Centre (Universitat Autònoma de Barcelona) his research focus was on the legacy of the Olympic Games, sport and communication, and sport policy and multiculturality. Currently he is Director of the Undergraduate Business School at La Salle (Universitat Ramon Llull) in Barcelona and is undertaking ongoing research into new technologies, media and the sports industry.

Ling-Mei Ko is an Assistant Professor of the Department of Leisure, Recreation and Tourism Management in the College of Business at Southern Taiwan University of Science and Technology. Her current research interests lie in issues relating to sport and leisure policies and sport management, particularly in the area of human capital.

Ping-Chao Lee is Professor of the Department of Physical Education at National Taichung University of Education in Taiwan. He has published papers both in English and Chinese in leading sport management journals. His current research interests include sport politics and the governance of professional baseball in Asia.

Clemens Ley, PhD, is currently working at the Sport Science Institute, University of Vienna. He researches and publishes in the field of sport, physical activity and health, focusing on motivational and volitional processes, social–cultural determinants, participatory approaches and psychosocial effects. He lectures in the fields of sport and health psychology, sport for development and research methodologies at various universities. Previously, he conducted intervention studies in the fields of HIV, community development and psychosocial intervention through movement, games and sports, while implementing various projects as a postdoctoral researcher in South Africa and as a member of the Group for Cooperation DIM (Universidad Politécnica de Madrid) in Guatemala, Ethiopia, Burundi and Mozambique. He obtained a Master's degree in cooperation for sustainable development and humanitarian aid and a degree in sports sciences with a specialization in prevention and rehabilitation.

Ming Li is Professor in Sports Administration and interim Executive Director of the Center for International Studies at Ohio University. His research interests are in financial and economic aspects of sport, and management of sport business in a global context. He has published a number of textbooks in sport management, including *Economics of Sport, Research Methods in Sport Management* and *International Sport Management*. He is on the editorial board of both the *Journal of Sport Management* and *Sport Marketing Quarterly*. Li used to serve as President of the North American Society for Sport Management (NASSM).

Iain Lindsey is a Reader in Sports Development at Edge Hill University. Iain's primary research interests concern the policy and practice of sports development with a particular focus on youth and community programmes. Within this general focus, Iain has three main areas of interest: the role of partnerships as part of sport policy making and delivery systems; the use of sport for development in the Global South; and the sustainability of sport development programmes. Iain has published various articles and book chapters on all three areas and his first monograph, *Sport Policy in Britain*, co-authored with Professor Barrie Houlihan, was published in 2012.

Oscar Mwaanga is a Senior Lecturer and Course Leader of the MA in Sport and Development at Southampton Solent University (UK). Oscar holds a PhD in sociology from Leeds Metropolitan University and an MSc in the social psychology of sport from the Norwegian University of Sport Science. He is a renowned international Sport for Development and Peace (SDP) activist and an indigenous leader of the sub-Saharan Africa SDP movement of the last decade, especially after founding the EduSport Foundation as the first SDP organization in Zambia in 1999. Oscar is also the founding Chairman of the Zambian Institute of Sport and also a pioneer of a number of world-renowned SDP initiatives, including Kicking AIDS Out and the SDP peer leadership approach.

Matthew Nicholson is an Associate Professor within the Centre for Sport and Social Impact at La Trobe University, Australia. His research interests focus on sport policy and development, the contribution of sport to social capital, health and well-being, and the relationship between sport and the media. His most recent books include *Sport Management: Principles and Applications* (2012), *Participation in Sport* (2011), *Sport Policy: Issues and Analysis* (2010) and *Sport and Social Capital* (2008).

Juan Luis Paramio-Salcines is a Senior Lecturer in Sport Management and Leisure Studies at Universidad Autonoma de Madrid, Spain. He has a PhD in sport management from the University of Loughborough, UK after completing an MA in sport management at Complutense University of Madrid. His principal scholarly interests include sport facilities and event management, commercial development and accessibility provision of stadiums, the economic impact of sport events and corporate social responsibility in sport. His work has been published in *Sport and Society*, *Soccer and Society*, *American Journal of Economics and Sociology*, *Urban Affairs* and *Sport Management Review*.

Joe Piggin completed his PhD at the University of Otago in New Zealand. Joe is currently a Lecturer at Loughborough University's School of Sport, Exercise and Sciences, where he teaches in various management and policy undergraduate and postgraduate courses. Joe's research interests are in the dynamics of sport and health policy production, with respect to the management of discourses throughout the policy process and promotion process.

María Rato Barrio, PhD, lectures, researches and publishes in the fields of urban segregation and violence, community development, interculturalism, sport for development, and research methodologies, mainly at Universidad Politécnica de Madrid (UPM), where she is also well a member of the Advisory Council of Cooperation for Development, and of the Group for Cooperation DIM. She finished her PhD at UPM in 2009, with a thesis about physical activity and sport as a tool to promote interculturalism in post-war contexts. She obtained degrees in physical activity and sport sciences, in social and cultural anthropology, and in teacher training; a specialist professional degree in Latin American studies; a Master's in culture, society and development in Latin America; followed by a Master's in cooperation for sustainable development and humanitarian aid. Since 1999, she has been involved in field assessment, implementation, evaluation, research and coordination in different development projects, especially in Latin America and Africa.

Sally Shaw is a Senior Lecturer in Sport Management in the School of Physical Education, University of Otago, New Zealand. She has published widely in the key journals in the field, including the *Journal of Sport Management*, *European Sport Management Quarterly* and *Sport Management Review*. Sally is a Research Fellow of the North American Society for Sport Management. In 2012, she was the Invited Speaker for the Tucker Center for Women and Girls in Sport Distinguished Lecture Series, University of Minnesota. Her research areas are gender relations, organizational partnerships and governance, and volunteer management in sport organizations.

Simon Shibli is a graduate in physical education, sport science and recreation management from Loughborough University. He joined Sheffield Hallam University in 1999 as a Senior Lecturer in Sport Management and is currently Director of the Sport Industry Research Centre and Professor of Sport Management. Simon is a qualified management accountant with the

Chartered Institute of Management Accountants (CIMA). He specializes in the finance and economics of the sport industry, and has a particular interest in elite sport policy and performance.

Eivind Å. Skille is Professor of Sport Sociology at the Section for Social and Cultural Studies at the Norwegian School of Sport Sciences, and at the Department for Sport Studies at Hedmark University College. His research is in the overlap between sport sociology and sport management, and he has published in sports policy, sport organization and sports participation. His most recent studies focus on sport organization at the level of local sport clubs, young leadership at the Youth Olympic Games, the history and sociology of Telemark skiing, and indigenous/Sámi sport in relation to policy and organization.

Wei-Chun Tai is an Assistant Professor of the Department of Information and Management in the College of Digital Design at Southern Taiwan University of Science and Technology. His research interests include information management, social networking and media.

Tien-Chin Tan is an Associate Professor of Sport Sociology and Policy at National Taiwan Normal University. His main research interests are public policy for sport, particularly in the areas of sport development, elite sport development, youth sport, and school-based sport policy in Taiwan and China. He has published articles in a variety of journals, including the *China Quarterly*, *Journal of Sport Management*, the *International Review for the Sociology of Sport*, *Journal of Sport and Social Issues*, *International Journal of the History of Sport* and *International Journal of Sport Policy*. He serves on the editorial board of the *International Review for the Sociology of Sport*. Dr Tan is also associate editor of *Asia Pacific Journal of Sport and Social Science* (published by Taylor & Francis) and *Journal of Physical Activity and Exercise Science* (published by Taiwan Society of Physical Activity and Exercise Science).

Lucie Thibault is Professor in the Department of Sport Management at Brock University (Canada). She is former Editor of the *Journal of Sport Management* and continues to serve on its editorial board, as well as the editorial boards of the *International Journal of Sport Policy and Politics* and the *European Sport Management Quarterly*. She specializes in the fields of sport policy, global issues in the sport industry, inter-organizational relationships between public and nonprofit sport organizations, and the Canadian government involvement in sport. She has been an invited keynote presenter featuring her research at many conferences around the world.

Maarten van Bottenburg is Professor of Sports Development at the Utrecht School of Governance of Utrecht University. In his research, he has focused on themes such as the globalization and commercialization of sport, elite sport policy, sports participation trends, the societal meaning of sport, and sport management. He has published several books and articles in journals such as the *American Behavioral Scientist*, *Leisure Studies*, *Journal of Sport Management*, *Sport Management Review*, *European Sport Management Quarterly* and the *International Review for the Sociology of Sport*. In addition to this, Van Bottenburg has undertaken contract research projects for governments, sport organizations and companies. As excursions outside his main discipline, Van Bottenburg has published jubilee volumes of significant Dutch institutions in the realm of labour relations, health care and social security.

Kong-Ting Yeh is Dean and Professor at the College of Management, National Taiwan Sport University, Taiwan. His major is sport management, focusing on the specific fields of sport economic analysis, sport industry management, sport facility management and sport mega-event management. Dr Yeh has done various academic research projects in the above-mentioned fields and has published the textbook *Mega Sport Event Management*. He is now working with IOC Olympic Studies Centre to develop the project Olympic Athletes Welfare and serving the Asian Association for Sport Management (AASM) as Secretary General.

Marie Therese Zammit has been involved in sports management in Malta since 1989, including positions of Vice President of the Malta Basketball Association (1997–2001) and on the Executive Board of the Maltese Olympic Committee (2001–8). A MEMOS IX graduate in 2006, she is presently reading for a PhD in sport management at the Centre for Olympic Studies and Research at Loughborough University. Her research addresses the development of Olympic Solidarity.

ACKNOWLEDGEMENTS

As editors we would like to thank all of the contributors to this volume for their patience and forbearance with our editorial approach, and for the quality and thought-provoking nature of their contributions. The volume has pulled together a rich interdisciplinary and inter-cultural expertise, and the end product is one with which we hope all our contributors will be pleased.

The ideas behind this book grew out of discussions we had had while working together as colleagues at Loughborough. Simon Whitmore at Routledge initially approached our team with the proposal that we work on a handbook for sport management (a task that our colleagues Leigh Robinson, Guillaume Bodet, Paul Downward and Packianathan Chelladurai took on, producing the *Handbook of Sport Management* last year). However, although we recognized the gap in materials relating to sport management we were also acutely aware that probably even less literature existed in the sport policy field, and we thus proposed two contributions to the handbook series, one for management and one for sport policy. The latter is the text published here.

We would like to thank Simon Whitmore for his positive engagement with the commissioning and developing of this text, and, together with his colleague Joshua Wells, for his assistance in bringing the project to fruition. The professionalism of the Routledge team has proved an excellent resource for us as editors.

Finally, we would like to thank our colleagues and research students who have contributed to our understanding of many of the ideas addressed by contributors in the text. We hope the book will, as intended, inform, stimulate and provoke further discussions in the analysis and evaluation of sport policy.

Ian Henry and Ling-Mei Ko

ABBREVIATIONS

AASM	Asian Association for Sport Management
ABA	Australian Broadcasting Authority
ACCC	Australian Competition and Consumer Commission
ACES	European Capitals of Sport Association
ACF	advocacy coalition framework
ACSF	All-China Sports Federation
AFC	Asian Football Confederation
AFL	Australian Football League
AMSD	Audiovisual Media Services Directive
ANOCA	National Olympic Committees of Africa
ASC	Australian Sports Commission
ASTRA	Australian Subscription Television and Radio Association
BCR	benefit–cost ratio
BMR	black and minority ethnic group
BRICS	Brazil, Russia, India, China and South Africa
BUCS	British Universities and Colleges Sport
BUPs	Basic Universal Principles of Good Governance of the Olympic and Sports Movement
BUSA	Bauleni United Sport Association
BWC	Baseball World Cup
CAAWS	Canadian Association for the Advancement of Women and Sport and Physical Activity
CAS	Court of Arbitration for Sport
CBA	cost–benefit analysis
CBO	community-based organisation
CEA	cost-effectiveness analysis
CFA	Chinese Football Association
CFIDC	China Football Industry Development Corporation
CFMC	Chinese Football Management Centre
CJEU	Court of Justice of the European Union
CNAAF	China's National Amateur Athletic Federation

COC	Chinese Olympic Committee
CPBL	Chinese Professional Baseball League
CSD	community sport development
CSF	critical success factor
CSL	Chinese Super League
CSLC	China Football Association Super League Company
CSP	County Sports Partnership
CVM	contingent valuation method
DCMS	Department for Culture, Media and Sport
DCSF	Department for Children, Schools and Families
DG Comp	Directorate General for Competition Policy
DPP	Democratic Progressive Party
EASM	European Asociation of Sport Managment
EU	European Union
FDI	foreign direct investment
FIFA	Fédération Internationale de Football Association
FLM	Front Libération Nationale
GAISF	General Assembly of International Sports Federations
GANEFO	Games of the New Emerging Forces
GAS	General Administration of Sport
GDR	German Democratic Republic
GRECO	Group of States against Corruption
GSO	global sports organisation
IAAF	International Association of Athletics Federations
IF	international federation
IGO	intergovernmental organization
ILO	International Labour Organization
INSEP	Institut national du sport, de l'expertise et de la performance
IOA	Indian Olympic Association
IOC	International Olympic Committee
IRR	internal rate of return
ISF	International Sports Federation
KMT	Kuomintang
KPI	key performance indicator
LAA	Local Area Agreement
LSA	local sports alliance
MNC	multinational company
MOU	memoranda of understanding
NASSM	North American Society for Sport Management
NBL	National Basketball League
NCCP	National Coaching Certification Program
NFL	National Football League
NGB	national governing body
NGO	non-governmental organisation
NOC	National Olympic Committee
NOPES	New Opportunities for PE and Sport
NPM	New Public Management
NPV	net present value

NRL	National Rugby League
NSA	non-state actor
NSC	National Sport Council
NSMC	National Sport Management Centre
NSO	national sport organisation
OECD	Organisation for Economic Co-operation and Development
PAR	participatory action research
PAT 10	Policy Action Team 10
PBRF	Performance Based Research Fund
PCT	Primary Care Trust
PDM	partnership development manager
PESSCL	Physical Education School Sport Club Links
PESSYP	Physical Education and Sport Strategy for Young People
PIDE	Programa Intercultural a través del Deporte (Intercultural Programme through Sport)
PLA	People's Liberation Army
PSC	Politburo Standing Committee
RBM	result-based management
REF	Research Excellence Framework
ROC	Republic of China
RSB	Regional Sports Board
RTP	Right to Play
SAC	Sport Affairs Council
SDO	Sport Development Officer
SDP	Sport for Development and Peace
SEA	Single European Act
SEM	Single European Market
SEU	Social Exclusion Unit
SNA	social network analysis
SOC	sense of coherence
SPARC	Sport and Recreation New Zealand
SPLISS	sports policy factors leading to international sporting success
SROI	social return on investment
TASS	Talented Athlete Scholarship Scheme
TCM	travel cost method
TFEU	Treaty on the Functioning of the European Union
TML	Taiwan Major League
UEFA	Union of European Football Associations
UKA	UK Athletics
UN	United Nations
UNESCO	United Nations Educational, Scientific and Cultural Organization
UNICEF	United Nations Children's Fund
UNODC	United Nations Office on Drugs and Crime
UPM	Universidad Politécnica de Madrid
USOC	United States Olympic Committee
USSR	Union of Soviet Socialist Republics
VSC	voluntary sports club
VUB	Vrije Universiteit Brussels

WADA	World Anti-Doping Agency
WCP	Workplace Challenge Programme
WCPP	World Class Performance Programme
WHO	World Health Organization
WSIA	World Sports Integrity Agency
WTO	World Trade Organization
WTP	willingness to pay

PART I

Theoretical perspectives and methodologies

1

ANALYSING SPORT POLICY IN A GLOBALISING CONTEXT

Ian Henry and Ling-Mei Ko

Introduction

The literature in policy analysis has traditionally incorporated a wide range of foci; for example, in the study of policy institutions, policy processes and policy outcomes (Parsons, 1996). It encompasses both analysis *for* policy (i.e. analysis that makes a direct contribution to the policy process, clarifying the criteria against which policy is to be judged or enhancing decision-making against agreed criteria) and analysis *of* policy (i.e. the study of the policy process itself and explanation of how the policy process operates, considering for example issues such as in whose interests does policy operate, and to what ends; Ham and Hill, 1993).

The scale of policy analysis also varies from the micro level often associated with understanding the nature and impact of incremental change in a specific context; to the meso level which may focus on policy making within a limited cultural, social, political or economic horizon; to macro-level concerns with global phenomena or with widespread, general or 'universal' impacts such as feminist concerns with impact of policy on gender relations (Marshall, 1999).

The range of concerns outlined above has become increasingly evident in the sport policy literature, interest in which has grown rapidly over the last decade or so. The appearance of articles on sport in journals addressing generic policy domains, and of a significant journal dedicated specifically to the analysis of sports policy (*The International Journal of Sport Policy and Politics*), bear witness to the growing volume of the literature, the diversity of theoretical bases on which it draws, and its widening comparative, international and transnational foci (Bergsgard, Houlihan, Mangset, Nødland, and Rommetvedt, 2007; Green and Houlihan, 2005b; Henry, Al-Tauqi, Amara, and Lee, 2007).

However, rarely has the range of methodologies, theoretical orientations and geographical foci been explicitly considered, in particular in relation to sports policy. This book seeks to redress this imbalance, focusing on different disciplinary and theoretical traditions, different methodological foundations both in terms of methods adopted and the ontological and epistemological foundations or assumptions on which such methods are based, and different geopolitical constituencies, bridging the analysis 'for' and analysis 'of' policy approaches.

Analysis 'for' sport policy and analysis 'of' sport policy

The distinction we note above, between analysis for/of policy seems to imply two polar opposites, but this is an unhelpful claim. Underlying this notion of 'two poles' of policy analysis is an oversimplification of the distinction between theory and practice. Much of the work undertaken in the field of sports policy is undertaken to directly inform, enhance and justify particular sports policies or programmes of action. Policy evaluation to inform the implementation of policy is a classic example. However this is not to say that such approaches are not informed by theory – theories of power, theories of social change, theories of policy formulation and implementation. Indeed we would argue that no practical statement is completely free of theoretical implications.

While practice cannot be theory-independent, theory itself, particularly social theory, carries with it practical implications. This was famously reflected by Kurt Lewin in epigrammatic style when he suggested that 'there is nothing so practical as a good theory' (Lewin, 1951: 169). This statement may have reached the status of platitude in the contemporary context, but some theorists, critical theorists for example, would claim that one of the criteria on which a theory should be judged is its potential to make a positive practical improvement to the real

Figure 1.1 Selected examples of approaches to sports policy analysis in this collection

Analysis for policy	Methodologies for policy evaluation
↑	• Cost–benefit analysis in the analysis of sport policy (Chapter 5)
	• Meta-analysis, analytic logic models and the assessment of impacts of sport policies
	• Sport and international development: methodologies for evaluating the use of sport in post-conflict societies
	• The economics of sport policy
	Defining critical policy success factors
	• Identifying 'success factors in elite sports policy systems'
	• Measuring and forecasting elite sporting success
	• Bidding policy for major sporting events
	Analyses of types of policy programme
	• Promoting student athlete interests in European elite sports systems
	• Sport and urban regeneration
	• Sport and social inclusion
	• Sport development and community development
	Analyses of policy structures
	• The development of a world anti-doping system
	• Global governance of the Olympic System
	• The developing roles of the European Union and the Council of Europe
	• Models of policy in the European Union
	• Non-governmental organizations (NGOs) in sport for development and peace
	Analyses of key policy concepts
	• Sports governance
	• Sports policy and social capital
	Social theory and policy analysis
	• Clientelism and sport policy
	• Feminist analyses of sports policy
	• A postcolonial approach to sport policy: case study of the Maghreb region in North Africa
↓	• Theorising the analysis of sport policy
Analysis of policy	• Discourse analysis and its application to sport policy analysis

world, its emancipatory potential. Thus, we would argue that it is more appropriate to see this distinction between analysis of and for policy as a continuum, and that the contributions to this book reflect the full range of types of contribution one might expect to see even though the contributors to the volume are largely drawn from the academic world rather than that of policy practitioner.

Theoretical (and meta-theoretical) foundations of sports policy analysis: a typology of approaches to sports policy comparison

Much of the work incorporated in this book is (either explicitly or implicitly) comparative. Indeed, as Durkheim remarked, all social analysis is comparative even if it deals only with a single case since analysis invariably deals with how unique or typical a particular case is. We have argued elsewhere that comparative analysis in sports policy can be encompassed within a fourfold typology (Henry *et al.*, 2007), and Table 1.1 summarises the allocation of studies to this typology, though individual studies may overlap between these ideal type descriptions.

The first of the types we term 'seeking statistical similarities' in which, at its simplest level, descriptive statistical approaches seek to identify the similarities between policy systems. This might address research questions such as 'what are the main features of the sports systems that enjoy the highest levels of adult participation in sport', seeking to identify the characteristics of national systems that have high and low levels of participation. Such an approach for example underpinned the COMPASS project (Compass, 1999), a partnership between researchers in a number of European states that sought to ascertain the nature and level of statistical association between adult participation rates in sport as a variable, with a range of other variables, whether economic (e.g. level of GDP per capita; level of per capita spending on sport), cultural (distinctive cultures in Scandinavia, Northern and Southern Europe, Europe), political (centralised versus decentralised policy systems) or organisational (sports policy systems which are public sector, commercial sector or voluntary sector led). The aim of this type of approach is to produce accurate statistical operationalisation of key factors related in this case to participation, and to develop nomothetic, law-like generalisations about the association of participation with such factors in order to develop explanations of why some national sports systems produce greater levels of participation than others.

Table 1.1 Chapters exemplifying different types of comparative analysis of sport policy in this collection

Comparative Type	Exemplars
Type 1: Seeking similarities statistically	• Methodologies for identifying and comparing success factors in elite sport policies (Chapter 16: De Bosscher *et al.*) • Measuring and forecasting elite sporting success (Chapter 17: Shibli *et al.*)
Type 2: Describing difference	• Sport and urban regeneration (Chapter 22: Paramio Salcines) • Clientelism and sport policy in Taiwan (Chapter 13: Lee and Jiang)
Type 3: Theorising the transnational	• Non-governmental organisations (NGOs) in sport for development and peace (SDP) (Chapter 8: Mwaanga) • A postcolonial approach to sport policy: case study of the Maghreb Rregion in North Africa (Chapter 25: Amara)
Type 4: Defining discourse	• Discourse analysis and its application to sport policy analysis (Chapter 3: Piggin)

The approach however faces major difficulties in terms of the measurement and application of variables at national levels. A major difficulty is that data are not always produced by national systems in truly comparable ways. Thus differences in the way adult sports participation is measured, or in the way governments sports expenditures are accounted for, the extent and nature of types of decentralisation and so on, are so great that meaningful statistical comparison becomes at best difficult and at worst positively misleading. Furthermore, even with statistically significant relationships between the dependent variable and other independent variables, this does not of itself constitute an explanation of the relationship between them, which will often require qualitative research approaches to develop a convincing account of the nature of causal or mediating relationships explaining levels of adult participation. In short these type 1 approaches suffer from the traditional limitations of positivist analysis.

A key problem for such approaches is the 'black box' problem, where statistical measures of policy inputs (e.g. financial and human resources) and of outputs (rate of adult participation), and the levels of statistical association between them, are known but the explanation of how the input variables result in changes in the output variable, is 'hidden' within the black box of policy process. In order to understand how the policy system is able to convert inputs into outputs we need some detailed account of how the policy system works – how the policy system is shaped, of the nature, range and interaction of interest groups and elites in the deciding of policy priorities, and so on. Statistically significant associations of themselves do not constitute explanations of how outcomes are achieved.

Although there are limitations of this type of approach, there are significant potential benefits also since it allows the researcher to summarise relationships across a large number of policy systems. Perhaps the best-known and most rigorous attempt to apply a type one approach in recent years has been that by De Bosscher and her colleagues (De Bosscher, De Knop, and Heyndels, 2003), who have focused on developing a framework by which to explain the dependant variable of 'national success in elite sporting performance'. They have developed the SPLISS framework (Sports Policy factors Leading to International Sporting Success) which identifies nine 'pillars' of sporting success (see Chapter 16), each composed of a range of operational indicators. Notwithstanding the sophistication of their approach and the development of batteries of indicators rather than reliance on a small number of higher level indicators, the approach still has to overcome the difficulties of explaining why and how these inputs achieve the measures of elite sporting success that they do, which requires some detailed qualitative analysis of policy systems.

The second type of policy comparison we have entitled 'describing differences' to maintain the use of alliteration in their naming of types, but which also involves describing differences (and similarities) in policy systems. Such an approach involves the use of middle-range accounts often based on ideal typical accounts. Houlihan and Green in their various accounts of comparative policy and policy change present such an approach in for example Houlihan's analysis of similarities and differences in policy systems in Bergsgard *et al.* (2007), Green and Houlihan (2005b) and Houlihan (1997).

Houlihan and Green's use of ideal types is perhaps even more explicit in their adoption and testing of middle range theoretical accounts of policy change involving for example the advocacy coalition framework (Houlihan and Green, 2006). Other examples from within this book would include Lee and Jiang's development of political clientelism as an explanatory frame to account for the development of policy in Taiwanese sport.

A key issue for such approaches is the extent to which they move beyond the descriptive to identify 'real' structures underpinning sport policy. In essence this is a debate between interpretivist and constructivist approaches on the one hand, and realist/critical realist claims on the other. The latter lays claim to identifying real structures that may be socially constructed but that exist independently of the actors who constructed them, and that exert causal influence in the sense of enabling and constraining certain forms of social (in our case policy) action.

The third type is that of 'theorising the transnational', referring to those studies that go beyond national level analysis to locate their accounts of policy development in the context of theories of global change. A range of the chapters in this book relate to transnational analysis. Oscar Mwaanga's account of the nature and role of NGOs in the international development through sport movement (Chapter 8) is one such example. In addition, in terms of seeking to develop an explanation of the transnational influences on national sports systems by reference to post-colonial perspectives on policy development, Mahfoud Amara's research on the development of sport policy systems in the Maghreb region (Chapter 25) represents a theoretically informed analysis of the development of policy systems within the context of a wider transnational theoretical frame. This approach has the strength of not constraining explanation of policy formation and change by reference to a local or national frame but recognising the influence of (and influence on) global factors in relation to local policy outcomes.

The fourth and final type of approach to analysis of policy systems we had termed 'defining discourse' and is related to the recent developments in the study of policy as discourse (Hewitt, 2009; Leow, 2011). The use of this label is intended to encapsulate a double meaning. It refers to both the ways in which some discourse analysts see discourse as reflecting underlying ways of seeing, explaining, or understanding a particular policy context, policy problem or policy action, that is reflecting realities or different actors' understandings of those realities. Here, discourse is a reflection of the individual or group's perception of policy realities, and the researcher's task is to define the nature of those different reflections by defining the discourse that relates to them. A key concern here is often with identifying 'power over discourse', explaining whose account (and thus whose values) are dominant.

The second meaning relates not to whether the discourse used *reflects* the ways in which actors understand policy but rather how discourse *determines* the way they do so. Discourse in this sense *defines* reality. In this second somewhat more radical approach to discourse analysis the researcher is often more concerned with the 'power of discourse', its ability to define policy realities.

The application of discourse analysis to sport policy analysis is the focus of Piggin's discussion in Chapter 3. He identifies ways in which discourse analysis of different types allow for the identification of how dominant and subordinate voices in policy debates reflect/reproduce the nature of dominant interests in that process.

This brief discussion of types of approach to the analysis of sports policy serves to illustrate the rich vein that runs through work in this field and, we would argue, is represented in the nature of the contributions to this book.

Ontological and epistemological premises of policy analyses and policy evaluations

One set of issues that is rarely explicitly addressed even in those studies that fall at the 'analysis of policy' end of the spectrum of policy analysis, relates to the ontological and epistemological positions adopted in particular studies and the consequences of these positions for the application of the analysis. We have discussed this in more detail elsewhere (Henry *et al.*, 2007; Henry, Amara, Al-Tauqi, and Lee, 2005) but it is worth briefly highlighting key elements of this discussion in order to clarify the differing nature of claims that might be made on the basis of these assumptions.

Ontologies relate to what beliefs may be held, or claims may be made, about what exists, and in particular whether structures exist independently of the actors involved or are simply social constructions of those actors. Realists claim that though we do not observe underlying social structures directly, we observe the consequences of the existence of such structures, and thus can imply their existence on the basis of what we do observe (for the purposes of brevity a simplified framework of ontological and epistemological positions is used here; for a fuller account of the range of realist positions see Blaikie, 2010: 92–104). Idealists by contrast hold the view that reality is a product of socially constructed and shared interpretations of the world. As such, social 'reality' is a contingent feature of social action and thus can be modified by the actions of actors.

Between these two positions lies a third, that of critical realism (or social realism), which to some degree represents a current orthodoxy. Critical realists argue that social structures are real, they exist independently of individual actors and exert causal influence, but that they are socially constructed, that is they are the product of previous social action (and, though relatively permanent, may under the right circumstances be modified in the future). Thus, for example, gender structures that exist in any given society independently of particular men and women, enable and constrain the options available to particular actors (male and female) but they can be modified based on further social action (witness for example the impact of the suffragette movement on the political structures).

In line with the principal ontological positions are the various epistemological approaches that relate to the means by which knowledge is acquired, and claims as to the nature of acquisition of knowledge. Classic positivism seeks to identify social 'facts' about patterns of behaviour at an observable level in an 'objectivist' fashion. Interpretivism approaches the task of understanding social reality by the analysis of actors' own understanding of the significance and meaning of their own behaviour. A radical strand of this line of thinking is the position of certain discourse analysts who wish to argue that all that can be said to exist (or at least all that is available for primary analysis) are the discourses produced by social actors and that analysis of discursive construction therefore is the primary research task of social analysts.

Critical realism draws on both qualitative and quantitative forms of data but defines the nature and roles of that data in relation to its retroductive research strategy. The retroductive approach defines a process whereby empirical observation of events involves the identification of 'patterns' (statistically or in qualitative accounts) that are used in the positing or building of hypothetical models of structures and mechanisms that will explain the empirical observations made, and the patterns observed. These models allow the identification of structures and mechanisms in ways that will causally explain the empirical phenomena observed and will allow further testing of the power of explanation of empirical phenomena.

How does this impact on the practical activities of sports policy analysts? Chen, Henry and Ko (Chapter 4) refer to the work of Pawson (2006) and Pawson and Tilley (1997), who adopt a realist approach to policy evaluation, arguing cogently that policy explanation, since it is dealing with social systems that are open and generally dynamic, is about providing evidence to support claims that certain mechanisms produce particular outcomes (or classes of outcome) within one or more specific (types of) social context. Pawson and Tilley are scathing in their dismissal of experimental design/scientific method, pragmatic evaluation and constructivist evaluation, which they rehearse as alternatives to their own realist model.

In relation to the first of these alternatives, they critique the logic of experimentation in policy evaluation, which relies on pre- and post-intervention testing with a group that has been subject to the intervention or 'treatment' and a control group that has not. The principal objections to this are twofold. Social situations are not like laboratory conditions where all relevant variables can be controlled so that the impact of change in the single variable 'subject to treatment'/'not subject to treatment' can be observed. Laboratory conditions represent a (relatively at least) closed system, whereas almost all policy evaluation takes place within open, dynamic social systems in which it is not possible to maintain stasis in all variables except the policy intervention itself. Social policy accounts have to take into consideration not just the mechanisms for producing policy outcomes but the conditions under which, or the environments within which, such mechanisms can come into play.

The pragmatist model of evaluation begins not with a set of ontological and epistemological principles but rather, taking Weiss as their major proponent with principles of utility, feasibility, propriety and accuracy (Mark and Weiss, 2006; Stufflebeam and Welch, 1986). Any approach to policy evaluation under this set of criteria is acceptable if it is useful to the political decision makers, is feasible (within budgets and physical capacities), and is ethically acceptable. However the criterion of 'accuracy' prompts the question: accurate under which criteria? Accuracy is relatively easy to define in relation to simple tasks (counting the number of beans in a pile), but rather less so in complex contexts where the nature of what is to be measured is subject to challenge or complex articulation. Ultimately in pragmatic evaluation we end up defining our problems in the way decision makers see them in order to speak in the decision makers' own language and thus be more likely to impact on their policy behaviour. If the policy makers' perspective, however, is limited or wrong-headed we run the risk of never challenging such limitations and our evaluations certainly cannot be said under this approach to be founded on soundly argued ontological and epistemological principles.

The third target for Pawson and Tilley is constructivist policy evaluation which seeks to understand policy in the terms of the various stakeholders involved. The problem with radical constructivist accounts is that in their wish to avoid privileging the account of the policy maker or implementer, and to provide a space for the voice and perceptions of other stakeholders, they are obliged to argue that no account can be given special status (and this includes the account of the policy evaluator, which thus has to be viewed as no better or worse than any other). There is therefore a central problem with concepts of truth. Pawson and Tilley (1997: 21) thus describe the constructivist approach as 'throwing out of the objectivist baby with the relativist bathwater'. In addition to problems of the truth-claims of the argument, the scope of the application of constructivist applications will be limited since 'neither problems nor their solutions can be generalised from one setting to another' (Guba and Lincoln, 1989: 45 quoted in Pawson and Tilley, 1997: 22). Such a statement militates against the establishing of results that are valid in more than one situation resulting in hopelessly narrow claims with regard to whether policies 'work'.

In terms of analysis 'of' policy perspectives on how policies and their consequences are socially constructed, constructivist approaches may provide privileged insights into other perspectives, but in terms of analysis 'for' policy its applications are severely limited. Pragmatic approaches remind us of the need to engage with the real world if we want to contribute positively to the policy process, but to avoid the dangers of accepting the ways in which policy problems are conceptualised, and framed in ways that limit the scope of our research questions or the range of possible answers.

In contrast to these three limited approaches to policy analysis and evaluation, the realist approach thus argues for identifying real causal mechanisms but that are context contingent. Thus the core questions they seek to address are 'What works? For whom? In what circumstances? And why?' Most of the contributions that address *analysis for policy* in this text generally share a realist perspective. They may be concerned with focusing more specifically on one or other of the realist's core questions, identifying the relationship between contexts, generative mechanisms of change, and the ability to achieve change through policy. However, others that address *analysis of policy* also address more centrally issues of power in terms of questions such as: whose interests are served by particular policies? How are policy problems conceptualised or discursively constructed? How do such constructions constrain or enable certain courses of action? Why do certain forms of policy emerge at particular points in time? Both types of endeavour are important if we are to understand policy analysis in the domain of sport. Each has its place in this volume which is intended to make a contribution to the reader's understanding of how policy analysis in sport can aid our understanding of how the policy world is shaped within, and impacts upon the wider social context.

2

THEORISING THE ANALYSIS OF SPORT POLICY

Barrie Houlihan

Theory and theorising

At its worst, theory obscures and confuses, often due to multiple definitions, cryptic application and an approach to theorising that values complexity over parsimony: at its best, theory guides research, constructively challenges research findings and helps to make sense of social phenomena. Whether one's engagement with theory has been positive or negative, it is not possible to investigate and make sense of the sport policy process without theorising. Theory may be broadly defined as general statements that describe and explain the relationship between variables: such statements are often concerned to identify causes and effects arising from the relationship. Examples of such relationships would include that between age or gender and levels of sport participation, or the relationship between particular sports and the generation of personal social capital.

The criteria for determining 'good' theory vary according to one's ontological and epistemological assumptions. For those researching from within a positivist paradigm a good theory is generally one that: allows for categorisation; enables explanation of relationships between variables; facilitates prediction; and generates testable, ideally falsifiable, hypotheses. One example would be the application of rational (or public) choice theory (Niskanen, 1971) to government sport agencies (such as the Australian Institute of Sport, UK Anti-Doping and the Irish Sports Council), which would suggest that the members of these organisations would be more concerned with the pursuit of their rational self-interest (e.g. larger organisational budgets and staffing which give greater opportunity for personal benefit) than with the pursuit of public policy objectives. A second example would be the testing of Robert Michels' 'iron law of oligarchy' (Michels, 1911; Tolbert and Hiatt, 2009) in relation to the development of national governing bodies (NGBs) or international federations. The 'law' suggests that as organisations grow in membership the greater organisational complexity results in a concentration of power in the hands of a small leadership group.

Those working within an interpretivist paradigm are more likely to see theory as emerging from the analysis of data, that is, an inductive process often referred to as 'grounded theory'. Here the concern is less with predicting the course of future events than in explaining social complexity. Analyses of the way in which social discourse shapes perceptions of gender and of the body and, by implication, public policy are illustrative of this type of theorising (Markula and Pringle, 2006). A good theory for the interpretivist is one that explains a case satisfactorily and a good theorist is one who is sensitive in his/her 'reading' of data such that s/he is able to identify important variables in the explanation of the case.

Critical realists operate in territory between the two previous paradigms. On the one hand they accept the possibility of causal explanations (e.g. the causal relationship between social class and patterns of sport participation) while also accepting that we cannot see the world as it really is and thus need to employ theory 'as a sensitising device to reveal the structured reality beneath the surface' (Hay, 2002, p. 122). For Danermark *et al.* (2002), 'good' critical realist methodology moves through a number of stages that begin and end in the more concrete. The stages of analysis move through: description of the focal event or situation; identifying key aspects of the event/situation; abduction/drawing inferences; development of potential explanatory theories; resolution between theories and data.[1]

Types of theory

Ontological and epistemological assumptions provide the context within which theorising takes place. However, theory, particularly in relation to its application to the analysis of policy, can take a number of different forms. Abend (2008) distinguishes between seven meanings of theory, four of which are particularly relevant to our present discussion. The first is what Abend (2008, p. 179) refers to as 'a Weltanschauung ... an overall perspective from which one sees and interprets the world'. Feminism, Marxism and neo-Marxism, pluralism and neo-pluralism and rational choice theory are all examples of this type of theory. Each of these macro-level theories provides a conceptual language and usually a set of propositions about the world which informs and structures social investigation. At times macro-level theories can become so dominant in a branch of social science (for example the realist perspective in international relations) that they assume paradigmatic status in the Kuhnian sense (Kuhn, 1996). However, such paradigmatic dominance is rare outside the natural sciences; within the social sciences theoretical pluralism is much more common. In the practice of policy analysis it is not uncommon for researchers to choose to operate within a particular macro-level theory such as feminism (Orloff and Palier, 2009), neo-pluralism (Lindblom, 1977) or neo-Marxism (Hill, M., 2009), or to eschew a commitment to a particular perspective and to use them as competing worldviews that sensitise empirical research and inform research design. An important variant on this first meaning of theory is that view of the world that rejects the aspiration to detachment and disinterestedness and embraces a fundamental normativity. Such theories would include critical theory, post-colonial theory and feminist theory.

The second meaning of theory that Abend identifies and that is relevant to sport policy analysis, although in a slightly modified form, is theory as 'an explanation of a particular social phenomenon' (2008, p. 178). While Abend would restrict this definition to specific cases, such as explaining the decision by China to support the establishment of the Games of the New Emerging Forces (GANEFO) as a rival to the Olympic Games in the early 1960s, the definition could be expanded to refer to the explanation of a particular class of social phenomena and would thus, for example, apply to theories specifically designed to explain the (sport) policy-making process. Such meso-level theories would include the advocacy coalition framework (Sabatier and Jenkins-Smith, 1993), multiple streams (Kingdon, 1984), punctuated equilibrium (Baumgartner and Jones, 1993) and policy network theory (Marsh and Rhodes, 1992). Each of these theories is concerned to explain how policy is made although each tends to emphasise particular aspects of the policy process such as agenda-setting, the role of individuals or specific catalysts for change.

The third meaning of theory of especial relevance to the study of policy concerns the analysis of specific problems or aspects of the policy process such as the relationship between structure and agency, path dependency, or the significance of policy learning and transfer. This type of theory is an element within a number of macro theories such as the variants of Marxism and pluralism as well as some meso-level theories. For example, in Marxist theories of capitalist policy making there is a long-standing debate about whether the policies produced by governments within capitalist economies are *structured* to benefit capital or whether policy is more the outcome of the interplay of class interests with the possibility that policy that benefits the working class might, on occasion, be produced. A second example would be the discussion of path dependency (the idea that previous policy decisions narrow future policy choices) which is relevant to the advocacy coalition framework, network theory and neo-institutionalism.

The final meaning of theory relevant to our discussions is 'a general proposition, or logically connected system of propositions, which establish a relationship between two or more variables' (Abend, 2008, p. 177). For example Robert Michels's 'iron law of oligarchy', discussed above, suggests a relationship between the variable 'organisational complexity and size' and the variable 'concentration of power in the hands of an oligarchy'. Similarly, Anthony Downs in his 'issue attention cycle' argued, *inter alia*, that recognition by the public of the cost and complexity of an issue often leads to the gradual downgrading of an issue and its move down the policy agenda.

In undertaking an analysis of sport policy it is likely that the researcher will be using some or all of the four types of theory discussed above. However, the particular combination of theory adopted will depend primarily on the research question under consideration, but will also be influenced by the researcher's own ontological and epistemological assumptions. Most analyses of sport policy tend to utilise middle-range or meso-level theory as the focus tends to be on the interaction between state agencies and other national-level organisations and on specific issues such as elite athlete success, gender inequity in the leadership of sport organisations, the bidding process for major sports events or the impact of lottery funding on sports club development. However, even when the focus is on a substantive and clearly defined policy issue, many researchers find reference to macro-level theory (*Weltanschauung*) useful in sensitising the researcher to broader explanatory themes that might have shaped the behaviour of organisations involved in the policy process within the substantive area of interest. Indeed it is possible to argue that there is an under-utilisation of macro-level theorising in relation to sport policy and that by focusing on the meso level we run the risk of downplaying or even ignoring the deeply rooted societal forces that discretely, but effectively, shape day-to-day policy decisions.

The discussion thus continues by looking more closely at some examples of macro-level theory and how they might be used to analyse sport policy and also how they might inform analysis at the meso level.

Using macro-level theory in the analysis of sport policy

The range of macro-level theories is extensive and only a selection will be reviewed here to illustrate the contribution that this level of theory can make to the analysis of sport policy. The macro-level theories of particular interest are those that deal more explicitly with the distribution of power in society and/or the relationship between the state and society. Although the two categories overlap significantly in the former category, one would include Marxism and neo-Marxism, globalisation, pluralism and neo-pluralism, feminism, and in the latter category one would include governance and public choice theory. There are a number of excellent reviews of this body of theory (see for example Dryzek and Dunleavy, 2009) and also a number of reviews that examine individual theories or selections of theories in relation to sport, though not explicitly in relation to sport policy (see for example Hargreaves, 1986; Sage, 1990; Morgan, 1994; Jarvie and Maguire, 1994; Giulianotti, 2004; Carrington and McDonald, 2009).

Table 2.1 summarises four theories that are either among the more commonly adopted or are among those considered to have the greatest potential to inform analysis. Each theory is described and evaluated in terms of their unit of analysis, their conceptualisation of the role of the state, their view on the dynamic for public policy, the meso-level theories/frameworks with which they are particularly compatible and their primary focus in relation to sport. As can be seen, each directs the researcher to give emphasis to different analytic variables (for example, social class, interest groups, networks or markets) and each directs attention to a different set of key research questions, such as social control and commodification for the Marxist and the regulatory significance of the state for the market liberals.

It is certainly not impossible to address questions relating to particular substantive policy issues utilising macro-level theory. Using feminist theory to examine the policy outcomes of NGBs of sport, governments and international federations or using neo-pluralism to examine the application of competition (anti-trust) policy to the sale of broadcasting rights would undoubtedly be insightful. However, I would argue that while macro-level theory can account for particular policy outcomes they are less useful in understanding the process by which those outcomes were generated or, in other words, the way in which macro-level systemic orientations or biases were articulated in the day-to-day operation of organisations. In order to achieve this finer level of understanding it is argued that it is necessary to augment macro-level theory with analytic frameworks and theories specifically designed to provide insights at the meso level and, as is indicated in Table 2.1, there are a number of meso-level theories that have a strong compatibility with theories that are intended to provide the researcher with a *Weltanschauung*.

Using meso-level theory in the analysis of sport policy

As was the case with macro-level theory, there is a wide range of theories available at the meso level. Sabatier (1999) identified eleven frameworks for analysis and explored seven in detail which included the stages heuristic, institutional rational choice, multiple streams, punctuated-equilibrium and advocacy coalition. John (1998), in a similar review of the field, identified five broad theoretical approaches to policy analysis – institutional, group and network, socio-economic, rational choice and ideas-based. Three meso-level theories will be discussed in this section – punctuated equilibrium, the advocacy coalition framework and multiple streams. These theories have been selected because they fulfil the following criteria:

- a capacity to explain both policy stability and policy change;
- a capacity to illuminate a range of aspects of the policy process such as agenda setting, policy selection and policy implementation;
- an applicability across a range of issues within the sport policy sub-sector;
- a capacity to provide a longitudinal perspective on policy change (Houlihan, 2005a).

Punctuated equilibrium
Developed by Baumgartner and Jones (1993), the punctuated equilibrium theory of the policy process emphasises the simultaneous presence of pressures for change and stability where long periods of stability are followed by periods of, often rapid, change. They argue that the forces that create stability (i.e. the interaction of ideas, institutions, interests and socio-economic factors) are also those that are responsible for the rupture in policy stability and the onset of a period of policy change. The model shares many common characteristics with Lindblom's

Table 2.1 Selected major macro-level theories and sport policy

Dimension	Neo-Marxism	Governance	Neo-pluralism	Market liberalism
Unit of analysis	Social classes	Policy networks and sub-systems	Interest groups	Markets and individuals
Role of the state	Under Marxism the state is an instrument of the ruling capitalist class: under neo-Marxism the position and role of the state is less clear with some arguing that the state's role is to manage capitalism which might involve short term actions which go against the interests of capital accumulation (e.g. provide welfare services through taxation to enhance legitimation).	Due to increasing complexity of social issues, governments seek to act in partnership with civil society organisations. Rhodes (1994) sees this as a loss of power (the hollowing out of the state) whereas Rose (1999) argues that we are witnessing an extension of state power (i.e. a 'rolling out' of state power).	The state is an active participant in making policy, partly mediating between rival groups, but also protecting and promoting its own interests (especially in relation to problem definition and preferred solutions). The state has a bias towards business interests.	Argued that markets maximise social welfare and that individuals are rational utility maximisers. The role of the state is to enable markets to operate effectively (with as little regulation as possible). Market liberals, especially rational (public) choice theorists, have a deep suspicion of state action and argue that politicians and state officials will act rationally and consequently seek to maximise their budgets (through taxation) to secure organisational growth and therefore larger personal rewards. The role of the state should be limited to activities such as protecting property rights, defence, providing basic infrastructure and services (in cases of market failure) and regulating monopolies.
Dynamic for policy-making	Class conflict and/or the inherent instability of capitalism (e.g. the 2008 global banking crisis).	Accumulation of evidence and/or external event (e.g. financial crisis).	Interaction between groups with unequal influence.	Market competition and the pursuit, by individuals, of personal interest.

Continued

Dimension	Neo-Marxism	Governance	Neo-pluralism	Market liberalism
Associated meso-level frameworks and approaches	None clearly, but elements of network theory in which business dominated or business oriented networks would manage policy sub-systems; and institutionalism in which dominant power relations become institutionalised in the state.	Policy communities; institutionalism.	Advocacy coalition framework; punctuated equilibrium theory; institutionalism.	Multiple streams.
Primary focus for the study of sport policy	Sport as a form of social control (i.e. diverting attention from the ills of capitalism) or sport as a source of profit (e.g. through broadcasting and commodification).	Sport policy networks/community and their membership, values and decision processes.	Existence and influence of advocacy coalitions for interests such as elite, women, youth and community sport.	The regulatory role of the state. The relationship between the state, the market and the not-for-profit sector.
Orientation/key questions	How is the tension between sport as a 'new industry' and as an element of welfare provision managed?	What are the dominant values in the community? How is the membership of the community decided? How insulated is the community from other policy sub-sectors?	To what extent do advocacy coalitions exist in sport? If they do, what is their relative strength and what is their relationship to government?	Is the state competing with the commercial sector by providing sports facilities? Is the expansion of state involvement in sport evidence in support of the public choice critique of public officials (seeking personal benefits – increased salaries – rather social welfare)?
References	Offe 1984; Brohm 1978; Jessop 1990; Morgan 1994; Girginov & Sandanski 2011	Pierre & Peters 2000; Houlihan & Groeneveld 2011; Rose 1999	Lindblom 1977; van den Berg & Janoski 2005; Green & Houlihan 2004	Friedman and Friedman 1962; Niskanen 1971

Source: Houlihan and Lindsey (2013)

(1959; see also Braybrooke and Lindblom, 1963) theory of incremental policy making and its emphasis on political compromise and satisficing rather than optimising and gradualism. It also shares common ground with the literature on policy communities (Heclo and Wildavsky, 1974; Marsh and Rhodes, 1992), which emphasises the role of communities in dealing with 'normal' issues, the maintenance of boundaries between insider organisations and outsiders, the role of ideas in maintaining community cohesion and the collective interest of community members in maintaining the broad status quo. In the punctuated equilibrium theory ideas (for example, about what constitutes a problem and what constitutes a solution to a problem) that reinforce the interests of power elites become institutionalised in the policy sub-sector.

However, the stability within a policy sub-sector can be undermined by a number of forces. First, there can be the steady accumulation of pressures for change which might come from changing patterns of behaviour (for example the accumulation of evidence in the 1960s and 1970s in the UK that the rules regarding amateurism in sports such as rugby union, tennis and athletics were being ignored) or from changes in values and ideas (for example, regarding the importance of success at the Olympic Games). A second source of destabilising pressures can come from the actions of policy entrepreneurs who are looking for opportunities to promote their (or their client's) interests which are currently not being met by the existing policy community. An example of this type of pressure might be the lobbying (largely unsuccessful so far) by football supporters' groups within the European Union for a greater voice regarding the governance of clubs. A third force for change is the media which, when for example it picks up on the ideas of policy entrepreneurs or 'whistle-blowers', can add considerable momentum to forces undermining policy stability, creating a bandwagon effect. One such example is the debate about the governance of some of the major international federations, FIFA in particular, which has received considerable media attention and forced the organisation to modify, if only marginally, its governance procedures. A second example would be the way in which child protection issues related to sport, and especially the sexual abuse of young athletes, were initially a concern limited to discussion among a small number of academics, but when adopted by the media became major issues that NGBs were forced to address more urgently. In other words the media are important in turning a private concern into a public issue.

The coherence and intuitive appeal of the theory is acknowledged, but it is not without its critics. John (1998) points to its descriptive nature and its confidence in the effectiveness of grass-roots politics and opinion to challenge institutionalised policy communities, thus ignoring the capacity of those interests to manipulate public opinion. Perhaps of more significance when applying the model to sport policy is the fact that much sport policy is spillover from contiguous policy sub-sectors such as education, health and economic development. For example, in most countries it is unlikely that sports interests will have had significant influence over decisions about the status of physical education in the school curriculum, the decision to bid for the Olympic Games or the football World Cup, or the investment by public bodies in community sport. It is much more likely that these decisions were influenced by education, economic/diplomatic, and health/welfare sub-sectoral interests, respectively. Sport is arguably distinguished from many other policy sub-sectors by being characterised by policy taking rather than policy making (Dery, 1999; Houlihan, 2000).

These criticisms notwithstanding, the punctuated equilibrium theory has much to recommend it for the study of sport policy. Not only does it require the researcher to address questions relating to *both* policy stability and change, but it also foregrounds the issue of the relationship between structure and agency – the third meaning of theory outlined above. By drawing attention to the tendency for interests to institutionalise their power and also to the long term-fragility of that institutionalisation, the model allows for a more subtle analysis of the interaction between established interests, outsider interests and the role of policy entrepreneurs. Overall, the punctuated equilibrium theory provides substantial scope for the generation of hypotheses in the study of sport policy.

The advocacy coalition framework

The advocacy coalition framework (ACF) is, like the punctuated equilibrium theory, rooted in broadly pluralist macro-level assumptions about the distribution of power and the competitive nature of the policy process. It also shares assumptions about the capacity of ideas/evidence to influence the behaviour of decision makers and, at times, to prove more significant than organisational or sectoral self-interest. According to Sabatier and Weible (2007, pp. 191–2), the ACF is founded on three important assumptions:

- the macro-level assumption that most policy making occurs among specialists within a policy subsystem but that their behaviour is affected by factors in the broader political and socio-economic system;
- a micro-level 'model of the individual' that is drawn heavily from social psychology; and
- a meso-level conviction that the best way to deal with the multiplicity of actors in a subsystem is to aggregate them into 'advocacy coalitions'.

The ACF rests on a number of operational assumptions, namely:

- The increasing complexity of the problems facing governments has resulted in increasing specialisation both within government (by public officials and by politicians) and also in civil society (i.e. specialist interest groups).
- Policy subsystem participants hold strong beliefs which they hope to translate into action.
- Policy beliefs are slow to change and consequently a time frame of ten years or more is required for the analysis of policy change.
- Subsystems involve actors from different levels of government and increasingly from international bodies and from other countries.

Within policy subsystems it is common to find between two and four coalitions competing for influence over policy although they are rarely of equal influence, with one coalition often clearly in a dominant position. As with much of the literature on policy communities (Marsh and Rhodes, 1992), shared beliefs and values give the coalition its coherence and continuity. Similar to work by Benson (1982) and Peffley and Hurwitz (1985), Sabatier and Jenkins-Smith (1993) argue that a hierarchy of beliefs can be identified as follows:

- Deep core beliefs that affect most policy subsystems and refer to normative assumptions (for example about the proper role of government in sport) and ontological assumptions about human nature (for example whether the propensity to cheat in sport is normal or aberrant). These beliefs are slow to change.
- At a more shallow level are policy core beliefs that refer to the operationalisation of deep core beliefs within specific subsystems. For example, at the deep core level a common belief was, and still is in some countries, that men and women should fulfil different roles in civil society. In sport this has often been interpreted to mean that women's participation in competitive sport should not be encouraged. A second example might be deep core beliefs about the use of the countryside and its romantic conceptualisation as a pastoral idyll which

is in stark contrast to urban life. The operationalisation of this deep core belief in relation to sport might be to limit the use of the countryside for non-traditional/noisy sports such as powerboat racing and motocross.

- The final, shallowest, level concerns secondary beliefs that tend to be narrow in scope and related to quite specific issues in the sub-sector. Examples from the sport policy sub-sector might include how participation strategies vary from one NGB or municipality to another. As these beliefs have a much narrower focus they tend to be much more amenable to change.

Policy change is driven by conflict between coalitions and often a policy broker will mediate between coalitions to generate policy outputs. However, the ACF assumes a high degree of rationality in the policy process as it is argued that policy change is also driven by policy-oriented learning which refers to the relatively slow accumulation of evidence and experience that can make the defence of the policy status quo increasingly difficult. Thus, while coalitions will be resistant to accepting the implications of evidence that challenges their core beliefs and consequent policy preferences, the accumulated weight of evidence will gradually undermine the status quo.

The ACF is arguably more convincing when explaining the persistence of policy stability (through the dominance of particular coalitions possessing a coherent set of core beliefs) than in explaining policy change (the impact of a mix of exogeneous factors, rationality and policy learning). Perhaps most importantly, the framework under-theorises the nature of power and the extent to which protection of interests undermines the willingness to accept contrary evidence. However, the ACF has been applied in a large number of policy analyses including some in sport (Parrish, 2003d; Green and Houlihan, 2004) and has proved a useful heuristic tool.

Multiple streams framework

Unlike the ACF and the punctuated equilibrium theory the multiple streams framework is more sharply focused on one aspect of the policy process, namely, agenda setting. In his review of the utility of the multiple streams framework, Zahariadis (2007, p. 65) argues that a good theory (focused on policy selection) will provide answers to three questions:

- How is attention rationed?
- How and where is the search for alternatives conducted?
- How is selection biased?

John Kingdon (1984) argues that these questions can best be answered by conceptualising the policy process as comprising three conceptually distinct 'streams' (problems, policies and politics), each of which has its own dynamics and rules. Interconnection between streams occurs at critical points in time when policy windows open (due, for example, to crisis or to the regular cycle of policy review, such as the annual budget-setting process) and/or through the actions of policy entrepreneurs. It is on these occasions that the three streams are likely to intertwine and produce policy change. Four assumptions underpin the framework, the first of which is that decision makers operate in conditions of ambiguity. Ambiguity may be manifest in relation to the definition of problems. For example, is the low or declining levels of participation in organised sport a health problem, an educational problem or a sport problem? Similarly, is doping in sport primarily a health problem, a sport problem or a problem of law and order? The second assumption is that, unlike individuals for whom problem processing is serial, that is, individuals tend to focus on one problem at a time, organisations, such as governments, are parallel processors, that is, they deal with many issues, some of which overlap. In governments, not only do problems overlap and blur into one another, but solutions also overlap and can themselves create or be overtaken by new problems. The third assumption is that policy makers operate under significant time constraints, not simply because of the queue of other problems vying for their attention but also because of the public expectation that a policy response should follow quickly once a problem has been publicly acknowledged. The final assumption is that the three streams are relatively independent.

The three streams are summarised in Figure 2.1. The problem stream consists of a range of issues that the public and policy makers want tackled. Issues are brought to the attention of policy makers in a variety of ways including through indicators (e.g. surveys of levels of partici-pation in sport or the prevalence of obesity among the young), focusing events (e.g. evidence of corruption in an international federation, an incident of doping involving a high profile event or athlete or a significant failure to win medals at an Olympic Games) and feedback (e.g. from existing programmes, indicating a lack of progress in raising the participation levels of a particu-lar target group). The politics stream comprises a number of elements including party ideology where a change of government between social democrat and neoliberal parties can have a sub-stantial impact on the willingness to recognise problems as legitimate business for government. Another element in the politics stream is the strength and activity of interest groups and would include NGBs of sport and national Olympic committees. A third element is the national mood (towards the quality of school sport opportunities or the adequacy of the performance of the team in a country's national sport) and is often reflected in the strength and activity of interest groups, but also refers to the reflection of the national mood in the media. The policy stream comprises a complex mix of ideas that are competing for acceptance within policy networks. Competition might be in relation to talent identification and development programmes such as the Long Term Athlete Development programme, ways of funding sports participation, coach training programmes, or the degree of autonomy to be granted to sports organisations. The criteria according to which policies are selected will include their compatibility with the values of the governing party and technical and financial feasibility.

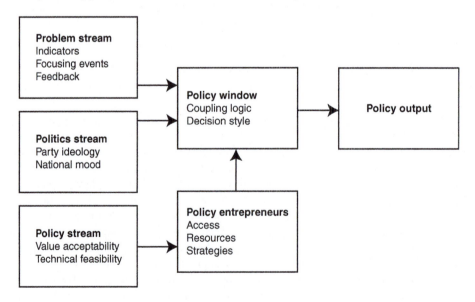

Figure 2.1 The multiple streams framework

Source: Adapted from Zahariadis (2007)

The multiple streams framework with its emphasis on ambiguity, complexity and messiness is in marked contrast to the analytic frameworks that emphasise an underlying rationality in the policy process. As well as being a thought-provoking challenge to the other frameworks such as the ACF and punctuated equilibrium, multiple streams is of interest because it can be combined or integrated with other theories. Not only does it clearly fit within a pluralist macro-level theory, but it also prompts an analysis of the relationship between structure and agency by the emphasis given to the role of policy entrepreneurs.

Using theory

It is rare in the social sciences for researchers to question the value of theory. However, far more open to discussion is what kind of theory and how much theory is appropriate to incorporate into a research design. Unless one is specifically concerned to test the utility of a specific theory then the primary purpose of theory is to guide the various stages of research from the generation or identification of research questions and the generation of hypotheses through the collection of data to the interpretation of data. The appropriate use of theories guides research (i.e. identifies what is important when undertaking fieldwork data collection) for, as Stoker observes, 'Theories are of value precisely because they structure all observations' (1995, p. 17, quoted in Grix, 2004). Without theory or some other means of discriminating and classifying empirical data it would be impossible to separate the trivial from the crucial observations. However, theory must be proportionate to the complexity of the research questions. Parsimony in theory is always preferable to, and more effective than, complexity: while the former should lead to clarity of data collection and its interpretation, the latter often leads to confusion in explanation if not paralysis. Furthermore, theory must be used with a degree of scepticism and especially in relation to research into (sport) public policy where the commitment to utilising one theory, such as Kingdon's multiple streams with its underlying pluralist assumptions about the relative openness of the policy agenda, might prevent the recognition of the extent to which particular interests are institutionalised. In this respect there is a case for seeing meso-, and indeed macro-level theories, providing the researcher with a repertoire of resources on which they can draw. In addition, it is important for the researcher to acknowledge the interconnection between macro- and meso-level theories.

As was made clear in Table 2.1, it is possible to nest meso-level theories within the broader macro-level theories of the state and society. More importantly, it should be stressed that all meso-level theories are the encapsulation of theoretical assumptions that have their origin in macro-level theorising. Just as the multiple streams framework resonates most clearly with the assumptions underpinning pluralist and neo-pluralist theorising, both the ACF and the punctuated equilibrium frameworks are based on a series of macro-level assumptions about the nature of power and particularly the distribution of power in society (both national and global), the relationship between civil society and the state, and the scope for agency. At the very least, analyses located at the meso level should demonstrate a clear awareness of the macro-level assumptions that inform their adopted analytic frameworks. As Green (2005) demonstrated, a research strategy that aims to integrate macro- and meso-level theories offers the prospect of substantial insight into the sport policy process.

In summary, the analysts of sport policy have at their disposal a rich, challenging and diverse body of theory. Admittedly, almost all theory development in relation to policy analysis has been stimulated by research focused on other, usually more substantial policy sub-sectors. In general, the adaptation of these theoretical frameworks has not proved problematic, but there is certainly scope for theory development and refinement prompted by insights derived from the study of sport policy. The challenge for the coming years is to develop and publicise those insights, and thus to contribute to the refinement of theory.

3

DISCOURSE ANALYSIS AND ITS APPLICATION TO SPORT POLICY ANALYSIS

Joe Piggin

Introduction

We are all discourse analysts. Whether we are reading, debating or writing policy we are attempting to understand the political dynamics at play in its construction and predict the ramifications of its implementation. However, formalised discourse analysis of sport policy requires the application of a theoretical framework, and the selection of a specific method. This chapter offers a way of thinking about discourse in sport policy, and provides methodological considerations for undertaking a research approach that is inherently political. The focus is on the application of discourse analysis as a means of understanding how policy agenda are set and policy decisions (and realities) are produced. First the chapter defines and discusses *discourse as a form of knowledge*. Second, it delineates the theoretical origins of discourse analysis and discusses how a researcher's *understanding of power* will influence the type of analysis undertaken. Third, it highlights *some important principles* when thinking about discourse in public policy and illustrates these by highlighting some of the recent and emerging discourse analyses in the sport policy realm. Fourth, a *range of methodological considerations and techniques* are offered with regard to implementing a study of sport policy discourse. This section also considers the inherently political stance researchers take by undertaking such analysis.

Policy decisions affect both people's opportunities to participate in sport and how we understand the sporting opportunities available to us. As Forester (1993) argues, public policy, 'by patterning social interaction, could … be seen to shape not only the distribution of "who gets what", but the more subtle constitution of ways we learn about and can attend to our concerns, interests and needs' (p. ix). These concerns are of special import for those involved in the sports realm, since there is a wide array of stakeholders competing for finite (and often scarce) resources, and at any moment there exists perceived power imbalances, distrust and a lack of understanding within and between state, voluntary and corporate institutions that are involved in sport. Knowing more about these dynamics will allow policy writers, readers and those involved with sport to understand the complexities involved in sport policy. Further, as an inherently political terrain, sport policy is an important site for stakeholders to challenge or resist potentially debilitating assumptions and decisions, particularly since those with policy-making power often ignore or design knowledge at their convenience (Flyvbjerg, 2001). Potentially debilitating policy decisions that determine such things as resource distribution and status can be challenged and resisted by those unfairly affected. Many scholars attempt to explain these dynamics by studying discourse (Foucault, 1972; Fairclough, 1989; Ball, 1993; Hodge and Kress, 1993; Chalip, 1995; Taylor, 1997; Bacchi, 2000; Wodak and Meyer, 2001).

Discourse as a form of knowledge

Despite often disagreeing about the specific uses and effects of discourse, there is general acknowledgment in academia that discourses are forms of knowledge about the world. These knowledges play a significant role in how we understand the social world, the people within it and how we and others should behave. For example, one of the original writers on discourse, Michel Foucault, explains that what we know about madness (as an example of a discourse) has been:

> constituted by all that has been said in all the statements that named it, divided it up, described it, explained it, traced its developments, indicated its various correlations, judged it, and possibly gave it speech by articulating, in its name, discourses that were to be taken as its own.
>
> (Foucault, 1972, p. 35)

Therefore, a discourse (such as madness, neoliberalism, health promotion or coaching) governs the way a topic can be meaningfully talked about, reasoned about, and it influences how ideas are put into practice. While a discourse produces a way for a topic to be discussed, and defines an acceptable and intelligible way to talk, write and conduct oneself, it also rules out, limits and restricts other ways of talking and conducting oneself. This is not to say that only one discourse is present in each social setting. Indeed, it is the interplay of different discourses that is often of interest for discourse analysts.

Discourse and critical analysis

Sport policy, not unlike other areas of social policy, is a site where struggles over resources, status and identity, occur frequently. Significant problems for policy makers include how to distribute resources (not merely physical resources, but also those such as the granting of legitimacy and status), *and* how to justify to stakeholders vying for these resources that the decisions are the 'correct' or 'best' ones. According to Parsons (1995), policy writing 'involves creating a plausible story which secures the purposes of the plotter" (p. 15). Because these policy stories might unfairly exclude stakeholders or citizens, many scholars believe critical analysis is needed. Chalip (1996) argues critical policy analyses are useful because they furnish interpretations and critiques that can be used by undervalued or excluded stakeholders to challenge debilitating policy assumptions. Similarly, Forester (1993) advocates that a *critical* approach to analysing public policy can assist in understanding the workings of power since 'neither incremental-based or utilitarian [approaches] help us to understand how policy making and policy implementation reshape the lived worlds of actors [or] restructure social worlds in ways that alter actors' opportunities, capacities to act, and self conceptions' (p. 12).

Since the policy terrain is inherently political, its analysis must be undertaken with a methodology that acknowledges and accommodates this. Danziger (1995) writes that policy analysis (and analysts) cannot be unbiased or objective:

Because standards of judgment, canons of evidence, and normative measures are prescribed by his or her professional community, the potential for professional scientific objectivity, political neutrality, or substantive change are, by definition, curtailed significantly ... the givens of any field of activity, are constructed socially and politically ...

(Danziger, 1995, pp. 436–437)

While all policy analysts have a desire (either stated or latent) to improve the effectiveness of policy, these have historically been considered either positivist or post-positivist analyses. As DeLeon (1998) points out, neither of these main approaches are necessarily useful on their own. That is, most people would find it virtually worthless to write public policy without doing some form of quantitative research and similarly would find it impossible to deconstruct a policy using only a positivist framework. Whereas positivist policy analysts have traditionally clung to the idea that 'knowledge would replace politics' (Torgerson, 1986, p. 34), post-positivists acknowledge and examine the crucial role that language and argumentation play in the framing of policy problems and in the assumptions, facts and criteria that generate potential solutions (Danziger, 1995). Schram (1993) argues such a constructivist approach is beneficial because:

[M]ore so than conventional approaches, a post-modern policy analysis offers the opportunity to interrogate assumptions about identity embedded in the analysis and making of public policy, thereby enabling us to rethink and resist questionable distinctions that privilege some identities at the expense of others.

(Schram, 1993, p. 249)

Power and discourse

To undertake a discourse analysis is to make some assumptions about how power operates in society. Popular Western analyses of power tend to posit power as inherently problematic for individual actors. For example, Steven Lukes (2005) asks, 'is it not the supreme exercise of power to get another or others to have the desires you want them to have ...?' (p. 23). This parallels Gramscian sentiments about powerful institutions imposing a 'false consciousness' on citizens. Pierre Bourdieu's (1986) attention was focused on how symbolic power (or 'capital') influences citizens. While each has distinct areas of focus there is significant overlap in their concerns, foremost is how power relations influence rules (policies) in society, the effect these have on individuals, and how individuals and organisations can act despite these rules. While these theorists all provide interesting and useful frameworks with which to analyse power, this chapter proceeds by focusing on Michel Foucault's concept of discourse to explain how power operates through sport policy.

How power operates is the central concern for many discourse analysts. What is created by the workings of power? What are the effects? What resistance occurs? Foucault conceives power existing in numerous forms: 'power must be understood in the first instance as the multiplicity of force relations ... as the process which, through ceaseless struggle and confrontations, transforms, strengthens or reverses [relations of power]' (1978, pp. 92–93). This line of thought is clearly different to an emancipatory understanding of social action, whereby theorists aim 'to liberate human beings from the circumstances that enslave them' (Horkheimer, 1982, p. 244). A Foucauldian approach does not make such claims. Discourse analysis might draw attention to or try to minimise or replace dominating discourses but 'emancipation' is not necessarily total from a Foucauldian perspective. Instead, discourses are ceaselessly reinvented and replaced by others.

Michel Foucault explains that his goal is to 'criticize the working of institutions which appear to be both neutral and independent' (in Rabinow, 1984, p. 4). Foucault's concepts can help policy analysts for various reasons. First, the exercise of power, Foucault argues, 'is a "conduct of conducts" and a management of possibilities' (1994a, p. 341). This is also a fitting definition of public policy from a critical perspective. Questions of discipline and freedom are central to Foucault's theories, and are of great importance for sport policy contexts, where judgements are made about the allocation of resources and criteria of inclusion and exclusion. Second, Foucault's ideas about discourse and power range from governing entire populations to individual action with institutional settings. Third, Foucault's interest in the body and pleasure also usefully inform sport policy analysis, which is of course concerned with ideas about athleticism and human movement, physical education and leisure. Fourth, Foucauldian concepts can be thought of as specific 'tools' with which to investigate and understand particular aspects of sport policy.

Underlying assumptions in policy discourse analysis

There are a multitude of discourses (but some dominate in policy)

Discourse analysis proceeds on the assumption that competing discourses vie for prominence in the writing and implementation of policy. For instance, while crime prevention has at times been used to legitimise investment in government sport funding, it has now lost favour (perhaps because there is little evidence that crime is prevented with increases in funding). Meanwhile, with the ever-expanding literature on the physical health/disease prevention benefits of physical activity, these rationale are now central to the prefaces and introductions of state sport documents, as are statements about national identity and economic benefits to be derived from sport investment.

Some discourses complement each other, some collide

Foucault (1978) writes that 'power operates through ceaseless struggles and confrontations …' (p. 92). Discourse analysts reject the idea of policy making and implementation as a rational and linear process. By examining the underlying assumptions of evidence offered to support policy decisions, the researcher can illuminate problems that are usually not explicitly acknowledged by the policy writers. As Piggin, Jackson and Lewis (2009a, 2009b) point out, evidence used by policy makers is often contradictory, and often clashes with other ways that people make decisions and articulate a policy.

The effects of dominant discourses need to be exposed

Fairclough states 'ideology is most effective when its workings are least visible' (1989, p. 85). Exploring and acknowledging these subtle or hidden shifts in policy is a common practice for discourse analysts. For example, recently, many state sport agencies have engaged in practices that echo wider neoliberal shifts in society, resulting in policy informed by ideas about performance, efficiency and accountability. For instance, Green and Houlihan (2006) argue that recent ideological shifts towards neoliberalism in the Australian and UK sport sectors affect 'the capacities and liberties of NSOs [national sport organisations] to act in ways that might diverge from the "desired directions" of government' (p. 67). Such is the influence of these discourses that they can spread. A study of 'New Public Management' (NPM) impacting on sport policy in Trinidad and Tobago concluded that recent state reforms towards NPM 'bore similarities at the discursive, decisional and practical levels of convergence with those undertaken in several more advanced western countries' (McCree, 2009, p. 475). While of course there will be many positive impacts of changes to management structures, discourse analysts tend to focus on the problematic, hidden aspects of policy decisions.

Marginalised voices/subjugated knowledges should be illuminated

Green and Houlihan (2006) argue the effect of policy is primarily discursive; it changes the possibilities we have for thinking 'otherwise', with inherent power relations hidden within the contours of sport policy debates. Discourse analysts aim to problematise and 'uncover' subtleties, assumptions and apparently common sense ways of organising sport. Indeed rather than considering only policy documents, which are typically written utilising the language of the dominant discourse, marginalised voices should be investigated. In other words, Foucault suggested that, in order to understand what power relations are about, 'we should investigate the forms of resistance' (1994b, p. 329). Shehu and Mokgwathi (2007) encourage scholars to adopt a critical stance towards national sport and recreation policies as they are texts bound to specific meaning and learning, with potential to impact on roles and subjectivities.

Recent studies have attempted to identify alternative knowledges. Piggin, Jackson and Lewis (2009b) argue that policy makers utilise multifarious sources of knowledge in order to construct national sport policy, despite ostensibly being informed by 'evidence'. Green (2004a, 2004b) considers some of these marginalised and alternative voices in English and Canadian sport policy discourse, and asks whether the current structures mean that 'we are in danger of losing sight of "other" meanings attached to sporting activities' (2004a, p. 380). While ways of knowing do not necessarily transform radically in a short period of time, discourse analysts who are concerned with issues of fairness and marginalisation usually hope that the act of researching can build momentum towards new, progressive understandings of previously unfair policies.

Discourses can change

In 1982, Johnson wrote that governments of the future will find it increasingly necessary to limit the 'autonomy' of sport. The extent to which this has occurred has been a central theme in many recent discourse analyses of sport policy. For example Harvey, Thibault and Rail (1995) investigate how the Canadian federal government has adopted a neo-corporatist approach to manage the number of interest groups in both fitness and amateur sport. Adopting a discursive policy analysis, the researchers concluded that pluralism within public policy was ultimately replaced with neo-corporatism (or neoliberalism). Similarly, Bercovitz (1998, 2000) problematises that the seemingly taken-for-granted nature of an 'Active Living' (physical activity) policy in Canada contained hidden political agendas and provided a vehicle for 'the rapid retreat of the welfare state' (2000, p. 19). Also, Green (2006, 2007b) considered how the sport-for-all policies have gradually been eroded in various countries in favour of elite sport priorities.

Power is both oppressive and productive

Power should not be thought of only in a negative sense. Power also produces in that it contributes to achievements and advances in many aspects of society. Foucault writes: 'One should not assume a massive and primal condition of domination, a binary structure with "dominators" on the one side and "dominated" on the other, but rather a multiform production of relations of domination' (Foucault, 1980b, p. 142). It is apparent that while Foucault includes the productive capacities of power relations, it is the oppressive aspects that are most often the concern of policy critics and researchers. For instance, it is common for citizens and various organisations that interact with government agencies to consider themselves subordinated by a system of domination, thus aligning more with a Gramscian, hegemonic understanding of power than a Foucauldian one (see Pringle, 2005; Olssen, 1999).

Resistance is not futile

A discursive approach to policy analysis contends that people and groups are not powerless. Instead, they can be active in and crafting different ways of knowing, performing and challenging instances of domination. Some studies have recently addressed such challenges. In a study focusing specifically on moments where dominant policy is resisted, Sam and Jackson (2004) argue that an emphasis on 'rationalisation' and 'integration' raises a variety of paradoxes that may create opportunities for some previously marginalised groups to voice issues and problems. In another study, Piggin (2010) suggests that despite feeling powerless in the face of government sports policy, citizens can influence public policy through 'public' criticism.

Eschewing pretence of perfect solutions to social problems, the goal of studying discourses is not to try to eradicate power relations. Since discourses transmit and produce power, they reinforce social arrangements, but they can also be used to expose power relations (Foucault, 1978). Researchers can highlight areas of inequity and unfairness in a discourse, making it possible to act against it. For Foucault, there is no such thing as absolute power, for he claims that where there is power there is resistance.

The positivist assumption of a distinct measurable reality (which much evidence-based public policy is based on) is a popular target for analysts using discourse. Smith and Leech (2010) show that individuals involved with the implementation of sport policy do not necessarily comply in the way policy makers would have intended. Teachers who were required to provide statistical evidence of their sport and physical education teaching sometimes manipulated data in order to assemble evidence in support of their achievement of a self-assessment score that would 'look good' in their school's prospectus, and, therefore, satisfy the priorities of their head teacher. While this may not be considered a noble form of resistance to dominant policy systems, it is illustrative of the idea that there are many types of resistance.

Discourses transcend individuals

While policy writers might hold a certain amount of legitimate authority, they are only in the position because of their unique context. Markula and Pringle (2006) explain that Foucault's position on the workings of power is such that powerful individuals, groups and nations 'do not arrive at their position because they have power, but they become influential due to the contingent workings ... and tactical usages of "discourses"' (p. 34). Therefore the analysis of power:

> should not concern itself with power at the level of conscious intention or decision ... it should refrain from posing a labyrinthine and unanswerable question: Who then has power and what has he in mind? ... Let us ask, instead, how things work at the level of ongoing subjugation ... which subject[s] our bodies, govern[s] our gestures, [and] dictate[s] our behaviours.
>
> (Foucault, 1980a, p. 97)

The power of discourses comes from the fact they are used (or put into practice) by individuals or groups. Sam and Jackson (2006) illustrate how individuals are not always powerful by considering how certain practices can shape New Zealand sport policy. They argue that despite a New Zealand sport policy Taskforce 'giving the impression that it had voiced the shared beliefs, mutual understandings, and common interpretations of the problems in New Zealand sport' (p. 383), these beliefs do not necessarily manifest themselves in successful and popular policies, since institutional constraints significantly limit the agency of those involved in its production.

A focus on governing processes

Many recent analyses of sport policy discourse are informed by a concern about the mechanics of governing a population (such as citizens of a state, or participants in a sport). As such, many researchers have utilised ideas about governmentality (Foucault, 1994c; Rose, 1990), whereby a population is 'the object that government must take into account in all its observations and knowledge in order to govern effectively' (Foucault, 1994c, p. 217). Governmentality is concerned with how a population should 'be ruled, how strictly, by whom, to what end, [and] by what methods' (Foucault, 1994c, p. 202). Rose explains this process as 'interlocking (although not necessarily synergistic) apparatuses for the programming of various dimensions of life ... through which we are urged, incited, encouraged, exhorted and motivated to act' (1990: p. xxii). Green and Houlihan (2005a) discuss governmentality in the context of UK and Australian National Governing Bodies of Sport (NGBs) and argue that some neoliberal reforms have favoured the pursuit of particular goals.

> In recent years, the 'particular objectives' for the sport of athletics have closely mirrored the importance placed upon elite success set out in the Lottery Strategy 2002–05, which stated that 'winning medals is just as important as getting people to take part in sport'. Governing processes such as these ensure that citizens believe in 'a kind of regulated freedom'.
>
> (Rose, 1990, p. 174)

Method

What do we analyse?

Discourse analysts pay attention to one of two themes in their analyses of sport policy. The most popular method is to examine the discourses within policy, such as articulations of healthism, nationalism, economic philosophies (in particular neoliberalism), and gendered or ageist discourses to name a few. The other is to examine the discursive processes through which policy is formed, and focuses on discourses contributing to the policy process itself, such as notions of transparency, efficiency and fairness.

Broadly, Scheurich (1997) provides four dimensions around which to guide the discourse analysis. These include an analysis of the social construction of a policy problem, an investigation of how policy choices are shaped by social regularities (or rules of formation), an examination of a discourse's ability to define solutions, and an analysis of the legitimatisation process and effect of the new discourse. It seems common practice for discourse analysts to focus on and develop one of these themes through the research process. For example Piggin, Jackson and Lewis (2009a) focus on 'games of truth' and 'transparency' in order to understand the definition of policy solutions, while Green and Houlihan (2006) focus on disciplinary effects of sport policy. Determining an aspect (or aspects) of policy discourse to problematise is an important step, since the entire network of power relations cannot be explored in detail. Therefore, it is useful to consider which aspects the researcher believes is most problematic/marginalising in terms of power relations. Indeed, the final theme/s analysed are not necessarily those from the beginning since there are often movements and discoveries throughout the research process.

The researcher usually arrives at the research project with a predetermined interest in a particular policy and discourse. From this point, in order to investigate a theme or discourse in detail, the researcher should consider *both* more and less overt discursive practices can be illuminated. Thus, it is both times of conflict and 'common sense' that critical researchers use as sites for investigation, since the 'connections between the use of language and the exercise of power are often not clear to people, yet appear on closer examination to be vitally important to the workings of power' (Fairclough, 1995, p. 54). Policy writers do not necessarily intend to mislead or be unfair through policy. As Gee (2001) points out, we 'always assume, unless absolutely proven otherwise, that everyone has "good reasons" and makes "deep sense" in terms of their own socio-culturally-specific ways of talking, listening, writing, reading, acting interacting, valuing, believing and feeling' (p. 79). As with other research approaches, it is important to 'ring-fence' the scope of the study, while simultaneously acknowledging new perspectives may emerge throughout the research process.

How do we analyse?

Discourse analysis, like all research, faces numerous challenges to be successful. These include the researcher addressing issues of incorporating text, context *and* discourse, the selection of texts, deciding how to analyse the data, making a highly subjective analysis persuasive, and determining the best way to write it up (Phillips and Hardy, 2002).

As a starting point, it is useful to consult the policy documents that relate to the issue being explored. Fairclough (1995) sums up the relevance of texts, such as policy documents, in the (re)production of dominance when he wrote that any text is always simultaneously constitutive of social identities, social relations and systems of knowledge and belief, as well as constituted by them. Therefore, policy documents themselves are a useful starting point to identify dominant discourses.

Depending on the focus of the research, a range of data collection techniques are available. Of course, since public policies (and their effects) are articulated in many ways, a wide range of sites might be useful to explore, including speeches, media interviews, policy press releases, media presentations, electronic media, talk-back radio, letters to the editors of magazines and newspapers. Also, semi-structured interviews and participant observation can also be useful. The discourse analyst must consider what texts are the most important in constructing the object of analysis, which texts are available for analysis, and what texts are produced by the most powerful (or marginalised) actors.

In *choosing the particular sites* for the research, Phillips and Hardy (2002) have some helpful suggestions. These include asking: Does the research site have characteristics that make it likely to produce useful results? Has a good source of discursive data presented itself? Has a 'crisis' occurred that will reveal insight into discursive activity? Once the researcher has decided on the terrain for analysis, questions can begin to be asked about the discourses. Of course, these questions will be informed by the researcher's specific interest in the policy area. A critical exposition of the researcher's assumptions can be useful throughout the analysis. As there is no set of criteria that must be followed, here is a variety of questions which might be useful in developing an analysis.

Policy production

- What are the political antecedents to the policy?
- Which organisation/s ratified the policy's construction?
- Who wrote the policy? What were the mechanics of its production?
- What explicit and subtle reasons are used to justify the policy?
- How are causes or a problem conveyed? Who is identified as causing, and able to fix the problem?
- Who is the intended audience of the policy?
- What style of language is used to communicate ideas?
- What values can be ascribed to the type of language used?
- What role do various organisations have in implementing the policy?
- How are individuals/groups framed? Who is bestowed with authority, and who is not?
- How forceful are declarations/suggestions?
- How are metaphors, synecdoche and numbers employed?
- To what extent do stories/narratives frame the policy in different ways at different times?
- How are identities constructed throughout the policy background?
- What elements of the policy are emphasised/marginalised/omitted? Why?
- How is evidence used in the policy? To what extent is the evidence persuasive?
- What sources of knowledge (aside from statistical evidence) does the policy utilise?

Policy dissemination

- How is the policy manifested into programmes and what is the effect of these?
- How is the policy measured?
- How is the policy defended?
- What are the ramifications of targets not being met?
- Who is able to criticise? What is criticised? What are the assumed consequences of criticism?
- Is there coherence between the policy and other texts, such as press releases, advertising and interviews?
- To what extent do discourses conflict and contradict one another? What are the implications of this? Whose interests are served by the deployment of certain discourses?
- What discourses are created or opposed throughout the policy process? How does the policy sustain/disrupt/question existing structures of power?

Considerations in analysis

During the data collection and analysis phases of policy discourse analysis, the researcher needs to keep in mind a variety of factors or questions that inform the analysis. First, the post-positivist framework that discourse analysis tends to utilise assumes that any data gathered will be partial, situated and relative. Acknowledging this will mean that policy makers (and citizens) also engage with many other discourses at the same time. Of course, the entire range of discourses that contribute to the entire corpus of sport and recreation policy rhetoric could never be covered. Just as policy makers might be unaware of various discourses at work by others involved in sport and recreation, stakeholders are rarely granted access to meetings, discussions, conflicts, confrontations and editing processes that contribute to final articulation of a policy. Thus, only 'parts' of the sphere of policy production can be analysed.

Second, an important concern is determining who chooses the discourse that should be used to minimise unfair domination. Favouring one interpretation over another might merely result in more unfair domination. Giving some thought to this throughout the research process is important; asking how *should* policy be written?

Third, it is important to consider the day-to-day effects of policy discourse on citizens' experience with sport. It is apparent many of the aforementioned studies have an interest in 'alternative' voices, though often these do not explicitly examine opportunities for the enactment of these voices in sport policy contexts. Foucault argues that studies of power could only take place 'on the basis of daily struggles at the grassroots level ... where the concrete nature of power became visible' (1994a, p. 116). Given the recent economic climate which has lead to cutbacks to spending on sport and leisure provision in various countries, there is scope for analysis of the discourses that arise with the turbulent terrain. In March 2009, for example, the UK government implemented a policy that gave free swimming pool use to people aged 16 and under or 60 and over in England. However, in 2010, the government ended the scheme. Indeed, this is a site where there will be daily struggle for citizens who did use such opportunities, and knowing more about their experiences would surely assist in future policy decisions. Similarly, the apparent increasing prominence of corporations promoting physical activity and healthy diets is worthy of analysis from a governmental perspective.

Fourth, Henry, Amara, Al-Tauqi and Lee (2005) write that Foucauldian notions of discursive power exercised by those who control the means of policy expression and discussion are difficult to accommodate in comparative analysis if one holds the hard-line view that discourse is situated. However, Henry *et al.* argue that as researchers, policy writers and lecturers we do work across language communities on the notion of nearest approximations most of the time. Indeed, since there appears to be a homogenising of sport policy discourses in international sport with particular regard to many aspects of Olympism and professional sport, research may well be useful for comparative purposes.

Concluding comments

Making policy recommendations on the basis of discourse analysis is usually done with relatively polite suggestions about recommendations or reconsiderations of public policy goals or statements. This is perhaps due in part to the expected style of academic journal articles. However, there is space beyond research articles that can be explored to suggest change. Indeed, working with the organisations or policy makers who were the subject of study is one way of creating change, as is promoting the findings through media interviews and articles.

The ongoing problem for undervalued and excluded stakeholders is to address how to effectively resist debilitating policies and practices. As an inherently political endeavour, discourse analysis is one element of resistance, since it can expose and illuminate unfair practices. However, it is not necessarily sufficient as the only form of resistance. Researchers would do well to consider what can be done with the discourse. Can it be changed? If so, how could this be accomplished?

An interest in analysing discourse comes from an interest in power relations. The researcher should ask: which ideas dominate? Which ideas are marginalised? What are the results? By analysing these elements, we attempt to make policy fairer. Understanding both the discourses that inform sport and recreation policy and the ways in which its public policies are argued about and contested will enable a citizenry to be less constrained than they might otherwise be.

4

META-EVALUATION, ANALYTIC LOGIC MODELS AND THE ASSESSMENT OF IMPACTS OF SPORT POLICIES

Shushu Chen, Ian Henry and Ling-Mei Ko

Introduction

The period since the 1970s has seen a considerable growth in policy evaluation research in volume, diversity and sophistication. The major dimensions of such change may be summarised under five categories.

- Evaluation has moved from simple input–output approaches, which were primarily concerned with efficiency (cost per unit of output) often based on statistical association, to explanations that look 'inside the policy-making black box' to develop causal explanations of how particular policy interventions can bring about the changes desired (Leeuw and Vaessen, 2009).
- There has been an increasing recognition in social policy research that classical evaluation approaches associated with experimental logic are often inappropriate for evaluating change in social contexts in which the open system nature of those contexts militates against isolation of the impact of a particular 'treatment'. Thus, in such complex social settings, the context-specific nature of outcomes needs to be understood (Pawson, 2006; Pawson and Tilley, 1997).
- Related to this recognition of the limitations of experimental method has been the development of critical or social realist ontologies (Archer, 1995; Bhaskar, 1978, 1986) which have promoted 'depth realist' explanations of the causal influence of real social structures. Such structures, though not amenable to direct observation, exert causal influences whose effects may be observed. Pawson and Tilley (1997) codify a realist approach in their promotion of 'realistic' evaluation, where they contrast this with the experimental, but also pragmatic, and constructivist models of evaluation, arguing for an approach that explains policy change by reference to the operation of 'real' social mechanisms and how these produce outcomes in specific contexts or types of context.
- These advances at the conceptual level as to what constitutes an adequate explanation of policy impact, have been accompanied by the promotion of greater precision in terms of specifying both intended and actual outcomes of policy intervention, in particular in the case of the former, through the growing prominence of the use of analytic logic models (Cooksy, Gill and Kelly, 2001), and in the latter, developments associated with the operationalising of impact through assessing additionality (Luukkonen, 2000).

- Finally, advances in understanding and application of techniques of aggregation and synthesis of data and policy explanations have taken place in the field of meta-evaluation such that not only statistical aggregation of findings (meta-analysis) but also synthesis of qualitative claims explaining outcomes (meta-synthesis) have been developed in ways that allow the strength of explanation of collections of studies to be assessed.

The growth of both academic and policy-related interest in the analysis of sport policy has also grown alongside these developments. The aim of this chapter therefore is to illustrate and evaluate three of the key developments in policy evaluation and their application to the sports field by reference to existing studies. These are analytic logic models, meta-evaluation and the estimation of additionality.

The application of logic models in sport policy analysis

The use of logic models came to prominence in the 1990s and 2000s with the growing emphasis on evidence-based policy practice (Head, 2009). It is used widely across government, not-for-profit organisations and profit-based entrepreneurial activity (Dodd-Butera and Broderick, 2011; Jordan, 2010; Lenihan, 2011), providing a means to articulate and illustrate the intended relationship between *policy content* and *inputs*, *activities* (throughputs), *outputs* (the immediate products of the activities), *outcomes* (longer-term effects) and *impacts* (the intended and unintended consequences of the policy initiative).

As defined by Conrad and Randolph (1999), a logic model is a 'graphic representation of a program that describes the program's essential components and expected accomplishments and conveys the logical relationship between these components and their outcomes' (p. 18). It is a picture of how a programme works and to what end, with the provision in the case of analytic logic models of a theory or theories of change.

Logic models are used for the purpose of programme (or project) design and planning, when intended linkages between inputs and activities and longer-term goals are open to multilevel stakeholders and evaluators. It helps to build up a shared understanding of the programme concepts and approach. They are also used for programme implementation, the developing of an action plan against intended goals. Using the logic model to identify and collect the needed data in order to monitor and improve programming (if necessary). Finally, they are used for programme evaluation and reporting where the model provides a set of measures against which elements may be reported. By developing a logic model, with an aim of learning and programme improvement, key results (positive and negative) of a particular programme can be presented.

The structure and key elements of a logic model

The elements that go to make up the logic model vary slightly in terminology and content from one author to another, but perhaps classically incorporate the six elements identified in Table 4.1.

As we have suggested, a number of authors employ different modifications of this framework (see e.g. Stake, 1967; Stufflebeam, 1971). For example, Taylor-Powell (1999) conflates *inputs* and *activities/throughputs*. There are good reasons, however, for retaining these as separate aspects of a logic model, since not only what activities are undertaken, but also how the activities are provided may be critical to the achievement of intended outcomes. Thus, if we consider a logic model underpinning an intervention to promote the engagement of young girls in sports activities, in certain types of community, it will be important to have the programme delivered

Table 4.1 Key elements of a logic model

Key elements	What are they?
Context/environment	These will include contextual factors such as the size and nature of the problem; the political, economic, social and organisational context relevant to the programme; the objectives of the programme which have been set out by stakeholders.
Inputs/resources	The inputs refer to the financial, human, and organisational resources provided to address the policy problem.
Activities (throughputs)	The throughputs refer to the kinds of actions which have been taken by policy implementers. These incorporate both what is done (in terms of activities undertaken), and how these activities are undertaken since these may be critical to success. For example, activities aimed at increasing participation in sport for young girls from conservative and traditional communities may, for a variety of reasons, be effective only when these activities are delivered by female leaders as coaches.
Outputs	The outputs summarise what direct and immediate results of inputs and activities are, such as numbers of participants attracted, regularity of their participation, and so on.
Outcomes	The outcomes refer to subsequent changes in behaviour triggered by delivering the programme, which can be divided into *short-term* and *long-term* outcomes as it may continue for many years after a project has been completed. For example, specific changes may include changes in participants' skills, behaviours, sense of self-efficacy and propensity to act in certain ways.
Impact	The broader *intended* and *unintended* changes which occur in organisations or communities as a consequence of the programme/project.

by female leaders. In effect female leadership may be a necessary, though not sufficient, condition of success, since it provides role models for the girls themselves, and reassures parents from conservative communities that concerns about aspects of required 'modesty' will not be infringed. Simply providing the *'activities'* themselves in such social contexts may be unlikely to result in the desired changes to girls' (and as they grow older) to young women's behaviours. How the activities are delivered and by whom may be a critical success factor.

Analytic logic models can be more than a programming tool

Recently, a question has been raised in relation to the extent of the effectiveness of the logic model framework. In order to answer this question, it is important to make a distinction between, on the one hand, the descriptive outline of the stages of policy development and implementation, and on the other the specification of the causes of changes, which in effect represent implicit and/or explicit assumptions underpinning the model.

In respect of the role of logic models, one can identify two main different types: the *descriptive* logic model and the *analytic* logic model. A *descriptive logic model* focuses on simply presenting and describing the above key elements in chronological order. One of its functions is to map out a proposed programme that helps stakeholders and evaluators visualise and understand, at a very basic level, how financial and human investments represent a precursor to achieving intended programme goals. *Analytic logic models*, by contrast, highlight causal relationships between inputs, activities, outcomes and impacts which may thus be subject to evaluation. In effect, theories of change (or conceptual frameworks) are built into analytic models such that the reasons for the desired change being achieved can be tested and evaluated in ways that can contribute to future policy and practice. This function provides rich explanation of the reasons for exactly which types of inputs or resources can contribute to the change desired. It also identifies the problems or issues that are addressed by the programme, and provides a rationale for selecting certain solution strategies and providing potential activities.

An example of a descriptive logic model for a project relating to HIV/AIDS education through sport is given below (see Figure 4.1), and its more developed equivalent, an analytic logic model, is provided to illustrate the difference between the two types (see Figure 4.2). This is not taken from a specific case but is simply used here to illustrate the mechanics (and some of the limitations) of developing and applying both types of model. Figure 4.1 merely outlines the flow of events anticipated – from provision of AIDS education through sport, to enhanced knowledge, to intentions to modify behaviour, to reduced infection rates.

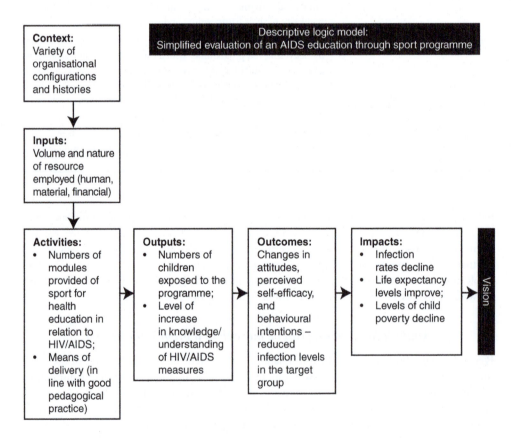

Figure 4.1 An example of a descriptive logic model

Figure 4.2, however, makes explicit the assumptions on which the expectations of change are premised. The principal assumptions/theoretical premises might be defined as follows:

1 Young people are likely to engage with education through sports and games more enthusiastically than through traditional educational methods. Of course we know that this will not be true for all children (some children are alienated by sport), or for all sports (competitive games may be alienating for some children where they have little chance of 'success').

2 Developing self-efficacy through sport can enhance self-efficacy in wider social contexts. Perceived self-efficacy relates to peoples' beliefs about their capacities to produce effects – in short, their perception that by their own efforts they may be able to affect their own lives. Teaching sporting skills can produce high levels of perceived self-efficacy (if appropriate positive experiences of sport are provided) and this is the claimed mechanism here. However, such causal claims need to be tested or challenged in terms of internal logic or empirical evidence. In this case for example, negative experiences may produce the opposite where in competitive sport the individual perceives that no matter how hard they practice they will not be able to affect the sporting outcome. In addition, it is by no means clear in the literature that enhancing self-efficacy in sport will result in enhanced self-efficacy in other domains (Biddle, Hagger, Chatzisarantis and Lippke, 2007).

3 It is further assumed that improved knowledge and understanding on the part of the young people targeted will increase the likelihood of (intended) behavioural change. While one

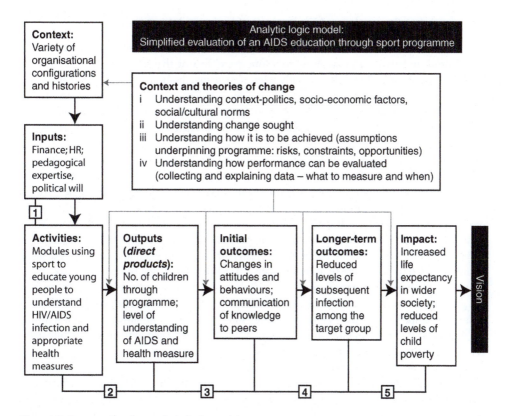

Figure 4.2 An example of an analytic logic model

might argue that improved knowledge and understanding of sexual health matters will be a necessary condition of behavioural change, it is not necessarily a sufficient condition for such change for all individuals. The availability of resources through which to implement behavioural change (for example, the availability of condoms, or of clean needles for drug users) may well also be required.

4   Behavioural change will reduce levels of infection and thus increase life expectancy. Here the assumption is that the key behaviours in transforming HIV/AIDS infection have been identified, and knowledge about such behaviours transmitted during the education through sport programmes.

5   Higher parental life expectancy will reduce child poverty. Here, there is an assumption that a major cause of child poverty is the lack of an adult/parent to provide care/shelter and some financial resource for children in societies with a high adult mortality rate through AIDS, though this may be only one factor in the production of child poverty, even in societies in which HIV/AIDS is prevalent.

Thus, we can see that the underlying logic and the supporting theoretical assumptions are made explicit and can be subject to challenge in the articulation of the logic model in complex projects/programmes such as that described above. The assumptions are laid bare in the process of articulating the model, and the potential for developing measures against which reporting and evaluation might take place is clearly evident.

Strengths and limitations of logic model approaches

The key advantage of the logic model approach is that it distils detailed descriptions of the assumptions underlying a programme to a 'one-page' format that can be easily read and followed (Cooksy et al., 2001). It explicitly depicts conceptualisation of each step of the whole chain, and helps to demonstrate a logical flow from a belief structure to related interventions, to outcomes, and then to impacts. In addition, the process of developing conceptualisation of the theory of the intervention is valuable as it helps to leverage greater insight into programme operations and effectiveness.

Supporters of logic models believe that the process of collaboratively developing logic models together helps the often multilevel stakeholders and programme evaluators (at the beginning of the evaluation process) to reach a common understanding of the programme in order to define more clearly its vision and objectives, and to envisage whether the designed actions would accomplish the goals. It is useful in the sense that it is a mutual educational process which may help to avoid misuse of the theory by the programme operators (Patton, 1997).

Furthermore, having all the components clearly articulated in graphic form helps evaluators to link theory to practice and to accommodate changes in knowledge (Alter and Murty, 1997). The planned operation theory in the logic models may change in practice due, for instance, to the growing availability of resources, or the emergence of knowledge of unintended effects. It is therefore important for the evaluators and key stakeholders to constantly revisit and scrutinise the defined assumptions in line with ongoing activities and achieved outcomes along the delivery process, making changes to the model if necessary.

Although the logic model approaches provide benefits, as identified above, concerns in relation to its application have also been raised. For example, as Yin (1998) suggests, efforts need to be made in order to make the logic models more clearly articulated analytic strategies. He emphasises that most current logic models do not specify clearly enough the substantive processes between inputs, throughputs, outputs and outcomes. Clearly, without this articulation, logic models are simply a sequential pattern of events that do not aid understanding of how outcomes are actually produced.

When it comes to practice, some operational issues have also been identified. For example, debates around the costing of developing logic models have emerged, with some commentators suggesting that the process can take up a lot of resources (e.g. Bickman, 1989), while others have argued that the cost can be justified by benefits to programme stakeholders above and beyond their use to the evaluators (Patton, 1978), and that it is actually a way of avoiding costly evaluation in situations where evaluation efforts will not be made if there are unlikely to be observed effects as identified by the logic models (Wholey, 1994). Another concern, as C.H. Weiss (1997) has pointed out, is that logic models may depict rigid statements that limit the programme's responsiveness to new information. In particular, programme evaluators may only concentrate on those listed outcomes and thus ignore unintended effects that are not part of the programme theory.

Furthermore, it is important to recognise that different stakeholders may have different logics. Given that a social intervention often involves different levels of stakeholders (national, regional and sub-regional) each with their own interests and targets, there is a need to understand the way that different stakeholders view the world (and the policy problem, its intervention and so on). Adopting a single logic model may thus deny the possibility of other views. Nevertheless, debates around establishing a logic model for a particular programme may well serve to bring to the surface underlying differences in assumptions, and even desired outcomes between different stakeholders.

Notwithstanding these limitations, logic models have significant potential as integrative frameworks that not only combine pattern matching and time-series analysis techniques (Yin, 1998), but also provide a unique tool in explicating underlying causal relationships in a simple picture, hence its usefulness for case study evaluation (e.g. Mulroy and Lauber, 2004; Yin, 2009).

Meta-evaluation and policy analysis

Meta-evaluation is an increasingly recognised approach for evaluating a number of evaluation studies. It initially emerged as a result of evaluators being required to appraise their own evaluations (Stufflebeam, 1974), particularly in the education area, such as in the Advanced Technological Education (ATE) Evaluation project described by Gullickson, Wingate, Lawrenz and Coryn (2006). Nevertheless, the number of meta-evaluation studies appearing in the literature is not substantial, despite a growing recognition of the need for evaluation of evaluations. This was highlighted by Nilsson and Hogben (1983) in the early 1980s, and has been further emphasised in the past decades by a number of commentators, for example, Cooksy (1999), Scott-Little, Hamann and Jurs (2002), Bustelo (2002), Madzivhandila, Griffith, Fleming and Nesamvuni (2010). In addition, some studies entitled 'meta-evaluations' are rather more in the nature of cross-case analysis rather than meta-evaluations (e.g. Ashworth, Cebulla, Greenberg and Walker, 2004; Russ-Eft and Preskill, 2008).

The concept of 'meta-evaluation' was first introduced by Michael Scriven, writing in the late 1960s (Scriven, 1969), and was subsequently developed in his *Evaluation Thesaurus* (Scriven, 1991), in which he lays emphasis on 'The evaluation of evaluations – [and] indirectly, the evaluation of evaluators' (Scriven, 1991, p. 228).

Subsequent definitions of meta-evaluation include for instance that of Patton (1997, p. 193), for whom meta-evaluation is the answer to the following questions: 'Was the evaluation well done? Is it worth using? Did the evaluation meet the profession's standards and principles?' Bustelo (2002) suggests that meta-evaluation is a systematic gathering, analysis and assessment of a predetermined set of evaluation processes, while Stufflebeam, based on his experience in leading the development of professional standards for evaluations in the US, defines meta-evaluation as:

> the process of delineating, obtaining, and applying descriptive information and judgmental information – about the utility, feasibility, propriety, and accuracy of an evaluation and its systematic nature, competent conduct, integrity / honesty, respectfulness, and social responsibility – to guide the evaluation and / or report its strengths and weaknesses.
>
> (Stufflebeam, 2001, p. 185)

The application of meta-evaluations

The demand for evidence-based policy/practice followed on from the development of the evidence-based medicine approach to clinical practice in the early 1990s in which the demand for clinical decisions was to be based on the best available scientific evidence rather than intuition. This philosophy was quickly adopted and adapted to other fields, reinforcing an emphasis on quantitative rather than qualitative analysis and positivistic methods. The evidence-based practice movement also reinforced the need for scrutiny of the quality of evidence and thus the demand for evaluators to ensure the quality of their methods and analysis. The prominence of meta-evaluation was a product of this movement since it could provide recommendations in relation to how evaluation studies should be designed to produce technically adequate, useful and cost-effective results. In addition, the conducting of meta-evaluation serves to enhance the accountability of evaluators themselves, controlling potential evaluator bias, and increasing evaluation credibility.

It is important to distinguish between different types (forms and functions) of meta-evaluation. Figure 4.3 seeks to clarify the distinction between the related terms of meta-evaluation, meta-analysis, meta-synthesis and quality assurance in the form of evaluation of evaluations. The diagram incorporates a basic distinction between, on the one hand, evaluation synthesis (the synthesis of quantitative, or qualitative or mixed evidence of outcomes of particular policies/interventions), and on the other, assessment of the process of evaluation adopted (the ontological and epistemological foundations of approaches adopted, internal logic, methods employed, treatment of data and robustness of conclusions). A comprehensive and rigorous meta-evaluation will be required to address both evaluation of process and synthesis of outcomes.

An example of a meta-evaluation of sport policy is provided by the London 2012 Meta-evaluation commissioned by the Department of Culture, Media and Sport, the first three reports of which outline the scope and methodology adopted (Grant Thornton, ECORYS and Centre for Olympic Studies and Research Loughborough University, 2011b, 2011c, 2012). The study, which is reputed to be the largest study to date of legacies of a mega-event, seeks to evaluate and synthesise the results of the evaluations of individual projects or programmes that are a product of London's hosting of the 2012 Olympic Games.

The approach adopted in this study illustrates the potential but also a number of the practical difficulties in applying the meta-evaluation approach. The study as a whole is premised on a logic model designed to capture the intended legacy outcomes from the Games, and employs methods consistent with governmental advice on policy evaluation (Government Social Research Unit, 2007; HM Treasury, 2003) and requirements from the Department for Culture, Media and Sport (DCMS) in terms specifically of the assessment of legacy (Department for Culture, Media and Sport, 2008a).

Reports 1 and 2 in the study (Grant Thornton *et al.*, 2011b, 2011c) outline the scope, research questions, strategy and methods adopted. The study aims to synthesise into a single

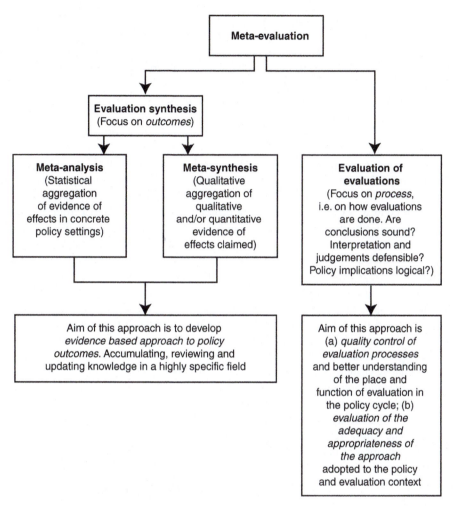

Figure 4.3 A comprehensive meta-evaluation graph

over-arching study 'the findings of individual "project-level" evaluations – commissioned out-side of the meta-evaluation study – in order to provide a comprehensive initial evaluation of the additionality, outputs, results, impacts and associated benefits of the investment in the Games' (Grant Thornton, ECORYS and Centre for Olympic Studies and Research Loughborough University, 2011a, p. 5). The four principal legacy themes or impacts identified for evaluation are: sport; the economy; community engagement; and the regeneration of East London. In each of these areas:

Evaluations will … be synthesised using a common set of output, result and outcome indicators, in order to answer a core set of research questions, paint a picture of the activ-ity underway across each legacy theme and aggregate the impacts wherever possible. This 'bottom up' research approach will be supplemented with a combination of:

- Analysis of management information data, monitoring reports and case studies, par-ticularly for major projects lacking evaluation;

- 'Top down' analysis of secondary data from National Statistics and established surveys, in some cases involving the inclusion of additional questions to aid the interpretation of the drivers of 'high level' trends;
- Economic modelling to assess wider and longer term economic impacts, including effects on nations and regions outside London;
- Limited primary research of different types, including both survey work and a programme of consultations.

(Grant Thornton *et al.*, 2011a: p. 6)

Among the points to emphasise here is that meta-analysis which broadly attempts to aggregate the effect size of the impact of particular interventions, while useful in the aggregation of data on effect sizes in randomised control studies prevalent in the medical field, is inappropriate in this kind of context. The synthesis is thus a matter of integrating material from 'top-down' data with 'bottom-up', project-level evaluation data. To take a concrete example, an intended legacy of the Games was that it would inspire greater levels of participation in sport and physical activity. National level cross-sectional data on participation across time from the Taking Part Survey developed by DCMS and the Active People Survey developed by Sport England provide a picture of participation using different operational measures of participation in sport. This can be compared with data on the impact of individual projects or programmes that have developed or perhaps intensified as a result of the winning of the bid to host the 2012 Games. Bottom-up evaluations are much more likely to reveal what types of intervention are effective in leveraging additional participation in sport and why they are successful, since they can incorporate qualitative analysis of the project and its impact. However, the rigour and relevance of both top-down and bottom-up evaluations in terms of, for example, transparency, credibility, rigour and accuracy need to be appraised before inclusion in the overall evaluation.

Figure 4.4 demonstrates the nature of the strategy adopted, which will involve the detailed appraisal of the nature and quality of the monitoring and management information systems, and of the evaluation of individual projects and programmes. It will also incorporate attempts to estimate in quantitative terms the impact of the Games on participation levels, not by meta-analysis but rather by an intelligent synthesis of the data.

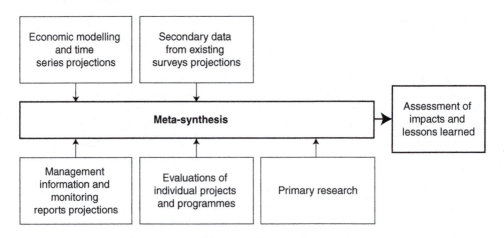

Figure 4.4 Meta-synthesis strategy

Source: adapted from Grant Thornton *et al.* (2011a, p. 6)

At the time of writing (Report 4 is about to be published), a major concern is with reconciling the fact that top-down, national-level studies indicate a fairly flat profile for sports participation (with little or no indication of increased participation from the period before the London bid was initiated, to 2011, though this does not include the immediate post-Games period) and the evidence of bottom-up data from individual (and sometimes quite large) interventions that suggests that these projects have provoked significant increases in participation. Several explanations might be mooted to reconcile such data. First, it is unclear whether participation in new projects represents *substitution* for other forms of participation which thus does not result in increases in overall levels of participation. Second, there may be displacement if the new 'Olympic initiatives' replaced other initiatives that would otherwise have been provided. Third, in many instances such projects may impact on those who already participate in sport, intensifying their rate of participation but not increasing the numbers of participants significantly. Where the project is intended to bring in new participants, this attraction of existing participants may be described as a form of *leakage*. Fourth, the national data from the *Active People* and *Taking Part* surveys only capture adult participation (for those aged 16 or more), while the growth in participation may have been greatest among younger people. For this reason the UK government has decided to lower the age range for which data are sought (and incidentally also to merge the two national surveys into a single data source).

'Additionality' and related concepts in the assessment of impact

Of course, in order to assess the legacy of the 2012 Games for London and the UK, an assessment is required of the extent to which the staging of the Olympic Games in London produced inputs, throughputs, outputs and in particular outcomes that would not otherwise have occurred. In other words an assessment of the net impact of the Games requires an assessment of additionality.

The concept of additionality originally came from the evaluation of innovation and technology policy in which a justification for public support for technology development in private companies was needed to demonstrate that public funds did not simply displace private corporate investment in R&D, but was additional to that which would have happened anyway (Buisseret, Cameron and Georghiou, 1995). The framework of additionality was developed and refined in the UK in the early 1980s (Luukkonen, 2000). In practical terms, additionality has become one of the key concepts employed in public sector policy evaluation studies, together with, for instance, general impacts, effectiveness, efficiency and value for money (English Partnerships, 2008; HM Treasury, 2003).

In policy terms, the focus of a concern with additionality is on distinguishing the *net* impact of a project or programme; that is, what additional impacts (and outputs/outcomes) were achieved exclusively as a result of the programme/project rather than those impacts/outcomes that would have occurred anyway. This is a critical issue for a number of reasons. First of all, in terms of the validity of findings, the final assessment of the impacts created by a particular intervention does not stand up to scrutiny if only the *gross* impacts were captured. Without assessing additionality it is not clear what the intervention is adding over and above what would have happened anyway. As a result, it might present a misleading picture of the value of a programme owing to the fact that only the direct impacts of a programme are measured, and the wider impacts, or how the project may have impacted on other activities, are not taken into account. In addition, the process of teasing out the additionality of an intervention helps programme/ initiative developers and policy makers to gain a better understanding of all stages of an intervention's life cycle, to make a comparison between actual achievements and the objectives of a programme, and to thereby identify unintentional outputs/outcomes.

Overall, the process of defining, or calculating/estimating additionality is crucial to maxim-- ise the impacts of an intervention, and to ensure it delivers real results. At the end of the process, it draws lessons from the evaluated programme to inform the work of stakeholders, and also the development and evaluation of future similar projects.

Measuring additionality

English Partnerships (2008) provides practical guidance on the basic information of how to take into account the additionality of intervention with the purpose of ensuring the net impact could be assessed. The formula from Table 4.2 displays how to assess the net impact, and also presents how to calculate the additionality of the intervention. Here, the application of the additionality formula does not focus on precise calculation of every element, but does require clarity about the likely scale and nature of an intervention's additional impacts.

Estimation of the net impact involves adjustments to be made for *leakage, displacement, substi- tution* and *multiplier effects*. The first step of calculating additionality is to set out the counterfactual scenario, which means what would be the case if its antecedent were not true; in other words, what would have happened if the intervention had not gone ahead. For example, when cal- culating the impacts boosted by the UK hosting the London 2012 Games, the counterfactual scenario is defined as what would have happened without the London 2012 Games having taken place. The counterfactual scenario has two dimensions: (a) the policy counterfactual; (b) the outcome counterfactual.

(a) *The policy counterfactual*: refers to an assessment of the key strategies, policies and initiatives that would have been delivered in the absence of the Games. This would normally be done by reviewing the policy and strategic documents and conducting key stakeholder interviews to establish the nature, and direction, of travel of policy, before a given baseline date. In the case of the 2012 meta-evaluation study, for example, a baseline date of 2003 was adopted because it was in that year that the British Olympic Association, the City of London and the British government committed to submitting a bid to host the Games. There would clearly have been a range of interventions that would have been major drivers of changing people's behaviour in terms of sport participation even if the Games bid had been unsuccessful, and many of these policies would have been 'visible' before the baseline date. Even where policies were already in existence before the baseline, as a result of the London 2012 Games, the government may have paid more attention to the addressing of such issues, resulting in larger injections of funding and policy effort into some existing initiatives, and also the implementation of some new interventions. Thus, by contrasting the two policy scenarios, the additional impact of policy change can more readily be captured.

(b) *The outcome counterfactual*: relates to what results (outcomes) would have occurred on the ground in the absence of the Games. Thus, for example, the national and local levels of sport participation may be compared before and after the decision was taken to bid for hosting of the Games using data from national surveys. Only after the counterfactual analy-- sis has been identified can an estimation of the additional impact of legacy-related activities be made.

The assessment of net impact thus expressed in the formula:

net impact = additionality of information

Table 4.2 Net impact calculation

Net impact	=	Additionality of intervention
Net impact★	=	[Gross Impact × (1-Leakage) × (1-Displacement) × (1-Substitution) × (1+Multiplier effect)]

★After taking into account of the counterfactual effects.

In order to assess the net impact, one has to take into account four principal elements:

- *Leakage*: the extent to which the gross impact of benefits generated and intended for a particular group, region or country incorporates beneficiaries from other groups, regions and countries. An example here might be where the UK's coach development system training coaches at elite level, produces coaches who subsequently take up employment with teams from other countries.
- *Displacement*: where new provision displaced other activities or services that had previously been supplied; thus, where a provider of services launches an 'Olympic Fitness' facility but this has an impact on the market, displacing other providers.
- *Substitution*: when consumers of a service or beneficiaries of a project simply substitute the new service provision for what they had been previously using or benefiting from.
- *Multiplier effect*: the extent to which direct benefits from an intervention trigger further additional indirect benefits. For example, attracting a family member to a jogging club results in other family members participating informally in jogging.

We outline here an example of an approach to assessing additionality and demonstrating associated issues in relation to the Workplace Challenge Programme (WCP). The WCP evaluation formed part of another meta-evaluation research project of the impact of the London 2012 Games in a non-hosting English region (Leicestershire) (Chen and Henry, 2012), which incorporated a meta-synthesis of qualitative and quantitative evidence within a county of the impact of the 2012 Games.

In terms of assessing additionality, the first step was to set out the counterfactual scenario. It was indicated in interviews with key stakeholders that the existence of the WCP was not directly attributable to the London 2012 Games (in other words, it would have taken place anyway). Nevertheless, it was given a greater prominence because of the 2012 Games. In terms of the London 2012 impact, a survey of participants (n = 202 of whom 77 were reporting participation after the Games)[1] indicated that:

- 18% (+/− 8%) of the respondents either agreed or strongly agreed that '*the publicity material for the London 2012 Games had influenced their decision to participate in the WCP programme*'; thus, the Games appeared to impact upon participation rates for the WCP.
- 32% (+/−10%) of the participants either agreed or strongly agreed that '*the publicity surrounding the 2012 Games made them more aware of the benefits of taking part in sport and physical activity*'.
- quantitative evidence collected before and after the programme suggested there was a statistically significant increase in the level of physical activity participation [from Time 1 (i.e. before taking part in the programme) (M = 4.62, SD = 1.71) to Time 2 (post programme report) (M = 5.95, SD = 2.18), t (60) = −5.81, p < 0.000 (two-tailed)].[2] The mean increase

in the level of physical activity participation was 1.33 units (30 minutes of moderate intensity exercise). The eta squared statistic (eta squared = 0.36) indicated a large effect size. However, this was an increase largely on the part of people who already participated in sport.

In terms of exploring the additional *outcomes* of the WCP there are a number of issues to consider. First, the issue of *displacement* was not assessed in this case study, though interviews with stakeholders did review whether the WCP did displace or replace existing schemes or programmes. Second, there was leakage in the project in the sense that the major impact was on a group outside the target group since it was intended to get the less active to become more active, but in fact a disproportionate element of the response was by the already active. Substitution seems to have played little role in decision making by the target group. This is indicated by the fact that, regardless of whether there was any substitution, a net increase in participation was reported. However, attempting to pinpoint (a) whether increased participation in sport through WCP is of sufficient intensity to result in wider social and economic benefits, or (b) whether there is any impact on participation rates for individuals who are not on the WCP but who are influenced to participate by those who are on the WCP (i.e. the existence of *multiplier effects*), is problematic. Thus, in many respects the data on the WCP capture gross rather than net impacts.

The importance and issues of assessing the additionality

This brief example illustrates how, assessing additionality is not always a straightforward process. It requires a good understanding, judgement and knowledge of the intervention, together with sufficient information with which to assess claims along these four dimensions. Nevertheless, the establishing of additionality remains critical in relation to the question of whether there is a rationale for a given intervention (Georghiou, 1998).

The addressing of the issue of additionality in evaluation studies, where it is undertaken at all, is reported by McEldowney (1997) as tending to rely on only one or two simple counterfactual-type questions; and when reporting the results of additional impacts of a programme, often only crude measures of additionality (i.e. high or low) are employed. Furthermore, information is often collected on these dimensions through key stakeholder interviews, but given stakeholder interests these data may be prone to bias, especially when interviewees are members of organisations in receipt of funding assistance.

Conclusion

This chapter has sought to provide an outline of a range of policy evaluation techniques that have recently begun to be adopted more frequently in the sport industry, illustrating their application with practical examples, together with critical analysis of the strengths and weaknesses of each.

In the case of the application of logic models, these are regarded in the field as being effectively employed to expose the causal assumptions of policy makers and programme deliverers.

In terms of meta-evaluation, its nature and peculiarities make it suitable for large-scale and comprehensive evaluation projects that seek to develop evidence-based approaches to outcomes by gathering evidence from a range of projects or policy programmes. Such an approach invites the assessment of process (how adequate are the methods adopted to evaluate the policy programme?) and in terms of outcome (how robust are our assessments of the size and significance of impact). However, this approach has still not been widely adopted in sport-related evaluation, and certainly the use of meta-analysis is rarely likely to be appropriate in the open-system, dynamic policy contexts in which most sport policy interventions take place.

Similarly, in considering issues of additionality, while its importance has been underlined in the above discussion, it should be noted that operationalising the key concepts has proved difficult. Nevertheless despite such problems of operationalisation, taken together, these principles, mechanisms and models provide conceptual tools for identifying the questions that it is crucial to address in providing realistic evidence-based policy evaluation in practice.

5

THE ROLE, CONTRIBUTIONS AND LIMITATIONS OF COST–BENEFIT ANALYSIS IN THE ANALYSIS OF SPORT POLICY

Ming Li and Kong-Ting Yeh

An introduction to cost–benefit analysis

Cost–benefit analysis (CBA) has been frequently utilized as a technique intended to provide estimates on the monetary value of the costs and benefits of a public project to determine whether or not it is worthwhile, and ultimately to help in improving the quality of public policy decisions (Fuguitt and Wilcox, 1999; Kopp, Krupnick, and Toman, 1997; Treasury Board of Canada Secretariat, 1998). Specifically, it compares the costs of the project with the benefits derived from the implementation of the project in a quantitative way. The CBA technique is also commonly utilized by regulatory agencies to evaluate and identify public policy alternatives that are least costly but help achieve the set goal (Kopp *et al.*, 1997). With the help of CBA, the regulatory agency can screen all the alternatives and select the one accruing the largest overall net benefits.

Bergsgaard, Houlihan, Mangset, Nødland and Rommetvedt (2007: cover notes) point out that 'Over recent years there has been a steady increase in public investment in sport and frequently, as a consequence, a sharp debate about how public resources should be used'. In addition, the debate has addressed the question of how the usage of CBA is linked to the public interest. Thus, the analysis of the costs and benefits of public investment in sport has become an important tool for sport administrators to justify the necessity of such investment. This chapter is intended to outline and evaluate the methodologies of CBA, outlining its conceptualization, economic foundation and the basic protocol in performing it, as well as its applications in sports policy contexts. This chapter will also review the limitations of this particular analytical apparatus.

There is a wide variety of sport policy decisions that can be analysed with CBA. They include, but are not limited to, the appropriation of public funds in building sports facilities to be used by privately owned professional sports teams, to host an international sports event (e.g. an Olympic Games), to launch a sport lottery, to privatize or outsource sport operations to private entities, to empower quasi-governmental organizations/agencies in sport development, and so on. (Bergsgard *et al.*, 2007). A good example to illustrate the application of CBA in sport policy development is its use to justify government spending on the hosting of an Olympic Games. 'How should the costs and benefits of holding the Games themselves be distinguished from the costs and benefits of the capital investments required to hold them' (McHugh, 2006)? On the cost side, the analyst must seek answers to a number of questions, such as: what is the amount of funds required from government to subsidize the construction (costs)? How long will such subsidization last? What is the opportunity cost of the public investment? On the benefit side, questions to be examined include, what is the amount of tourism-related revenue that will be generated, for example by visitors' spending on event tickets, lodging and catering, entertainment, retailing, and so on. (Késenne, 2005)? And what are the external effects or nonmarket effects (e.g. improved city image, pride and volunteerism, improved attitudes towards sports activity, stimulated tourism demand, etc.) which will be created by the hallmark event? The sport policy decisions that can be analysed by CBA also include the enactment of a particular legislation for the protection of a particular sport industry segment or for the promotion of improving public health.

Conceptualization and economic foundation of cost–benefit analysis

Cost–benefit analysis defined

As mentioned previously, CBA is a type of analysis or, specifically, an umbrella term of a set of evaluative procedures that have been frequently used by public policy makers or regulatory agencies to evaluate proposed public investment projects (Fuguitt and Wilcox, 1999; HM Treasury, 2003; Kopp *et al.*, 1997; Ray, 1984; Sassone and Schaffer, 1978). It is defined as 'an estimation and evaluation of net benefits associated with alternatives for achieving defined public goals' (Sassone and Schaffer, 1978, p. 3). According to the Treasury Board of Canada Secretariat (1998), CBA 'is a hybrid of several techniques from the management, financial and social sciences fields' (p. 8). Based on the assumption that a CBA is used to determine whether a public policy can achieve the goal of identifying the 'greatest gains to the society', Fuguitt and Wilcox (1999, p. 35) present a comprehensive definition of this analytic technique:

> Cost–benefit analysis (CBA) is a useful approach to assess whether decision or choices that affect the use of scarce resources promote efficiency. Considering a specific policy and relevant alternatives, the analysis involves systematic identification of policy consequences, followed by valuation of social benefits and costs and then application of the appropriate decision criterion.

Owing to the challenging nature of assessing and measuring the non-monetary value or non-market effects of some public investment projects or owing to the difficulty in putting the benefits into dollars in some cases, cost-effectiveness analysis or CEA, as a subset of CBA has also been adopted (Kopp *et al.*, 1997; Treasury Board of Canada Secretariat, 1998). Owing to the constraint on page length, this chapter will not provide an in-depth review of this particular alternative to CBA.

Decision criteria

Public policy decision makers often adopt a number of criteria to determine whether a public policy is justifiable from the standpoint of costs and benefits (Brent, 1996; Fuguitt and Wilcox, 1999; Kopp *et al.*, 1997; Sassone and Schaffer, 1978). A survey of literature concerning CBA reveals that such criteria as *net present value, cut-off and pay-back periods, net average rate of return, internal rate of return, benefit–cost ratio, minimum average cost* and *equity* are frequently used in making decisions in CBA cases.

Net present value. Among the aforementioned decision-making criteria, the *net present value* (NPV) is the most commonly used and accepted criterion (Fuguitt and Wilcox, 1999; Sassone and Schaffer, 1978) in ranking and evaluating investment decisions. NPV is the difference between the present value of returns from an investment project (including present and future inflows of cash) and the present value of the cost of the project (including the present and future outflows of cash) (Brent, 1996; Investopedia, 2012). It is often used in capital budgeting to analyse the profitability of an investment or project.

To use this evaluation apparatus, the critical point is in deciding which discount rate to use in the calculation of the NPV. The discount rate should reflect society's time preference for goods and services. Treasury Board of Canada Secretariat (1998) maintains that it normally uses a discount rate of 8–12 per cent to assess investment projects. A recent CBA conducted for the 2010 Vancouver Winter Olympic Games used a discount rate of 10 per cent (McHugh, 2006). The European Commission (2008), however, suggests a much lower discount rate of 5 per cent. The UK Government even advises the use of a 3.5 per cent rate (see Annex 6 of the *Green Book: Appraisal and evaluation in central government* (HM Treasury, 2003) for details in terms of how the 3.5 per cent discount rate is calculated). The formula in calculating the NPV is shown as follows:

$$NPV = -C_0 + \frac{B_0 - C_0}{(1+r)^0} + \frac{B_1 - C_1}{(1+r)^1} + \ldots + \frac{B_t - C_t}{(1+r)^t} + \frac{B_n - C_n}{(1+r)^n}$$

where

> NPV = the net present value
> B_t = the monetary value of benefits incurred at time t
> C_t = the monetary value of costs incurred at time t
> r = the discount rate
> n = the life of the project, in years

To judge whether the NPV of an investment project is acceptable, the decision-making criterion is one of whether the project produces a positive NPV (in which case it is acceptable), or the project produces a negative NPV (in which case it should be rejected). When comparing two projects, the project that produces the greater or greatest NPV is the best option to choose (Sassone and Schaffer, 1978; Watkins, 2008). For example, if the initial cost of a project was $100 and there were $70 in benefits and $25 in costs for each of three years, and the annual discount rate was 10 per cent, then the NPV would be:

$$NPV = -\$100 + \frac{\$70 - \$25}{(1+0.1)^1} + \frac{\$70 - \$25}{(1+0.1)^2} + \frac{\$70 - \$25}{(1+0.1)^3}$$

$$= -\$100 + \$45.45 + \$41.32 + \$37.57$$

$$= \$24.34$$

Internal rate of return. The internal rate of return (IRR) method is used to screen a project to determine whether or not it meets certain pre-set criteria. 'The IRR of a project is defined as that rate of discounting the future that equates the initial cost and the sum of the future discounted net benefits' (Sassone and Schaffer, 1978, p. 17). In other words, it is the discount rate, r, at which the NPV of the project will be equal to zero. The formula used to calculate the IRR is based on that for the NPV. A good investment is thus one in which the IRR is equal to, or greater than, a pre-set level (the desired or required rate, or the social discount rate), in which case the project is deemed acceptable.

$$C_0 = \frac{B_1 - C_1}{(1+r)^1} + \dots + \frac{B_t - C_t}{(1+r)^t} + \frac{B_n - C_n}{(1+r)^n}$$

where

C_0 = the initial cost

B_t = the dollar value of benefits incurred at time t

C_t = the dollar value of costs incurred at time t

r = the internal rate of return

n = the life of the project, in years

The IRR is most often associated with comparison or evaluation of competing investment opportunities. While using the IRR as a decision-making rule, the decision maker must be aware of its limitations as the IRR is viewed in some quarters as an unreliable measure and a poor substitute for the NPV methodology (Treasury Board of Canada Secretariat, 1998). Such limitations are especially apparent if it is used in comparing two investment options of different sizes.

Payback period. The payback period is concerned with the amount of time it will take for cash inflows (benefits) to recover the cash outflows (costs) of a project. In other words, it is 'the time it takes for the cumulative present value of benefits to become equal to the cumulative present value of costs' (Treasury Board of Canada Secretariat, 1998, p. 44). In general, a project with a shorter payback period is one that should be preferred. The greater the payback period, the longer it takes to recover the investment made, and thus the less attractive the investment option. The following is the formula used to determine the payback period of an investment project.

$$P = \frac{C_0}{B_t}$$

where

P = the payback period

C_0 = the initial investment (cost)

B_t = the average annual cash inflows (benefit)

Although the payback method has the benefit of conceptual clarity it suffers from a number of shortcomings (Gitman and Zutter, 2012). It attaches no value to cash flow after the end of the payback period; makes no adjustments for risk; is not directly related to maximization of return as NPV and IRR are; and it ignores the time value of money.

Benefit–cost ratio. A benefit–cost ratio or BCR is the ratio of the present value of benefits to the present value of costs of an investment project. The project with a benefit–cost ratio of less than 1 should be rejected (Fuguitt and Wilcox, 1999; Watkins, 2008). The BCR is most appropriate for the condition where a number of investment options are under the consideration. While comparing several investment options, the decision maker should choose the one with the highest BCR value. For example, in a CBA study conducted by Christie, Crabtree, and Slee (2001), six improvement scenarios of recreational walking/biking trails were examined to determine their economic efficiency. The BCRs of all the scenarios were calculated to see whether they all provided positive welfare gains for the targeted community. Among the six proposed improvement scenarios, the BCRs of five of the scenarios were greater than one. The calculated BCRs were also used to assess the priorities of public investment in these recreational sports facilities. The BCR is calculated with the following formula:

$$BCR = \sum_{t=0}^{n} \frac{B_t}{(1+r)^t} / \sum_{t=0}^{n} \frac{C_t}{(1+r)^t}$$

where

BCR = the benefit–cost ratio
B_t = the monetary value of benefits incurred at time t
C_t = the monetary value of costs incurred at time t
r = the discount rate
n = the life of the project, in years

Principles and overarching issues in the application of cost–benefit analysis

In order to execute a CBA properly, it is suggested by economists that a number of practical principles be followed (Brent, 1996; Fuguitt and Wilcox, 1999, pp. 156–161; Watkins, 2008, p. 1–13). We focus here on the most critical of these principles.

Principle 1: Efficiency is only one of the several possible goals that decision makers might consider. As such, decision makers should focus their decisions on efficiency while considering other social objectives.

Principle 2: The CBA should identify all the positive and negative consequences caused by the implementation of a policy. The consequences are the real changes in economic value. The economic value is often measured by the sum of individual preferences as expressed by consumer willingness to pay (WTP). Individual preferences form the basis for measuring the social values of a policy.

Principle 3: The social benefits are the sum of individuals' WTP. On the other hand, social costs are the opportunity cost of the allocated resources or the foregone benefits of the resources' best alternative use. The foregone benefits are individuals' WTP.

Principle 4: The costs and benefits of a policy must be expressed in terms of a common unit so that there is a 'bottom line' for the desirability. In other words, an equivalent money value must be used to measure the costs and benefits.

Principle 5: The CBA of a policy should include a counterfactual ('with and without') comparison. The baseline scenario (i.e. without the policy) should be first constructed. The researcher will then be able to make comparison between the baseline information with the consequences (i.e. the demonstrated incremental costs and benefits) of implementing the policy.

Principle 6: Double counting of costs or benefits must be avoided. For example, building a sports stadium in a dilapidated area of a metropolitan location may enhance the value of the surrounding property. The increased property values are the benefits of the policy decision for such construction. The enhanced property values will lead to an increase in revenues from property tax collection. To include both enhanced property values and the increased revenues from tax collection would be considered double counting.

Methods of economic valuation

The public resource used in the implementation of a policy can be measured with a market price if the resource is demanded by consumers and has a market value. As mentioned above, assessing individual preferences allows the researcher to determine the degree to which individuals value the public resources invested. The market value of the consumer demand for a marketed public resource (i.e. the resource having a market price) can be used to estimate the social preferences for, and ultimately the society's valuation of the resource. Fuguitt and

Wilcox (1999, p. 177) maintain that 'a resource's total value is measured by society's WTP (or total WTP)', which is the sum of the consumers' total expenditure plus the consumer surplus. Consumer surplus can be defined as the difference between what consumers are willing to pay for a good or service and what they actually pay (i.e. the market price) (Brent, 1996). The concept of 'consumer surplus' is the focal point of the economic evaluation as it provides a theoretical foundation for valuing the preferences of the public on policies pertaining to their preferred social goals (Brent, 1996; Fuguitt and Wilcox, 1999).

The consumers' total expenditure can be determined by multiplying the market price of a particular resource in a particular geographical area by the quantity of the resource demanded or purchased by the residents residing in the area. The determination of consumer surplus (or consumers' WTP an additional amount for the resource over the marketed price) requires some sophisticated approaches. As such, economists often employ various statistical techniques, such as multiple regression analysis, to predict and/or estimate the total consumer demand and the total WTP of a marketed resource so as to determining the total benefits of the resource (Brent, 1996; Fuguitt and Wilcox, 1999).

If the use of public resources for achieving some social goals cannot be priced with a market value, the determination of the costs and benefits may then have to apply the valuation techniques that are designed specifically for valuing nonmarket effects of a public policy (Fuguitt and Wilcox, 1999). Two such techniques that are commonly used by economists in this regard are the contingent valuation method (CVM) and the travel cost method (TCM) (Oh and Hammitt, 2010). The former method solicits the decision-making behaviour (e.g. the WTP) under the hypothetical situation that a particular policy, which is pertinent to the consumers, would be adopted. The CVM is appropriate to assess the willingness of taxpayers to pay for a project invested with public funds (e.g. hosting a sports tourism event) and is especially used in the environmental CBA and environmental impact assessment (Venkatachalam, 2004). The latter method, however, determines the costs by comparing the actual price paid by the consumers for a good and service and the latent price that they are willing to pay.

Contingent valuation method

To determine the nonmarket effects of a public policy with the use of the CVM, a contingent valuation survey must first be developed (Crompton, 2004; Rahmatian, 2005). The survey contains three essential components: a hypothetical market scenario, valuation questions, and respondents' demographic information and preferences to be used to test the response validity and reliability (Crompton, 2004; Fuguitt and Wilcox, 1999; Rahmatian, 2005).

The hypothetical market scenario is normally presented at the beginning of the survey instrument. It provides the survey participants with information about a condition under which the hypothetical scenario occurs. For example, assume that the local recreational authority of XYZ county has successfully obtained some funding from the state government to build a skate park. However, the amount of funds provided by the state is only sufficient to cover the construction costs. The maintenance and management of the facility then requires an additional source of funding. It is decided that a user fee be assessed to cover such expenses.

The hypothetical market scenario must be pretested to ensure that it can be understood easily by the survey participants. Immediately following the hypothetical market scenario are valuation questions. In the valuation, the respondents are asked to express their WTP for the hypothetical scenario (Christie *et al.*, 2001; Johnson and Whitehead, 2000). A typical valuation question looks like this: 'What is the maximum amount you are willing to pay for a resource benefit (e.g. to use the skate park)'? or 'Are you willing to pay for the use of the skate park? If yes, in what amount $_'.

To answer the first question, the respondents are expected to provide an amount that they feel is acceptable in exchange for the use of the facility. To address the second question, they would have to choose a 'Yes' or 'No' answer first and then provide an amount they are willing to accept as the cost. The respondents may also be asked whether or not they accept a value presented to them. For example, the valuation question may state: 'Would you be willing to pay $4 for the use of the skate park'? A dichotomous answer choice ('Yes' or 'No') is provided.

The valuation question can be designed with multiple levels of bidding. Instead of simply providing a 'Yes' or 'No' answer to a dichotomous CVM question as mentioned previously, the respondent could be asked to answer additional follow-up questions (Crompton, 2004; Fuguitt and Wilcox, 1999). For example, assume the researcher learned via a pretest that the maximum amount of the user fee to be considered acceptable by the local residents for the use of the skate park is $12. The researcher can then include a set of valuation questions in the questionnaire. The following flowchart helps illustrate the process of how the respondents' WTP are determined with multiple levels of valuation questions.

Before presenting the hypothetical scenario and the valuation questions to the population to be surveyed, it is critical for the researcher to address a number of issues that could affect the accuracy of the results. These issues include the sampling method and sample size. While probability sampling method is most preferred, it is strongly recommended that the researcher use appropriate statistical procedures to estimate a sample size meeting the desired degree of accuracy (Fuguitt and Wilcox, 1999; Rahmatian, 2005).

A number of statistical techniques are used to analyse the collected WTP data, which include mean or median of WTP, frequency of WTP and multiple regression analysis with WTP as the dependent variable. There is insufficient space here to consider the various statistical techniques that may be employed. However, it is worth stressing that in all such cases issues of validity and reliability will be critical in assessing the usefulness of results.

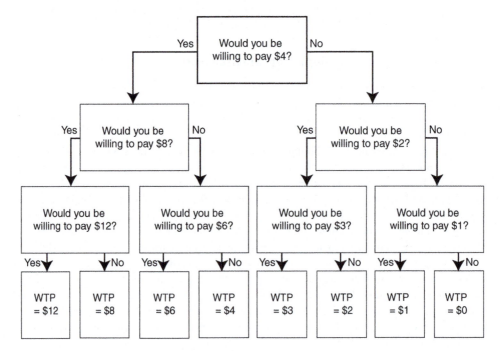

Figure 5.1 Contingent valuation approach

Travel cost method

The TCM is used to assess the time and resources that visitors spend to travel to and from a particular site (e.g. a recreational sports site) as it is assumed that the visitors will incur a variety of travel costs. The amount of such costs will affect their future decisions to revisit the site (Brent, 1996; Fuguitt and Wilcox, 1999).

To apply the TCM, the researcher first needs to define clearly the concept of 'travel cost'. In general, such costs as (1) admission or user fee to access the site, (2) transportation expenses, and (3) costs associated with the time incurred while travelling to and from the site and the time staying in the site (opportunity cost), are regarded as part of the travel costs (Brent, 1996; Clawson, 1966; Fuguitt and Wilcox, 1999). The researcher must take a comprehensive perspective while assessing the transportation expenses if a private vehicle is used during the travel. The transportation expenses that may be incurred with the use of a private vehicle include parking cost, tolls, and vehicle operating costs such as gasoline, maintenance, tires, insurance, licence and registration, depreciation, etc.).

A protocol for performing a cost–benefit analysis

To help decision makers in the public sector properly utilize CBA in assessing their sport-related policy options so as to prescribe one that will yield maximum economic return to the public, economists have recommended a number of protocols that should be observed while performing a CBA (European Commission, 2008; Fuguitt and Wilcox, 1999; Hanley and Spash, 1993; Treasury Board of Canada Secretariat, 1998). For example, the Treasury Board of Canada Secretariat (1998, p. 9) suggests a 9-step process to conduct a CBA:

- Examine needs, consider constraints, and formulate objectives and targets.
- Define options in a way that enables the analyst to compare them fairly.
- Analyse incremental effects and gather data about costs and benefits.
- Express the cost and benefit data in a valid standard unit of measurement.
- Run the deterministic model (using single-value costs and benefits as though the values were certain).
- Conduct a sensitivity analysis to determine which variables appear to have the most influence on the NPV.
- Analyse risk by using what is known about the ranges and probabilities of the costs and benefits values and by simulating expected outcomes of the investment.
- Identify the option that gives the desirable distribution of income.
- Considering all of the quantitative analysis, as well as the qualitative analysis of factors that cannot be expressed in dollars, make a reasoned recommendation.

On the other hand, the European Commission (2008) proposed a six-stage process using CBA to appraise public investment projects. The six stages are:

- a presentation and discussion of the socio-economic context and the objectives;
- the clear identification of the project;
- the study of the feasibility of the project and of alternative options;
- financial analysis;
- economic analysis;
- risk assessment.

Stage 1	Define the project
Stage 2	Identify costs and benefits
Stage 3	Quantify costs and benefits
Stage 4	Apply decision-making criteria
Stage 5	Conduct a sensitivity test

Figure 5.2 Steps common to a range of the protocols employed in CBA

Fuguitt and Wilcox (1999, p. 37) suggest that 'When analyzing a specific policy, cost–benefit analysis involves several components', which can be expressed in three steps. The first step is to identify the positive and negative social consequences of the policy, followed by the step in valuing the costs and benefits of these consequences. The next step is to apply the decision criteria to determine whether the policy promotes efficiency. A close examination of all the protocols proposed for conducting a CBA reveals a number of common elements or steps, which are all contained in the following CBA framework.

Stage 1: Definition of the project

To conduct a CBA, it is critical for the researcher to first have a clear picture of what policy is being evaluated and why it needs to be evaluated. In other words, what is the situation under which a CBA is called for? To answer these questions, a base situation must be established so that all future decisions can have a base to compare. For example, to support sport development in a state, a sport lottery could be introduced as a means to raise the needed funds. To establish the baseline, the current funding situation for sport development in the state should be described in detail. The description not only depicts the status quo before the implementation of the lottery, but also substantiates the needs for the implementation of public-driven fundraising projects, such as the issuance of a sport lottery.

In addition, it is critical for the researcher to define the scope of society, as CBA is a technique for assessing the social costs and benefits from a perspective of all the members of a given population (Sassone and Schaffer, 1978). Does the policy affect the residents of a county, a city, a state or even a country? The definition could profoundly impact the results of a CBA. For example, the main reason why a CBA is conducted for an Olympic Games is to examine the effectiveness of the decision to bid for the right to host the Games and the subsequent investment of public funds into preparing for the event as the residents of the host city would be profoundly affected by the decision. Furthermore, it is equally critical to define when the policy begins, that is, when 'resources are first committed and begin to generate opportunity cost' (Fuguitt and Wilcox, 1999, p. 150).

It is also suggested that a project scenario be constructed (Sassone and Schaffer, 1978). The project scenario unambiguously recognizes and estimates the resources needed to implement a policy or project and the expected outcomes of the policy implementation.

Stage 2: Identify the costs and benefits

The next crucial step in conducting a CBA is to identify both the tangible costs and benefits (e.g. direct costs and benefits), and intangible costs and benefits (indirect costs and benefits such as externalities). As mentioned by Mules and Dwyer (2005), sports tourism events often bring with them a variety of 'intangible' costs and benefits to the host communities.

According to Fuguitt and Wilcox (1999), there are a number of different classifications of the costs and benefits incurred as a result of implementing a public policy. This chapter will mainly present the classification commonly used in CBA studies (Fuguitt and Wilcox, 1999; Sassone and Schaffer, 1978), which divides the costs and benefits into two groups: internal effects and external effects. Internal effects consist of marketed resource costs (i.e. the values of the market-priced resources or input used in implementation of the policy, such as 'capital, start-up costs, operating expenses, and maintenance expenses'), marketed output benefits (i.e. 'the increased value of physical goods and services that are created by the policy and sold in the market', such as the value created from the reuse of sports facilities constructed for a mega event), and marketed output costs (i.e. the negative consequences for some individuals in the community, such as an increase in parking fees caused for the duration of a local event) (Fuguitt and Wilcox, 1999, p. 167).

The external effects are the 'uncompensated gain and loss in welfare' to individuals in the affected community. They are in fact non-market effects as they can be valued but cannot be priced (Sassone and Schaffer, 1978). The external costs are referred to by economists as technological externalities (Fuguitt and Wilcox, 1999).

Let us use an example to illustrate the costs and benefits as a result of hosting an Olympic Games. According to McHugh (2006), an Olympic Games incurs costs and brings in benefits respectively in two areas: event and infrastructure (see Figure 5.3 for details). Many of the event costs (e.g. bid costs, security, administrative costs, advertising, etc.) and infrastructure costs (e.g. the construction of housing and support transit infrastructure, competition venues, etc.) are marketed resource costs. The congestion externalities are part of the external effects. On the other hand, the mega event usually creates a variety of marketed output benefits, such as TV revenue, revenues generated from tickets sold to visitors, revenues generated from lodging and catering services provided to visitors, sponsorship revenues from nonlocal corporations, etc.) (Késenne, 2005). The future reuse of the event-related legacies (e.g. the future use of the housing facilities constructed for the Games, the transit infrastructure, the competition venue, increased tourism demand, etc.) should also be treated as part of the marketed output benefits. Promotion of sporty lifestyle, viewing pleasure of local residents, volunteerism surplus and other pride externalities are external benefits to the host community.

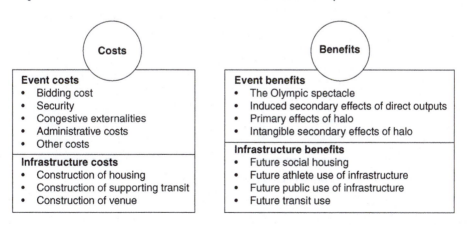

Figure 5.3 Cost–benefit analysis of staging an Olympic Games

Source: Adapted from McHugh (2006)

There are a number of tasks that need to be performed to execute Stage 2. While identifying the costs and benefits, it is critical to determine the timing of all the costs (i.e. when does each of the incurred costs begin?) and benefits (when do the benefits begin and end?). For example, when examining the costs and benefits of hosting a particular Olympic Games, the researcher must realize that the costs incurred by the host city for the mega event begin long before its commencement, and even before the International Olympic Committee (IOC) awards the city the right to host the event seven years prior to the beginning of the Games. In general, costs and benefits of an Olympic Games can be examined in three phases: the pre-games phase (i.e. soon after the city has decided to bid for the Games, up to a decade prior to the actual event), the Games phase, and the post-Games phase (at least a decade after the Games) (Preuss, 2004b).

Stage 3: *Quantify the costs and benefits*

To quantify the costs and benefits, the researcher should first identify appropriate economic valuation methodologies to be used. Such decisions have to be based upon the nature of the resource used in the implementation of a policy; that is, whether or not it can be measured with a market price or needs to be estimated with the valuation techniques used specifically for valuing nonmarket effects of a public policy if the resource cannot be priced with a market value.

It is suggested by the Treasury Board of Canada Secretariat (1998) that all analyses must be performed using the same analytical framework in order to provide fair and consistent assessment of all public projects. The analytical framework usually contains such components as a parameters table, and a table of costs and benefits over time. The parameters table is a table that lists all the important variables used to calculate the costs and benefits. One such variable is the discount rate to be used in determining the NPV of all the costs and benefits. Discounting the future value of benefits is a critical part of this step. It is important to consistently use the same discount rate while comparing the costs and benefits of several projects. It is also important to choose an appropriate discount rate as it affects the value assigned to future benefits.

On the other hand, the table of costs and benefits over time contains information about net costs and benefits in both nominal and constant dollars, the net present value in each period of time, and the NPV of the entire project. Table 5.1 is an example of a simplified table of costs and benefits over time.

Table 5.1 A simplified illustration of the calculation of costs and benefits over the life span of an investment project

Periods	Costs		Benefits	Net	Net	Present
	Materials	Labour	Sales	Nominal $	Constant $	Values
1st Year	($100)	($67)	$40	($127)	($124)	($113)
2nd Year	($212)	($34)	$90	($156)	($148)	($123)
3rd Year	($455)	($84)	$600	$67	$57	$43
4th Year	($734)	($52)	$1,150	$364	$295	$201
NPV = $8						

Source: Adapted from Treasury Board of Canada Secretariat (1998)

Stage 4: Apply the decision-making criteria

Once all the identified social costs and benefits are quantified, one can compare the costs and benefits to determine whether the policy leads to a net increase in social welfare. This is done with the application of one or several aforementioned decision-making criteria, such as NVP, BCR, etc. If a number of investment options are involved in the implementation of the policy, the investment option that brings in the best NVP or BCR will undoubtedly be preferred and selected. This principle is exemplified in the case mentioned by Christie *et al.*'s (2001) study that compared six improvement scenarios of recreational walking/biking trails.

Stage 5: Conduct selective sensitivity analysis

The last step included in the CBA framework is the sensitivity analysis, which assesses the impact of potential risks and uncertainty on a number of select variables and on the assessment of the policy during the course of implementation. Specifically, the analysis shows how fluctuated values of costs and benefits affect the decision criteria, such as NVP or BCR (Fuguitt and Wilcox, 1999). To perform the sensitivity analysis, the researcher will first need to identify the variables: (1) whose values are most likely to fluctuate when the policy is being carried out; (2) that have a high degree of uncertainty; and (3) that have the greatest impact on the decision criteria. Once the variables are selected, a range of values will be assigned to each of them at three levels, the lower-bound or worst-case scenario, the likely value, and the upper-bound or best-case scenario. In the next step, the decision criteria are calculated. Table 5.2 is an illustration of a sensitivity analysis conducted on a number of key variables for a study designed to examine costs and benefits of physical activity using bike/pedestrian trails. The analysis shows that equipment and travel cost in the worst-case scenario has the lowest cost–benefit ratio of 1.65. The benefit still outweighs the cost by 65 per cent (Wang, Macera, Scrudder-Soucies, Pratt and Buchner, 2005).

Table 5.2 Cost–benefit ratios of extreme cases of physical activity using bike/pedestrian trails in 1998 (US$)

Variables	Worst-Case Scenarios		Best-Case Scenarios	
	Value	*Cost–Benefit Ratio*	*Value*	*Cost–Benefit Ratio*
Cost of Trail Construction and Maintenance	$0.78/user	2.08	$0.20/user	3.12
Equipment and Travel Cost	$300/year	1.65	$0/year	13.40
Direct Health Benefit	$365/year	1.90	$763/year	3.97
Life of Trail	10 years	2.22	50 years	3.14
Number of Trail Users	50% below actual number	3.39	50% above actual number	3.63

Source: Wang *et al.* (2005)

Conclusions and limitations of CBA

In conclusion, this chapter reviews the conceptualization and economic foundation of CBA as an analytical technique to assess the appropriateness of public policies. Specifically, a number of essential topics concerning the application of this analytical technique, such as the decision criteria, the principles and overarching issues, and methods of economic evaluation, are reviewed. We have also discussed the basic protocol used in assessing the costs and benefits incurred from the implementation of a policy, and in comparing the costs against the benefits to render a decision regarding the appropriateness of the policy. The basic protocol suggested for use in performing a CBA include: defining the project, identifying costs and benefits, quantifying costs and benefits, applying decision making criteria, and conducting sensitivity analyses.

We conclude, however, by highlighting the limitations of a cost–benefit approach to the evaluation of policies. Many of these are summarized by Kopp *et al.* (1997) and include:

- The difficulties of conducting economic valuation of nonmarket effects.
- The problem of assessing the impact of a public policy on the change of environment as the environment represents a public good. Any attempt to assess environmental value is inappropriate as there is no market established for the valuation of 'property rights' over environmental resources.
- The problem of incorporating all stakeholders in assessing costs and benefits. Not all stakeholders affected by a public policy are likely to be examined in the CBA, and thus some individuals or groups in the affected communities are excluded from the decision process. For example, CBA often neglects the future generations, and 'non-human' stakeholders.
- The fact that CBA rarely engages with equity considerations. Costs and benefits mean different things to different income groups. Benefits gained may often be worth more to the poor. Those receiving benefits and those burdened with the costs of a project may not be the same.
- The differences between social welfare and individual welfare. What individuals want may not be necessarily the same as what the society collectively wants.
- Fsinally, that some measurements of benefits require the valuation of human life. Many people are intrinsically opposed to any attempt to do this. This objection can be partly overcome if we focus instead on the probability of a project 'reducing the risk of death' – and there are insurance markets in existence that tell us something about how much people value their health and life when they take out insurance policies.

The above list is not exhaustive but is sufficient to underline the difficulties inherent in undertaking cost–benefit analysis. While the techniques involved hold out the prospect of 'rational', empirically grounded attempts at a 'felicific calculus' that can inform policy, and thus are deemed by some commentators to be essential to rational policy making, others find it difficult to accept a less than perfect approach to the quantitative measurement of costs and benefits with 'value' reduced to financial value in an attempt to find the lowest common denominator for evaluating decisions.

PART II

Globalisation, governance, partnerships and networks in sport policy

6

THE GLOBAL GOVERNANCE OF SPORT

An overview

Jean-Loup Chappelet

From a pastime reserved for a few privileged amateurs in Europe at the beginning of the twentieth century, sport has since become a phenomenon that concerns millions – whether they practise sport or are fans of it – and that continues to develop throughout the world. Globalisation both drives and strengthens it (Maguire, 1999). Sport is a major social phenomenon, and thus has major economic, environmental and political consequences.

Despite its importance, however, sport is subject to very little state regulation, notably on the international level. Since its emergence in England in the eighteenth century, it has in fact been taken in hand by a wide spectrum of self-governed, private organisations on a local and national level (clubs, leagues, national federations or governing bodies, National Olympic Committees (NOCs), organising committees of events), and also on an international level (International Olympic Committee (IOC), the International Sports Federations (IFs)). Certain clubs date from the mid-nineteenth century, and many national Olympic sports federations were established in Europe at the end of the same century. The IOC was founded in 1894, and most of the IFs were created at the beginning of the twentieth century. Nowadays, as several authors have suggested, these global sport organisations have self-governance problems (e.g. Sugden and Tomlinson, 1998; Forster, 2006; Chappelet and Kübler-Mablott, 2008).

This chapter is divided into four parts. The first part outlines the organisation of global sport as it developed over the twentieth century in an autonomous fashion. The second shows how governments and intergovernmental organisations intervened in this self-governed system at the end of the twentieth century. The third part explains how the global sports organisations reacted to governmental intervention by advocating their specificity and autonomy, and by adopting principles of good governance. The last part maps the way beyond the governance of sports organisations to a global governance of sport seen as a global policy outcome.

The Olympic System and the *Lex sportiva*

Most of the above-mentioned sports organisations – including the IOC – have taken the form of non-profit associations under the law of the country where their headquarters are located, and it is today possible to classify them in the category of national or international non-governmental organisations (NGOs). They are strong players within civil society, and constitute what

Chappelet (1991) has termed the 'Olympic System' since their *raison d'être* revolves around the organisation of competitions at all levels, of which the most prestigious has been the modern Olympic Games, first held in 1896. Since the 1980s, new, private and profit-making actors have entered the scene: notably sponsors, the media, and professional leagues of athletes (such as the Association of Tennis Professionals) or teams (such as the National Basketball Association), in order to participate in and/or finance the System (Chappelet and Kübler, 2008).

The Olympic organisations have gradually created a 'private international regime' (Cutler *et al.*, 1999: 13), namely, 'an integrated complex of formal and informal institutions that is a source of governance for an economic issue area as a whole'. Over the years, the Olympic System has developed a series of rules related to sport that govern all those wishing to take part as competitors, organisers or officials. There is no alternative open to them: either they comply with the said rules or they cannot take part in competitions. Certain authors refer to this set of sports rules for all types of sport (over 140 disciplines are recorded) at all levels of jurisdiction (local, national and international), as the *Lex sportiva* (e.g. Latty, 2007; Kolev, 2008). This is not legislation in the classical sense of the term (as in that voted on by parliaments), but 'soft laws' accepted by a community: in this case, that of athletes and officials. These rules are transnational since they are often applicable beyond national frontiers. Any club, federation or country declining to apply them would rapidly find itself excluded from international competitions.

The Olympic Charter is intended as the ultimate authority within this legal edifice: it is a kind of constitution for global (Olympic) sport. The text and its annexes lay down the principles and rules that apply to all organisations and individuals within the Olympic System. It also constitutes the statutes of the IOC, which amends them regularly at its annual 'Sessions' (General Assemblies). A major revision of the Charter was undertaken in 1999, following the scandal that arose with regard to the candidature by Salt Lake City for the 2002 Olympic Winter Games, which had undermined the legitimacy of the IOC. This resulted in a new form of organisational governance of the IOC as described by Chappelet (2012).

This private international regime has its own judiciary in the form of the Court of Arbitration for Sport (CAS) based in Lausanne (Switzerland). Like any court of arbitration, it permits two parties engaged in a dispute (in this case related to sport) to submit their case for a decision on the part of one or three arbitrators (depending on the significance of the case). The arbitrators are chosen from a list of around three hundred legal experts who are familiar with sport, nominated by an International Council of Arbitration for Sport, which is a foundation under Swiss law. The entire structure works within the framework of Chapter 12 of the Swiss Federal Law on Private International Law even though the parties may choose to apply law other than that of Switzerland. The decisions issued by the CAS can only be appealed against before the Swiss Federal Tribunal (the country's Supreme Court) and only in the case of procedural errors. Since its foundation in 1983, the CAS has issued hundreds of such decisions, which constitute a kind of jurisprudence for the governance of sport. For the first time, in 2012, a CAS decision was declared 'unlawful' by the Swiss Federal Tribunal (Matuzalém case). The highly particular role played by Swiss law should be noted since, in addition to the CAS, a very large number of international sports organisations are based in Switzerland: notably the IOC and most IFs for major sports such as football, basketball, volleyball, cycling, aquatics, skiing and skating. (Basketball also has its own arbitration tribunal under Swiss law for disputes between players, agents and clubs.)

With the exception of the Catholic Church (and its Canon Law), international trade (and its *Lex mercatoria*; see Cutler, 2003) and the internet (and its ICANN Regulations), there are not many other organisational equivalents to the Olympic System. It is a typical case of global governance; that is, 'rule making and exercise of power at global level, but not necessarily by entities authorised by general agreement to act' (Keohane, 2002). It existed well before this concept became topical, for example via the Commission on Global Governance that was chaired, as of 1992, by former German Chancellor Willy Brandt. The case of the Olympic System is even more interesting because it above all brings together private organisations (most non-profit and some profit-making) that have always wished to preserve their autonomy with regard to governments. The concept of governance was in fact proposed, in the 1990s, as a means of fostering more participation of private corporations and civil society organisations with regard to the provision of public services in parallel – or even in competition – with the traditional governmental actors. As far as sport is concerned, however, the process is the exact opposite to this: it is the state that wants to intervene in the Olympic System.

Intervention on the part of the state

Since the 1960s, European states have begun to take more and more interest in sport and in trying to regulate it by establishing a legislative framework for sports organisations at a national level. The objective was to promote the benefits of sport in terms of education, health, social integration, and so on, but also to combat forms of abuse that have been historically related to it such as doping and hooliganism. This interest took the form of adopting constitutional provisions (for example in Switzerland in 1970) and national laws on sport (in 1972 in Switzerland), regularly adapted to the evolution of the phenomenon. Many countries followed the example of Europe, such as Canada in 1961, the USA in 1978, Brazil in 1993 and China in 1998. Even in those countries where a law on sport does not (yet) exist (for example the United Kingdom, Germany, Australia), state intervention is considerable in terms of public financing of the national, regional and local sports system (Chalip *et al.*, 1996).

On the level of international law, states and intergovernmental organisations became interested in sport at specific moments as of the 1970s, and more systematically since the 1990s, with the increase in certain types of abuse linked to sport that already existed including doping and violence, or that had recently emerged such as corruption, financial excesses, match fixing and illicit betting. These governmental interventions are now briefly presented.

The United Nations (UN) adopted a declaration (1977) followed by a Convention against Apartheid (1985) which led to South Africa being isolated on a sporting level before returning to the Olympic Games in 1992 following a change of regime. Some embargos imposed by the UN have also affected international sport, notably that against Yugoslavia in 1991. In 1978, the United Nations Educational, Scientific and Cultural Organization (UNESCO) adopted the International Charter of Physical Education and Sport. A statement of principles that does not have the force of a convention or even a recommendation, it was intended to compete with the Olympic Charter at a moment when the Olympic System was in a period where boycotts were affecting the Games (from Munich 1972 to Seoul 1988). Today, it has no practical consequences but nevertheless remains a legal instrument under international law, which is not the case for the Olympic Charter.

Since the early 1990s, the UN has once again become interested in sport via resolutions adopted by its General Assembly concerning the Olympic Truce, and which, since the 1994 Winter Games in Lillehammer, have been tabled by the host countries one year prior to each edition of the Summer or Winter Games. These symbolic resolutions nevertheless denote a certain degree of recognition of the Olympic System on the part of the UN System. In 2001, the UN Secretary-General appointed a Special Adviser on Sport for Development and Peace for the first time. A resolution on development through sport was adopted in 2003, and cooperation increased between UN agencies, the IOC and other international sports organisations in order to achieve the 'Millennium goals'. In 2005, and at the request of sports organisations, UNESCO adopted the International Convention against Doping in Sport, which has today been ratified by nearly all the Member States and thus incorporated within their national legislation. The said convention notably recognises the World Anti-Doping Code and the World Anti-Doping Agency (WADA), a foundation under Swiss law created in 1999 as a parity organisation in which the power is shared equally between the Olympic System and governments.

In 2009, the IOC was given observer status at the UN General Assembly – an honour awarded to a very small number of NGOs such as the International Committee of the Red Cross and the Sovereign Order of Malta. The following year, the UN General Assembly passed a resolution on 'Sport as a means to promote education, health, development and peace'.

On the European level, the intergovernmental organisation that has been the most active with regard to sport (since the 1970s) is the Council of Europe, which, during the Cold War, united only countries in western Europe, but today includes most nations on the continent (47 by 2012). This Council adopted two international treaties concerning sport that have been ratified by many countries (including non-members): the European Convention on Spectator Violence and Misbehaviour at Sports Events (1985) and the Anti-Doping Convention (1989). The Council's Committee of Ministers (its highest decision-making body) also adopted the European Sport Charter and the Code of Sports Ethics (1992) – which succeeded the European Sport for All Charter (1976) – as well as several other specific recommendations: on the role of sport in furthering social cohesion (1999); on granting visas to athletes (1999); on the prevention of racism, xenophobia and intolerance in sport (2001); on improving access to physical education and sport for children and young people in all European countries (2003); on the principles of good governance in sport (2005); on the fight against the manipulation of sports result (match fixing) (2011); plus numerous resolutions (cf. www.coe.int/t/dg4/sport). These legal texts have a certain weight with regard to sports organisations and states, and have at times been cited during various cases that athletes have brought before the European Court of Human Rights in Strasbourg (France).

In matters of sport governance, the Council of Europe recommends that the governments of Member States:

1. adopt effective policies and measures of good governance in sport, which include as a minimum requirement:
   - democratic structures for non-governmental sports organisations based on clear and regular electoral procedures open to the whole membership;
   - organisation and management of a professional standard, with an appropriate code of ethics and procedures for dealing with conflicts of interest;
   - accountability and transparency in decision-making and financial operations, including the open publication of yearly financial accounts duly audited;
   - fairness in dealing with membership, including gender equality and solidarity;
2. ensure that these principles of good governance are integrated into sports policies and practiced at national level, both in governmental and in non-governmental structures;
3. use these principles as the basis for setting an equitable partnership between the public authorities and the sports movement;
4. call upon all national institutions, non-governmental organisations and other groups concerned in sport to devise, implement, strengthen and support initiatives based on the principles of good governance in sport;

5. invite all sectors – non-governmental sports organisations, civil society groups and voluntary institutions – to cooperate closely with the national authorities in order to achieve and implement the principles of this Recommendation;
6. set up mechanisms to monitor the implementation of good governance in sport principles, and put in place mechanisms to deal with inappropriate or unethical behaviours in sport, including prosecution where necessary.

(COE, 2005)

The European Union (27 countries in 2011) has been guided by a twofold vision of sport (García, 2011). On the one hand, the sociocultural vision of sport was emphasised in the so-called Andonino Report (European Commission, 1984) which saw sport as a tool of European integration and led to some significant actions such as the Eurathlon programme (1995–98) and the use of European symbols at the Barcelona and Albertville Olympic Games (1992). The suggestion made in the report to form European teams for major sport competitions was rejected by the Olympic System (Rogge, 1995, 1997). On the other hand, the economic vision sees sport as a growing industry that must respect European (Community) law in particular competition law and the four freedoms (free movement of people, goods, capital and services). This dominant vision has considerably affected the governance of sports organisations in the European Union (and beyond through the agreements passed with many non EU countries).

Since the 1970s, but above all from 1995 with the Bosman ruling, the Court of Justice of the European Communities has been called upon to judge numerous cases related to sport that were brought before it by athletes lodging complaints against their sports organisations based on European law. Although many cases were won by organisations within the Olympic System, a certain number of sports rules had to be modified in order to be compatible with European law: for instance in 2001, the rules relating to the transfer of footballers regulated by the International Football Association (FIFA). In 2006, in its ruling on the Meca–Medina case (2006) the Court recalled that the rules and conditions for practising a sports activity came fully within European law once the said activity had an economic dimension (Chappelet, 2010).

The reaction by the Olympic System

After the Bosman ruling in 1995, the organisations within the Olympic System started to protest against sport being assimilated with economic activity, and claimed exemption from European law. This proved impossible, despite considerable political pressure in the form of various political statements (such as the Nice Declaration by the European Council in 2000 that recognised the social role of sport), but that had negligible practical effect. In 2009, however, the European Union finally adopted the Lisbon Treaty which, for the first time, provided the EU with competence in matters related to sport in its Article 16 and Article 165, on education and sport, which states:

1. [...] The Union shall contribute to the promotion of European sporting issues, while taking account of the specific nature of sport, its structures based on voluntary activity and its social and educational function.
2. Union action shall be aimed at: [...] developing the European dimension in sport, by promoting fairness and openness in sporting competitions and cooperation between bodies responsible for sports, and by protecting the physical and moral integrity of sportsmen and sportswomen, especially the youngest sportsmen and sportswomen.

3. The Union and the Member States shall foster cooperation with third countries and the competent international organisations in the field of education and sport, in particular the Council of Europe.

4. In order to contribute to the achievement of the objectives referred to in this Article:
   - the European Parliament and the Council, acting in accordance with the ordinary legislative procedure, after consulting the Economic and Social Committee and the Committee of the Regions, shall adopt incentive measures, excluding any harmonisation of the laws and regulations of the Member States,
   - the Council, on a proposal from the Commission, shall adopt recommendations.

   (www.lisbon-treaty.org; the parts concerning education are not cited)

As one can see, however, the competencies of the EU regarding sport are restricted to incentive measures and recommendations. In particular, harmonising the legislation relating to sport in the 27 countries of the EU is not envisaged, which would have caused problems for the transnational supremacy of *Lex sportiva*. The European Commission is, however, creating a basis for a European policy on sport whose main focal areas are described in the *Action Plan Pierre de Coubertin*, published as an accompanying document to the *White Paper on Sport* (2007), and the more recent Commission's communication *Developing the European Dimension in Sport* (2011).

Faced with growing interest on the part of European or global intergovernmental sports organisations, and in the wake of an ever-increasing number of cases of governmental interference in the functioning of sports organisations on a national level, sports organisations are today claiming the right to preserve their autonomy, that is, the capacity for self-government that has been their prerogative since the beginning of the twentieth century. Following a first seminar organised by the IOC on the subject in 2006, the sports organisations came to realise that their autonomy could only be maintained if they respected the rules of good governance (International Olympic Committee, 2008). They are encouraged in this effort by the EU institutions (García, 2011: 33).

In February 2008, Basic Universal Principles of Good Governance of the Olympic and Sports Movement (BUPs), drawn up by an IOC working group, were presented at a second seminar on the autonomy of sport. They were inspired by those adopted by the Council of Europe the previous year (see above), but are more far-reaching. Table 6.1 shows the seven dimensions of these principles.

The BUPs were presented at the Olympic Congress held in Copenhagen in 2009, during an address by an IOC Vice President, Thomas Bach (International Olympic Committee, 2010: 114–118), and are stated as having been adopted in the final resolution of the said Congress (International Olympic Committee, 2010: point 41 of the Final document, p. 250). In 2010, they were made mandatory ('in particular transparency, responsibility and accountability'') by the IOC Executive Board, which incorporated them within the IOC Code of Ethics. This indicates that the IOC, beyond its own organisational governance, shows concern for the good governance of other organisations within the Olympic System throughout the world, since it states that these are basic, universal principles. It considers, in fact, that the reputation of the Olympic and sports movement depends on that of all its members, notably the IFs and the NOCs.

The IOC is nevertheless treading on somewhat sensitive ground because of the proclaimed autonomy of each sport organisation. Certain IFs in fact preserve their prerogatives protectively. They have, moreover, already adopted their own rules of good governance: for instance the International Cycling Union (UCI, 2004), and/or codes of ethics, for example those of FIFA (football), FILA (wrestling), and FIVB (volleyball) (Chappelet, 2005). This leads to the issue of harmonising these various texts.

Table 6.1 Dimensions and sub-dimensions of the Basic Universal Principles of Good Governance of the Olympic and Sports Movement

Dimensions	Sub-dimensions
1 Vision, mission and strategy	1.1 Vision
	1.2 Mission
	1.3 Strategy
2 Structures, regulations and democratic process	2.1 Structures
	2.2 Clear regulations
	2.3 Governing bodies
	2.4 Representative governing bodies
	2.5 Democratic processes
	2.6 Attribution of the respective bodies
	2.7 Decision-making
	2.8 Conflicts of interests
	2.9 Duration of the terms of office
	2.10 Decisions and appeals
3 Highest level of competence, integrity and ethical standards	3.1 Competence of the members of the executive body
	3.2 Power of signature
	3.3 Internal management, communication and coordination
	3.4 Risk management
	3.5 Appointment of the members of the management
	3.6 Code of Ethics and ethical issues
4 Accountability, transparency and control	4.1 Accountability
	4.2 Processes and mechanisms
	4.3 Transparency and communication
	4.4 Financial matters – applicable laws, rules, procedures and standards
	4.5 Internal control system
	4.6 Education and training
5 Solidarity and development	5.1 Distribution of resources
	5.2 Equity
	5.3 Development
6 Athletes' involvement, participation and care	6.1 Right to participate and involvement of the athletes in the Olympic and Sports Movement and governing bodies
	6.2 Protection of athletes
	6.3 Health
	6.4 Fight against doping
	6.5 Insurance
	6.6 Fairness and Fair play
	6.7 Athletes' education and career management
7 Harmonious relations with governments while preserving autonomy	7.1 Cooperation, coordination and consultation
	7.2 Complementary missions
	7.3 Maintain and preserve the autonomy of sport

Source: International Olympic Committee (2008)

Furthermore, several NOCs have also adopted such codes of ethics: for example those of Italy, the Netherlands, the USA, Slovenia and Switzerland (Chaker, 2004: 29). The NOCs are nevertheless far more dependent on the IOC than the IFs. According to the Olympic Charter, their statutes (and thus their governance mechanisms) must be approved by the IOC. Should their statutes fail to comply with the IOC's requirements, the recognition of a NOC may be suspended or withdrawn by the IOC, thus preventing them from sending a team to the Olympic Games. A NOC and the national sports federations that are members thereof are, however, independent legal entities (usually associations) under the law of their countries and thus forced to respect national legislation and in particular – if it exists – national law relating to sport.

The recent case of India reveals the difficulties of reconciling autonomy with good governance and also the *Lex sportiva* with national laws. In 2010, a few months before the Commonwealth Games in Delhi, the Indian Minister for Sport proposed a new Sports Development Bill imposing a maximum age of 70 and a limited number of periods in office for the unpaid heads of national sports federations. Many sports officials in India are elderly and have been in office for over 20 years, notably the President and Secretary General of the NOC of India (IOA – Indian Olympic Association). The IOA immediately filed a complaint with the IOC, claiming political interference. In accordance with the Olympic Charter, the IOC requested the Indian Government to respect the autonomy of the Indian sports organisations, and at the same time took the opportunity to request the IOA to bring its statutes into compliance with the Olympic Charter, yet without demanding that a mandatory age limit or a restriction regarding periods in office be imposed. The Indian Minister for Sport replied (GOI, 2010) that the IOC's position appeared 'strange' to him since in 1999 it had imposed an age limit on its own members (70) and a limit to the periods in office for its President (8 + 4 years at most), and for the members of its Executive Board (4 + 4 years at most). He did not, however, mention point 2.9 of the BUPs adopted by the IOC that suggests in the conditional that 'the terms of office [in sports organisations] should be of limited duration in order to allow renewal of office bearers on a regular basis. Access for new candidates should be encouraged.' In parallel, a group of former Indian participants at the Olympic Games, baptised 'Clean Sports India' sent an open letter to the IOC President criticising the collusion between sports leaders and politicians, which undermined the autonomy and the good governance of sports organisations on the subcontinent.

Following a meeting in Lausanne in June 2010 between the Indian Ministry of Youth Affairs and Sports, the IOA and the IOC, the IOA agreed to modify its statutes. The modifications that were made several months later at a general assembly still did not, however, include a restriction to periods in office or age limits (since principle 2.9 is only a suggestion and not compulsory). The Minister threatened to impose the said limits by law since the Indian courts have long considered the country's sports organisations to be virtually public institutions. The IOA claimed its right to autonomy as regards establishing its own regulations. In April 2011, the IOC Executive Board stated that the attitude of the Indian Government could prevent Indian athletes from taking part in the 2012 London Games. In May 2011, the President of the IOA suspended himself from his office after he was jailed on corruption charges concerning his position as Chief of the 2010 Commonwealth Games Organising Committee in Delhi. Consequently the IOC requested that he be permanently dismissed but it did not happen before the Games in London.

Although the threat of preventing India from participating in London 2012 did not become reality, the case demonstrates the difficulty of reconciling good governance and autonomy – a concept that is acknowledged in Europe (Chappelet, 2010) but difficult to impose elsewhere, and notably in countries with authoritarian regimes. More generally, the question is one of ensuring that national (and at times international) law can cohabit and be harmonised with the

Lex sportiva. Without mentioning the Indian case, the IOC President, in his speech to a gathering of NOCs representatives and sport ministry officials which took place in Acapulco in 2010, declared that the IOC:

> fully recognises and accepts the need to act within the framework of national and local laws, which when approved, must take into consideration the international sports law (in accordance with the Olympic Charter) in order to avoid any potential future conflict.
>
> (Rogge, 2010)

This position is in fact asking that new national laws on sport be subordinate to the *Lex sportiva* (here under the name of 'international sports law') while tolerating existing laws that provide limited autonomy for the national sports movement (for example in France or in China).

From the governance of sports organisations to the global governance of sport

If we now turn to the nature of the principles adopted by the IOC (see Table 6.1), one can note that they are based on two approaches: that of corporate governance and that of political governance. Corporate (or organisational) governance is an approach that has developed since the 1980s following major financial scandals in companies quoted on the stock exchange, with a view to obtaining better control over their top management and protecting their shareholders. It was taken up again and adapted during the 1990s by intergovernmental organisations such as the World Bank and the Organisation for Economic Co-operation and Development (OECD) in order for it to be applied to governmental and non-governmental organisations with stakeholders rather than shareholders. The approach, which coincided with the New Public Management movement (Hood, 1991) that aimed to apply management techniques used for private companies to public administration, can be called political (or democratic) governance. These two approaches to governance are situated in a broader framework that Henry and Lee (2004) call systemic governance (see Figure 6.1) and in which sponsors, the media, sport equipment suppliers, private fitness clubs and others intervene in addition to non-profit sports organisations and the public authorities.

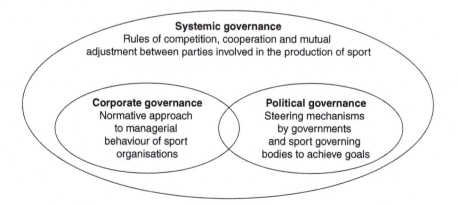

Figure 6.1 Three interrelated approaches to governance

Source: Adapted from Henry and Lee (2004: 27)

BUPs nos 1, 2, 3 and 4 stem from classical corporate governance with the exception of principles 2.4 (Representative governing bodies) and 2.5 (Democratic processes) which belong more to the world of political governance where stakeholders are more important than shareholders. In certain sports clubs with numerous fans or members (for example, the *socios* of FC Barcelona), they can go as far as highly contested elections, which give the elected officials a considerable degree of legitimacy.

BUP no. 5 (Solidarity and development), 6 (Athletes' involvement, participation and care) and 7 (Harmonious relations with governments while preserving autonomy) clearly stem from political governance. Compared with principles proposed for other governmental and non-governmental organisations, they have a sporting dimension (for example, fair play, the protection of athletes, and solidarity regarding the sharing of revenues from sport). Principle 1.2 (Mission) also addresses topics specific to sports organisations (Development and promotion of sport through non-profit organisations, Promotion of the values of sport, Ensuring a fair sporting contest at all times, etc.). Although essential from a political governance point of view (Kidd and Donnelly, 2000), the respect for human rights and fundamental freedoms by sports organisations is not listed in the BUPs, probably for political correctness. It should also be noted that certain BUPs are broad. The one regarding equity (5.2), for example, unites notions as varied as the fair distribution of resources to sports organisations, the opportunities for athletes to take part in competitions at their level, the possibility of organising major competitions, and the transparency of the selection criteria for awarding sports events.

It is, in fact, hardly surprising that the BUPs adopted by the IOC draw on both the world of private enterprise (and corporate governance) and that of the public authorities (and public governance), since non-profit sports organisations are typically situated between the two. Their main partners are sponsors and television networks (which purchase commercial rights to the competitions and the athletes), but also their sports fans and the governments (which finance sport for all and elite sport). Sports organisations wish to preserve their autonomy with regard to these private and public partners, even if BUP no. 7 (Harmonious relations) only mentions governments.

Now that the BUPs have been adopted by the IOC, the question of respect for them arises, including by the IOC itself. Assessing this compliance is the task of the IOC Ethics Commission, since the BUPs have been made mandatory under the IOC's Code of Ethics, and the said Commission is tasked with its application. The sanctions are stated in Rule 23 of the Olympic Charter (notably suspension or withdrawal of recognition for NOCs or IFs, withdrawal of the Games for Organising Committees, or exclusion from the IOC or from the Games for individuals). It is not clear whether a specific surveillance mechanism has been set up. The Ethics Commission's problems with regard to transparency and independence are known (Chappelet, 2011a; Pieth, 2011: 33–34). It would appear, however, that the IOC and FIFA presidents exchanged opinions on the occasion of awarding the Football World Cup for 2018 and 2022: a process marred by rumours of corruption that were finally judged to be unfounded by the FIFA Ethics Committee. Moreover, the IOC Ethics Commission and NOC Relations Department have organised presentations of the BUPs on the occasion of continental meetings of NOCs under the aegis of Olympic Solidarity (for example in Malta, in May 2010). The IOC decided in 2011 to focus on the most important principles for implementation rather than on the whole list of BUPs.

Questions of ethics, governance and corruption are closely linked. Several authors have suggested the creation of an agency to fight corruption in sport (for example Chappelet, 2002; Bourg and Gouguet, 2006). For several years, the Danish organisation *Play the Game* has been proposing a 'Global Coalition for the Good Governance in Sport' (Andersen, 2007). These ideas have again become topical as the result of a new form of abuse in sport, namely, the fixing of sports results linked to irregular or illegal betting (Chappelet, 2011b). The IOC has devoted two seminars to the issue in 2010 and 2011 (International Olympic Committee, 2010b) and has modified its Code of Ethics accordingly. It is endeavouring to have the problem addressed by governments on a national level and to finance the fight against the fixing of results by means of lottery companies purchasing the rights to use data from sports events (as has been the case in France since 2010). Since 2011, WADA has been calling for the creation of a World Sports Integrity Agency (WSIA), which would be the equivalent (or an extension) of WADA for questions of corruption which, moreover, also include doping (Howman, 2011). Other stakeholders (for example Transparency International, 2008) feel that it is possible to apply current conventions against public and private corruption that have been ratified by numerous States, notably those of the UN, the Council of Europe and the OECD. This would involve cooperation with such organisations as the UN Office on Drugs and Crime (UNODC), the Council of Europe's GRECO (Group of States against Corruption), the G7's Financial Action Task Force and Interpol, the international criminal police organisation. In 2011 the IOC signed a memorandum of understanding with UNODC to identify possible areas of work particularly related to drug abuse as well as corruption in sport. The Council of Europe decided in 2012 to start the process of drafting a convention against result manipulations in sport which would be open to non-European states. This would provide a first international law framework for this issue.

The organisations within the Olympic System are for the most part against the creation of an external agency that they will not closely control or for the extension of WADA's role. The UEFA (Union of European Football Associations) President has been calling for a European football police for several years (Rasmussen, 2010). FIFA gave US$ 20 million to Interpol in 2011 for a ten-year football anti-corruption training programme. But at the same time, UEFA created an in-house unit to monitor football betting, while the IOC and FIFA are using small external companies founded for the purpose in 2009. In order to respond to expectations from the outside world and to help its smaller member IFs, SportAccord (formerly GAISF, General Assembly of International Sports Federations) created in 2010 an in-house Sports Integrity Unit that provides advice and will soon launch a prevention programme. The Olympic System is still looking for a proper response to the global threat of match fixing which endangers the image of sport.

Conclusion

Beyond all these actions and proposals, how can sport – an increasingly important sector of human activity – be governed and regulated? Although they call for harmonious relations with governments, the sports organisations of the Olympic System appear to believe that they can achieve this alone as long as they respect the 'Basic universal principles of good governance' and as long as their autonomy is fully respected. Although they were not involved in the regulation of the sport sector to a great extent in the past, governments are coming to realise that they must intervene more and more in order to fight major areas of abuse linked to sport (such as doping, violence, corruption, the fixing of results, etc.) if the traditional benefits of sport (education, health, social integration, economic development, etc.) that justify the financial support provided are to be preserved. This growing awareness on the part of governments is taking place within a context of the ever-growing 'commodification' of sport (Auweele, 2010) brought about by its commercial partners (sponsors, the media, equipment suppliers, sports lotteries). Although these partners bring in considerable resources for the sports organisations (particularly the global ones among them), they are also the source of major risk, including for the autonomy of sports organisations, for example when they request sporting rule changes.

Faced with these new challenges, and beyond the (good) governance of the sports organisations, it is also necessary to address the issue of the global governance of sport as an important factor within local, national – but also European and international – public policies. This networked governance must involve all producers of sport, whether (non-profit) associations, or public and private entities, and notably those operating on a global level. Within this context, transnational sports organisations will only be capable of playing a leading role if they accept the need to partner more with governments and intergovernmental organisations involved in the regulation, financing and promotion of sport.

7

THE DEVELOPING ROLE
OF THE EUROPEAN UNION

Borja García

Introduction

Sport in Europe is traditionally a competence of national, regional or local authorities. However, supranational institutions such as the European Union (EU) have developed an increasingly important role. The relationship between the EU and sport policy is, however, quite complex. This is due to a series of circumstances that it is necessary to mention by way of introduction. First, a constitutional constraint conditioned for a long time any EU approach to sport. The EU had no direct competence on sport until very recently. Legally, sport in Europe was an exclusive competence of the Member States and, some would also argue, of the so-called sporting movement (sport non-governmental organisations). This, however, did not prevent sport from appearing in the EU political agenda relatively often, especially following the well-known Bosman ruling in 1995. This constitutional constraint disappeared with the entering into force of the Lisbon Treaty in December 2009. The new Treaty on the Functioning of the European Union (TFEU) includes for the first time a direct mandate on sport for the EU in Article 165. This is, however, a very 'thin' competence, where the EU can only coordinate and support the actions of the Member States.

Second, given the existence of constitutional constraint until 2009, the EU tended to approach sport indirectly through the regulatory policies of the Single European Market (SEM). This leads Tokarski *et al.* (2004) to differentiate between direct and indirect EU sports policy, the former being relatively modest and patchy, while the latter focused on the economic and legal aspects of professional sport.

Third, policy making in the EU involves a great number of actors and it would be wrong to assume that their preferences are easily aligned. In the case of sport, the Court of Justice of the European Union (CJEU), the European Parliament, the Commission and the Member States (meeting either in the Council of Ministers or the European Council) have differing views on sport. Even within the European Commission one can find contrasting internal approaches to sport. The result is a heterogeneous policy community that makes generalisations about EU policy on sport very difficult.

Fourth, it is now acknowledged and accepted that, despite diversity, there are basically two main (and contrasting) views of sport among EU institutions that have developed over time (Parrish 2003a, b): sport as an economic activity in need of regulation when it affects the SEM, and sport as a sociocultural activity with important implications for civil society, identities and culture throughout the EU. Owing to the complex institutional structure of the EU, none of these visions has real prevalence over the other. This depends on the circumstances of each particular case. Thus, the implications, tensions and evolution of these two views can explain a large majority of EU decisions in sport. Given the aforementioned lack of legal base to develop a fully fledged policy, there is heterogeneity in decisions and regulations. It might be argued that, to a certain extent, all those decisions together might amount to a sort of EU sports policy, but it would be quite an amorphous sport policy. Thus, the very nature of EU sport policy and the institutional structure of the EU make policy difficult to analyse in this case.

For the sake of clarity, this chapter will adopt a structure based on the division used by the European Commission since its 2007 White Paper on Sport. That document is considered to be an attempt to rationalise the EU approach to sport and, therefore EU sports policy. It was drafted by the Commission in preparation for the adoption of the TFEU, which includes an article on sport. In the White Paper, the Commission followed a threefold structure under three headings: the economic impact of sport, the sociocultural dimension of sport and the organisation of sport. The same structure was replicated by the Commission in its 2011 Communication setting up the policy priorities for a new EU sports policy under Article 165 TFEU (European Commission 2011). Thus, it seems sensible to build on this division to offer some clarity on the evolution of the role of the EU in sports policy. First, this chapter will explore the role of the EU as a regulator of sport. This focuses mainly on sport as an industry and a market place. Therefore, it affects mostly professional sports and it deals with issues of working conditions, broadcasting and commercial exploitation of sport. Second, the chapter will analyse the role of the EU as a partner of sport organisations in developing and/or protecting the sociocultural values of sport. This more directly affects amateur sport, volunteerism and activities linked to social inclusion or education through sport. Finally, the chapter will focus on the role of EU institutions in the governance of sport in Europe, which is invariably linked to the concepts of autonomy and specificity of sport.

The EU as a regulator of sport

In one of his seminal works on EU policy making, Giandomenico Majone (1994) characterised the European Union as a 'regulatory state'. In essence, Majone explains European integration as a process whereby Member States delegate regulatory powers in specific sectors to supranational authorities in order to insulate those areas from political pressures. This avoids sub-optimal policy outcomes induced by structural, political or social pressures at national level, such as time inconsistency in policies owing to changes in government. Thus, the power of the EU is described by Majone as mainly regulatory in nature, which links well with the largely economic nature of the European Union and its core SEM. Building on some of Majone's concepts, one can explore the impact of the EU in the regulation of the economic and commercial activities of sport. This is certainly a possibility to understand and to explain the role of the EU in sport policy. It is generally acknowledged that most EU sport-related decisions to date fall within this 'category', forming the above-mentioned indirect EU sports policy.

The regulation of sport by the EU has affected three main areas, which Parrish (2003a: 120–139; see also Parrish and Miettinen 2008) has defined as the exploitation market, the supply market and the contest market. The 'exploitation market' refers to the commercial activities of sport organisations in the marketing of their competitions. While it includes a variety of issues such as merchandising of ticketing arrangements, the core interest of this area lies on the attempts of the EU to regulate the selling of broadcasting rights for competitions. The 'supply market refers to the buying and selling of players' (Parrish 2003a: 138). This can be more generally understood as the EU regulation of the sport working market; that is the labour relations in professional and semi-professional sport between employees (athletes), and employers (clubs and/or governing bodies). Finally, the 'contest market' refers to the organisational structures of the game (Parrish 2003a: 132). This focuses on the impact of EU decisions on sport governance and the extent to which governing bodies might be trapped in a conflict of interest between their role as sport regulators (i.e. deciding on the rules of the game) and a commercial actor (i.e. selling broadcasting rights). EU incursions in what Parrish called 'the contest market' have developed significantly with a focus on sport governance worldwide. For that reason it seems appropriate to treat them in a section on their own further ahead, rather than in this opening section.

Regulating the players market

The European Union has had a profound impact on the regulation of athletes' working conditions, mostly through the judgements of the CJEU. Back in the 1970s the Court established in *Walrave*[1] and *Donà*[2] that athletes ought to be considered as 'workers' and therefore European regulations apply to their employment conditions as far as this is a matter of economic activity. But it was the well-known *Bosman* case[3] of 1995 where sport severely felt the regulatory power of the Single European Market. In *Bosman* the Court considered that football regulations on nationality quotas and international transfers were illegal in view of the freedom of movement provisions of the Treaty of Rome. Nationality quotas for EU nationals were abolished relatively rapidly by the Union of European Football Associations (UEFA) and national Football Associations. The issue of transfers was slightly more complicated, as sport stakeholders resisted implementing the Court's ruling. It took an investigation, and the threat of further legal proceedings, by the European Commission (European Commission 2001b, 2002) for the governing bodies to modify international transfer regulations. Yet, in the case of international transfers, the EU regulatory powers were mediated by the intervention of Member States (Prime Minister's Office 2000, 2001), which persuaded the Commission to reach a negotiated settlement with the football bodies rather than imposing the full liberalising rigour of EU law. Thus, the issue of international transfers resulted in a certain deregulation of this market, but it is generally acknowledged that the final agreement between FIFA (Fédération Internationale de Football Association), UEFA and the European Commission was a compromise, mostly favourable for the governing bodies' positions.

Even with the reduced impact in the transfer system issue, the effect of these twin cases has been that of a major transformation of the players market, which is now mostly liberalised. The European Union has played an important part in the deregulation of the transfer market, but it has to be noted that it was an indirect participation. These cases were brought before the European institutions by aggrieved parties (i.e. the players), whose struggle with other actors could not be solved within the internal structures of sport. Thus, the role of the EU as a regulator of sport came about virtually by default, rather than by the EU's own choosing. In that respect, regulation by the EU of sport in general and of football in particular could be considered another spillover (Haas 1968) of the process of economic integration and of the completion of the single market.

Regulating the broadcasting market

The commercial activities of sport, especially the exploitation of broadcasting rights, have also been subject to the attention of the EU, especially the Commission's Directorate General for

Competition Policy (DG Comp). Again, this was more of an indirect interest, because the Commission's main objective was the liberalisation of the audiovisual market. The television market in Europe was dominated for a long time by public broadcasters. When the EU liberalised the audiovisual market as part of its efforts to complete the single European market, new private satellite and digital broadcasters emerged throughout Europe (e.g. BSkyB, Canal+, Mediaset). These new operators soon realised the importance of live football broadcasting to secure new subscribers, thus facilitating entrance and domination of the new TV market. The Commission, in turn, noticed that a monopoly of any of these operators on live football broadcasting rights could result in excessive dominance of the recently liberalised market. DG Comp promptly identified the practices of sport bodies selling their broadcasting rights for competitions as a risk of market closure (European Commission 1999b, 1999c).

The European Commission has dealt with a number of cases investigating the way in which sport organisations sell their broadcasting rights. Among those, the high profile of the proceedings against UEFA (European Commission 2003), the English Premier League (European Commission 2006) and the German Bundesliga (European Commission 2005) is especially relevant. The regulation of the European Commission obliged the owners of the rights to sell broadcasting and other commercial rights divided in small packages, so several operators can buy rights for each specific market. In the case of the United Kingdom, the Commission went even further, obliging the Premier League to sell its TV rights to at least two different operators. The EU Competition authorities dedicated most of their attention to the broadcasting of sport, but they also dealt with issues such as licensing of official products[4] or the commercial exploitation of competitions by governing bodies.[5]

These interventions in sport-related cases were not driven by an interest in sport itself, but on the consequences for other sectors of primary importance for the Commission, such as the audiovisual market (European Commission 1999b). These decisions were underpinned by the fact that certain policies and commercial operations of sport organisations could be in breach of basic principles of competition policy or the single market's four fundamental freedoms.[6] The consequences of the EU's regulatory impetus for sport have been very direct and far reaching. In terms of policy, sport is subject to the full application of EU law. In institutional terms for the EU, this definition certainly favours DG Competition or DG Internal Market within the Commission and, more generally, the Commission over the European Parliament because the latter is a more political institution. Finally, for the governing structures of sport, the economic definition favours those that try to maximise economic profits, mainly top professional clubs and leagues. Governing bodies, such as the IOC, UEFA or FIFA, are penalised by this definition because their power to formulate policies would be subject to full EU competition law restrictions.

The EU as a social actor

In the mid 1980s the European Communities were starting to recover from a long period of what has been characterised as Euro-sclerosis, marked politically by Charles de Gaulle's 'empty chair policy' and economically by the financial and oil crisis of the late 1970s. Despite having completed a customs union in 1968 as a result of the Treaty of Rome, European leaders felt there were still too many protectionist regulations deterring the recovery of Europe's economy. A decision was taken to launch a far-reaching six-year programme to remove all those obstacles to create the single market. The Single European Act (SEA) was signed in February 1986 and it was intended to revise the Treaties of Rome in order to add new momentum to European integration. At the same time, the political leaders felt that it was necessary to procure social support for the European project if the citizens were to accept the increased levels of integration and the possible negative consequences of the single European market. For these reasons, the European Council commissioned a group of experts to draft a report on the social aspects of European integration. It was titled *Report on a People's Europe*, although it subsequently became known as the Andonino Report (European Commission 1984). The Andonino Report explored different ways in which to increase social support for European integration, and one of the suggestions was the use of sport. The Andonino report proposed the sponsoring of sporting events in which EC logos could be present, the formation of European teams for major sporting competitions, the promotion of sport for athletes with special needs, or the increased exchange of athletes within the EC (European Commission 1984).

These suggestions were well received by the European Council meeting in Milan in 1985 and also embraced by the European Parliament. The European Commission embarked for a few years on the sponsorship of selected sporting competitions such as Antwerp's tennis tournament (included in the professional tennis circuit), the Tour de l'Avenir (an under-23 version of the Tour de France, which was renamed as Tour of the European Communities from 1986 to 1990), and the 1992 summer Olympic Games (which received a grant from the Commission to display prominently EU flags and emblems during the games). Other initiatives included the Eurathlon programme, whereby the Commission, between 1995 and 1998, funded sport-related projects. This was an instrumental use of sport rather than a policy about sport in Europe. However, it demonstrates that there was some awareness of the social and cultural implications of sport.

One can connect this political discourse of 'an even closer union among the peoples of Europe' with an attempt to create a bottom-up Europhile sense of belonging. The generation of social capital through sport appears to be one of the tools identified by European leaders to do this. In this respect, the introduction of sport in the Andonino report and the idea of the social construction of Europe, can be linked to Putnam's democratic stream of social capital (see Putnam 1993, 1995b, 2000). Certainly, this is an analysis *ex post*, as the EU leaders never expressed their thinking in these terms, but the links seem apparent. Robert Putnam has a positive view of social capital, which he defines as 'connections among individuals, social networks and the norms of reciprocity that arise from them' (Putnam 2000: 19). In this vision, the association of individuals has the capacity of generating mutual trust, hence facilitating social stability. One could argue that, without mentioning it, the Andonino report and the EU leaders identified sport as a generator of European social capital because it can be a vehicle to facilitate exchange and people's connections.

A policy with an uncertain future

In this sociocultural vision of sport, the definition of the European Model of Sport by the European Commission was an important milestone. In an internal working document, the Commission referred to a European Model of Sport based on concepts such as solidarity, grassroots, local identity and tradition (European Commission 1998a). The value of sport as an element of social capital formation appears to underpin the Commission's thinking. It is perhaps for that reason that the *Helsinki Report on Sport* suggested in 1999 that excessive commercialisation of sport could put at risk its most characteristic social values and, therefore, it was necessary to act, if there was a political will, to protect the social features of sport (European Commission 1999a). Yet the *Helsinki Report on Sport* never translated into concrete policy actions and it was severely criticised as an unnecessary intervention of the Commission in an area where it had no competences (Weatherill 2009).

In terms of concrete policy decisions, while initiatives such as student exchange (e.g. the Erasmus programme) have matured to become a clear success, projects in the field of sport linked to this idea of generating social capital have realised very modest results. Proposals, such as the Eurathlon Programme mentioned above, languished slowly until the Court of Justice in 1998 ruled that the Commission could not fund any programmes or initiatives in areas where the EU has no direct legal basis, which was the case of sport.

It is only very recently, with the adoption of the White Paper on Sport (European Commission 2007b) and the inclusion of an article on sport in the Treaty of Lisbon that new policy initiatives and funding programmes are being proposed (see European Commission 2007a). In the last years the European Commission has funded research to acquire knowledge on which to base the development of the new EU sports policy under Article 165 TFEU. Studies on nationality discrimination in individual competitions, on the funding of amateur sports, on sport agents, on the economic impact of sport, or on sport governance have been funded.

In preparation for the new competence, EU institutions, under the initiative of the Commission are completing an action programme (European Commission 2007a) and they are funding the so-called 'Preparatory actions in the field of sport'. These actions have provided some funding (around €300,000 per project) to networks of civil society organisations that presented projects in areas such as the fight against doping, sport and physical activity, racial and gender integration in sport and through sport. These are probably the first steps of a cohesive EU sports policy, and they are heavily focused on the social dimension of sport. The Commission has so far funded projects between 2009 and 2011, and the results have yet to be evaluated.

Building on these preparatory actions, at the time of writing, the European Commission has agreed to propose an important initiative in the field of sport to implement the newly acquired competence of Article 165 TFEU. The Commission aims to propose a multiannual programme on education and culture, which will embed a part dedicated to sport on its own. If successful, this initiative will provide funds in the region of €30 million per year to implement initiatives that can develop 'the European dimension of sport', as required by Article 165 TFEU. This new programme will follow the political priorities set in the White Paper on Sport and the communication *Developing the European Dimension of Sport* (European Commission 2007b, 2011), with a heavy focus on social aspects of sport such as the educational role of sport, sport and social inclusion, amateur and grass-roots sport, gender and racial discrimination in sport, etc.

However, the entering into force of this programme is subject to two important obstacles. First, the Heads of State and Government of the Member States (meeting in the European Council) need to agree the EU Financial Perspectives for the period 2013–19, and that is not going to be an easy process. Sport policy could be a casualty if the leaders decide to reduce drastically the EU budget. Second, providing the adoption of the financial perspectives, the mentioned funding programme will have to be adopted by the Council of Ministers and the Parliament through the usual co-decision procedure. The latter aspect is less likely to be a problem, and it might well be the case that the Parliament increases the level of funding.

Thus, EU sport policy can also be analysed from a sociocultural perspective. The concept of social capital can help to explain the willingness of the EU to get involved in sport and social issues. It is only with the adoption of Article 165 TFEU that a fully fledged EU sport policy is developing, and it appears that it will focus on the sociocultural aspects of sport. However, it is still early days, and much will depend on the level of funding agreed within the new Financial Perspectives in 2013. This makes policy prognosis extremely difficult.

The EU and the governance of sport

Finally, the importance of the EU in sport policy can also be analysed through the concept of governance, especially systemic governance, which looks at the divisions of power and competences between public authorities and sport non-governmental organisations in the governance of sport. This is a difficult territory for EU institutions to negotiate. On the one hand, sport bodies are eager to vindicate the so-called autonomy of sport (see for example Blatter 2007; FIFA 2006). The concept of autonomy calls into question the necessity for public authorities to get involved in sport regulation, and especially in sport governance. This, of course, also applies to the EU. On the other hand, EU institutions, while acknowledging sport autonomy (see European Council 2000; European Parliament 2007), are not willing to relinquish their duty to protect the correct application of the provisions of the EU treaties to sport (European Commission 2007b). It is fair to affirm that EU institutions are reluctant to dictate which governance structures should be adopted in sport (García 2009a). That was especially evident in the *White Paper on Sport*, where the European Commission (2007b: 12) considered it 'unrealistic' to define one single model of sport governance in Europe and it acknowledged the complexities of new stakeholders gaining importance in sport. It is quite evident, however, that EU institutions are keen to be vigilant and they will make their support of the autonomy of sport conditional to the adoption of the highest standards of good governance (García 2009b, 2010).

To analyse the implications of EU sport policy in terms of governance, it may be useful to use the work of Ken Foster on the regulation of sport by the EU (Foster 2000). Foster analysed three alternative models of sports regulation by the European Union (Foster 2000: 43): first, the enforcement of private rights through the European Court of Justice (Foster 2000: 46); second, the regulation of sport by the Commission through competition policy, which allows for exemptions to be granted in particular cases (Article 101.3 TFEU) – this was conceptualised as 'supervised autonomy' (Foster 2000: 58); third, a more political approach that would accept sports self-regulation without the intervention of EU law (Foster 2000: 60).

Building on Foster's argument one can suggest three alternative visions of sports governance and, consequently, three different roles for EU institutions in those systems of governance: first, a direct or regulatory approach, where EU institutions would be an essential part of sports governance formulating policies about structures in sport; second, an approach that would recognise the total autonomy of sport and sport would be granted an exemption from the application of EU law. In this approach EU institutions would have no regulatory role in sports governance, but ideally they would endorse, support and facilitate sports governing bodies' initiatives (e.g. giving them political recognition or creating funding initiatives). In this model the role of EU institutions could be categorised as partnership; finally, a level of 'supervised autonomy' (Foster 2000: 58), where the sporting movement recognises the fundamental principles of EU law, but EU institutions do not have a proactive role in directly regulating sports governance, which is left to self-regulation. In this model, however, EU law adds a further layer of complexity because it is recognised that it applies to the activities of sports organisations.

It seems as if the undeniable importance of the EU in sport policy terms is lately moving towards this 'supervised autonomy' paradigm. On the one hand, EU institutions are not going to relinquish their powers under the EU Treaty to regulate sport activities if they affect the single market. Such regulation, however, will take into account the concept of the specificity of sport, which features in Article 165 TFEU. On the other hand, the new EU sport policy will be implemented in close cooperation with sport organisations, as the European Commission has already outlined. Thus, EU institutions have now become important actors in the governance of sport and their relevance is likely to increase, especially if the new sport programme goes ahead as planned by the Commission.

In this governance network, EU institutions play a double role. First, EU institutions (especially the Court of Justice and the Commission) will be supervising the application of EU law to sport, as explained in the White Paper. Second, they are happy to identify concrete areas in which their actions can add value to the work of federations and other stakeholders. This role can be characterised as partnership. The debate is open, however, as to where to put the stress – on the supervision or on the partnership.

Conclusion

The European Union is a supranational organisation whose initial remit was totally unrelated to sport. However, over the last two decades the EU has got involved in a number of far-reaching sport-related decisions, despite its lack of direct competence in sport. It is this lack of a constitutional mandate that makes it especially difficult to analyse EU sport policy, for it is an amorphous entity with no clear remit and objectives. The rising importance of the EU in sport can be analysed through three different concepts: the EU as a regulator, the EU as a social actor and the role of the EU in the governance of sport.

Although the initial regulatory impetus of the Court of Justice of the European Union and the Commission as regulators has been slightly modified by the political intervention of the Member States and the Parliament, it is still an important role. EU institutions are not going to relinquish their power under the Treaties and EU sport policy can still be understood as a regulatory policy. The adoption of the Treaty of Lisbon and the inclusion of Article 165 TFEU have opened the possibility of developing, for the first time a direct and coherent EU sport policy. Such policy is likely to focus on sociocultural issues. If the plans of the European Commission are not derailed by political or budgetary negotiations, the EU will increase its importance even more in sport, for it will have significant funds to implement its policies. Yet, this will still be accompanied by a regulatory role. The 'supervised autonomy' of sport is unlikely to be modified. Actually, the new programmes and the budget to be allocated by the European Commission might prove a very useful resource to secure compliance of sport organisations with good governance principles.

8

NON-GOVERNMENTAL ORGANISATIONS IN SPORT FOR DEVELOPMENT AND PEACE

Oscar Mwaanga

Introduction

The intensification of the Sport for Development and Peace (SDP) movement may be evidenced through the 'over 400 non-governmental organisations implementing Sport for Development and Peace interventions' in marginalised communities around the world (Hayhurst *et al.*, 2010, p. 3). According to Kidd (2008), non-governmental organisation (NGO) involvement within the SDP sector has grown apace and vastly expanded its enterprise, particularly through the medium of partnerships. This escalation of SDP initiatives has consequently generated considerable interest with various researchers examining the broad utility of sport in promoting social change (e.g. Armstrong, 2004; Burnett, 2010; Darnell, 2010; Hognestad and Tollisen, 2004; Kay, 2009; Levermore, 2008; Lindsey and Banda, 2010). Given that, on the whole, SDP initiatives are realised through or by means of SDP NGOs, it can be argued that these actors make up a significant driving force within the SDP movement. However, while constituting perhaps the prime driving force, NGOs are by no means lone players in this movement (Giulianotti, 2011; Levermore, 2008). Other organisations that are not classed as NGOs including government agencies, intergovernmental organisations (IGOs) and transnational corporations, all of which may be few in number but have a significant impact on the SDP movement in their own right. Notable examples include the United Nations (UN), the International Labour Organization (ILO), the United Nations Children's Fund (UNICEF) and the World Health Organization (WHO). For instance, the SDP expansion in part led the UN to declare the year 2005 as the International Year of Sport and Physical Education. By doing so, the UN clearly demonstrated its belief in the capacity of sport to be an effective tool for furthering the UN's development initiatives, particularly its Millennium Development Goals (United Nations General Assembly, 2006). Other UN related and specialist agencies have also recognised sport as a tool for international development, notably, UNICEF and WHO, which recognise that sport can improve the physical and mental health of specific populations (e.g. children and people with terminal illness), and have developed partnerships with NGOs, private interest groups and community-based organisations to encourage sports participation. Moreover, some governments in the Global North[1] (e.g. the Netherlands, Switzerland, Canada, Norway, the UK and Australia), through their respective development agencies, have not only provided funds but contributed towards the development of SDP policy. Equally, a number of Global South governments and intergovernmental institutions (e.g. the African Union) have taken particular interest in the capacity of SDP interventions to deliver development.

However, a lack of investigative studies focusing on SDP-related NGOs ensures that their roles and impacts remain elusive; indeed, a dearth of publicly available data regarding, for example, NGO impact assessments, further compounds the need for clarification (Horton, 2011). Furthermore, SDP research has been focused on examining sports impacts with limited considerations being given to wider social cultural approaches (Kay, 2009). Also, SDP discourse and research has not fully engaged the political, ideological and 'transnational complexity of the SDP sector' (Giulianotti, 2011, p. 51). Hence, the contention of this chapter is that in order to achieve positive transformative change in SDP, the politics relating to SDP NGOs and SDP in general has to be brought out of the 'closet'.

In this vein, then, using power, ideology and postcolonial theory as a theoretical framework of analysis, this chapter examines two related areas: first, the nature of SDP NGOs and their remit; and second, the relationship between SDP NGOs and how such relationships underpin SDP policy processes and outcomes. The chapter ends with the application of the theoretical framework to suggest and elaborate new insights into positive transformation of the SDP sector.

What are SDP NGOs?

A logical point of departure in trying to estimate the nature and identity of SDP NGOs is to elucidate what is meant by the term NGO in this context. NGOs are heterogeneous organisations that are linked to alternative terms such as the independent sector, volunteer sector, civil society, grass-roots organisations, transnational social movement organisations, private voluntary organisations, self-help organisations and non-state actors (NSAs). In wider usage, the term NGO can be applied to any non-profit organisation that is independent from government. NGOs are typically value-based organisations that depend, in whole or in part, on charitable donations and voluntary service. While ambiguity surrounds the definition of NGOs, the principles of altruism and voluntarism remain key defining characteristics. The World Bank defines NGOs as 'private organizations that pursue activities to relieve suffering, promote the interests of the poor, protect the environment, provide basic social services, or undertake community development' (Duke University Libraries, n.d.). Willets (2006, p. 2) recognises that 'at the UN virtually all types of private bodies can be recognised as NGOs ... so long as they are ... independent from government control, not seeking to challenge governments as a political party, non-profit-making and non-criminal'. Though this definition has broad distinguishing features, it is vague and leads to wide range usage of the term. However, Green (2008, pp. 90–91) highlights that NGOs are, characteristically, 'not driven solely by financial motives and may have imprecise objectives', and are accountable to diverse parties and heavily driven by volunteers. In sum, NGOs can be distinguished from government and profit-making or private sector institutions, but due to their wide ranging remit and sometimes imprecise objectives it is difficult to clearly distinguish between NGOs based on rigid definitional parameters.

Within the SDP sector the wide ranging usage of the term 'NGO' in trying to capture the multifarious organisational forms prevalent within the movement, together with the organisations' various contextual and purpose-related idiosyncrasies, becomes an issue when attempting to comprehend the characteristics and contributions of NGOs (Lewis, 2007). In addition, the ambiguity surrounding the meaning of the term 'sport for development' itself further compounds the difficulties of conceptualisation of NGO involvement within the movement. For example, Houlihan and White (2002) differentiate between development *of* sport (that is, interventions in which organisations aim to enhance participation and performance in sport as an end in itself; e.g. the International Football Association) and development *through* sport (signifying those interventions or organisations designed to use sport as a vehicle to achieve a range of social development goals). For example, Sport in Action is an indigenous Zambian SDP NGO founded in 1999 with the primary purpose of using sport as a tool to address community development goals. Other commentators have added to this debate; for instance, Coalter (2007b) introduces the terms 'sport plus' and 'plus sport'. Accordingly, 'sport plus' refers to initiatives primarily focused on the development of sport whereas 'plus sport' initiatives chiefly focus on social development through sport (Coalter, 2007b). Levermore and Beacom (2009) add a useful dimension that problematises the general categorisations of 'development through sport' and 'sport for development'. They assert that such conceptualisations assume that the use of sport in the development process is overwhelmingly positive, thus precluding the possibility of sport being detrimental to development. Against this backdrop, they advocate the use of 'sport-in-development' as representative of the perception that the use of sport *may* assist in the development process (Levermore and Beacom, 2009). Notwithstanding what may seem a useful debate that takes analysis beyond mere terminologies, a number of questions still remain unanswered, owing to the diversity of SDP NGOs.

SDP NGOs represent a myriad of forms and purposes for involvement in the SDP movement (Black, 2010). For example, SDP non-governmental organisations may be local, national, regional, transnational or international in their operational capacity, while also being based either in the Global North and/or in the Global South (Yeates, 2009). A local NGO can be localised to a particular community, in which case they may be called community-based organisations (CBOs). SDP CBOs will usually carry the name of a specific geographical community. An example here would be the Bauleni United Sport Association (BUSA), an SDP CBO using sport to address wide-ranging developmental issues facing young people in a geographically defined community: Bauleni (Zambia). Bauleni is a shanty compound located on the outskirts of Lusaka, the capital city of Zambia. The Rwandan 'Football for Peace' can be considered an example of a national SDP NGO. 'Football for Peace' encourages co-ed football, teaches self-responsibility, improving capabilities in conflict resolution and countering the negative impacts of the ethnic divide of the Rwandan population. Open Fun Football Schools has a similar remit to 'Football for Peace' in Rwanda, but because it concentrates on the Balkans region, it can be considered a good example of a regional SDP NGO. An apparent example of a transnational or international SDP NGO is the Toronto-based organisation Right to Play (RTP), which runs projects in over 20 Global South countries. RTP uses Western volunteers to run sports activities and programmes aimed at promoting physical health and life skills.

NGOs will naturally occupy variegated positions of what could be termed the 'vertical hierarchy' of the SDP movement (Nicholls, 2009, p. 158). In addition, SDP NGOs are further diversified when considering their location either in the Global North or South. Also based on the organisation's foci may be SDP NGOs categorically placed within funding (i.e. donor and/or recipient) SDP NGOs, performing advocacy and/or programme implementation (Levermore, 2008). In line with the above categorisation, the Laureus Sport for Good Foundation is an example of a Global North and predominately funding SDP NGO, while the Tegle Loroupe Peace Foundation, which promotes peace in the Greater Horn of Africa, can be categorised as a Global South and recipient SDP NGO. Furthermore, Levermore (2008, p. 185) suggests the following descriptive clustering of SDP NGOs based on the development objectives they seek to achieve:

1. Conflict resolution and intercultural understanding.
2. Building physical, social, sport and community infrastructure.

3. Raising awareness, particularly through education.
4. Empowerment: direct impact on physical and psychological health, as well as general welfare.
5. Economic development/poverty alleviation.

However, although the above classifications appear to situate SDP NGOs within distinctive categories, in reality these categories, more often than not, become blurred (Coalter, 2008). Certainly, examples of NGOs imbued with the SDP movement's main premises noted in the introduction may be found in all the diverse categorisations highlighted above (Beacom and Levermore, 2008). Despite these variations in SDP NGOs, at a fundamental level there is consensus on the basic notion that SDP NGOs use sport (and other forms of physical recreation) to facilitate social betterment in targeted communities and nations (Coalter, 2007b; Hognestad and Tollisen, 2004; Levermore, 2008). However, this consensus discourse has become so pervasive as to overshadow the realities of SDP as a complex and holistic set of changing processes simultaneously framed by tension and (re)production. The following statement crystallises the aforementioned consensus-based discourse: 'Sport for Development and Peace efforts catalyse global partnerships and increase networking among governments, donors, NGOs and sport organisations worldwide' (Sport for Development and Peace International Working Group, 2008, p. 12).

The assumption that harmony and order is a prerequisite of progress is without doubt based on Western development ideologies, including modernism and neoliberalism. However, such assumptions misrepresent the realities of SDP as a social construction shaped holistically by order and tension and heavily predicated by particular historical events, wider social factors and political ideologies. Indeed, SDP is a strongly contested set of practices that must be understood in relationship to both global and local arrangements in development and sport. These assumptions are taken often uncritically as received truth in contemporary SDP discourse. Notwithstanding this, some have begun to question the limited criticality and theoretical reflection in SDP (e.g. Black, 2010; Kay, 2009; Kidd, 2008). For example McDonald (2005, p. 582) critiques the allegedly harmonious SDP partnerships, which purport to build on 'equality, shared values and high trust, creating an illusory unity which masks fundamental differences of power and resources between the network organisations'.

Indeed, the SDP sector may arguably be described as a policy community, with many overlapping and sometimes competing interest groups, linked together by resources and common concerns, working in a sometimes crowded policy space. Given the complexity of the field, this chapter advocates theoretical approaches that deconstruct the received wisdom concerning SDP NGOs.

Theoretical frameworks

In order to disinter the nature, role and the relations of SDP NGOs, this section examines and applies three theoretical concepts and frameworks, namely, ideology, power and post-colonial theory, bringing to the fore some important historical, social and political issues that must be examined to achieve the kinds of critical understanding we have advocated.

SDP NGOs and ideology

All actions undertaken by SDP NGOs reflect particular assumptions and taken-for-granted 'truths', sets of beliefs (or ideologies) about the purpose and vision of SDP. Ideology informs the philosophical foundations (or worldviews) that construct social works. As Eze (1998) holds, the philosophical foundations of any society provide the meaning to what it is to be alive and to thus guide our views on development. Indeed, the SDP policy arena is not ahistorical or apolitical nor does it exist in an ideologically neutral vacuum, because it is socially constructed in a particular time, place, with specific purposes and in conformity with prevailing 'rules' for knowing, principles and values to support 'truth' and policy positions (Eakin *et al.*, 1996; Guba, 1990). Ideology as a social construction is an essential frame of reference which SDP NGOs use to define or make sense of their identity and roles.

The international milieu of SDP and its variegated sport NGOs operating between the Global North and South necessitates attention to the 'politics of development knowledge and development practice', together with the philosophical ideas this politics underpins (Black, 2010, p. 125). Cognisance of the historicity and ideologies that permeate the cultural exchanges that naturally occur within this internationally contoured movement is crucial. For example, SDP must take cognisance of the slave trade, colonialism and the 'destructive contact' between the North and South that comes to bear on the movement's architecture (Shivji, 2007, p. 3). These are essential in understanding the nature and role of SDP NGOs because they directly and indirectly inform certain actions.

For instance, what are the ramifications, of the view that SDP practice is framed inherently by neocolonialist, neoliberal and modernist ideologies that originate in the Global North (Darnell, 2010; Girginov and Hills, 2009)? The response is simply that international SDP practice aligns itself rather crudely to Global Northern notions of development that comprise 'a set of knowledges, interventions and world views which are also powers to intervene, to transform and to rule' (Sidaway, 2008, p. 16). Nicholls highlights that: 'Partnerships between north and south, donors and recipients, as well as between policy makers and practitioners, are fundamentally shaped by the pervasive discourses of [Northern] development' (Nicholls, 2009, p. 45).

The North, owing to its hegemony over the South, has the power to 'name, represent and theorize'; to produce knowledge on people and their lands and thus to recommend the 'best' courses of action in order for development to occur (Blunt and McEwan, 2002, p. 9). By implication, the naming or theorising of the South by the North takes away a fundamental right of Global Southern SDP NGOs to construct their own identity. Consequently, SDP becomes a place of ideological contest since Global South NGOs can be assumed to engage the movement based on the terms of their indigenous ideology.

For instance, the sub-Saharan African ideology of Ubuntu is important in the way many sub-Saharan African Sport NGOs approach their work. In short, Ubuntu 'is an ancient African worldview with roots deeply anchored in traditional African way of life' (Broodryk, 2002, p. 56). Ubuntu is often translated through the common African aphorism as: 'a person is a person through other persons' (Ramose, 1999, p. 49; Shutte, 1993, p. 46). This brings the ideal of being-with-others and coexisting in humility and compassion at the core of the Ubuntu worldview (Broodryk, 2002). Indeed, social relationships and community frame the idea of 'being and identity' for the sub-Saharan African (Forester, 2010, p. 244). To put this in a practical context, the EduSport Foundation[2] explicitly adopts Ubuntu as the organisational philosophy that it translates in its community development and empowerment-focused approach to SDP (EduSport Foundation, 2011). When SDP is understood as a development approach that is a 'powerful language which has historically functioned as a tool to ... replace one reality with another' (Wai, 2007, p. 73), one clearly sees how SDP is an ideologically contested policy arena. To build on the previous example, the EduSport Foundation as a Global Southern NGO is in apparent resistance to neoliberal and modernist assumptions of development when it explicitly or implicitly promotes Ubuntu. For instance, neoliberal and modernist assumptions of development more often than not have resulted in individualist (e.g. behaviour change) focused SDP interventions as opposed to community or collective orientated interventions that are framed within the Ubuntu worldview.

The view that hegemonic Northern ideologies frame SDP prevailing practice and assumptions is in itself not problematic because ultimately a particular ideology will influence a given society at a particular time in history. However, what is problematic is that SDP practices and assumptions are too often implicit, rendered invisible because they are perceived as self-evident truths or 'facts' rather than as socially derived conventions (Raphael, 2000). In addition, ideology also places a hierarchy on certain views and the holders of such views as congruent to 'universal truth'. This perpetuates the idea of privileged and uncontested positionality for some SDP NGOs and not others. Within the SDP context, they follow de rigueur, granting precedence to those SDP NGOs that occupy positions close to the Global North as the source of 'universal truth'. This is what Nicholls (2009, p. 158) terms SDP's 'vertical hierarchy'. In effect, those situated at the bottom of the hierarchy (i.e. indigenous or Global South NGOs) and their worldviews become further marginalised on the pretext that their views are not on based on factual knowledge. Consequently, the 'production and reproduction of misrepresentation' of the Global South NGOs is maintained. This chapter argues that the systematic and theoretical analysis that allows deconstruction of ideology unlocks opportunities for marginalised SDP NGOs to present their take on SDP which provides a unique and radical transformational development opportunity that is rarely seen in traditional development circles. Ideology is closely linked to power whose centrality in understanding the SDP NGOs cannot be disputed. We therefore turn in the section that follows to examine the role of power in the identity and role of SDP NGOs.

SDP NGOs and the role of power

The Global North/donor and Global South/recipient power relationship and the hegemonic colonising practices that pervade SDP, like other domains of international development, necessitate an interrogation of power and its manifestations (Rail, 2002). We can safely contend that not only is SDP mitigated by issues of power, but that its development and daily practices hinge on the workings of power. In fact, it is difficult to fully comprehend the nature and interactions of SDP NGOs outside the theoretical framework of power. Moreover, when SDP is viewed as a cultural endeavour designed in the North and implemented in the South, then SDP can be considered as closely related to resistance and (re)production of oppressive social relations (Brace-Govan, 2004; Shaw, 2001). Power relations in development have been approached from a range of theoretical vantage points (Rossi, 2004). Relevant for this current examination is the Foucauldian theory that focuses on development as a 'discursive formation'. According to Rossi (2004, p. 26) a 'discursive formation is a historically rooted system in which particular statements and acts make sense' more than others. When applied to SDP, 'this approach looks at development as a historically and culturally specific form of rationality which is inseparable from related regimes of practice and configurations of power' (Rossi, 2004, p. 1).

However, to fully appreciate the notion of discursive formations it is imperative to familiarise oneself with a more fundamental Foucauldian concept of discourse. Discourse can be defined as a system of ideas or knowledge linked to a specific text that is used to identify and legitimise the privileging of power of one person over another (Fairclough, 2003), or, simply a 'body of language use that is unified by common assumptions' (Abercrombie et al., 2000, p. 99). This analysis of discourse is divorced from its strictly linguistic roots to focus on its application in the specific social domain of development. Its application here coincides more with the general definition provided by Grillo: 'A discourse [for example, of development] identifies appropriate and legitimate ways of practising development [and SDP] as well as speaking and thinking about it' (1997, p. 12).

Clearly, discourse and discursive formation are productive in supporting the understanding of the ways in which discourse transmits power (Rail, 2002). This is largely because SDP NGOs do not work or 'exist without a certain regime of rationality' (Foucault, 1991, p. 79) that is 'historically rooted; and that ... works as a structure of knowledge, allowing, at any particular time, certain events and patterns of agency [for example, the sending of sport volunteers from the Global North to the Global South by Right to Play], and rendering unthinkable, unsayable and undoable others [for example, zero acceptance of innovative approaches in SDP from the Global South]' Rossi (2004, p. 2). Undoubtedly, it is within discourse that the identities, meanings and power relationships of SDP NGOs can be reinforced or challenged. As previously mentioned, discourse concerning SDP practices privileges a particular form of rationality or 'legitimates' relations of power whereby the Northern development paradigms dominate SDP practice. For example, only Western sport is used predominantly as a tool for fostering SDP interventions, as if their Global Southern communities do not have forms of physical recreation of their own. The discourse approach analysis of power relations in SDP practice also urges us to think in terms of a plurality of discourse. In his analysis Foucault (1975, p. 15) raises questions pertinent to understanding SDP NGOS and the work they do:

> What individuals, what groups or classes have access to a particular kind of discourse? How is the relationship institutionalised between the discourses, speakers and its destined audience? How is the relationship of the discourse to this author indicated and defined? How is the struggle for the control of discourse conducted between classes, actions, linguistic cultural or ethnic collectivises?

In the preceding quotation, Foucault (1975) acknowledges the hierarchically stratified subjectivities reacting to and manipulating discourses, but he does not reconcile these views. Levermore and Beacom (2009) identified the EduSport Foundation and Sport in Action as two indigenous NGOs that showed some evidence of practice that runs counter to the dominant SDP practices. Nevertheless, it should be noted that resistance is a form of power and that marginalised discourses have the opportunity to resist dominant discourses and subsequently force change (Pringle, 2005). Resistance is the mechanism whereby those who experience oppression on the basis of race, gender, age and sexual preference can challenge the multiple axes of power. This is well captured in Rossi's (2004, p. 26) articulation:

> This is particularly evident in the field of development, where actors [especially the 'recipients' of policies and 'interventions'] are faced with discourses to some degree external to their language, culture, and society. Relative 'distance' from the sources of development rationality increases the room for manoeuvre available to the actors involved ... But negotiations do not take place between equals. While it is important not to characterise less powerful actors as passive, there is a difference between framing the terms of reference for discursive struggles and being at best able to manipulate dominant orders of discourse subversively.

The hegemonic dominance of the Western development ideologies in framing the SDP NGOs and SDP policy in general leaves very few examples to refer to when trying to contextualise how an alternative SDP development perspective can shape SDP policy.

However, although Foucault (1975) offers very useful ways of conceptualising power in the SDP context, the actualities of power in framing the identities, work and social relationships of SDP NGOS are far too comprehensive and multidimensional to be captured in a single theory of power. Hence, other theoretical vantage points must be explored in order to understand the different formations of power in the SDP milieu. For instance, when trying to understand how Global South SDP NGOs foster resistance to hegemonic ideologies, the structural perspective of power that entails power as dominance provides an appropriate critical insight (see Deem, 1988). Likewise, the post-structuralist, examined above, helps to explore how power is embedded in social actions and relations within the SDP context (Foucault, 1978, 1981).

In gaining understanding of how SDP NGOs interpret and engage with the power issues in the framing of their identities and work, Lukes's (1974) dimensional analysis of power framework provides some insights. Lukes's (1993) framework is a useful way through which to meaningfully engage power dynamics and formations. In his analysis, Lukes (2005) identifies three dimensions of power: power as an overt dimension; power as subtle expression; and power as covert dimension. First, by viewing power as an overt dimension, we can begin to consider how alternative SDP views, ideas and issues are brought into focus through repressive direct, active and explicit methods (Eakin *et al.*, 1996). For example, Global South SDP NGOs are familiar with this overt dimension of power when their funding bids are explicitly turned down for reasons framed in development discourse with which they are not conversant. Another relevant example that highlights overt power is that it took over ten years for the Norwegian Confederation of Sport sponsored Kicking AIDS Out Network to formally acknowledge that the author, representing a Global South SDP NGO, was the founder for the Kicking AIDS Out approach (see Kicking AIDS Out Network History, 2010).

The second dimension of power helps us to understand the manifestations of power in more subtle ways. For instance, we can consider how alternative issues are brought to the table, but instead of being actively or overtly suppressed, they may be defused through negotiation, compromise or co-optation. A familiar example is how SDP initiatives pioneered in the South, such as the Kicking AIDS Out approach (Mwaanga, 2001), when co-opted into northern paradigms end up taking a mainstream behaviour focus as opposed to, say, a focus on poverty eradication (Eakin *et al.*, 1996). Finally, and most critical, is the covert dimension of power. This is the 'most insidious dimension of power because of its relative invisibility' (Eakin *et al.*, 1996, p. 159). This dimension of power works below the radar system in determining the general direction and formulations of SDP policy. To expose this type of power we must ask the question 'Whose interests are promoted by the adoption of particular SDP policies and actions? The Global Northern NGOs are viewed as powerful by virtue of the fact that their interests are served by the particular actions, policies, knowledge approaches etc. Alternative approaches, views and knowledge, for example, by indigenous Global South NGOs, are not brought to the SDP table because they are not even perceived as worthwhile. For example, one can apply this notion in trying to understand why many Southern SDP NGOs with non-Western development rationalities are not considered favourably for funding support and hence are disqualified from funding. Clearly, by evoking Lukes's (2005) framework we not only illuminate the different formations but also open up the possibility that marginalised SDP NGOs can be understood, and (more importantly) be understood based on stories told by themselves.

The following section presents and examines post-colonial theory as tool for debunking power and ideological formations and underpinnings that frame the identity and work of SDP NGOs as transnational SDP actors.

Post-colonial theory

Post-colonialism (post-colonial theory) is a specific intellectual discourse that consists of reactions to, and analysis of, the cultural legacy of colonialism (Sharp, 2008; Young; 2003). This conceptualisation of post-colonialism is useful in so far as it locates post-colonialism as a continuation of colonialism, albeit through different or new relationships concerning power and the control/production of knowledge (Sharp, 2008). Conceptualising post-colonialism as a temporal concept, meaning the time after colonialism has ceased, or the time following the politically determined independence day on which a country breaks away from its governance by another state, can be problematic because the 'once-colonized world' is full of 'contradictions, of half-finished processes, of confusions … and liminalities' (Dictionary of Human Geography, 2007, p. 561). For example, colonialism involves interruption and destruction of native culture by European [Western] imperialism (Smith, 1999). Gilbert and Tompkins (1996) urge that the debate and understanding of post-colonialism must be less a chronological construction of post-independence, more of a discursive experience where we engage and contest the colonial discourses, power structures and social hierarchies. The above conceptualisation of post-colonialism implies structural domination, meaning a system of control and discursive oppression whereby the dominant discourse privileges white, patriarchal knowledge and deems inferior the knowledge stemming from the non-whites (Darnell, 2007). Post-colonialism touches on one of the central issues within development – the concept of power and how it shapes development thinking and policy (McKay, 2004).

For example, the concept of representation and the power to dominate representations, among others, finds itself central to the post-colonial theoretic (Amselle, 2006; Said, 2006). Post-colonial studies have unmasked how (neo)colonial representations 'implicitly assume Western standards as the benchmark against which to measure' all things: this includes ontological assumptions, knowledge and the effectiveness of SDP interventions (Escobar, 1995, p. 8; Hettne, 1995; Smith, 1999). This is significant for the current analysis in that, fundamentally, organisations represent 'sets of collective action … undertaken in an effort to shape the world and human lives' (Czarniawska-Joerges, 2004, p. 407). In this sense, NGOs that support sustainable sports development (for whatever purpose, in whatever form and to whatever degree) do so in a distinctive manner; prescribing and describing according to their particular organisational constructions, perceptions and visions 'about the purpose of human life' and thus the nature of social development (Girginov and Hills, 2009, p. 165).

Post-colonial insights attend to the globally defined inequalities that exist and that undeniably permeate the SDP movement, giving (Northern) NGOs the influence 'to have particular truth effects' (Knights, 2004, p. 16; Nicholls *et al.*, 2011). Indeed, these unequal power relations determine which NGOs hold the privilege to 'define and shape [the movement's] constitution, identity and practices' (Giulianotti, 2011, p. 211). Following Chomsky, one might argue that the SDP movement and its interests are somewhat 'defined by power centres, operating in closed chambers' (Chomsky, 1999, p. 137). These closed chambers are evinced in the disparity of rhetoric and actual representativeness vis-à-vis stakeholder influence within the international SDP policy process (Beacom and Levermore, 2008; Nicholls *et al.*, 2011). Furthermore, in that an organisation's culture[3] (indeed guided by the wider cultural context within which it is situated) determines, somewhat, the processes and projects it realises, and given the diversity of NGOs within the movement, why is it that there is an increasingly 'homogenised SDP agenda'?

> This raises important questions about how to balance attempts to respect local SDP knowledge with attempts to promote a global agenda … SDP scholars and activists might

consider whether a cohesive movement might neglect issues of colonial histories, domina-tions, marginalisation, material poverty and inequality.

(Hayhurst *et al.*, 2010, p. 12)

This evokes otherwise mitigated considerations pertaining to the epistemological distances that may exist between the globally dispersed NGOs involved in the movement (Jammulamadaka and Varman, 2010). Moreover, in highlighting the exclusionary tendencies regarding repre-sentation, one may begin to comprehend that 'NGO action is ... based on certain theoretical premises and philosophical outlooks' (Shivji, 2007, p. 35) and particular ideological foundations.

Conclusion

The theoretical analysis applied in this chapter brought to bear the centrality of power and ideology, and how their deconstruction allows critical understanding of SDP NGOs and SDP practice in general. Deconstruction of ideology and power also provides practical approaches for engaging and understanding prevalent actions and decisions in SDP. In addition, this approach unlocks opportunities for marginalised SDP NGOs to enhance their voice, which provides unique opportunities for positive and transformative change. Exposing the implicit ideological and power formations entails at least that variegated identities and roles of SDP NGOs can be contested and (re)constructed on grounds other than those provided for by the hegemonic ideology (Tesh, 1990). For example, it allows us to see how 'ideology leads to concentration upon certain factors, variables or issues to the exclusion of others' (Raphael, 2000, p. 362). This allows us to question the rules of exclusion; for instance, as evidenced via SDP discourse which rhetorically endorses the involvement of indigenous SDP NGOs while excluding their input in decision-making processes and views in the construction of SDP (Burnett, 2010; Hayhurst *et al.*, 2010).

Finally, post-colonial theory was introduced as a discursive experience in engaging and contesting the colonial discourses, power structures and social hierarchies as they present in the construction, remits and interaction of SDP NGOs. We have sought to demonstrate how post-colonial theory helps to deconstruct the SDP discourse that purports political neutrality and consensus and yet is predominantly perpetuating and privileging hegemonic Global North values, principles and visions. The post-colonial theoretical analysis prospective provides hope for a decolonised future SDP practice that renders explicit the ideology and power structures at play in shaping the field.

9

EVALUATING OLYMPIC SOLIDARITY 1982–2012

Marie Therese Zammit and Ian Henry

Introduction: the role and function of Olympic Solidarity within the Olympic movement

Olympic Solidarity manages and administers the share of IOC income allocated to the National Olympic Committees from the sale of the television rights of the Olympic Games, providing sport aid programmes to meet their specific needs. Its primary function is thus an expression of solidarity between the developed (in sporting and in economic terms) and the developing world, within the Olympic movement through the redistribution of funds. Indeed the aim of the Olympic Solidarity Commission is stipulated in Chapter 1, Rule 5 of the IOC Charter as follows:

> The aim of Olympic Solidarity is to organise assistance to NOCs, *in particular those which have the greatest need of it.* This assistance takes the form of programmes elaborated jointly by the IOC and the NOCs, with the technical assistance of the IFs, if necessary.
>
> (International Olympic Committee, 2011, pp. 17–18; emphasis added)

It is the aim of this chapter to evaluate whether Olympic Solidarity can be said to meet this aim through a progressive redistribution of funds.

Figure 9.1 illustrates the primary sources of funding within the Olympic movement of which broadcasting revenue is by far the most significant. However, the sources of funding for Solidarity were not always so significant. Starting off with a few programmes in the early 1970s, with little finance and few administrative or technical staff, it has evolved into a distributor of multimillion dollar funded sport aid programmes, created for specific areas of the Olympic movement. In collaboration with the relevant International Federations, Olympic Solidarity seeks to provide better conditions in which athletes and officials may develop; and to spread Olympic values within the NOCs by funding values-related projects. Apart from its redistributive function, Olympic Solidarity is regarded by commentators as performing a number of other key roles. These include the generating of loyalty to the International Olympic Committee (1993), providing continuity in Olympic activity in the years between the games (Miller, 1979, p. 157), reducing threats from a number of other international sports organisations such as the Games of the New Emerging Forces (GANEFO) (Al-Tauqi, 2003), as well as seeking to ensure autonomy for the NOCs in their own countries (Chappelet and Kübler-Mabbott, 2008). Olympic Solidarity has facilitated the expansion of the Olympic Movement by developing and integrating new National Olympic Committees, particularly those from Asia and Africa, and later South America, Oceania and the former Soviet Union and Yugoslavia. The gradual development of the management of sport both in the NOCs and in the International Federations has risen in tandem with an overall increase in the level of technical expertise required in administration and coaching and in the volume of participation of athletes in the Olympic Games (Toohey and Veal, 2007).

In its early days from 1973 as an IOC consultative body (rather than a Commission), sport aid was made up of courses in the form of 'itinerant lectures', courses in coaching, and scholarships in sports administration (Miller, 1979, p. 152):

> The Solidarity programme takes two forms, the first is a Symposium … where people are gathered from many nations on a regional basis and will hear lectures and have discussions with experts on a number of subjects … The other part of the Solidarity programme is the running of special courses … either by sending special instructors or coaches to areas to give courses for people who may themselves become instructors, … or by bringing people from different countries under the aegis of the NOC and/or IF concerned to a centre for specialised courses.
>
> (International Olympic Committee, 1974, p. 393)

By 1974/75 at least five types of programmes were available. These consisted of missions of experts covering subjects in different areas such as 'organisation, financing, training of staff and specialists, relations with public authorities, sports infrastructure, sports medicine, etc.', with

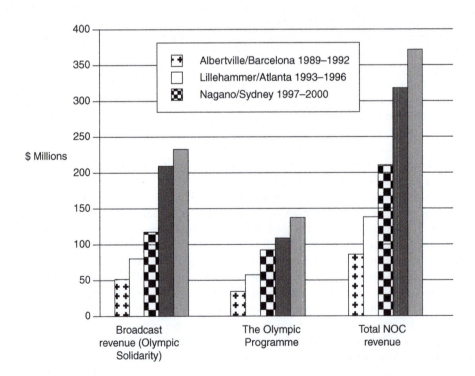

Figure 9.1 Sources of Olympic funding

courses lasting between 7 and 30 days; itinerant missions mostly to conduct technical courses, and scholarships for coaches, of one to eight months, for 'the perfecting and specialisation'; the publication of handbooks and brochures; and an advisory service for sports infrastructure (Olympic Solidarity, 1975, pp. 27–30). By June 1976, Olympic Solidarity had carried out 371 schemes of assistance and cooperation in 85 countries (Wieczorek, 1976).

In 1982, however, the budget was raised to US$2,900,000 (International Olympic Committee, 1981), and the Commission, which until then had been only a consultative body, took full responsibility for Olympic Solidarity, and in particular for the approval of accounts and budgets, and for proposals by the Director of Olympic Solidarity in respect of all its activities (International Olympic Committee, 1993). The nature of the Commission and its significance was revolutionised when in 1984 the Los Angeles Games attracted the first of the IOC's huge broadcasting contracts and sponsorship deals, the profits of which could be shared with NOCs and IFs. Olympic Solidarity therefore became the vehicle for redistribution of major sums worldwide. As a consequence, Olympic Solidarity proposed a four-year plan for the Olympic Solidarity programmes, starting from the quadrennium 1985–1988, which aimed to achieve the following:

- To give all of the world's NOCs a budget guaranteed in advance for a four year period;
- To oblige the NOCs and the National Federations to rethink the programming of their medium-term activities while avoiding improvisation;
- To simplify administrative norms as much as possible but with the least possible intervention, with a view to promoting effective thorough and responsible work.

(Olympic Solidarity, 1986, p. 8)

This was the beginning of Olympic Solidarity's increasingly systematic quadrennial planning approach, and when we consider changes in the development of Olympic Solidarity policy and funding later in the chapter we take as our point of departure this first quadrennium.

Although most of the Olympic Solidarity programmes had previously been directed towards countries with developing NOCs in Africa, Asia and the Americas, in 1984 some Olympic Solidarity programmes were made available for all NOCs, not simply those that were new or developing.

Following the 2000 IOC reforms, Olympic Solidarity was restructured. Many of the subsequent programmes were similar to what had been previously on offer, or only slightly modified or extended, but some new ones were also added. All the Olympic Solidarity programmes were reclassified into three distinct categories and budgeted for separately:

World programmes, which cover and reinforce all areas of sports development
Continental programmes, designed to meet some of the specific needs of each continent
Olympic Games subsidies, which complement the range of programmes and offer financial support to NOCs, before, during and after the Games.

(Olympic Solidarity, 2009, p. 6)

By 2001, Olympic Solidarity offered 21 world programmes and five continental programmes, one for each continent, and this is the pattern of funding that remains to date, though priorities may vary from one quadrennial to the next. Nine of the world programmes were new in comparison with those in the previous plan (Olympic Solidarity, 2001). The world programmes and the Olympic Games subsidies are managed by the International Olympic Solidarity Office in Lausanne, whereas an Olympic Solidarity office set up in each continental association in 2005 is responsible 'for managing the continental programmes and coordination with the International Olympic Solidarity Office in Lausanne' (Olympic Solidarity, 2005, p. 8). The decisions on what activities and which NOCs to fund for the continental programmes is however largely devolved to the continental associations, devolution and empowerment of NOCs and other stakeholders, having been a theme of the 2000 Commission's reforms introduced after the Salt Lake City scandal (International Olympic Committee, 1999).

The current structure of Olympic Solidarity funding programmes

The size and distribution of Olympic Solidarity funding in the last three quadrennia is illustrated in Figure 9.2. For the last quadrennium 43 per cent of expenditure was allocated to the world programme, 39 per cent to the continental programmes, 14 per cent to Olympic Games subsidies and 4 per cent to administration.

World programmes cover four distinct sectors: athletes, coaches, NOC management and Olympic values. The first three sectors provide different options in relation to a targeted group, while the Olympic values programmes target different areas related to sport: Sport Medicine; Sport and Environment; Women and Sport; Sport for All; the International Olympic Academy; Culture and Education; and Olympic Legacy. All NOCs now have access to all 19 world programmes for the 2009–2012 quadrennium.

Continental programmes began with decentralisation in 1997, when a budget for activities, an annual grant to partially cover operating costs, and financial assistance for meetings and assemblies of the continental associations was administered by each continental association of NOCs. Official decentralisation, of Olympic Solidarity funds, targeting aid for individual NOCs, took place in 2001, and by 2005 representatives of the five continental associations were allocated to liaise with Olympic Solidarity. Since the situation is different for each continent, 'the level of responsibility for these programmes and their management varies according to agreements drawn up at the beginning of the quadrennium' (Olympic Solidarity, 2001, p. 80).

Through the *Olympic Games subsidy* each NOC receives funding directly related to its participation in both the summer and winter Olympic Games. This was originally conceived to

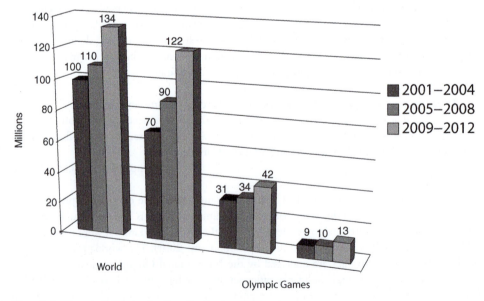

Figure 9.2 Olympic Solidarity funding distribution (US$ m.)

help the less affluent NOCs to attend the Olympic Games, particularly after finance was cited as a significant reason for non-attendance at the Moscow Games. Starting off as funding to cover travel and accommodation for a number of athletes and officials from each country, it has steadily increased and now includes:

- travel expenses for attendance at the Chef de Mission meeting before the Olympic Games;
- logistical subsidy;
- funding for the transport of a number of athletes and officials;
- funding for transport and accommodation for one youth camp participant;
- subsidy for every participating athlete.

These Olympic Games participation subsidies are directly related to the size of the participating contingent, since funding is decided largely on a per capita basis for a team. In the larger, more affluent countries, the number of participating athletes can be in the hundreds (the largest to date being the US contingent of 654 athletes in Atlanta 1996) while some small countries participate with a mere handful of athletes. All NOCs benefit from these subsidies, and according to the Olympic Solidarity reports, NOCs who do not send athletes to the Games have still received aid for participation of their officials, as was the case for Djibouti and Brunei, whose athletes did not participate in Athens 2004 and Beijing 2008 respectively. A concession is given to host countries for each edition of the Games for an increased number of participating athletes, for which they get a subsidy. This source of funding can reach very high values for a small number of countries in comparison with that available to most countries through all the other Olympic Solidarity programmes.

This then is the policy framework within which we set out to evaluate the extent to which Olympic Solidarity accomplishes its progressive, redistributive function. We address two of the three main programmes, the world programme and Olympic Games subsidy. Data on the continental programmes are extremely limited and in the sense that Olympic Solidarity as an organisation is not directly involved in deciding spending priorities for continental programmes, this is less relevant to an evaluation of whether Olympic Solidarity achieves its redistributive goals. Nevertheless should such data become available it would allow an interesting addition to the analysis reported here.

The approach to statistical analysis of Olympic Solidarity funding

In order to address our research question we review the distribution of funds for the world programmes and the Olympic Games subsidy across the period from the beginning of quadrennial planning (1985–8) to the most recently reported quadrennial distribution 2005–8. Data for the analysis was sourced by the review of annual and quadrennial reports published by Olympic Solidarity across the period.

Our analysis progresses in three stages. The first is a *descriptive* analysis of financial disbursements, on a quadrennial basis, to individual National Olympic Committees worldwide from 1985 to 2008. The second stage involves *analysis of the correlations* between, on the one hand world programme grant and Olympic Games subsidy levels, and, on the other, selected variables chosen as indicators of NOC characteristics in order to establish the levels of funding received by different kinds of NOC. The third stage involves standard multiple regression of world programmes grant and Olympic Games subsidy grant as dependent variables to identify the contribution of selected independent variables to the explanation of variance in the levels of grant awarded to NOCs under both categories (Figure 9.3).

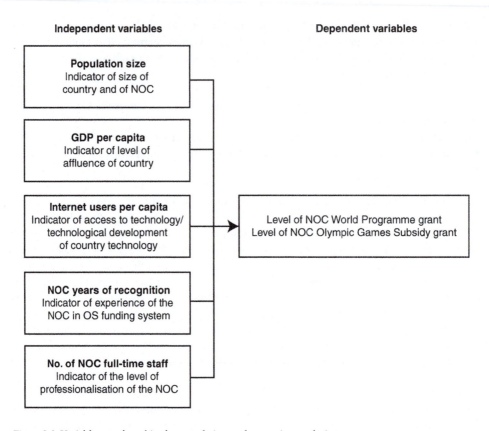

Figure 9.3 Variables employed in the correlation and regression analysis

The use of the indicators allows us to test the extent to which there is a relationship between what NOCs receive under both types of grant and the size of a country (population size); its relative affluence (GDP per capita); the number of full time staff in its NOC (and by implication the level of professional support available within the NOC in making applications); and the experience of the NOC within the Olympic System (number of years as an IOC recognised NOC).

Descriptive statistical analysis of the distribution of Olympic Solidarity grant aid

Figure 9.4 shows the relative growth of funding in both programmes. While it is clear that the average world programmes grant received by NOCs is considerably greater than the Olympic Games subsidy, nevertheless, as an analysis of the relative size of awards in the 2005–8 cycle illustrates, for some countries with large teams entering the Games (notably the USA, Russia, Germany, Italy, China, Japan and Australia) the level of Games subsidy can be in considerable excess of the average level of world programmes award (see Figure 9.5).

The rapid growth of funding in particular of the world programmes is a reflection of the growing value post Los Angeles 1984, of the broadcasting contracts that the IOC has been able to secure.

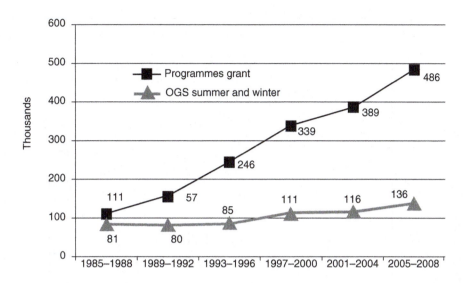

Figure 9.4 Means of world programme grant and of Olympic Games subsidy awarded by Olympic Solidarity (US$)

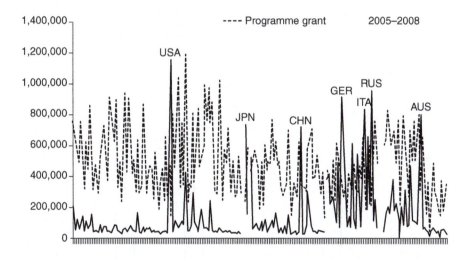

Figure 9.5 Comparison of world programme grants and Olympic Games subsidy disbursement levels for 2005–8 (US$) with named countries receiving highest Olympic subsidies

The relative distribution of world programme grants for the first and the last quadrennia in our sequence is illustrated in Figure 9.6. In the boxplot we see the median value marked by the black line in the box, while the box itself contains 50 per cent of the cases. The range is marked by the distance between the whiskers on each box, with outliers indicated by either a circle (plus a label) for those cases more than 1.5 times the length of the box outside the box or by a star (plus a label) for those lying more than three box lengths outside the box.

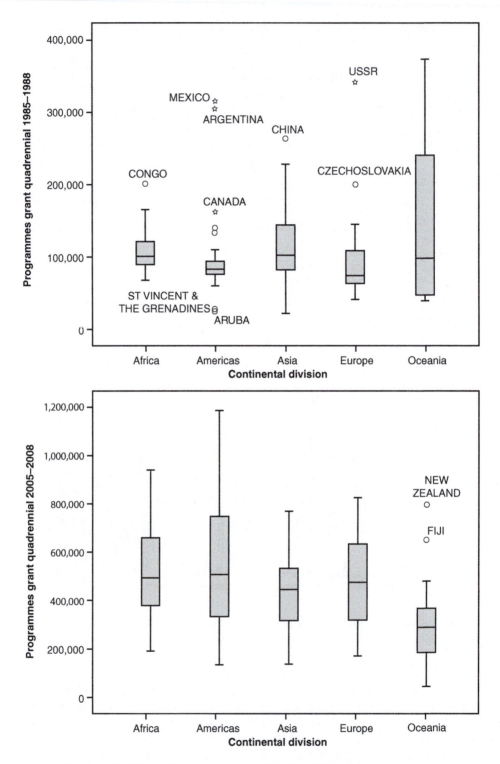

Figure 9.6 Boxplots of NOC world programme grants 1985–8 and 2005–8 by continent

For the quadrennium 1985–8 the distribution of grant is more widely dispersed for the Americas. At the high end in the case of the Americas are relatively large nations, Argentina, Mexico, Canada, the USA and Chile, while the outliers in terms of low levels of grant aid are micro states, St Vincent and the Grenadines and Aruba. In the 2005–8 quadrennium, however, values for each of the continents are more closely grouped around the median and there is only one continent (Oceania) with two outliers, New Zealand and Fiji.

In 2005–8 Oceania and Asia have the lowest median values, which in the case of the former is understandable since the continent contains a high proportion of micro states whose relatively small grants would reduce the median value.

The second set of boxplots in Figure 9.6 for 2005–8 represents a picture of a more closely regulated and normal distribution of grants, a pattern that may be attributed to the growing maturity of the grant aid system. The lack of large nation state outliers above the median suggests that the gap between large and small states in terms of world programme grants size is much less marked than it had been in the earliest quadrennial.

The distribution of Olympic Games subsidy by continent is not provided here for reasons of space but the pattern in all continents for the later quadrennials is one of highly dispersed values with 23 outliers across all continents, and a marked difference in terms of large state outliers above the median, and small state outliers below the median, demonstrating that large states benefit disproportionately from Olympic Games subsidy.

Analysis of correlation between grant aid levels and NOC/country characteristics

If we review the statistically significant correlations in Table 9.1 ($p \leq 0.01$) the table indicates that although in the first two quadrennia in the series, larger countries with older NOCs tended to receive larger world programme grants, there is a negative correlation between internet users and level of grant received for the middle three quadrennia.

Table 9.1 Pearson product moment correlation of selected variables with size of NOC world programmes grant 1985–8 to 2005–8

	Population size	Years in operation NOC	F/Time NOC Employees	Internet Users	GDP per capita
1985–1988	0.339**	0.210**	0.038	−0.003	−0.084
1989–1992	0.282**	0.203**	−0.054	−0.197**	−0.288**
1993–1996	0.063	−0.026	−0.008	−0.246**	−0.342**
1997–2000	0.004	−0.094	−0.136	−0.254**	−0.404**
2001–2004	0.103	0.116	0.008	−0.094	−0.385**
2005–2008	0.046	0.098	0.036	−0.099	−0.286**

** $p \leq 0.01$; * $p \leq 0.05$

Note: For Tables 9.1 and 9.2, for the variables incorporated here, preliminary analyses were undertaken to ensure that there was no violation of the assumptions of normality, linearity and homoscedasticity.

The relationship between population size and size of world programme grants is statistically significant in the early years but is not significant in later quadrennia as suggested by the existence of outliers in Figure 9.6 for the first but not the last quadrennium in the series. Similarly the more established (older) NOCs receive statistically significant higher grants in the two first quadrennia only. The information technology level of the country (number of internet users) is actually negatively related to the level of grant received for the second to the fourth quadrennium, and the size of the NOC in terms of employees is not significantly related at all to world programme grant levels. There is thus no support for the claim that the better resourced NOCs (in terms of numbers of employees) with a stronger national background in information technology are better able to make successful applications for world programme grant aid.

Indeed, the Pearson product moment correlation for GDP per capita is the variable most strongly associated with the size of the world programme grant. This is a *negative* association, indicating that the less affluent nations receive a statistically significantly higher level of grant aid under this programme for all but the first quadrennium. The variance explained is between 8 and 16 per cent for each of the second to the fifth quadrennia, providing support for the claim that for world programme grants at least, Olympic Solidarity is distributing money in ways consistent with its aim to provide assistance to those 'who have greatest need of it'.

A comparison of the relationship between levels of Olympic Games subsidy received and their correlation with the indicator variables (see Table 9.2) provides a stark contrast with that for the world programmes. Here all variables are *positively* and significantly correlated with Olympic Games subsidy. Effectively, the older NOCs, with larger staff sizes, from countries with larger populations, in more technologically developed contexts receive significantly higher levels of subsidy. Even more significant from the point of view of the concerns of this chapter, GDP per capita is *positively* correlated to Olympic Games subsidy level, meaning that the NOCs from more affluent countries will tend to receive higher subsidies. We will return to discuss the significance of this point in our conclusions.

Table 9.2 Pearson product moment correlation of selected variables with size of Olympic Games subsidy grant 1988–2006

	Population size	Years of recognition NOC	F/T Employees	Internet Users	GDP Per Capita
Calgary 1988 + Seoul 1988	0.206★★	0.642★★	0.517★★	0.556★★	0.379★★
Barcelona 1992 + Albertville 1992	0.252★★	0.526★★	0.518★★	0.484★★	0.304★★
Lillehammer 1994 + Atlanta 1996	0.267★★	0.463★★	0.548★★	0.470★	0.300★★
Nagano 1998 + Sydney 2000	0.262★★	0.489★★	0.542★★	0.399★★	0.306★★
Sydney 2000 + SLC 2002	0.264★★	0.493★★	0.551★★	0.499★★	0.385★★
Athens 2004 + Torino 2006	0.313★★	0.486★★	0.580★★	0.386★★	0.282★★

★★ p≤0.01; ★ p≤0.05

Standard multiple regression with dependent variables levels of world programmes grant, and Olympic Games subsidy grant

The application of standard multiple regression analysis is employed here to allow us to analyse the level of variance that can be explained in the two dependent variables (level of world programmes grant and level of Olympic Games subsidy received by NOCs), and in addition to establish the unique contribution to explanation of variance made by each independent variable. Independent variables were employed in the regression analysis after checking for multicollinearity, outliers, normality, linearity, homoscedasticity and independence of residuals to ensure that requirements were not violated.

While the overall level of explained variance of the world programmes grant is lowest in the latest quadrennium at 15 per cent, the unique contribution to explained variance of GDP per capita is 11 per cent in 2005–8 and 14 per cent in 2001–4 (see Table 9.3). Thus the level of affluence of a nation is negatively correlated to the level of world programme that it receives and this explains 11–14 per cent of the variance in the dependent variable for the last three quadrennia.

Table 9.3 Contribution of independent variables to explanation of the variance of world programmes grant level (unique contribution to explained variance is given in brackets)

Selected independent variables	1985–1988	1989–1992	1993–1996	1997–2000	2001–2004	2005–2008
Population size	0.379** (12%)	0.310** (8%)				
NOC years of recognition	0.284* (6%)	0.459** (14%)			0.298** (5%)	0.257*(4%)
F/time NOC employees		−0.274* (5%)				
GDP per capita		−0.328* (5%)	−0.356** (8%)	−0.479** (11%)	−0.522** (14%)	−0.488** (11%)
Total variance explained (R^2)	18%	31%	14%	19%	19%	15%

Note: The unique contribution to explained variance of an independent variable is calculated by squaring the part correlation (also referred to in some texts as the semi-partial correlation coefficient). The sum of unique contributions to explained variance of the various independent variables should thus (normally) be less than the total variance explained (since in addition to the unique variance attributable to each of the independent variables alone, there may be shared variance between independent variables). However, there are occasions on which 'IVs [independent variables] which correlate positively with [dependent variable] Y correlate negatively with each other (or equivalently the reverse) being negative involves a portion of the variances in the IVs all of which is irrelevant to Y: thus when each variable is partialled from the other, all indices of relationship with Y are enhanced' (Cohen and Cohen, 1995, p. 90). This is referred to as 'Cooperative suppression' and has occurred in a number of the regressions above (indicated by the cases in which zero-order correlations are bigger than part correlations). The size of the unique contribution to variance explained may thus be marginally inflated in all but the middle two quadrennials.

Table 9.4 Contribution of independent variables to explanation of variance of the Olympic Games subsidy received (unique contribution to explanation of variance in brackets)

	1985–1988	*1989–1992*	*1993–1996*	*1997–2000*	*2001–2004*	*2005–2008*
Population						0.160★ (2%)
NOC years	0.388★★ (10%)	0.423★★ (12%)		0.210★ (3%)	0.203★ (3%)	0.199★ (3%)
GDP per capita						
F/T employees	0.250★ (4%)	0.179★ (2%)	0.350★★ (8%)	0.329★★ (7%)	0.326★★ (7%)	0.356★★ (9%)
Internet users	0.393★★ (7%)	0.401★★ (8%)	0.389★★ (8%)	0.397★★ (7%)	0.408★★ (8%)	0.380★★ (7%)
Variance explained R^2	58%	56%	46%	47%	69%	70%

The regression data for the dependent variable Olympic Games subsidy (see Table 9.4), however, provides a starkly different picture. A combination of four independent variables, population size of country, the age of the NOC, the size of its workforce and the level of technological development (number of internet users), explains 69–70 per cent of the variance in the last two quadrennia. The mildly progressive pattern of grant distribution evident for the world programmes is absent from the pattern for Olympic subsidy grants and as Figure 9.5 shows (for the quadrennium 2005–8) despite the average Olympic Games subsidy being much lower than the average world programmes grant, for some of the larger countries (the USA, Germany, Russia, France) the Olympic Games subsidy is much larger than world programme grants received by most or all countries.

Conclusion

The data above illustrate two aspects or dynamics of revenue distribution. The first is that, in line with its mission for the world programme, Olympic Solidarity is successful in maintaining a progressive distribution of funding to the NOCs from less affluent countries. The second is that, in supporting every athlete attending the Games, funding is steered disproportionately to the larger more technologically developed nations with bigger NOCs in terms of staff numbers. In effect, one fund favours the developed nations and one the less affluent.

What is not clear (and is not directly controlled by Olympic Solidarity) is the nature of the distribution of the continental programmes. Here, expenditure may be influenced by Olympic Solidarity through advice offered and guidance provided when sought, but it is certainly not controlled by Solidarity. However, the continental associations do not necessarily declare how allocations are made and the total amounts disbursed, and this seems to be a significant governance failing.

Finally, it is worth acknowledging that one NOC (the US Olympic Committee – USOC) receives a significant proportion 'top sliced' from the IOC's earnings (12.75 per cent of US broadcast rights and 20 per cent of IOC global sponsorships), an arrangement established in 1984 as a contract in perpetuity, which the IOC has subsequently sought to renegotiate with minor amendments being agreed in 1996 and 2007. Thus, redistribution of funding through the world programme pales into insignificance in comparison with the USOC deal.

With reference to our initial research question, Olympic Solidarity *is* progressive in redistribution of the funds over which it exercises most control, while in relation to the Olympic Games subsidy, because of the flat rate funding approach per athlete attending the Games, inevitably the larger teams benefit most. Finally, the benefits received by USOC from the two major sources of IOC income, broadcasting and the TOP (The Olympic Programme) sponsors programme, dwarf the income received by other NOCs from world programmes, Games subsidy and continental programmes combined.

10

MULTICULTURALISM AND FEDERAL SPORT POLICY IN CANADA

Wendy Frisby, Lucie Thibault and Kathryn Cureton

Introduction

Canada is one of the most multicultural nations in the world. According to 2006 census data, nearly 6.2 million Canadians were born outside of the country (Statistics Canada, 2008b). Recent newcomers now originate largely from Asia including the Middle East, followed by Europe, and Central and South America. The largest urban centres, Toronto, Montréal, and Vancouver, are home for the majority of new Canadians, and for 70 per cent of them, their mother tongue is not one of Canada's official languages of English or French (Statistics Canada, 2008b). The fastest growing segments of the population are Aboriginals and new immigrants, some of whom experience lower levels of economic and social integration and are likely to have sport interests that differ from the Eurocentric activities historically offered in Canada (Department of Canadian Heritage, 2010). These statistics raise questions about how federal sport policy makers and leaders of sport organizations are responding to shifting population demographics.

For the purposes of this chapter, multiculturalism and sport policy in Canada are examined. While multiculturalism policy has a unique and long history in Canada, there are no policies tying it directly to sport at the federal level (Donnelly and Nakamura, 2006). This is surprising given that, according to Statistics Canada (2010), within the next 20 years, 60 per cent of the Canadian population will be foreign born. In their quest to address changing demographics, Canada's 1988 Multiculturalism Act made it clear that multiculturalism is a responsibility of all departments of the federal government (Ryan, 2010).

While newcomers bring different political, social, and cultural understandings of sport that could enrich and enhance Canada's physical culture, little is known about how their different circumstances and interests are being accommodated to promote their inclusion (Coakley and Donnelly, 2009). By inclusion, we are not simply referring to an assimilationist approach that consists of 'opening the doors' and expecting newcomers to leave their past behind and adopt a new dominant sport culture (Frisby and Ponic, forthcoming). Rather, we are referring to an intercultural approach to inclusion built on the capacity to acquire, interpret, and apply knowledge about each other's cultures (Omidvar and Richmond, 2005; Sandercock, 2004; Wood and Landry, 2008).

Based on the analysis of interviews conducted with seven federal sport policy makers as part of our larger *Multiculturalism, Sport and Physical Activity Study* (2006–2009),[1] selected media accounts, and relevant literature, this chapter discusses debates about the need for policy that addresses multiculturalism and sport, as well as the challenges that could be encountered when developing and implementing such a policy. Examples of the few initiatives that are being undertaken by Canadian sport or immigrant service organizations to promote inclusion, despite the lack of federal sport policy, are presented as a starting point for envisioning what a multiculturalism and sport policy could entail.

Brief history of multiculturalism policy in Canada

Canada's multiculturalism policy must be understood in relation to the country's history and policies on Aboriginal people and its early English/French settlers. In Canada, the term Aboriginal includes Native or First Nations, Inuit, and Métis people, whose population exceeds one million and is growing much faster than the non-Aboriginal population (Statistics Canada, 2008a). Although Aboriginal people were the original inhabitants of Canada, their rights were not officially recognized by law until the 1982 Canadian Constitution Act. Paraschak (1989) argued that native and non-native relations in sport have been characterized by exploitation and racism, owing to ethnocentric distortion, which is when assumptions are made about native cultural practices from a Euro-Canadian perspective. As an example, Robidoux (2006) explained how the use of native imagery in the logos of some North American professional sport teams is mostly perceived as unproblematic by non-native people, but is considered to be offensive to many native people because it positions them as 'less civilized'.

Under federal jurisdiction, Canada is officially a bilingual country. The work of the Canadian Royal Commission on Bilingualism and Biculturalism (1963–1969) led to the formal recognition of two official languages and distinct cultures of the early English and French settlers. Historical tensions in English and French relations are apparent in sport, as Francophone Canadians are often under-represented as athletes, coaches, and sport executives. As well, concerns have been expressed about Francophone athletes' and coaches' limited access to services and programmes in their own language (cf. Adam, 2007; Office of the Commission of Official Languages, 2000; Sport Canada, 2007; Svoboda and Donnelly, 2006). Svoboda and Donnelly (2006, p. 34), have noted that 'despite the efforts of Sport Canada and many national sport organizations, the Canadian sport system continues to function almost exclusively in English'. Furthermore, Francophone athletes and coaches must learn English to function and progress at the high performance level (Svoboda and Donnelly, 2006). Coakley and Donnelly (2009) have attributed this under-representation to differences in political, cultural, and economic power between English and French Canadians.

Given this brief historical backdrop, the original 1971 Canadian Multiculturalism Act was aimed at enhancing the sense of belonging for immigrants who were primarily of European descent – not Aboriginal people or English and French settlers who were considered in other legislation – because foreign residents from non-European countries made up just 3.2 per cent of the Canadian population at that time (Ryan, 2010). Changing source countries and rising immigration rates led to a revision of the 1971 Canadian Multiculturalism Act that came into effect in 1988. This revised Multiculturalism Act set out to 'recognize and promote the understanding that multiculturalism reflects the cultural and racial diversity of Canadian society and acknowledges the freedom of all members of Canadian society to preserve, enhance and share their cultural heritage' (Government of Canada, 2011, p. 3). The Act describes multiculturalism as an invaluable resource in the shaping of Canada's future which is also fundamental to the country's heritage and collective identity (Government of Canada, 2011). The federal government's role, according to the Multiculturalism Act, is to promote equitable participation in society by eliminating barriers; to assist social, cultural, economic, and political institutions to be respectful and inclusive of Canada's multicultural character; and to foster the recognition and appreciation of diverse cultures (Government of Canada, 2011). At the same time, the government sought to strengthen the status and use of English and French as the two official languages. The multiculturalism policy was not only a response to shifting immigration patterns, but was also meant to signal that freedom of choice is possible within an official bilingualism framework (Ryan, 2010).

Canada's federal multiculturalism policy is commonly referred to as a *mosaic* where people from varied backgrounds have the freedom to live as they see fit (Bibby, 1990; Lock Kunz and Sykes, 2007). According to Ryan (2010), in his evocatively titled book *Multicultiphobia*, the policy has been polarizing as some perceive it as destroying the country, while others believe it is one of Canada's most cherished characteristics. A conclusion drawn from a series of round-tables on Canada's multiculturalism policy was that there is strong support for its underlying principles which include equality, respect for diversity, human rights, and full participation in society (Lock Kunz and Sykes, 2007).

However, as is the case for other countries, there have been criticisms of the multiculturalism policy. Some believe newcomers should discard their previous cultures and conform to the dominant Canadian culture, even though the country is not characterized by a single monolithic culture or shared history (Ryan, 2010). Others are concerned that it encourages people to 'stick with their own kind' in ethnic enclaves, thus creating social divisions and a weakened national identity (Bissoondath, 2002). Another criticism is that multiculturalism policy diminishes the position of mostly French speaking Québec within Canada and turns attention away from the historically poor treatment of Aboriginal people. There have also been objections to the use of taxpayer dollars to provide accommodations to newcomers (e.g., language training, access to social services, and health insurance), because some argue that immigrants should pay for these services themselves as part of adapting to a new homeland (Ryan, 2010). Similar concerns have been raised in other countries, for example, when German Chancellor Angela Merkel and British Prime Minister David Cameron claimed that multiculturalism policy in their respective countries has totally failed (Corbella, 2011, p. A9).

The critics appear to be in the minority, however, as national opinion polls have consistently shown that the majority of Canadians agree that multiculturalism is a national asset and that government should assist immigrants in developing the skills and knowledge required to integrate (Ryan, 2010). There may be intergenerational differences though, as younger Canadians are less likely to see the relevance of multiculturalism policy (Lock Kunz and Sykes, 2007). This may be because more of them come from families with mixed ethnic backgrounds and they have grown up in a technologically linked-up multicultural and global environment (Lock Kunz and Sykes, 2007).

Canada's Multiculturalism Act is closely tied to immigration policy which has historically oscillated between actively encouraging international migration to overcome labour shortages and implementing strict controls, owing to fears that immigrants are taking jobs away from Canadian born residents (Elliott and Fleras, 1990). An example of the latter was the imposition of the 'head tax' on Chinese immigrants once their labour was no longer needed to help build the Canadian Pacific Railway in the early 1880s (Guo and DeVoretz, 2006). These fears become heightened when linked to threats to security, for example, when Japanese, Italian, and German Canadians were interned during World War II, and following September 11, 2001 when it was suspected that some of the terrorists who killed thousands of people in their destruction of the World Trade Center entered the United States through Canada (Ryan, 2010).

Over time, Ryan (2010) found that negative media accounts of multiculturalism policy have outweighed positive ones, even though the criticisms have not been widely taken up by Canadian adults according to national opinion polls. The following news account in *The Vancouver Sun* illustrates the ongoing and heated debates about whether newcomers should adapt to their new environment or whether Canada should be accommodating diverse religions and cultures.

> A dozen families who immigrated to Canada and are living in Winnipeg are demanding that their children be excused from music and co-ed physical education programs for religious reasons. They believe music is un-Islamic and that physical education classes should be segregated by gender. The school division is facing the music in a typically Canadian way – bending itself to try to accommodate these demands, even though across Canada, music and physical education are compulsory. The school district is trying to adapt the curriculum (e.g., by having students doing a writing project on music to meet the requirements) instead of having families fit into the school and Canadian culture.
>
> (Corbella, 2011, p. A9)

It is these types of media accounts that position newcomers as 'others' and fuel tensions between ethnic groups. Religious beliefs are the aspect of diversity with which policy makers and the public are most ill at ease because of a lack of knowledge, according to the report based on the multiculturalism round tables held across the country (Lock Kunz and Sykes, 2007).

Developments in Canadian sport policy

Tensions over multiculturalism have also transpired in sport (cf. BBC, 2010; Cable News Network, 2011; Henry, 2005). Before addressing these tensions, it is important to provide a brief overview of how sport is organized in federal government. Sport Canada is housed in the Department of Canadian Heritage, whereas responsibility for newcomers lies with the Department of Citizenship and Immigration. While neither Canadian Heritage nor Sport Canada refer specifically to multiculturalism in their mission statements, they both refer to the importance of culture. The federal government's Department of Canadian Heritage is 'responsible for national policies and programmes that promote Canadian content, foster cultural participation, active citizenship and participation in Canada's civic life, and strengthen connections among Canadians' (Department of Canadian Heritage, 2011, para. 1). Sport Canada's mission focuses on 'strengthen[ing] the unique contribution that sport makes to Canadian identity, culture and society' (Sport Canada, 2010, para. 1).

In 2002, Sport Canada, after an extensive pan-Canadian consultative process with key sport stakeholders, published the Canadian Sport Policy. This policy is focused on the achievement of four priorities: enhanced excellence, enhanced participation, enhanced capacity, and enhanced interaction. The priorities of excellence and participation are foundational to Canada's sport system, while capacity[2] and interaction[3] are support goals for these other two priorities (Sport Canada, 2002). As noted in the Canadian Sport Policy, 'barriers to sport participation in sport [should] be identified and eliminated, making sport accessible to all' (Sport Canada, 2002, p. 8). Furthermore, the policy document emphasized how 'certain groups such as girls and women, people with a disability, Aboriginal peoples, and visible minorities continue to be under-represented in the Canadian sport system as athletes/participants and as leaders' (Sport Canada, 2002, p. 8). Given that research has shown immigrants participate less in sport and physical activity than those who are Canadian born (Tremblay, Bryan, Perex, Ardem, and Katzmarzyk, 2006), and 'visible minorities'[4] are one of four underrepresented groups targeted by the Canadian Sport Policy, we sought to understand why a specific federal policy targeting multicultural participation in sport has not been developed.[5] As a result, in this section and in subsequent sections of the chapter, we rely heavily on interviews with seven Sport Canada policy makers who participated in our Multiculturalism, Sport, and Physical Activity Study to illustrate their perspectives and approaches regarding this policy issue.

In understanding Sport Canada's policy-making process, it was first important to understand why the federal government has included sport participation as a priority when it has historically focused almost exclusively on high performance sport. One interviewee offered the following explanation:

> It's a matter of equity and fairness. I mean, there is recognition that there are certain populations who face barriers to participation and Canada is a country that wants to be inclusive and so we're going to focus on those groups who aren't participating to the same degree as others.
>
> (Federal sport policy maker)

At the same time, it was clear that some policy makers found it easier to deal with Sport Canada's long-standing endeavours in sport excellence:

> Ironically, we have completed an excellence strategy, which started after the participation strategy was initiated, in part because it is a more exclusive responsibility of the federal government. It's a bit easier to articulate the excellence strategy. The sport participation strategy, we needed to do more thinking and lots of consultation on it, as they are not the same thing.
>
> (Federal sport policy maker)

The 2002 Canadian Sport Policy was seen as both a challenge and a basis upon which multiculturalism and sport policy could be developed:

> The Canadian Sport Policy is so broad, it doesn't matter what you do and you can say that you're helping advance it. So in some ways, what's good about it is also what's bad about it. It is all encompassing but it also doesn't focus.
>
> (Federal sport policy maker)

In a discussion paper released as part of the Canadian Sport Policy Renewal process (Sport Canada, 2011), it was acknowledged that the impact of the 2002 Canadian Sport Policy on increasing the participation of underrepresented groups remains questionable. This is especially true for visible minorities:

> The 2002 Canadian Sport Policy focused on increasing participation for four underrepresented populations: women, aboriginal people, persons with a disability, and visible minorities. Out of those four groups, the [federal, provincial and territorial] governments devoted meaningful attention to only the first three of these populations.
>
> (Sport Canada, 2011, p. 1)

This sentiment was reiterated by some of the federal sport policy makers we interviewed, as illustrated in the following quotation:

> So there are the four priorities listed in the Canadian Sport Policy [women, visible minorities, Aboriginal people, persons with a disability], definitely where we've done the least

amount of work, and some may argue where we've done no work as of yet, is with visible minorities. That's a gap in our work right now.

(Federal policy maker)

As will be addressed in the next section, this gap was occurring despite the fact that federal sport policy makers perceived this as an important policy area.

Reasons for developing multiculturalism policy in sport

Several reasons were identified to warrant the development of a policy on multiculturalism and sport. First, one policy maker acknowledged that Sport Canada was not fulfilling its responsibilities related to the Multiculturalism Act and considered this as a compelling reason for developing policy:

> It's my belief and has been for a number of years now that Sport Canada has been silent on this issue for far too long and that we need to be developing some kind of policy perspective on this. And there's been reluctance to do that in Sport Canada and I'm not sure where the reluctance is coming from. We have a responsibility as a department in the Multiculturalism Act and we are not owning up to that. To me that is the strongest argument for a policy.

(Federal sport policy maker)

In addition, other policy makers pointed to the diversification of Canada's skill base and physical culture as a driving force behind policy development:

> We need to value these groups for the richness that they bring into the sport system so that if we're not embracing and creating a welcoming environment, then we're missing out on skills that we could otherwise be accessing. And from a pragmatic point of view, that means our sport system is not as strong as it could or should be.

(Federal policy maker)

Another reason identified by policy makers was that national, provincial, and local sport organizations are turning to Sport Canada for leadership, especially when high profile incidents of racism have been reported in the media.

> I think that we are all aware of incidents that have grabbed the newspapers' sport headlines, particularly the girls who wear the hijab. There was another case this weekend in Manitoba about a young girl being barred from a judo tournament. And it grabbed the headlines. Yesterday it was all over the newspapers. And this is further to other incidents that happened in Québec. And we don't really have a policy position on this, other than to say that Sport Canada encourages the greatest participation for all Canadians in sport. Besides saying it is rather general wishful thinking, we don't have the position to which sport organizations can turn back to us for leadership.

(Federal sport policy maker)

Research is beginning to show how racial and ethnic discrimination is being experienced in Canadian sport. For example, Tirone's (2000) study with children of immigrants from India, Pakistan, and Bangladesh demonstrated how these children had been bullied while participating in sport, but sport leaders failed to intervene on their behalf. Similarly, Doherty and Taylor (2007) reported that newly arrived immigrant youth often felt excluded from activities because of rejection by other youth and little action was being taken by sport leaders to counteract this problem.

Sport has also been a mechanism of social control, such as when Muslim teenage girls were prohibited from playing soccer and participating in taekwondo in Canadian communities because they were wearing their hijabs (under protective headgear for taekwondo) even though this practice is allowed in other countries' local sport systems (Tirone, 2010). This is one of the reasons why some immigrants may prefer to participate with those from the same ethnic background. There are, however, others who choose different routes and assimilate into the dominant culture or develop subcultures within their own ethnic communities that are characterized by certain values, political associations, and dress styles (Stodolska and Alexandris, 2004). Donnelly and Nakamura (2006) found few examples of interculturalism, whereby Canadian and foreign born residents learn from each other about different sport practices.

Policy development in multiculturalism and sport could also drive improvements in the education and training of leaders (i.e., coaches, officials, volunteers, administrators). The need for better education and training was evident in Livingston, Tirone, Miller, and Smith's (2008) study on the involvement of newcomers in coaching and their involvement in the Coaching Association of Canada's National Coaching Certification Program (NCCP). The researchers showed that officials, coaches, and athletes did not know how to connect with minority groups or how to accommodate their participation in sport. Immigrant-serving agencies may be in the best position to understand the needs of newcomers because they have the knowledge and experience providing support services and programmes. Unfortunately, sport and physical activity are rarely part of their organizational mandates (Frisby, 2011).

The other compelling reason for developing policy is the 'healthy immigrant effect', even though none of the federal sport policy makers we interviewed referred to this effect. The healthy immigrant effect is a term coined by researchers who have shown that immigrants tend to have better health than Canadian born residents prior to immigration, but their health tends to decline upon arrival (Health Canada, 2010). Sport has a role to play in health promotion, but this connection is not articulated in the Canadian Sport Policy. As we demonstrate below, structural silos in government is one likely explanation for the lack of policy that connects sport to health and immigration.

Challenges in addressing multiculturalism policy in sport

Structural divisions, complexity, a lack of data, and the lack of capacity of sport leaders to implement policy were cited as challenges that Sport Canada is facing in developing a multiculturalism and sport policy. In terms of the structural challenge, Canadian Heritage, Health Canada, and Citizenship and Immigration are all separate departments in federal government. Graefe (2006, 2008) contends that attempts to improve intergovernmental relations to develop more integrated social policies are often fraught with inertia and dysfunction because each governmental unit has a vested interest in working within its own policy domain to solidify their positions as different political parties come in and out of power. Another structural issue is that there is no umbrella sport organization that represents the interest of multicultural sport, making it difficult for Sport Canada to work with one major stakeholder as they have done in other policy areas. For example, Sport Canada has worked with the Canadian Association for the Advancement of Women and Sport and Physical Activity (CAAWS) on their policy for women and girls; the Aboriginal Sport Circle for their policy on Aboriginal people's participation; and the Canadian Paralympic Committee, Special Olympics Canada, and other organizations for their policy on sport for persons with disabilities. Sport Canada policy makers are faced with the enormous challenge of developing a multicultural sport policy that represents the interests of the over 200 ethnic groups that are part of the Canadian cultural mosaic.

In addition to structural divisions, complexity surrounding conceptualizations of diversity made it overwhelming to contemplate how to proceed. Diversity is defined by Sport Canada as:

> the richness of human differences and encompasses both the visible and invisible differences among people with respect to, but not limited to, gender; age; ethno-culture; socio-economic status; mental, cognitive and physical abilities; sexual orientation; religion and spiritual practices; world view; family status; educational background; appearance; group affiliation; and organizational affiliation.
>
> (Sport Canada, 2011, p. 1)

As a result, underrepresentation cannot be attributed to one single factor such as ethnicity and targeted groups cannot be treated as homogeneous, making it difficult to avoid very general policy statements. This is illustrated in the following comment from a policy maker:

> When we talk about multiculturalism or visible minorities, it's sort of a grab bag of so many different cultures and backgrounds. Each may have their very specific views about sport and different needs as to how sport could be adapted to better attract these populations. Definitely, I think this is going to be quite an interesting and challenging issue for us when we look at it.
>
> (Federal sport policy maker)

As acknowledged by Sport Canada (2011), another challenge is that sport participation rates and trends among ethnocultural groups are not well known because the data needed to make informed policy decisions are currently unavailable. The following statement illustrates that not being able to defend a new policy position to politicians may, in part, be responsible for the reluctance Sport Canada has shown in this policy area:

> When you asked what factors facilitated or hindered the implementation of the policy and the strategy, the need to have better data gathering is major because we just don't have it. We need to mount the evidence base so we can put forward policy that we have confidence in and that we can defend if it gets challenged.
>
> (Federal sport policy maker)

Another policy maker pointed out that some data are often difficult to measure and only gathering participation data is insufficient:

> The difficulty with that is the participation data tell you how many people are participating, but it does not tell you why. It doesn't tell you what the barriers are, so they are limited in their usefulness. We also recognize that some social factors like socio-economic status are really hard to measure.
>
> (Federal sport policy maker)

It was suggested that qualitative and quantitative data are needed, including evaluations of the impact that targeted policies and programmes are having:

> We need to have research in order to make better policy decisions but also to assist us in the policy development process. Research will guide the identification of issues and the analysis of those issues, the identification of options and analysis of the options. And it will help demonstrate impact too.
>
> (Federal sport policy maker)

Another concern is that 'volunteer-based sport organization may lack the resources, knowledge and expertise, or the commitment to develop and implement strategies for the inclusion of under-represented groups' (Sport Canada, 2011, p. 2). We would counter that enhancing capacity is precisely why Sport Canada needs to take a leadership position in policy development.

Next steps in policy development

When contemplating next steps in policy development, there was great uncertainty about how to proceed as illustrated in the following comment:

> Is the objective to not have barriers or if there are barriers to address them or to remove them? Is the objective that we are able to find in sports what we find in Canadian communities? That means that if in the Canadian mosaic there is 15 per cent representation of visible minorities, is our objective then to put 15 per cent visible minorities in sports? Is our objective to make sure that initiatives are put in place, an approach that is a little more proactive than to just say: there are no barriers? Should there be incentives? For me, this is not at all clear.
>
> (Federal sport policy maker)

One policy maker argued for a strategic policy approach, but admitted that there had been very little discussion about what that would entail:

> It would be better if we had sort of a strategic policy approach to this, and essentially said, OK, here's the big picture, here's the sections that we're going to put our initial focus on and why. And if someone were to challenge us as to why we do it this way, we would have a rationale to provide us with. But you could ask me right now the question of why have we not done visible minorities or a multiculturalism policy and I wouldn't be able to give you a very sound rationale, as this is not one that we have had a discussion about.
>
> (Federal sport policy maker)

While federal multiculturalism and sport policy is lacking in Canada, we did uncover an example of a national sport organization that is devising strategies to increase Aboriginal and immigrant participation in their sport. This example could inform policy development. A strength of Hockey Canada's programme (i.e. ice hockey) is their multilingual communication materials that are being distributed to households across the country. However, media accounts of the programme appeared to question the motives of Hockey Canada. More specifically, increasing memberships by assimilating youth into one of Canada's most popular sports was the motivation for the initiative, rather than making meaningful changes to the sport at the grass-roots level in order to accommodate a wider range of ethnocultural circumstances and interests (Canadian Television Network, 2011; Oviatt, 2011; Pap, 2011). As noted by Oviatt:

Alarmed by sliding enrolments in minor hockey programs across the country, Hockey Canada is launching an offensive in a dozen languages, targeting the households of recent immigrants and First Nations families to boost the number of Canadian kids strapping on skates. Minor hockey registration continues to be on a downward spiral and there are concerns that in the next 10 years, there could be 200,000 fewer kids playing the sport. In 2011, Hockey Canada had 560,000 members after peaking at 584,679 members in 2008–09. For the first time, its annual planner, which is mailed to registered minor hockey players under the age of ten, is available in twelve languages including English, French, Arabic, Chinese (Cantonese and Mandarin), Cree, German, Inuktitut, Italian, Portuguese, Punjabi, Spanish and Tagalog. Hockey Canada used census figures to determine their focus. The planner includes a personalized season planner, hockey-related activities, comic strips, pins and stickers. According to Hockey Canada's Vice President, the mail out serves three purposes: an affinity to the national sport body, a recruitment angle as other kids are seeing it and getting excited about playing, and it may help kids already involved stay in the sport longer.

(Oviatt, 2011, p. C9)

Another example for encouraging sport participation among newcomers is the Inclusive Recreation Model for Immigrants and Refugee Youth developed by the Ontario Council of Agencies Serving Immigrants (OCASI, 2005). Key features of the model include involving youth in decision making, preparing them for athletic competitions and coaching certification, encouraging parental involvement, and building partnerships with a wide network of community partners. The report by Donnelly and Nakamura (2006) features a number of other national and international examples that could serve as a starting point for developing multiculturalism and sport policy.

The need for dialogue should be central to the policy development process, as the federal sport policy makers acknowledged. Two-way dialogue was fostered in our Multiculturalism, Sport, and Physical Activity Study when Chinese women were brought together with local, provincial, and federal sport policy makers in a two-day workshop to share their stories about migrating to Canada and the role that participating in community programmes had in their lives. They provided a number of recommendations, with the assistance of interpreters from an immigrant service agency, on how to foster their inclusion and the inclusion of other newcomers. These recommendations included multilingual communications through cultural groups and immigrant service agencies, providing multilingual instructions by ethnically diverse staff, and providing opportunities for them to teach and lead activities in which they had participated before immigrating (Frisby, 2011). It is this type of dialogue that can lead to informed policies that promote intercultural understanding, increased participation, and the diversification of Canada's physical culture.

Conclusions

Developing and implementing multiculturalism and sport policy could foster opportunities to enrich Canada's physical culture when foreign and native-born people learn from each other's sporting traditions. Most policy makers understood the need for a multiculturalism and sport policy, given changing demographics, low participation rates, and the potential benefits of increased participation. However, they pointed to challenges related to structure, complexity, and a lack of data that have stalled their efforts to move forward.

The key will be to foster diversity without divisiveness. Roundtable discussants proposed that multiculturalism policy should not just target visible minorities, but should be inclusive of Aboriginals, persons with English and French heritage, and all other immigrants regardless of their skin colour (Lock Kunz and Sykes, 2007). The identification of promising practices to build upon, working with other departments in government (e.g., health, citizenship and immigration), and having direct contact with new Canadians and different ethnocultural groups are important first steps that could inform future policy making. However, developing policy alone will not be sufficient. It must be accompanied by capacity building and a willingness to develop related programmes and services at the federal, provincial, and local levels.

Given that one of our goals in this chapter was to give voice to the federal bureaucrats who are responsible for policy development in the area of multiculturalism and sport, we felt it was fitting to give them the last word.

> I really feel that the sport community, generally speaking, has not done a very good job of addressing Canada's changing diversity and we need to wake up and do something about it. There are just a lot of good reasons to do it and we shouldn't not do it just because it is so hard to do.
>
> (Federal sport policy maker)

11

EUROPEAN MODELS OF SPORT

Governance, organisational change and sports policy in the EU

Ling-Mei Ko, Ian Henry and Wei-Chun Tai

Introduction

In this second section of this book, there are a number of references to the development of governance networks and transversal governance. The shift from bureaucratic hierarchical (traditional) forms of governance to transversal networks is one that, while remarked on in the literature as a general tendency (Henry and Lee, 2004; Hoye and Cuskelly, 2007), is particularly clear in the British context. This chapter seeks to tease out the nature of this change and the policy thinking that underpins it, and evaluates an attempt to introduce networked approaches to the development and delivery of sports policy at the local level through County Sports Partnerships undertaken in England in the later stages of the New Labour administration.

We start by situating the discussion in a debate about sport policy change in Europe that we have developed elsewhere (Henry and Ko, 2009), outlining a fourfold typology of European policy systems developed by Jean Camy and his colleagues (in VOCASPORT Research Group, 2004) in the VOCASPORT project. Drawing on this typology we subsequently seek to tease out aspects of governance and policy delivery that relate to each of the types and to outline some of the tensions experienced within European policy systems in the ways in which they are subject to forces for change. This provides the context for a discussion of a case study of sport policy change in England that seeks to influence and steer policy through networks and partnerships at the local level in ways that are consistent with what Camy terms the social model.

A typology of European sport policy systems

Our starting point is the outlining of a typology of sports policy systems briefly introduced by Jean Camy and his colleagues in the VOCASPORT Project (VOCASPORT Research Group, 2004) which groups together European policy systems into four clusters or configurations.[1] The first of these is what Camy *et al.* term the *bureaucratic configuration*, which exhibits high degrees of state involvement (15 states exhibit this type of policy system: Belgium, Cyprus, Czech Republic, Estonia, Finland, France, Hungary, Latvia, Lithuania, Malta, Poland, Portugal, Slovakia, Slovenia, Spain):

> The 'bureaucratic configuration' is characterised by the very active role that the public authorities take in regulating the system. There is almost always a legislative framework specific to the field (law on sport). This is a system characterised by rules from a public authority which, with its political/democratic legitimacy, does not necessarily negotiate to any great extent with other players.
>
> (VOCASPORT Research Group, 2004: 53)

The second ideal type is the *entrepreneurial configuration*, which Camy *et al.* describe as being characterised by a high level of involvement of market forces, both in terms of direct provision, and also through contractual engagement by the state to manage publicly owned facilities (through for example competitive tendering procedures). Market discipline is thus evident on both public and private sectors. Two states are identified as incorporated within this configuration, namely Ireland and the UK.

The *missionary configuration* incorporates those states for whom the voluntary sector acts with delegated powers (six states fall within this type: Austria, Denmark, Germany, Italy, Luxembourg, Sweden):

> The 'missionary configuration' is characterised by the dominant presence of a voluntary sports movement with great autonomy to make decisions. The state or regional authorities delegate it much responsibility for orienting the sports policy, even though they may become gradually involved in a contractual logic with it.
>
> (VOCASPORT Research Group, 2004: 53)

While the missionary configuration involves delegation to the sport movement, the fourth group, the *social configuration* builds on involvement of civil society more generally. The social configuration (for which only one instance is identified by Camy *et al.*, namely, the Netherlands) has high levels of interaction with partners such as trades unions, voluntary and commercial sector providers:

> The 'social configuration' is characterised by the presence of the social partners within a multifaceted system. This type of system is not univocally dominated by one player, but instead is subject to cohabitation/collaboration between public, voluntary and commercial players.
>
> (VOCASPORT Research Group, 2004: 53)

Camy *et al.* go no further than identifying the four configurations and argue that, while there are tendencies for change or stresses and strains in terms of conforming to these types, the characterisation of states as falling into these categories broadly captures aspects of the system.

Camy's description of the four types of configuration can, we suggest, be further enhanced as an explanatory framework, in particular by drawing on the generic literature on local governance. For example the relationship between the four configurations can be effectively illustrated along the two dimensions that Janet Newman (2001) employs in distinguishing approaches to governance in public sector services (see Figure 11.1). The vertical axis relates to the role of the state – centralised versus decentralised power. The horizontal axis relates to the promotion of innovation and competitiveness at one end of the continuum (by employing the commercial or voluntary sectors in the delivery of sports services), to continuity (through state regulation) and sustainability (by engaging wider social involvement).

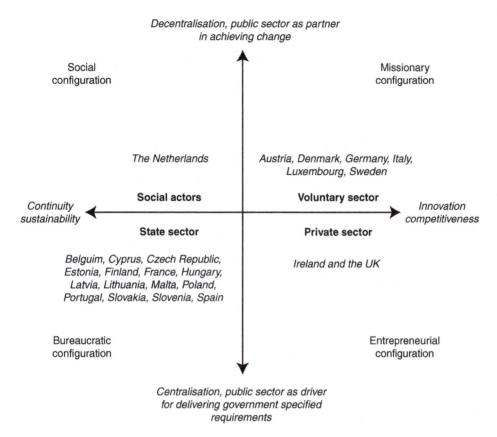

Figure 11.1 The relationship between the four VOCASPORT types of national sports policy system

An important feature to note about these four types is that they imply a different focus in terms of service delivery. The bureaucratic configuration places emphasis on regulation of processes, rules and requirements concerning how to proceed – in short, on *accountability* through following required processes. By contrast, the entrepreneurial configuration focuses almost exclusively on *outputs*, particularly in the context of public sector bodies contracting commercial entities to manage services, where contracts will stipulate the kinds of output to be achieved.

The focus of the missionary configuration is on maintaining the broad social *outcomes* of a healthy voluntary sector in sport, rather than on government specifying the nature of direct outputs to be achieved. The voluntary sector, it is assumed, should be relatively independent of direct government pressures, and when given selective autonomy will produce public benefits.

The social configuration is somewhat different. It is an approach that is premised on the notion that for policy solutions to be sustainable and implementable they have to have the commitment of all major stakeholders. This approach is thus focused on a long-term commitment to social, political, and economic inclusion as a broader outcome, the building of *social capacity* in each sector such that multi-perspectival analyses of policy may be undertaken producing better, more sustainable, and joined-up policy.

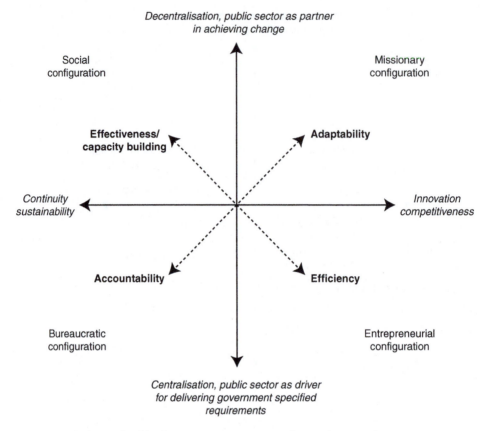

Figure 11.2 The key goals of the four VOCASPORT types of national sports policy system

These differential foci imply fundamentally different approaches to policy. They are in effect based on the achievement of different goals, and there are tensions between these. The core goal of the bureaucratic model is to secure accountability, while the missionary model's insistence on freeing the sports sector from state control is to ensure flexibility and adaptability, the ability to respond to changing circumstances unfettered by the bureaucracy of the traditional state apparatus, and free from party political interests. Similarly, while the core concern of the entrepreneurial model is to secure efficiency, in terms of cost per unit of output, the social configuration is concerned with securing the social engagement of all stakeholders to maximise the benefits of consultation in terms of the quality of decisions made, but also the subsequent ownership of, and commitment to, policy by these key actors. In short, the social model seeks to promote active citizenship, and to enhance the strengths of civil society more broadly.

In effect, in the discussion of the empirical work that follows, we will seek to argue that the English sport policy system moved on under New Labour in terms of the form of sports policy model adopted, moving away from the commercial culture of the entrepreneurial model to adopt an approach that is based on local partnership and governance much more closely aligned to the social model as articulated in the VOCASPORT study. The New Labour concern to develop third sector initiatives that promoted policy facilitation through partnerships within and beyond sport, we would argue, was most prominently promoted through the introduction and development of County Sports Partnerships.

The literature on policy change: governance, networks and social capital

There are perhaps three related literatures that might be highlighted as directly informing and reflecting New Labour's broad policy goals in relation to local governance in the context of its attempts to define a new policy path, or what came to be termed in the 1990s a Third Way. These are the literature on governance itself; on networks generally, and policy networks in particular; and on social capital.

The growing significance of the literature on governance became highly visible in the literature on the UK policy system following the Thatcherite programme of market-based initiatives. The hierarchical top-down bureaucratic structures that characterised local government in the 1970s were to be replaced by a range of contract-based initiatives that displaced considerable decision making into the commercial sector and voluntary sectors, replacing a set of unified hierarchical structures with a network of relationships between actors drawn from different sectors. In effect, this represented the UK's shift from a bureaucratic to a market-based entrepreneurial model. As Rhodes (2007: 1244) argues, 'In the 1990s ... the study of networks mutated into the study of governance' since networks 'are the defining characteristic of governance'.

These shifts reflect what is described more broadly by commentators as a move away from direct *government* (government control of policy and service delivery) towards a network from of *governance*. Hill and Lynn, for example, addressing the international arena, argue that 'the shifts away from hierarchical government toward horizontal governing reflect ... a gradual addition of new administrative forms that facilitate governance within a system of constitutional authority ...' (Hill and Lynn, 2005: 173), while Kooiman also emphasises the fact that such forms extend well beyond the traditional boundaries of the state when he defines governance as:

> The totality of interaction in which public as well as private actors participate aimed at solving societal problems and creating societal opportunities; attending to the institutions as contexts for these governing interactions; and establishing a normative foundation for all these activities.
>
> (Kooiman, 2003: 4)

The nature of this change is regarded as more than merely a subtle shift in policy approach, and is described by some commentators as revolutionary:

> Indeed we seem to be going through a revolution in the governance of public production systems as governments seek to reach beyond their borders to find additional resources, additional operating capacity and even additional legitimacy to achieve their assigned goals.
>
> (Moore and Hartley, 2008: 5)

The development of the policy literature on governance is clearly linked to the development of networks. Rhodes (2007: 1244) indeed defines networks as 'the defining feature of governance' and identifies governance systems as manifesting four key characteristics: interdependence between organisations; continuing interaction between network members; game-like interactions 'rooted in trust and regulated by rules of the game negotiated and agreed by network participants' (Rhodes, 2007, p. 1246); and implying a significant degree of autonomy from the state. Policy networks are, however, a special species of the network phenomenon, since:

> Policy network analysis stresses how networks limit participation in the policy process; decide which issues will be included and excluded from the policy agenda; shape the

actors through the rules of the game; privilege certain interests; and substitute private government for accountability.

(Rhodes, 1997: 1251)

The research on, and advocacy of, networks and governance is clearly related to the influence of communitarian thinking (Etzioni, 1993) in New Labour's ideological programme to establish a 'Third Way', one that lay between traditional Labour's emphasis on a strong public sector, and the neoliberal move towards market-based solutions (Giddens, 1994, 1998) and which would be replaced by the development of inclusive networks incorporating actors from across the public, commercial and third sectors.

In addition to New Labour's attraction to networks and governance as policy concepts, the concept of social capital as promoted by Putnam (2000) was embraced in New Labour's policy thinking from the beginning of the decade. Putnam's own focus was on the atomisation of civil society which he ascribes to a lack of social capital, that is a lack of norms of mutual trust and social reciprocity in contemporary civil societies. He operationalised this in his research as a weakening of social ties as evidenced by declining membership of social organisations and decreasing political participation. However, while Putnam's major preoccupation is with linkages in society in terms of 'bonding' (intra-group connections), and bridging (inter-group connections), extended by Woolcock (1998) to include linking (inter-institutional connections), the concept of social capital was taken up enthusiastically in the management and policy fields in the analysis of intra- and inter-organisational linkages, as well as those between policy domains (in ways that are thus analogous to the concern with bonding, bridging and linking).

Lee (2009) undertakes a systematic review of the literature on the application of the concept of social capital to management contexts and concludes that there are three dimensions to the concept of social capital as applied in the literature, namely, structural, cognitive and relational. The structural dimension relates to network ties and configurations that are predominantly assessed in terms of size/volume (the number of ties individual elements have) and centrality (the relative number of direct links in the network between one individual or group of individuals and those other groups in the population. Relational social capital relates to 'underlying normative conditions of trust, obligation, expectation and identity that guide actors' network relations' (Lee, 2009: 257). Cognitive social capital involves the ability to engage in shared languages, codes and narratives. As Lee describes this:

> Individual social actors who share values for implementing codes of conduct and attitudinal similarities can also repeat efficient verbal exchange …. These language forms develop perceptual codes and provide a frame of reference. In other words, shared language helps create codes of conduct for establishing appropriate conversation patterns.
>
> (Lee, 2009: 258)

Thus, for example, in discussions between professionals who are members of the sports policy network and the health policy network, respectively, the use of certain terminology (physical exercise or activity) rather than others (e.g. sport) might be seen as contributing to dialogue that will ensure a sense of 'inclusion' of policy communities and 'commonality' and thus promote trust and reciprocity.

The three core concepts we have outlined above thus represent complementary elements in the developing policy ideology of New Labour following its election in 1997. The concept of 'networks' relates primarily to the constitutive framework of policy actors, 'governance' to the normative prescription and the description of the nature of the preferred system of policy delivery and control, while social capital reflects the individual and organisational 'glue' by which the framework (network) and policy approach (governance) are to be held together and sustained.

Methodology for the empirical case studies.

While our study is limited to a focus on two local networks in sports policy in England, there is a growing international literature on the development of forms of network governance. Hill and Lynn point out that there is 'widespread ... belief that the focus of administrative practice is shifting from hierarchical government toward greater reliance on horizontal, hybridised and associational forms of governance' (2005: 173). They go on to point however that 'Recent arguments to this effect however made limited recourse to the body of empirical evidence that might shed light on the actual extent of this transformation' (Hill and Lynn, 2005: 173).

While Hill and Lynn seek to operationalise measures of what constitutes a governance approach and seek to apply this in a positivistic analysis of the level of prominence of these operational measures, Bevir and Richards (2009) argue for a qualitative, 'decentred' analysis of the changing policy environment. Some such studies exist, including for example Fleming and Rhodes (2005) on policing policy, and Hardy and Rhodes (2003) on the health service, but despite a growing treatment in the literature of sports governance and partnerships (Henry and Lee, 2004; Hindley, 2002; McDonald, 2005), there is a relative absence of detailed empirical evaluation of the operation of network governance in relation to sports policy. The aim of this article is therefore to evaluate the extent to which the attempt to introduce a network-based approach to local governance of sport policy was successful. We thus seek to locate our analysis in an empirical evaluation of two case study County Sports Partnerships in the English regions that draws on secondary quantitative, and primary qualitative, data.

Following the introduction of County Sports Partnerships (CSPs) in 2002, a study was commissioned in 2006 from Loughborough University by the DCMS, funded by the Treasury, to review the application of three interventions in two CSP case study areas designed to evaluate and enhance network interaction in relation to sport policy (Henry, Downward, Harwood, and Robinson, 2008). One of the interventions involved the implementation of a social network analysis in both CSPs using a commercial service provider. The policy evaluation team was responsible for the analysis of the perceived usefulness and accuracy of the social network data that emerged and in particular the extent to which these data and the associated network maps informed any policy action subsequently taken to improve network interaction and policy delivery. This was accomplished via 98 qualitative interviews with CSP members and members of other stakeholder organisations in the network.[2] These interviews were undertaken at two points. The first was from February to April of 2006 immediately after the social network analysis findings had been communicated to stakeholders, and the second approximately 18 months later September to November 2007.[3]

The social network analysis undertaken by the service provider was designed to test the nature and strength of relationships between actors from the various stakeholder groups. This was accomplished by first establishing with CSP personnel a list of individuals and their organisations who were (actually or potentially) significant actors in local sport-related policy (227 individuals for Leicester-Shire and Rutland CSP and 225 for Lincolnshire CSP). The individuals and their stakeholder organisations were organised into constituencies by the CSPs that were used by the social network analysis (SNA) providers in reporting results of the SNA. These constituencies were conceptualised slightly differently in the two CSPs (see Table 11.1).

Having identified the individual stakeholders, each was contacted by email and asked to complete an online questionnaire with five questions as follows:

1   Who do you go to or talk to, to help get day to day work done around sport and physical activity?
2   Who do you go to or talk to when you need a decision relating to work around sport and physical activity?
3   Who do you go to or talk to when you need expert advice relating to work around sport and physical activity?
4   Who do you go to or who do you talk to when exploring new ideas or new ways of working around sport and physical activity?
5   Who do you talk to, to keep up to date with what's going on in the world of sport and physical activity?

For each question respondents were asked to indicate who they had contacted and how frequently (daily, weekly, monthly, less than monthly). Response rates were high – 72.9 per cent in the case of Leicester-Shire and Rutland, 74 per cent in relation to Lincolnshire CSP. The maps of interaction between the individual stakeholder and their organisations and/or constituencies were then made available to each of the respondents.

The particular approach adopted for the social network analysis and its limitations are not discussed here for reasons of space (for a full account see Henry, Downward, Harwood, and Robinson, 2008b: 1020). Our concern here is with how the results were perceived; in effect, whether they reflected the intuitive picture of the network that interviewees held, and whether this picture of network interaction informed subsequent attempts to strengthen appropriate interaction between different constituencies. Our concern is therefore less with the quality and objectivity of the social network analysis itself than it is with the ways in which reported results of the SNA are accommodated in the discourses of the actors involved from the different constituencies.

Table 11.1 provides a breakdown of the interviewees in terms of the constituencies from which they are drawn. A total of 98 interviews were conducted with 58 interviewees. Thus, in 40 cases repeat interviews were conducted at both points. Two thirds of the interviews were conducted with CSP personnel.

The interviews were digitally recorded and subject to analysis employing Nvivo software to identify key themes emerging in interviewees' accounts of the developing relationships between stakeholders from the various constituencies.

Table 11.1 The schedule of interviews

Constituency	Stakeholder Organisation	No. of interviews
Sport	County Sports Partnerships	58
	National/Regional Governing Bodies	8
	Sport England East Midlands Regional Office	4
Local Government	Local Authorities	14
Education	School Sport Partnership Development Managers	8
Health	Primary Care Trusts	6
Total		98

Analysis of findings: social network analysis and the nature of partnership in the new local sports governance system

The social network analysis

Following completion of the SNA, participants were introduced by the SNA provider (or in some instances by one of the authors) to visual representations or network maps of the links between all nodes (individuals) in all stakeholder organisations and thus between each policy constituency. These network maps were supplemented at interview by data provided by our interviewers on the level of connectedness of the interviewees compared with others within his or her own organisation, and across the different stakeholder organisations and the different policy constituencies. The basic measure employed for this purpose was the density of ties, calculated for each individual, each stakeholder organisation or group of organisations, and each policy constituency. The measure of density employed was the number of direct ties between nodes as a proportion of the maximum number of potentially available ties. Nodes, or groups of nodes reflecting greater density of ties are thus regarded as more central to a network. Table 11.2 presents a summary of these data for the network as a whole and the major policy constituencies – education, local government, sporting governing bodies, health and the voluntary sector.

As the table indicates, the density of links is greater in the case of the Leicester-Shire and Rutland CSP than it is for the Lincolnshire CSP for virtually all groups, with the exception of density of four of the categories of links for national governing bodies of sport, and even here the differences are minimal. This difference might have been anticipated given the more geographically compact nature of the former. Although strictly speaking the rankings of the stakeholder groups and policy constituencies cannot be directly compared (since some of the groups are aggregated differently in the two counties) nevertheless the overall pattern seems clear. The CSPs themselves reflect the greatest density of links, followed by Sport England East Midlands Region, and the education constituency, and local government sports contacts. The health constituency shows the lowest level of density of links for Lincolnshire, and the second lowest for Leicester-Shire and Rutland. Perhaps the only exception in the pattern of density measures relates to partnership development managers (PDMs) in sports colleges in Leicester-Shire and Rutland (0.2592). This was second only to that of the CSP organisation itself for 'work links' and actually exceeded the CSP on the other four categories of links. However, because in the case of Lincolnshire the PDMs were not differentiated from other categories of education links, direct comparison was not possible between the data for both counties along this dimension. However, interview data suggested that there was a difference in the 'embeddedness' of the PDMs in the Lincolnshire system, and it was possible at the individual level to illustrate this.

Following the communication of the initial SNA findings in the form of maps shown to and discussed with stakeholders, the research team focused interviews on relationships among stakeholders and between stakeholders and the CSPs from four major constituencies. These constituencies were selected because they reflected poor connectivity (the health sector), reflected stronger connectivity (the sports sector), manifested differences between the counties in terms of connectivity (the education constituency), or reflected a polyvalent, multiservice constituency (local government). Interviews took place at two points, immediately after the communication of the SNA results and a period some 18 months later as described above in the methodology section. The interviews focused on the nature of interaction, or the types of interaction sought, between individuals in these stakeholder organisations in the different policy constituencies.

Table 11.2 Social network density in five domains for both county sports partnerships

Density of links in Leicester-Shire and Rutland CSP						
	Individuals responding	Work links	Decision making	Expert advice	Innovation	Social links
County Sports Partnership						
Leic's and Rutland CSP	18	0.2604	0.0656	0.0578	0.0544	0.0914
CSP shadow board members	8	0.0839	0.0282	0.0267	0.0221	0.0328
National/Regional sport bodies						
Sport England EM	11	0.1227	0.0714	0.0680	0.0586	0.0887
Sports governing bodies	22	0.0608	0.0169	0.0158	0.0128	0.0239
Sports coach UK	2	0.0706	0.0368	0.0337	0.0337	0.0552
Other regional sports bodies	4	0.0615	0.0062	0.0138	0.0108	0.0200
Education						
Sports college partnership development managers	10	0.2592	0.1048	0.0827	0.0932	0.1232
Schools and colleges	18	0.0517	0.0233	0.0216	0.0253	0.0288
School sport coordinators	10	0.0762	0.0158	0.0110	0.0219	0.0225
Local authorities						
Council sport contacts	22	0.1114	0.0457	0.0365	0.0351	0.0513
Council non sport contacts	10	0.0570	0.0374	0.0306	0.0239	0.0368
Cultural services chief officers group	9	0.0568	0.0192	0.0171	0.0130	0.0199
				Density of links		
	Individuals responding	Work links	Decision making	Expert advice	Innovation	Social links
Voluntary sector bodies						
Voluntary sector sport	4	0.0675	0.0230	0.0000	0.0199	0.0307
Voluntary sector non sport	3	0.0245	0.0102	0.0000	0.0123	0.0164
Health Sector						
Health organizations	6	0.0256	0.0031	0.0061	0.0020	0.0082
Others	7	0.0307	0.0061	0.0053	0.0044	0.0061
Total	164	0.1035	0.0254	0.0213	0.0210	0.0317

Table 11.2 Continued

Density of links in Lincolnshire CSP						
	Individuals responding	Work links	Decision making	Expert advice	Innovation	Social links
County Sports Partnership						
Lincs CSP	19	0.2194	0.0583	0.0470	0.0372	0.0577
National/Regional sport bodies						
Sport England EM	11	0.1192	0.0855	0.0958	0.0686	0.1105
Sports governing bodies	27	0.0495	0.0211	0.0189	0.0144	0.0275
Sport patrons	1	0.0240	0.2216	0.2515	0.1737	0.2874
Venues	3	0.0319	0.0739	0.0818	0.0579	0.0958
Other sport partners and agencies	9	0.0858	0.0220	0.0259	0.0180	0.0299
Education						
Schools and colleges	21	0.0870	0.0225	0.0179	0.0176	0.0236
Local authorities						
Council sport contacts	32	0.0786	0.0216	0.0186	0.0193	0.0229
Council non sport contacts	12	0.0343	0.0065	0.0060	0.0085	0.0065
	Density of links					
	Individuals responding	Work links	Decision making	Expert advice	Innovation	Social links
Voluntary sector bodies						
Clubs and volunteers	10	0.0220	0.0107	0.0071	0.0083	0.0113
Voluntary sector non sport	13	0.0201	0.0041	0.0023	0.0018	0.0018
Health Sector						
Health organizations	5	0.0071	0.0012	0.0000	0.0036	0.0000
Others	5	0.0096	0.0012	0.0024	0.0000	0.0012
Total	168	0.0776	0.0198	0.0179	0.0152	0.0218

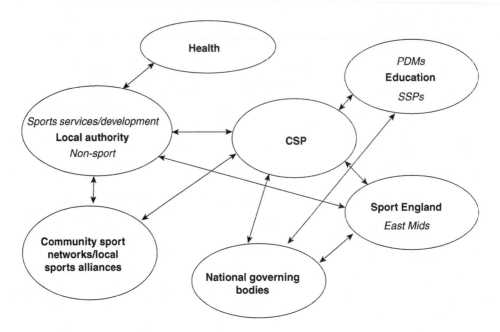

Figure 11.3 Constituencies of interest in CSPs as a basis for SNA round 2 interviews

Interview data qualitative accounts of links between constituencies

The health constituency

Members in the health sector who were part of the social network identified were predom-inantly members of the Primary Care Trusts in both counties which had oversight of the delivery of local medical and health services. At the first set of interviews, the SNA itself and interviewees' subsequent comments (with one major exception in a particular local authority) highlighted the lack of interaction between the health and sports sectors.

In the interim between completion of the SNA and the second set of interviews, significant moves towards change were reported as having taken place in the health sector by a number of health sector and other interviewees. In both counties the National Health Service Primary Care Trusts (PCTs) had been rationalised into fewer, larger units. Apart from any potential economies of scale, the new arrangements were said to mediate the severe financial problems from which some of the smaller PCTs had previously suffered.

Among the reasons for enhanced partnership activity was the growing involvement of PCTs in Local Area Agreements and Local Strategic Partnerships,[4] where partnership working with the local authorities in what was termed the 'healthier communities' and 'older people' policy blocks had involved jointly funded projects. As one interviewee put it:

> I think the Local Area Agreement has generally spurred on much more partnership, much more feeling that we ought to do things in partnerships. The LAA only came in here this year and so links haven't been good between us and sport has definitely not been a priority for us at all but will be more so in the future.
>
> (PCT representative)

A Local Authority interviewee stressed that although such initiatives may have an 'exercise' rather than 'sports' label or emphasis, there were opportunities to enhance support for both health and sports purposes:

> The PCT themselves are bringing a significant amount of funding. ... they're giving 70 per cent of the funding .... But the real trick is, is for example some of the health trainers ... they're meant to go out, they give advice on physical activity with a local sports club, what to eat, how best to get access to a physical activity environment. But the skill sets on which we manage to sort of get these people on board, they're not just the archetypical health trainer as it says on the job description, most of them are sports coaches, most of them are sports professionals, most of them have a sports degree background and they're actually adding to our own sports infrastructure. ... it's supposed to be a PCT health thing, but on a sports system it's bringing added value to the team and vice versa as well.
>
> (LA interviewee)

Nevertheless there were clear examples given by this individual of how targets were beginning to be integrated in certain contexts:

> We're doing that in conjunction with a mental health project with the PCT. We're now taking referrals for people with mild cases of depression into sports development programmes. ... We're tracking 138 people in the district on how that's actually improving their health.
>
> (LA interviewee)

This local government officer had seen his team grow considerably over the life of the project, with increasingly diverse roles performed by his team to match the increasingly diverse funding:

> I mean it's certainly grown in the last 12 months. I mean my team when I spoke to you before, we were probably about eight. We're now 32 ... which is sports development officers, active arts officers, coaches, leisure and play officers, play officers, sports fitness trainers, food for life trainers, extended exercise people, mental health people and ten physical ... ten fitness trainers and three GP referral officers.
>
> (LA interviewee)

The Public Health Directors claimed that there was a growing concern among health professionals to use non-clinical interventions. These had been well recognised in terms of exercise and its impact on obesity for which exercise (rather than necessarily sport-based) programmes were increasingly evident. However, other benefits were also increasingly acknowledged:

> I think health professionals are much more amenable to non-NHS interventions to improve health than in the past. I mean you mentioned depression, I know the evidence that exercise for mild to moderate depression can be as effective as drugs. We haven't anything specific on exercise but we have had a scheme of a sort of book loan prescription system for people with depression. ... five practices have been involved in that and they are very enthusiastic. So it's an example, it's nothing to do with sport, but an example of where general practitioners are keen to try out something that is different rather than just write out a prescription for antidepressants.
>
> (PCT interviewee)

However, some of those outside the medical profession commented on the fact that they perceived a significant difference between the attitudes of those within the PCT who came from a *clinical* background, and those who came from a *public health* background, in terms of their willingness to champion non-clinical interventions:

> It's about that background as well. There are three key people within our current PCT who I can identify as key advocates for preventative measures. ... all of those people have come from a public health background as opposed to a clinical performance background.
>
> (CSP interviewee)

There was, thus, recognition in both counties that although interaction between PCTs and the health sector on the one hand and local authorities on the other, in relation to health and exercise, had grown considerably, this was from a small base and the focus was largely on physical activity and exercise, rather than sport.

However, despite this progress, the setting of priorities for medical professionals was derived from key performance indicators (KPIs), and physical activity targets were not always to the fore even among non-clinical interventions where anti-smoking and healthy eating programmes had often been more directly linked to health gains.

> We're performance managed, ... we have reduced the gap in life expectancy, infant fatality, teenage conception rates, between 20 per cent of local authorities that are most deprived, which includes Lincoln. So we expected to improve life expectancy overall but to improve more in Lincoln so that the gap between Lincoln and the rest of the county, which is about a couple of years, on average is reduced. So all our lifestyle activities, smoking, diet, exercise and so on are all heavily focused, or increasingly heavily focused on Lincoln as seen as being down as the way first to meet those particular public health targets.
>
> (PCT interviewee)

Thus, in summary, themes developed by the interviewees suggest that the health sector is more evidently linked in with the other constituencies with the advent of the new local Primary Care Trusts and the growing impact of Local Area Agreements. Interventions however tended to be exercise-related rather than sports-related, though there is evidence of these focusing on mental as well as physical health. PCT intervention was dictated by the nature of KPIs, and although there is some evidence of a change in culture in the health sector, this tends to be where non-clinical public health-focused individuals are present in senior roles counterbalancing the dominant culture which valued clinical over public health promotion interventions.

The education constituency – School Sport Partnership Development Managers

In this policy constituency there seemed to have been a clear difference between the connectivity of some members of the education constituency – notably Partnership Development Managers (PDMs) based at Specialist Sports Colleges – in each of the two counties. While the other sectors (particularly the health and local authority sectors) had seen a fair amount of change in the interim between both sets of interviews, the situation in respect of the education sector seems to have further reinforced some practices in particular in the Lincolnshire context where there was a culture of focusing exclusively on this group's own KPIs.

Well one thing that social network analysis did show us was that PDMs were not neces-sarily networking and they were very insular in the way that they are dealt with and if anything anecdotally that's got worse. ... you could say they are very focused in achieving what they need to achieve and the systems and processes that they use they are very clear about. ... That also means that there is a downside against that which is that the develop-ment of partnership working is on their own terms always, to their advantage always. So it's not partnership in that sense.

(CSP interviewee)

This perception in respect of the Lincolnshire Partnership Development Managers is consistent with those of other interviewees (from the CSP, the local authority sector, and the Partnership Development Manager group). A local authority representative in Lincolnshire noted the prob-lem in these terms:

One of the frustrations that I see sort of leading with sport in Lincolnshire is ... the relation-ship between district, School Sport Partnerships and the County Sport Partnership. I think the schools see ... [themselves as] an isolated little group ... I think they also see that the facilities belong to the schools in the first instance and the community in the second, which to my under-standing should be the other way round. And I think they're a little bit sort of head in the sand.

(LA interviewee)

The general consensus was that the tendency to work in isolation on the part of Lincolnshire Partnership Development Managers was in part a product of the objectives and performance indicators that formed part of their monitor and evaluation system (such as the percentage of children experiencing five hours of quality physical education in and out of school, the quantity of school–club links etc.) that were specific to the school sector.

Most of the PDMs are driven into a silo, a bunker mentality by what is piled on to us from the Youth Sport Trust [the NGO charged with monitoring the PDMs' and schools' perfor-mance], from DCSF [Department for Children, Schools and Families]. ... You've got to do this, this and this and looking wider [at other policy goals] becomes more and more difficult.

(PDM interviewee)

This implied that Partnership Development Managers' involvement with the County Sports Partnership was perceived in the case of Lincolnshire not merely as a relatively minor con-cern on the part of the County's Partnership Development Managers, but as something that might potentially 'get in the way' of achieving the goals established in the PESSCL[5] (Physical Education School Sport Club Links) monitoring system developed by the Youth Sports Trust.

Unless the County Sport Partnership can actually be perceived to help with the things that we are being given to do all the time there won't be a great deal of interaction ... I had a meeting yesterday with my Youth Sports Trust area rep ... and one of the topics for discussion was to decrease the amount of external stuff I do e.g. things like this, [working with] the County Sports Partnership, that I shouldn't be doing those things, that I should just be focusing on what I am doing as a PDM ... and that sort of mentality is sort of pushed at us the whole time. So we tend to interact very closely with the people that we feel can facilitate our direct outcomes.

(Partnership Development Manager interviewee)

The pressure to consider wider County Sports Partnership activity as a distraction was thus in part a product of supervision by other entities, not simply the Youth Sports Trust but also the heads of those schools that housed the Partnership Development Managers and who acted as their line managers.

> Most of the time there isn't pressure from any of the schools other than the one you are based in which is all the time banging on about the fact that you cost them money because you're based there and they want more out of you than anybody else because you are based in their school and they want that to happen.
>
> (Partnership Development Manager interviewee)

As a consequence of such pressures, it is argued that these Partnership Development Managers felt unable to commit to wider social development goals – they were, for example, not well represented in the Children and Young People element of Local Area Agreements, nor were sports development goals for those beyond school age seen as a priority. For example, in relation to Sport England's target of an increase in adult sports participation of 1 per cent per annum:

> That doesn't apply to us, we're funding 5–16 year olds. Your 1 per cent increase is 18+, you can possibly switch it down to 16 on one or two things but generally speaking it's 18+. … that's not our concern anymore. If you want to sit back in your silo … actually why am I spending time doing anything with that, that's not hitting any of my targets.
>
> (Partnership Development Manager interviewee)

By contrast, the Partnership Development Managers in Leicestershire were seen as receptive to partnership activity which, though they have priorities defined by the same system of performance indicators (Physical Education School Sport Club Links), their approach generally took them beyond the bounds of a PESSCL related agenda. A local authority representative related how cooperation had been long established.

> I think we overcame [the PESSCL focus] because way before PESSCL started we had the Hinckley and Bosworth school sports group where every term all the Heads met and we would go to one of their meetings and just talk about what we're doing and what we've done and what we had achieved and then from that we developed our own where all the interested teachers would come together once a term and really from there we were able to identify four Heads who were real sporting champions and were able to work with them and then they would influence a wider circle. So we got Hinckley Rugby Club involved, we got the tennis clubs involved, we got the hockey clubs involved so every term we would have one club going into some interested schools. We got awarded some money for it, we even got the group their own constitution so they could bid for funding.
>
> (LA interviewee)

In the Leicester-Shire and Rutland CSP context, one significant difference with Lincolnshire particularly at the time of the first survey was that the Local Sports Alliances (known in some localities as Community Sport Networks, district level committees of sport-related interest groups) had been developed earlier. The Leicestershire Partnership Development Managers tended to be well integrated into this form of local, sub-county-level network.

I think nationally our local sports alliance network is looked on with some envy really and the fact that we've got nine established with terms of reference and nine with action plans. Six or seven probably delivering on those action plans I think strong plans, other counties are going to compare themselves with us. ... The PDM who is the Chair [of the Local Sports Alliance] has really bought into the concept and he has partners that have been consistently around the table for the last 12–18 months. ... a number of the LSAs have active PDMs.

(CSP interviewee)

In summary, while the structural context of the two county community sports systems differs to some degree (Lincolnshire having a different tradition in terms of its education system and perhaps having less developed Local Sports Alliances), the cultural context is also very different in terms of organisational culture between the two counties, and a number of interviewees emphasised that in the Lincolnshire context trust and shared vision and mission between Partnership Development Managers and the CSP or the sports development sector of local authorities was low.

Sports development officers and the local government constituency

Perhaps the major factor to affect local authority work in sport in the period between the two sets of interviews was the growth of Local Area Agreement activity. This had provided some momentum in the shifting of local authority roles away from sport development per se and into various aspects of community development, and transversal policy agendas.

Well up until recently most had sports development backgrounds but I think what we are seeing is ... a move away from sports for sports sake, ... what we're seeing is the development of community strategies at a local authority level which feeds into community cohesion ... we have got the community strategy for the county, which develops the Local Area Agreement, and then you've got community strategies at each level developing that. So what we're seeing is that people are looking and saying right, okay, it's not just about sport, it's about the development of local communities.

(CSP interviewee)

This tendency is reflected, for example, in the case of one of the Lincolnshire District Councils where the development of posts that were associated for example with promoting healthy eating as much as with physical activity, was a new phenomenon.

I am actually beginning a slight role change ... we are doing a lot of work on the Choosing Health initiative. We have got a lot of dual funded posts on physical activity, education, food and healthy lifestyles and sort of targeted activity to the over-fifty-fives. Those roles are coming on line as we speak ... they are targeted on the LAA target areas, which again is obviously an additional thing, we do it above, beyond the actual sports leisure strategy which we worked to.

(LA interviewee)

In contrast with the Partnership Development Managers, the local authority agenda was considerably broader. The sharing of goals with the CSPs, for example, helped in the development of a common line of action or at least greater empathy between the local authority personnel and the CSP. Sporting goals were also seen as complementing, rather than competing, with the wider social goals of the local authority.

We've adopted the Sport England targets in regard to volunteers and in regard to [sports] participation and certain subsections within those, which you can break down to district level .... So I mean I certainly regard the stuff that I've done with the CSP here as very, very fundamental, ... my overall goal for my sports team is to reach the Sport England targets, because if we do that we'll make the district healthier, we will have an impact on crime, etc., etc. and those performance indicators are most definitely interlinked.

(LA interviewee)

The use of sport and exercise to address a variety of agendas had allowed some local authorities that were quick off the mark to enhance their recruitment, as noted earlier. This focus on Local Area Agreement generating non-sporting, healthy lifestyle factors, however, does mean that to some extent the local authority sports development staff who are converted to undertake lifestyle advocacy roles may be less likely to engage with CSP staff since the focus of their work has changed.

In summary, the local authority sport development context was under pressure to adapt to the promotion of transversal agendas that cut across sport such as social inclusion, health, or community safety. This in turn demanded the formation of new types of partnership. However, ironically the CSP was perhaps less likely to engage with the local authority in some of these new partnerships since its defining function is sport (and physical recreation) rather than, for example, healthy eating.

The sports constituency – national governing bodies

The involvement of national governing bodies (NGBs) in local networks is in part a function of size and resource dependency. The smaller NGBs had an incentive to work in partnership in order to achieve their goals with a small resource base, and although larger NGBs had the resources to work with partners at local level they tended to lack the resource incentive.

The smaller ones – we do a fair bit of work with triathlon because we run the [local] triathlon ... we work with them and we did the first disability triathlon last year. Their big problem is resources. I mean the poor development officers can't be in ten places every evening to tell them what's going on.

(LA interviewee)

So, for example, England Netball is allocated £5,600 to work in Leicestershire to deliver its aims. So clearly they are going to need to do some partnership working to be able to enhance that to deliver on the outcomes of their Whole Sport Plan because £5,600 is nothing and ... for the likes of hockey, basketball, athletics, and it makes it really difficult to deliver at a local level. So it's probably those sports that are more proactive, seek partnerships including our own whereas with the likes of the FA they don't need us.

(CSP interviewee)

I think football is still trying to get their heads round LSAs [local sports alliances]. I was at the local football partnership a few weeks ago and they still can't get their heads round engaging this sporting alliance .... I think football is so big. I think they've been arrogant with how they engage and how they communicate with people.

(LA interviewee)

However, the difficulties for CSPs of engaging with the smaller NGBs were reflected in the fact that when Lincolnshire CSP adopted a system of memoranda of understanding (MOU) with individual NGBs, even where such agreements had been formalised, active cooperation did not always result. A similar approach was being adopted with School Sport Partnerships by NGBs.

> I do believe many governing bodies have gone down the line of trying to almost contract a level of service within the School Sport Partnership and we'll do this if you do that and mini service level agreements are beginning to sort of roll out between governing bodies and School Sport Partnerships ...
>
> (CSP interviewee)

In respect of partnership working with local authorities, the NGB representatives interviewed pointed to the fact that as local authorities became more engaged with wider social agendas, rather than with sport per se, NGB involvement with local authorities was on the decline with greater priority being attributed to links with education:

> But I see the local authority SDO [Sport Development Officer] as the poor relation in that communication and they seem to be the last to know whereas five years ago, before, school sports partnerships they were right at the heart of that debate with the national governing bodies.
>
> (CSP interviewee)

> [My priorities now are] schools and competitions ... My two key areas for the coming year, two years, three years, whatever, the really topical ones are schools. Work with schools, particularly with ... competitions. And increasing the competitive structure, improving the competitive structure ... The SDOs ... I don't attend their meetings.
>
> (NGB interviewee)

However, while the picture of NGB networking with other constituencies may be variable, in relation to networking within the NGB sector between sports where cooperation might provide benefits, this appeared to be lacking. One of the CSP officers, for example, observed that:

> I don't think governing bodies work together particularly well and I think that's mainly because it means a change in the way in which they view life and a change in a way in which they work so there is no sort of cross referencing or sharing certainly not for resources or even ideas at this particular point in time.
>
> (CSP interviewee)

There is in addition a major contrast in terms of physical location that has a bearing on relationships between CSPs and NGBs. On the one hand Lincolnshire has a widely dispersed population and thus increased travel times are involved simply in meeting with NGB representatives, while Leicester-Shire and Rutland is privileged by virtue of the shared location of the offices of the CSP and many NGBs regionally on a central, sports-based university campus that facilitates interaction on the part of the CSP with NGB representatives.

Conclusion

The social model of sport policy, seeking to build on communitarian ideals of the development of social capacity across sectors and across policy domains, may well be a reasonable characterisation of the direction of policy change that was sought by New Labour, drawing on the well documented advocacy of governance-based approaches to policy design and delivery, but to what extent was this reflected in policy change at the grass-roots level? As Hill and Lynn (2005) remark, empirical analysis of whether governance changes (rather than changes in policy rhetoric) are actually evident in policy systems is still relatively rare, and this gap is one this chapter seeks to address.

In broad terms the evidence accumulated through the two case studies suggests that although there has been some movement towards cooperative engagement in a governance/partnership approach, this is limited. Where such shifts have been evidenced has been in contexts where situations make stakeholders' resources dependent on one another. The experience associated with Local Area Agreements in the English system provided one such example in which the local partners by committing to and achieving specified common policy goals, can secure resources for their organisation. A further example was that of smaller national governing bodies of sport that do not have the resources to achieve desired policy outputs and thus outcomes locally, and that are therefore dependent on local partners. In addition to cases of resource dependence, where there had been a local culture of cooperation, this engendered trust and facilitated cooperation (as was the case in the description of the Partnership Development Managers in Leicester-Shire and Rutland).

However, by contrast there were powerful countervailing influences. Perhaps the most significant was that of competing professional cultures. This was particularly marked in the case of the health constituency where clinical medical culture has traditionally dominated over a public health culture. Thus, sport, or more accurately exercise, as an alternative to clinical forms of intervention had less powerful advocates, and thus, leveraging of partnership activity between health and sport constituencies was not easily accomplished. Some education professionals and even sports administrators in NGBs also appeared to operate on a different set of priorities from those engaged in local government sports development departments. The gap remained unbridged between a culture of development of sport (sports professionals), development of young people through sport (education professionals), development of health through exercise (public health professionals) and the contribution of sport to cross-cutting policy goals such as social exclusion, community safety, or economic development (local government officials including sports development officers).

In addition to this lack of joined up policy across policy domains, there was also a lack of evidence of engagement across the public, private and third sectors. This lack of coordinated effort was less the case for the public and third sectors where in sport there has been a tradition of public/voluntary sector cooperation with, for example, sports clubs using publicly owned facilities at subsidised rates. However, in our two cases, apart from some commercial management of publicly owned facilities, and with the exception of an arrangement for medical practitioners to refer patients to commercial health and fitness clubs for exercise prescription as an alternative or complement to prescribed drugs, there was very little evidence of engagement with commercial providers to deliver on policy goals

Finally, the reported impacts of separate KPIs for each constituency militated against cooperative working. KPIs in the education sector (which rewarded schools and Partnership Development Managers for enhancing provision and opportunities for school age children) conflicted with those for NGBs (which focused on sporting excellence and enhancing largely adult participation), medical KPIs (predominantly associated with clinical practice) and local authority KPIs (which related to both increasing adult participation, the perceived quality of services, as well as indicators for cross-cutting policy agendas). Thus, the fact that sport ranged across such a wide spectrum of policy activity was both an incentive to, and an inhibitor of, partnership working.

In our review of the literature we cited three dimensions of social capital identified by Lee (2009) from his systematic review. The first dimension, structural social capital, relates to network ties and configurations. The variable engagement of different stakeholder organisations and policy constituencies was clearly illustrated in the results from the social network analysis. The lack of interconnectivity of some groups was marked and allowed us to explore the reasons for this lack of structural social capital in our qualitative data. The second dimension, relational social capital, deals with conditions of trust, obligation and identity that inform and mediate the actors' relations in network. In our cases, the relative strength and the exclusionary nature of some professional cultures would seem to undermine relational capital. Cognitive social capital relates to shared codes and narratives, in effect language games employed between actors, stakeholder organisations and policy constituencies. In our cases, the lack of a shared narrative is evident in the treatment of sport, health, development and other policy goals. If social capital is the 'glue' that bonds the 'governance through partnership' system together it is clear that this was underdeveloped or absent in parts of the system, and that while constructing a social model approach to policy represented an attractive policy goal, its implementation presented significant challenges.

When the Coalition Government came to power in 2010, New Labour's attempts to generate cross-cutting policy agendas or joined-up policy thinking and action, and delivery of policy outcomes across public, private and third sector boundaries, which constituted a shift in the direction of the 'social configuration' of sports policy, was abandoned. In government rhetoric the proposal of a 'Big Society' philosophy which placed more emphasis on, among other things, self-provision and volunteerism replaced joined up approaches to policy thinking and delivery. However, though New Labour's experiment in seeking to break down divisions between policy domains and sectors may have been relatively short-lived, afflicted by political change, and by the onset of large-scale recession, nevertheless the experience provided by this initiative in sport provides valuable insights into the strengths and limitations of attempts to steer the policy system towards a social model.

12

GLOBALISATION, SPORT POLICY AND CHINA

Tien-Chin Tan

Introduction

The aim of this chapter is to operationalise concepts or theories of globalisation in order to analyse China's engagement in global football through an examination of Chinese elite football. There are several reasons for identifying this particular research aim, namely, the political, economic, cultural and academic importance of this process of engagement in the global context.

Considering first the political aspect, the People's Republic of China is one of the five permanent members of the UN Security Council and the world's largest developing country under a Communist regime (Zhang, 2006). Any decision the Chinese government makes in relation to global affairs would arguably have some impact on the rest of the world. Noting the increasing number of governmental and non-governmental organisations in the global context (Chan, 2006), it is important to investigate the role and importance of the Chinese state within these organisations in general and those concerned with global football, such as the IOC and FIFA in particular. Indeed, this research echoes Houlihan's (2005) argument which highlights that, in addition to the economic and cultural dimensions, a third, but less commonly explored, dimension of globalisation is the development of a global organisational infrastructure for sport, evident in both the governmental and non-governmental spheres.

Second, regarding the economic aspect, China's economy has maintained an average annual growth rate of 9.4 per cent since it adopted the open-door policy in 1978. Since 1993 it has ranked first in attracting foreign direct investment (FDI). The total value of its imports and exports rose from US$20.6 billion in 1978 to US$1,150 billion in 2004, ranking third in the world, and of this over half was from foreign investments (Zhang, 2006). In 2010 China's GDP pushed ahead of Japan to make China the world's second biggest economy after America (McCurry, 2011). With the movement of goods, capital and labour across borders, we are interested in the role of the national government in dealing with the challenge from foreign investment (multinational companies) in the Chinese elite sport system. Quoting from Jackson *et al.* (2005: 207), a possibility exists that 'These multi-national companies are contributing to the advancement of post-industrial capitalism – a political, economic and cultural system that is fundamentally changing the nature of the nation state and the international flow of people, products and ideas.' Furthermore, other authors such as Hall and Soskice (2001), Garrett (1998), Weiss (2003) and Scharpf (2000) also remind us to 'bring institutions back in' to the study of globalisation and, indeed, into capitalism more generally. It is argued that, while nations may experience common pressures, the existence of different institutional and cultural environments means that they respond in different ways and achieve different outcomes. In this sense, Weiss (2003: 27–28) argues that 'domestic institutions, depending on their characteristics, can hinder or enable states to respond to new challenges and accomplish new tasks, thus softening, neutralizing, or exaggerating the potentially constraining effect of the global market'. The argument of these authors suggests that it is very important to focus on Chinese domestic sport institutions, such as the General Administration of Sport (GAS), the Chinese Olympic Committee (COC) and the Chinese Football Association (CFA).

Third, regarding the cultural element, when Communist China under the leadership of Mao Zedong initiated the Cultural Revolution (1966–76), Western cultural products, such as competitive sports, were regarded as reflecting the values of 'evil capitalism' which could contaminate the ideological purity of Chinese Communism (Fan and Xiong, 2003; MacFarquhar, 1997). After the Cultural Revolution, China practised the 'open door policy' and embraced world capitalism by joining the World Trade Organization (WTO) and bidding to host the 2008 Olympic Games in Beijing. Regarding sport as an important cultural practice (Houlihan, 2005b; Giulianotti and Robertson, 2007; Jarvie, 2006), we are interested in the process whereby these Western cultural flows of elite sport reached into the Chinese state and the ways in which the Chinese government responded to them. John Tomlinson claims that 'the de facto common denominator of both the process and the experience of globalisation is the global capitalist economic system' (2007: 164). He also reminds us that 'the issue of the increasing general *commodification* of culture deserves most attention' (Tomlinson, 2007: 164, original emphasis). Houlihan (2005b: 52) raises the same issue as Tomlinson and reminds us to refocus on the issue of 'the spread of particular cultural practices', or 'the recognition of global commercial interests in major sports events such as the Olympics and the soccer World Cup' when carrying out research in relation to sport globalisation.

Finally, and most importantly, we attempt to echo the argument of Houlihan (1994) and Maguire (1999) in which they point out the need to develop criteria by which to judge the 'reach' and 'response' of global flows in local cultures. Thus, our biggest challenge is to contribute to current academic debates by developing indicators that will help examine the phenomenon of sport globalisation in the Chinese context. These indicators will be outlined and demonstrated later in the chapter. In addition, in relation to the concepts of 'reach' and 'response', Houlihan (2005b) highlights the problem that, although many studies of globalisation exhibit a quite proper concern with the extent to which the deep structure of culture is affected by sports globalisation, they generally fail to give significant consideration to the role of the state, owing to too great a focus on the arguably shallower impacts of globalisation such as the commercialisation of cultural commodities. We therefore attempt to refocus on the role of the state to investigate the trajectory of its relationship with global football.

Research phases in relation to indicators and the analytical framework

The indicators generated and the analytical frameworks adopted for this research are the key tools for this paper. There are five research phases in relation to the indicators and analytical framework: (1) review of the literature on globalisation to generate research questions and identify indicators; (2) data collection and initial analysis by indicators; (3) second round analysis adopting the framework of Houlihan (1994, 2003); (4) third round analysis adopting the framework of Held *et al.* (1999); and (5) evaluation of these two frameworks by using the four criteria suggested by Jarvie (2006).

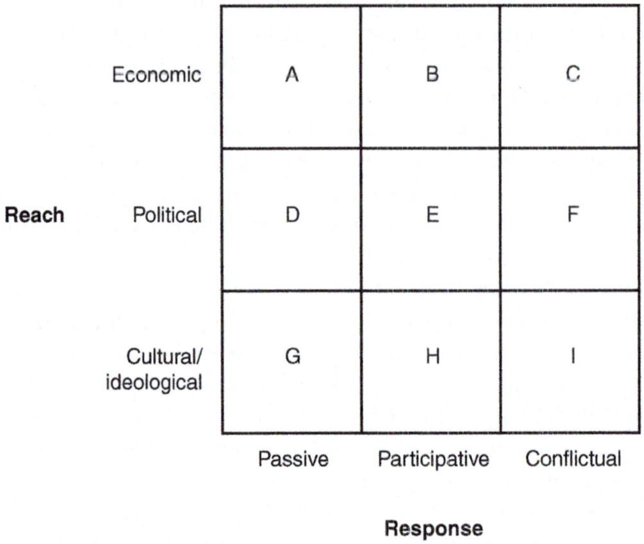

		Passive	Participative	Conflictual
Reach	Economic	A	B	C
	Political	D	E	F
	Cultural/ ideological	G	H	I

Response

Figure 12.1 Patterns of globalisation
Source: adapted from Houlihan (1994: 371; 2003: 360)

In the first and second phase, the researcher drew on theories at the macro level (from the three main schools of thought on globalisation) to identify concepts and approaches that would be helpful in guiding preliminary decisions, including the selection of the case study of the Chinese elite football and the selection of relevant documents to review. Thus, we conducted the literature review in relation to the globalisation theories, which not only helped us to grasp the main debates among the three main schools of thought on globalisation (hyperglobalists, sceptics and transformationalists), but also assisted us in deductively generating the indicators for the collection and analysis of relevant data. In the third phase, the framework of the patterns of globalisation (see Figure 12.1) developed by Houlihan (1994, 2003) was adopted to help us grasp the complexity, trajectory and momentum of the relationship between China and global football.

In order to capture and embody the concept of globalisation, Houlihan (1994, 2003) adopts the concepts of 'reach' and 'response'. For Houlihan, 'reach' refers to the depth of penetration by the global culture of the local culture, whereas 'response' refers to the reaction of the recipient culture. He emphasises that 'reach' might be total or partial and response might be passive, participative, or conflictual, and that it is likely that a country might be located in one or more of those categories and that they will respond to different elements of globalisation in slightly different ways, which might cover two of those types of response. To identify the depth of reach, Houlihan borrows Hannerz's terminology of globalisation in terms of cultural flows:

> cultural commodities, the actions of the state in organizing and managing meanings (such as developing, maintaining, and refining national identity), 'form of life' (the dissemination of habitual perspectives and dispositions) (Hannerz, 1991: 111–116), which represent economic, political and social aspects.
>
> (Houlihan, 1994: 370)

Table 12.1 The summary of 'reach' of global culture

	Meaning	Example
Economic	Consumption of commodities	The reception of satellite television sports broadcasts
Political	Actions of the state	The development, maintenance, and refinement of national identity by involvement in major international sports events such as the soccer World Cup and the Olympic Games
Cultural/ ideological	Deep structure of cultural processes	The extent to which the values the of global capitalist sport individualism and commercialism are adopted by local athletes or local clubs

Source: adapted from Houlihan 1994: 370-371; 2003: 360)

Regarding the social aspect, this aspect is difficult to define since Houlihan calls it 'social' but very often is referring to a broader set of cultural and ideological values. For Houlihan, what he refers to as the 'social' aspect covers the broad cultural values of a society; thus, social ideology is not just the ideology of political parties and other formal groups but rather reflects the dominant ideas within a society and its everyday values. According to this, we modify the denotation of the term – 'social' – in Houlihan's framework to refer both to the cultural values and everyday ideology of the population. In addition, Houlihan (1994: 370) argues that total reach would imply a penetration of all three cultural flows, while partial reach would suggest that the impact of globalisation could be confined to one or two flows. The concept of depth of reach is summarised with examples in Table 12.1. Regarding the three types of response to reach, these are summarised with examples in Table 12.2.

Table 12.2 The three types of response

	Passive	Participative	Conflictual
Meaning	Either an enthusiasm for the external culture or an inability to challenge the global culture	A process of negotiation, bargaining, and accommodation between the global culture and local cultures; a sufficient control over resources to provide recipient cultures with leverage	Not only the possession of sufficient resources to enable resistance but also a set of values that leads to rejection or attempted rejection of the global culture
Example (Actions of the state)	Unable to challenge the foreign clubs or MNCs that exploited or abandoned their young talented athletes	Shifts in public funding to protect/promote particular sports	Olympic boycotts or advocating and organizing GANEFO (Games of the New Emerging Forces)

Source: adapted from Houlihan (1994: 370–371; 2003: 360).

In the fourth phase, the framework of the theorisation of globalisation developed by Held *et al.* (1999) is used to focus on the debate over the state's role in the global process, which is very firmly focused on what the government did and the policy of government regarding its relationship with globalisation. In addition, the indicators that were generated to measure the relationship between the Chinese state and global football were inspired by, and derived from, the works of these three main schools of globalisation theorists as mentioned in the first phase. In the final phase, the analysis of China's relationship as reflected in this paper and Jarvie's 'four useful values of theory to analyse sport phenomena' (2006: 19) were used in order to examine the utility of the frameworks of Held *et al.* (1999) and Houlihan (1994, 2003).

Globalisation frameworks and theories

The frameworks of Held *et al.* (1999) and Houlihan (1994, 2003) are thus important analytical tools for this study. They have strong theoretical implications but they are not theories that have clear causal drivers and a sense of causal process (Sabatier, 2006). Schlager argues that 'Frameworks provide a foundation for inquiry by specifying classes of variables and general relationships among them' (2006: 294). In that sense, Houlihan provides a framework of the 'patterns of globalisation' (see Figure 12.1), identifies a set of variables (such as 'global reach' at economic, political and cultural/ideological levels and varieties of 'local response' – passive, participative and conflictual) and provides guidance to how to investigate and conceptualise the complexity, trajectory and momentum of the relationship between China and global football. However, as Schlager reminds us, 'Frameworks organize inquiries, but they cannot in and of themselves provide explanations of behaviour and outcomes. Explanation and prediction lie in the realms of theories and models' (2006: 294). Indeed, we do not attempt to explain 'a sense of causal process'; rather, we investigate and analyse the complexity, trajectory and momentum of the relationship between China and global football by utilising Houlihan's framework.

In addition, Schlager notes that 'frameworks provide a metatheoretical language that can be used to compare theories, allowing policy scholars using different theories to use a common language, to learn from one another, and to identify pressing questions to pursue' (2006: 294).

Table 12.3 A framework for the theorization of globalisation

	Hyperglobalists	*Sceptics*	*Transformationalist*
Advocates	Ohmae (1990, 1995); Reich (1991), Strange (1994, 1996) and Albrow (1996)	Hirst and Thompson (1998), Weiss, L. (1997), Vogel (1996) and Gilpin (2001)	Held *et al.* (1999), Held and McGrew (2002, 2007) and Giddens (1990, 1991)
Driving forces	Global market and technology	States and markets	Combined forces of modernity
Power of national governments	Declining or eroding	Reinforced or enhanced among developed countries	Reconstituted, restructured
Summary argument	The end of the nation-state whose role will be replaced by MNCs and IGBs (international governing bodies)	Internationalisation depends on state acquiescence and support	Globalisation transforming state power and world politics

Source: adapted from Held *et al.* (1999: 10)

The framework of Held *et al.* (1999) is adopted to compare three main schools of globalisation theory, to target the emphasis of the state-centred focus and to highlight certain questions, such as the three key theoretical research questions and the debate over the state's role in the global process. As Ostrom argues, 'frameworks bind inquiry and direct the attention of the analyst to critical features of the social and physical landscape' (quoted in Schlager, 2006: 294). This is the rationale for adopting the framework of Held *et al.* (1999), namely, to help maintain a focus on an analysis of the state's role in the global process.

There are three main schools of globalisation theory summarised in the framework of Held *et al.* (1999) (see Table 12.3): hyperglobalists, sceptics and transformationalists. This tripartite schema is intended as a preliminary way of understanding the general contours of scholarly debates, rather than as a rigid template into which all writers must be neatly located. What is at stake in the debates between these three positions is not simply what globalisation means, but whether, and in what senses, it is present at all (Holton, 2005). According to the hyperglobalists, cross-border economic relationships engendered by free trade and the increased mobility of capital and labour render national economies outmoded and undermine the role of national governance (see for instance Albrow, 1996; Ohmae, 1990, 1995; Reich, 1991; Strange, 1994, 1996). A number of influential scholars have also been interested in cross-border interdependencies, such as Immanuel Wallerstein and world systems theorists, and these have helped to stimulate the hyperglobalists and worked in parallel with them (Holton, 2005: 7). Indeed, Ohmae (1995: 5) argues that globalisation is a phenomenon has led to the 'end of the nation-state'.

As for the sceptics, such as Hirst and Thompson (1998), Weiss, L. (1997), Vogel (1996) and Gilpin (2001), they argue that theories of hyper-globalisation have mistakenly concluded that cross-border activity is intrinsically transnational. Instead, the sceptics consider that nations remain alive and well (Holton, 2005). Even if some functions are lost, others are gained (Mann, 1993). National markets and national policies in domains such as education, training and infrastructural planning remain of considerable importance, and this throws doubt on theories of the imminent decline of the nation state (see also Weiss, L. 1997). Indeed, sceptics have had a good deal of success in scrutinising and evaluating speculative propositions in the light of more considered accounts that are better grounded in evidence than those of the hyperglobalists. They usually take an 'approach' in order to begin a process of seeking out clearer and more plausible concepts in an effort to avoid the pitfall of applying simplistic theories to very complex social changes. This has required a measure of scepticism towards propositions that are regarded as self-evident by many and cherished as articles of faith by some (Holton, 2005).

The view taken by the transformationalists, such as Held *et al.* (1999) and Held and McGrew (2002, 2007), is that the world of nation states cannot contain or have within its structure all the many significant elements of global life, including the ordering of territory. The case for using the term 'globalisation' is that it enables us to understand the extent to which many forms of transformation are no longer containable within or fully controlled by inter-national arrangements. These include mobility of finance and technology, which create and re-create complex spatial divisions of labour, global communications technology, and the operation of global social movements (Held *et al.*, 1999). The transformationalists' line of argument is critical of certain aspects of both the hyperglobalists' and sceptics' approach. Put simply, their position is twofold. First, transformationalists agree with the hyperglobalists' contention that the world is undergoing a fundamental transformation, but they disagree with their claim of 'the end of the nation-state', owing to the important role of the state during the globalising process (Marsh *et al.*, 2006: 175). Second, transformationalists consider that the sceptics' thinking is too 'sceptical'. The power of national governments is not necessarily diminished by globalisation, but, on the contrary, is being reconstituted and restructured in response to the growing complexity of the process of governance in a more interconnected world (Held *et al.*, 1999).

Finally, as far as this research is concerned, we are in sympathy with the definition of globalisation advanced by Hay and Marsh (2000). Their version of the concept requires thinking of globalisation as something other than a singular and inexorable process causing change – a juggernaut beyond human control. Rather they see globalisation as a trend, and the effect of a range of processes such as cross-border interconnection and interdependence, but a trend that is reversible by counter-trends. Globalisation is the *explanandum*, which means 'that to be explained', not the *explanans*, which means 'the explanation of change'. Globalisation, in short, is an effect not a cause (Hay and Mash, 2000; Holton, 2005). Thus, it is the state's response to the globalisation of football and the values associated with elite football development that is the central focus of this paper.

The nature of China's attempts to manage its interaction with global football

In order to manage its relationship with global football, the Chinese government took strategic approaches in the political, economic and cultural/ideological fields. These were: (1) transforming the domestic administrative structure so as to use its political power more effectively and efficiently in the international and domestic elite football arenas; (2) setting up a Competition Division in the Chinese Football Management Centre (CFMC) and amending sport regulations in order to be able to control, or at least influence, commercialisation; and (3) strengthening Chinese communist ideological education to manage the consequences of commercialisation.

Indeed, the indicators that were generated to measure the relationship between the Chinese state and global football were inspired by, and derived from, the works of the three main schools of globalisation theorists (see Table 12.3), as mentioned before.

As for the indicators, all those we generate are strongly linked to each other (see Appendix, page 153), which helped us to look for consistency and logic between the variables, such as commercialisation and globalisation. This means that we are not relying on one indicator alone, but on a cluster of indicators that are all moving in the same direction. The values of indicators help to identify tensions, particularly between clubs and country, and also to analyse the relationship of the PRC to globalisation. Although we have made every effort to maintain high levels of validity for this study, Maxwell still reminds us that 'validity is a goal rather than a product; it is never something that can be proven or taken for granted' (1996: 86).

As for the political aspect, we used indicators such as the following:

- formal engagement with international sport as a participant country (including membership, joining competitions, ranking, bidding for, or hosting FIFA World Cup);
- the number and position of Chinese sports representatives in FIFA;
- the distribution of the national sports budget to elite football;
- the number and purpose of special elite universities or training centres for elite football;
- the resource of coach development programmes for elite football;
- the ownership of special elite training facilities for football in China;
- the number of people or local clubs that participate in elite football;
- the structure of the Chinese Football Association.

Utilising the above indicators, we are able to identify four main political strategies adopted by the Chinese government to deal with the challenges from global football. These four political strategies are: (1) taking more seriously the aim of obtaining a leadership position in the Asian

Football Confederation (AFC) and desiring to have more influence in FIFA; (2) transforming the administrative structure; (3) strengthening the athlete selection, training and competition system towards the Olympics and FIFA World Cup; (4) preventing the seven major football clubs from organising a new super league.

In the case of Chinese elite football, the momentum to adopt and maintain these strategies came from the sheer dominance of the Central Committee of the Chinese Communist Party (State Council), particularly the key actor, Li Tieying, a member of the Politburo Standing Committee (PSC) and a State Councillor (1988–98), who encouraged the adoption of a Western approach (in particular, capitalist principles) to revitalise the Chinese elite football system. The design of 'two in one' agencies was and is paramount in the state's construction of a centralised and simplified political and sporting administration that underpins the country's system of elite football development. For example, the CFMC was created by the GAS in the 1990s, but the leadership and general function was exactly the same as in the CFA. The title 'CFA' was used to connect with international organisations and 'CFMC' was used to interact with the domestic political system. Under this design, the Chinese government was able to transform its football administrative structure in three ways: (1) by setting up a highly institutionalised and rationalised Chinese football system; (2) by introducing the club system; and (3) by establishing football companies as commercial agents. The primary concern of the CFMC (CFA), as with the other National Sport Management Centres (NSMCs), is to oversee and manage the training and monitoring of its seven national teams respectively. By centralising and simplifying its football administrative structure, the Chinese government could drive its elite footballers in the Chinese Super League (CSL) clubs to strive for success in the Olympic Games and the FIFA World Cup and could also encourage them to develop government's values of raising national pride, increasing national cohesion and demonstrating the superiority of socialism. It also helped high-ranking officials in the CFA (such as CFA vice President, Zhang Jilong) to obtain leadership positions in the AFC and to take FIFA seats in order to influence the decision making in the international sport regime. By so doing, the PRC could use its political power more effectively and efficiently in the international and domestic elite football arenas.

As for the economic aspect, we employ indicators such as the following:

- the attitudes and values of football players towards material rewards;
- the distribution of the national sports budget to elite football;
- the structure of the Chinese Football Association;
- the resource of coach development programmes for elite football
- the values and attitudes of the government towards commercial football
- the tensions between the professional football clubs and government.

By utilising these indicators, five main economic strategies adopted by the Chinese government to respond to global football can be identified, namely: (1) generating multiple sources of income for elite football systems; (2) introducing a system of financial rewards; (3) intervening in players' transfer affairs; (4) controlling the CFA; and (5) manipulating the domestic professional leagues (such as the CSL). These economic strategies were supported by the setting up of a Competition Division in the CFA and a Marketing Department and by amending football regulations to act as constraints on football commercialisation.

In 1993 high ranking officials in the National Sport Council (NSC) and the State Council highlighted the view that 'Following the development of Chinese sport, the problem of investing more in the national sport budget and generating more extra sport income is a highly critical issue' (Li, 1996: 5–6). Following the words of these political leaders the NSC issued two internal official documents in 1993, which not only gave the CFA a green light to learn from advanced capitalist countries, but also empowered the CFA to generate multiple sources of income by establishing 'economic bodies' (*Jingji shiti*) to subsidise elite football and basketball systems. After this, the Chinese government allowed the CFA to establish different economic bodies or companies including the China Football Industry Development Corporation (CFIDC) and the China Football Association Super League Company (CSLC) and to sign contracts with international sport management companies (such as IMG (International Management Group) and Infront Sports and Media) in order to generate multiple incomes from the football market. After introducing a capitalist football system, the national football budget was considerably reduced to the level of a few million yuan which was used to directly subsidise the national teams and Olympic squads. As a result, the Chinese elite football system became heavily dependent on investment from commercial football clubs and the commercial income of the CFA, which was more than 50 times the size of the national football budget in 2005. However, when the Chinese government decided to adopt a market mechanism and sponsorship to generate commercial income, it faced a serious struggle over priorities between the emergent commercial sector (particularly clubs and sponsors) and national team development, and also between highly paid and internationally mobile football 'stars' and the state-controlled elite (Olympics and World Cup) development system.

In order to manage the consequences of commercialisation, the Competition Division and two companies, the CFIDC and the CSLC, in the Chinese Football Association were set up under the supervision of the GAS. By creating these new governmental commercial agencies, the Chinese government could generate commercial incomes from the CFA, national teams and individual sports stars, but more importantly, ensure that all their commercial contracts and activities would not endanger the national priority of the performance of the national teams. Indeed, by 'updating' the instructions and regulations in football, the GAS, particularly its finance department, played a key role in reducing the perceived negative impact of commercialisation on Chinese elite football development in four ways, namely, by setting a limit on the salaries and transfer fees that professional clubs could offer their players and their buyers; by creating a special procedure for dealing with the domestic transfer market; by controlling the CFA; and by manipulating the CSL. By integrating these four strategies and updating the regulations in the 'One Protocol and Two Licences'[1] policy in football, it allowed the CFA to own the exclusive commercial rights of domestic football leagues and recruit any club player unconditionally. It also allowed the CFA to shorten the season of CSL and intervene in players' transfers in order to support their main mission – 'Olympic and World Cup success first'. In the words of Cui Dalin (the Vice Sport Minister) and Ma Chengquan (the director of the CFA Competition Department), 'The premier mission of the 2007 CSL season is to fully support the 2008 Beijing Games. Stabilising the development of the CSL is secondary' (Wang, 2007).

As for the cultural/ideological aspect, by examining the indicators, particularly 'the attitudes and values of football players towards material rewards' and also 'the values and attitudes of the government towards commercial football', we can identify how 'ideological education' was adopted to reduce the negative impact of commercialisation, particularly among star players. Indeed, the danger of creating 'peculiar men' who were commercially and financially self-centred was highlighted by political and party leaders in 1995 after the embrace of the principles of Western capitalism. In addition to instigating suitable rules to regulate the material interests of clubs, coaches and players, the responsibility for carrying out intense ideological indoctrination was given to a senior manager of each national squad. 'Ideological education' took the form of teaching relating to patriotism, collectivism and revolutionary heroism, in order to dilute and reduce the allure of materialism and money. Moreover, in line with the new policy, one to two weeks military training with the People's Liberation Army (PLA) became a new form of training strategy to 'discipline' and 'inspire' these highly paid footballers and basketball players to work as hard as their PLA counterparts, in order to fight wholeheartedly for their country in international matches, especially in the 2008 Olympic Games. Indeed, the whole purpose of 'ideological education' was to firmly fix the value of 'national pride first and personal interest second' in the mind of Chinese footballers in order to prevent star players or 'peculiar men' from having a negative impact by adopting the values of global capitalist sport, namely individualism and commercialism.

Theoretical implications of the nature of China's interaction with global football

From the perspective of Houlihan's framework (1994, 2003), China's position, in terms of the depth of 'reach' in the economic, political and cultural/ideological fields should probably be located somewhere between participative and conflictual (see Figure 12.1). But the problem is that in a country such as China it is very difficult to distinguish the cultural/ideological and economic from the political, because the political system is still very dominant. Although we have attempted to assess the depth of penetration of global values using Houlihan's three categories of reach, all the evidence in the economic, political and cultural/ideological spheres appears to point to the fact that these changes were led by the Chinese government and were political decisions (embracing capitalism and transforming administrative structures). However, even though government struggled against the implications of capitalist sport in terms of the impact on players, ironically it also promoted these phenomena, such as social transformation (emerging individualism and commercialism in star players, particularly the phenomenon of 'peculiar men') and economic changes (emphasis on commercial rights and sponsorship). The trend towards sport globalisation in the Chinese context is so complicated that it is difficult for us to locate the global reach and local response in the case of football in just one category of reach and one precise response. Using Houlihan's framework, we are able to summarise China's attempts to manage its interaction with global football in Table 12.4.

By taking strategic approaches in the political, economic and cultural/ideological fields, the Chinese government demonstrated its capacity, to some degree, to successfully find effective ways to manage its relationship with global football. This was shown particularly by: (1) the setting up of new governmental commercial agencies (such as the CFA Competition Division, CFIDC and CSLC); (2) updating sport and football regulations; and (3) strengthening Chinese communist ideological education.

From the perspective of the transformationalists, rather than globalisation bringing about the 'end of the state', it has encouraged a spectrum of adjustment strategies – by setting up new governmental commercial agencies, updating sport and football regulations, and strengthening Chinese communist ideological education – and, in certain respects, has produced a more activist state. In addition, the sceptics share a similar viewpoint to their transformationalist counterparts. Vogel contends that 'regulatory reform by definition involves reformulating the mechanisms of policy implementation' (1996: 19) and is amply illustrated by the updating of sport and football regulation and the influence of the policies of 'One Protocol and Two Licences' in football. Modification of implementation mechanisms in turn affects the very ability of state actors (GAS, CFA Competition Division, CFIDC, CSLC) to perform their functions, which is why they insist on giving their own needs and preferences high priority (Olympic and World Cup glory) as they pursue regulatory reform (Vogel, 1996).

Table 12.4 Summary of China's attempts to manage its interaction with global football

Key Indicators	Main Strategies Adopted to Manage Globalisation and Commercialisation	Patterns of Reach and Response	Theoretical Implication
Economic aspect: 1. The structure of the Chinese Football Association; 2. The values and attitudes of the government towards commercial football; 3. The tension between the Chinese professional football clubs and government.	*Economic aspect:* 1. Set up Competition Divisions in the CFA to generate multiple sources of income for the Elite Football System; 2. Introduced a system of financial rewards; 3. Updated sport and football regulations to control football commercialisation in three ways: (i) Intervened in footballers' transfer affairs, (ii) Controlled CFA and (iii) manipulated Chinese Super league (CSL).	*Economic aspect:* 1. Located somewhere between 'participative' and 'conflictual' responses.	1. Part of the transformationalists' argument was supported but more evidence backed the case of the sceptics.
Political aspect: 1. The number and position of Chinese sports representatives in FIFA and the Asia Football Confederation; 2. The structure of the Chinese Football Association; 3. The distribution of the national sports budget with in elite football; 4. The tension between the Chinese professional football clubs and government.	*Political aspect:* 1. Took more seriously the aim of obtaining a leadership position in the Asia Football Confederation (AFC) and desired to have more influence in FIFA; 2. Transformed administrative structure; 3. Strengthened athlete selection, training and competition system regarding towards World Cup and Olympics; 4. Prevented seven major clubs from organizing a new super league.	*Political aspect:* 1. Located somewhere between 'participative' and 'conflictual' responses.	
Cultural/ideological aspect: 1. The attitudes and values of football players regarding material awards; 2. The values and attitudes of the government regarding commercial football.	*Cultural/ideological aspect:* 1. Used 'ideological education' and 'military training' to prevent star players from becoming 'peculiar men'.	*Cultural/ideological aspect:* 1. Located somewhere between 'participative' and 'conflictual' responses.	

How useful are the frameworks of Houlihan (1994, 2003) and Held *et al.* (1999) for analysis of the development of sport policy in China?

Houlihan's framework is a useful tool to act as a starting point in the process of analysing the relationship between the Chinese government and global football, but it was not adequate for capturing the trajectory, momentum and complexity of globalisation. Unfortunately, Houlihan's framework fails to locate the global reach and local response in the Chinese elite football case in just one category of reach and one precise response. Indeed, as discussed, the trend of sport globalisation in the Chinese context is so complicated that it is difficult to reach a clear-cut conclusion at the political, economic and cultural/ideological levels, and to indicate one pure response in the passive, participative and conflictual aspects. In addition, the fact that Houlihan's framework appears to be unsuccessful in capturing the trajectory and momentum of the relationship between China and global football, also encourages the researcher to locate relationships as either participative or conflictual when the reality is more complex and subtle.

Furthermore, Houlihan's 'reach' and 'response' model is static and resembles a snapshot of China in the mid to late 2000s, but it does not really explain how this situation came about and, more importantly, what the trajectory of China's relationship with globalisation has been? Houlihan's framework is an heuristic device that was useful as a starting point for this research on sport and globalisation in Chinese football, but it does not capture the ambiguity, the exception and trajectory of China's relationship with globalisation. In order to overcome these problems, we suggest two ways in which to refine Houlihan's framework. The two ways are to remove the distinction between three types of response and among three levels of reach, and to locate the different responses in economic, political and cultural/ideological levels, which allow us to capture the momentum and trajectory of the relationships between the Chinese government and global football (see Figure 12.2).

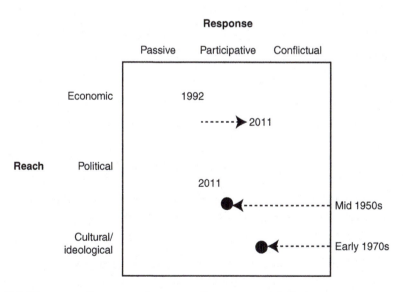

Figure 12.2 The suggested movement in patterns of responses to globalisation

1 The arrows indicate the extent of change from the date indicated. The line in the political level is longer than the one in the cultural/ideological level, suggesting the movement has been greater from conflictual to participation.

2 Dots (●) indicate the location of the relationship between the PRC and global football in 2011.

After refining Houlihan's framework and plotting the result of China's response to global football, it is possible to mitigate the limitations of Houlihan's framework in terms of capturing the ambiguity, the exceptional nature and direction of China's relationship with globalisation. We use the football case to illustrate the momentum and trajectory of the relationships between the PRC and global football at the economic, political and cultural/ideological level. From Figure 12.2, the relationships within these three levels in 2011 can be illustrated diagrammatically using arrows to identify the direction of travel and point of origin so as to attempt to capture the direction and dynamism of such change.

First, at the economic level, the motivation of the Chinese government in introducing the Western club system was 'to catch up with advanced football countries in a short period of time' and 'to generate commercial income to support its elite football system'. As a result of the calculations of a group of Chinese leaders, the club approach, in particular the European one, with the support of private and state-owned enterprise and wider society, was adopted in 1992 in order to develop a strong national football team. But the ambition of the Chinese government, which attempted to maintain the socialist ideal and take advantage of capitalist elements at the same time as reforming its elite football system, turned out to be problematic. The point of conflict occurred because both sides (government and club owners) had very different priorities when running the Chinese professional football league. From the government's point of view, it regarded the professional clubs not only as a 'talent pool' to support national teams unconditionally, but also as a 'money tree' through which about 95 per cent annual budget of the CFA might be covered. As for the perspective of the club owners, their main purpose for running a commercial club is to make a profit without intervention from the government.

Indeed, most Chinese professional football clubs in the early 1990s were transformed from provincial football teams under the guidance of the Chinese government. Up to that time, most CSL clubs were owned by large companies. With their different priorities, the relationship between government and club owners became increasingly conflictual as football in China became more and more of a business. According to a top manager of one of the CSL clubs, although the plan for organising a new super league was finally abandoned because of governmental opposition, it was recognised that the plan might be revived after the 2008 Beijing Games. Taking the football case at the economic level, we suggest that the dynamism of the relationship between the Chinese state and global football began in a participative way in 1992 but moved towards a conflictual approach in 2011 (see Figure 12.2 at the economic level).

Second, at the political level, the trajectory of the relationships between the Chinese government and global football can be divided into three phases. During the first phase, China rejected global football and sought to participate in the GANEFO[2] after failure to resolve the 'two Chinas issue'[3] with the IOC. During the second phase, the Chinese government re-engaged with global football but appeared to be less interested in football and more interested in the leverage that FIFA and the (AFC could give it in relation to its dispute with Taiwan. In the final phase, China participated in global football and focused on winning medals in the Olympic Games and FIFA World Cup, hosting the Women's World Cup twice (1991, 2007), possibly bidding to host the 2026 World Cup, being a 'good' FIFA member, adopting the European club system, introducing a system of financial rewards, and generating most of its income to support its elite football system from the market by means of football sponsorship. An analysis of these three phases suggests that the dynamism of the political relationship between the PRC and global football began from a conflictual stance in the late 1950s but moved towards the participative approach in 2011 (see Figure 12.2 at the political level).

Third, with regard to the cultural/ideological level, we have attempted to focus on the trajectory of the values and attitudes of the Chinese government towards its athletes and others involved in sport whose way of life appeared to change after the open-door policy in the late 1970s in general, and the introduction of the commercial football club system in the early 1990s in particular. It is possible to divide the process into three phases to capture the trajectory of the cultural/ideological relationships between the Chinese government and global football. During the first phase, China rejected global football socially during the Cultural Revolution. Not only did Vice Premier He Long, who was accused of 'taking the bourgeois road' (*Zhou ziben zhuy daolu*), die in jail in 1969, but also numerous elite players, coaches and administrators were purged, persecuted and tortured, football facilities were abandoned or destroyed and international sports contacts virtually ended. During the second phase, China reintroduced the modern football system after the end of the Cultural Revolution. All footballers in national squads (World Cup team, Olympic squad, U16, U19) were selected from 22 'significant cities and areas for football in China' in which footballers were prevented from being transferred and prohibited from being involved in commercial activity. During the third phase, from the establishment of the commercial club system, the free movement of Chinese elite footballers between domestic and foreign clubs became possible, although the Chinese government was still uneasy about their materialist-orientated attitudes and behaviour (shown by its views on 'peculiar men'), and attempted to manage them by imposing ideological education, army training, limited salary, limited transfer fees and limited movement of players. In characterising these three phases, we suggest that the dynamism of the cultural/ideological relationship between the PRC and global football began from a conflictual point during the Cultural Revolution but moved towards somewhere between a participative and conflictual dimension in 2011 (see Figure 12.2 at the cultural/ideological level).

As for the framework of theorisation of globalisation developed by Held *et al.* (1999), Jarvie's 'four useful values of theory to analyze sport phenomena' is a significant starting point for the examination of the usefulness of the framework of Held *et al.* (1999). Jarvie's four key uses of theory are: asking theoretical questions to explain or generalise about sport, culture and society; allowing theoretical testing; illuminating circumstances or equally destroying certain cherished myths; and stimulating new ideas (Jarvie, 2006: 19).

First, with respect to asking theoretical questions, the three main schools of globalisation theorists highlighted in Held *et al.*'s framework (1999) focus on the debate over the state's role in the global process, which is very firmly focused on what the government is doing and the policy of government towards its relationship with globalisation. The emphasis on state-centred analysis in this framework allows us to raise a main theoretical question, namely, in what ways does the Chinese government seek to manage its relationship with sport globalisation? In addition, the indicators we have generated to measure the relationship between the Chinese state and global football are inspired by, and derived from, the work of these three main schools of globalisation theorists as discussed in the previous section. Indeed, these three main schools of thought on globalisation identify concepts that make us sensitive to certain questions. For example, the sceptics, such as Vogel (1996) and Weiss (2003), constantly remind us of the ability of the state to adapt and retain its power through its capacity for re-regulation and transformation of administration. The argument of hyperglobalists forces us to address questions that are sometimes taken for granted. Of course, globalisation is transforming the world and the argument that the state is being undermined by the power of finance and capital is plausible but there was little evidence in our case study to support the hyperglobalists' perspective. In addition to the arguments of the hyperglobalists and sceptics, the perspective of the transformationalists also forces us to address certain different questions about globalisation and helps us come to the same view as the sceptics or sceptics–transformationalists enabling us to have a much more sophisticated view of, and produce more sophisticated answers to, all three of our questions.

Second, in terms of allowing theoretical testing, both Houlihan's (2005b) and Held *et al.*'s (1999) frameworks provided a unique opportunity to evaluate their utility. As mentioned previously, with the empirical evidence generated from indicators that were derived from our interpretation of the work of these three main schools of globalisation theory, we were able to evaluate Houlihan's framework and even refine it. In respect of Held *et al.*'s framework, the empirical evidence displayed in this case study suggests that the argument of hyperglobalists (such as Albrow, 1996; Ohmae, 1990, 1995; Strange, 1994, 1996 who not only see the end of the nation state and its role being replaced by MNCs and international federations (IFs), but also argue that in a borderless world traditional national interest has no meaningful place) is problematic and unpersuasive. Instead, the position appears to be closer to the arguments of sceptics, such as Hirst and Thompson (1998), Gilpin (2001) and Vogel (1996), who stress that, far from the nation state being undermined by the processes of internationalisation, these processes strengthen the importance of the nation state in many ways. Indeed, the Chinese state continues to use its power to implement approaches (such as the 'One Protocol and Two Licences' policy) to channel economic forces in ways favourable to their own national interests (Olympic and World Cup success) and to secure a favourable share of the gains from international economic activities (particularly by setting up new governmental commercial agencies such as Market Promotion Divisions in the COC and NSMCs, and CFIDC and CSLC in the CFA).

Third, with regard to illuminating circumstances or destroying certain cherished myths, Held *et al.*'s framework (1999) provides an opportunity to illuminate the circumstances of globalisation. From our one main theoretical research question and the empirical evidence gathered, we illustrate how the Chinese government not only made its own choice in becoming involved in global football and demonstrated its capacity to manage the four main tensions that arose from commercialisation, but also had specific strategies (administrative transformation and re-regulation) to manage its relationships with global football at the economic, political and cultural/ideological levels. All the evidence indicates that the taken-for-granted argument of hyperglobalists who proclaim 'the end of the state' can be regarded as illusory. Indeed, regarding the role of the Chinese state in this case study, building state capacity rather than discarding it would appear to be the lesson of dynamic integration. It appears to suggest that the world we are living in is far from *globalised*, rather, the term *globalising* or *internationalisation* are more appropriate in connection with the elite football case in the Chinese context.

Finally, in terms of stimulating new ideas, it may be time for Held *et al.* (1999) to refine this framework because there is something of an overlap between the sceptics' and transformationalists' point of views. For example, these two groups of theorists agree that the government would take the approach of administrative transformation and re-regulation in order to manage its relationship with globalisation (or internationalisation). Although both groups argue that the state plays a key role in the process of globalisation (internationalisation), the main difference is that the sceptics argue that the state has done so voluntarily, having calculated its own national interest. The transformationalists, however, contend that the state has been forced to become involved under pressure from globalisation. Indeed, it appears that considerable empirical evidence supports the sceptics' point of view with the Chinese government demonstrating its capability to make choices over its relationship with sport globalisation and making up its own mind to reach out and incorporate or embrace global influences, rather than global influences forcing their way into the Chinese football system. However, a slightly different interpretation could argue that some of the evidence, such as permitting player transfer, and allowing high payment for sport stars, might possibly be regarded as evidence of a transformationalist trend because it is difficult to identify the difference between the state simply 'adjusting' and the state 'giving in'. Although the framework of Held *et al.* (1999) is a useful tool to help us understand and analyse the relationship between the Chinese state and global football, it has further potential for development and greater sophistication, given the evidence of sport globalisation generated in this study. It could well be that Houlihan, a theorist of sport globalisation, is right in claiming that we should underline the importance of treating globalisation as an open-ended set of processes that do not necessarily lead to a fixed destination (2008b). Essentially, Houlihan, who was inspired by these three main schools of globalisation theorists, particularly Hirst and Thompson (1998), attempted to develop a similar model (Houlihan, 2008b) by identifying 'sport and the outcomes of globalisation' in three stages: internationalised sporting world, multinationalised sporting world, and globalised sporting world. Although Houlihan modestly acknowledges the problematic nature of his model, he reminds us that there is a pressing need to refine the concept of sport globalisation and give it a greater degree of precision, thus allowing for the identification of the process and the criteria that represent necessary conditions for the identification of globalised sport to be possible (2005).

Indeed, in this paper we have attempted to utilise different frameworks (such as Held *et al.*, 1999, and Houlihan 1994, 2003) to help us understand the role of the state in shaping domestic engagement with international sport. Substantial and consistent evidence suggests that the Chinese government has played a dominant role as a mediator of the commercialisation and globalisation of sport in the case of elite football, by adopting normative orientations and organisational arrangements in the context of the Chinese state. This conclusion endorses the suggestion that increased regulation is the most likely consequence of intensive globalisation. In the words of Vogel (1996: 2–3), 'the rhetoric of globalisation ... serves only to obscure what is really going on ... liberalism requires reregulation ... I find stronger markets but not weaker governments'. Vogel also concludes that globalisation has brought with it 'regulation not deregulation'. In terms of the case of football in the context of the PRC, we echo Houlihan's argument in concluding that in terms of football in China 'it is more accurate to talk of internationalised, rather than globalised, sport' (2005: 69).

Appendix: indicators of engagement with global football

'Hard' indicators:

- formal engagement with international sport as a participant country (including membership, joining competitions, ranking, bidding for or hosting FIFA World Cup);
- the number and position of Chinese sports representatives in FIFA;
- the number and purpose of football facilities in China;
- the distribution of the national sports budget to elite football;
- the number and purpose of special elite universities or training centres for elite football;
- the resource of coach development programmes for elite football;
- the ownership of special elite training facilities for football in China;
- the number of people or local club they participate in elite football;
- the tensions between the professional football clubs and government.

'Soft' indicators:

- the extent to which the Chinese government accepts the values and attitudes of commercial football;
- the attitudes and values of the Chinese government and Chinese professional football clubs in relation to the rights of elite athletes (for example, the transfer and players);
- the attitudes and values of football players towards material rewards;
- the structure of the Chinese Football Association;
- the values and attitudes of the government towards commercial football.

13

CLIENTELISM AND SPORT POLICY IN TAIWAN

Ping-Chao Lee and Ren-Shiang Jiang

Introduction

Political clientelism and its related concepts (patron–clientage, political patronage, relations of patronage) have long gained considerable attention in political studies. Political and social analysts have regularly commented on the existence of political clientelism, which in Taiwan has prevailed for several decades (Chen, 2009; Chien, 2008; Chu and Lin, 2001; Hood, 1996; Hsu, 2009, 2010; Kau, 1996; Kuo, 2000; Roy, 2003; Solinger, 2006; Tsai, 2009; Wang and Kurzman, 2007; Wu, 2003). In relation to the approach of the political literature on clientelism, it argues that the clientelistic network/relation is an important factor affecting strategy choice, because of its influence both on the legitimacy of the government and on the nature of the goods that it is optimal for a government to provide (Kurer, 1996). Additionally, 'clientelism cannot be meaningfully considered apart from the setting in which it exists. The forms which it takes depend to a considerable extent on the structure of the society and on the political system in which it operates' (Lemarchand and Legg, 1972, p. 156). Reflecting on this point, the authors consider the political development of Taiwan, where strong clientelistic relations have existed since the Kuomintang (KMT) regime retreated to Taiwan after its defeat by the Communists in 1949. Because of the immigrant KMT elite's lack of roots in Taiwan, the KMT secured its rule through a comprehensive patronage system reaching out and co-opting the local elite. Effectively, clientelism became one of the major principles of KMT rule to control national politics (Chen, 2009; Chien, 2008; Tsai, 2009). At the grass-roots level, existing patron–client networks were incorporated into the party structure (Chu and Lin, 2001). Without challenging either the KMT's political legitimacy or its domination of the political scene, local factions have monopolized local political and economic privileges through a patronage system (Wu, 2003). The patron–client system of sharing economic and political interests between the KMT and local factions provided a foundation for the island's political stability and the legitimacy of the regime (Matsumoto, 2002; Tang, 2003).

Recently, the political context has changed as the Democratic Progressive Party (DPP) ended half a century of KMT control of central government in 2000 (Sullivan, 2010; Zhu and Chung, 2010). Although democracy has provided opportunities for political representation and accountability, it has also created incentives for maintaining and nurturing clientelistic bonds (Szwarcberg, 2009). Consequently, the DPP itself, even though in the past it had denounced

154

the patron–client relations between the KMT and its supporters, as a new regime, began to adopt similar behaviour to turn meritocratic/bureaucratic administration into patronage positions in order to consolidate and defend its power (Hsu, 2009; 2010). In 2008, by failing to deal with economic and political problems, also caused by the suspicion of political corruption, the DPP government had to accept a huge loss of confidence which provided a political opportunity for the KMT's candidate Ma Ying-jeou to become the new president of Taiwan after the Presidential election (Ferstl, 2010). 'Ma made his political reputation in large measure as a clean candidate who adamantly opposed corruption. The KMT won the election because of Chen administration sleaze' (Copper, 2009, p. 478).

Within this context, by taking one particular set of ideas and examining the way clientelism has been applied in the study of Taiwan's specific political and social context, our intention here is to undertake an analysis of how its dynamics have been experienced in relation to sporting politics. We focus on the strategic relations at play in Taiwan's professional baseball system in politically 'turbulent' periods, and specifically on the phenomenon of clientelism in sporting politics, since it indicates the nature of the clientelistic network that has developed, in the Taiwanese context, with its own specific cultural characteristics.

During a period of political change (1997–2003), Taiwan's government sought to deal with the development of a merger between two professional baseball leagues and the aftermath of a major corruption scandal concerning gambling and the fixing of matches in 1997. Moreover, the success of staging the Baseball World Cup in 2001 re-established the game as the country's major sporting obsession. The merger of the two leagues in 2003 illustrates specifically the interconnection of professional sporting business with political parties. More precisely, it provides us with the opportunity to evaluate how sociopolitical actors (including state agencies and individuals) and business elites (owners of clubs in two leagues) behaved in order to achieve strategic goals.

What is political clientelism: meanings in Taiwanese context

The concepts of 'patronage' and 'clientelism' and the 'patron–client' relationship, which have a long history in various philosophical and religious literatures, were further transferred to politics, sociology and anthropology for the discussion of various phenomena in both primitive and modern societies (Zhanga, Ding and Baoa, 2009). Clientelism, then, is seen as a set of 'structured relations that can change over time with the changes of social configuration reflecting political and socio-economic development' (Cheol, 2008, p. 115). It involves 'strategies for the acquisition, maintenance and aggrandisement of political power on the part of patrons, and strategies for the protection and promotion of their interests on the part of the clients' (Piattoni, 2001, p. 2). Such strategies are possible, in part, because of the structural context of politics in given societies, and thus can be regarded as a specific form of strategic relations (Henry and Nassis, 1999). Clientelistic relations between political parties and organizational forms in civil society, in certain contexts, perform a strategic function in mediating the state's role.

The two principal forms that clientelism takes are those of traditional, dyadic relationships between individuals (Cheng, 1988), and 'modern', political party-directed clientelism. Explanations of political clientelism have tended to fall under two headings. The first is that of 'culturalist' accounts. In such accounts clientelism is characterized as a feature of Gemeinschaft-type societies, based on Weberian notions of traditional power, where individuals and groups are bound into relations of reciprocity, with social and material benefits being disbursed in exchange for commitment and support (Henry and Nassis, 1999). Clientelism is thus seen as a form of politics that is the product of local culture. In parallel to the European phenomenon, in the Asian context the traditional concept of 'guanxi', reciprocal relationships based on notions of trust, face and hierarchy (Gold, Guthrie and Wank, 2002) has characterized business and political relationships, particularly in situations such as that of Taiwan with (until recently) its authoritarian system where mistrust of strangers and reliance on personal relationships and networks were fostered by political exclusion of ethnic Taiwanese (Solinger, 2006). In fact, the existence of clientelism in the Taiwanese context is related to traditional 'guanxi' sets of relations. As 'a particular form of Chinese social governance mechanism, guangxi's [sic] nature refers to social networks that an individual builds and a form of social ties and connectiveness popular in Chinese culture' (Gu, Hung, and Tse, 2008, pp. 13–14). Essentially, Chinese cultural roots in Confucianism emphasize 'the importance of interdependent social connections as Chinese people inhabit an intricate web of personal and social inter-connections. Their incentive structures and enforcement mechanisms tend to be informal rather than formal' (Dunning and Kim, 2007, pp. 329–330). Taking on a special significance in Chinese societies, guanxi is thus a central concept in Chinese culture and a product of the contemporary, political and socio-economic system. 'With its cultural embeddings guanxi, as the social norm of conduct, functions as complex adaptive systems that expand and interconnect to become well-knit social networks' (Wong, 2010, p. 419). Such social networks/connections between or among individuals and/or interactive behaviours are based on these connections (Zhuang, Xi and Tsang, 2010). Guanxi relates to the network of social relations and obligations in which an individual or group of individuals is implicated. Such networks form the basis of guanxi which 'encompasses implicit mutual obligation, assurance, trust, and understanding, and governs Chinese attitudes toward long-term and social business relationships' (Hwang, Golemon, Chen, Wang and Hung, 2009, p. 235). Therefore, being introduced into a network by an already known and respected party is critical. Indeed, the personal relationships so nurtured are based implicitly on mutual interest and benefit, and on an expectation that a favour entails a debt to be repaid; they thus have a binding power and primacy (Solinger, 2006).

The second type of explanation of clientelism is 'developmentalist' in that it is explained as a function of the distorted or incomplete development of particular political systems. Those who have articulated a modernization thesis, whether of Marxist, or liberal orientation, have implied that clientelism, and similar kinship, friendship, or community-based relations, represented a transitory stage in the development of class-based or interest-based politics (Roniger and Gunes-Ayata, 1994). Such explanations have assumed that patronage based on familial patterns would be replaced by rational allocation of resources on the basis of universal (rather than personal) rights and that these rights would be administered through the organizational form of state bureaucracy and the political form of the liberal democratic, welfare state (Kurer, 1996). Actors and their interactions are interdependent, with relations between actors being regarded as channels for transferring useful resources. Ultimately, the network of these interactions may provide opportunities for human action. The patron–client relationship is, therefore, seen as 'an interest-coordinating mechanism that allocates power and distributes resources' (Wong, 2008, p. 183).

As Lewis (2000, p. 250) claims, 'All human activity takes place within the context provided by a set of pre-existing social structures.' The political perspective is that, in Taiwan, the KMT party constructed a patron–client relationship with local factions and business leaders (Tsai, 2009) and such a clientelistic system, party clientelism, has been developed to maintain nation-wide networks with capitalists as well as with civil groups (Tang, 2003). While different political regimes always impeded the development of civil societies, as we have noted, central political leaders regularly used patron–client relationships to co-opt local elites. In turn, these elites provided favours to their followers in exchange for political support. As a result, relation-oriented social interactions had prevailed throughout the history of the Taiwanese state (Chen, 2009). Since the lifting of martial law, Taiwan's political system and the ways in which people can participate in or affect it have changed radically. More specifically, it is the 'dynamic and continuing process of democratization that has changed all important elements of policymaking in respect to agenda setting, interests and ideas formation, actors and networks involved' (Ku, 2010, p. 98). However, the 'bureaucratically entrenched form of clientelism has not disappeared with the transition to democratization' (Bernstein, 2008, p. 935). Indeed, 'democratization did not obliterate the former authoritarian structures, but merely altered them and thus increased the channels through which businesses could use finance to affect the political process' (Tsai, 2009, p. 369). Having only recently been restored to democracy, the historical context of Greek politics reveals that clientelistic relations have remained a significant feature of contemporary politics (Henry and Nassis, 1999). Regarding Korea in East Asia, its democratization of politics in 1987 provided momentum for changing the political configuration of the clientelist map (Cheol, 2008). At a similar point, South American states such as Argentina have seen a new pattern/development of political clientelism following the move away from more authoritarian regimes (Paradiso, 2010; Szwarcberg, 2009). As Paradiso (2010, p. 49) argues, 'The practice of patronage politics has expanded since the 1990s, when Menem introduced neo-liberal reforms that allowed politicians to develop strong networks of clientelism' (Paradiso, 2010, p. 49). In Taiwan's case, the legacy of patronage politics, patron–client relations and informal networks capturing formal structures of authority was widely used by the DPP's administration (Hsu, 2009; 2010). The change of government did not end clientelistic relationships but simply replaced the actors at both ends of the chain. Zhu and Cheng point out that with 'The "third wave" of political democratization in many emerging economies, the establishment of new political parties is allowed, leading to intense party competition and even rivalries' (Zhu and Chung, 2010, p. 6). Social and economic leaders and political actors interact with each other for exchange of information and resources. Therefore, even though Taiwan has twice experienced a change of ruling party, the 'clientelism rooted in KMT authoritarian rule has not been dismantled with democratization but was re-framed by new means of regulation in the name of liberalization in the sweep of global neo-liberalism' (Chien, 2008, p. 192).

The development of political context in Taiwan

The political system in Taiwan has grown from the context of the imposition of what was essentially a one party state by the Chinese nationalist forces headed by Chiang Kai-shek and his political party the Kuomintang, with opposition in the early stages of the establishment of the nationalists on Taiwan being brutally suppressed (Roy, 2003). Indeed, Taiwan's society moved from a pre-modern form, at the time of Chiang Kai-shek's arrival in 1949, through rapid economic development and authoritarian political control, to an advanced economy and an emerging multi-party democracy. 'Modern' forms of governance, thus, were simply not available in the early stages of the KMT control. Martial law and domination by the military elite were the norm. Ethnic/familial relations were crucial features of a Taiwanese society, whether in overt terms (such as the crushing by the Nationalists of Taiwanese resistance in the 'massacre' of 28 February 1947) or in hidden ways as in the development of the links between the military elite and business interests. Such links were generally ethnically or family oriented (Cheng, 2001; Chu and Lin, 2001; Kau, 1996; Kuo, 2000).

Taiwan's politics and economy were dominated by the KMT up until 1987 when the greatest wave of political democratization in Taiwan's modern history took place (Zhu and Chung, 2010). Political liberalization has been in transit for a relatively shorter period since the lifting of martial law in 1987, the development of multi-party politics, and the introduction of popular elections for the presidency in 1996. In effect, Taiwan has developed into a dynamic capitalist economy with decreasing state intervention. When the Nationalists took control of the island, the economy was significantly reliant on agricultural production (32 per cent of GDP in 1950). Throughout the 1960s and 1970s Taiwan enjoyed rapid growth and industrialization as one of Asia's 'tiger economies'. This has been followed by rapid growth in the service sector, which by 2010 accounted for 67.2 per cent of GDP (Directorate-General of Budget, Accounting and Statistics, 2011). Moreover, the country enjoys a major trade surplus, and its foreign reserves are the world's third largest. However, global forces are mediated in local contexts, and invariably local responses to global contexts will vary in political, social, cultural and economic terms. The form of clientelism in Taiwan's case is clearly characterized by local forces. As political activity was 'normalized' with the relaxing of martial law in 1987, it is not surprising that the emerging political system did not conform to the modernist ideas of liberal pluralism, but rather maintained a strongly clientelistic character (Bernstein, 2008; Hood, 1996; Kau, 1996; Kuo, 2000; Wang and Kurzman, 2007; Wu, 2003). Because 'policymaking had to rely on the votes and financial support of key local politicians and businesspeople, the authoritarian developmental regime gradually lost its arbitrary power and had to win the support of the local factions and business groups that arose during the liberalization process' (Hsu, 2010, p. 7). Thus, the strategic context for the development of professional baseball in the 1990s was one of both emerging political liberalism (with the arrival of a challenge to KMT dominance and the development of new political parties, in particular the DPP), and enduring clientelistic relations.

It is clear, then, that the preconditions for political clientelism existed in Taiwanese society from the outset of the nationalist regime. Strong, central control of the economy by the state was a fact of life under martial law, and 'trust' in the mechanisms for social distribution of benefits was clearly lacking. Redistribution and welfare took place through family and ethnically based mutual aid organizations (Kau, 1996; Kuo, 2000). As politics liberalized, spaces were opened up for numerous interest groups, but their development took place in the context of a social system with more than simply residual clientelistic links between the military, political, social and economic elites. Retrospectively, it appears that clientelistic relations have had a clear geographical/spatial character as well as an ethnic basis in Taiwanese political context (Hsu, 2010). It might be claimed that the uprooting of Chiang Kai-shek's supporters in their retreat from the mainland, with its loss of links with traditional community, provided a fertile context for the development of clientelism. When the Chinese mainlander-dominated KMT government was in power (1947–2000), the military elites (drawn largely from the ethnic mainland Chinese communities) operated through cooperation with business elites drawn largely from mainland Chinese groups who predominated in the Northern part of the island, as opposed to native Taiwanese groups who predominated in the Southern part. When the Nationalists first migrated to Taiwan in 1946 it was hardly surprising that politics should be constructed on ethnic links. In a context of military struggle against the Communists, and once on the island, one of military suppression of Taiwanese resistance, it was a matter of trusting those who were 'one's own kind'. However, part of the legacy of importing traditions of politics from the mainland was the import of links between political elites and crime, which had been a feature of the pre-communist state (Reaves, 2002). Such practices of doing business with one's own kind were reinforced by the fact that welfare provision by the state was from the early days minimal, and social provision was made in large part through the extended family and also through ethnically based social organizations (Goodman and Peng, 1996).

While mainlander groups dominated the KMT, and the KMT dominated Taiwanese politics, the main thrust of policy towards mainland China was the goal of reuniting Taiwan with

China. However, with the lifting of martial law in 1987, a native Taiwanese President Lee was elected. The KMT under Lee's leadership, in which he began to consolidate his interests by developing political coalitions against established interest groups, has achieved an impressive start at clearing the roadblocks of the old, conservative forces and moving down the road of democratization (Chu and Lin, 2001). However, as the process of reform and democratization set in, the weakening of KMT control coupled with the growing strength of its followers began to change the nature of the traditional patron–client relationship in Taiwan politics (Kau, 1996). Though the DPP in the past had denounced the KMT's long-term manoeuvring of local factions and economic favours, 'the DPP now pursues a faction-based electoral strategy of the increased political and economic privileges associated with patronage' (Wu, 2003, p. 106). Indeed, with the emergence of the DPP and its subsequent coming to power in 2000 and 2004, locally, this party has so far been unable to clean up its factionalism because DPP politicians 'have also built up their own networks in different localities so that such informal arrangements remained operative and influential long after the democratic transition' (Tang, 2003, p. 1035). In addition, the period of the DPP's regime allowed the rise of new elite groups based on political and business networks, while businessmen developed and strengthened friend/family networking in order to cope with sociopolitical transformation. For instance, former President Chen Shui-bian, who has been seen as an implacable opponent of 'money-politics in Taiwan's democracy, encountered criticism and queries about his "political charisma" because of his close relationships with Taiwan business tycoons' (Shaw, 2010, p. 7). Indeed, there were significant implications for anti-corruption efforts in Taiwan involving both political power and business interests. Particularly serious, were the revelations of the financial scandal in relation to former President Chen Shui-bian's family members, especially his wife, officials appointed by Chen, and business associates on charges of corruption who through a close guanxi network engaged in nefarious activities such as insider trading, money laundering, embezzlement, business interest exchanges, and the obstruction of justice (Gold, 2010; Hwang *et al.*, 2009). Having been indicted on corruption charges and jailed pending trial, this indicated that 'the Chen era, begun with so much promise, at least to some, had ended with Taiwan in rather bad shape domestically and internationally' (Gold, 2010, p. 92). Moreover, 'the ghost of corruption that collapsed the KMT regime in 2000 haunted the DPP in return' (Hsu, 2009, p. 307). Chen's own implication in a corruption scandal was a particular disappointment to supporters who saw him as breaking with the alleged endemic corruption of the KMT (Copper, 2009). On the one hand, in three respects, political reform, civil/political liberties and corruption, Taiwan witnessed stagnation or backsliding after 2000 and, thus, one might contend that Taiwan's democracy regressed during the Chen era. This is supported by more general assessment of Taiwan's polity during the same period of time (Copper, 2009, pp. 476–477). On the other hand, 'sustainability of political influence affects the persistence of the clientele networks. If politicians can maintain sustained political power, clientele networks persist over time' (Cheol, 2008, p. 117). In the case of Taiwan, Chen, who once stood at the top of the clientele networks, stepped down from the post of president after his term in office. Politicians strategically adapt to changing social configurations, which has resulted in historical changes in clientele networks surrounding politicians.

The dynamics of the political clientelistic relations: the case of the 2003 merger between two professional baseball leagues in Taiwan

There are limitations on the state's capacity to pervade and control society, and a certain power on the part of members of a society to insulate themselves from, and exert influence upon, the state (Duan, 2005). 'Political action takes form within a matrix of social relations. Those who try to mobilize disruptive power must overcome the constraints typically imposed by their multiple relations with others' (Piven, 2008, p. 12). In the post 2001 Baseball World Cup (BWC) period, the prestige of success in the BWC (Taiwan performed exceptionally, achieving third place) assisted political powers in driving the process of merger of the two professional leagues to completion. Given a context of domination and a property of social interaction (Giddens, 1976), President Chen's direct involvement, fuelled by varying combinations of political, ideological and nationalist considerations, was able to 'sway the actions of another actor or actors' (Piven, 2008, p. 3). President Chen's direct involvement brought about a radical change in the confrontational positions taken by the leagues and was instrumental in ending the history of controversy between the two leagues:

> May 2002, President Chen declared that he hoped to guide reconciliation between the two opposing professional baseball leagues .... And he assigned a specific assistant, who had a close family connection to Chairman Chen of the CPBL, to accelerate negotiating the merger after receiving a letter, which was described as an appeal for the government to involve itself in the professional baseball industry, from an owner of a professional baseball club.
>
> (Tseng, 2003)

In Taiwan, baseball can evoke the strongest feeling in the majority of the public and give expression to collective passion (Yu, 2007). Baseball, it is thus argued, is not just sport but is interwoven closely with Taiwan's politics. In short, baseball was too important in terms of national identity and pride to disappear from the market. As one commentator put it:

> For Taiwan, baseball is politics ... The game has been utilized as a means to exercise the governments' political hegemony ... No matter how much people may want the game [to be] free from politics, whilst power networks exist, baseball is never going to be free from politics.
>
> (Lin, 2003, p. 232)

The emergence of the merger between professional baseball leagues has provided the DPP government with an opportunity to link its political goals through fans' support of baseball, to promote Taiwan's national identity. A DPP legislator acknowledged this comment regarding Taiwan's consciousness among its citizens, which highlighted the importance of the discussions that took place in the 2003 merger case, and explained:

> Baseball is our national sport which is an important facet of claims to nationhood, and national pride on the part of the Taiwanese. Most of our citizens, in particular our DPP supporters from Southern Taiwan, where it has been seen as the most important region for developing baseball, are satisfied with this merger because of the President's and DPP government's involvement.
>
> (Interview with DPP legislator, 2 May 2007)

The 2000 presidential election resulted in the KMT, the party that ruled Taiwan for more than half a century, turning power over to the DPP. 'Most of the major winning constituencies were located in the southern regions and rural areas, and thanks again to electoral support from the South, the DPP won re-election in 2004' (Hsu, 2010, p. 9). Indeed, the Southern region is crucial for the DPP's election victory. 'The DPP government had to respond to the demands of its supporters, who were mostly based on the Southern region' (Hsu, 2009, p. 303). Although the KMT has long 'since "indigenized" and ethnic cleavages have weakened with democratization, the DPP's dogged pursuit of an explicit Taiwanese national identity and its implications for future relations with China, remains a point of contention' (Sullivan, 2010, p. 474). While DPP politicians referred to the achievements of the merger, the KMT politicians tended to criticize DPP's involvement with 'strategic considerations' and maintained that:

> The major implication for completing the merger by the DPP government was to serve fans' and baseball leagues/clubs' needs ... Professional baseball will flourish and thus benefit baseball development. KMT was seen as of secondary importance because of the President's involvement in this merger.
>
> (Interview with KMT legislator, 9 May 2007)

At the level of political legitimacy and party politics, the complicated relations between political parties, individual politicians and professional baseball leagues had a significant effect on the merger. Despite those very evident party affiliations, the DPP government and its president succeeded in persuading its supporters who owned the Taiwan Major League (TML) to swallow the bitter pill of a one-sided merger in which only two of the TML's four clubs survived. The only overtly partial move made by the government in favour of the TML position was to promote a motion for the Chinese Professional Baseball League (CPBL) to compensate the TML to the tune of NT$80 million for each of the two teams that would go out of existence. This move was rejected by the CPBL. As clientelism perceives interested actors as:

> Aggregations of clientelist networks attracting individual benefits for particular individual members by influencing policy implementation, policy choice is thus the result of individual demands for individual benefits, and a strategy emerges only post hoc, as an accidental consequence of these pressures.
>
> (Kurer, 1996, p. 651)

Inevitably, the merger took place on CPBL terms, which, from the TML perspective, was a better outcome than simply allowing the weaker of the two leagues to wither and die. The interrelated politic–economic relationships between them were acknowledged as a crucial factor contributing to the pressure for the merger, since the key actors in this issue were seen to be closely linked in political, economic and familial terms. In fact, there had been a complicated relation between political parties and professional baseball league, as a comment by Krich illustrates:

> Only in Taiwan, where connections to political parties are crucial in operating franchises and constructing ballparks, would a baseball official, TML Executive Director Robin Tseng, explain: our league is more DPP while the other league (CPBL) is more KMT.
>
> (Krich, 2002, p. 10)

In addition, the ties between actors are entirely informal, going beyond the relationship that may exist by virtue of their officially sanctioned social roles (Kurer, 1996). While looking at the relations between leaders of political parties, CPBL and TML, the following comment is able to tell the story:

The Chairman of the CPBL, Chen, has close family connections with the president of the Naluwan Corporation (TML) Chen. The friendship between them has helped to push this merger. In addition, it is recognized that the Chairman of the CPBL Chen and the president of the Naluwan Corporation (TML) Chen have close connections with the President.

(Tseng, 2002)

'Human agency inevitably takes place within social figurations of power, networks of inter-dependent human beings with shifting asymmetrical power relations. These figurations produce competitive tensions that shape both individual action and the goal of their actions' (Brandtstädter, 2003, p. 92). As we can see a 'specific link' within or outside the professional baseball system, it is not hard to understand that owners of professional clubs were concerned not only about overcoming worsening financial deficits but also with maintaining their political and economic relationships with the government. Such sociopolitical connections are linkages between individual business leaders and political actors such as party leaders and elected legislators that reflect the idea in the social networks literature that interpersonal linkages can serve as conduits of resources and influence (Chung, Mahmood and Mitchell, 2009). When we look at the political circumstances surrounding the CPBL, to some degree, this League was established and sponsored by some companies with strong connections to political interests, in particular to the KMT (Liang, 1993). In KMT's Taiwan before 2000, the authoritarian political system and socio-economic system, with its attached clientelistic features, was the social figuration of power within which individuals and groups acted. Having seen the power of clientelism of the KMT regime, the DPP aimed to break up the dominance of the local KMT factions and engaged in destroying such client networks after democratic transition (Hsu, 2009, 2010; Tang, 2003). Because of their 'relatively weakened' KMT affiliation, leaders of the CPBL attempted to restructure this industry, and sought to establish good political relationships with the DPP ruling government in terms of access to relevant resources for the future. Because 'resources and capabilities are interrelated, actors need resources to elaborate their capabilities and, in the process of doing so, reproduce the resources' (Hiss, 2006, p. 86). What the leaders of the CPBL considered important was the long-term development of the industry and they clearly felt that the government's attitude would play a vital role in the future.

As Raeymaekers points out, 'Elias argues, no "zero-point" can be identified with regard to the emergence of social relationships within and between social groups: rather, society should be depicted "like a dance", where several social groupings gradually create their structured action over time' (Raeymaekers, 2007, p. 21). The restructured professional baseball system implicated its new 'content and form' since it had added on new meanings and served new ends that responded to the sociopolitical regime of DPP's Taiwan. Personal relationships with government and party officials are also frequently considered highly significant for doing business in Taiwan (Ledeneva, 2008). Businessmen have a strong interest in extending their networks of personal relationships to public officials for a wide variety of business-related activities (Bickenbach and Liu, 2010). As 'guanxi can be used to contact influential persons, particularly government officials who can help with beneficial business opportunities, contacts play an important role in establishing personal relationships with patrons, partners, and clients' (Ledeneva, 2008, p. 140). Thus, the established interest groups, without regard to their party afflictions, have the incentive to utilize their existing structural relationships in order to minimize the risk and uncertainty in the new democracy (Kuo, 2000). On the other hand, though the state's position retains monolithic power over social issues, it attempts to bind business elites into its economic–political patronage (Matsumoto, 2002). Political leaders 'unavoidably have to establish a relationship with businesses in order to get enough financial support for political purposes' (Tsai, 2009, p. 370).

Political clientelistic relationships, guanxi and culturally specific features of the sport system in Taiwan

In highly competitive contexts, long-standing patterns of interaction provide a social figuration with a level of power and control that new forms of interaction or association lack. Therefore, this allows for a better chance to occupy strategic positions and resources. 'The power of a group or social figuration increases not only because of an accumulation of resources or power chances, but also [by virtue of] the more internal coordination between a complexity of social positions it achieves' (Brandtstädter, 2003, p. 96). Much more important are the personalized, affective bargaining relationships found among the political and economic elites in the sporting system. In the exchange between patron–client ties, 'each side requires some resources and opportunities such as political resource, discourse power, fame, economic status etc. from the other, setting up interdependent relationships in different degrees' (Zhanga *et al.*, 2009, p. 403). Negotiations between business social networks and political actors in the system shape the terms of 'new patronage' and interests. New 'clientele networks are thus developed into 'strong bonds through which political leaders can exercise discretionary power in distributing positive benefits' (Cheol, 2008, p. 116). Responding to the fact that a 'contribution' of President Chen had successfully promoted the merger, the (previously KMT-orientated) CPBL adjusted its position to some extent with the announcement of the way in which the CPBL named the Championship Series in 2003. This reflects the DPP position with emphasis on Taiwan as an independent entity, a core difference with the KMT. For the first time, the Taiwanese national identity (with the use of the term Taiwan in the title of the event – and wording/discourse in the naming of the nation is of critical importance in the Taiwan context) was promoted by the CPBL (Chinese Professional Baseball League, 2003).

There are a few conceivable strategies to respond to the exit of the clienteles/partners and one would be to develop ties to new clienteles, which might be a strategy of flexible adaptation to survive historical changes (Cheol, 2008; Giddens, 1998). 'Structures are socially constructed, reproduced and changed through the actions of people in real time, but that, at given points in time, actors occupy different interest and power positions within structures, giving them different goals, levels of autonomy and clout' (Wood and Gough, 2006, p. 1698). The patron–client relationship is conceived as 'the cognitive and social structures for the agents to engage each other and act upon them in their everyday reflexive pursuit of self-interest, which can be flexibly redefined circumstantially' (Wong, 2008, p. 183). In fact, the patron–client relationship has both constraining and enabling properties (Giddens, 1984). Results of the merger are increasing interdependencies and new pressures to behave in accountable and predictable ways. 'The larger and more powerful a figuration, the more likely a shift from external constraints into self-constraints and the emergence of a new habitus' (Brandtstädter, 2003, p. 96). In a specific 'clientelistic environment' such as Taiwan, both patrons and clients have an interest in adopting and pursuing benefits, since 'agents observe the patron–client rules and, therefore, reproduce the differential status between the patron and the client purposefully while they rationally pursue their own interests' (Wong, 2008, p. 183). They are unlikely to be abandoned permanently without changes in the political structure. Hence, one could see a set of reciprocal dependencies that connect people in multiple directions (Mennell and Goudsblom, 1998). Agency and clientelism may coexist and be co-constitutive of social action (Giddens, 1984). This means that the owners of CPBL are increasingly concerned with attracting particularistic benefits for themselves where their KMT oriented political ideology has no import in 'political' decisions. The leading members of corporations are tempted to join political clientelistic networks as a way of influencing administrative decisions. Thus, whatever the type of regime, when the patron fails to perform, at that moment his/her clients would also decide to change and attach themselves to a new patron.

Patron–client ties are important in Chinese political culture. Such ties between the 'business elites and the state are oiled via informal channels of personal relationships (*guanxi*). Guanxi, the essential element in linking Chinese social networks, 'has been a way of life from time immemorial. Therefore the personal investment required to develop and maintain good social relations is accepted as an unavoidable fact of life' (Wong, 2010, p. 1080). These personal ties of reciprocity between bureaucrats and business elites are characterized by mutual exchanges between allocation of resources and political support (Duan, 2005, pp. 83–84). The concept of guanxi is 'inherent to Chinese social life since it is defined by personalized networks of influence and relationships among the Chinese people for centuries' (Gu *et al.*, 2008, p. 12). From a cultural perspective, the influence of traditional Chinese culture is the fundamental reason for the use of guanxi in Chinese society and such Chinese cultural heritage over thousands of years has favoured social relations as a means to coordinate mutual exchanges (Shaomin, 2004). The relationships established through 'the performance of reciprocal obligations tend to be seen as perpetual, with one repayment requiring yet another expression of favor or consideration' (Dunning and Kim, 2007, p. 330). 'By developing personal relationships to other persons that may also develop personal relationships among each other the development of individual relationships ultimately leads to a network of relationships' (Bickenbach and Liu, 2010, p. 19). In Taiwan's sporting system, '*guanxi* decisions often have the goal to serve oneself or to serve others ... and represent its own or the organization's interests' (Ferstl, 2010, p. 117). As Ferstl points out, it is a common phenomenon for Taiwan's sport leaders in the SAC to favour their own party members, county magistrates or city mayors while distributing the national sport budget. One of the most vivid examples here is that political calculation and consideration became key criteria in deciding the distribution of funding for the two world mega-events to be held in Taipei and Kaohsiung cities (the Deaflympics, and the World Games). Owing to Taiwan's politically polarized environment, the organizer of the 2009 Taipei Deaf Olympic Games only received NT$200m from the Sport Affairs Council (SAC). According to a senior official in the SAC Department of Competitive Athletics, 'most of the SAC directors had a very strong party ideology [supportive of the DPP] when DPP became the ruling party after 2000' (Tan, Cheng, Lee and Ko, 2009, p. 109). He highlighted that:

> The reason that Kaohsiung municipal government could be granted such a huge sum of money was because its mayor belonged to the DPP camp. In contrast, the director of SAC was unwilling to subsidize Taipei city [the host of the 2009 Deaf Olympic Games] because its mayor belonged to the DPP's rival party, the Kuomintang (KMT).
>
> (Tan *et al.*, 2009, p. 109)

Thus, because of the strong political affiliation among these SAC leaders to the DPP, Kaohsiung received around NT$6.9 billion from the SAC, almost 25 times more than its counterpart, Taipei city.

The above example serves to illustrate nature/phenomenon which meets the conditions under which political clientelism is expected to flourish as it lacks 'objective criteria for resource allocation and public confidence in the objectivity of measures and processes employed in resource allocation' (Henry and Nassis, 1999, p. 49). In the case of merger, it reflects that clientelism is a persistent feature of social and political relations in Taiwan and affects a wide range of domestic affairs including sport. Actors always attempt to construct a network of links with other centres of social power that have decision-making capacities directly affecting the realization of their objectives. Within the sociopolitical relationship, political leaders, in this case President Chen, have a great potential for exerting influence, owing to the intrinsic power of their position. They were mainly people closely connected to local factions or the leaders of business groups who were able to mobilize financial and political support for the political parties. Indeed, political ties to the ruling party enable businessmen to enjoy information advantage and acquire resources that are under the ruling party's control (Zhu and Chung, 2010, pp. 15–17). Family/friend networks help the elite secure 'state positions', permitting them to exercise economic and political influence (Krznaric, 2006). These allied political and economic elites may share the same vision of the baseball's future in accordance with their own interests and implement that vision to a certain degree.

Conclusions

In Taiwan, political parties form an alternative basis for individual identity, particularly when traditional forms of solidarity are undermined by 'modernizing' phenomena such as urbanization and industrialization. However, an additional feature of Taiwan's political system, which goes some way to explaining the strength of personal affiliation to a party (or the distrust of the 'other' parties), is the relatively recent role which party affiliation played in internal civil strife. The (initially brutal) imposition of the KMT in 1949 reinforced a form of distrust, or at least an unwillingness to trust, which helps to perpetuate reliance on the political patronage of one's own party, or reliance on guanxi networks, which helped to define relationships with political entities. As the memory of civil struggle recedes, and there is an opening out of business and political relations beyond the local, different attitudes may be developed. Nevertheless, it is difficult to wholly disengage from political, business and social cultures that have been so deeply rooted even if different regimes (parties) with dichotomous political ideologies have taken power.

There's a point to highlight here, which is that the business leaders spontaneously adapted to the new democratic system and found crucial channels of interest maximization. An implication of the patron–client analysis is that this relationship is derived from the political and economic 'benefits' that accumulate along with professional baseball development. It is from professional baseball development that the patrons and the clients create their resources and opportunities for each other. As previously noted, support of individual business and other interests groups exerted influence through political parties, and politicians, on government to precede the merger. The weaker financial grouping, the TML, had links to the stronger political grouping, which also sought to secure the kudos of finding a solution to professional baseball's parlous situation. The state machinery sought to impose a solution on the various parties by requiring the CPBL (associated largely with KMT) to compensate the TML (associated largely with DPP) with the sum of NT$ 80 million. Here, political influence was successfully resisted by the CPBL, the power of its market position allowing it to hold out against state influence. Financial links across political parties between members of the business elite were crucial to finding a solution to this problem. The DPP's action in promoting a solution to the baseball merger of the leagues provides an example of one side conceding ground and persuading its supporters (TML owners) to accept a deal that principally benefited sports entrepreneurs (CPBL owners) associated with the KMT. However, this example is one in which the DPP affiliated owners would have inevitably lost out more heavily if a merger had not been agreed.

Finally, a conclusion that one might draw is that political clientelism, as a set of political provisions, is classically coupled with societies in the shift from traditional, kinship/community-based social configurations to the organic solidarity of modern social and political configurations. In political terms, it is apparent that Taiwan has been transformed from martial law to democratic elections, to a multi-party system, and that aspects of political modernity were being developed. The level and process of modernization of the society, the political culture, had shaped the very nature and behaviour of various actors in this system and, to some extent, diluted the circumstances under which clientelism might continue to thrive. As democratization reveals a constant interplay between structural factors and strategic factors, the understanding of strategic context (and in particular the political clientelism characterizing the Taiwanese sport business context) that exists as resources and constraints on the social action of any actor involved, is essential if we are to understand the opportunities and limits that are provided for those actors in the political sporting system. Thus, the existence of political clientelism that has survived for generations is unlikely to terminate, but rather may re-emerge in new forms of social regulation fostered and/or constrained by the social and economic structures of Taiwan's society, in which sport is inevitably subsumed.

14

SPORT AND MEDIA POLICY

Matthew Nicholson and Russell Hoye

Introduction

The relationship between sport and the media is a significant arena of government policy and arguably subject to more government intervention than other facets of sport. Government policies in the arenas of elite development or participation, for example, often seek to ensure an outcome that is directly related to the performance of a sport organization (such as a national governing body or a community sport organization). Ensuring that a sport, such as rowing or cycling, achieves more Olympic gold medals or attracts more grass-roots participants is typically achieved by improving the systems, human resources, training, facilities or talent identification processes. The policies, in the form of increased financial assistance or the requirement to develop 'whole sport plans', for example, are focused directly on sport organizations and their operations. By contrast, government policy in the sport media arena is typically focused on ensuring outcomes that sport organizations can either facilitate or hinder, but that relate very little to their daily practices and processes. These issues will be discussed in greater detail below, but the example of listed events[1] will serve to provide context. By listing events that are unable to be broadcast exclusively on pay or cable television, governments seek to ensure access to a specific form of entertainment for the majority of the population. This policy restricts the commercial activities of a sport organization seeking to sell its product in the marketplace, yet the activities of the sport organization are only of relevance to the government in terms of the indirect impact on its citizens.

The importance of sport to both the modern media industry and consumers has resulted in government seeking to implement policies and regulation across four major areas of the sport media relationship. First, government regulation attempts to prevent the broadcast rights to sport events migrating exclusively from free-to-air television to pay or subscription television. Second, governments have developed regulatory policy aimed at ensuring that sport and media organizations do not engage in anti-competitive behaviour in the buying and selling of these broadcast rights. Such behaviour can lead to monopolies being created that will necessarily restrict supply, which in turn will raise prices to a level that will exploit consumers (New and LeGrand, 1999). Third, governments regulate to prohibit certain types of advertising being associated with sports broadcasting, such as tobacco advertising. Finally, government regulation attempts to limit or prevent any negative consequences of the vertical integration of the sport and media industries, such as the purchase of a sport team or league by a media organization. This chapter examines each of these policy areas, drawing on examples from a number of countries, in order to identify the reasons cited by government for undertaking such direct intervention in regulating the relationship between sport and the media, to identify whether sport is central to determining the nature and extent of such interventions, the variety of regulatory instruments used, and to make some assessment of their impact on sport.

Sale of broadcast rights

Hoehn and Lancefield (2003: 566) noted:

> the pre-eminent position of sports programming in a channel's offering and as a key driver of a TV delivery/distribution platform has forced governments to intervene in media merger proposals, sports-rights contract negotiations, and disputes among TV distribution systems over access to content.

The importance of sport has been enhanced by a shift in the broadcasting industry paradigm, from one in which content, such as sport, was competing for broadcast time on media outlets that were scarce, to one in which a multitude of outlets and forms are competing for scarce content (Cowie and Williams, 1997). In the latter paradigm a range of products are considered to be 'premium content', with sport often viewed as the most valuable because it not only attracts large audiences, but is relatively cheap to produce and its commercial potential is often not hindered by cultural and language barriers. The competition between broadcasters to secure the rights to sport events is based on their perceived value in:

> (i) generating advertising and programme sponsorship revenue, particularly by attracting the most difficult to reach, and high-disposable-income consumer group, the 16–34 ABC1 males; (ii) driving subscription penetration and reducing churn by building loyalty, and, increasingly, driving interactive revenues (such as betting) in digital pay-TV and online distribution markets, which can also have positive spillover effects to the broadcaster's overall brand, as well as demand for other content and products; and (iii) achieving public-service obligations, including the coverage of a wide range of sports, minority sports, and 'national games'.
>
> (Hoehn and Lancefield, 2003: 554)

The value of sport rights, specifically broadcast rights for football, are derived from what are considered to be their unique characteristics:

> First, football is an ephemeral product as viewers are often only interested in live broadcasts. Next, substitution is very limited, because viewers who want to see a given football event are unlikely to be satisfied with the coverage of another event. Finally, the exclusive concentration of rights in the hands of sports federations reduces the number of sellers on the market.
>
> (Toft, 2003: 47).

The value of sport broadcast rights has grown considerably over the last 15 years and as Hoehn and Lancefield (2003: 556) argued, 'major rights have tended to migrate to pay-TV platforms in Europe and premium cable and satellite services in the USA'. The policy response by various governments to protecting the interests of broadcasters, sport organizations and consumers has been varied but, as Noll (2007: 400) highlighted, governments have tended to focus on three issues related to sports rights:

> whether pay-TV should be allowed to capture rights to events that historically have been broadcast on free-to-air stations, whether rights to team sports should be sold by leagues or by teams, and whether a single buyer should be permitted to acquire all of the rights to a major sport. Reflecting conflicting views about these issues, different leagues around the world have adopted different policies and practices regarding the sale of broadcast rights and the distribution of the revenues from rights fees among their members.

The first of these issues, the migration of rights from free-to-air TV to pay TV, is addressed in the next section of this chapter. The remaining two issues are central to determining the value of rights, as Noll (2007: 419) concluded:

> The performance of sports broadcasting depends on the market structure for rights, which in turn is determined by two competition policy decisions. The first is whether the power to sell rights is reserved for teams or given to leagues. The second is the policy of national governments with respect to competition in broadcasting.

In the European market, the objective of the European Commission is to prevent sport leagues, clubs and broadcasters engaging in anti-competitive behaviour. Their view is that 'effective competition in these markets is likely to improve the functioning of broadcasting markets and give viewers access to TV services that are reasonably priced, innovative, of good quality and with a variety of offers' (Toft, 2003: 47). The selling of rights by leagues such as the Union of European Football Associations (UEFA) on behalf of their member clubs to a single broadcaster in each European Union (EU) state was considered, in 2003, to contravene the European Commission's policy on competition:

> The joint selling arrangement which UEFA initially notified meant that all TV rights were sold to a single free-TV broadcaster in each Member State and on an exclusive basis for periods up to four years. Some rights could be sub-licensed to a pay-TV broadcaster, subject to UEFA's prior consent and against payment of 50% of the sub-licensing fee to UEFA. Sub-licensing arrangements can do little to alleviate the restrictive effects of a joint selling arrangement. Football clubs had no access to exploit any TV rights. Neither UEFA nor the football clubs exploited Internet or mobile telephone rights. The notified arrangement thereby contained most of those negative aspects of joint selling which it is the Commission's policy to counter.
>
> (Toft, 2003: 48)

The Commission's objections centre on their view that this form of 'packaging and manner of sale of football TV rights can distort the competitive process by favouring the business methods of particular broadcasters or by raising barriers to entry on the market' (Toft, 2003: 48). So, while the Commission acknowledges that the joint selling of sport broadcasting rights is an accepted practice and in many instances facilitates exclusivity, which in turn maximizes the return that sport leagues and their clubs can achieve, they consider that joint selling also facilitates long-term contracts and if the broadcaster is dominant in the marketplace, this can lead to market foreclosure. Their response has been to influence the selling arrangements used by leagues such as the UEFA Champions League by insisting on shorter contract periods, the sale of discrete parcels of rights, rather than the entire league 'bundle', and enabling clubs to sell certain rights if leagues are unable to sell them.

Nicholson (2007) noted that various European governments responded differently to the challenge of regulating the practice of joint or collective selling of sports rights by their respective national leagues. France enabled the national football federation to be the sole authority responsible for the sale of broadcast rights (Cave and Crandall, 2001; Rumphorst, 2001). In direct contrast, the Netherlands competition authority prohibited the joint selling of rights by the Dutch Football Association. In Italy, a similar ban on the collective selling of live rights by the national football federation was imposed in 1999 by the Italian competition authority (Tonazzi, 2003). However, the collective sale of highlight packages was allowed owing to the logistical difficulties in selling these rights on an individual basis (Rumphorst, 2001).

This tension between leagues or clubs being empowered to sell broadcast rights is most evident in the USA. Nicholson (2007: 89) noted that:

> Court rulings in 1953 and 1960 determined that league wide television contracts that benefited the collective at the expense of the rights of individual teams were a violation of the Sherman Act. In response, the government enacted the Sports Broadcasting Act in 1961, which gave sport leagues the ability to offer rights as a package to a national network on the grounds that it was in the interest of spectators and the leagues' health and competitive balance (Cave and Crandall, 2001; Sandy, Sloane and Rosentraub, 2004). As a result, the National Football League (NFL) signed its first national television contract in 1962, which was worth US$4.7 million annually.

Such direct government regulatory intervention in the USA via the creation of the Sports Broadcasting Act has allowed the National Football League to offer collective rights to national networks since 1962 (Nicholson, 2007). Cave and Crandall (2001) noted that no other professional sport in the US relies solely on national rights and that the NFL has the highest proportion of total revenue derived from broadcast rights. Nicholson (2007) argued that a governing body's capacity to limit or prevent the sale of individual rights by teams to local and regional broadcasters is related to their ability to argue that collective selling of rights is necessary to maintain competition within the League. In reality, this is a difficult argument to sustain with the result that almost all basketball, baseball and hockey teams in the United States sell individual broadcast rights rather than their leagues maintaining control over the collective rights (Noll, 2007).

The other issue related to the sale of sports rights is the extent to which broadcasters can monopolize sports rights by purchasing them via extended contracts or through controlling the majority of the market. In relation to this, the International Competition Network's 'Unilateral Conduct Working Group' reported in 2008 that foreclosure, in which competition is weakened when the actions of a dominant business or organization hinder or eliminate actual or potential competitors in the marketplace, is more likely when businesses are able to enter into arrangements of exclusivity and when these arrangements are long term. In the sport broadcasting context, the issue of foreclosure is most significant when media organizations are able to obtain the exclusive rights to premium sport content. In the Italian response to the Unilateral Conduct Working Group Questionnaire on predatory pricing and exclusive dealing, they cite the example of where a major broadcaster displayed anti-competitive behaviour:

> Telepiù, the incumbent firm in pay-TV market, signed long-term contracts for exclusive broadcasting rights with a significant share of Italian soccer teams. The Authority first

ascertained the existence of Telepiù's dominant position in the Italian pay-TV market, as indicated by its market share (the entire market through 1997, 93 per cent of all subscribers at the end of 1998 and 82 per cent at the end of September 1999). The Authority concluded that Telepiù had violated Article 82 of the Treaty. It was found that the acquisition of exclusive rights to top sports events for a lengthy period, just at the time when the conditions for effective competition in pay TV were being established (entry of a new operator, the approaching expiry of Telepiù's exclusive rights to league matches), reinforced its dominant position and raised the already high barriers to entry into the relevant market, so making likely a harm to consumer welfare. The Authority also deemed Article 82 of the Treaty to be violated by the clause according to a right of pre-emption to Telepiù or its subsidiaries for acquisition of exclusive rights for the period following the expiration of initial rights, as this would enable the dominant firm to further prevent competitors from gaining access to the most important program contents.

(Autorità Garante della Concorrenza e del Mercato, 2008: 15–16).

Efforts by governments to prevent such behaviour are again mixed. In Italy, for example, regulation 'prohibits a single broadcaster, irrespective of distribution platform, from owning the rights to more than 60 per cent of live football matches' (Hoehn and Lancefield, 2003: 562). This is in contrast to Germany 'where the government intervened to ensure that the collective sale of premium football was exempted from national competition law' (Hoehn and Lancefield, 2003: 562). In countries such as Australia, New Zealand and the UK, no such restrictions on the purchasing rights of media companies exist.

Access to sport broadcasts

As noted earlier in this chapter, the migration of rights from free-to-air TV to pay TV has also been subject to a high degree of government intervention. Prior to the introduction of pay-per-view or subscription TV, the general public were able to access sport via the state and commercial free-to-air broadcasters. The public benefits of this system have generally been considered to be of social and cultural significance. Nicholson (2007) argued that governments have assumed that the migration of sport from free-to-air to pay television will cause market failure, whereby the cost imposed on the sport product, which was previously delivered at no cost, is likely to result in significantly fewer people having access to the product. Many governments regard sport events of national and international significance to be merit goods, where community demand for the product is high because of social benefits, 'but the normal market cost would be intolerable for an individual consumer' (Michael, 2006: 63). The government intervention in this instance has come in the form of protecting some rights for sport events being sold to the highest bidder without first testing whether free-to-air broadcasters wish to purchase the rights. In member states of the European Union these legal measures are enshrined in something that Parrish (2008: 82) claims is 'where issues of sporting autonomy, commerce and public interest collide' – the Television Without Frontiers Directive ('the Directive'), and a later revision known as the Audiovisual Media Services Directive (AMSD). The Directive was established in 1989 and then amended in 1997. Article 3a of the 1997 version of the Directive states:

Each Member State may take measures in accordance with Community law to ensure that broadcasters under its jurisdiction do not broadcast on an exclusive basis events which are regarded by that Member State as being of major importance for society in such a way as to deprive a substantial proportion of the public in that Member State of the possibility of following such events via live coverage or deferred coverage on free television. If it does so, the Member State concerned shall draw up a list of designated events, national or non-national, which it considers to be of major importance for society. It shall do so in a clear and transparent manner in due and effective time. In so doing the Member State concerned shall also determine whether these events should be available via whole or partial live coverage, or where necessary or appropriate for objective reasons in the public interest, whole or partial deferred coverage.

The European Commission argues that events such as the FIFA World Cup, the European Football Championship and the Olympic Games are of major importance to society. Article 3a of the Directive is therefore designed to prevent instances where events such as these are broadcast exclusively on pay television. Under Article 3a, individual member states are able to construct a list of events that should be made available for the purchase by free-to-air broadcasters. Individual country lists reflect different national sporting and cultural preferences. For example, Austria includes the FIS World Alpine skiing championships and the World Nordic skiing championships, Belgium includes football and cycling, while the list for Ireland includes culturally specific events such as the All-Ireland Senior Inter-County Hurling Finals, Irish Grand National, Irish Derby and the Nations Cup at the Dublin Horse Show.

The revised list of sports events protected under Part IV of the Broadcasting Act 1996

Group A (Full Live Coverage Protected)
- The Olympic Games
- The FIFA World Cup Finals Tournament
- The European Football Championship Finals Tournament
- The FA Cup Final
- The Scottish FA Cup Final (in Scotland)
- The Grand National
- The Derby
- The Wimbledon Tennis Finals
- The Rugby League Challenge Cup Final
- The Rugby World Cup Final

Group B (Secondary Coverage Protected)
- Cricket Test Matches played in England
- Non-Finals play in the Wimbledon Tournament
- All Other Matches in the Rugby World Cup Finals Tournament
- Six Nations Rugby Tournament matches involving home countries
- The Commonwealth Games
- The World Athletics Championship
- The Cricket World Cup – the final, semi-finals and matches involving home nations' teams
- The Ryder Cup
- The Open Golf Championship

Figure 14.1 List of protected events, UK
Source: Department for Culture, Media and Sport (2009)

Listed events in the UK are divided into group A and group B events, depending on their perceived importance (see Figure 14.1). Like many European nations, the UK's Group A listed events comprise sport events that are considered to be of global importance, such as the Olympic Games, the FIFA World Cup Finals Tournament and the Rugby World Cup Final; regional importance, such as European Football Championship Finals Tournament; and local importance, such as the FA Cup Final, the Grand National and the Wimbledon Tennis Finals. The UK Television Broadcasting Regulations of 2000 state that Group A events must be made available for acquisition by a free-to-air broadcaster and that the channel or broadcaster must have a minimum 95 per cent penetration. By contrast, Group B events are those that may not be broadcast live on an exclusive basis unless an adequate provision has been made for secondary coverage. The minimum acceptable service in this respect is edited highlights or delayed coverage of the event of at least 10 per cent of the event or 30 minutes of coverage for an event of one hour or more in duration, whichever is greater.

A similar approach is adopted by the Australian government through part seven of the Australian Broadcasting Services Act of 1992 that gives the responsible government minister the power to protect the free availability of certain types of programmes. In reality the list, known as the anti-siphoning list, is comprised of sporting events that are considered to be nationally significant (see Figure 14.2). Like the UK listed events, this list gives free-to-air broadcasters the first option to purchase the rights to these events, but does not compel them to do so. If no free-to-air broadcaster purchases the rights to an event, the event is automatically delisted 12 weeks prior to its commencement (previously six weeks), at which time the rights are able to be purchased by a pay television provider. The Australian regulations also contain anti-hoarding provisions, which essentially provide protection against commercial free-to-air television networks acquiring the rights to broadcast sport events, but then not exercising these rights. The anti-hoarding provisions are required in large part because of the extent of the anti-siphoning list, both in terms of the number of sports and also the number of single games or matches within a single event (e.g. the number of matches at Wimbledon).

In 2001 the Australian Broadcasting Authority (ABA, now the Australian Communications and Media Authority) reviewed the anti-siphoning provisions on behalf of the government. The ABA (2001: 13) concluded that 'Australia's anti-siphoning scheme and its list of events are both more extensive and restrictive than those in operation overseas'. The explanatory statement to the Broadcasting Services (Events) Notice (No. 1) 2004 (Commonwealth of Australia, 2004), claims that industry reaction to the ABA's report was generally negative. In other words, neither the free-to-air commercial broadcasters nor the pay television providers were satisfied with the outcome of the review. The report recommended some changes to the list, including the deletion and addition of certain events, as well as the extension of the anti-siphoning provisions for a period of five years (Australian Broadcasting Authority, 2001). According to the government, following the release of the report it was lobbied by free-to-air commercial broadcasters that wanted the list extended for ten years, in order to provide commercial certainty in rights negotiations. On the other hand, pay television providers lobbied to have the list reduced in size, or an alternative regulatory regime imposed (such as a dual rights scheme, in which there are tier 1 and tier 2 events listed, similar to the A and B events in the UK scheme discussed previously).

The ABA's investigations not only revealed that the anti-siphoning provisions were highly contentious, but that there was little agreement within the sport and broadcasting sectors about the purpose and impact of the regulations. For example, the Australian Football League (AFL) argued in its submission that the anti-siphoning provisions were anti-competitive, that they prevented sport organizations from maximizing their revenue and that they should be abolished entirely. Similarly, the Women's National Basketball League argued that a proposal to include

Olympic Games

1.1   Each event held as part of the Olympic Games.

Commonwealth Games

2.1   Each event held as part of the Commonwealth Games.

Horse Racing

3.1   Each running of the Melbourne Cup organised by the Victoria Racing Club.

Australian Rules Football

4.1   Each match in the Australian Football League Premiership competition, including the Finals Series.

Rugby League Football

5.1   Each match in the National Rugby League Premiership competition, including the Finals Series.
5.2   Each match in the National Rugby League State of Origin Series.
5.3   Each international rugby league 'test' match involving the senior Australian representative team selected by the Australian Rugby League, whether played in Australia or overseas.

Rugby Union Football

6.1   Each international 'test' match involving the senior Australian representative team selected by the Australian Rugby Union, whether played in Australia or overseas.
6.2   Each match in the Rugby World Cup tournament.

Cricket

7.1   Each 'test' match involving the senior Australian representative team selected by Cricket Australia played in either Australia or the United Kingdom.
7.2   Each one-day cricket match involving the senior Australian representative team selected by Cricket Australia played in Australia or the United Kingdom.
7.3   Each one-day cricket match involving the senior Australian representative team selected by Cricket Australia played as part of a series in which at least one match of the series is played in Australia.
7.4   Each World Cup one-day cricket match.

Soccer

8.1   The English Football Association Cup final.
8.2   Each match in the Fédération Internationale de Football Association World Cup tournament held in 2006.
8.3   Each match in the Fédération Internationale de Football Association World Cup tournament held in 2010.

Tennis

9.1 Each match in the Australian Open tennis tournament.

9.2 Each match in the Wimbledon (the Lawn Tennis Championships) tournament.

9.3 Each match in the men's and women's singles quarter-finals, semi-finals and finals of the French Open tennis tournament.

9.4 Each match in the men's and women's singles quarter-finals, semi-finals and finals of the United States Open tennis tournament.

9.5 Each match in each tie in the Davis Cup tennis tournament when an Australian representative team is involved.

Netball

10.1 Each international netball match involving the senior Australian representative team selected by the All Australian Netball Association, whether played in Australia or overseas.

Golf

11.1 Each round of the Australian Masters tournament.

11.2 Each round of the Australian Open tournament.

11.3 Each round of the United States Masters tournament.

11.4 Each round of the British Open tournament.

Motor Sports

12.1 Each race in the Fédération Internationale de l'Automobile Formula 1 World Championship (Grand Prix) held in Australia.

12.2 Each race in the Moto GP held in Australia.

12.3 Each race in the V8 Supercar Championship Series (including the Bathurst 1000).

12.4 Each race in the Champ Car World Series (IndyCar) held in Australia.

Figure 14.2 Anti-siphoning list of events, Australia 2006–10

Source: Australian Communications and Media Authority (ACMA) (2009)

the League's finals on the anti-siphoning list would curtail its ability to negotiate a suitable broadcast rights deal. The notion that sport organizations could be disadvantaged by the anti-siphoning provisions was also raised by the Sport 2000 Taskforce, when it argued in its review of the Australian sport system at the end of the 1990s that the removal of the anti-siphoning laws would be likely to significantly increase the TV broadcasting revenues of the major sports (Commonwealth of Australia, 1999). Subsequently, in submissions to a Senate Committee investigation into the anti-siphoning provisions, the AFL, National Rugby League (NRL) and National Basketball League (NBL) all claimed that the regulations did not allow sports to maximize the benefits of rights negotiations (Commonwealth of Australia, 2005). By contrast, the Confederation of Australian Motor Sport submission to the ABA suggested that the list served motor sport well, while Tennis Australia wanted to safeguard the free-to-air coverage of the most popular tennis tournaments and matches, but also wanted to enable pay television operators to acquire the rights to lesser events. Sport Industry Australia took the middle ground by recognizing that public interest was served by the anti-siphoning list, but argued for a new system in which sport organizations could negotiate with free-to-air and pay television broadcasters as required.

In 2003 the Australian Competition and Consumer Commission (ACCC) presented a report to government on the impact of emerging market structures on competition in the communications sector. As part of its investigations, the ACCC examined the anti-siphoning provisions, and concluded that:

> potential costs of the current anti-siphoning regime include: possible reduction in the number of sports programs that may be broadcast; less consumer choice for consumers; less competition between FTA and pay TV broadcasters in both acquiring rights and at a retail level; and increased barriers to entry for pay TV operators.
>
> (Australian Competition and Consumer Commission, 2003: 72)

In many respects the ACCC's conclusion mirrored the Australian Productivity Commission's (2000: 444) finding that 'the anti-siphoning rules are anti-competitive and that the costs of the current scheme to sporting organizations, the broadcasting industry and the community as a whole, exceed their benefits' and its subsequent recommendation that 'broadcasters in one form of broadcasting should not be allowed to acquire the broadcast rights of sporting events of major national significance to the exclusion of those in other forms of broadcasting'. In 2003 the ACCC recommended that a dual rights regime be adopted in place of the existing anti-siphoning provisions, but in 2004 the government resolved to extend the existing anti-siphoning regulations, because they best achieved the original intentions of the legislation, which was to ensure free-to-air access to significant sporting events. One of the arguments since 1992 has been that pay television penetration has not been sufficient to justify allowing the potential migration of sporting events, yet in the UK it has been demonstrated, in particular through the example of BSkyB and their acquisition of rights for the English Premier League, that the migration of sport events can be an important driver of pay television take-up. Thus, the rationale and implementation of the Australian regulations have created what is essentially an anti-competitive catch-22 for pay television broadcasters.

Two of the most influential and outspoken actors in the sport broadcasting policy community in Australia are two industry organizations that represent free-to-air commercial television broadcasters (FreeTV, previously the Federation of Australian Commercial Television Stations) and pay television broadcasters (Australian Subscription Television and Radio Association, ASTRA). Both these organizations have been vocal in support of and in opposition to the anti-siphoning regulations respectively, through formal mechanisms such as government and government agency enquiries, as well as informal publicity and promotional campaigns. Both have established websites to advocate their case and encourage the Australian public to contact their local member of Parliament in support of their causes. The information provided by both organizations is essentially contradictory; ASTRA claims that of the 1,300 events on the anti-siphoning list, only 23 per cent are covered live by free-to-air broadcasters, while FreeTV claims that 838 events are actually matches at the Australian Open and Wimbledon tennis tournaments and that free-to-air coverage of the AFL, NRL, cricket and motor sports is substantial.

In short, the anti-siphoning law protects the interests of commercial free-to-air broadcasters through ensuring that sport is available to the Australian population at little cost rather than via pay television. The Australian government has therefore placed pay television operators at a commercial disadvantage. When pay television was introduced to Australia in 1995, free-to-air television networks expressed concerns that pay television would capture the rights to sport and free-to-air television would lose advertising revenue. In 2002 pay television advertising revenue was less than AUS$100 million, while free-to-air advertising exceeded AUS$2,000 million.

Advertising content associated with sport broadcasts

Governments also seek to regulate media content in order to protect their citizens, most commonly referred to as 'the consumers'. Perhaps not surprisingly, governments are most concerned about media content that has the potential to cause harm. For example, the Canadian Television Broadcasting Regulations of 1987 note that a licensee shall not broadcast:

> any abusive comment or abusive pictorial representation that, when taken in context, tends to or is likely to expose an individual or a group or class of individuals to hatred or contempt on the basis of race, national or ethnic origin, colour, religion, sex, sexual orientation, age or mental or physical disability ... nor ... any obscene or profane language or pictorial representation.
>
> (Canada Department of Justice, 1987)

Governments also seek to regulate which types of content are appropriate for broadcast at particular times of the day, with a view to protecting particular segments of the community and children in particular. In many nations governments have applied classification standards that categorize television programmes and films on the basis of their content (most commonly the amount and degree of sex/nudity, violence and profane language). In the case of films, these standards are used to prevent access to people on the basis of their age, while in the case of television they are used by broadcasters to determine when they are able to be broadcast, as well as providing parents with a guide to regulate their children's viewing.

Governments also seek to regulate media content in order to maximize benefits that accrue to citizens or consumers. The Canadian Broadcasting Act of 1991 refers to the purpose of the Canadian broadcasting system:

> [S]afeguard, enrich and strengthen the cultural, political, social and economic fabric of Canada (and) encourage the development of Canadian expression by providing a wide range of programming that reflects Canadian attitudes, opinions, ideas, values and artistic creativity, by displaying Canadian talent in entertainment programming and by offering information and analysis concerning Canada and other countries from a Canadian point of view.
>
> (Canada Department of Justice, 1991)

Similarly, one of the aims of the Australian Broadcasting Act of 1992 (Commonwealth of Australia, 1992) is 'to promote the role of broadcasting services in developing and reflecting a sense of Australian identity, character and cultural diversity' (S3). Local content regulations are the most prominent form of regulation in this context and serve to both enshrine and protect a nation's cultural values. In Canada, public and private broadcasting licensees are required to devote 60 per cent and 50 per cent respectively of evening broadcasts (between 6pm and midnight) annually to Canadian programmes. Similarly, the Australian Content Standard requires 55 per cent Australian content during evening broadcasts on commercial television stations, with specific sub-quotas for Australian children's programmes, documentaries and drama. Being relatively cheap to produce in comparison to other programming genres, sport events are important in assisting broadcasters reach these quotas.

Government regulation of media content as it relates to sport is apparent in both of the categories summarized above: harm mitigation and benefit maximization. Sport organizations tend not be to be involved in the policy communities formed to develop policies and regulation to mitigate harm in the media, and in general the impact of these regulations on sport organizations, although there are important exceptions, is low. On the other hand, in order to maximize social and cultural benefits available to media consumers, broadcasting policies across a range of nations often focus on sport organizations and events. Sport organizations are often heavily involved in the policy communities that coalesce to debate and develop these policies and regulations, although it is clear that they are rarely the most influential.

As previously noted, government regulations designed to minimize the potential harm to consumers through exposure to media content generally have little influence on sport organizations. There are, however, notable exceptions, although it is evident that the regulations are not applied consistently across national jurisdictions. Harm mitigation regulations that have the greatest impact on sport organizations are in the area of prohibitions on tobacco advertising and sponsorship. In this context, government regulation of media content is designed to mitigate the harm that consumers do to themselves by consuming products advertised through the media, rather than consumption of media itself. The content regulations that govern tobacco advertising are akin to content regulations or standards regarding alcohol advertising, but are inherently different to content regulations that govern appropriate levels of sex or violence in the media (despite arguments that exposure to sex and violence might make people more predisposed to sexually deviant or criminal behaviour).

The Australian government effectively banned all tobacco advertising on radio and television in 1976 through amendments to the Broadcasting and Television Act. A further amendment in 1990 made it illegal to advertise tobacco products in newspapers and magazines. One of the unintended consequences of these regulations was that tobacco companies began allocating far more of their promotional budgets to sporting events, leagues and teams, as a way of maximizing their public exposure and circumventing advertising regulations. Rothmans sponsored motor racing, Marlboro sponsored the Australian Open Tennis Championships, Escort sponsored the Victorian Football League, Winfield sponsored Australian Rugby League, while Benson and Hedges secured the marketing rights for international cricket played in Australia (Stewart, Nicholson, Smith and Westerbeek, 2004). In response, the Australian government, through the Tobacco Advertising Prohibition Act of 1992, made it illegal not only for Australian media organizations to broadcast or publish a tobacco advertisement, but also for tobacco companies to sponsor sport. As a result of this legislation, Australia became one of the 'darkest' markets in the world for tobacco manufacturers and one of the first democracies in the world to ban tobacco advertising and sponsorship (Chapman, Byrne and Carter, 2003). The concept of a 'dark market' is a euphemism used by British American Tobacco executives, which refers to the dichotomy between media and no media and restrictive advertising regulations that make it impossible to use standard marketing practices across major media outlets (MacKenzie, Collin and Sriwongcharoen, 2007).

The Australian Tobacco Advertising Prohibition Act allowed existing tobacco sponsorships to run for the duration of their contract, which meant that most tobacco sponsorship of sport in Australia was eliminated by the end of the 1990s. The impact of the Tobacco Advertising Prohibition Act on Australian sport organizations was significant. It was estimated that the value of tobacco sponsorship of sport in the early 1990s was AUS$20 million, which represented approximately 30 per cent of all private sport sponsorship in Australia (Furlong, 1994). However, the Act also contained provision for sporting or cultural events of international significance to be granted an exemption if it was likely that the event would not be held if an exemption was not granted. Most notably, Australia's round of the Formula One Grand Prix was granted an exemption until 2006 on the grounds that a ban would have meant the event would not have continued, such was the importance of tobacco sponsorship to Formula One.

As a result of the Tobacco Advertising Prohibition Act of 1992, Australia was regarded as being in the vanguard of tobacco advertising regulators. In many respects this was a result of its stance on sport sponsorship. Of all the national tobacco advertising regulations introduced throughout the world in the 1990s, very few banned tobacco sponsorship of sport. As a result, in many developed countries with highly commercialized sport systems, tobacco companies focused their promotional activities on sport and sport organizations subsequently benefitted from artificially inflated sponsorship revenues. For example, the advertising of tobacco products in Canada was banned under the Tobacco Products Control Act of 1988, but the tobacco sponsorship of sport was allowed until 2003. However, the Canadian ban on tobacco sponsorship of sport contained no provision for exemptions, meaning that it could be argued that the Canadian government's regulations were even stronger than Australia's. As a result of the 2003 regulations, the Canadian round was dropped from the international Formula One Grand Prix circuit in 2004. This decision was consistent with Formula One's role in lobbying against tobacco advertising controls and negotiating exemptions from national laws and prohibitions.

In Europe, a directive banning tobacco advertising and sponsorship was first proposed in 1989; it was adopted in 1998, before being annulled in 2000. A subsequent European Commission directive was proposed in 2001, which eventually took effect in 2005. Neuman, Bitton and Glantz (2002) have argued that the significant delay between the initial proposal and adoption, as well as the annulment, were due in large part to the sustained lobbying and strategic tactics of tobacco companies such as Phillip Morris and British American Tobacco. They identified that one of the strategic tactics employed by the tobacco companies was establishing alliances with groups that represented industries throughout Europe, including Formula One Racing, a sport organization that benefitted substantially from tobacco advertising. Corporate documents obtained by Neuman *et al.* (2002: 1328) revealed that Phillip Morris established a programme in the early 1990s to strengthen relations with the then 300 Formula One journalists, 'in order to sensitize them to the issue and make them react against the proposals of restrictive legislation'. Neuman *et al.* (2002) did not analyse the relative successes of the variety of tactics employed; however, it is clear that sport organizations such as Formula One played a relatively minor role in what was a very large policy community, particularly when compared to other actors such as national governments, the World Health Organization, the World Bank, major national and regional health agencies, tobacco companies, media organizations and (what became) the European Union.

Sport organizations might rarely be influential actors in the policy communities that develop regulations that determine whether and how tobacco products can be advertised, but there are examples where sport has been deliberately used to subvert government regulations and been drawn into the policy community by default. In these instances sport's significant media coverage, as well as its existence as a product in its own right (that can be sponsored and named), result in the role of sport and sport organizations being highly ambiguous. The use of sport sponsorship by tobacco corporations in Thailand is a good example of sport's ambiguity in terms of media regulation, as well as the often unintended consequences of government regulations. In 1992, the same year in which Australia adopted its Tobacco Advertising Prohibition Act, Thailand enacted legislation that comprehensively banned tobacco advertising. According to MacKenzie *et al.* (2007), transnational tobacco corporations attempted to undermine the regulations because they considered Thailand an important growth market and feared it would become a regional model of tobacco control. One of the primary ways in which the tobacco corporations attempted to do this was through sport sponsorship. Through their analysis of British American Tobacco's internal corporate documents, MacKenzie *et al.* (2007) argued that the company sponsored regional sport teams and events in order to exploit what was considered a loop-hole in the government regulations (which primarily dealt with national media), as well as attempted to influence the way in which the events and competitions were covered in the media (in order to safeguard their investment). One of the unintended consequences of the Thai legislation was that sport teams and events, particularly in motorsport, received additional financial and political support that would not have been expected or warranted, which in turn raised issues of equity and morality. Unfortunately, sport organizations are often no more than pawns in a larger battle between health regulators and tobacco corporations, and arguably will continue to be so as long as they accept tobacco sponsorship.

Although in many instances tobacco advertising regulations throughout the world have resulted in an ambiguous role for sport, broadcasting standards regulation and its relationship to sport are even less well defined. For example, the Hong Kong Broadcasting Authority's (2007) code of practice for television broadcasting contains guidelines for various types of content. The code of practice notes that real-life violence takes many forms, including physical violence in which blows are exchanged and that 'the depiction of violence on television should be handled with extreme care by the licensee' and that 'the degree and type of violence and the detail which can be shown depend upon context and the service on which it is shown' (Hong Kong Broadcasting Authority, 2007: 18). The vast majority of the violence section of the code of practice appears to regulate the dramatic representation of violence in television broadcasting, rather than violence in other areas of television programming. While it might be assumed that sport is a 'context' in which violence is deemed acceptable, the degree and type of violence is likely to vary depending on the sport and the individual contest. In this respect, the broadcast of kickboxing or ultimate fighting during hours when children are likely to be watching might be considered unacceptable or at very least dubious in light of the code of practice.

Media ownership

The final area of government regulatory intervention in relation to sport and the media is in the area of preventing the vertical integration of the sport and media industries, whereby sport franchises are purchased by broadcast corporations. Hoehn and Lancefield (2003) and later Nicholson (2007) used the case of the UK Competition Commission blocking the takeover by media company British Sky Broadcasting (BSkyB, a News Corporation subsidiary) of the high profile football club Manchester United in the late 1990s to highlight government's concerns of such vertical integration effects on consumers. On 29 October 1998 the British Secretary of State referred the proposed acquisition of football club Manchester United by BSkyB to the United Kingdom Competition Commission (formerly the Monopolies and Mergers Commission). In its final report the Commission noted that BSkyB was:

A vertically integrated broadcaster which buys TV rights, including those for sporting events, makes some of its own programmes, packages programmes from a range of sources into various channels, and distributes and retails these channels to its subscribers using its direct-to-home satellite platform as well as selling them wholesale to other retailers using different distribution platforms.

(Competition Commission, 1999: 3)

At the time of the inquiry, BSkyB was essentially the only provider of premium sports channels on pay television and as a result of the limited number of sports rights available to the market, BSkyB's high market share delivered it an effective monopoly. Any acquisition of Manchester United by BSkyB was therefore likely to enhance its ability to raise prices above competitive levels with impunity. The Commission noted that the influence of the highly successful Manchester United team over other Premier League clubs would lead to excessive influence over other clubs to support the sale of rights to BSkyB. The notion that BSkyB could be both a club owner and a bidder for the broadcast rights was just one of the anti-competitive impacts of the proposed merger that led the Commission to conclude that it should be prohibited. Nicholson (2007) noted that the decision of the Competition Commission to prohibit the purchase of the club by BSkyB was based mainly on the effects on competition between BSkyB and other broadcasters but that it would also lead to undue influence over the football league.

Conclusion

The first of our four questions we have sought to address in this chapter is what are the reasons government has intervened in the relationship between sport and the media through regulatory policy? We conclude that governments have done so to overcome concerns about (1) the potential lack of competition in the marketplace through either sport governing bodies exerting control over the market by collective selling of rights or, alternatively, media organizations enjoying a monopoly through the acquisition of the majority of rights to a particular league or event; (2) the potential loss to consumers of their 'free' access to viewing what are considered significant cultural events; and (3) the potential harm that may come to consumers through their exposure to inappropriate health or behavioural messages associated with sport broadcasts. To effectively combat competition issues governments have developed regulatory measures to restrict the conditions under which broadcast rights can be sold and purchased, the types of events that may be shown exclusively on pay TV, and the advertising of tobacco through many media forms associated with sport.

Our second question focuses on how central sport has been in determining the nature and extent of such regulatory interventions. In relation to policies designed to minimize harm, sport is rarely directly involved and if it is, it is restricted to engaging as an interested lobbyist. In relation to the regulatory policies designed to maximize social and economic benefits, these are usually formed in consultation with sport organizations, although they remain on the margins of the debate as evidenced by the recent Australian reviews of the anti-siphoning list, where certain organizations argued for anti-siphoning to be dropped, or at least to have their events removed from the list, yet the government persisted in maintaining the current list.

The third question we have sought to answer is to identify the variety of regulatory instruments employed by government to achieve their policy objectives. These instruments have focused on the broad issues of competition and content. In terms of the Baldwin and Cave (1999) framework, these have been in two categories: command and control strategies and market harnessing controls. The use of command and control strategies is evidenced by governments seeking to regulate content in order to protect consumers via such things as prohibiting tobacco advertising or sponsorship of sport, as well as seeking to regulate access to free to air sport broadcasts in order to protect consumers (i.e. anti-siphoning provisions that allow consumers access to content), although the supposed benefit is hard to quantify in this instance. Governments have also employed market harnessing controls such as allowing leagues an exemption from competition policy to enable them (in some instances) to act as a cartel and thereby prevent individual clubs auctioning off the rights, or ensuring that sporting leagues offer non-exclusive rights contracts to ensure competition between media organiza-tions and prevent monopolies.

Our final question relates to the impact on sport of these regulatory policies. In simple terms, the listed events regulations mean that some sports are unable to maximize the value of their rights by not being able to auction them off to the highest bidder. As Parrish (2008: 94) concludes:

> Regulation diminishes the value of sports rights and this is a major concern for the govern-ing bodies. Two public interest arguments must be balanced. The first is that of ensuring public access to major sporting events on free-to-air television. The second is allowing sufficient commercial freedom for the governing bodies to attain maximized revenues from rights in order to support re-investment in sport at all levels. Article 3a impacts upon these solidarity mechanisms by limiting the commercial freedom of the governing bodies. Therefore, regulation may potentially have the perverse consequence of penalising active participants at the grassroots of sport in favour of inactive television viewers.

Similar concerns can be expressed for the effect on sport consumers:

> This is reflected in the nature of the regime which affords consumers limited influence on the composition of national lists. It cannot be convincingly argued that the lists reflect actual consumer demand ... [but rather consist of] ... events which are assumed to be of major importance to the public.
>
> (Parrish, 2008: 95)

In other words, at least in relation to regulating the sale of broadcast rights, it can be argued that both sport and sport consumers are worse off than if no such regulations existed. In regard to other regulatory measures, such as restricting advertising of tobacco, the vertical integration of sport and media companies, or the packaging of rights, sports would consider themselves worse off because such regulations diminish the prospective value of their broadcast rights and access to much-needed revenues.

Acknowledgement

A version of this chapter has previously been published in Hoye, R., Nicholson, M. and Houlihan, B. (2010) *Sport and Policy*, Oxford: Elsevier Butterworth-Heinemann, an imprint now owned by Taylor & Francis. This material has been used with permission of Taylor & Francis.

15

LEVERAGING SPORT EVENTS

Fundamentals and application to bids

Laurence Chalip and Bob Heere

There is an emerging paradigm shift in the ways that the public sector has come to think about sport events. Public investment in events needs to be justified by the benefits that those events provide to the host destination. In the past, that has been ascertained with reference to the *impacts* of events. Thus, each event has been treated as a potential economic and/or social stimulus in-and-of itself. The question was, 'What does this event do for us?' The emerging paradigm asks, 'What can we do with the event to optimize the benefits that we seek to obtain?' This question asks how we can leverage an event to best advantage. It invokes a set of strategic planning concerns when building a sport event into the destination's portfolio of services. Events can be leveraged to optimize attainment of economic, social, and/or environmental objectives.

The leveraging paradigm

Economic leverage

The first leveraging model (Chalip, 2004), which derives from work on the Sydney Olympic Games (Brown, Chalip, Jago, and Mules, 2002; Faulkner *et al.*, 2000) and the Gold Coast IndyCar race (Chalip and Leyns, 2002), focused on economic leverage. The model (presented in Figure 15.1) recognizes that the portfolio of events at a host destination is a leverageable resource. In other words, through strategic action, each event provides opportunities to create economic advantage through event visitors and trade, as well as through event media. Further, events can be cross-leveraged so that they create synergies, particularly in marketing the host destination. Specifically, event visitors and event trade provide opportunities to optimize total trade and revenue by enticing visitor spending, lengthening visitor stays, retaining event expenditures, and enhancing business relationships. Event media provide opportunities to showcase the destination via event advertising and reporting, and to use the event in destination advertising and promotions. The original model (Chalip, 2004) details the model's logic, the means to pursue opportunities, and the steps to enable formulation of the requisite strategies and tactics. A more detailed specification of the strategies and tactics for enhancing the host community's image by building its brand through events, particularly event media, is provided by Chalip and Costa (2005).

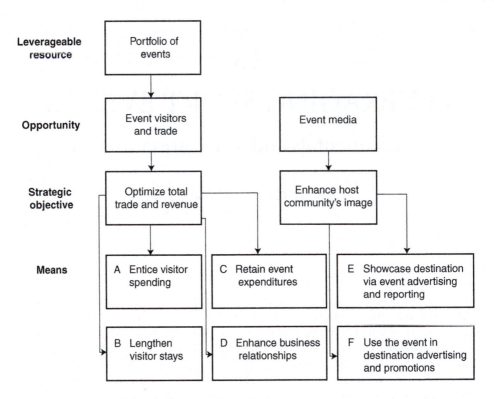

Figure 15.1 Economic leverage of sport events

Source: adapted from Chalip (2004)

The model's logic rests on two established tenets regarding economic returns that events can provide. The first tenet holds that events can build future economic growth by enhancing the destination's overall brand. This is furthered to the degree that event advertising, public relations and broadcasting showcase the destination in combination with the event. Similarly, featuring the event in destination advertising and promotions, even outside the period of the event, can enhance the brand by underscoring associations between the event and its host destination.

The second tenet holds that event visitors from outside the local economy and the trade associated with an event generate new spending in the local economy, which is how events render an immediate and tangible economic effect. To optimize that revenue, visitors can be enticed through promotions to spend more (e.g. for souvenirs, dining, tourism). If they lengthen their stays to include pre-event or post-event tourism, then their total spend will also be enhanced. Of course, spending associated with an event only has an effect on the local economy if it is retained, so it becomes essential to use local suppliers and local labour wherever possible. Finally, if new relationships can be forged between local business people and visiting business executives during the event, then new trade can be obtained.

Empirical research into economic leverage is still in its infancy, although leverage is clearly becoming a generative paradigm. Early research demonstrated that event organizers and local government officials may make strong claims and have strong ambitions about the economic outcomes for the events they host, but do little planning to attain those outcomes (Bramwell, 1997). Subsequent work (Chalip and Leyns, 2002) demonstrated that businesses may also fail to leverage, thereby obtaining little benefit from an event. They can even be hurt by an event if it deflects or sidetracks regular customers. However, that same research demonstrated substantial benefits for businesses that do seek to leverage, and it found particularly strong benefits for businesses that form local alliances to enable precinct-wide leveraging tactics. Research comparing the leveraging initiatives employed by Australian cities hosting acclimatization training for visiting national teams prior to the Olympic Games also demonstrated that the greater the level of strategic leverage, the greater the benefits obtained (O'Brien and Gardiner, 2006). In short, although economic leverage is rarely observed, it can be effective when it takes place. O'Brien (2007) showed that this can apply as much to small local events as it does to hallmark or mega events.

Further work has explored the potentials and outcomes of economic leverage. Much of that work has had an avowedly marketing orientation. The work has demonstrated that many (but not all) event attendees do want to combine attendance at a sport event with tourism activities, particularly following the event (Chalip and McGuirty, 2004). This is especially true for first-time visitors (Snelgrove and Wood, 2010), but it requires that they be enabled and encouraged to seek information about the host destination while planning their trip (Taks, Chalip, Green, Késenne, and Martyn, 2009). In other words, in order to enhance visitor spending at an event, it is essential that tourism opportunities be promoted in source markets long before the event, possibly including offers for bundles that combine tourism and event attendance in a manner that appeals to the unique psychographics of event tourists.

It appears that tourism marketing to event visitors may need to be somewhat different than marketing to other leisure tourists. The economic benefits from an event derive from the spending of event tourists, and are optimized when event tourists engage in tourism beyond the event. However, tourism marketers have typically endeavoured to market to event tourists in the same ways they market to other leisure tourists. The problem is that sport event attendees may be less interested in normal tourism icons than in activities that are consistent with the sport subculture that initially attracted them to the event (Chalip and McGuirty, 2004), particularly if the activities allow them to celebrate, strengthen, or parade their involvements with the sport subculture (Green and Chalip, 1998; Snelgrove, Taks, Chalip, and Green, 2008). There is also evidence that first-time visitors who have engaged in long-haul travel to attend an event may be more interested in tourism activities through which they might learn about the local culture than in the kinds of pilgrimages to tourist icons that are typically marketed to leisure tourists (Kim and Chalip, 2004). These findings may explain why tourism marketers often complain that they are unsuccessful when marketing touristic activities to sport event visitors.

Sport events are also expected to generate sufficient media to enhance the host destination's tourism brand, even among those who do not attend the event (Chalip, 2005). Thus, sport events should ideally be integrated into an overall marketing communications plan that fosters interest in the destination among potential tourists. By stimulating tourism through an effect on the destination brand, events would be expected to render an indirect economic benefit. Early work demonstrated that sport event marketers and destination marketers often do seek to find ways to use events to build the host destination brand (Jago, Chalip, Brown, Mules, and Ali, 2003), but that is by no means universal (Misener and Mason, 2009). Further, effective use of events for destination branding can be compromised by the failure of sport managers, event organizers, and destination marketers to work together productively (if at all) because they function in independent spheres and lack shared frames of reference (Weed, 2003). As a result, the marketing value of events for the host destination is reduced (Chalip, 2005). Indeed, events can have negative (as well as positive) effects on the host destination brand (Chalip, Green, and Hill, 2003; Green, Lim, Seo, and Sung, 2010; Xing and Chalip, 2006). This is because host destination imagery and mentions are incidental elements of event media, which become paired in haphazard ways with event occurrences.

Nevertheless, the interest and visitation that an effectively marketed event generates can render business opportunities. Events are poor places to do business (except business that has to do directly with running the event), but they can be effective places for building business relationships. O'Brien (2006) studied the ways that Australian business development strategists capitalized on the Sydney Olympic Games to foster new opportunities for Australian businesses. The plan required two elements. First, it was necessary for those who sought to use the Sydney Olympic Games for business development to generate public and private sector support and partnerships to enable formulation and implementation of a strategic plan. Second, it was necessary to identify or construct opportunities through which to capitalize on the Olympics (before, during, and after the Games) to create business networking and to nurture overseas relationships for Australian businesses. There had been no similar attempt previously, so the planners operated primarily on intuition. Although the strategy did not yield all the hoped for outcomes, it was sufficiently effective that the Australian government has continued the initiative through other events. They have even capitalized on Australian teams competing internationally to extend the effort to events outside Australia.

The potentials for obtaining new business through events, even when not the host destination, have also been of interest. There are demonstrable opportunities for non-host destinations to benefit from events, particularly by hosting visiting teams for acclimatization training. However, hosting visiting teams brings little economic benefit unless the host destination formulates and implements a strategic leveraging plan that enables new business relationships to be formed between local businesses and businesses from the countries represented by teams or athletes undergoing acclimatization training (O'Brien and Gardiner, 2006).

Findings to date demonstrate that the economic leverage of events requires substantial strategic planning and monitoring. There is a great deal still to be learned. Among the significant research questions are these:

- How can the necessary alliances among businesses, across industries, and between sectors be formed and sustained locally to enable effective economic leverage of sport events?
- How should sport events best be synergized with the total product and service mix at the host destination to foster tourism by event attendees, particularly before and after an event?
- What are the most effective means for capitalizing on sport events to build the host destination's brand?
- What are the most efficient and effective means to enable and encourage information seeking about the host destination from prospective event attendees?
- What strategies and tactics best enable local businesses to utilize sport events to identify and build relationships with potential business partners?
- How can events in the event portfolio be cross-leveraged?

Social leverage

Communities often seek to use events for purposes of social development, as well as for economic development (Jago *et al.*, 2003; Misener and Mason, 2009). Chalip (2006) developed a model for social leverage of sport events, which was subsequently given further elaboration, and integrated into a more general framework for which environmental leverage was identified as a special instance of social leverage (O'Brien and Chalip, 2008). The resulting model (presented in Figure 15.2) recognizes the liminality generated by a sport event as the core leverageable resource. Liminality is a feeling of celebration and the accompanying sense that social rules and social roles are relaxed or possibly even suspended. Liminality has been widely demonstrated and much studied by anthropologists. They view it as the heart of events' capacity for social effect (Handelman, 1990). When events create a liminoid space, they enable exploration of social possibilities that might seem threatening if tested outside the liminoid frame. Liminality can enable new social conditions to become attainable.

When an event creates a liminoid frame, there are two outcomes that engender opportunities for social leverage. The first is the feeling that new energy is flowing through the communal atmosphere. The sense of community among those enjoying the event is consequently elevated. Anthropologists call this '*communitas*'. The second outcome is the content and volume of media that are generated. Celebrations and consequent liminality enable media presentations that identify and can even explore social conditions in ways that might be less well received outside the liminoid frame of events. Together, these provide opportunities to align the event with targeted social issues, to do so with reference to the target sport subcultures, to entice engagement with targeted social issues, to enhance social interactions by lengthening visitor stays, to showcase social issues via event advertising and reporting, and to use the event to publicize target issues.

The original model (Chalip, 2006) draws from the anthropological literature to identify means to engender liminality and *communitas*. That model describes the steps necessary to elevate a sense of celebration and to cultivate social interaction among event attendees. Theming and the inclusion of ancillary events can elevate celebration. Creation of spaces and opportunities (both formal and informal) to socialize with other event attendees can cultivate socialization. Purposefully designing these into events needs to be at the core of event planning if social leverage is to be enabled.

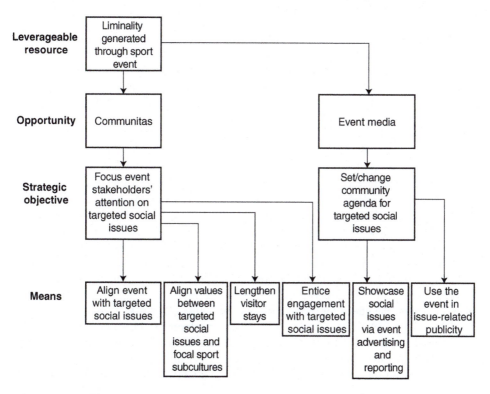

Figure 15.2 Social leverage of sport events

Source: adapted from O'Brien and Chalip (2008)

Surprisingly, the vast majority of research on social leverage does not derive from a social leveraging model – perhaps because matters of liminality and *communitas* have remained the provenance of anthropologists, and have otherwise been conspicuous by their absence from mainstream literatures on event management and marketing. There is substantial work on cause marketing (aka: cause-related marketing) through which sport events form partnerships with a cause. However, research about cause marketing typically examines its effects on consumer attitudes or intentions with reference to the event and/or its sponsor, rather than in terms of any effects it may have for the cause. One apparent exception is a study of charity sport event attendees which found that an association between an event and a cause could enhance the sense of camaraderie at the event, which might then be used to enable social change in those communities (Filo, Funk, and O'Brien, 2009).

The work on sport for development is another venue in which studies have sought to show that sport (including but not limited to sport events) might be useful for nurturing social development. There are a number of organizations that now seek to use sport for development. None yet uses a clearly articulated strategic model for leveraging sport to achieve its aims, and sport for development programmes have not been subjected to rigorous evaluation (Coalter, 2010).

Of course, the social leverage model presupposes that leverage is both feasible and effective. That presupposition has been tested. Smith, A. (2010) studied the initiatives pursued by Deptford in southeast London (UK) to foster social development through the 2007 Tour de France. He concluded that multiple strategic initiatives involving multiple stakeholders could facilitate achievement of urban development objectives. Kellett, Hede, and Chalip (2008) compared the ways that two communities neighbouring Melbourne, when it was host city for the Commonwealth Games, made use of opportunities to engage with visiting teams before and during the Games for the social benefit of their communities. One city engaged in substantial strategic planning in the years leading up to the Commonwealth Games, and successfully obtained new relationships, cultural insights, and improved organizational networks. The other city had no strategic vision for engaging with visiting teams, and consequently obtained no social benefit. These studies clearly demonstrate that social leverage is feasible, and that it can be effective.

In the only direct test of the social leverage model, Ziakas and Costa (2010) studied a recurring event in a small Texas town, and examined the ways that liminality and *communitas* were produced. They showed that event organizers combine sport and the arts to celebrate local heritage and to engender a shared sense of community among all who attend. They found that undercurrents of discord that might otherwise disrupt the community could be explored symbolically and resolved during the event, and they argue that the event consequently strengthens the community's social fabric. They note that the event is so meaningful to those who attend that it attracts the majority of town residents, as well as former residents who thereby re-establish their social ties to the community and to one another. Ziakas and Costa contend that this level of social value has evolved over time through effective strategic planning.

Social leverage of sport events requires a great deal more research. To date, research has either focused on the effects for sport or its sponsors, rather than for the community, or it has proceeded without reference to a general model of social leverage. There are clearly important questions to be addressed having to do with the creation and use of liminality and *communitas*, particularly for purposes of social development or social change – as anthropologists have recognized for some time (Handelman, 1990). Ziakas and Costa's (2010) finding that sport and the arts can be blended effectively to achieve social objectives recommends further research, particularly since other work demonstrates that sport event organizers can be ineffectual when mingling the arts with sport (García, 2001). The means to create synergy between social and economic leverage also require further study. Finally, although O'Brien and Chalip (2008) suggest that environmental leverage is simply a special application of social leverage, processes and potentials for environmental leverage need further exploration.

Coordinating leverage

In order for leverage to proceed, the relevant stakeholders must be coordinated. That requirement emerges consistently as a key variable differentiating successful from unsuccessful leverage (Chalip and Leyns, 2002; Jago *et al.*, 2003; Kellett *et al.*, 2008; O'Brien and Gardiner, 2006; Smith, A. 2010). The challenge is exacerbated by the difficulties that organizations often have when working across industries or economic sectors (Bramwell, 1997; García, 2001; Weed, 2003). Event organizers are typically too busy staging their event to be tasked with formulating and implementing leverage, although they clearly need to support leveraging efforts. Yet there is no single entity for which event leverage is necessarily a natural assignment.

Past successes have resulted from the strategic vision of local business alliances (Chalip and Leyns, 2002), the creation of ad hoc organizations responsible for leverage (Faulkner *et al.*, 2000; O'Brien and Gardiner, 2006), the strategic vision of particular public servants who push their vision through their particular agencies (O'Brien, 2006), or a combination of these (O'Brien, 2007; Kellett *et al.*, 2008). The fact remains that coordinated strategic leverage of sport events is much more the exception than the rule, despite a great deal of rhetoric from event promoters to the contrary. It occurs when there is entrepreneurial vision somewhere in the system, and when conditions enable that vision to be realized. If strategic leverage of sport events is to become more commonplace, then more systematic organization to enable leverage is essential (Misener and Mason, 2009). Further research is necessary to establish the necessary and sufficient conditions to foster the requisite structures to enable consistent and effective leverage.

Event leverage is grounded in a logic that distinguishes it from legacy planning

Sport events – particularly mega sport events – often fail to yield the benefits claimed for them (Burbank, Andranovich, and Heying, 2001; Cashman, 2006), leave facilities that are unneeded and possibly unsustainable (Kissoudi, 2008; Searle, 2002), or simply function as an income transfer from one social class or one business group to another (Putsis, 1998; Terret, 2008). The disappointments associated with events have generated a great deal of interest in post-event legacies – that is, the tangible benefits that a sport event might leave behind. The core insight is that events should be planned and implemented in a manner that will render positive legacies.

Stimulated in particular by the International Olympic Committee's project entitled 'Olympic Games Global Impact', which was launched in 2000, there has been a flurry of interest in the nature and means for improving event legacies. As a result, several models have been forthcoming that suggest ways for event organizers – typically with help from government – to design and implement mega events in a manner conducive to positive legacies (e.g. Girginov and Hills, 2009; Kaplanidou and Karadakis, 2010). The most comprehensive model (Gratton and Preuss, 2008) argues that legacies should be considered with reference to those that are planned and unplanned, tangible and intangible, and negative as well as positive. It suggests that compulsory and optional measures intended to create legacy should be imposed on cities that bid for events. It argues that event infrastructure, knowledge, image, emotions, network, and culture represent opportunities to enhance tourism, business development (including attracting or creating new industry), hosting future events (including conventions and trade fairs), and the quality of local life.

It is particularly noteworthy that the discourse concerning legacy is couched in a rhetoric that focuses on event organization and on the franchisor/franchisee relationships that characterize relationships between mega event owners and candidate host cities (MacAloon, 2008). In other words, the focus is on event organizing committees and event components, with particular reference to mega events (typically the Olympic Games). Although organizing committees and event components certainly matter when leveraging, models for strategic leverage of sport events do not put the onus on event organization, reify franchisor/franchisee relationships, or limit themselves to mega events. Rather, event leveraging models focus on strategic planning for which events become added resources in the host destination's entire product and service mix. Consequently, strategic goals are pursued by synergizing each event (and the destination's portfolio of events) with the array of products and services that the host destination can offer.

Extending leverage to event bidding

One limitation of leveraging (and legacy) models is that they focus on ways to optimize event outcomes given that a particular event will occur. Yet, event organizing begins before there is any assurance that the event will take place. For mega events, the process begins with the bid.

It can be quite expensive to bid for a mega event (GB Editor, 2010; Kelly, 2010; Kelso, 2011), but there is no guarantee of winning. Consider, for example, that Sochi spent US$27.5 million to win hosting rights for the 2014 Winter Olympic Games, while PyongChang spent US$21 million and Salzberg spent US$8.5 million in their losing bids. These costs were up from the previous round of bids, wherein Vancouver spent US$21.5 million to win rights to the 2010 Winter Olympic Games, while Salzberg spent US$6.5 million and PyongChang spent US$2.4 million on their losing bids.

The numbers are even more substantial for the Summer Olympic Games and the FIFA World Cup. London spent US$48 million to win rights to the 2012 Olympic Games, while Madrid, Moscow, New York, and Paris each spent almost US$25 million in their failed bids. Similarly, Russia spent over US$30 million to win the right to host the 2018 FIFA World Cup, outclassing three other bids ranging from approximately US$10 million to US$24 million. Estimates of Qatar's costs to win rights to the 2022 World Cup put the amount well in excess of US$80 million.

There has been substantial research purporting to ascertain the necessary characteristics for winning bids (e.g. Emery, 2002; Ingerson and Westerbeek, 2000; Persson, 2002), such as overall quality of the event as proposed, quality of the bid committee, and public support. However, bid expenditure data suggest that winning bids are typically those with the highest total spend. In other words, spending more seems to grant the illusion of superior quality and support. As a result, it has become incredibly expensive to bid for a mega event, and bid costs continue to rise – even for losing bidders.

The derivative question is whether bids to host mega sport events might be leveraged in a manner analogous to the ways that events can be leveraged. There is tantalizing evidence that bidding can be beneficial under the right circumstances. Alberts (2009) claims that Berlin's failed bid to host the 2000 Olympic Games stimulated an array of development initiatives that ultimately complemented the city's overall development. Beneworth and Dauncey (2010) argue that Lyon's failed bid to host the 1968 Summer Olympic Games helped Lyon to advance proposals establishing its significant role in European political and spatial planning. These studies suggest that a failed bid can advance political and planning agendas, but the studies do not demonstrate that those outcomes are unambiguously positive.

Recent economic modelling (Rose and Spiegel, 2009) demonstrates that bidding for a mega event, such as the Olympic Games, can boost trade, even if the bid fails. Further, the boost in trade is as high if the bid is lost as it is when the bid is won. This result is attributed to the signalling effect of mega event bids such that the mere fact of bidding indicates upcoming social, political, and/or economic liberalization. If that is the basis for the trade effect, then the value of losing bids will be higher for developing nations than for developed economies in democratic societies.

Taken as a whole, the three studies examining failed bids demonstrate that bidding for a mega event can generate potentially leverageable opportunities. Those opportunities are the media attention, networking and relationship building, and consequent learning that are elicited by a mega event bid. Drawing on studies of event leverage, it is clear that each opportunity can support pursuit of several strategic objectives, each of which can be pursued using multiple tactics. The consequent model is provided in Figure 15.3. The model is avowedly hypothetical; it is presented here to stimulate future research, ideally as action research wherein efforts to apply the model are evaluated and lessons are drawn and shared.

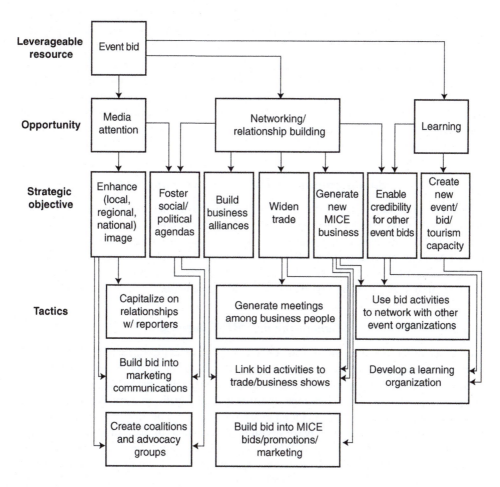

Figure 15.3 Bid leverage

Capitalizing on media attention

International media follow the bidding for mega events with substantial interest. For example, a simple LexisNexis search by the authors on recent media uses of the phrase 'Olympic bid' generated over 1,000 hits, as did a similar search on the phrase 'World Cup bid'. Media attention can be used to enhance the local, regional, or national image. This can be furthered if standard marketing and public relations tactics are applied. Reporters who are covering a bid require backgrounders and sidebars that add local colour to their coverage. By helping them to identify and research such stories, the bid destination can enhance its overall brand. Similarly, promotions for the host city can enhance the image by (sometimes) highlighting the fact that the city is a candidate to host the event for which it is bidding. Coalitions and advocacy groups that come together to support the bid can also become channels through which to communicate favourable images of the host city both nationally and internationally.

Fostering social/political agendas

Research on failed bids (Alberts, 2009; Beneworth and Dauncey, 2010) demonstrates that bids for mega sport events stimulate a great deal of enthusiasm, media, and social networking which then undergird planning and development. Although this effect could readily be misused to support the political agendas of elites in a manner that is not in the best interests of local citizenry (Whitson and Macintosh, 1996), it could also be put to positive use. Bids clearly have effects on local, regional, and national politics. Once bidding is under way, the best means to assure that media, social networking, and public enthusiasm are directed to ends that serve the public interest is to bring uses of the bid into public strategic planning processes. Coalitions and advocacy groups are one useful tool.

Building business alliances and widening trade

Coalitions and advocacy groups can also bring businesses together. Similarly, business leaders' interests in the ways that an event might foster business opportunities can provide the necessary stimulus to bring business people together for joint strategic planning. Trade shows and business conventions provide another opportunity for business people to capitalize on interest in the destination that has been furthered by a bid. Each of these tactics can provide a platform for building business alliances and negotiating new trade agreements.

Generating new MICE business

'MICE' stands for meetings, incentives, conventions, and exhibitions. Each of these is another kind of event that can generate economic returns (Boo and Kim, 2010). A city's claim that it is capable of hosting a mega sport event also communicates that the city can successfully host large meetings, conventions, and exhibitions, and that it is potentially an attractive destination for incentive travel. Consequently, a bid for a mega sport event can be used to enhance the attractiveness of the city to those who make decisions about where to place their MICE business. This can be used in bids to host MICE business, and when networking with decision makers at trade shows. Further, since bid city representatives must travel and meet decision makers, it is not uncommon for them to interact with those who make decisions about MICE business for their companies or for associations in which they are members. Those interactions provide additional opportunities to promote the bid city as a MICE destination.

Building capacity and enabling credibility for other event bids

It is popularly claimed that Manchester's losing bids to host the 1996 and 2000 Olympic Games created the expertise, relationships, and credibility that enabled the city to bid successfully to host the 2002 Commonwealth Games. Indeed, it is a commonly held view among bid cities and bid organizations that bidding is a skill that is learned, and that bidding for one event creates relationships with elites that can support bids for other events. Learning and networking with other event organizations therefore become potentially useful tools for leveraging.

The future of event leverage

Public servants are under increasing pressure from businesses and citizen groups to cultivate benefits from sport events. At the same time, event owners and event organizers are legitimately concerned that public support for their events will become eroded if event costs are not compensated by sufficient aggregate economic and social gain. Although business leaders, local residents, public officials, event owners, and event organizers operate under disparate contingencies, and may consequently have different perspectives, each is being compelled to recognize that a sport event must have value beyond mere entertainment if it is to be sustained. It is a matter of practical accountability. If there are public expenditures to seek or host sport events, then there must be sufficient public returns on those expenditures. Although planning and implementation of sport event leverage require investment of time and creative energy, the investment is worthwhile when it enhances the economic and social benefits that an event or an event bid provides.

PART III

Elite sports policies

16

METHODOLOGIES FOR IDENTIFYING AND COMPARING SUCCESS FACTORS IN ELITE SPORT POLICIES

Veerle de Bosscher, Maarten van Bottenburg and Simon Shibli

This chapter outlines the methods explored as part of a large-scale project called the SPLISS study, which is an acronym for sports policy factors leading to international sporting success. This study aimed to improve the development of theory concerned with key success factors of an elite sport policy as well as the methods employed to compare elite sport policies more objectively and less descriptively (De Bosscher, 2007; De Bosscher, De Knop, Van Bottenburg, Shibli, and Bingham, 2009). To reach this aim, the SPLISS study mirrored the economic literature, where the measurement of world competitiveness is routinely used to provide a framework to assess how nations manage their economic future (e.g. Depperu and Cerrato, 2008; Garelli, 2008; Porter, 1990). This approach was replicated in an elite sport setting to assess how nations manage their future success in international sport competition (De Bosscher, Shibli, Van Bottenburg, De Knop, and Truyens, 2010), in an international comparison with six nations (extended in 2012 to a new study involving 15 nations). In this regard, the study was inspired by the way in which economic competitiveness is measured quantitatively as 'the determinants of productivity' and thus it explored the development of a scoring system to analyse and compare elite sport policies of nations as they relate to international sporting success. As competitiveness inherently refers to the relative position of an organisation *vis-à-vis* its competitors (Önsel *et al.*, 2008), international comparisons are the only way to identify and compare the SPLISS. Elite sport is therefore seen as 'international by definition' (Van Bottenburg, 2000), and an international comparison of a theoretical framework was done in order to improve the development of theory and methodology. Special attention is paid in this chapter to how mixed methods research has made a valuable and suitable contribution to the study and to the evaluation of policies in general and elite sport policies in particular.

Background and problem definition of the SPLISS study

The key research question of the SPLISS study was to define the relationship between elite sport policies (inputs and throughputs) and international sporting success (outputs). This research question refers to a causal analysis identifying *cause* (elite sport policies), and *effect* (international success). Many authors (e.g. Russo and Williamson, 2007; Shadish, Cook, and Campbell, 2002) have pointed out that cause and effect relationships can be very complex (Rudd and Johnson,

2010). As a consequence researchers believe that causal relationships cannot be fully known because we do not operate in a closed system (House, 1991).

In elite sport studies correlations and other statistical techniques are often used in large sample size studies to analyse the influence of macro-level factors (of which population size and wealth are identified as the most important), on international sporting success, especially with regard to the Olympic Games. These factors do not explain causal relationships directly (for example through elite sport spending, infrastructure, number of talents and athletes, etc.). While these macro-factors can be easily measured and explain more than 50 per cent of international sporting success (e.g. Bernard and Busse, 2004; De Bosscher, De Knop, and Heyndels, 2003), these factors cannot be influenced in the short term, for instance by national authorities. According to Houlihan, Bloyce, and Smith (2009) the decline in macro-level theorising of the policy process is a welcome correction to the over-simplification of complex social processes that has frequently accompanied analysis, the inflated generalisations that were generated and the all-too-easy dismissal of counter-factual cases. A gap in the literature emerges when it comes to explaining the meso-level factors of sporting success, namely the level of sports policies. These factors are the focus of the SPLISS study, to determine the sport policy factors leading to international sporting success (De Bosscher, 2007; De Bosscher, Bingham, Shibli, Van Bottenburg, and De Knop, 2008). Here, statistical relationships are more complicated and theory development is still at an early stage. This latter in particular is related to the complexity of international comparative studies (e.g. Dacosta and Miragaya, 2002; Henry, Amara, Al-Tauqi, and Lee, 2005; Porter, 1990). In sport the issue is even more complex because sports systems are closely enmeshed with the culture of a nation and therefore each system is unique. Cultural factors shape the environment surrounding sports: they are integrated with the determinants and not isolated from them. Such factors change only gradually and are difficult for outsiders to replicate (Porter, 1990). Furthermore (elite) sport development is dominated to a large degree by a nation's political system. Politics determines policies (Houlihan, 1997; Houlihan and Green, 2008). These are all extraneous and uncontrollable factors that make comparability problematic. Accordingly, much discussion exists about the suitability of nations as units to be compared (De Bosscher, 2007). Moreover, there appears to be a lack of standardisation of methods used for comparative research, as well as limited publicly available and quantifiable data on sport policies (Henry *et al.*, 2005). As a result, there is not very much research on comparative sports studies in the public domain, other than those that are primarily descriptive and that either have non-comparable data from different nations, or use qualitative methods to examine general trends and similarities among nations. Bergsgard, Houlihan, Mangset, Nødland and Rommetveldt (2007) observed that many international comparative studies fail to establish analytical relationships between variables. Many comparative sport policy studies, such as the Advocacy Coalition Framework (Sabatier and Jenkins-Smith, 1993) used by Green and Houlihan (2005b) to compare elite sport policies in three nations, are more associated with qualitative issues and examining statistical relationships is not the purpose of such studies. As in general comparative public policy studies, they are mainly concerned with: 'what governments do, why they do it and what difference it makes' (Wolf, 2010). As Houlihan *et al.* (2009) state, there is also need for the development of robust, evidence-based empirical research on the impact of sport policy. While it may be unrealistic to provide a complete solution to this problem, the SPLISS study attempts to close this gap.

In this chapter we highlight the use of *mixed methods research* as a potential solution for reducing problems relating to the comparability of international data and the objective evaluation and measurement of policies in general and of elite sport policies in particular. While there has now been a trend towards triangulation and mixing methods in comparative public policy research, after a considerable period of qualitative–quantitative confrontation (Wolf, 2010), this is not yet the case in international comparative (elite) sport policy research, nor in sport management research. The use of numbers in qualitative research is controversial (Maxwell, 2010) and relatively few sport policy researchers have used numerical data in their work for both pragmatic and philosophical reasons. Rudd and Johnson (2010) also point out that where mixed methods research has been applied in sport management, research designs are not fully developed and involve only limited or weak use of the methods; for example, simply involving a questionnaire with open and closed questions.

By illustrating the different steps used in the SPLISS study we will reflect on what value mixed methods research has added or not added (or not yet added) to answer our research questions, as well as discussing how the use of mixed methods research extends the current methodologies in our field.

Mixed methods research design used in the SPLISS study

Mixed methods have been embraced by a growing list of academic areas, including psychology, social work, nursery, medicine, health sciences, management, organisational studies, evaluation and education (Creswell, 2009; Tashakkori and Teddlie, 2003). Despite this broad acceptance of the technique, mixed methods have not yet been fully explored as a means to reduce problems related to (in)comparability in international comparative policy research. Researchers have been mixing qualitative and quantitative approaches for decades, but to put both forms of data together as a distinct research design is relatively new (Creswell and Plano Clark, 2007; Tashakkori and Teddlie, 1998). Design classification systems such as defined by Cresswell and Plano Clark (2007) that outline the procedures and variants of four major mixed methods designs were considered to be very useful tools in assisting the design selection process of the SPLISS study. Nonetheless, as indicated by Vrkljan (2009), determining which design to use can be a daunting process. In the SPLISS project different design types were blended: a *concurrent triangulation* design (data transformation model, Creswell and Plano Clark, 2007, p. 63) was embedded as an intermediate step in a *sequential exploratory design:* a (mainly) qualitative phase followed by a mixed quantitative and qualitative phase (see Figure 16.1). This means that:

- In phase 1, a conceptual model was developed on the sport policy factors leading to international sporting success (SPLISS), because of an identified gap in the literature and the lack of an empirically grounded theory on the factors that determine international sport success. The study is *exploratory* because of the premise that 'an initial qualitative exploration is needed for the reason that measures or instruments are not available, there is no guiding framework or theory and the variables are unknown' (Creswell and Plano Clark, 2007, p. 75).
- In phase 2, this conceptual framework was tested in an empirical environment by comparing it in six nations. The aim of this stage was to improve construct, criterion and content validity of the conceptual model. This stage consisted of obtaining *concurrent* qualitative and quantitative data on the elite sport policies of the sample nations. Subsequently, mirroring economic competitiveness studies, the data were translated into a quantitative scoring system. At all of the data collection, data analysis and interpretation stages, qualitative and quantitative methods were mixed.

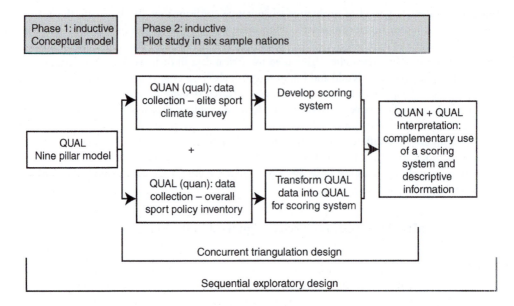

Figure 16.1 Summary of the mixed research methods design used in the SPLISS study

Source: adapted from De Bosscher *et al.* (2010)

A third phase is planned in future research: a deductive method to validate the theory; using factor or cluster analysis to validate the subscales; reliability analysis to assess the internal consistency; and correlations to discover possible causes and effects. These phases will be outlined in more depth in the next part.

Phase 1: development of a conceptual model on the sports policy factors leading to international sporting success

The development of the SPLISS model was based on mainly three kinds of sources, related to the aim of increasing validity: face validity, content validity, construct validity, criterion validity (see De Bosscher *et al.*, 2010 for more information):

1   a comprehensive body of literature on sport systems and policy analysis. This literature was supplemented by studies at the micro level, which attempted to understand the determinants of success for individual athletes rather than nations (De Bosscher, De Knop, Van Bottenburg, and Shibli, 2006);
2   a survey with international coaches from 22 nations to approach key success drivers from an expert perspective;
3   a survey with 114 Flemish (i.e. the northern, Dutch speaking part of Belgium) elite athletes, 99 coaches and 26 performance directors to approach key success drivers from a consumer perspective.

These latter surveys used simple open-ended questions to identify the external factors that make the most significant contribution to the international sport success of athletes.

Two independent researchers employed inductive procedures to cluster relevant raw data into first order and second order themes until interpretable and meaningful key categories were found (Gliner and Morgan, 2000). This is illustrated in Table 16.1 for one pillar (pillar 4, talent identification and development). Subsequently, to increase validity and interpretive consistency (Tashakkori and Teddlie, 2003), the list of different items and (sub)themes, derived from both the literature and preliminary research, was presented to an international consortium group of seven researchers with expertise in elite sport policy research (the SPLISS group), who were asked, independently, to cluster the items into categories. This categorisation was compared and discussed during a two-day meeting. Where different interpretations emerged, the items were regrouped and discussed until consensus was achieved.

Finally, it was concluded that a total of 144 key success drivers, or critical success factors (CSFs), which can be influenced by policies, can be distilled down into nine key areas in elite sport policy or 'pillars', situated at two levels: (a) inputs (financial support) for elite sport, which are quantitative and are reflected in pillar 1; and (b) throughputs, or the processes of how inputs can be managed to produce the required success (outputs), reflected in the remaining eight pillars, which are mainly qualitative. This model – presented graphically in Figure 16.2 – was the starting point of the international comparative study in phase 2. Methods to collect and analyse data during this stage were merely qualitative, except from counting numbers from the content analysis.

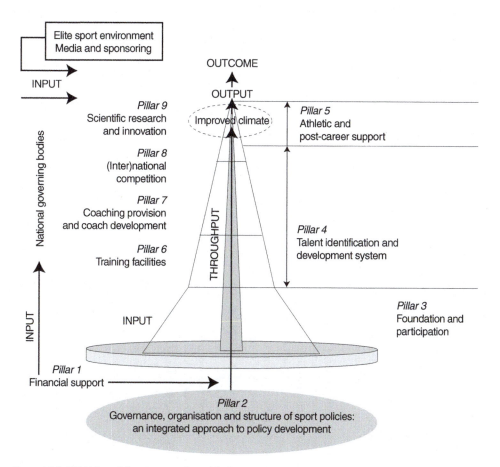

Figure 16.2 SPLISS model: a conceptual model of nine pillars of sports policy factors leading to international sporting success

Table 16.1 Fraction of the inductive content analysis with regard to the sports policy factors leading to international sporting success

Source	Detailed indicators	SPLISS Critical Success Factors	SPLISS pillars
(1)	4.1.1 System for talent detection/recruitment of young talents (n = 3)	4.1 There is an effective system for the detection of young talented athletes, so that the maximum number of potential top-level athletes are reached at the right time	Pillar 4 Talent identification and development system (22 sub–CSF)
(3)	4.1.2 Early talent spotting through schools (as typical in former communist nations)		
(3)	4.1.3 Right age of talent identification		
(3)	4.1.4 Talent recognition system that is informed and covered by sports scientists		
(3)	4.1.5 A testing battery to identify young talents and a monitoring system		
(3)	4.1.6 Planning of talent spotting within the NGBs		
(3)	4.1.7 Funding specifically for the identification (recognition and scouting) of young talented athletes		
(3)	4.1.8 An effective system for the statistical identification and monitoring of the progress of talented and elite athletes		
(1)	4.2.1 Effective talent development programme: from sport to all to elite level (n = 4)	4.2 There is a nationally coordinated planning towards NGBs in order to develop an effective system for the development of young talents	
(1)	4.2.2 Knowledge about the different development stages of a (tennis) player at the highest level (n = 1)		
(1)	4.3.1 (Individual) long–term training programme (n = 2)	4.3 Young talents receive multidimensional support services appropriate to their age and level that are needed to develop them as young athletes at the highest level	

Source	Detailed indicators	SPLISS Critical Success Factors	SPLISS pillars
(2)	4.3.2 Staffing/coaching during talent development (n = 4)	4.4 and 4.5 Young talents receive nationally coordinated support for the combination of sports development and academic study during secondary education (12–16/18 years), and higher education (>18 years) and where relevant primary education (for early specialisation sports where such a system is required)	Pillar 4 Talent identification and development system (22 sub-CSF)
(3)	4.3.2 Sufficient training opportunities at a high level; training with a selected group of talents		
(3)	4.3.3 Training camps at club level and with the national squad		
(3)	4.3.4 Specialised training, long-term and systematic from childhood to adulthood; training methods adapted to the age of the talents		
(2)	4.4.1 General support services to combine high level training with study (n = 13)		
(1)	School system: combination of tennis with studies (n = 1)		
(2)	4.4.2 Sufficient training facilities at school (n = 4)		
(2)	4.4.3 Study support (n = 3)		
(2)	4.4.4 Flexible arrangements at university level (n = 3)		
(2)	4.4.5 A positive attitude towards elite athletes at school and to get support services from school (n = 8)		
(2)	4.4.6 Support services in the federation for the combination of elite sport and study (n = 9)		
(3)	4.4.7 High frequency training within the school system (as typical in former communist nations)		
(3)	4.4.8 Programmes combining sport with education (including study support, flexible study programmes and training facilities at school)		

Note: Talent identification and development systems (Pillar 4) as an illustration, based on three sources: (1) literature analysis, (2) a survey with international coaches from 22 nations in one sport (tennis) and (3) a survey in Flanders including 26 sports, with elite athletes (n = 114), elite coaches (n = 99) and performance directors from national governing bodies (n = 26) (the exact quotes from the surveys have already been clustered into a/b level).

Phase 2: A pilot study in six sample nations, to test the model in an empirical environment

In order to test the conceptual model and its critical success factors in an empirical international environment, and thus to improve construct validity, the nine pillars were compared in a pilot study of six nations: Belgium (separated into Flanders and Wallonia[1]), Canada, Italy, the Netherlands, Norway and the United Kingdom. The selection of these nations was based on: first, the sport performances (to include good, medium and poorly achieving nations with the aim of observing differences in policies); second, the countries' socio-economic nature (Western industrialised countries); and third, a broadly comparable cultural background (De Bosscher *et al.*, 2009). Furthermore, with regard to improving criterion validity of the critical success factors and their relationship to success, this second stage attempted to explore a method to measure the elite sport policy determinants (also called the components of productivity or competitiveness determinants in economic studies) (Depperu and Cerrato, 2008; Porter, 1990), quantitatively. This stage was crucial to assess the extent to which nations with good elite sport policies perform better in the international arena than nations with less developed elite sport policies. This study reflected mainstream economic studies to obtain methodological insights concerning the measurement of competitiveness, such as the IMC World Competitiveness Yearbook (Garelli, 2008) and the Global Competitiveness Report (World Economic Forum, 2007).

During this second stage, triangulation of methods was used, a type of design in which different but complementary data are collected concurrently and analysed against the conceptual model (Creswell and Plano Clark, 2007). These quantitative and qualitative data are subsequently transformed into a quantitative scoring system, assisted with qualitative descriptive background information that measures the competitive position of the six sample nations in the nine pillars of the conceptual model. We will briefly explain the different stages of this diagram and the manner in which the mixed methods were combined (Wolf, 2010). For more detailed information on the SPLISS study see De Bosscher *et al.* (2008, 2009, 2010).

Data collection: qualitative and quantitative

The data to be collected on elite sport policies in nine pillars, were, with the exception of pillar 1, essentially qualitative in nature. Critical success factors (CSFs) in the nine pillars from the first stage were operationalised into instruments for data collection in the six sample nations.

In order to collect data on all of these factors, two different research instruments were used:

1   An overall elite sport policy inventory, which was a comprehensive research instrument in its own right, was used to collect mainly qualitative data on all pillars identified. It was completed by the relevant researchers in each country through interviews with policy agencies and analysis of existing secondary sources such as policy documents. This inventory contained 84 open-ended and closed questions in the nine pillars including their evolution in the past ten years. Open-ended questions primarily sought to gain insight into each country's policy system for each pillar, closed questions were added to ensure a degree of comparability across nations for the various sub-criteria. Space was left for additional comments that might be helpful in refining the conceptual model.

2   The second instrument was called the 'elite sport climate survey', completed by athletes, coaches and performance directors (national governing bodies) of each nation as main stakeholders in elite sport. In the six countries combined, a total of 1,090 athletes, 253 coaches and 71 performance directors completed these questionnaires. Here, mainly quantitative information was

collected through objective dichotomous (yes/no) questions to assess availability (for example, the kind of information that stakeholders had received); and subjective questions on a five-point Likert scale, to assess how stakeholders perceived the CSF (for example whether stakeholders perceived the information that they had received as sufficient). This survey served two purposes: first, to gather information through stakeholders on objective indicators or 'facts' that cannot easily be measured (De Pelsmacker and Van Kenhove, 1999); and second to assess the quality of elite sport development as it is perceived by the primary users. These methods also derive from the marketing and services' literature, which assumes that it is the consumers who best know the quality of a service as they experience it (Chelladurai and Chang, 2000) and the effectiveness literature which states that the primary stakeholders in sport organisations should be involved (Chelladurai, 2001; Papadimitriou and Taylor, 2000; Shilbury and Moore, 2006). Different competitiveness studies in the field of economics, such as the World Competitiveness Yearbook (Garelli, 2008; Rosselet, 2008), use similar methods.

Data analysis: transformation into quantitative data to develop a scoring system

During this stage, the SPLISS study aimed to develop a measurement system, or 'scoring', basically for two reasons:

- to move beyond the descriptive level of comparing the elite sport policies of nations in order to objectify comparison in nine pillars and to recognise patterns of well-developed elite sport policies;
- and, secondly, to find possible relationships between elite sport policies (independent variables) and sporting success (dependent variable) or to increase criterion validity on the conceptual model.

We refer to Sandelowski, Voils and Knafl (2009), who state that quantifying qualitative data is done in qualitative research 'to facilitate pattern recognition or otherwise to extract meaning from qualitative data, account for all data, document analytic moves, and verify interpretations' (p. 210). In addition, Sandelowski *et al.* (2009) stated that the purpose of quantifying qualitative data sets for integration with quantitative data in mixed-methods studies 'is to answer research questions or test hypotheses addressing relationships between independent (or explanatory or predictor) variable(s) and dependent (or response or outcome) variable(s)' (p. 211). In this respect, the scoring system aimed to express the general assessment of each pillar for each nation by consolidating different criteria into one final percentage score, which is suggested by De Pelsmacker and Van Kenhove (1999) as a typical methodology for measuring competitiveness in market research.

In summary, Figure 16.3 is an example of how the scores for different critical success factors in one pillar (pillar 5: athletic and post athletic career support) were aggregated into one final percentage score for the six sample nations. We refer to De Bosscher *et al.*, 2010 for more details on the development of the scoring system. The main difficulty in transforming data to create a measurement system concerning construct validity is because of the absence of clear standards to rate an elite sport system objectively. The basis of the methodology in this respect is: first, data collection through a survey, which delivers quantitative data about qualitative items; and, second, the involvement of an international consortium group as a team of experts in developing the research instruments and assessing each critical success factor. As there is no general consensus on the use of scales (Ochel and Röhn, 2006), it was decided to allocate all CSFs a score on a one-to-five point scale, with 'one' indicating little or no development and 'five' a high level of development. Depending on the source (elite sport climate survey or overall sport policy questionnaire) and type of question (open-ended, dichotomous, or assessment), the standards for this five-point scale differed. Generally there were three types of ratings:

- qualitative ratings derived from the overall policy questionnaire, where qualitative information on the elite sport systems for each pillar had to be transformed into a score for a five-point scale;
- quantitative ratings derived from the objective dichotomous (yes/no) questions in the elite sport climate survey;
- quantitative subjective ratings derived from five-point Likert scale questions in the elite sport climate survey.

W	Weights for each CSF	Critical Success Factors (CSF)	CAN	FLA	ITA	NED	NOR	UK	WAL
	Stage 1: the career of elite athletes: individual lifestyle support								
2	Athletes receive direct financial support (a monthly wage) to become a professional/full-time athlete		4	scores on a 1–5 scale; questions deriving from the overall policy questionnaire (black text)		5	4	4	5
2	Coordinated support programme for elite level athletes (apart from financial support)		5			5	4	5	2
1	*Total gross annual income (non-student athletes)*		*3*	scores on a 1–5 scale; questions deriving from the elite sport climate survey (grey text); dichotomous questions		*5*	*4*	*5*	*na*
1	*Gross annual income from sport activities of athletes (non-student athletes)*		*2*			*na*	*3*	*5*	*na*
1	*Kinds of facilities that athletes can make use of (according to athletes)*		*na*			*2*	*3*	*na*	*3*
	Stage 2: the post-athletic career								
3	Support for athletes at the end of their career		4	1	3	4	4	4	1
	Sum of (the points for each nation × weight)	**TOTAL points**	35	21	27	39	38	40	17
	Maximum score that each nation can have, taking into account the number of 'non-available' answers (= weight for each CSF ×5)	**Max**	45	45	35	45	50	45	35
		Number of times NA	1	1	1	1	0	1	2
	Percentage scores = total points/MAX	Total score for pillar 5	77,78	46,67	77,14	86,67	76,00	88,89	48,57

na: date not available; W: weight

Italic text: results from elite sports climate survey; non-italic text: results from deriving from the overall sport policy questionnaire

NB: Wallonia supplied data on relatively few criteria

	Assessment by athletes, coaches and coordinators (pillar 5)								
W			CAN	FLA	ITA	NED	NOR	UK	WAL
5	*General satisfaction with the support package that athletes receive*		*4*	*3*	*na*	*5*	*4*	*na*	*na*
1	*Rating level of sport specific coaches (acc. to athletes)*		*na*	scores on a 1–5 scale; questions deriving from the elite sport climate survey, based on net ratings		*5*	*5*	*na*	*na*
1	*Rating level of (para)medical coaches (acc. to athletes)*		*na*			*5*	*4*	*na*	*na*
1	*Rating level of social & business support (acc. to athletes)*		*na*	*4*	*na*	*3*	*1*	*na*	*na*
1	*Satisfaction with attitude of the employer (acc. to athletes)*		*5*	*5*	*na*	*5*	*5*	*na*	*na*
	TOTAL points for assessment		25	34		43	35		
	Max		30	45		45	45		
	Number of times NA		3	0	4	0	0	4	4
	Total score for assessment of pillar 5		83,33	75,56	NA	95,56	77,78	NA	NA

na: date not available; W: weight

Grey text: results from elite sports climate survey; **black text: results deriving from the overall sport policy questionnaire**

NB: Canada supplied data on relatively few criteria and scores were not calculated for the UK, Wallonia and Italy due to the low number of responses from coaches in the survey

CAN	Canada	ITA	Italy	NOR	Norway	WAL	Wallonia
FLA	Flanders	NED	The Netherlands	UK	United Kingdom		

Figure 16.3 An illustration of the scoring system in the SPLISS pilot study, in pillar 5: aggregation of scores of several CSFs into one overall percentage score

Overall, one-third of the CSFs were developed through the elite sport climate survey and two-thirds through the overall sport policy questionnaire. This balance is similar to the World Competitiveness Yearbook (Rosselet, 2008).

Results

The results section consisted of a general score for each nation on each pillar, expressed as a 'traffic light' where nations are divided into five categories according to their score, complemented with descriptive and qualitative information on elite sport systems (De Bosscher *et al.*, 2008, 2009). The second added value on 'how' and 'why' questions, rather than simply 'whether' and 'to what extent' a critical success factor was available. The use of mixed research methods enabled comprehensiveness and a more reflexive analysis of data.

Without dwelling on the comparison of elite sport policies, the main point of note in the SPLISS study was that the implementation of transforming qualitative data into quantitative scores improved our understanding on the extent to which nations are developed in managing their elite sport success. The results of what was a pilot study were inconclusive in terms of a possible relationship between elite sport policies and success, which was in part attributable to the small sample size. Nonetheless, the analysis of the six sample nations did lead to some interesting findings about this input–throughput–output relationship that would probably not have been discovered with qualitative analysis alone. It facilitated pattern recognition as indicated by Sandelowski *et al.* (2009). In summary, for example, the study contended that successful countries in international elite sport incorporated more of the key success factors than the unsuccessful countries, which indicates the probability that elite sport success is increasingly the result of investing in a blend of pillars. Mainly four pillars were identified as key areas of effectiveness in which the three most successful nations from the sample in summer sports have invested most: pillar 1 (financial support), pillar 5 (athletic and post career support), pillar 7 (with regard to the coach development) and pillar 6 (training facilities). Furthermore, the scores showed that three pillars are still underdeveloped in all the sample countries and may be areas where nations can gain a competitive advantage over others: pillar 4 (talent identification and development), pillar 7 (provisions for coaches) and pillar 9 (scientific support and innovation). This study did not, however, yield evidence for the importance of each CSF in relation to success, nor for their weight within the pillars. Further research is needed to explore the scoring system more in depth and with more nations and other cultures. Conversely, from a theoretical viewpoint, the analysis also showed that nations that do not perform well in one or a few policy pillars can still be successful in Olympic sports. It may, therefore, be argued that there are different models at the meso level to explain elite sporting success and that it is unrealistic to look for a convenient truth about the successful production of elite level athletes.

Discussion: strengths and limitations of the SPLISS study

This chapter highlighted the use of *mixed methods research* as a potential solution for reducing problems relating to the comparability of international data and the objective evaluation and measurement of policies in general and of elite sport policies in particular. Drawing its influences from economic competitiveness measurements, the SPLISS methods are based on three essential features that attempted to address these issues:

1   the development of a theoretical model of success determinants in elite sport with the identification of clear critical success factors that are used for international comparison;

2   the development of a scoring system to measure competitiveness of nations in elite sport for each dimension of the theoretical model to express the general assessment of each pillar for each nation by consolidating different criteria into one final percentage score;

3   the involvement of the main stakeholders in elite sport – the athletes, coaches and performance directors – as the evaluators of policy processes in elite sport.

In this respect the SPLISS study distinguishes itself from and is complementary to, both in methodological and theoretical terms, the work done by Bergsgard *et al.* (2007), Digel, Burk and Fahrner (2006), Green and Houlihan (2005b) and Houlihan and Green (2008). These studies aim to compare nations and describe qualitative issues in elite sport development. Examining relationships is not the purpose.

Table 16.2 below provides an overview of the strengths, weaknesses, threats and opportunities as they are seen by the SPLISS consortium group. Accordingly, the SPLISS group has planned to repeat its study in 2011 and 2012 at the overall sports level, including some of these weaknesses and with more nations involved.

Taking this SWOT analysis into account, the use of mixed methods research in the SPLISS study provided strengths that offset the weaknesses of both quantitative and qualitative research as argued by supporters of the methods (e.g. Creswell and Plano Clark, 2007; Rudd and Johnson, 2010). They were seen as a useful tool in the SPLISS study for several reasons:

- It helped to strive for completeness and to provide a better understanding of research problems than either approach alone (Creswell and Plano Clark, 2007); it enabled comprehensiveness and a more reflexive analysis of data. Accordingly the SPLISS study also tried to assess the 'black box' of throughput both in terms of the existence of various system components and also the rating that athletes, coaches and performance directors give to these system components.

- Different approaches were useful to increase internal and external validity of the SPLISS model.

- The scoring system was a useful tool (a) to move beyond the descriptive level of comparison and thus to extract meaning from qualitative data and to verify interpretations, (b) to facilitate pattern recognition that relate inputs and throughputs to outputs (Sandelowski *et al.*, 2009) and, accordingly, (c) to improve criterion validation of the conceptual model.

- By including diversity of views from people with different rationales, namely policy makers, elite sport experts, coaches and elite athletes, quality of elite sport development is evaluated as it is perceived by the primary users and data were included that are not easily measured.

However, the potential of mixed research methods has not yet been fully realised in this study. More research is required to expand the techniques for quantifying qualitative data and to develop the analysis options for data transformed this way (Creswell and Plano Clark, 2007), to determine weightings for each CSF and the importance of different pillars. Discovering how policy causes success is yet another step to take, as there are clearly different paths to success. Further planned quantitative research and a SPLISS-II study with more nations and particular attention to the 'why' questions are just a few elements that can contribute to increased insights and causal inference. As Morgan (2007, p. 71) suggests, by moving 'back and forth' between induction and deduction, one can convert observations into theories and then assess those theories through action. In this way, understanding based on shared meaning can benefit from the different approaches to research. Despite its potential, mixed methods research can also be a particularly demanding research strategy and this also raises questions about feasibility. Mixed research methods are time consuming (Creswell and Plano Clark, 2007) and this, in combination with the fact that the use of surveys in an international context is expensive, makes comparative studies very labour-intensive, and increases the need to deal carefully with the boundaries inherent in such cross-national comparisons.

Table 16.2 SWOT analysis of the SPLISS methods

Strengths

General

- reflects economic/management competitiveness measurements; and involves literature from different areas in (elite) sport, effectiveness and strategic management (De Bosscher *et al.*, 2010)
- uses standardised methods to compare nations (De Bosscher *et al.*, 2010)
- development of a conceptual model, based on comprehensive literature analysis, complemented with surveys to address the viewpoints of users (athletes, coaches, performance directors) and experts;
- measures of inputs–outputs, but also throughputs: the processes of an elite sport policy; attempts to identify possible relationships
- the use of mixed methods research to address the problems associated with cross-national research, related to operationalisation, comparability, measurement, explanations of causality, validation, reliability, interpretation, moving beyond the descriptive and balancing between global and local factors (De Bosscher *et al.*, 2007; Henry *et al.*, 2005) and the lack of standardized and measurable data; 'mixed methods provides strengths that offset the weaknesses of both quantitative and qualitative research and it enabled comprehensiveness and a more reflexive analysis of data' (Creswell and Plano Clark, 2007)
- methodology complements and advances existing comparative elite sport studies.
- involves key stakeholders in the evaluation of policies to obtain both hard data and perceived data: measurement of data that are difficult to measure (De Bosscher *et al.*, 2009; 2010)
- role of the consortium group: an international cooperative research, with experts from different fields increases reliability of international comparisons and validity of research instruments (De Bosscher *et al.*, 2010)
- clear definition of success, using different methods to measure absolute success and relative success to compare countries under ceteris paribus conditions (De Bosscher, 2007; De Bosscher *et al.*, 2008; De Bosscher, De Knop & Heyndels, 2003)

The SPLISS model (De Bosscher *et al.*, 2006)[a]

- athlete centred model (based on a wide range of micro- and meso-level literature, best practices and expert interviews)
- complete model, which can be operationalised pillars into measurable concepts by identifying 144 critical success factors (De Bosscher *et al.*, 2009; 2010)
- has been validated in/can be applied to other contexts: sport-specific level as measured in athletics (Truyens, De Bosscher, Heyndels and De Knop, 2011), ice skating (Bogerd, 2010), tennis (Brouwers, 2012), at the local/city level (Van Rossum and De Meyer, 2012)
- attempts to identify possible relationships between inputs, throughputs and outputs in elite sport

Measurement

- method goes beyond the descriptive level of comparison; the scoring system is a supportive and tangible way of understanding elite sport policies more broadly in relation to sporting success (De Bosscher *et al.*, 2009), helping in pattern recognition and increasing criterion validity

Note:
a quantitative findings alone are not sufficient to generalize the quality of elite sport systems (De Bosscher *et al.*, 2010).

Weaknesses

General

- can competitiveness in elite sport be comparable to economic competitiveness (De Bosscher *et al.*, 2009): with regard to profitability, rules of demand and supply; dependence on government funding
- practice often develops at a faster pace than theory (De Bosscher *et al.*, 2010)
- 'instant picture': the SPLISS study evaluates elite sport at one moment from a static perspective, while elite sport development is dynamic and changing continuously (Bogerd, 2010)
- SPLISS uses a short-term evaluation, while elite sport is the result of, among other factors, long-term policy evaluation (De Bosscher , 2007), as it takes on average at least ten years to develop elite athletes (Ericsson, 2003).

SPLISS model

- the model uses a functionalistic and rationalistic approach (Bogerd, 2010): the critical success factors are related to success and winning, without taking into account unintentional side effects of these factors (e.g. drop outs, increased commercialization, increased gap between elite sport and sport for all), which in turn may have regressive effects on success in a longer term
- the SPLISS model focuses at the overall sports level, without taking into account the specificity of sports: each sport requires specific criteria for evaluation (SIRC, 2002; De Bosscher *et al.*, 2009); further validation processes are needed
- the environment of elite sport ('pillar 10') is not included (De Bosscher *et al.*, 2009, 2010): e.g. sponsorship and media, because it is less obvious that the can be directly influenced by policies and merely because data are not available on an international comparable level
- substantial focus on government-funded sports, mainly Olympic sports
- does not include policy networks and interdependent relationships between different actors and organizations
- top-down model: assumption that elite sport policy is a condition for success (e.g. in contrast to the United States) there is no evidence for the importance of each CSF in relation to success, nor for their weight within the pillars (De Bosscher *et al.*, 2009)
- construct validity (De Bosscher *et al.*, 2009)
- subjectivity: the construct of the model is to a large extent based on expert opinion
- inter-correlation among the criteria is difficult to avoid (overlap in the pillars)

Measurement

- the definition of standards in the scoring system is arbitrary for qualitative data: largely based on expert opinion and constant comparison of meanings (SPLISS consortium group); weights are subjective
- criterion validity (related to the small sample size): an international comparison with only six nations does not allow correlations between each CSF and success; the purpose of the scoring system is limited to general pattern recognition (De Bosscher *et al.*, 2009, 2010) due to the lack of a larger empirical data set; this is planned in future research

---

Opportunities

- need for a long-term evaluation of elite sport policies in each pillar, including the political and social context of nations and explain 'why' elite sport policy decisions are taken, looking for more evidence based empirical research (Houlihan *et al.*, 2009)
- criterion validity: a quantitative analysis involving more countries could highlight possible statistical relationships (correlations) between policies and success
- construct validity: factorial analysis and cluster analysis to reduce and cluster the different CSF into meaningful dimensions or pillars in order to refine the construct validation of the critical success factors used to measure each pillar; construct validation is a continuing process of experimentation and modification leading to the refinement of the instrument that measures the construct (Gliner and Morgan, 2000).
- provides a tool that can be applied to other contexts (sport-by-sport comparisons and national governing bodies, local level, private sport academies); they may also reveal that certain pillars are more conditional than others; clusters of similar models may be found, for example, for early versus late specialisation sports, for team sports versus individual or dual sports, for more sports that are organised on a market-led basis, summer sports and winter sports, and so forth (De Bosscher *et al.*, 2009)
- institutionalisation and governmentalisation of the SPLISS model: the model is based on the assumption that governments/policies can influence success; therefore it is possible that this model is less applicable to more commercialised sports and to sport contexts where government involvement is not predominantly attendant (e.g. United States); a validation of the model to commercial sports and other sport contexts would enrich the theory development
- SPLISS is based on a resource-based approach, focusing on those (production) factors which can be influenced by policies and whereby countries can determine their own competitive position; these methods leave an opportunity for an outside in approach, whereby the market structure (characteristics of the global sporting market) determines the outcome and position of countries in international competition (Truyens *et al.*, 2011)
- SPLISS-II: the SPLISS study is repeated in 2011–2012 on a larger scale, including more nations and going into more depth on each pillar; furthermore, other SPLISS projects are developing (SPLISS judo, SPLISS winter sports, SPLISS Paralympics)

Threats/points of attention

- there are many extraneous factors influencing success and which cannot be controlled (as they are intangible) (De Bosscher *et al.*, 2009): cultural factors, nationalism or traditions, historical developments, path dependency (Houlihan and Green, 2008, referring to Kay, 2005)
- there are several ways to skin a cat (De Bosscher *et al.*, 2009): because of country specific, historical and cultural reasons, nations may find different answers to implement the proposed successful elite sport systems; is it realistic to develop a theoretical model on the SPLISS factors?
- construct validation is never really reached (De Bosscher *et al.*, 2009)
- scoring system may not be isolated from the general sports context and historical development, e.g. path dependency and the general political context (Houlihan, 1997)
- interpretation of the results: elite sport policies does not take part in a closed system; danger of generalizations (De Bosscher *et al.*, 2010)
- feasibility: mixed methods research in an international context is expensive, labour-intensive and time consuming (De Bosscher *et al.*, 2010)

Source: based on De Bosscher (2007)

17

MEASURING AND FORECASTING ELITE SPORTING SUCCESS

Simon Shibli, Veerle de Bosscher and Maarten van Bottenburg

Introduction

In this chapter we consider two key challenges that face nations seeking to achieve success in elite-level sport. As a proxy for what is meant by the term 'elite-level sport', we use summer Olympic Games, which in 2012 involves 26 sports, 39 disciplines and 302 events. The first challenge is the issue of measuring the performance of nations in elite sport in a consistent manner such that the efficiency and effectiveness of a system can be measured. By the term 'efficiency' we mean the ratio of inputs to outputs, for example the amount of money that is invested in a sport in order to win an Olympic medal. As a contrast, the term 'effectiveness' is a measure of output, that is the extent to which stated goals are achieved, without reference to inputs such as cost. The second (and perhaps somewhat controversial) challenge is the notion of forecasting how nations might be expected to perform in elite level sport. These two issues require some contextualisation and should not necessarily be accepted as valid concerns without further explanation. Why would nations be interested in measuring their performance in elite sport and what justification can there be for attempting to forecast performance?

The International Olympic Committee (IOC) has been consistent about the purpose of the Olympic medal table for some time. In its 2003 study into European sporting success UK Sport reported the IOC's position as quoted below:

> The International Olympic Committee (IOC) does not recognise global ranking per country; the medal tables are displayed for information only.
> [and]
> The medal tables by country are based on the number of medals won, with gold medals taking priority over silver and bronze. A team victory counts as one medal.
> (UK Sport, 2003, p. 35)

While the IOC might regard the medal table as being information only, this is not a view that is universally accepted by nations taking part in the Olympic Games. There is no more explicit example of this than the United Kingdom for whom UK Sport, the national agency for elite sport, described its 'ultimate goal' for the London 2012 Olympic and Paralympic Games as being 'top four in the 2012 Olympic medal table, and second in the Paralympic medal table'

(UK Sport, 2011). Prior to the UK there have also been other nations that have set targets for Olympic success, notably China in 2008 (Shibli and Bingham, 2008) and East Germany in 1972 (UK Sport, 2003).

The major reason why nations might set performance targets for elite sport systems is because typically it is public money, raised in the form of taxation or the profits of lotteries, that is used to fund such systems. Politicians are often (or should be) held to account for their use of public money and for this reason it is considered legitimate to measure the efficiency and effectiveness of their elite sport system in the same way that they would for any other publicly funded services such as hospitals or the police. Furthermore, the funding of elite sport may also be linked to wider societal goals such as encouraging more people to engage in sport and physical activity. Again London 2012 is a good example of how the perceived inspiration effect of elite sport success was a component of a wider initiative to encourage one million people to play more sport and a further one million to take up physical activity in a more general sense. The legitimacy for politicians to measure elite sport success can be appreciated by looking at a process diagram as shown in Figure 17.1.

The logic underpinning Figure 17.1 is that in return for financial support from public sources (inputs) in order to deliver elite sport development systems (processes), there must be immediate tangible results (outputs) which in turn are instrumental in delivering longer-term benefits (outcomes). If the system can be seen to be working, it provides the basis for continued or indeed enhanced support. By contrast, if the system is not working then it may be forced to improve or even experience a reduction in funding. The UK provides a good example of how the relative efficiency of investment can be measured. Following the Athens Olympiad, the National Audit Office conducted a review of UK Sport's World Class Performance Programme and found that the average cost for each medal won in Athens was £2.4m (National Audit Office, 2005). These types of metric provide benchmarks against which informed value for money assessments can be made.

Almost as a logical extension of measuring historical performance, it would seem appropriate to forecast future performance and to set targets for future performance, however much this is contrary to the IOC's position. In return for an investment of £264m in the London Olympiad, the elite sport system in the UK was charged with delivering a top four finish in the medal table for which a haul of around 60 medals was thought to be necessary. Similarly, in Paralympic sport an investment of £48m was designed to achieve second place in the medal table. In the remainder of the chapter we examine how performance in elite sport can be measured and we also demonstrate how forecasting techniques have been used to predict how nations will perform in future events.

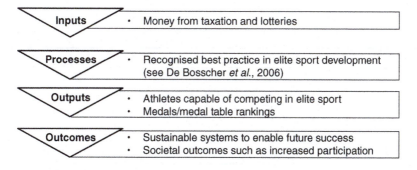

Figure 17.1 Elite sport systems as a process

Measuring performance

While the notion of measuring performance might be contrary to the ideals of the IOC, the reality is that most nations view the Olympic medal table as an order or merit and not as a something that is provided for 'information only'. However, the Olympic medal table should not be viewed as the starting point for measuring performance, nor should it be accepted on its own as a valid measure of performance. These two issues are dealt with in greater depth below.

In 2011 the world's population was estimated at around 6.9 billion people. In the Olympic Games the number of athletes taking part is capped at around 11,000. Thus, in simple terms, the likelihood of an individual being an Olympian is around one in 627,000. If we assume that athletic talent is distributed evenly across the world, then it becomes possible to compute some basic measures of performance, for example the number of Olympians 'produced' by each nation. This figure can in turn be related to the expected number of Olympians we might expect each nation to produce. Table 17.1 shows the performance of selected nations in producing Olympians for Beijing 2008.

China has a population of more than 1.3 billion people and in its host Olympic Games of 2008 had a team of 639 athletes. Had team sizes been based on their relationship to population, then China's team size would have been around 2,131 athletes. This was not the case for two key reasons. First, through the Olympic Games the IOC is trying to achieve what its president Jacques Rogge (2002) described as 'a real universality', by which he meant the Olympic Games being relevant to the 200+ recognised National Olympic Committees. One method to achieve this 'real universality' is by rationing places at the Olympic Games via the use of a continental quota system whereby qualifying places are allocated, in part, on the basis of geography rather than absolute ability. This type of policy legislates against large nations such as China dominating the event at the expense of smaller nations. Second, the rules for many sports in the Olympic Games deliberately limit the number of athletes from any one nation taking part. For example, in boxing in 2008 there were 11 events with four medals available in each event. However, although 44 medals were contestable, each nation could only enter one boxer per weight category, thereby limiting each nation to a maximum of 11 boxers. This approach also has the effect of being inclusive towards smaller nations and diluting the influence of larger nations – an approach economists refer to as diminishing returns to scale. Consequently, in the case of China, the largest team in Beijing 2008, the number of athletes was 639 which was 30 per cent of what might have been expected if places were allocated on the basis of population (2,131). The United States is an example of a large nation that managed to produce more Olympians than might be expected (index score of 119), whereas Brazil did not quite 'punch its weight' in 2008 (index score of 85). The USA has a long-established record of achievement in

Table 17.1 The production of Olympians by selected nations

Nation	Population	Actual Olympians	Expected Olympians	Index Score[a]
China	1,336,000,000	639	2,131	30
USA	313,000,000	596	499	119
Brazil	203,400,000	277	324	85
United Kingdom	62,800,000	312	100	312
Jamaica	2,800,000	56	4	1254
Cayman Islands	51,000	4	0.1	4918

a Index score = (Actual Olympians/Expected Olympians) × 100

most Olympic sports, traditionally performing well in athletics and swimming – these are two sports in which qualification is based on merit to a greater extent than most other sports. For example, the USA qualified three athletes for the men's 100m event and in so doing effectively competed for the gold, silver and bronze medals. Brazil, by contrast, is an emerging nation in Olympic sport, having won fewer medals in the period 1920 to 2008 (91) than the USA won in 2008 alone (110). The United Kingdom qualified more than three times as many athletes as its population would otherwise predict. This can in part be attributed to the large-scale investment made in Olympic sport by the government via Exchequer and National Lottery funding. Furthermore, the UK has pursued a strategy of sporting diversity (concentrating on a wide range of sports) rather than specialisation (concentrating on a narrow range) which enables it to contest more of the 302 events available than other nations. In 2008 Jamaica competed in four sports (athletics, swimming, cycling and equestrian) out of a total of 28; and of its 56 athletes who took part in the event, 51 were track and field athletes. This is a good example of a highly specialised approach to elite sport. Because track and field enables nations to compete for more than one medal per event (team relays excluded) it is possible for Jamaica to produce strength in depth in what is clearly a very important sport to the nation. The success of Jamaica's track and field programme can be appreciated by the finding that its index score of 1,254 indicates that it produced more than 12 times as many Olympians as would have been expected on the basis of its population. Finally, the Cayman Islands has an index score of 4,918, meaning that its production of four Olympians was more than 49 times higher than would expected on the basis of population. With a population of 51,000, the Cayman Islands would only be expected to produce one Olympian every ten editions of the Olympic Games. It is precisely for this reason that the IOC pursues its 'real universality' approach to ensure that the Olympic Games, and its associated commercial property rights, are as relevant to as many of the world's 6.9 billion people as possible. Thus, smaller nations tend to qualify proportionately more athletes than larger nations. In addition, the event cannot be said to be truly meritocratic as the continental qualifying quota system and the rules within each sport may prevent the best athletes from taking part. It could be possible that the best two heavyweight boxers in the world are both from China. However, as nations can only enter one athlete per weight category, the second best heavyweight boxer would be excluded from taking part. For the (hypothetical) boxer who is allowed to take part, it could be argued that qualifying for the Olympic Games was actually harder than winning the gold medal. It is this type of anomaly that results in the Olympic Games being a compromise between meritocracy and universality.

The number of athletes who qualify to take part in the Olympic Games is a good starting point in demonstrating the point that the medal table is but a partial measure of performance. Only around one in four nations taking part will win a gold medal and the majority of nations (around 120 out of 200) will return home without a medal of any colour. Nonetheless, for many nations there are positives to be taken simply from athletes qualifying to take part that will justify the investment made in developing them. However, once qualified there are other measures of performance that fall short of winning a medal that can also be viewed as evidence of relative success. The 100m in Beijing 2008 provides numerous examples of athletes and nations who can all draw positives from their experiences. The headline memory will always be Usain Bolt breaking the world record in spectacular style to win the gold medal, but for the 80 athletes who entered the first round of the event there are alternative measures of success as shown in Table 17.2.

Table 17.2 Beijing 2008 100m – measures of success

Round	Athlete	Nation	Time	Achievement
1	Nawai	Kiribati	11.29	Season best
1	Jurgen Themen	Surinam	10.61	Personal best
1	Okilanu Tinilau	Tuvalu	11.48	National record
2	Naoki Tsukahara	Japan	10.23	Season best
2	Churandy Martina	Dutch Antilles	9.99	National record
Semi-final	Naoki Tsukahara	Japan	10.16	Season best
Semi-final	Churandy Martina	Dutch Antilles	9.94	National record
Final	Michael Frater	Jamaica	9.97	Personal best
Final	Churandy Martina	Dutch Antilles	9.93	National record

None of the athletes listed in Table 17.2 won a medal and only two made the final, yet all of them could find reasons to be satisfied with their efforts for having achieved milestones such as a season's best, a personal best, a national record and in most cases progression beyond the first round. It is difficult not to feel a degree of sympathy for Churandy Martina of the Dutch Antilles who broke his national record three times in the competition and ultimately came fourth in the final. Overall, for all of the athletes featured in Table 17.2 (and many others as well), it is reasonable to argue that within their own contexts, the athletics 100m event in Beijing 2008 showed clear evidence of progression and success for the athletes concerned. This type of analysis illustrates that the final medal table on its own is only a partial measure of performance, notably for the 120 nations that do not win any medals.

That the Olympic medal table itself is a less than complete measure of performance is well demonstrated by reviewing the top five nations in the Beijing 2008 table as shown in Table 17.3.

It has been a question of some debate as to which nation was the most successful in Beijing. Using the IOC ranking system, which the IOC presents for 'information' only, China is the top placed nation with 51 gold medals compared with the USA's 36; whereas using total medals, the USA has claimed that its total of 110 is a superior performance to China's 100. When asked about this issue Jacques Rogge is quoted in Jeffery (2008) as having said: 'I am sure each country will highlight what suits it best – one will say the gold medal tally counts, and the other will say the total medals count, we take no position on that.' A problem with both the IOC and total medals as measures of performance is that they ignore the totality of achievement by not distinguishing between the different values of medals. One method to combat this weakness is to award points such as three for gold, two for silver and one for bronze as shown in Table 17.4.

Table 17.3 Beijing 2008 top five nations

Rank	NOC	Gold	Silver	Bronze	Total
1	CHN	51	21	28	100
2	USA	36	38	36	110
3	RUS	23	21	28	72
4	GBR	19	13	15	47
5	GER	16	10	15	41

Table 17.4 Beijing 2008 top five measured by points

Rank	NOC	Gold	Silver	Bronze	Total	Points	Market Share
1	CHN	51	21	28	100	223[a]	12.0%
2	USA	36	38	36	110	220	11.8%
3	RUS	23	21	28	72	139	7.5%
4	GBR	19	13	15	47	98	5.3%
5	GER	16	10	15	41	83	4.5%

a China 223 points = $((51\times3)+(21\times2)+(28\times1)) = (153+42+28) = 223$.

In Table 17.4 the point system shows that China (223) achieved a marginally better performance than the USA (220) and thus the average quality of medals won by China was superior to that of the USA. The use of points can be developed to enable time series analysis of a nation's performance. By dividing the points won by a given nation by the total number of points awarded at a particular event, it is possible to compute a measure of 'market share'. As the number of events contested at the Olympic Games has grown steadily from 237 in 1988 to 302 in 2008, market share is an effective way of standardising performance to analyse performance over time. For a more detailed look at performance measurement in elite sport, see De Bosscher *et al.* (2007). Figure 17.2 shows the market share of China and the United Kingdom over the period 1984 (when China first took part in the Olympic Games) and 2008 (the last data point available at the time of writing).

In 1984 China arguably over performed because of the Eastern Bloc boycott of the Olympic Games. Seoul 1988 was viewed as a national humiliation for China (see Hong *et al.*, 2005) which led to subsequent large-scale investment in sport. This investment led to a spectacular increase in performance in 1992 followed by consolidation and growth in the

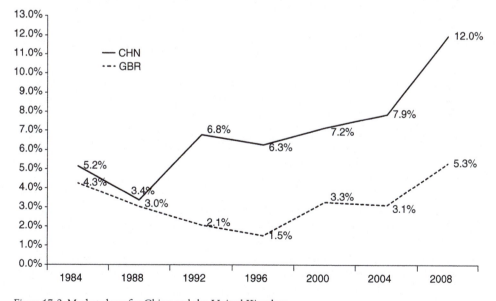

Figure 17.2 Market share for China and the United Kingdom

period 1996–2004 and finally a large spike in performance as host nation in 2008. By contrast, the United Kingdom experienced three editions of continuous decline after a good showing in 1984 before reaching its low point of 1996, which, like China in 1988, was perceived as being a humiliating performance. Changes to the rules in the way National Lottery funding in the UK could be used, saw significant investment in elite sport from 1997 leading to significant improvement in 2000, consolidation in 2004 and sharp improvement in 2008. It was by examining patterns of performance in the Olympic Games such as those shown in Figure 17.2 that provided the encouragement for us to develop our work from seeking to explain what had happened in the past to forecasting what was likely to happen in future events. This issue of trying to forecast future performance in the Olympic Games is the subject of the next section.

Forecasting performance

Rationalising and justifying the performance of nations in the Olympic Games has been of interest to academics for many years. The use of macro-economic measures to forecast the performance of nations in the Olympic Games has been an area of considerable interest for academic researchers since the 1950s (see for example: Jokl et al., 1956; Jokl, 1964; Shaw and Pooley, 1976; Colwell, 1982; Baimbridge, 1998; and Johnson and Ali, 2002). In the literature it has been the trend over the last 60 years for economists to use models that are based upon the two key variables of population and wealth. Many of these studies show that population and wealth are the two most important socio-economic variables that impact positively on success (see, for example, Novikov and Maximenko, 1972; Levine, 1974; Kiviaho and Mäkelä, 1978; Suen, 1992; Van Bottenburg, 2000; De Bosscher, De Knop and Heyndels, 2003; Johnson and Ali, 2002; Morton, 2002; Bernard and Busse, 2004). These two variables typically account for, or 'explain', over 50 per cent of a nation's success in the Olympic Games. Wealth on its own of course does not explain sporting success. It does, however, provide the wherewithal for nations to create the conditions necessary for elite athletes to be produced as outlined in the 'nine pillars' model in the previous chapter. More recently, providers of media content, for example, The Associated Press, Sports Illustrated and USA Today have sought to forecast how nations might perform in the Olympic Games. Indeed the number of academics and organisations making such forecasts has grown to such an extent that Dutch academics Kuper and Sterken (2008, 2010) evaluated the forecasts of six organisations after the Beijing 2008 and Vancouver 2010 Olympic Games. What they concluded was that forecasts based on short-term form, that is, within the current Olympic cycle, tend to be more accurate than those based on econometric modelling. Furthermore, econometric models that include variables that factor in an element of performance in elite sport (such as at recent world championships) outperform those that rely on macro-economic variables only, but are still less accurate than form-based models.

In 2008 Shibli and Bingham used an alternative approach to forecasting the performance of China in its host Olympic Games. Using a combination of simple regression and judgement they forecast that China would win 46 gold medals and would be ranked first in the medal table. If regression can be described as 'science', then judgement is perhaps best described as 'art'. There were two key judgements used in the Shibli and Bingham forecast. First, the boycott-affected 1984 data point overstated China's performance because the non-attendance of the Eastern Bloc nations reduced the level of competition and enabled China to win more medals than it would have won had the Eastern Bloc nations been present. Second, that home advantage in the Olympic Games conveys a quantifiable benefit in terms of the host nation, over and above the extrapolation of a trend line of performance. By regressing China's performance over time from 1988 and extrapolating to 2008 it was found that China was expected to win 39 gold medals. To this total was added the quantifiable benefit of host nation status, which was found to be seven gold medals, to give an overall forecast of 46 gold medals. In practice, China actually won 51 gold medals but the forecast of 46 was more accurate than those of Johnson and Ali (44), Bernard (38), Italian expert Luciano Barra (37) and the American media outlets such as *Sport Illustrated* and *USA Today*.

When this regression-based forecasting approach is applied to other nations the results remain encouragingly accurate. If we replicate the analysis on the top five nations from Athens 2004 to project ahead to Beijing 2008 we achieve results that are closely in line with what happened in practice as shown in Table 17.5.

Despite the weakness in the Russia forecast, the total number of gold medals forecast for the five nations in Table 17.5 was 139, which in total was six more than actually achieved by the nations concerned. What the findings discussed above seem to indicate is the influence of past performance and host nation effects as factors that are likely to impact positively upon future success rather than macro-economic variables. As increasing numbers of nations take a strategic approach to elite sport development, it is likely that factors such as population and wealth will reduce in importance and policy factors such as the 'nine pillars' (see De Bosscher *et al.*, 2006) will increase in importance. Past performance seems to perform a useful role in acting as a proxy for the efficacy of policy factors.

On the basis of the encouraging results achieved with the summer Olympic Games we applied the same techniques to the 2010 Winter Olympic Games. There is less literature on the Winter Olympic Games than the summer edition, but the macro-economic determinants are essentially the same as for the summer Games with the addition of 'climate' as a winter-specific variable. The evidence, perhaps not surprisingly, is that nations from colder climates tend to perform better in the Winter Olympic Games than nations from warmer climates. Using a model based on population, wealth, political structure, past performance and climate, Johnson (cited in Futterman, 2010) forecasted that the host nation Canada would win five gold medals and 27 medals in total. Other forecasts for Canada based on form by the British Olympic Association (6 gold and 30 medals in total) and Luciano Barra (6 gold and 29 medals in total) were also made public in the run up to Vancouver 2010 (see Williams, 2010).

Table 17.5 Shibli/Bingham forecast gold medals compared with actual in Beijing

Nation	Forecast Gold Medals	Actual Gold Medals	Variance
China	46	51	-5
USA	36	36	0
Russia[a]	29	23	+6
Japan	11	9	+2
Australia	17	14	+3
Total	139	133	+6

a The forecast for Russia is based on three data points as Russia has only competed in the Olympic Games in its own right since 1996. In 1992 Russia competed as part of a Unified Team and up until 1988 Russia was part of the Union of Soviet Socialist Republics team (USSR), which was an amalgamation of 15 different nations. It is not really appropriate to conduct a linear regression on three data points, so for the purposes of this exercise a simple average of Russia's three last scores has been taken (26 gold medals in 1996, 32 in 2000 and 28 in 2004).

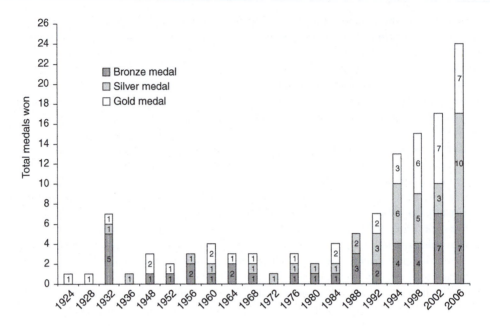

Figure 17.3 Canada's performance in the Winter Olympic Games 1924–2006

Our own analysis of past performance revealed that Canada was on something of an upward trend in terms of its performance in the Winter Olympic Games as shown in Figure 17.3. This indicates that since 1980 Canada had followed a path of continuous improvement in terms of medals won and since 1992 had also been increasing its number of gold medals won. As the host nation in 2010 it would be reasonable to expect Canada to perform even better than it had done in 2006. Since 1980 home nation status in the Winter Olympic Games has been worth two gold medals and five medals overall compared with the host's performance in the previous edition of the event. This finding alone would be enough to propel Canada from seven gold medals in Turin 2006 to nine in Vancouver 2010 and from 24 medals overall to 29. However, in addition to the benefits of home advantage, Canada's performance in the Winter Olympic Games has been on an upward trend. Our forecast using linear regression of past performance suggested that Canada would win at least 10 gold medals and 30 medals overall. So why was our forecast for gold medals so much higher than those of other forecasters?

We felt that the most significant factor in Canada's favour was the massive increase in investment it has made in winter sports. In the four years leading up to Turin 2006 Canada's investment in winter sports was around £12m. This yielded 24 medals at an average cost of £0.5m. In the four years leading up to Vancouver 2010 Canada invested £60m and won 26 medals in total, at an average cost of £2.3m per medal. So, a fivefold increase in funding and a near fivefold increase in the cost per medal seemed like a good starting point to expect a significant improvement in performance. Money alone does not buy success and there were other factors at play. First, there are positive psychological effects for the host nation. Many people believe that playing at home gives athletes a lift and enables them to perform at their best. This is unproven scientifically and is equally likely to hinder athletes who may become riddled with self doubt under the weight of national expectation. Crowds do help, but it tends to be the more subtle impact of crowds on officials in subjectively scored events that create benefits for the host nation (see UK Sport, 2008). Judges might be subconsciously influenced to award

Table 17.6 Summary of forecasts compared with actual for Canada at Vancouver 2010

Forecaster	Forecast Gold	Actual Gold	Variance	Forecast Total	Actual Total	Variance
Johnson	5	14	−9	27	26	+1
B.O.A.	6	14	−8	30	26	+4
Barra	6	14	−8	29	26	+3
Authors	10	14	−4	30	26	+4

higher marks to host nation athletes and referees inadvertently tend to favour home teams. The second key benefit of home advantage is that Canadian athletes had the opportunity to train on the facilities that were used during competition. This provides particular advantage in technical sports where familiarity with sliding tracks for example can provide a distinct competitive advantage. There was controversy surrounding the Whistler Sliding Centre to which Canadian athletes had unfettered (approximately 300 runs) access in advance of the event, while the athletes from other nations had minimal access (approximately 30 runs). Finally, the favourable qualifying conditions offered to the host nation often means that it does not have to play its full hand in international competition in the lead up to the event. There is sometimes an element of surprise as home nation athletes keep innovative techniques under wraps in the lead in to the Games, and then unleash their 'A game' when it really matters. At the end of Vancouver 2010, Canada had won 26 medals in total of which 14 were gold medals. An analysis of the accuracy of the forecasts reviewed above is shown in Table 17.6.

All forecasts underestimated the number of gold medals won as Canada set a new record for the number of gold medals ever won by a nation at the Winter Olympic Games. The most accurate gold medal forecast was the one based on past performance and host nation effect which, as discussed above, appears to be a reasonable proxy for the impact of policy factors. Interestingly, all forecasts overestimated the total number of medals that Canada actually won with the most accurate being +1 for the Johnson model. The finding that the two form-based forecasts overestimated by +4 and +3 total medals suggests that some home nation athletes did not achieve their full potential. Overall, all forecast methods achieved reasonably accurate results for total medals won, but tended to underestimate the number of gold medals won. Canada's increase in gold medals from seven to 14 comfortably exceeded the historical home advantage increase in gold medals of two. Perhaps the key finding from the research is that there is clear evidence that Canada's elite sport policies were effective in generating improvement on a continuous basis. It is unlikely that Canada will be able to maintain such levels of performance in Sochi 2014.

Having demonstrated that our forecasting approach delivers respectable results for what are now past events, we turn our hand to making a forecast for how Great Britain and Northern Ireland will perform in London 2012, which at the time of writing (March 2011, was still a future event). Figure 17.4 illustrates that for the United Kingdom 1996 was something of a pivot point.

It was the low point of three editions of continuous decline and the launch pad for three editions of continuous growth in terms of total medals won. Atlanta 1996 was for the UK what Chalip (1995, p. 5) describes as a 'focusing event' in the sense that policy towards elite sport changed following what was perceived to be a nationally traumatic event 'that can symbolise an issue and focus policy makers' attention on proposals to redress the issue'. Some focusing events in national sporting performance have led to increased investment in elite sport, often as a means of overcoming perceived failures, for example Australia in 1976 and China in 1988. As was the case with China, we make the judgement to exclude the 1984 data point in the regression and to use from 1988 onwards. Our regression is based on the number of gold medals won in previous editions and assumes that there will be 302 gold medals contested in London 2012.

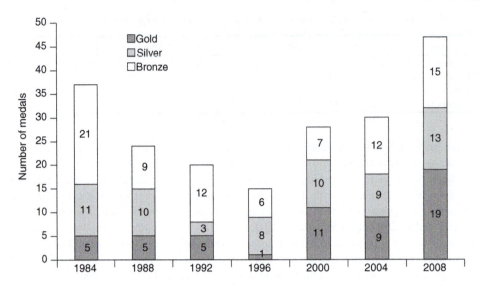

Figure 17.4 The United Kingdom in the Olympic Games 1984–2008

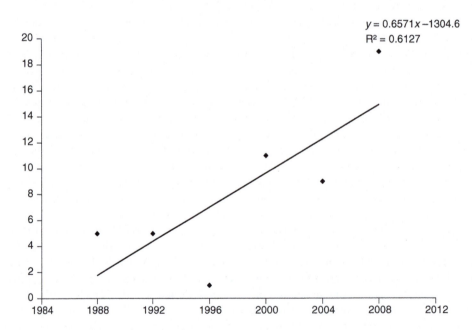

Figure 17.5 Proportion of gold medals won by the United Kingdom 1988–2008

Using the equation for the trend line shown in Figure 17.5 enables us to extrapolate that in 2012 we expect the United Kingdom to win 17 gold medals.

$y = 0.6571x - 1304.6$; if x equals 2012 then

$y = (0.6571 \times 2012) - 1304.6$

$y = 1322.1 - 1304.6 = \mathbf{17.4}$

The R^2 score of 0.61 (coefficient of determination) is equivalent to a correlation of 0.78 which can be interpreted as a 'strong' relationship. To this initial forecast of 17 gold medals we also need to factor in a home advantage effect to allow for the investment made in elite sport during the London Olympiad, the special qualifying concessions offered to the host nation by the international sport federations, and the other aspects of home advantage such as crowd effects on judges and familiarity with facilities. The value of the host nation effect that we apply is simply the average increase in gold medals won by the host nations since 1988. The application of the recent average increase in gold medals won is simply a judgement call based on our observations of the accuracy of the same technique in prior editions of the Olympic Games. In Figure 17.6 we show the increase in gold medals won and the change in medal table ranking of the last six host nations.

All six of the most recent hosts have increased their gold medals won and their ranking in the medal table and are consequently placed in the top right-hand quadrant of Figure 17.6. The average number of gold medals won relative to the previous edition of the Olympic Games is nine. Therefore we complete our forecast by adding nine to the extrapolated figure of 17 from the regression to arrive at an overall forecast of 26 gold medals. Repeating the analysis for total medals won using exactly the same approach, but simply substituting total medals for gold medals, provides an overall forecast of 57 medals. History will judge how accurate these forecasts proved to be!

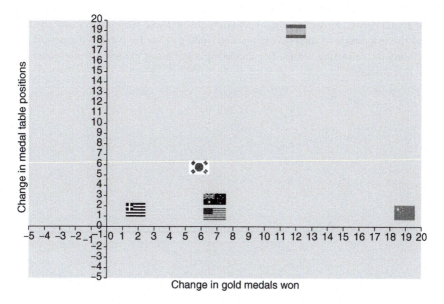

Figure 17.6 Change in gold medals won and medal table ranking 1988–2008

While our forecasting model performed well for the host nations in Beijing 2008 and Vancouver 2010 it does not follow that it can be applied mechanistically to other events. To derive our approach we looked at how nations' performance varied from edition to edition and sought to find a way of describing this numerically in order to test it at future editions of the same event. When we applied our methods to the Paralympic Games and the Commonwealth Games we found that there was much less strength in the relationships between performance and time. As a result, the forecasts produced were not particularly accurate as the patterns of performance by nations were more random than they were for the Summer and Winter Olympic Games. In search of a possible explanation, one key finding we found for both the Paralympic Games and the Commonwealth Games was how much the programme of events changes between editions. Paralympic sport is unique in the way in which there are different categories of event for people with different types of disability within the same sport. In the Commonwealth Games the host city has a significant degree of influence over the range of sports that are contested. In Delhi 2010 53 per cent of events were in 'core' sports that must be contested and 47 per cent were in events chosen from a list of approved sports by the organisers. India enjoyed its best ever Commonwealth Games, finishing second in the medal table for the first time, largely because of its success in wrestling and shooting. These were two optional sports that were specifically included in the programme to improve India's chances of success. By contrast, the programme of events in the Summer and Winter Olympic Games is relatively stable and is set by the IOC rather than the host nation. As a result, the fluctuating patterns of performance seen in the Commonwealth Games and Paralympic Games are not replicated in both versions of the Olympic Games. What this type of analysis reveals then is the importance of exercising judgement and not relying solely on mechanistic processes. While a mechanistic process may have been shown to be reliable in one set of circumstances, it should not be generalised more widely without a clear understanding of the new context to which it is to be applied. As we found with attempts to replicate our model elsewhere, there may be other factors at work that undermine the accuracy of a forecasting technique. Traditionalists and idealists may have reservations about measuring performance and even greater reservations about attempting to forecast performance in major sports events. However, the benefits sought by those who make investments in elite sport and the magnitude of such investments are such that we have entered a period of public accountability for delivering results. For increasing numbers of nations it is no longer the 'taking part' that matters.

18

PROMOTING STUDENT–ATHLETE INTERESTS IN EUROPEAN ELITE SPORT SYSTEMS

Dawn Aquilina and Ian Henry

Introduction

The analysis of sports policy often focuses on a limited set of stakeholders, and relatively rarely engages in the discourse of rights (as opposed to, for example, discourses of effectiveness, efficiency and economy). There are exceptions, although these tend to relate to general claims such as the UN assertion of the child's 'right to play'. This chapter seeks to evaluate through a review of student–athlete lived experience of different systems of provision of higher education services for elite student athletes, whether the individual student–athlete's rights as 'student' and as 'national representative' in elite sport are differentially met within the different systems of provision in European Member States.

The background to this discussion is the demonstration by the European Union of a significant and growing concern for the protection of athletes in relation to education and training and their integration into the workforce in a post athletic career. This is explicit for example in a number of statements in documents such as the sporting Annex to the Nice Treaty, the conclusions of the French Presidency delivered in Nice in 2000, the White Paper on Sport (European Commission, 2007b) and the recent Communication adopted by the European Commission, entitled *Developing the European Dimension in Sport* (European Commission, 2011). Promotion of equity or at least good practice thus remains a key concern. The EU has been actively seeking to find alternative means of engaging in dialogue with other global stakeholders to discuss this matter. Presidency Conclusions (11–12 December – Council of the European Union, 2008) in Brussels stated that the European Council Declaration on sport has acknowledged the 'need to strengthen the dialogue with the International Olympic Committee and representatives of the world of sport, in particular on the question of combined sports training and education for young people' (17271/08 Annex 5). By including this issue on the agenda, the European Council has demonstrated the increasing importance attributed to the effective management of a dual career of elite sport and education by young sportspersons. Indeed, in 2011–12 the European Commission established an Ad Hoc Expert Group to develop guidelines for Dual Career Athletes, motivated in large part by the wish to protect the rights of young elite sportspersons.

While it will be noted that the European Union has to date had limited scope in influencing policy at the nation state level within this context, responsibility to ensure that student–athletes have access to opportunities and support to combine a dual career successfully has thus lain with the nation state. Bergsgard *et al.* (2007: 253) observed that the level of 'priority given to elite sport varies considerably between countries, due in part to different national cultural values and traditions, political and administrative structures, and relationships between governmental and civil society sport organisations'. Thus, it is a matter for each nation state to decide how important sporting achievement is, usually by taking a local democratic decision on whether to invest in promoting elite athletes. However, one of the principal arguments presented in this chapter is that if nation states do invest in elite sport and build on the efforts of elite sportspersons, as demonstrated by the three approaches in Finland, France and the UK investigated by Aquilina (2009) and reported here, nation states have a moral responsibility towards their elite athletes. A critical message here is that nation states should not leverage sporting success by mortgaging the future of student–athletes, and in particular by diminishing their access to educational rights. The athlete may serve the interests of the state, the national federation, or the educational institution by attaining high level performance, and these bodies may serve the athlete's purposes in developing their athletic potential, but such a system implies a set of mutual obligations in which the interests of all parties (particularly of young athletes who may be most vulnerable) should be protected.

Elite sport systems and the education of young athletes: a brief review

With the increasing level of investment in national elite sporting systems it is not surprising that governments, the principal investors, have been keen to learn from successful sporting nations, and this has led to researchers trying to identify 'models that work' in this domain. Oakley and Green (2001) had observed that national elite sporting systems of historically successful nations such as the UK, the US and Australia, among others, seemed to be converging at various points offering very similar services to their elite athletes and employing similar strategies. The analysis of the policy literature is particularly useful as it provides insight into the broader network of systems and professionals surrounding the elite athlete. Most of the research reviewed in this area has adopted a 'top-down' approach to map out the diverse elite sporting systems established in various nation states, with little emphasis on 'bottom-up' studies of athletes' own experiences of such systems. For example, in an attempt to try and identify the key aspects that make up a successful sporting nation, Oakley and Green (2001) observed that there were a number of convergences between countries, including the type of educational services provided for elite athletes. This observation was confirmed in a broader comparative study by De Bosscher and her colleagues (De Bosscher, De Knop, and Van Bottenburg, 2009) as they identified nine policy dimensions that were deemed critical to ensure sporting success. (See also Chapter 16 of this volume.)

One of the ways in which nation states continue to secure sporting success is through the development of student–athletes, which is a phenomenon of growing importance to individual nation states as the proportion of elite athletes in higher education continues to increase. The term 'student–athlete' has been used extensively throughout the writing of this chapter and although various definitions are provided in the literature, in the context of this chapter it refers to those individuals who are undertaking university-level education and who are also actively involved in elite-level sport. This term is therefore often used to reflect the direct link between being a full-time athlete and a university student.

The importance of student–athletes to the elite performance of a nation state is illustrated by the British experience. Official statistics released by the British Universities and Colleges Sport (BUCS) website indicate that over 60 per cent of the Great Britain team participating

Table 18.1 Contribution of British student/graduate–athletes to the medal tally at the Beijing Olympic Games, 2008

	GB Total	*Students/graduates contribution*
Number of elite athletes	311	180
Medals won at the Beijing Olympic Games 2008	77 Gold – 19 Silver – 13 Bronze - 15	42 Gold – 12 Silver – 7 Bronze – 7
Gender	168 (men) 143 (women)	87 (men) 93 (women)
Events entered by GB team	20	16

Source: adapted from British Universities and Colleges Sport (2008)

at the Athens Olympic Games, 2004 were in fact 'products' of the higher education system (British Universities and Colleges Sport, 2008). Statistics on the Beijing Olympic Games, 2008, indicated that 58 per cent of Team GB consisted of current and former student–athletes. There were 77 British competitors in total who won a medal in Beijing with 42 (55 per cent) of these having come through the university system. Table 18.1 shows the demographics of those elite athletes with a higher education background. More recent statistics from the London Olympic Games, 2012, confirm that 61 per cent of Team GB was once again composed of either current or alumni of higher education institutions. Perhaps what is even worthier of note is the fact that since the Barcelona Olympic Games, 1992, 65 per cent of all gold medal winners had gone through the higher education system (British Universities and Colleges Sport, 2012).

In France the statistics are comparable to those of the UK. Bayle, Durand and Nikonoff (2008: 153) observed that almost half of France's medallists (16 out of 33) from the Athens Olympic Games were in fact student–athletes based at INSEP (Institut national du sport, de l'expertise et de la performance). The authors suggest that the elite training centre, (which also provides academic programmes) is regarded as a highly successful system as it consistently

Table 18.2 Contribution of French student/graduate–athletes based at INSEP to the medal tally at the Beijing Olympic Games, 2008

	France Total	*INSEP Students'/Graduates' contribution*
Number of elite athletes	323	98
Medals won at the Beijing Olympic Games 2008	41 Gold – 7 Silver – 16 Bronze - 18	21 Gold – 3 Silver – 9 Bronze – 9
Gender	198 (men) 125 (women)	Not known
Events entered by French team	23	13

Source: adapted from INSEP website (www.insep.fr)

manages to produce exceptional athletes who have contributed towards France's traditionally strong performance in medal tables for both the Olympic Games (e.g. seventh in London 2012) and various World Championships. Table 18.2 illustrates the contribution of INSEP's current and alumni student–athletes to the medal tally (21 out of 41) during the Beijing Olympic Games.

From a survey conducted by the Finnish Olympic Committee investigating 425 athletes' educational and vocational profiles, it was concluded that 65 per cent of their elite athletes were also going through the higher education system. The survey also revealed that not only do Finnish elite athletes follow the same educational paths as their non-sporting peers but they even had a higher level of educational attainment than the rest of the population (Merikoski-Silius, 2006).

Methodology for the study of elite student–athlete experiences

The study outlined in this chapter (which is reported more fully in Aquilina, 2009), involves the selection of 18 athletes, six from each of three different national systems of provision of higher education opportunities for elite athletes. The selection of the three exemplar policy systems draws on the findings of a study of sport and the education of elite young sportspersons undertaken by the authors and their colleagues for the European Commission in 2004 (Amara, Aquilina, Henry, and PMP Consultants, 2004) which identified four types of policy response by European Nation States. The current study selected one national system as an exemplar from each of the first three types of policy system. From each of these three exemplar systems six athletes were selected as cases for analysis. Selection of athletes was designed to reflect diversity in terms of age; individual/team sport; gender; age at which specialisation in the sport normally took place; whether the athlete had graduated or was still a student; and whether the athlete was still active or had retired.

The four types of athlete/education policy system were as follows.

State-centric/statutory action

In such cases the state has placed a legal obligation on universities to make special educational provision for student athletes. Examples from the 2004 study included France, Hungary, Spain and Portugal. France was selected from those countries exhibiting 'State Centric Provision' as our source for case study student–athletes. In the case of France, a central institution, INSEP, established by the state under the Loi Mazeaud in 1975 (and with forerunners going back to the mid-nineteenth century) provides educational services for elite athletes directly or negotiates a link with other education providers under the umbrella of the services managed by INSEP.

The choice of French athletes to interview in order to investigate their experience of the system was restricted mostly to those student–athletes who were formerly or currently training and studying at INSEP in Paris. Interviews took place in November, 2007. As Table 18.3 illustrates, four of the interviews were carried out with student–athletes in athletics, badminton, swimming and synchronised swimming. The retired judoka in the sample had been based at INSEP but was working in the UK at the time of interview. The handball player held a professional contract with one of the top teams in France. Handball is a professional sport in France but it is not included in the INSEP programme. The interview therefore took place at the player's home club's office in Paris.

Table 18.3 Selection criteria for French student–athletes

	Age	Individual/ team	Male/ female	Early/late age of specialisation	Active/ retired	Student/ graduate	University degree/other qualifications
Athletics	28	Individual	F	Late	Active	Graduate	• Bachelor's in Sports Science • Masters in Coaching • Professorat de Sport
Badminton	31	Ind. / Team	M	Late	Active	Student	• Bachelor's in Sports Science • Professorat de Sport
Handball	21	Team	M	Late	Active	Student	• Bachelor's in Business and Management
Judo	27	Individual	F	Early	Retired	Graduate	• Bachelor's in Sports Science • FIFA Masters • Masters in Sport Management
Swimming	22	Individual	M	Early	Active	Student	• Information Technology Diploma • Coaching diploma
Synchronised swimming	20	Team	F	Early	Active	Student	• Bachelor's in Sports Management

State as facilitator/sponsor of measures

The second type of approach was one in which the state, acknowledging student–athletes' needs, provides permissive legislation or regulations, authorising but not requiring universities to make special educational provision for student–athletes at the elite level. Examples of this approach include Belgium (Flanders), Denmark, Estonia, Finland, Germany, Latvia, Lithuania and Sweden.

Finland is selected as the exemplar of this second approach. In Finnish higher education all fields of study apply *numerus clausus*, in which entrance examinations are a key element. The Finnish Ministry of Education awards grants for athletes proposed by the Olympic Committee and the Paralympic Committee who on the basis of their international performance have potential for winning a medal in the Olympic or Paralympic Games, or in the World Championships. The level of the tax-free sport grant in 2004 was either €12,000 or €6,000 per year. Grants were allocated in both summer and winter Olympic sports as well as in non-Olympic and Paralympic sports. The total amount awarded in sports grants for the year 2004 was €558,000 (Merikoski-Silius, 2006).

The criterion for allocation of a full (€12,000) Athlete's Grant was that the athlete had reached sixth–eighth place in the individual competition of the season's main event (Olympic Games, World Championships or World Cup overall competition). The criterion for the grant of €6,000 was that the athlete had finished in eighth–twelfth place in individual competition

Table 18.4 Selection criteria for Finnish student–athletes

	Age	Individual/ team	Male/ female	Early/late age of specialisation	Active/ retired	Student/ graduate	University degree/other Qualifications
Athletics	32	Individual	M	Late	Active	Student	Masters in engineering
Basketball	28	Team	F	Late	Active	Graduate	Masters in environmental economics
Football	42	Team	M	Late	Retired	Graduate	Masters in media technology (engineering)
Gymnastics	32	Individual	M	Early	Active	Student	Masters in sports sociology
Ice-hockey	20	Team	F	Late	Active	Student	Masters in food technology-chemistry
Judo	22	Individual	F	Early	Active	Student	Masters in adult education

for these same events. The criterion for the award of a young athlete's grant (€6,000) was that the athlete had attained twelfth to fifteenth place in the corresponding competitions. An athlete awarded a grant was required to sign a training contract with the given Sports Federation and the Finnish Olympic Committee, in which the athlete agreed to follow the existing anti-doping rules as well as other requirements such as having a personal study programme (Kanerva, 2004).

Of the elite Finnish athletes selected, five of the six were currently active in the following sports: athletics, basketball, gymnastics, ice-hockey and judo, and were at various stages of their sporting careers, with three planning to retire within the coming year. The retired professional football player had moved on to coach a top division team. Three of the interviews took place at the Finnish Olympic offices in Helsinki while the other three were carried out in a central hotel cafeteria as requested by the participants.

Most of the interviewees were studying or had studied at Helsinki University, but one athlete was registered at Jyväskylä University (the only university in Finland offering sport-related degrees) and another at Tampere University. Owing to the nature of university education in Finland, all of these athletes had graduated or would soon graduate with a master's degree. It was unanimously agreed by all Finnish interviewees that leaving university directly after graduating with a bachelor's degree did not afford them any realistic opportunities to gain the employment of their choice, and it was generally accepted that they needed to study up to a master's level in order to have better opportunities in the labour market.

National Sport Federation/Institution as intermediary

The third type of approach is one in which the sporting and educational development needs of the individual are overseen (sometimes loosely) by sporting institutions such as National Federations and where sporting representatives act as advocates on behalf of the student–athlete, negotiating flexible arrangements and variations in study plans with the university in order to ensure that the requirements of sport and of the education system are not mutually exclusive. Examples of this type of approach are Greece and the UK.

The exemplar chosen for the selection of interviewees was the UK. A number of universities in the UK have traditionally informally offered elite student–athletes special concessions in terms of exam dates, location for holding examinations, assignment deadlines, waiving of attendance requirements and flexible duration of programmes of study. However, at the elite level those athletes on UK Sport's World Class Performance Programme have access to the services of a 'Performance Lifestyle Advisor' employed by one of the National Institutes of Sport in the UK, and where necessary this individual would negotiate directly with teaching staff on behalf of the student–athlete.

While the UK system had thus traditionally had an informal element of negotiation (often by the National Sports Federation or the Performance Lifestyle Advisor), as preparations for the hosting of the London 2012 Games intensified, government activity in this area increased and there was an evident shift in the UK system from that of '*National Sport Federation/Institution as Intermediary*' to '*State as facilitator/sponsor of measures*'. The Talented Athlete Scholarship Scheme (TASS) introduced in 2004 had been further formalised and extended. This scheme serves athletes below the World Class Performance Programme. The programme provides government funding that is designed to promote a partnership between NGBs and Higher Education/Further Education institutions. Its stated aims are to promote a balance between academic life and training as a performance athlete, thus reducing the drop-out of talented athletes from sport due to academic and financial pressures. The focus is thus on maintaining sporting performance and the scholarships, which amounted to up to £3,500 per year, are generally intended for supporting sporting expenditure on services such as coaching, physiotherapy, sports science, nutritional advice and sports psychology, rather than on educational services or materials.

An addition to the TASS scheme in 2009 were TASS 2012 scholarships aimed at those with potential to progress towards the World Class Performance Programme. This provided annual grants of up to £10k but again these were intended for sports support services rather than educational services. Nevertheless, TASS advisors may negotiate with university staff on behalf of their student–athletes to achieve some flexibility in requirements.

The top tier of elite athletes on the World Class Performance Programme (WCPP) receive the services of a Performance Lifestyle Advisor who provides advice and support for all non-sporting aspects of lifestyle including educational and vocational preparation support. The WCPP at the time of the interviews in 2007 was divided into three categories of athlete, namely 'Podium', those with genuine potential to win Olympic/World Championship medals; 'Development', those who will be competitive for medals in 2016; and 'Talented', athletes identified as those likely to progress through the World Class pathway. A total of 1,200 athletes in the top two categories had benefited from government investment of £100m. per year for sports performance support.

Five out of the six athletes interviewed in the UK were training and either currently studying or had recently graduated from Loughborough University, the country's leading higher education institution specialising in sports science and elite sport support. The sports in which the interviewees were competing were athletics, golf, gymnastics and triathlon. In addition, the sample included a professional rugby player who held a professional contract with one of the top Scottish rugby teams and had previously been registered as a student at Edinburgh University.

Table 18.5 Selection criteria for British student–athletes

Sport	Age	Individual/ team	Male/ female	Early/ late age of Specialisation	Active/ retired	Student/ graduate	University degree/other qualifications
Athletics	23	Individual	F	Late	Active	Graduate	Bachelor's in psychology
Athletics	23	Individual	F	Late	Active	Student	Bachelor's in English and publishing
Gymnastics	22	Individual	M	Early	Active	Student	Bachelor's in business studies
Golf	22	Individual	M	Late	Active	Student	Foundation degree in sports science
Rugby	26	Team	M	Late	Active	Graduate	Bachelor's in sports science
Triathlon	23	Individual	F	Late	Active	Student	Bachelor's in fine arts

Laissez-faire – few or no formal structures

The fourth approach is one where there are few or no formal structures, and arrangements (where these prove feasible) are generally restricted to individually negotiated agreements. This category is broad in so far as these individually negotiated educational routes had been accommodated for a range of athletes in some institutions in for example the Netherlands and Cyprus but in other countries in this category, such as Italy, Ireland and Malta, education systems had traditionally been quite rigid in nature in relation to student–athletes' needs. In addition to Cyprus and the Netherlands, states whose systems fall within the *laissez-faire* approach included Austria, Czech Republic, Ireland, Slovakia and Slovenia.

For pragmatic reasons of resource, no country was selected as an exemplar from this type of system, though case studies of how student–athletes had negotiated or failed to negotiate their way through the sporting and educational systems with no formal guidance might well prove instructive in terms of whether athletes' rights are breached.

As we have already commented, much of the analysis of policy relating to elite sport has employed a 'top-down' approach addressing policy from a predominantly institution-based position. The principal aim of this study therefore was to redress this imbalance and to gain insight into the elite athletes' worldviews, and their perceptions of the significant factors in personal educational decision making. To this end, detailed interviews were conducted employing a life-story approach (Miller, 1999) with the elite athletes selected who had experience of university-level education, to understand what constraints and opportunities existed for them, and to establish how these have been negotiated by athletes in different sporting contexts and in different types of educational system, with what kinds of outcome. By identifying examples of good practice in the three European contexts together with constraints hindering the student–athlete's academic and/or athletic development, the research sought to identify ways in which some of these difficulties may be addressed, with policy implications in terms of informing thinking in relation to how policy makers, administrators, educators and coaches might enhance the student–athlete experience in higher education.

Thus, central to this study was the importance of choosing a strategy and method that enabled the gathering of data related to these athletes' own perceptions and experiences. A life-story method of interviewing was adopted, as advocated by among others (Gearing, 1999; McGillvray and McIntosh, 2006; Roderick, 2006; Smith and Sparkes, 2009) as a means for gaining a deeper understanding of the lives and experiences of the athletes interviewed. The approach also gave 'voice' to the interviewees, empowering them from the very start of the interview process to take greater control of the narrative provided.

While our approach to the selection of national systems was as a result in part of a wish to evaluate the impact of such structures on the experiences of student–athletes, the use of a life-history approach provided a counterbalance against any tendency to give too much weight to a structural (institution/policy structure) account that explains outcomes solely or predominantly as a product of the policy structures set up to achieve such outcomes. Although all the athletes interviewed inhabited, or had inhabited, the world of elite sport and of higher education, there were still elements that were particular to specific individuals, such as the type of sport they practised with its particular sporting culture, the athlete's gender, and the life stage (and sporting life-cycle stage) that they had reached. At a more complex level, one also had to take into consideration that there were further differences from one culture to the next in a transnational study of this nature (Crotty, 2003). Thus, listening to the student–athletes' stories in their own words, with the flow and direction of the interview negotiated with, rather than imposed on, the interviewee was critical to accessing the interviewees' worldview.

Research findings and discussion

A thematic analysis of student–athletes' interviews sought to highlight critical factors that interviewees identified as being instrumental in how effectively they managed their dual career. These factors were outlined under three dimensions: the personal – relating to the participants' own disposition and skills and their ability to strike a balance between the two careers of athlete and student; the support network of people including but not limited to parents, coaches, teaching staff and other sport professionals; and the wider structures, the institutional and policy setting, encompassing both academic and sporting institutions surrounding them.

At a personal level, the student–athletes argued that they must have a favourable disposition themselves towards their dual career and have to be proactive to progress successfully. As the British gymnast commented, athletes not only have to be in the right mindset to want to combine their education and sport but, more importantly, be capable and skilful enough to organise and manage their life well in order to be able to sustain it in the longer term. All student–athletes interviewed emphasised the importance of developing a wide range of skills, whether it was to help them balance the daily demands of a dual career or whether they needed to cope with a critical situation. The perceived value that student–athletes placed on their skill set was clear throughout each interview as they traced the major decisions that guided their dual career. This finding resonated well with the main arguments in the literature that fostering skills such as leadership, teamwork, effective decision making and mature career planning can help to 'counterbalance the negative aspects of the elite performer's experience' (Miller and Kerr, 2002). Miller and Kerr extend this argument as they observe that such skills are not only critical tools to manage a dual career in academia and sport but have lifelong value, as such skills 'address the whole person issues including psychological, emotional, personal, social, moral, and intellectual development' (Miller and Kerr, 2002: 144).

A central recurring theme that came through the interviews was the concept of balance and the relative importance that all 18 student–athletes interviewed attached to their own definition of this concept. It is important to note at this stage that what constituted a 'balanced lifestyle' implied a series of different things at different times to these student–athletes and therefore made it increasingly hard to conceptualise. Student–athletes were quick to concede that balance did not mean a 50/50 split between their two careers but thought of it more as a varying degree of balance depending on their priorities, and this included balancing not simply sporting and educational demands but also family and the social dimensions of their lives. At times when an assignment was due or an exam was coming up, student–athletes gave priority to their academic career while their sporting career took precedence during competition time. At times when sporting and academic demands clashed, student–athletes tended to choose the former. From the interviewees' comments it was clear that achieving a degree of balance between the two components (athletic/academic) was paramount in order to sustain a dual career in the longer term, yet what these student–athletes understood by the term a 'balanced lifestyle' contrasted starkly with how their own university friends, coaches, family members and other friends regarded it. However, the general consensus remained that a degree of balance must be attained as student–athletes experienced mutual benefits of pursuing both careers (see Aquilina, 2013). These findings were largely consistent with the main observations made in the literature that the critical factor identified by a number of researchers in successfully combining an elite sporting career with an academic one is balance (McKenna and Dunstan-Lewis, 2004; Miller and Kerr, 2003). The second point that has been highlighted in the literature with regard to this concept of balance is that both the support network of professionals and the support system surrounding the student–athlete must be conducive to helping these individuals find and, more importantly, maintain a level of balance throughout their careers (Miller and Kerr, 2002).

The key people surrounding the 18 student–athletes, who were considered to be the most influential in their life, included the parents, partners, coaches, peers, academic staff and other professional sport staff. Having the support and understanding of these key people has been described by athletes as one of the significant factors in determining how well they coped with specific transitions and transitional periods (from school to university; from living at home to moving away; from junior to senior athlete; from national to international level competition etc.). This support was manifested in a myriad of ways, ranging from emotional support to financial assistance and all athletes felt indebted in some way to these people. Coaches in particular have been identified as having a critical role to play in ensuring that they provide the support needed to the student–athletes they coach. As the participants noted during the interviews, training and competing at such an elite level often meant that they spent most of their time with their coaches. There were different types of relationships that student–athletes had developed with their coaches, with the most effective being where responsibilities such as the organisation and planning of training schedules and decisions over which competitions to compete in were equally shared. By encouraging their student–athletes to discuss issues and strive towards mutual goals, coaches facilitated the effective management of a dual career. However, in order for this to be possible the coach had to develop certain personal characteristics that would enable him/her to provide the right support. The French judoka explained how the coach should be of a certain disposition and philosophy himself/herself to be able to support a student–athlete in combining a dual career. She described how her club coach, being also a university lecturer, understood better her concerns and could openly discuss with her various aspects of her two careers as he understood both worlds.

At a wider level, the student–athletes identified also the academic and elite sporting structure/environment surrounding them as being instrumental in facilitating the way they managed their dual career. Being in a system that supported both their academic and athletic development provided these student–athletes with the 'right environment' not only to help them manage their dual career on a day-to-day basis but also be successful at it in the longer term.

The roles that some universities have adopted in order to sustain their student–athletes can be best described in the type of support they are providing. This support related to both academic and sporting opportunities but also had implications for the choice of post-athletic career. Where such academic provision existed student–athletes took advantage of a series of services such as the opportunity to schedule their own timetable (as in the case of the Finnish students), extending the final year over two years to ease the academic work load (as in the case of the two British track and field athletes) or having access to individual tutoring (as was the case for the French athletes who might have missed an important lecture because of training camps and competitions during term time). Some universities, in particular the University of Jyväskylä in Finland and Loughborough and Edinburgh universities in the UK, are also continuing to invest in elite sporting infrastructure to meet the increasing sporting demands of their student–athlete populations. Furthermore, by liaising with national sporting federations such as the Finnish Gymnastics Federation whose national training centre is located at the University of Jyväskylä, or establishing partnerships with National Governing Bodies such as those of netball, cricket, badminton and gymnastics in the case of Loughborough University, universities were able to develop a number of initiatives that could benefit the student–athlete. Having both NGBs coaches and administrators based on campus facilitates a constant exchange of ideas and knowledge with Loughborough University staff who specialise in key areas of elite sport through their research. Thus, making use of professionals in fields such as physiology, psychology, physiotherapy, nutrition and lifestyle management universities are available to provide quality elite training programmes and support while making it increasingly more manageable for student–athletes to cope with their sporting and academic commitments more efficiently.

In the United Kingdom 'sport advocates' (national governing bodies or national institutes of sport) tend to act on behalf of the student–athlete to negotiate flexible educational provision with academic institutions. In this case there are members of staff such as performance lifestyle advisers within national institutes of sport, who are responsible to guide student–athletes as to how to manage a dual career effectively. However, from the findings of this study it appears that the participants interviewed in the United Kingdom preferred to negotiate flexible measures with academic staff personally. There were a number of provisions that student–athletes availed themselves of, such as extending the number of years to complete their degree and getting special permission to attend training camps and competitions abroad; however, for all of the six British interviewees special arrangements were agreed on a case by case basis. National governing bodies were only occasionally consulted to provide documented evidence of the international training camps and competitions that the interviewees were attending. This particular finding might suggest that 'sporting advocates' have limited scope in the day-to-day management of student–athletes' lives, but as five of the British student–athletes interviewed argued it was important for them to have access to the range of services that were provided by the various national institutes of sport. The key services identified were medical assistance from doctors and physiotherapists, sports science support and in one case the service of a sport psychologist. Although all of these services were directly linked to the athletic development of the participants, having the right support in their sporting life was deemed to have a positive impact on their academic career, and therefore contributing to the successful management of a dual career.

In the case of those French student–athletes who were based at INSEP it was generally agreed that the training centre offered them an extensive range of opportunities to develop their dual career in a very positive way. Being part of a large student–athlete community, having access to both high performance facilities and quality academic programmes was considered to be an ideal milieu to facilitate the achievement of their athletic and academic potential. Moreover, having a number of flexible measures in place together with access to a support network of academic staff, facilitated significantly the student–athletes' lives. Interviewees participating in this research study were fully aware of their right not to be discriminated against while they were studying at university.

The French handball player, who was not based at INSEP, explained how his professional club went a step further and had become actively involved in his academic development through a type of apprenticeship scheme, set up between the university, the athlete and the club. This negotiation was not the same as other nationwide apprenticeship schemes that are established within professional sporting clubs (e.g. football) in France but was individually negotiated to meet the athlete's specific needs. In France most university students are encouraged, and in some degrees it is even mandatory, to have a work placement in industry to gain practical experience. Since the handball player was currently studying for a degree in business studies, he needed to gain work experience in an environment where he could develop and use his managerial skills. Therefore his handball club gave him the opportunity to work both at an administrative level and also help market the club. This had proved to be such a positive partnership that at the time of interview the athlete was currently preparing a detailed proposal on how this apprenticeship could be converted into a permanent post within the club structure, once he graduated from university.

From the understanding of these student–athletes lived experiences it became clear that institutional structures in their own country only go some way to explaining how they facilitate the management of their dual career and there were other significant sport-specific aspects that were more significant than these structures. For instance a common concern voiced by all student–athletes was the excessive sporting demands on their time. It has been widely acknowledged that with the increasing competitiveness in international sport and the growing professionalisation of elite sport more time is being invested to ensure that elite athletes achieve their sporting targets (Conzelmann and Nagel, 2003; International Olympic Committee, 2008). Having to attend training camps and competitions away from university also has been found to add pressure for student–athletes and thus various alternative measures had to be explored. Research by INEUM and TAJ (INEUM Consulting and TAJ, 2007) has already highlighted some of the extremes that exist in the quality and quantity of training hours demanded of athletes, yet no clear guidelines have been agreed upon to date and this remains an issue for each individual elite student–athlete to negotiate with her/his coaching staff. The case of the French swimmer is an illustrative example of this type of policy concern as he struggled to complete his academic degree owing to the increasingly high demands being placed on his time by his sport. He noted how following his best sporting performance at the Athens Olympic Games in 2004 he was constantly being pursued by sponsors and other individuals from the elite sporting world which put a strain on both his sporting career and personal life. He admitted that in retrospect he would have appreciated having some guidance/support on how to handle such success as it subsequently led to a negative experience. Being at an institution such as INSEP presented a slightly more complex challenge for two other French student–athletes because they were aware that their sporting demands and commitment would always have to be given priority because of the nature of the institutional structure. Being essentially a training centre some coaches did expect their athletes to give sport precedence at all times and this did conflict with the successful management of a dual career for some of the French athletes. In the context of France, Bayle *et al.* (2008) observed that an increasing number of French athletes are finding themselves in similar vulnerable situations as more demands on their time are being made by sport federations/elite training centres on the one hand, and private/commercial organisations on the other. There does not seem to be any regulatory framework to help the athlete decide on how much time s/he can dedicate to each of these entities and therefore the authors envisage a situation where 'different organisations – clubs, national teams, and national, regional, and world organising bodies – keeping a tally of the number of dates that accrue to each' (Bayle *et al.*, 2008: 160). This situation calls for a reassessment of the demands made by each of the stakeholders involved, such that the 'ownership' of an athlete's time is reclaimed by the athlete and, where appropriate, support is provided to guide the negotiations made by the athlete.

Issues revolving around time management affected not only French athletes as four out of the six Finnish athletes were also finding it challenging to manage the number, timing and duration of training camps and competitions. As the Finnish gymnast observed, if an athlete was at the peak of his/her sporting career, they were usually required to spend around eight months of the year away from home and/or university. Timing was critical with such events and therefore at times student–athletes observed that they were unable to progress as consistently in their academic career as anticipated, owing to clashes in commitments. Regrettably, for athletes, many of the annual international sporting events were usually scheduled during the same period, which at times interrupted term time at university year on year. Thus, even in Finland where students have the opportunity to schedule their own academic timetable to fit their individual needs, from a student–athlete's perspective this still remained problematic as the same modules were offered during the same period of the year and these would continue to clash with the period of peak seasonal sporting demands.

This problem was further exacerbated for those student–athletes who were competing in Winter Olympic sports and whose greater sporting demands fell during the European winter season, with the top international tournaments culminating in early spring. As the Finnish ice-hockey player attested, other than having to be away for a week at a time on a monthly basis for training camps, the most challenging period was during the World Championships, where the national team members had to spend a whole month away from their home country every year.

As the Finnish and British athletes noted, it was at times problematic for student–athletes to plan for their academic career in advance, owing to the nature of decision-making that characterised elite athletics. A Finnish athlete explained how, at the time of interview, he was finding it a challenge to plan his academic workload as final selections for international tournaments take place just a short time before the actual competition. Student–athletes were therefore constantly being held back by this feeling of uncertainty, not knowing whether they would be competing or not, whether they had to travel for competitions, how many hours they would need to dedicate to their athletic preparation and other similar factors, all of which needed to be taken into consideration. Consequently, short-term planning in sport made it increasingly hard to plan ahead in other aspects of their lives since most decisions revolved primarily around their sport.

Other types of challenge related to the specific 'status' and 'culture' of certain sports where there were marked gender differences and where academic attainment was not fully valued. Two Finnish female athletes observed how there was a disparity between the professional status of the game in their home country and the semi-professional status of the female players. They explained how there was a much higher proportion of men who achieved full professional status and could earn a living from their sport, while the proportion of women who were able to do so remained sparse. This had implications for the effective management of a dual career as women were still expected to work either part time or full time to support themselves financially. Both the Finnish basketball and ice-hockey players drew comparisons between the relatively professional set-up of the men's leagues and the semi-professional nature of the women's game. They commented that there were only a few women playing team sports who had managed to secure professional contracts in Finland and therefore for the rest it was imperative that they were either in education or employed to be able to maintain their lifestyle.

Student–athletes across the three nations were aware that in some sporting contexts, for example in combat sport and football among others, the sporting culture inculcated in such settings is at times to the detriment of the educational development of some of their athletes. The Finnish judoka explained how she had to overcome a number of challenges to effectively cope with the dual demands of her careers since she became part of the national selection. She described how some of the national team coaching staff opposed her furthering her studies at university since they thought that this would interfere with her athletic development. In spite of her many attempts to convince her national team coach otherwise, by the time of the interview they had still been unable to come to a mutual understanding of her choice of lifestyle. This particular resistance to academic involvement on behalf of the sporting staff echoes earlier recommendations made by Bourke (2003) and McGilvray and McIntosh (2006) who exposed the detriments of such practices and argued for a comprehensive strategy in continual professional development and developing career transition policies within elite sport contexts.

Conclusion

In our sample all of the athletes had chosen a dual career as students (who one might argue are already a privileged group who have the capability to articulate their narrative to serve their own interests) who have 'made it' into higher education; thus, the research may be missing out on a substantial segment of the elite athlete population. By not interviewing elite athletes who did not pursue higher education the researchers may be overlooking a population whose experience (for example those focusing exclusively on sporting careers) may be markedly different from those who opt for a dual career. However, it should be noted that in the case of the UK, 61 per cent of Olympic athletes from the Barcelona Olympic Games (1992) to London Olympic Games (2012) had had experience of higher education (British Universities and Colleges Sport, 2012) while 50 per cent of the French medallists at the Athens and Beijing Olympic Games had been students at INSEP (Bayle *et al.*, 2008: 153).

Being a student was something that the students chose to do for various reasons, and in many cases they reported the fact that doing so made them better athletes and helped them sustain the demands of an elite sporting career for longer:

> When I was finishing the Baccalaureate it was very hard to juggle everything at the same time so then in my second year I decided to focus on sport over education, since we got all the good results. I stopped classes for a semester but it was not a good option! I needed to study because I was going a bit crazy!
>
> (Synchronised swimmer, France)

As has been discussed earlier in this chapter the range of life skills that student–athletes drew on to manage their dual career was very wide, encompassing organisational and time management skills, leadership, goal-setting and analytical skills:

> I think it's important because when you are interested in going to school in developing yourself and getting to know new things you develop your analytical ability and that's what you need in football and you also need the hard work in the long term. If you think of a football player it takes years to learn how to play football and it's the same with school, there's a learning curve you follow and I think those two things support each other.
>
> (Footballer, Finland)

Bolles (1996) defined transferable skills, which can also be termed as life skills, 'as those sets of skills that are potentially transferable to any field or career, regardless of where they were first learned or developed' (cited in Mayocchi and Hanrahan, 2000: 95). Congruent to this definition student–athletes confirmed that they had developed their set of skills in a number of ways, whether it was through formal learning at school or training in a sporting environment and they tended to consistently draw on these transferable skills to manage their dual careers successfully.

From the findings of this research there was no evidence that one particular system was in effect more successful than others in allowing the individual to meet the demands of a dual career and thus to secure his/her right to education and the fulfilment of sporting potential. As the Finnish gymnast observed, while he was aware of other national systems of combining education and elite sport, he still believed that his own national system was equally functional and effective as it had allowed him to perform, gaining a gold medal in the World Championships. He did not think that an 'ideal' model existed and was convinced that the key to managing a dual career successfully ultimately relied on the individual:

> I haven't come across any system that's ideal or is any way better than what is on offer here in Finland. I think it all depends on the individual and his personal commitment towards his studies. You have to take the initiative. There are some countries which allow you to go at a slower pace or else negotiate special arrangements on your behalf but I don't think it's necessarily better than what's on offer here. I know in the US for example they have a good scholarship system but I wanted to stay in Finland, as I said we have good training facilities and good level of education.
>
> (Gymnast, Finland)

This same logic was argued by three of the British student–athletes interviewed who had been offered full sport scholarships at North American colleges/universities but who all declined as they did not want to realise their sporting potential at the expense of their academic development. All of the interviewees were aware of the risks associated with signing a formal contract with a high profile sports college, where student–athletes may be obliged to compete in a stipulated number of events, travelling over long distances for training camps and events on a regular basis, and be expected to dedicate a substantial amount of their time for training purposes, compromising the time needed to fulfil the academic demands to a good standard. When an athlete is recruited to a university the implicit contract is one in which the university will provide appropriate educational experiences and enhance the individual's stock of intellectual capital. Recruitment of athletes onto programmes from which they are unlikely to benefit and in which they have little chance of completing successfully is a practice highlighted in the US college system but which there could be some danger of reproducing in a European form. It is thus recognised that in Europe more effort should be invested to continue to protect the academic interests of student–athletes at university.

The placing of excessive demands and expectations on young elite sportspersons by the nation state (usually in the form of national institutes of sport or national elite training centres, e.g. INSEP) or by national federations, in terms of commitment of time and other resources, can effectively deny these young people access to educational opportunities that may be critical to their future well-being and ironically also to their performance as athletes. When nation states are funding bodies that place such individuals in positions where educational opportunities have to be sacrificed, one would argue that there is a moral obligation to compensate athletes with privileged access to resources to ensure that their rights as ordinary citizens to appropriate educational opportunities are not prejudiced. The nation state therefore has to assume greater responsibility to ensure that student–athletes have access to opportunities and support to combine a dual career successfully. The European Union with its competence in sport's 'new role under the Lisbon Treaty is to support and coordinate sport policy in member states. Action is foreseen in areas where challenges cannot be sufficiently dealt with at a national level alone' (European Commission, 2011: 4). Such areas will incorporate protection from commercial interests (Aquilina and Henry, 2010), avoiding discrimination (Aquilina and Henry, 2010), developing guidelines on combining sport training and general education(European Commission, 2011) and innovative approaches to dual career management (Ooijen, 2010).

However, the approach adopted in our study was not simply to review policy structures and approaches, but to seek to understand the worldview of the student–athletes themselves. A clear theme in the argument of the elite athletes in these studies suggests that what is provided in terms of sporting or educational policy structure is likely to be most effective if it is complemented by coaches, educationalists, sports administrators and other members of the entourage who provide options, but who also facilitate the decision making of the student–athlete so that s/he can make informed decisions about their sporting and educational careers, and thereby become an 'architect', rather than a 'victim', in shaping their own destiny.

19

ANTI-DOPING POLICY

Historical and contemporary ambiguities in the fight for drug-free sport

Paul Dimeo and Thomas M. Hunt

Introduction

Definitions and uses of the term policy can refer to a range of strategic or operational activities. It can be an area of politics (for example, environmental policy or housing policy) – and consequently infer governmental objectives. It can be a broad vision tied to stated objectives, such as having a policy on child development or on health in the workplace, in which case policies can be driven by single organisations with sufficient resources to enable significant social change. Policies can also be concrete rule-based outcomes such as, for example, the regulations for parking at universities. These might be single or multiple organisations but differ from other forms of policy in that the requirements are highly specific and therefore the results can be monitored clearly.

A number of theorists have examined the policy process: the activities by which policies are made, implemented and changed (for example, Kingdon, 1984; Sabatier, 1999; John, 2003). Although detailed analysis of policy theory is beyond the scope of this chapter (see Nowlin, 2011 for such a discussion), two key points are identified here that will help to set the conceptual framework behind contemporary anti-doping policy. The first is that policy rarely occurs as a linear set of functions; instead it is best understood as a series of overlapping policies that are fluid, adaptable and dependent on local and global power relations. The second is that the early stages of the policy process under which a vision is rationalised and developed set the context for the planning, implementation, monitoring and eventual success or failure of the policy.

Public, private or third sector organisations often have policies that set out their visions and/or mission statements. Within the sports sector, policy documents tend to refer to those constructed by governmental or public sector organisations that have stated aims around sports development (Houlihan, 2008a; Green, 2009). These might be aspirational ideas for collectively engaging related organisations, such as is the case in recent efforts to improve health through sports participation. Or they may be evidence-based with incremental and realistic plans for improvement (Coalter, 2007b). Stating that a country has won a specific number of medals at international competitions and aims to improve upon that by a specific percentage over a given time period serves as one prominent example of such a document.

By tracing the chronological development of anti-doping policy since 1960, the aim here is to present and discuss the most significant aspects of the substance and process of anti-doping policy in order to enhance understanding of the past, present and future of the subject. More specifically, this essay argues that the ambiguities of earlier historical periods in the policy process continue to haunt contemporary anti-doping policy makers.

Anti-doping policy development: 1960–80

Anti-doping policy crosses over the definitional types noted above. It began as (and remains) an aspirational policy based on vague assertions of sport and morality that lacked a clear sense of vision and a realistic ambition that could be achieved and monitored (Dimeo, 2007). It developed from a situation where rumour and speculation outweighed actual evidence. While the point of origin for anti-doping policy cannot be objectively identified – there were brief statements by leading sports organisations prior to the Second World War – it was around the late 1950s/early 1960s that it gathered momentum, ideological shape and institutional support. Around this time, the policy leaders did not know what the drugs involved would actually do to the human body or the extent to which they were used. Many of the rumours focused on professional cycling, and public denouncements of doping had come through such voices as those of the American Medical Association (Dimeo, 2007). The IOC's attention was sharpened by the death of Danish cyclist Knud Enemark Jensen in the 1960 Rome Games (Hunt, 2011), rumoured to be linked to amphetamine use (a claim later proven to be unfounded; see Møller, 2005).

Nonetheless, the 1960s witnessed the shaping of drug use within sport as a problem. A number of leading campaigners argued that 'artificial stimulation' was immoral, that it undermined the values of sport, that it posed health risks for athletes and that it represented the sort of degradation commonly associated with 'deviant' drug use in society. Yet, these assertions were social constructions rather than absolute truths; sport was largely understood as a different field that required its own set of rules. It was not enough for sports authorities to follow public criminal laws; instead they took it upon themselves to establish criteria for wrongdoing and punishments for violators of those criteria that were independent of those imposed by the law and police systems (Koller, 2008; Hunt, 2011). Indeed, this point was of fundamental importance to the development of anti-doping policy in sport.

The consequence was that the agreed objective of anti-doping policy became to rid sport of drugs completely. In other forms of drug regulation there was flexibility depending upon the classification of the drug and their potential uses and abuses. Alcohol, amphetamines, morphine, heroin and antibiotics received different treatment by medical and criminal policy makers. Yet, within sport there was little scope for any flexibility. The practice of taking amphetamines, using alcohol during competition, and so on, were uniformly treated as immoral within the policy framework. Athletes were considered to have acted unethically and to have contravened the values of sport. Astonishingly, this was the case for events that took place well before the first policy criteria for wrongdoing were even established. When the IOC President Avery Brundage commissioned Arthur Porrit and then Prince Alexandre de Merode in the 1960s to lead the fight against doping (Dimeo, 2007), he expressed an opinion that anti-doping was something of a public relations exercise and that the IOC could not fund and resource a comprehensive international anti-doping policy (Hunt, 2011). Yet, Porrit and de Merode both made public statements that doping was a serious ethical problem that, if left alone, could have drastic consequences. As such, anti-doping efforts through the 1960s took place in the context of significant internal discord as to how best to organise and implement the desired aim of drug-free sport.

By the late 1960s, the Council of Europe, a handful of European governments, and a number of national sports organisations had established the issue as a substantive policy concern.

In doing so, these bodies exerted considerable pressure on the IOC – the organisation that alone possessed the international prestige and authority needed to establish meaningful leadership on anti-doping. Once a definition of doping was put in place, a list of banned substances was created and testing implemented during events (Todd and Todd, 2001). The aspiration of drug-free sport had mutated rapidly into an operationalised policy with written documents and manifest outcomes for those who transgressed the rules. By this time period the term 'policy' could be read in a number of ways – anti-doping was a broad vision defined only in terms of violations under a socially constructed set of legal rules that were themselves created external to public institutions. In short, sport at this point had gone a considerable way towards monopolising legislative, executive and judicial power over anti-doping in sport. Athletes, as a consequence, steadily lost their rights to contest the fairness of anti-doping rules or the punishments handed out for their violation.

The first experimental tests concerning the effectiveness of anti-doping policy were conducted in Italy in the early 1960s and, though far from conclusive, they seemed to show a reduction in amphetamine use owing to the potential penalties (Venerando, 1964). Following this, a group of scientists ran a modest number of unofficial tests at the 1964 Olympics, mainly on cyclists who were seen as a problem group at this stage (Hunt, 2011). Anabolic steroids were at the time emerging as a drug for weightlifters and other power athletes, but no test existed to detect their presence in the human body until 1975 (Brooks *et al.,* 1975; Ward *et al.,* 1975). Testing for amphetamines and alcohol was conducted in single-sport events in 1965 and 1966, then at the Olympics in 1968. The objective of drug-free sport was given further impetus after the death of English cyclist Tom Simpson in 1967, though many elite cyclists saw doping as part of their profession and resisted the testing system (Dimeo, 2007; Thompson, 2008). However, we can see that the period between 1960 and 1970 revolutionised the world of sport with respect to doping and anti-doping. The former had evolved from a small problem in a handful of sports, mainly referring to in-competition use of stimulants such as amphetamines and caffeine. The latter had grown from little more than a vague idea into a legalistic policy based on an oversimplified, idealistic notion of the impact of drugs on athletes and on the moral virtues of sport.

The nature of anti-doping policy at the beginning of the 1970s was such that a socially constructed dichotomy had been put in place between those who supported drug-free sport and those who supported cheating. Yet, this was a false dichotomy that served to mask a range of ambiguities that would continue to challenge the development of anti-doping policy.

The first of these was that the anti-doping framework of testing and punishment had little chance of succeeding, as the leading authorities simply did not possess sufficient economic or persuasive power to make it effective. The use of steroids was actively promoted in East Germany and the Soviet Union by the late 1960s and into the 1970s (Ungerleider, 2001), and other countries turned a blind eye to doping among their athletes (Todd, 1987; Voy, 1991; Hoberman, 2005; Hunt, 2011). Professional cyclists remained entrenched in a culture of systematic doping through team networks. There were no out-of-competition tests and steroids could be 'washed' out of the athlete's system within three weeks, making it easy to avoid detection (Beckett and Cowan, 1979). Yet, the IOC's anti-doping leaders, such as the Chair of the Medical Commission, Prince Alexandre de Merode, would regularly claim that the war on drugs was being won (Dimeo and Hunt, 2011).

The second ambiguity was that the rules designed to detect cheating produced several unintended consequences. The initial plan had been to stop athletes from using stimulants and thus end doping; however, the response to regulation was innovation within a black market of new drugs and masking agents that increased health risks while promoting doping. Since the 1960s, the list of banned substances has grown to the point that it is extremely hard for an athlete to understand the chemical compounds that are presented to them (Chambers, 2009). A related problem has been that in the attempt to prevent the use of certain stimulants like ephedrine, their employment in the treatment of legitimate medical issues has been difficult to judge in policy terms. There have been accusations made against athletes who took such substances to combat conditions such as asthma – one of the early cases being the 16-year-old American swimmer Rick de Mont who tested positive at the 1972 Munich Games after being cleared to use an inhaler by American team physicians (Hunt, 2011).

And a third ambiguity concerned an inconsistent application of anti-doping rules, either within sports or within countries (Houlihan, 1999). As noted above, East Germany (the German Democratic Republic – GDR) and the USSR maintained formal policies to dope their athletes in order to gain Olympic success. Other countries wanted to ensure that communist governments did not achieve those symbolic victories and so took a passive stance on anti-doping. Still others, such as the UK and Norway, possessed strong anti-doping policies. However, another problem was that of how developing countries could fund anti-doping education and internal testing while struggling to fund sport in general. There seemed to be an assumption that all countries would be able to make the same commitment to anti-doping. However, if athletes were not educated about the rules or tested out-of-competition then they faced higher risks of being caught at major international events. Equally, if they did not know what supplementation was legal then they were at a disadvantage to their rivals. The policy thus created a range of unintended variations that actually undermined the concept of a 'level playing field'. As a number of critics said through the 1970s and 1980s, the Olympics had become a battle between doctors, and thus the countries with the most resources and the highest level of determination to succeed could better 'support' their athletes and identify strategies to beat the system. The GDR, for example, tested athletes' samples before they left the country, allowing a system that provided steroids to over 10,000 athletes to produce only two positive tests over a 20-year period (Franke and Berendonk, 1997; Ungerleider, 2001).

Therefore, the ill-conceived policies designed to crack down on drugs that began in the 1960s led to the dramatic developments of the 1970s and the creation of an uncontrollable doping problem. The definition of doping and the efforts to create a global policy to rid sport of drugs had created a crisis. The weaknesses in the regulatory framework for dealing with the issue were exploited by unscrupulous athletes and governments in the context of increasing commercialisation and politicisation in sport. The traditional amateur ethos that decried 'artificial' means of enhancing performance now appeared anachronistic, and the attempts to defend that ethos through anti-doping seemed futile. Yet, the rhetoric of anti-doping remained powerful as sports authorities and leaders defined doping as a serious threat that extended beyond sport to wider humanity (Dimeo, 2007). For example, when Lord Killanin took over the IOC Presidency from Avery Brundage, he asserted that doping:

> in my view, is the greatest danger [to the future of the Olympic movement], far more serious than infractions of the Rules concerning amateurism or any insidious political intrusion. Anabolic steroids create false individuals, be they men or women – artificial people out of test tubes.
>
> (Descoeudres, 1979, p. 140)

Nonetheless, the reality was that anti-doping policy was beset by ambiguities that seriously weakened the fight against drugs in sport.

Crisis of policy and the creation of WADA: 1980–2000

Although a test for steroids was implemented at the 1976 Olympics, the historical record shows that doping was widespread throughout the 1970s and certainly in the 1980 Moscow Games (Todd and Todd, 2001). The IOC leadership continued a charade in which it could show the world what steps were being made to combat doping at the same time that athletes and their medical support staffs continued to consume and innovate. Perhaps the most significant policy development was the reliance on the testing system to somehow 'prove' that doping was being controlled by the international authorities. In other words, the IOC and others invested testing with an authority in order to establish their credentials in having achieved something. IOC officials could point to the fact that only a handful of athletes tested positive in the years 1968 to 1980 to prove that their policy was working – science was seen as the solution to the problem and too much trust was placed in that science. This had an ambiguous outcome: the IOC could claim success but since anecdotal evidence suggested athletes wanted to keep using banned substances, they could request more resources to keep the vigilant work going. As the British doctor and IOC anti-doping expert Professor Arnold Beckett said in 1980: 'We win some, we lose some. The war goes on' (Denlinger, 1980). Prince Alexandre de Merode, who had now been Chair of the IOC Medical Commission for 13 years, repeated the assertion that new research and better testing had meant the Moscow Games were 'clean'. Yet, he had developed a strategy of arguing that anti-doping required more research in order to respond to the innovations in the supply chain (Dimeo and Hunt, 2011). The war needed to be funded.

Yet this war had its limits: it could not be too successful or it risked fully exposing the extent of doping and thus undermining public support for the Olympics and other international events. This dilemma was exemplified when the IOC was accused of covering-up a set of positive lab results during the 1984 Los Angeles Games. Arnold Beckett was effectively asked to leave the Games after criticising de Merode's handling of this affair (Dimeo, 2007). However, the 1984 Games had invited a great deal of speculation in the media about the role of doping. New drugs had come onto the market and those motivated by success over ethics had advantages that others did not. While the Olympics struggled to keep the historical and amateur ideals in place, other sports also faced problems. Professional cycling and non-Olympic bodybuilding gained a reputation for doping. Outside of elite sport, steroids were becoming more common. In the USA, professional, college and even high school sports were increasingly suspected as being fertile grounds for doping. So, as the IOC tried to maintain its moral high ground, all around it the sports world was rapidly changing. Nonetheless the policy directive remained the same: more testing would help prevent doping. Every Olympic Games saw an increase in the number of tests conducted, yet the numbers testing positive remained low.

The 1988 Ben Johnson case has been well documented (see, for example, Kidd *et al.*, 2001), and it allowed the IOC to prove that it was taking doping seriously after the 1984 accusations. However, what emerged in Canada would be devastating to the anti-doping campaign. In the aftermath to the exposure of doping within elite athletes, the Canadian Government instigated an internal investigation into the matter. The Dubin Inquiry showed that doping was rife, not just in Canada but across international sport, supported by traffickers and doctors, and promoted by commercial and nationalist impulses. The ambiguities of the 1960s not only remained but actually undermined the vision of drug-free sport. It was clear now that the black-and-white dichotomy had only served to create two self-serving industries: doping and anti-doping. The more resources that went into anti-doping to fuel an unwinnable war, the more innovative and dynamic the doping suppliers and users became. Yet, even after the Johnson affair, IOC officials were increasingly seen as weak leaders on the issue of performance enhancement. Academic research during this period showed that doping remained widespread and that the anti-doping system was largely ineffective in combating the problem (Hoberman 1992; Goldman *et al.*, 1984; Todd, 1987; Voy, 1991).

Through the 1990s, a series of further scandals combined to make the IOC's position as leaders of international anti-doping untenable. When the Berlin Wall fell in 1989, Werner Franke and Brigitte Berendonk removed Stasi files from their storage facility and fled to a secure location from where they revealed details of the GDR's doping system. This led to legal cases in reunified Germany that told the shocking details of the ways in which young athletes, some as young as 12 years old, were given male hormone steroids without their knowledge or consent and without full understanding of potential side effects. Many women suffered severe short- and long-term health consequences. These details showed how ineffective anti-doping had been through the 1970s and 1980s. During the 1996 Atlanta Games, the IOC was accused of a similar cover-up as in 1984, when it seemed that too many positive tests would ruin the image of the Games. Moreover, details emerged of doping in American sports, Chinese swimmers were caught in possession of growth hormones and there were other high profile cases such as that of Michelle de Bruin. The world of cycling had been under scrutiny since Paul Kimmage's (1998) inside story of doping , and there were suspicions of doping in the high profile events. These were confirmed when Willy Voet, an employee of the Festina team, was caught at the Belgian border carrying the team's supply of drugs for the 1998 Tour de France (Voet, 2002). A subsequent police inquiry showed systematic, management led doping within that team, and others came under suspicion. Since then, professional cycling has been the focus of increased anti-doping efforts yet continues to be plagued by both scandals and an inconsistent application of policy (Møller 2010).

The IOC's position had become untenable by the end of the 1990s. While that organisa- tion had provided the leadership, the apparent moral guidance based on de Coubertin's ethical vision for international sport, the resources to fund anti-doping efforts and the quadrennial event to focus attention on the issue, it became increasingly apparent that another strategic policy was required.

In 1999, sports leaders were invited to a conference in Lausanne to discuss the future of anti-doping. Many were surprised when the outcome was an independent organisation with global authority funded by the IOC and a number of governments. The IOC retained a great deal of authority, not least in positioning former Vice-President Dick Pound as the first Head of the World Anti-Doping Agency (WADA). The headquarters had originally been in Lausanne, close to the IOC base, but was later moved to Montreal. As such, the 'independence' of the organisation could be criticised, at least in its early years.

Yet, even in the formation of WADA, there was little if any reflection on the policy vision that had so spectacularly failed in the preceding 25 years – namely, the achievement of drug-free sport. Similarly, the rationales for supporting and strengthening anti-doping policy remained the same: the health of the athletes and the fair play aspect of sport. In the face of growing scepticism about the motivation of athletes and the reality of short-lived professional careers vis- à-vis considerations of short-term ethics and long-term health, WADA simply reinforced the basic principles of anti-doping established in the 1960s. Indeed, given the lack of amateurism in sport (Beamish and Ritchie, 2004), the logic of modern sport (Møller, 2010), the increased medical supervision of athletes (Waddington, 2010), the failings of anti-doping (Hoberman, 2005), and the lack of athlete engagement with anti-doping, WADA's position seemed defen- sive, traditionalist and out-of-touch with reality.

WADA in the twenty-first century

In order to address some of the weaknesses of IOC-led anti-doping, the policy directives led by WADA were even more ambitious. The WADA Code, first published in 2004, included an extensive list of banned substances and provisions that more or less obliged countries to become signatories to the Code and to accept specific responsibilities for delivering education and testing to their athletes. The out-of-competition testing system was beefed up to include the 'whereabouts' system that required athletes to provide an hour each day where they would be in a specific place for testing officials to find them if required. Scope remains for 'accidentally' missed tests – athletes are not punished until they have missed three out-of-competition tests – but if they do so face a two-year ban from all competitions. This has provoked intense debates around surveillance and privacy, with many critics arguing that athletes' civil rights are overly infringed (Houlihan, 2004), and a group of 65 athletes took such a case to court in Belgium (BBC, 2009). Such is the intensity of debate around this issue that Waddington (2010) has argued, albeit perhaps unconvincingly, that athletes are being treated in a similar way to convicted paedophiles. Cases have also been overturned by the Court of Arbitration in Sport (CAS) in instances where athletes demonstrated legitimate reasons for missing a test. It seems that the more WADA tries to monitor athletes, the greater the number of problems that result.

A number of other problems remain in the new anti-doping framework, including the management of therapeutic use substances, the consistency of penalties and the struggle to keep abreast of black market innovations. More broadly, not all athletes have been persuaded of the value of drug-free sport, with regular cases of positive tests occurring. Professional cycling has perhaps been most affected by the 'crackdown' on doping, with many of the most successful riders either found guilty, strongly suspected or punished for relatively minor offences. The recent case involving Lance Armstrong and his colleagues from the US Postal Service Team shows the extent of doping through the 1990s and 2000s in this and many other teams. A central controversy in Armstrong's case was the failure of the UCI/WADA testing system to keep up with doping innovations and the avoidance tactics of dopers, and thus led to reliance on witness testimony. It also opened up the doping culture of the sport to public scrutiny and led to demands for anti-doping empowerment.

The spate of recent confessions from some of the world's most successful cyclists show the struggles faced in trying to enforce regulations in a sport where the athletes themselves have failed to engage with the ethical principles and practical rules of anti-doping. However, the obsessive zeal with which anti-doping has been pursued can have problematic consequences. For example, Michael Rasmussen was removed from the Tour de France for missing two tests when, in itself, this was not a doping violation; Alberto Contador was banned when his test sample featured trace amounts of clenbuterol that could have resulted from consumption of tainted meat; and scientists are now able to re-test samples that have been stored for up to 8 years thus undermining the certainty that a race winner is truly the winner. It can also be argued that Lance Armstrong has been treated unfairly since he is the only cyclist to be sanctioned without either a positive test or a confession. Cycling is fascinating because it shows us how the historical moralising efforts to enforce fair play can have a range of controversial outcomes and consequences.

WADA inherited the policy problems created by the visionaries and idealists of the 1960s. As outlined above, one ambiguity was that anti-doping could never succeed so long as the leading authorities did not have sufficient economic or persuasive power to prevent it. WADA has far greater resources and institutional power to enforce compliance – its budget for 2010 was

$26m. Yet, it cannot succeed in its objective of drug-free sport because there are still too many athletes who will turn to doping products to enhance their performance, or who will fall foul of the testing system or who will unintentionally use a banned product. A number of recent studies show that athletes are 'at risk' of doping when they feel under pressure to perform, are returning from injury or imagine that others in their sport are doping. Indeed, according to a recent Danish study, it is not ethics or health that prevents athletes from using doping substances but the fear of getting caught (Christiansen, 2011). The objectives of anti-doping do not seem to reflect or promote values; the anti-doping rules instead serve only to ensure athlete compliance to the rules. An interesting question which is still to be addressed is whether public support for anti-doping is dwindling as some have suggested (Hoberman, 2005), in which case the social stigma attached to the 'scandal' of doping may no longer prove a deterrent.

The second ambiguity was that the rules designed to detect cheating produced unintended consequences. There is no doubt that black market suppliers continue to innovate to allow athletes to cheat the testing system. The testimony of Victor Conte, head of the BALCO laboratory that supplied several athletes with a designer steroid known as THG, showed that there were several methods used to 'innocently' miss tests and to use drugs not yet on the list of banned substances. He also analysed the patterns of out-of-competition tests and judged his athletes' usage accordingly. Indeed, he accused the authorities of *naïveté* and showed that athletes and their medical advisors who were determined to cheat could do so with relative ease. In addition, there are no tests for genetic manipulation, despite warning that such practices have been occurring in elite sport for several years (Miah, 2004).

The third ambiguity noted above is that the policies were inconsistently applied. WADA has tried to recover this position by asking individual sports governing bodies and national governments to sign up to the Code. Some research shows that athletes feel there are geographical variations in the application of the educational and 'whereabouts' aspects of doping control (Hanstad and Loland, 2009). The issue of funding remains for developing countries who cannot afford to support elite athletes and have a resource-intensive anti-doping programme. As such, some countries are suspected of being less than committed to anti-doping and therefore lenient towards their athletes in terms of the use of doping products while training.

Conclusion

The world has changed since Knud Enemark Jensen tragically fell off his bike and focused attention, albeit misleadingly, on doping in sport. Social circumstances related to drugs have changed. In some ways, there are now much tighter controls on recreational and medical drugs, but there has clearly been a rapid expansion in research, knowledge and application of drugs. The trend, especially in the USA, towards anti-ageing and physical regeneration therapies (Hoberman, 2005) suggests that using drugs to improve bodies, minds and performances, may become more acceptable. If we can use Viagra in the bedroom then why not use low levels of testosterone in sports?

Sport has also changed since the 1960s, and the cultural values of inter-war middle-class athletes who took on post-war administration positions no longer seem relevant. International sport is a business, with athletes potentially earning enormous salaries over their careers, gaining sponsorship and becoming celebrities. Their view of what a career in sports means is no doubt different to that of previous generations.

However, anti-doping has remained fundamentally much the same. Policies have been based on the same principles, and over time have reasserted, reinforced and enhanced the strategies of testing and punishment based on scientific knowledge of drugs. Yet, the challenges faced by anti-doping authorities remain intractable dilemmas because they are trying to control groups in society when not all of these groups want to be controlled.

WADA has increasingly become a policing agency, determined to catch those perceived as criminals. In recent times, WADA has liaised with border control and other police forces to try to catch traffickers. They have encouraged national anti-doping agencies to 'target' tests on athletes suspected of doping; this has meant developing 'intelligence' and profiling specific athletes, coaches and doctors. In a globalised society increasingly dominated by surveillance and technology, WADA is keeping a watchful eye on suspects. It seems somewhat ironic that the tactics of the *Stasi*, which had been used to ensure doping remained a secret in the GDR, are used to pursue the ambitions of anti-doping authorities.

To conclude, the historical trajectory of anti-doping policy showed considerable variation depending on anti-doping leadership and the practices of 'dopers'. Yet, the problems have remained consistent and the policy responses have focused on growing the 'reach' of anti-doping. Doping and anti-doping have been interdependent forces, feeding off each other, and responding to each other's latest move. This is a war that cannot be won, but neither can it be lost. From the 1960s through to the present, it is a war for which the *raison d'être* has been, and continues to be, the continuing of the war.

Acknowledgement

Parts of this chapter appeared in Thomas M. Hunt, Paul Dimeo and Scott R. Jedlicka (2012) 'The historical roots of today's problems: a critical appraisal of the international anti-doping movement', *Performance Enhancement and Health*, vol. 1, no. 2: 55–60.

PART IV

Development, sport and joint policy agendas

20

THE EVALUATION OF SPORT AND SOCIAL INCLUSION POLICY PROGRAMMES

Chris Kennett

Introduction

The potential role of sport in tackling social exclusion received considerable attention from scholars and policy makers at the beginning of the 2000s (Collins *et al.*, 1999; Kennett, 2002; Collins and Kay, 2003; Coalter, 2007b; Bloyce and Smith, 2009; Hoye *et al.*, 2010; Waring and Mason, 2010) but relatively little research has been undertaken on the evaluation of policy interventions in this field. As the conceptual relation between sport and social exclusion has already been explored at length by other authors, this chapter will provide a brief theoretical overview before analysing literature on how interventions aimed at tackling social exclusion have been evaluated using two examples from the UK: Active England and New Opportunities for PE and Sport (NOPES). Building on the work of Tacon (2007), a realist evaluation approach is proposed for the evaluation of sport-based social inclusion projects. This analysis will be framed in the context of changing priorities in UK sport policy during the 2000s.

Social exclusion and sport: a conceptual overview

The origins of social exclusion can be traced back to Weberian and Durkheimian thought. Weber identified exclusion as a form of social closure that occurred as groups assumed positions of privilege over others. Meanwhile, contemporary discourses on social exclusion, particularly at the European Union level, are full of Durkheimian concepts such as inclusion, integration and cohesion. Indeed, contemporary notions of social exclusion have their origins in French social policy where *les exclus* was used as a label for those suffering from a breakdown in structural, cultural and moral ties that slipped through the welfare net in the mid-1970s (Levitas, 2005).

Exclusion was central to Townsend's study of deprivation and relative poverty, in which poor people were those whose 'resources are so seriously below those commanded by the average individual or family that they are in effect, excluded from ordinary living patterns, customs and activities' (1979: 32). Relative rather than absolute measures of poverty involve multidimensional factors that stretch beyond income to consider processes of deprivation and exclusion from mainstream society.

Some of these measures, such as Townsend's (1979) Deprivation Index, included leisure and recreation activities as part of the ordinary activities of people in modern society.

Although sport was not directly identified, its consolidated role as part of welfare provision in many societies has established sport as a social and economic good that people have the right to participate in.

By the beginning of the 1990s the concept of social exclusion had started to take over from traditional, more politically sensitive notions of poverty in EU policy discourse. Social exclusion was defined as a multidimensional and relational process that Room (1995) identified as requiring a joined-up policy response. At the Lisbon Summit in 1996, EU member states agreed to promote social inclusion and social cohesion, locating the need to tackle social exclusion at the centre of many countries' policy agendas. This was the case in the UK, where in 1997 the newly elected Blair government established its cross-departmental Social Exclusion Unit (SEU). The SEU defined social exclusion as: 'A shorthand label for what can happen when individuals or areas suffer a combination of linked problems such as unemployment, poor skills, low incomes, poor housing, high crime environments, bad health and family breakdown' (SEU, 1998 in Kennett, 2002). This definition relates social exclusion to individuals and geographic areas suffering from a multidimensional process that marginalizes them, but did not define exactly what the state of exclusion was. Certain groups were identified as being more at risk of exclusion, and particular focus was placed on excluded neighbourhoods or 'sink estates' as some were labelled.

Certain groups, such as unemployed people, disabled, young single mothers, immigrants, ethnic minorities, low skilled are identified as having a higher risk of experiencing social exclusion for a combination of social, cultural and economic reasons that compound the degree of exclusion an individual may experience. Therefore, a young, unemployed, single mother from an ethnic minority, living in an area of high deprivation would be more likely to experience social exclusion.

Similarly, social inclusion is also a contested concept and is often interpreted as the opposite to social exclusion. Rather, it is the complex process of overcoming challenges of social exclusion, involving the empowerment of certain groups and the development of excluded geographic areas, often through policy-driven interventions. Bailey (2005: 76) highlighted a series of inter-connected dimensions of social inclusion that included:

- spatial: social inclusion relates to proximity and the closing of social and economic distances between areas;
- relational: social inclusion is defined in terms of a sense of belonging and acceptance;
- functional: social inclusion relates to the enhancement of knowledge, skills and understanding; and
- power: social inclusion assumes a change in the locus of control.

Measuring the achievement of social inclusion according to these dimensions and relatively vague conceptual definitions creates important challenges for the sport policy makers, practitioners and researchers alike. How to establish realistic objectives and methodologies to measure spatial inclusion, the extent to which a group feels a sense of belonging or acceptance, to what extent knowledge and skill development occur, or identifying how power relations change in a community highlight the multidimensional complexity of demonstrating increased 'inclusiveness' in society.

Indeed, while common criteria for measuring social exclusion across EU member states have been defined (European Commission, 2009), there is no single definition of social exclusion. Levitas (2005) maintains that discourses on social exclusion are 'actively deployed as part of political projects, and the disputed meaning of exclusion is part of this political process; social exclusion is an essentially contested concept' that formed part of the ambiguous and contentious 'Third Way' approach to much British government policy in the late 1990s (Levitas, 2005: 3).

Sport was used as a policy tool for the wider achievement of social inclusion in the UK, but as will be discussed in the coming sections, relatively little research has been undertaken on its effectiveness.

Social inclusion policy in the UK: the role of sport

Since the inclusion of sport as part of wider welfare provision in the mid-1970s, the benefits of sport for individuals and communities have been well documented (Collins *et al.*, 1999). Sport has been used as a vehicle for achieving social policy objectives including improving health and creating active citizens, the inclusion of marginalized groups, building communities and developing citizenship, fighting crime, regenerating neighbourhoods, among others. While the social role of sport has been central to sports policy in the UK, so has elite sport. Policy has shifted between these two main policy priorities over the years, from Sport For All in the 1970s, to sport as means to economic regeneration in the 1980s and early 1990s, to sport's role in tackling social exclusion and poverty at the end of the 1990s.

At the end of the 1990s in the first term of the New Labour government, policy attention focused on social exclusion and sport quickly became part of the central government policy response to social exclusion through the formation of the Department for Culture, Media and Sport (DCMS) Policy Action Team 10 (PAT 10). PAT 10 commissioned a research report that identified sport as having a key role to play in increasing community development as part of wider neighbourhood renewal processes, and placed sport at the centre of social exclusion policy (Collins *et al.*, 1999).

Emphasis was placed on local authorities to strategically develop sport and leisure services that enabled disconnected groups to form part of society's mainstream. The PAT 10 report's findings informed the UK government's 2002 publication, *Game Plan: A strategy for delivering Government's sport and physical activity objectives*, which was co-authored by the Strategy Unit and the DCMS. *Game Plan* embodied New Labour policy of the time with a 'joined-up' approach to government involving 'cross-cutting' action aimed at 'Bringing Britain Together' and constituted what Coalter (2007b) identified as a much needed example of evidence-based policy.

Game Plan identified the social benefits of sport for health, education and tackling social exclusion as Tessa Jowell MP and the then Secretary of State for Culture, Media and Sport stated in her forward to the document, 'it [sport] can help us tackle serious health issues. It can also help to contribute to other areas, such as crime reduction, social inclusion and help with the development of young people in schools' (Strategy Unit, 2002: 7). The benefits of elite sport were also identified in social and cultural terms, with national sporting success producing a 'feel good factor' as well as economic benefits. The key aims were to increase participation in sport in general and in particular among disadvantaged groups, to improve performance at the elite level and attract major sporting events to the UK.

This two-pronged approach to sports policy with the social role of sport taking precedence over elite sport was in-line with attempts at the European level to establish a Europe-wide vision of sport's role in society. The European Commission White Paper on Sport (European Commission, 2007b) was heralded as a landmark moment in the developing relationship between sport and the European Union (Rogulski and Miettinen, 2009). The White Paper identified several roles for sport in European society, including its relationship with public health; the impacts of doping; sport's role in education and training; its role in tackling social exclusion; and sport as part of EU external relations.

The European Commission's policy commitment to the potential role that sport can plan in tackling social exclusion was clear, stating that:

> better use can be made of the potential of sport as an instrument for social inclusion in the policies, actions and programmes of the European Union and of Member States. This includes the contribution of sport to job creation and to economic growth and revitalization, particularly in disadvantaged areas. Non-profit sport activities contributing to social cohesion and social inclusion of vulnerable groups can be considered as social services of general interest.
>
> (European Commission, 2007b)

The priority groups identified in the White Paper were those subject to discrimination, disabled people and women.

However, policy priorities in the UK sport policy were about to change. London's winning of the 2012 Olympic bid saw central government sport policy start to shift to the point where in 2008 the DCMS published *Playing to Win: A new era for sport*. While the document applied to Sport England's strategy, much of the content was relevant to the UK. By way of contrast to Tessa Jowell's comments in *Game Plan*, Andy Burnham MP, then Secretary of State for Culture, Media and Sport, stated that the aim of *Playing to Win* was 'to get more people taking up sport simply for the love of sport; to expand the pool of talented English sportsmen and women; and to break records, win medals and win tournaments for this country' (Department for Culture, Media and Sport, 2008b: 1).

The vision of *Playing to Win* was to give more people of all ages the opportunity to participate in high quality competitive sport and to create a world leading sport nation. While this vision involved getting a million people to participate in sport regularly, the focus was on what was called a 'seamless ladder of talent development' that would take young people from school sport to the pinnacle of international sporting achievement. This was a far cry from the PAT 10 report's call to joined-up action and community development through sport.

Sport's main role changed from being that of a social instrument tackling the multidimensional problems of social exclusion in 2002 to being 'sport for sports sake' with a new emphasis on improving sporting performance and excellence in 2008. Green (2007a) stated that under New Labour elite sport discourse had strengthened significantly along with the development of active citizens.

Evaluating sport and social inclusion policy programmes

The PAT 10 report clearly stated that the evaluation of sport's role in achieving social aims was not only under researched, but that undertaking systematic evaluation was not a priority for policy makers and practitioners in the management of programmes and activities (Collins *et al.*, 1999). Eight years later, Tacon (2007) stated that decades of providing sporting programmes and activities had passed without developing 'hard' evidence that systematically demonstrates the benefits of sports in social terms (Bailey, 2005; Bloyce and Smith, 2009; Spaaij, 2009).

According to Tacon (2007), policy makers and practitioners still seemed to be working predominantly on the theoretical assumption that sport is a social good, without engaging in more informed, critical analysis of its role in tackling complex processes such as social exclusion. In the worst cases, Spaaij (2009) stated that social development through sport may be imposed on disadvantaged communities in a top-down manner. There is a clear need to maintain a critical approach when evaluating the impacts of sports interventions, which might be negative and in fact reinforce social inequalities and social exclusion.

Long *et al.* (2002) identified three levels of sports-related project evaluation: milestones, outputs and outcomes. Milestones are related to the ongoing evaluation of a project's progress and often involve key stakeholders such as sponsors. Outputs are short-term, generally quantifiable products such as number of participants, frequency of participation, measurements of performance. Outcomes are longer-term impacts that in the case of sport and social exclusion would involve changes in the lives of individuals, groups and communities that might result in greater levels of inclusiveness.

The measurement of outcomes is complex and the first challenge is to determine the meaning and then measurement of social inclusion. How, for example, do we know whether individuals or groups are experiencing increased inclusion as a result of participating in a particular sports programme?

The European Commission established 14 common criteria for measuring levels of social exclusion in European Union member states (European Commission, 2009) that involve multiple measures including: risk of poverty for individuals (poverty being defined as 60 per cent of national median income); levels of income inequality between the top and bottom 20 per cent of the population; health inequalities (including life expectancy); education outcome and human capital formation (share of people aged 18 to 24 with lower-level secondary education); financial sustainability of social protection systems; pensions adequacy (median disposable income of people aged 65+ compared to the rest of the population); inequalities in access to health care; improved standards of living (based on disposable income levels); employment levels among older workers; people in work that are experiencing poverty; labour market participation; deviations in employment rates between regions; and per capita health care expenditure.

It would be difficult, if not impossible, to demonstrate that any improvements in these, or more locally devised measures, were directly connected to a sports-related intervention. The indirect and intangible benefits of sport combined with the inability to separate sport from its wider socio-economic context are the key methodological challenges when evaluating its outputs and outcomes.

The PAT 10 report (Collins *et al.*, 1999) identified only 11 studies in the existing literature that involved what the authors described as rigorous evaluation systems that employed a variety of methodologies and were output focused. The main reason cited by this report for the overall lack of evaluation was a lack of resources dedicated to the process of identifying potential outcomes, gathering and analysing data.

Drawing on more recent studies, Tacon (2007) highlighted a series of factors that impeded the effective evaluation of social inclusion projects, including:

- an absence of a clear rationale or definition of measurable outcomes for the project (Collins *et al.*, 1999);
- use of inappropriate methods such as questionnaires that interfere with projects of a more sensitive nature (Taylor *et al.*, 2000);
- the contexts of inclusion may be multiple and difficult to separate, for example, extending beyond sport to education, work and wider leisure activities (Long *et al.*, 2002; Bloyce and Smith, 2009);
- collection of unreliable, anecdotal data from very limited and often unrepresentative samples (Nichols, 2007; Feinstein *et al.*, 2005; Bloyce and Smith, 2009);
- limited knowledge of initial participation rates and behaviour of excluded groups before intervention occurs (Coalter, 2007b);
- lack of consensus over the key measures related to inclusion and the establishment of causal relationships, e.g. the questionable importance of self-esteem and crime reduction (Emler, 2001; Nichols, 2007);

- inadequate funding of social inclusion projects, which limits their duration and therefore the ability to measure effects on social inclusion processes, or the inadequate allocation of funding to evaluation phases of projects (Collins *et al.*, 1999);
- as a consequence of the previous point, focus being placed on measuring milestones or outputs more directly related to funding objectives (Long *et al.*, 2002); and
- the duration of projects, which was also limited due to wider shifts in government policies and changes in ministerial terms (Walker, 2001).

Therefore many sport interventions were being designed and implemented uninformed by prior experiences due to an overall lack of systematic research caused by a lack of resources dedicated to evaluation activities.

Examples of sport and social inclusion evaluation practices in the UK

As part of the 2002 *Game Plan* strategy, considerable funding was directed towards sport programmes, activities and sport infrastructure developments with the aim of tackling social exclusion. The need to demonstrate the outcomes of sporting and social outcomes of various policies and programmes was becoming of increasing importance with those involved in sports development coming under increasing pressure to develop communities through sport as well as developing sport among people in their communities (Bloyce and Smith, 2009). This was reflected in the evaluation of some key programmes, such as Sport England's Active England programme (Sport England, 2009) and the NOPES programme (Hulme and Lee, 2009) and will be discussed in more detail in this section.

Active England

As part of the Active England programme (jointly funded by the Big Lottery Fund) 214 projects in total were funded, 107 of which were set up in areas that are among the most deprived 20 per cent in England and Wales between 2003 and 2008. The aim of the programme was to 'improve the health and well-being of individuals and communities as a whole, through actively promoting sport and other forms of healthy exercise' (Sport England, 2009: 1).

The Active England programme had three main objectives: to create sustainable, innovative multi-activity environments in areas of sport, social and health deprivation; increase participation in sport and physical activity among all the sections of society but particularly those sections of society underrepresented in sport and physical activity participation; and ensure the sports sector and key partners adopt new ways of working (Sport England, 2009: 1).

A focus on resource-based output evaluation criteria was also evident for underrepresented groups in the reporting of the programme's achievements (Sport England, 2009: 2). The evaluation was based on output key performance indicators (KPIs) such as the percentage of underrepresented groups among participants (such as black and minority ethnic groups (BME)); the effectiveness of the project related to costs (e.g. number of participants per £10,000); total numbers of key participant groups (e.g. coaches, leaders, instructors); participation frequency and intensity (e.g. number of participants during a one-month period); number of participants gaining sport-related and general qualifications (e.g. coaching certificates obtained by participants); number of jobs created and the securing of future funding for the project.

The evaluation of the individual projects was left to the organizing body, while Sport England conducted primary research that was analysed in combination with data collated from projects. Data collection methods included 'project surveys, project visits, qualitative research through developing case studies and sharing learning findings through learning exchange events and the Active England Learning Zone' (Sport England, 2009: 14). As part of the data collection process an innovative reporting information system called Value Mapping was used to gather data on outputs 'in real time' rather than just for milestones. Other evaluation that took place focused on programme learning and what could be improved for the future in ten 'Legacy Reports'. This formed part of what the report called the embedding of a self-evaluation culture.

Interestingly, the report contains a section entitled 'soft outcomes', for which there was 'no explicit objective for projects to contribute to' (Sport England, 2009: 29). These 'soft outcomes' included increased motivation; improved self-esteem; boosting confidence; and social engagement and interaction. Brief examples were provided from selected projects but little importance was given to them in the context of the report as a whole. The lack of commitment to outcomes reflects the overall concern with measuring and delivering on quantitative outputs.

The fact that the evaluation of the funded projects was the responsibility of the project managers, even though evaluation support activities and monitoring were undertaken by Sport England, must raise questions as to the objectivity of the data obtained. As identified by Bloyce and Smith (2009), many sports development practitioners were under intense pressure to secure funding for projects, which may result in overly positive reporting.

A further problem was that project managers had dedicated resources to the organization of activities, not their evaluation and 'did not have the time or resources to continued tracking people over time' (Sport England, 2009: 16). Apart from the fact that desired outcomes were not established as part of the KPIs, the way in which project managers allocated resources meant that the longer-term impacts of the projects were not evaluated.

Indeed, while this report stated that its roots lay in the *Game Plan* strategy there was a distinct lack of focus on achieving social inclusion in general (it is only mentioned once in the evaluation report). Rather, the focus seemed to be on justifying project funding based on short-term output measures. The report highlights the change in policy priorities at Sport England that occurred during the Active England programme with the publication of the 2012 Legacy Action Plan in 2008, which saw a shift away from promoting physical activity to funding sport in preparation for the 2012 Olympic Games.

NOPES programme

The NOPES programme received £751m funding from the Big Lottery Fund for the construction or development of sport facilities in deprived areas with the aim of contributing to community development, and was evaluated by the Loughborough Partnership (Hulme and Lee, 2009) between 2003 and 2009 and by Waring and Mason (2010). The main aims of the programme were: 'Through the provision of sporting facilities it was envisaged that increased *access to* and *use of* the facilities by all groups in society would promote inclusion, cohesion and, ultimately, equality' (Waring and Mason, 2010: 520). Funding was allocated to local authorities based on a range of criteria. The local authorities then identified a portfolio of projects to receive investment that corresponded to the desired outcomes stated in the NOPES programme. Each project proposal was evaluated by the Big Lottery Fund for approval. The majority of proposals were for new facilities to be built in schools for the benefit of students and the wider community.

The NOPES programme was evaluated over a six-year period, in terms of its impact on partnership, participation and wider social change. This was undertaken through a multi-method approach including baseline and annual surveys, case study visits to local authorities and projects, a discrete study about the design and management of facilities and a study about the impact of the programme on disaffected young people (Hulme and Lee, 2009: 4).

Waring and Mason's (2010) study involved 11 case studies of local authority portfolios comprising 105 projects, with between six and 20 projects per portfolio. Data were gathered through interviews with stakeholders on the three main strands of the evaluation process: partnership effectiveness, impact on participation and impact on wider social outcomes. The research was longitudinal with interviews taking place prior to the facility opening, one year after opening and three years after opening.

While the NOPES programme had six intended outcomes, the authors focused on the fifth: the promotion of social inclusion through access to, and use of, sports and outdoor adventure facilities by all groups in society.

The findings of this study reveal more in-depth insights into the changing perceptions and attitudes of key stakeholders over time. For example, the perception among stakeholders that not having the opportunity to participate was the problem – that is, the lack of a facility. Once the facility was opened, a commonly held belief was that social inclusion would take care of itself. A traditional Sport For All approach was evident in believing that the priority was to open the doors and let everyone have access.

Ongoing research revealed that the new facilities had important symbolic value for the local community. The facilities came to represent the regeneration of a community and an associated 'feel good factor' developed. These kinds of insights are difficult to obtain through short term, output-oriented evaluation.

Waring and Mason (2010) highlighted the importance of distinguishing between macro- and micro-level social exclusion as part of the evaluation process. Macro exclusion exists where systems and structures have resulted in the exclusion of certain groups or areas, such as migratory movements, deindustrialization processes, mass unemployment. The micro level focuses on the experience of an individual's perceived exclusion from a community connected not only to deprivation, but also to their life histories and relations (or lack thereof) with other community members. Thus, the authors recommended a re-examination of the power relations that create exclusion.

The evaluation reveals the need for a proactive approach that responds to the multifaceted nature of social exclusion as a complex process. The need for a longitudinal approach is also evident as stakeholders' views changed from pre to post opening of facilities. The initial belief that the building of a new facility and the opportunity this provided was sufficient to achieve desired outcomes had changed to recognize the need for a proactive outreach approach when the researchers returned after the facility had been in operation.

Evaluating sport and social exclusion policy: a realist perspective

According to the literature and more recent examples, the key issue regarding the evaluation of sport-based social inclusion projects is the overall lack of longitudinal, outcome-oriented research, which had primarily been caused by practical factors related to resources and the limited duration of projects.

Moreover, a wider debate exists over the use of appropriate methodologies in the evaluation of social inclusion projects. The use of controlled experimental methods with clearly defined interventions and the systematic comparison between control and experimental groups raised questions regarding the extent to which other variables can be controlled for or the degree of representativeness of selected participants.

Similarly, the administration of questionnaires was potentially invasive in the context of a sport-based initiative and could produce the effect of participants feeling like objects of research rather than feeling involved in the project itself. Surveys can also be questioned in terms of the quantification of complex, long-term, multidimensional processes related to inclusion.

Drawing on the work of Pawson and Tilley (1997), Tacon (2007) proposed the use of a realist evaluation approach when evaluating football-based social inclusion projects. This approach emphasized the need to take into consideration the specific context within which the project occurs and involves the following cycle:

- theory-driven hypothesis generation to identify potential outcomes;
- data collection using pluralist methods, appropriate to the hypotheses;
- rather than attempts at experimental generalization, a 'programme specification' occurs where conclusions are drawn from the programme in relation to the actors involved in the specific context (similar to within case analysis);
- the findings inform and potentially modify existing theories and imply a process of continuous improvement.

This methodological approach is influenced by case study research and action research (Eisenhardt, 1989; Yin, 2003). The context-based analysis of single or multiple programmes combines with the aim of producing some kind of social change for the participants by including them in communities. The theory-building focus is also characteristic of grounded theory (Glaser and Strauss, 1967).

Tacon (2007) provided several examples of the realist evaluation approach in action, including housing projects, crime reduction and drug rehabilitation programmes (Pawson and Tilley, 1997; Crabbe and Slaughter, 2007; Nichols and Crow, 2004). A realist approach was also advocated by Sport England, for example, in establishing guidelines for measuring the impact of interventions for National Governing Bodies of Sport.

This approach enabled the evaluation of multiple 'soft' factors ignored by many studies, including 'personal and social development, improved educational performance and engagement in the labour market … building trust, using community sports coaches as role models, and team-working' (Tacon, 2007: 15).

While being influenced by the qualitative approaches, realist evaluation advocates mixed method research designs and the use of data triangulation. It is important to gather objective data but with full consideration of the project's context and the complexity of actors and processes involved in it. This would appear to respond to the documented limitations of evaluation processes undertaken to date and implies a movement away from short-termism and the use of purely quantitative measurement of milestones and outputs, to a longitudinal approach that gathers data of different types from a variety of actors to explain and understand the achievement (or not) of outcomes.

This approach is particularly applicable to the field of social exclusion, poverty and deprivation where people's realities are far from static. Walker's (1995) research into the dynamics of poverty revealed how individuals move in and out of poverty, requiring policy makers to look beyond absolute poverty measures to consider a wider band of people whose circumstances fluctuate. The complexity of how and why people fall in and out of poverty forms part of a multidimensional structural context from which individuals cannot be extracted in the process of measuring the impacts of interventions such as sport-based inclusion projects.

Liu *et al.*'s (2009) facilities benchmarking study analysed sports facility usage data for 1997, 2001, 2006 and 2007 for the UK and statistically demonstrated that the most deprived groups in society and the 60+ age group remained underrepresented in sports participation, and that participation among young people aged 11–19 and disabled people had actually decreased although this was subject to facility type. The findings of this study in theory indicate that the efforts to socially include key target groups as part of the *Game Plan* policy had seemingly failed, at least in terms of facility usage.

While quantitative data can reveal important tendencies in terms of macro-level participation patterns, there is a need to simultaneously understand the micro-level reality of social exclusion for individuals and communities through a more qualitative approach.

A fuller understanding of the context of that increase and its 'quality' in terms of the degree to which that participation is inclusionary is needed. For example, if participation at a sport facility increases among target groups but that participation is divisive or conflictive among those groups, the degree to which the intervention tackles social exclusion can be questioned.

Simply bringing people together in shared sporting spaces can be seen as a small step in a much more complex process. Playing together is potentially positive, but it must have an impact beyond the moment when the final whistle has blown, and contribute to tackling deeper issues of inequality between groups in communities (Kennett *et al.*, 2008).

Indeed, it would be interesting from a research perspective to analyse the outcomes of sport-based projects as part of the evaluation of wider community development initiatives. This would contribute to overcoming the limitation of realist evaluation's case-specific approach by providing an understanding of the wider context.

Conclusions

The concepts of social exclusion and inclusion are characterized by their ambiguity and general vagueness, which were perhaps appealing for New Labour's policy makers seeking to address social issues but without having to engage in significant wealth redistribution. Levitas (2005) was highly critical of social inclusion policy under New Labour, stating that it was symptomatic of an overall policy approach that played to a neoliberal audience while engaging in enough redistribution to keep traditional supporters on board. Playing to these two audiences was sustained through 'spin' in which ambiguous rhetoric, such as that attached to the concept of social inclusion, had a crucial part.

While Levitas's (2005) critique of New Labour's policy approach to tackling social exclusion is specific to the UK context during the late 1990s and early 2000s, the message is clear: social exclusion had been used as part of a wider, shifting political discourse where it had formed part of party politicking and the case of sport was no different.

By including sport in social inclusion policy, this ambiguity combined with an unquestioning belief in the social benefits of sport to produce a policy approach embodied in the *Game Plan* strategy that set itself highly ambitious objectives that were extremely difficult to measure. The relatively scarce literature on social inclusion and sports programme evaluation posed an important question as to whether these programmes were aiming to include people *in* sports or to include people *through* sports. Programmes aimed at including people *in* sports were typically short term and output based, being organized with the fundamental aim of getting people (particularly underrepresented target groups) to participate in sport. The result of the participation was in this sense not a priority, as importance was placed on the relatively easy to demonstrate fact that participation had occurred. The programmes that aimed to include people *through* sports, requiring a long-term, more complex approach to evaluation that attempted to measure the outcomes of participation, were seemingly few and far between.

Indeed, in methodological terms it appeared that there was a significant gap in existing research that could begin to be filled by longer-term qualitative studies that focus on the life experiences of excluded individuals and the role sport plays in their lives. For this kind of evaluation to take place, the undertaking of objective, systematic, empirical data collection must be built in to the funding requirements for sports projects. In the UK case, focus had been placed until now on measuring outputs from the perspective of programme organizers, rather than the experiences of the participants. The adoption of a realist approach and the use of a combination of complementary data collection methods could provide a fuller insight into the complex, multidimensional process of social exclusion.

The wider macro sport policy context in the UK revealed a shift away from social inclusion towards elite sport performance in preparation for the London 2012 Olympic Games. It seemed that from a central government perspective sport policy evaluation focused more than ever on the UK's output in the medal table at the Olympic Games. This shift in priorities affected the context in which the evaluation of sport-based social inclusion programmes occurred, potentially limiting their continuity and the possibility of undertaking longer-term research. The ambitious, far-reaching plans laid out in the evidence-based *Game Plan* strategy were to be implemented up to 2020 but only six years later had been replaced by a very different policy vision.

Important conceptual and methodological challenges exist when attempting to analyse policy action evaluation systems related to sport and social exclusion, not only in terms of the lack of research undertaken in this area, but also for reasons that reveal more about the politicization of sport than the achievement of policy objectives.

21

SPORT DEVELOPMENT AND COMMUNITY DEVELOPMENT

Iain Lindsey and Andrew Adams

Introduction

The potential of sport to contribute to community development has increasingly gained global prominence in recent years. This alignment of sport with community development can be attributed to the general view of sport as morally benign (Coalter, 2007a) and its increasing salience to both international bodies and national governments as a mechanism to achieve particular local policy objectives (Houlihan and Green, 2009). The United Nations (2003: 5), for example, states its belief that 'sports programmes are also a cost-effective way to contribute significantly to health, education, development and peace and a powerful medium through which to mobilize societies'. Similarly Houlihan and Groeneveld (2011: 1) recognise the growing number of national governments seeking to utilise sport 'in the pursuit of a range of pro-social policy objectives such as social inclusion, health improvement and community integration and safety'. While these authors highlight governments in the Global North, it is also the case that governments in the Global South are in increasing numbers recognising the potential contribution that sport can make to individual and community development, as Banda (2010) identifies is the case in Zambia for example.

Much of the positioning of sport, and its capacity to deliver in relation to community development, resonates with broader policy themes. Many community-oriented policy objectives, such as those associated with well-being and sustainability are difficult to define and as a result remain vague and shifting (Jordan, 2006; Stoker, 2006). Similarly, authors such as Coalter (2007a) have raised concerns about the malleable way in which sport has been presented as contributing to a diffuse array of potential policy objectives. Sport also has links with the broader movement towards community and civil renewal, defined as 'giving people a stronger sense of involvement in their communities and a greater say over their lives' (Stoker, 2004: 7), that arguably rests on both active citizenship and partnership working. Likewise, positive representations of sport development have focused on the contribution of multiple policy actors and bottom-up process of implementation that may benefit individual citizens and communities simultaneously (Frisby and Millar, 2002; Bolton, Fleming and Elias, 2008; Charlton, 2010).

This chapter will critically analyse some of these important conceptual and policy themes that bind sport development to community development. The following section will examine the often simplistic use of the concept of community and outlines the theoretical architecture of social capital. The second section will identify the governance structures that are associated with sport and community development and consider the ways in which these structures may facilitate and constrain sport and community development efforts. These more conceptual and internationally relevant sections will inform an in-depth analysis of sport and community development policies in a specific country: the UK. The concluding section of the chapter highlights the importance of political structure and country-specific cultural determinants to be able to assess whether sport can contribute to community development.

Making sense of community

The term community can mean many things to many people. Community is not a single entity but is resplendent within its many dimensions, definitions and conceptualisations, and reflects cultural, political and social aspects of national and international concern. Certainly, in considering the many different uses of the term community, and in particular how it can be conceived alongside sport development, an understanding is required of both what is meant by the term itself and also how specific interpretations of community have been incorporated into particular policy agendas. It is worth noting that Plant, writing in the early 1970s, cautioned that community 'is so much a part of the stock in trade of social and political argument that it is unlikely that some non-ambiguous and non-contested definition of the notion can be given' (Plant, 1974: 13). Given this warning that community cannot easily be identified or specified as one single entity and can include a diverse range of individuals, the notion of a geographical community, in which 'very different world views can share the same geographical space' (East, 2002: 169–170), becomes especially problematic for policy makers. Indeed much of the literature that examines community development and sport participation tends to assume that geographical community is the community. Vail (2007), in her study of community tennis development in Canada, while extolling the virtues of community development models and need for empowered individuals operating within settings of appropriate capacity, makes no mention of what community is or can be taken to mean. Similarly, Frisby and Millar (2002) highlight the difficulties in defining community development, but do not consider the problematics of defining community per se.

Furthermore, Taylor (2003) has argued that the term community can be used descriptively (describing common interests that individuals might share becomes important), normatively (as a school of thought in making assumptions about the way individuals should live) and instrumentally (such that community becomes a proactive arm of policy implementation). In this sense a community may or may not be geographically located. Indeed Anderson (1991) has elaborated on the existence of 'imagined communities' which, as potentially large and dispersed groups of individuals, can develop high levels of group identification (particularly when pursuing a particular cause) that can lead to strong feelings of attachment and belonging (Whiteley, 1999). However, much of the literature concerning communities, their development and their involvement in development (Maloney, 1999; Nash, 2002; Taylor, 2003; Stoker, 2004) would suggest that communities once defined and clarified, will tend to operate in a normative way that dictates the moral climate of that community and consequently the behaviour of the individuals who are part of that community.

Taylor (2003) has argued that policy makers tend to confuse the descriptive and normative meanings of community, and then subsequently assume that this idea of community will 'naturally' facilitate the smooth implementation and execution of policy. For Taylor, policy makers make the assumption:

that common location or interests bring with them social and moral cohesion, a sense of security, and mutual trust. But they [the policy makers] also tend to go a step further and assume that norms will be turned into action; that is, that communities can be turned into agency, with people caring for each other, getting involved in collective enterprises and activities and acting together to change their circumstances.

(Taylor, 2003: 38)

This consideration has potentially important ramifications for thinking about the creation and development linkages within communities, and in particular it imposes a consideration of the means and methods of activating citizens within the community level approach.

Without a doubt the notion of community as non-uniform presents a challenge for governments and agencies that, in the application and implementation of social policy, often take an area-based approach. This approach has been dominant in Europe since the late 1960s (e.g. in the Netherlands – Van Harberden and Raymakers, 1986) and is exemplified by the many stand-alone (issue-specific) special initiatives aimed at addressing the particular problems of disadvantaged localities (Newton, 1999). Most of these types of initiatives have been relatively short-lived and often deployed in successive waves by governments focused on appealing to the electorate and winning elections (Hastings, McArthur and McGregor, 1996). In the UK, for example, the instigation from 2001 of Sports Action Zones (Frazer, 2002; Imrie and Raco, 2003) was indicative of both the dominance of geographical concerns for policy implementation and governmental belief in 'community' as a 'central collective abstraction' (Levitas, 2000). To be sure these targeted programmes emerging from the 'social investment state' placed a strong emphasis on the value of state investment in human and social capital (Lister, 2004).

Community development logically then takes the definition of community and adds an action process to it to achieve outcomes that are commensurate with one's starting point, which is the definition of community. For Biddle and Foster (2011), when discussing health behaviour change, development in a community is a proactive activity achieved by seeking out the target community. In essence, community development addresses commonality of interests to improve the 'life conditions' of those involved (Vail, 2007). Frisby and Millar (2002), in their study of low-income women's sport participation in Canada, refer to community development in terms of a social action process that aims to change individuals' economic, social, cultural and environmental situation. Many of the approaches to community sport development (CSD as it has been referred to in much of the literature; e.g. Frisby and Millar, 2002; Bolton *et al.*, 2008; Hylton and Totten, 2008) also involve the need for greater capacity building. The available literatures on community development and capacity building are both huge;[1] however, for this chapter it is sufficient to note that capacity building has been identified as a bottom-up process (Collins and Kay, 2003) that, while relying on skilled workers, allows development to be at the pace of local groups (Adams, 2011a). Furthermore, capacity building in sports development primarily concerns sustainability in the civic arena and to that extent is concerned with 'giving citizens the opportunity to engage with each other rather than directly with a public authority' (Stoker, 2006: 194). On a broader note, it is striking that according to development theory (Eade, 1997; Eade and Sayer, 2006), the ultimate aim of capacity building is empowerment which is vital 'if development is to be sustainable and centred in people' (Eade, 1997: 1).

To fully consider the impact of sport and community development it is also necessary to outline the influence and importance of social capital theory in promoting local policy outcomes. In so doing it is possible to argue that the concept has become influential for two reasons in particular. First, social capital has provided a theoretical basis for promoting and interpreting the social benefits of sport organisation and participation, which has helped to explain how sport can be viewed as contributing to developing tolerance, trust, social cohesion, and adherence to moral frameworks (Putnam, 2000; Smith and Waddington, 2004; Halpern, 2005). Second, the dominant conceptualisation of social capital, based primarily on the writings of Robert Putnam, has focused attention on the voluntary sector around which sport globally is predominantly centred.

Like community, social capital is a contested term. This chapter only considers the version promoted by Robert Putnam, largely because it was this version that caught the political zeitgeist at the turn of the century (Fine, 2010), and became the social capital theory of choice that served to influence social policy aimed at instigating its creation in many Western liberal democracies.[2] Thus, in this context many community development outcomes expected of sport development relate to policy-maker expectations that voluntary sport activity will have clearly recognisable societal-level outcomes. This policy focus may have suffered an Anglophone bias outside the UK. Canadian research on sport policy and social capital, for example, has highlighted how public policy can be informed and guided (see for example Canadian Policy Research Initiative, 2005) while also interpreting and informing on grass-roots sport experiences in light of policy applications of social capital (Donnelly and Kidd 2003; Sharpe, 2006; Perks, 2007). Similarly, Australian research has identified social capital as a key feature of sport and community development in rural communities (Tonts, 2005) and how policy intervention in football (soccer) can alter the community impact when creating social capital (Lock, Taylor and Darcy, 2008).

This approach to policy making driven by the work of Putnam (1993 and 2000 in particular) has been referred to as the 'democratic strain' (Lewandowski, 2006) of social capital. The key ideas that form the basis of much of the democratic strain of social capital are listed in Figure 21.1 below.

- Networks and connections are of primary importance.
- Bonding social capital occurs with people like us and reflects solidarity within groups.
- Bridging social capital occurs with people unlike us reflects linkages across social cleavages.
- Individuals create community via their normative capacity as social facts.
- Individualism can be reconciled into collective action.
- Normatively, trust and reciprocity are created or arise from social networks.
- Civil society is idealised and voluntary associationalism is identified as both indicator and creator of social capital.
- Voluntary associations (VSCs) and the volunteering occurring within them are privileged as the place and means to establish an active citizenry and a civic culture.
- Expansion of voluntary associations 'encouraged' to increase capacity to fulfil functions ascribed to civil society by government, in particular promoting a vision of a normalised and centralised community.
- Standardisation linked to modernisation is necessary to manage this aspect of civil society.

Figure 21.1 Key assumptions of democratic social capital

Governance, sport and community development

As identified in the previous section, the development of communities has been taken to be a legitimate concern of government and policy makers. As such, understanding of the broader context of governmental action is important when examining community development and its potential relationship with sport development. This is especially the case as it has been widely recognised that the dominance of neoliberal policy agendas in many countries from the 1980s onwards led to significant changes in the context of governmental action and, more generally, the relationship between states and societies (Sørensen and Torfing, 2008). Broadly speaking, neoliberal policies pursued by supranational bodies and national governments sought to 'roll back' the state with greater responsibility for public and collective action placed with private and voluntary sector organisations (Stoker, 1998). Two specific consequences of these policies have been that, first, the distinction between public, private and voluntary sectors has become blurred (Pierre and Stoker, 2000) and, second, the institutional landscape of public policy has become increasingly fragmented among a wide variety of organisations across these different sectors (Stoker, 2000). Each of these consequences has resonance with the institutions involved in sport and community development.

While international and national policies have provided impetus for much sport and community development work (Hylton and Totten, 2008), local state agencies are often key stakeholders in sport and community development. In the United Kingdom and Canada, which are just two examples cited in the literature, local public sector employees (Houlihan and White, 2002; Frisby and Millar, 2002) and local authorities more generally have commonly been strongly involved in efforts to use sport to address a variety of social objectives within local communities (Roberts, 2004; Bolton *et al.*, 2008; Thibault, Frisby and Kikulis, 1999). Beyond the local public sector, voluntary sector organisations are also often highlighted as important in contributing to sport and community development. In fact, it could well be argued that the history of voluntary sector sport clubs being central to the development of communities predates the current policy emphasis (Sports Council, 1988; Collins and Kay, 2003; Horch, 1998). A more recent additional trend, in line with neoliberal policies referred to earlier, has been the emergence of an increasing number of voluntary sector, or non-governmental, organisations specifically orientated towards utilising sport to contribute to aspects of community development. In the UK, for example, a voluntary sector organisation named Catch22 was commissioned to deliver the government-funded Positive Futures sport and community inclusion programme. Vail (2007) also describes the contribution that Tennis Canada, a national governing body within the voluntary sector, made to a leading community development project.

This description of the 'landscape' of institutional stakeholders in sport and community development is necessarily brief. It should also be recognised that this overview only captures a fraction of the array of organisations that could be considered to have influence on sport in specific communities[3] and has largely ignored the numerous organisations from beyond the sport sector that may have an interest, albeit sometimes a more indirect one, in sport and community development. What is clear, however, is the applicability to sport and community development of the broader recognition of the complexity and fragmentation that exists across different areas of public policy (Skelcher, 2000). In turn, this complexity is a key facet of the contexts in which a shift from government to new modes of governance has been recognised (Pierre and Stoker, 2000).

Within the literature on new modes of governance, many authors identify a transition from hierarchical 'government' or market-based modes of coordination to governance based upon 'self-organising, inter-organisational networks characterised by interdependence' (Rhodes,

1997: 15; Sørensen and Torfing, 2008). For Bingham (2011), the shift to network governance was not only a response to a fragmented institutional context but also a consequence of the realisation of the intractable nature of many so-called 'wicked issues' such as those associated with community development. Authors have commented on the applicability to sport of the concept of network governance (Green and Houlihan, 2006; Lindsey, 2010b). In respect of the governance of communities, this applicability is highlighted by the increasing prominence of local partnerships and other forms of alliances involving sport organisations in a variety of different countries (e.g. Thibault *et al.*, 1999, in the United States of America; Lindsey, 2009, in England; Alexander, Thibault and Frisby, 2008, in Canada). Moreover, in the United Kingdom in particular, Bolton *et al.* (2008: 94) consider that the development of network governance 'provided a new legitimacy to community sport development'.

In examining network governance, Bingham (2011) identifies a distinction between collaboration between organisations involved in the implementation of public policy and collaboration orientated towards public participation in governance. Both of these aspects are relevant to the contribution that sport can make to community development. The latter aspect has the more longstanding connection to community development that had its origins in 'relationships with the state (central or local) in which demands are made for services' (Sihlongonyane, 2009: 140). In this respect, some authors consider the transition to network governance to be a positive development that, through the inclusion of a wider range of actors and agents in the policy process, allows some transfer of power away from those who govern (in government) towards the governed (Rhodes, 1997; Bevir and Rhodes, 2003; Grix and Phillpots, 2011). With relevance to the topic of this chapter, however, Bingham (2011) strikes a more cautious note in recognising that the membership of governance networks may not always be representative of particular communities. Similarly, with respect to local community sport, voluntary sports clubs are often viewed as both a mechanism for community development and as an authentic voice of the community itself (Adams, 2011a). However, this is by no means necessarily or universally the case. Lynn (2011) suggests that community organisations may not have the capacity to identify community needs or have their own standards of representative democracy and Adams (2011a) argues that the mutual aid aspect of voluntary sports clubs can impede the manner in which a club may interact with its geographically located community. Certainly, voluntary sports clubs can themselves be exclusive (at the very least in informal ways) (Torkildsen, 2005). Moreover, the competition between clubs and even across sports in many communities means that identifying representative voices from the community and voluntary sport sector can be problematical.

It is also important to consider collaborations that involve organisations in the implementation of public policy and their (potential) relationships to sport and community development. Partnerships orientated towards development in particular communities have been initiated, often as a result of mandatory government instruction (Bingham, 2011) and almost universally in the area-based initiatives described earlier in the chapter. Collaboration in such partnerships may be more closely associated with the bonding and bridging forms of social capital that are outlined in Figure 21.1. It is here that something of a paradox exists, in that while bridging capital may be considered as more important to community development (Coalter, 2007a), the effectiveness of collaboration is dependent on the 'shared values and norms' (Bevir and Rhodes, 2011: 205) that are a feature of bonding forms of social capital.

Nevertheless, such collaboration may well be important to sports organisations that seek to contribute to community development. As has been recognised by authors such as Coalter (2007a) and Lawson (2005), sport is unlikely in isolation to make a significant contribution to development within communities. Therefore, linking with organisations from other policy sectors is essential for many sport organisations, not only to improve programmes but also to access resources (Thibault *et al.*, 1999; Frisby and Millar, 2002). The extent to which sport organisations are themselves effectively included in broader collaborations associated with community development remains open to question and probably a large degree of local variation. Despite the increasing prominence of the potential contribution that sport can make to community development in international and national policies, this is a view that is by no means a view universally shared within other policy sectors. Houlihan and Lindsey (2013) note that the health sector, and in particular the medical profession, in the United Kingdom has not reciprocated the enthusiasm demonstrated by stakeholders in the sport sector for mutual collaboration. Even where collaboration is established, organisations from better resourced sectors that are more established in community development work, such as health and regeneration, may hold greater power than those from the sport sector.

A further linked question that remains is the extent to which network governance may ultimately be effective and efficient in generating outcomes associated with community development. As Houlihan and Lindsey (2008) indicate, this is a question that presents significant methodological problems. Nevertheless, across literature associated with both sport and other policy sectors, a large range of factors are recognised as being important in contributing to the success or otherwise of collaboration. Bingham (2011), for example, identifies factors such as institutional design, leadership, trust building and shared understanding as important in contributing to effective collaboration. Organisational capacity is also required in order for effective collaboration and, in this regard, it is notable that a study in Canada by Frisby, Thibault and Kikulis (2004: 123) found that local government leisure organisations, a likely key component in ensuring sport contributes to community development, largely 'lacked the capacity to effectively manage the numerous and complex partnerships they were engaged in'. While this, of course, represents an isolated study in a single country, perhaps the best that we can say is that there is likely to be huge diversity in the contribution that collaboration involving sport organisations makes to community development.

The foregoing also largely ignores ongoing relations of hierarchical power that may sit alongside or operate within network governance arrangements. Despite neoliberal policies limiting the capacity of governments to directly deliver services and intervene in a number of policy areas, a number of authors suggest that governments retain a key role in attempting to 'steer' governance networks (Leach and Percy-Smith, 2001) and as a result influence practices such as those that may contribute to development through sport and within communities. It is also widely recognised that governmental steering uses a variety of distinctive policy tools or instruments, the implementation of which can also be widely identified in sport and community development. Particularly prominent among such policy tools are those associated with the New Public Management (NPM) movement that emerged alongside the neoliberal policies of the 1980s and 1990s. Despite the increased prominence of network governance representing something of a reaction to the fragmentation that resulted from NPM, the development of practices of performance management and measurement continues to have a 'far reaching and enduring' influence (Heinrich, 2011: 262). Across a number of countries, governmental target setting, monitoring and evaluation have become commonplace in sport development and have significant implications for practices within communities (Nicholson, Hoye and Houlihan, 2011). In the UK, for example, the priorities of local sport development partnerships have been significantly influenced by nationally developed targets for community participation in sport (Lindsey, 2010a). That this singular example may also be more generally relevant is demonstrated by Bevir and Rhodes (2011: 213) who state that systems of performance management and target setting have, in a number of countries, 'spread … to embrace the control of localities'.

Understanding of this control, and its relevance to sport and community development, is enhanced when we consider the combination of widespread systems of performance management with other governmental policy tools. The traditional policy tool of allocation of funding has been linked in many countries to successful adoption and achievement of performance management practices and targets (Cheung, 2011). Again, the UK represents an indicative example in which much lottery funding for sport and communities is distributed according to centralised application procedures and associated targets (Garrett, 2004; Lindsey, 2010b). However, as Coalter (2007a) recognises, the contributions that sport can make to aspects of community development are extremely difficult to evaluate, let alone capture in largely quantitative performance targets. While Frisby and Millar (2002) suggest that those involved in community development need to 'reconceptualise' the quantitative accountability systems inherent in NPM, an alternative interpretation is that the dominance of such systems limits the potential for community development through sport. Overall, as Peters (2008, cited in Le Galès, 2011) recognises, the possibilities of network governance for sport and community development may well be tempered by the centralising tendencies associated with the use of policy tools such as those identified.

The consequences for sport and community development of this balance of local responsibility and external control are impossible to judge without significant empirical research and are likely to be divergent in different localities and sites of community action. Both Vail (2007) and Frisby and Millar (2002) highlight that community development does not sit easily with the tradition of top-down management that exists within sport. In this regard it is notable that Sellers (2011) cites Skocpol (2003) to argue that increased centralisation may contribute to the weakening of social capital. Certainly, in the sporting context, authors such as Adams (2011a) have suggested that increased national direction of voluntary sports clubs may limit their capacity to independently address community needs. Nevertheless, there is also evidence from voluntary sector sports clubs and other local sporting organisations to support Bevir and Rhodes's (2011) assertion that local agencies may successfully resist centralising influence of modern policy tools. Such resistance to authority certainly is in line with a traditional concern of community development (Sihlongonyane, 2009) and Harris, Mori and Collins (2009) point to the resistance engendered among a proportion of voluntary sport clubs by the 'blanket approach' towards them adopted by national sport agencies in England.

UK policy contexts for sport and community development

It is in the context of active citizenship and civil renewal that New Labour's (1997–2007) record of producing policy geared towards including community action in the delivery of public services should be borne in mind (e.g. Home Office, 1998; Lewis, 2005; Kendall, 2005). The term community, used rhetorically, functionally and concretely from 1997–2010 by New Labour in a variety of political, policy and governance situations (Finlayson, 2003; Prideaux, 2005) facilitated a pragmatic approach to governing. Used rhetorically, community-signalled 'ways of thinking' (Finlayson, 2003) about governing and provided a naturalised and unifying collective response to a socially fragmented society. For former Prime Minister Blair, community thus implied a 'recognition of interdependence but not overweening government power. It accepts that we are better able to meet the forces of change and insecurity through working together' (Tony Blair cited in Levitas, 2000: 191).

The importance of New Labour's modernisation project should not be overstated, and the subject has been covered in some depth elsewhere,[4] but it was part of the fundamental architecture of governance that enabled collectivism, civil society, social capital, social inclusion to become wrapped up in sport and community development. Certainly, the idioms of pragmatism and eclecticism (Newman, 2001), when allied to social and public policy, enabled New Labour to redefine and re-energise a conceptualisation of community as both antidote to the excessive individualism of unfettered neoliberalism, and as a positive force for developing the collective values of reciprocity and solidarity (Avineri and de-Shalit, 1992; Arai and Pedlar, 2003). Thus, during New Labour's period of office (1997–2007) notions of sport development became closely allied to community development. This aspect of community sport development played to concerns for a normative and palliative commonality that was viewed as important for the well-being of all and not just as a residual service for the poor and excluded (Bolton *et al.*, 2008).

The emphasis on community and of community empowerment in delivering services has arguably come to have a somewhat hegemonic hold over notions of developing mixed economies of welfare in the UK. Indeed, under the auspices of the UK Coalition Government[5] and promoted in particular by the Prime Minister, David Cameron, 'Big Society'[6] offers clear potential for community development, in the guise of civil society, to become both the object and subject of governmental policy objectives (M. J. Smith, 2010; Alcock, 2010). Big Society as a political vision is replete with localist intentions to 'downshift' power and the operation of public interest decision making away from central government to citizens and organisations at the local and community level (Stoker, 2004; Cabinet Office, 2010; Bubb, 2011). Indeed, the notion of localism, where individuals, groups and organisations in a community are increasingly encouraged or empowered to deliver services locally for the consumption of local citizens, presents continuity in the British political establishment between consecutive governments of different political traditions. Certainly, New Labour's focus on the promotion of a modernised, self-regulating form of networked governance (Stoker, 2004), which focused on the creation of social capital, collaborative partnerships and a mixed economy of welfare (Jordan, 2006), presents itself as a forerunner to the 'Big Society' in meeting and facilitating local policy objectives. The key point in this respect is to note that these processes have become embedded within, and contiguous to, the role of sport development in the UK.

The local nature of sport development practice in the UK together with the importance of voluntary action signalled the importance that New Labour attached to sport policy 1997–2007. During this period the relationship between sport development, social policy and community development in the UK revolved around what former Sports Minister Richard Caborn referred to as the 'sport for good' agenda (cited by Collins, 2010: 368). Moreover, social capital was identified as the key mechanism to achieve societal level benefits via the mundane promotion of sport participation. In the UK 'new localism' (Stoker, 2006) became prominent in sport development structures, allowing for the devolution of power and resources to the front line. New localism also incorporated agreed national minimum standards and policy priorities (Corry and Stoker, 2002; Stoker, 2004) and prescribed a set of circumstances for the continual enhancement and maintenance of voluntary participatory experiences (see for example, Strategy Unit, 2002; Sport England, 2007).

It is where new localism, network governance and community development meet that social capital has had much purchase in recent years. It is arguably the case that the localist intentions of the governance narrative endorsed social capital as *the* tool to promote issues of connectiveness, trust, civic renewal and active citizenship (Levitas, 2000; Maloney, Smith and Stoker, 2000; Imrie and Raco, 2003; Sixsmith and Boneham, 2003; Stoker, 2004, 2006). To be sure, much of the focus of social capital and community development has been linked to Putnam's assertions that voluntary associationalism is the most favoured site of social capital formation in Western democracies. This position subsequently created the political framework for privileging sport development within civil society as a means of community development.

In the UK the emergence of the Conservative-led Coalition Government's ideological concern with reducing the size and scope of the state has further promoted an emphasis on the voluntary action of citizens (Smith, M.J., 2010). In short, individual citizens operating within the realms of civil society are viewed politically as policy agents who can provide services more efficiently and effectively for fellow citizens through a networked alliance, where governance seeks to simultaneously empower and enable. Certainly the emphasis on volunteerism and the potential for social benefits that may emanate from individual citizen involvement in collective activity has been taken up by sport and sport development policy with gusto (Adams, 2011b; Nicholson and Hoye, 2008; Coalter, 2007a; Blackshaw and Long, 2005).

The importance of social capital within a modernised policy context can be felt in the drive to mainstream and centralise active citizenship within a networked approach to establishing civic renewal and community development (Finlayson, 2003; Morrison, 2003). Certainly, the high dependence on volunteers in Britain to provide the majority of sport participation opportunities (Taylor *et al.*, 2003) highlights the importance of social capital theory to interpreting sport development practices in the UK. Moreover the creation of the Social Exclusion Unit in December 1997, the Neighbourhood Renewal Unit in 2001 and Active Community Unit in 2002 focused attention on government aspirations to empower and activate citizens and communities. This example of structural capacity building clearly illustrates the need to ally structural top-down policy frameworks with corresponding bottom-up policy tools. The implication for sport and community development is that to fully enable citizens to develop the capacity for the formation of social capital there must be an 'institutionally thick arena' (Imrie and Raco, 2003) surrounding the context of implementation. This brief overview of sport and community development in the UK has highlighted how and why social capital, under the gaze of NPM and allied to wider community development concerns, became a key fixture of the accountability culture in the UK during the period 1997–2007.

Conclusions

As the first parts of this chapter demonstrated, conceptualising 'community' is a notoriously 'slippery' task. That there are potentially multiple conceptions of 'community' leaves room for policy makers to appropriate and utilise particular favoured definitions and to conceive of the development of communities in particular ways. To some degree this has presented an opportunity for policy advocates to make the case for sport as a potential contributor to community development. For other sporting organisations, voluntary sports clubs in particular, notions of community espoused within policy do not necessarily correspond with those held by individual club members or by those representing the agencies allocated the task of making a contribution to community development. This potential dissonance has only been heightened by the increasing prominence of the equally slippery concept of social capital that has been commonly linked with both community and sport development.

Advancement of social capital theories is also strongly connected with the development of new forms of network governance. Certainly, the promotion of collaboration generally and within particular sport and community-orientated programmes in particular, can be strongly associated with and may potentially contribute to, closer ties within particular communities. Partnership and collaboration across different communities and interests is likely to be more challenging in practice. Furthermore, some 'traditional' notions of community development as resistance fit less easily with collaborative approaches to governance. Recognising that network governance may still sit within and alongside more established hierarchies of power (McDonald,

2005), therefore, presents both opportunities and threats to those who wish to use sport to contribute to community development.

In terms of these threats, in the UK at least, it can be argued that the association of network governance with governmental mechanisms facilitated the top-down steerage given to sport agencies such as national governing bodies (NGBs) and locally delivered sport opportunities via voluntary sports clubs (VSCs). Subsequently by imposing conditions on NGBs and VSCs, government sought to shape preferences (Hay, 2002) and exert control whilst not formally undermining the authority of particular actors (Green, 2007a). Moreover the focus of NPM on measurable evidence as the underpinning feature of policy development (Solesbury, 2001; Sanderson, 2002) also served to reinforce and legitimate the democratic strain of social capital, which itself has sought to identify 'causality', 'culprits' and solutions for policy problems involving perceived social capital deficits (Putnam, 2000). The conditionality associated with the promotion of social capital and community development through sport in the UK tended to reflect broader governmental concerns with democratic renewal and the strategic role of social capital. Consequently, the operational and strategic condition for sport development, at local and grass-roots levels has been located within a framework predicated on compliance and conformity. Based on this scenario, it is questionable whether community development, a process that enables and empowers (Vail, 2007) and which, according to Pedlar (1996: 14), allows for 'learning and doing for oneself', could occur in the UK, given the predominant need to generate evidence of efficiency and effectiveness to serve the top-down nature of sport policy (see Coalter, 2007a; Grix and Phillpots, 2011; Houlihan and Green, 2009).

These arguments and the illustration of the UK case certainly raise further questions regarding the potential contribution that sport can make to community development in the global context. A clear signal from this brief overview of sport development and community development is that policy makers need a clearer understanding and perspective on what sport can and cannot do in and for particular communities. Considering how community development outcomes may be achieved, and by whom, presents a further set of questions and challenges. Ultimately, there is unlikely ever to be agreement on these issues even from solely within the sport sector. Certainly, both sport and community need greater articulation between policy makers and practitioners if we are to move beyond simplistic, monolithic and one-dimensional accounts that offer little to those implementing sport at the community level.

22

SPORT AND URBAN REGENERATION

Juan Luis Paramio-Salcines

Introduction

The study of the relation between sport and urban regeneration and their effects on cities and their citizens has a long history in Western cities. While the chronology and aims may vary from city to city and country to country, since the Second World War sports-related projects have been increasingly employed as part of the regeneration strategies of many cities. There is neither a unique sport strategy linked to urban regeneration nor an accepted model to drive regeneration through sports initiatives as a feature of the postmodern city. The nature of sport has therefore the potential to contribute in various forms, both traditional and new, to the regeneration of urban areas, which is specifically examined in this chapter.

Focusing on a major sporting event such as the Olympic Games, the first signs of the use of a sport project as a key instrument to promote significant changes and other associated developments in cities may be found with the 1960 Rome Olympics. This event was successfully emulated by the city of Munich, which built and concentrated all the new sports venues required for the 1972 Olympic Games (including the distinctive Olympic Stadium designed by Günter Behnisch and Frei P. Otto, in a massive derelict area in the north of the city as part of the Olympic Park), which even today represent a significant legacy for the city.

Essex and Chalkley (1998), Coaffee (2007), Gold and Gold (2007) and more recently Smith (2012) coincide in noting that the Olympic Games of Rome 1960, Munich 1972 and especially Barcelona 1992 have been presented as showcases of sport-led urban regeneration. It is also worth pointing out that, since the 1970s, city leaders in Indianapolis have embarked on a long-term sports strategy to develop *amateur sports as an industry in the city*, and also to rebuild the city centre and change its image, a case that has been widely studied. Despite having been criticized for the limited impact on the development and economic growth of Indianapolis over the period 1974–92 (Rosentraub *et al.*, 1994), this strategy has been emulated by other cities worldwide. The cases of Indianapolis and other cities have opened a wide debate on the effectiveness of sport as a strategy to promote significant transformations in contemporary cities.

Despite differences about what features characterize contemporary urban regeneration and sport under post-Fordist economies, there appear to be some recurrent and inexorably linked trends. Consistent with much of the literature on urban politics, there is broad agreement that the nature and characteristics of contemporary urban policies and sport have gradually been reasserted as part of the shift from the '*managerial and social*' concerns of previous policies to local government being more '*proactive and entrepreneurial*', with the development of partnerships between business and political interests to shape urban politics, partly driven by experiences in North American cities, with the role and nature of sport being gradually undermined as part of the welfare agenda in favour of a growing emphasis on sport as a salient economic growth strategy consistent with urban entrepreneurialism (see, e.g. Atkinson and Moon, 1994; Burbank, Andranovich and Heying, 2001; Callicott, 2000; Coaffee, 2007; Harvey, 1990; Hall and Hubbard, 1998; Henry and Gratton, 2001; Henry and Paramio-Salcines, 1999; Osborne and Gaebler, 1992; Paramio-Salcines, 2000; Schimmel, 1995, 2001; Smith, 2012; Tallon, 2010; Thornley, 2002).

Marking a sharp break with the recent history of sport and urban regeneration, we have witnessed an emerging trend with more cities of developing countries[1] (either alone or as part of a wider national strategy), such as in Brazil (Rio, and the 2014 Football World Cup and 2016 Olympic Games), Russia (Sochi, and the 2014 Winter Olympic Games and the 2018 Football World Cup), India (New Delhi and the 2010 Commonwealth Games; Uppal, 2009), China (Beijing and the 2008 Olympic Games; Tien, Lo and Lin, 2011), South Africa (Durban and the 2010 Football World Cup; Maening and Schwarthoff, 2006; Maening and du Plessis, 2009) or Qatar (Doha, and the 2006 Asian Games, the 2020 Football World Cup and currently bidding for the 2020 Olympic Games), to name just a few. These have used (or are using) sports related projects as part of massive regeneration schemes. An overpopulated city such as New Delhi aspires to be, after the organization of the 2010 Commonwealth Games, a '*prospective bidder for international sporting events*' (Uppal, 2009: 8, original emphasis). Some of them are at the planning stage and others have embarked on (a serial reproduction of strategies as Harvey, 1990 claims) or major and minor related projects with considerable financial investment in those projects.

Contemporary cities and their political and economic elites justify the promotion of sports projects based on the combination of a myriad of accepted effects such as the promotion and revitalization of their local economy, the fostering of economic and social benefits, the enhancing of their cities' images worldwide in some cases and in others acceleration of the regeneration of derelict areas and other associated effects, which are less tangible but equally attractive (Coaffee, 2007; Essex and Chalkley, 1998; Henry and Gratton, 2001; Jones and Evans, 2008; Shoval, 2002; Schimmel, 2001; Zagnoli and Radicchi, 2009). As Nieto and Sobejano (2001) comment below, in reference to the expected implications that the bidding of Madrid for the 2012 Olympic Games (and later on included in the bid book of the 2016 and 2020 Olympic Games) would have on the city:

> Hosting the Olympic Games is an exceptional opportunity to define and co-ordinate the urban and architectural transformations required by big cities which are difficult to accomplish under normal circumstances. Paradoxically, a sporting event has the potential to make radical changes to the development of a city.
>
> (Nieto and Sobejano, 2001: 7)

A further development of the urban entrepreneurialism is the growing inter-urban competition between cities to reinvent themselves as *centres of consumption and entertainment* through a wide range of sports projects (an aspiration that was already described by the French sociologist Lefebvre in 1968) (Amendola, 2000; Burbank *et al.*, 2001; Harvey, 1990; Tallon, 2010). This situation is not completely new if we bear in mind that sport has traditionally been a key element in the economic regeneration strategies and in the re-imagining of many North American cities and to a lesser extent of European cities and other parts of the world.

Despite these common urban policy responses, urban leaders also recognize the need to promote their comparative competitive advantages and to differentiate from others by using particular sports events, infrastructure or projects, either alone or in combination. Therefore, the nature of sport offers opportunities in some cases to innovate which are not incompatible or mutually exclusive. As an example of this, Singapore used the organization of the 117th International Olympic Committee Session on 6 July 2005, which decided the winning city to host the 2012 Olympic Games (finally awarded to London), to gain more recognition internationally and to promote sport development at local level (Yuen, 2008). Even a small city such as Preston in the UK has used sports heritage through the English National Football Museum, opened in February 2001, to promote the physical, economic and social regeneration of a derelict area of the city, near the oldest football stadium in the world, the Deepdale stadium (Moore, 2008). The Preston City Council was not behind this project which was initiated and led by the private sector with a total (and limited if compared with other projects) capital cost of £15 million,[2] though subsequently the local council decided to back the project with £2 million per year. However, owing to financial problems, the Museum has recently been relocated to Manchester at one of its iconic buildings, Urbis.

There is not a hegemonic discourse on the influence of some of the processes mentioned on the nature and characteristics of urban policies and sport in different countries, but it seems that most developing countries have moved in the same direction (Burbank *et al.*, 2001 for the US, Harding and Le Galès (2000) for France, Amendola (2000) for Italy or Paramio-Salcines (2000) for Spain). Regardless of the size, economic base and political history of cities, common to all of them is their desire to promote and enhance economic growth and to promote the physical transformation of cities through sport related projects.

This contemporary global phenomenon cannot be analysed in isolation and is best understood in terms of its connection with a broad framework of post-Fordism, globalization, the role of spectacle in postmodern societies and the emergence of new practices and forms of urban governance, following North American models, such as the development of public–private partnerships at local level to influence decision making to support those projects (Cochrane *et al.*, 1996; Essex and Chalkley, 1998; Henry and Gratton, 2001; Paramio-Salcines, 2000; Schimmel, 2001). However, some commentators highlight the economic, social and spatial stresses inherent in the current redirection of urban and sport policy (Harvey, 1990; Hall and Hubbard, 1998; Lenskyj, 2000).

Some of the key questions at the heart of the sport and urban regeneration debate are what a sport project does and what contributions it makes to the city that hosts the project and to its inhabitants. Owing to the increasing complexity and massive (largely public) investments required to plan and manage contemporary sports events and infrastructure, another question is how to better evaluate the effectiveness of sports projects as a regeneration strategy of cities worldwide.

The primary thrust of this chapter is therefore to explain the relation between sport and urban regeneration through a wide variety of sporting projects in cities all over the world. The remainder of this chapter proceeds as follows. The first section focuses on understanding how academic literature has covered the development of the body of knowledge in relation to sports and urban regeneration and the range of approaches or strategies that have been adopted to drive the transformation of cities. The second covers a brief theoretical overview of how new urban theories understand contemporary urban decision making, including the promotion of sport initiatives to drive the economic development and the regeneration of urban areas. The chapter finishes by incorporating the recent experience of the city of Madrid, a case that examines the legacy and effects on the city, mainly in relation to sports venues and infrastructure, after the two recent consecutive failed bids to host the 2012 and 2016 Olympic Games, an issue that has received less attention in literature than it deserves.

Understanding the past, present and future relation between sport-related projects and urban regeneration

When we analyse the progress made in sport regeneration in contemporary cities, it is relevant to look back to the 1960s and to examine trends in research on this topic and the kind of strategies used mainly in North American and British cities. If we look at North American cities, for the last 50 years urban leaders, mainly politicians and economic elites, have adapted their cities to changing economies by restructuring land use in an attempt to regenerate their economic base (Logan and Molotch, 1987; Stone, 1989, 1993). Those leaders have valued the significant potential of professional sports teams and the building of stadia and arenas and major events, among others, for the revitalization and economic development of many North American cities; strategies that a 'new wave' of urban theories such as 'regime' and 'growth machine' approaches clearly support. Cities such as Baltimore, Detroit, Philadelphia and especially Indianapolis have been cited as successful examples of the use of sport as a regeneration strategy.

Since the 1980s, academics such as Baade and Dye (1988), Logan and Molotch (1987), Rosentraub *et al.* (1994), Sack and Johnson (1996) and Schimmel (1995) were pioneers in exploring the effectiveness of sport as a regeneration strategy and the development of coalitions between public and private actors to support those projects. Some of those issues, such as the effectiveness of sport to drive the regeneration of cities, have generated substantial debate between those that support the public funding of stadia and arenas on the basis that they provide a good return on local economies (Chema, 1996; Okner, 1974), while others, such as Baade and Dye (1988), Baade (1996), Coates and Humphries (1999), Euchner (1993), Rosentraub (1997) or Noll and Zimbalist (2000), take a contrary view and criticize public subsidy for its limited effects on overall economic activity and employment. Years later, the debate over the effectiveness of sport regeneration strategies is still open in many countries, with limited consensus on the effectiveness of those strategies, mostly relying on public funds, in North American cities.[3]

Britain also offers an interesting insight as it is at the forefront in the promotion of sport and urban regeneration to overcome social problems in inner cities. Among others, we should highlight the work of authors such as Caroline Pack and Sue Glyptis (1989) and Mike Collins (1989), which provided a useful benchmark for the state of this field in the UK, but with a different paradigm to North America. At the time of its publication, Pack and Glyptis's (1989) study entitled *Developing Sport and Leisure: Good practice in urban regeneration* aimed to identify and disseminate good practice in urban regeneration in British cities through sport and leisure. In that study, the authors pointed out that '*sport and leisure have a positive part to play in many aspects of urban regeneration*' (1989: 1, original emphasis). Those projects, funded through the Urban Programme (a national funding programme to support urban/community development initiatives), sought mainly to address community needs or welfare objectives rather than focusing on the economic dimension as was more common in North American cities. Though the initial and general concern focused on the social impacts of sport related projects, the work of Collins (1989) called also for examination of the role of sport, leisure and recreation in economic regeneration as reflected in the North American case. As mentioned above, the case of Indianapolis has inspired the strategy of other cities such as Sheffield (Henry and Paramio-Salcines, 1999), Birmingham or Manchester to use sports projects to drive their urban and economic regeneration. The volume of work covering the relation between sport and urban regeneration has subsequently increased in Great Britain as the latest work by Andrew Smith (2012) entitled *Events and Urban Regeneration: The strategic use of events to revitalise cities* illustrates.

Since the 2000s the analysis of sport and urban regeneration has increasingly gained broad attention among academics and practitioners, but we have witnessed a gradual change of paradigm in the relation between sport and urban regeneration. Indeed, the majority of the literature on sport and urban regeneration has gradually evolved away from a concern with sport being used to tackle social problems and deprivation in urban areas towards valuing *sport as an important economic development strategy*. Therefore, the broad relation and the effects that teams, sports stadia and facilities and events have on cities and their inhabitants have been studied from different perspectives beyond the sport management field. In fact, sport and urban regeneration has risen to prominence in recent years in a wide variety of disciplines, including geography (Alberts, 2009; Essex and Chalkley, 1998; Gold and Gold, 2007; Jones and Evans, 2008; Shoval, 2002), urban planning (Chapin, 2004; Coaffee, 2007; Smith, 2006, 2012; Thornley, 2002; Yuen, 2008), sociology (Lenskyj, 1996, 2000; Roche, 1994, 2000, 2008), political science (Levin, 2010), economics (Baade and Matheson, 2000; Maening and Schwarthoff, 2006; Uppal, 2009) and leisure and sport management (Davies, 2005, 2010, 2011; Henry and Gratton, 2001; Paramio-Salcines and Dobson, 2004; Sam and Hughson, 2010; Schimmel, 1995, 2001) reflecting also a recognition of the opportunities in this field for multidisciplinary approaches.

Academic literature has also grown significantly as there are more dedicated journals, books and conferences that fully integrate the relations between sports projects, infrastructure and events, urban regeneration and sport policy.[4] For instance, Henry and Gratton's *Sport in the City: The role of sport in economic and social regeneration* (2001) still provides today one of the best texts that examine in great detail the body of research in sport and cities and more recently Gold and Gold's *Olympic Cities* (2007) which is one of the few books focused exclusively on analysing the impacts of the Olympic Games in many cities that have hosted this mega event. There are many issues to consider and analyse linked to the planning and management of sport related projects. Among others, it is acknowledged that since the 1980s an increasing attention has been devoted to measuring the economic relevance of all types of sports events (Preuss, 2004b; Gratton *et al.*, 2005), considering that sports events can generate a range of sporting and non-sporting benefits that according to UK Sport (2005) is difficult to generate by other means. In the UK, for instance, the concern for analysing the economic and social impacts of major events at local and national levels led to the establishment of the Major Event Support Group – now the Major Events Steering Group – in 1994. As part of the growing economic potential of sports projects worldwide, in 2002 the UK government set up the UK Trade and Investment Sector Group to help large and small British companies to identify opportunities linked to bidding and organizing events worldwide. To illustrate the interests involved, Table 22.1 below shows the significant economic investment required for cities that bid either for the Winter or the Summer Games. This in itself is a topic worthy of further study and debate.

Table 22.1 Global sports projects sector

	Bid budget	Operational budget	Infrastructure Budget
Salzburg	$ 8.5m	$ 965m	$ 2.1bn
Sochi	$ 27.5m	$ 1.5bn	$ 8.8bn
Pyenongchang	$ 35.2m	$ 1.3bn	$ 7.1bn
Chicago	$ 49m		
Madrid	$ 40.4m		
Rio	$ 42m		
Tokyo	$ 48m		

Source: Bacchus (2009)

As part of this growing worldwide interest in sports projects, UK Sport (2005) has developed a holistic methodology to help British cities bid and subsequently host any sports events. However, there is still debate about how best to measure the impacts of events (Gratton *et al*., 2005). Work adopting a critical analysis of the limited impact of sport projects on overall economic activity and employment has also proliferated, mainly focused on American cities, though there are limited studies on European cities (Brunet, 1994; Gratton *et al*., 2005; Henry and Gratton, 2001; Gold and Gold, 2007).

Contributions of traditional and new urban theories to the debate of sport and urban regeneration

Each theory has its flaws and strengths. Are there competing theories when trying to understand the relation between urban policies and sport? Traditional urban theories such as pluralism, elitism or Marxism have been used to study urban political power since the 1960s. However, there are new urban theories, which originated in the North America context in the late 1980s, such as growth coalition or regime theory (Stone, 1989, 1993; Fainstein and Fainstein, 1986; Elkin, 1987) that have gained momentum in helping to understand the complexity of urban decision making and their implications for urban and sports policy changes (Misener and Mason, 2008, 2009; Henry and Paramio-Salcines, 1999; Paramio-Salcines, 2000; Schimmel, 1995, 2001; Smith, 2012). One of those theories is *regime theory*, which has been employed to evaluate the emergence and operation of new forms of urban governance, such as public–private partnership, as well as the role of those coalitions in the development of a sport strategy. Although academic literature on sport and economic development has grown over the last years, it is only recently that we have witnessed an increasing research effort to specifically identify the role of sport in coalition construction and the role of coalitions in the development of urban and sport strategies.

There are some exceptions that have focused on major sporting events such as the World Student Games 1991 in Sheffield (Henry and Paramio-Salcines, 1999; Paramio-Salcines, 2000), the analysis of three different cities that actively pursue sport development strategies – namely Edmonton, Canada; Manchester, UK; and Melbourne, Australia (Misener and Mason, 2008, 2009), cities that have hosted the Olympic Games or have actively pursued hosting the Games (Burbank *et al*., 2001) or even the effects of failed bids for the Olympic Games that have been analysed as the cases of Manchester 1996 (Cochrane *et al*., 1996; Law, 1994), Toronto 2000 (Lenskyj, 1996, 2000), Berlin 2000 (Alberts, 2009), Stockholm 2004 (Levin, 2010) or Cape Town 2004 (Hiller, 2000) show. In particular, authors such as Burbank *et al*. (2001), Cochrane *et al*. (1996), Henry and Paramio-Salcines (1999), Hiller (2000), Levin

(2010), Paramio-Salcines (2000) and Schimmel (2001) suggest that the process of bidding for sporting events facilitated the emergence of public–private partnerships in some of the afore-mentioned cities.

Traditional and new sport strategies linked to urban regeneration in cities

Most attention has traditionally focused on major sporting events such as the Olympic Games, the World Football Cup or even the European Football Cup, on sport facilities, mainly stadia and arenas, and infrastructure (Davies, 2010, 2011) and less attention has been focused on other innovative strategies related to sports-led regeneration such as Preston in the UK, which has recently used the English National Football Museum to this end (Moore, 2008). Evidence reveals that there is a growth in the number of cities worldwide bidding to host different types of sporting events, mainly the Olympic Games and the Football World Cup. Despite the fact that the International Olympic Committee itself warned that the increasing complex-ity and cost of the Games could discourage many cities from bidding (International Olympic Committee, 2002), the recent bidding process has led Whitelegg (2000: 801) to declare that '*the battle to stage the Olympic Games is now as competitive ... as the event itself*', a situation that extends to other sporting events.

As Table 22.2 illustrates, until 1992 the number of cities bidding to host the Summer Olympic Games remained relatively low. However, the commercial and managerial success of the Los Angeles Olympics of 1984 (Burbank *et al.*, 2001) and the significant urban transforma-tions associated with the 1992 Barcelona Games represented a turning point that stimulated the interest of more cities in this global mega event (Brunet, 1994; Emery, 2001; Gratton *et al.*, 2005; Roche, 2000; Payne, 2006; Smith, 2012).

Table 22.2 Number of cities bidding to host the Summer Olympic Games (1984–2020)

Year	Cities bidding for the Olympic Games	Olympic city
1984	Los Angeles (1)	Los Angeles
1988	Athens, Melbourne, Nagoya and Seoul (4)	Seoul
1992	Amsterdam, Belgrade, Birmingham, Brisbane, Delhi, Barcelona and Paris (7)	Barcelona
1996	Athens, Atlanta, Belgrade, Manchester, Melbourne and Toronto (6)	Atlanta
2000	Sydney, Beijing, Berlin, Brasilia, Istanbul, Manchester and Milan (7)	Sydney
2004	Buenos Aires, Cape Town, Istanbul, Lille, Rio, Rome, St. Petersburg, San Juan, Seville, Athens and Stockholm (11)	Athens
2008	Seville, Paris, Istanbul, Toronto, Havana, Osaka, El Cairo, Bangkok, Beijing and Kuala Lumpur (10)	Beijing
2012	Madrid, New York, Paris, Moscow, London, Leipzig, Havana, Rio de Janeiro and Istanbul (9)	London
2016	Doha, Chicago, Madrid, Tokyo and Rio de Janeiro (5)	Rio de Janeiro
2020	Baku, Doha, Istanbul, Madrid, Rome and Tokyo (6)	Due to be known at IOC session (7th September 2013)

Source: Own elaboration

This situation has led Shoval (2002) to state that we are at the beginning of a new phase in the development of the Olympic Games with more global cities participating as the 2012 and 2016 bidding process shows. As a plethora of authors agree, the growth in the number of cities bidding to host the Olympics, exemplified by Hall and Hubbard (1998: 8, original emphasis) as the '*major marshalling point for the urban boosterism and civic peacockery*', is the evidence that more cities worldwide now perceive major benefits to be derived from the Olympics as well as other events. Consistent with the literature on urban politics, the decision to bid for any sport project is made and controlled by the city's political authorities, backed by different tiers of government and business leaders. However, there is some criticism of the democratic process of the Olympic bids and of the expected benefits to cities and their citizens that the *boosters* of the Olympics promote (Lenskyj, 1996, 2000).

Not only have major sporting events been key elements of regeneration strategies, but also sport facilities such as stadia and arenas, either as part of the planning and organization of those events or as isolated projects, have played a central role in the regeneration of more cities around the world in the 1990s and especially in the 2000s. As part of the main fabric of urban projects, postmodern stadia and arenas have been commoditized as postmodern 'cathedrals of consumption', tourist attractions, leisure and business centres or icons of city marketing (Paramio *et al.*, 2008). As commented, in North American cities there are many examples of new stadia built as part of regeneration projects.

Evidence suggests that in the 1990s and 2000s we have seen the biggest 'construction boom' of the ultimate generation of more technological and commercial stadia in a great number of countries around the world, the first ranked in Europe being Britain, followed by Italy, France, Japan and Korea, Portugal, Germany,[5] and only recently by Spain (Paramio *et al.*, 2008); a process that has not ended. Brazil has plans for the construction and upgrading of 12 stadia for the World Cup 2014 with an estimated budget of £1.5bn and the construction of nine new venues, the upgrading of eight existing venues and the building of temporary venues with an estimated budget of £10bn.

After the study of Bale and Moen (1995), which was one of the first to analyse the impact of stadia on European cities, other authors have examined the impacts of contemporary stadia, some of them linked to bids for the Olympics, the Football or Rugby World Cups or other events such as the Commonwealth Games, as central elements of city-wide regeneration. Stadia have also formed part of the regeneration process of more European cities in the last decade. Examples of this relationship in Europe are, among others, the Millennium Stadium, Cardiff (Jones, 2001; Davies, 2005, 2010), Manchester City Stadium, Manchester (Davies, 2005), the Stade de France, Paris (Thornley, 2002), London and the Emirates Stadium and the new Wembley, the Amsterdam Arena, Amsterdam, Athens and the Olympic Stadium or Madrid and Estadio de Madrid (proposed Olympic Stadium as part of the failed bids of the city to host the 2012 and 2016 Olympics and which still forms part of the new bid project of Madrid for the 2020 Olympic Games) (Paramio *et al.*, 2008). Building costs that clearly rocketed after the building of two of the first examples of the latest generation of stadia such as Ajax's Amsterdam ArenA and the Stade de France Stadium, both examples clearly linked to the physical, social and economic regeneration of derelict areas in Amsterdam and Paris.

Data reveal that construction costs of most of stadia built in the 1990s were substantially overtaken by those of stadia built in the 2000s and specially the new Wembley Stadium at an astonishing cost of €1.1bn (see Table 22.3 below).

Table 22.3 The escalating costs of construction of selected new and proposed stadia in Europe, linked to major sport events and important elements of urban regeneration projects

Period	Name of stadium, capacity and year of opening	Cost (Euros)	Linked to sport events
The 1990s	Amsterdam ArenA, Amsterdam, Holland. 52.000 Amsterdam ArenA. 1996	€127m	Bid for the 1996 Olympic Games, Amsterdam
	Stade de France, Paris, France, 80,000, 1998	€407.3m	1998 Football World Cup, France
	Millenium Stadium, Cardiff, Wales, UK, 72,000, 1999		1999 Rugby World Cup
The 2000s	Veltins-Arena, Gelsenkirchen, Germany, 61,481, 2001	€190m	2006 Football World Cup, Germany
	Estádio da Luz, Lisbon, Portugal, 65,647, 2003	€119m	2004 European Football Championship, Portugal
	Allianz Arena, Munich, Germany, 69,901, 2006	€340m	2006 Football World Cup, Germany
	Wembley Stadium, London, UK, 90,000, 2007	€1.1bn	2012 London Olympic Games and bid for the 2016 and 2020 Football World Cups
	Estadio La Peineta, Madrid, Spain, 70,000 (still pending, to move to the proposed Madrid Olympic stadium)	€250m	Bids of 2012, 2016 and 2020 Madrid Olympic Games

Source: Own elaboration

Unlike the US and European cases, there are few studies elsewhere that examine stadia as urban development catalysts. For instance, Maening and Schwarthoff (2006) and Maening and du Plessis (2009) analyse the impact of nine stadia built for the South Africa World Football Cup 2010 or Uppal (2009) who examines the contribution of the 2010 Commonwealth Games to speed up the much-needed urban regeneration of New Delhi. There are other studies that focus on the stadium (Telstra Stadium, Sidney) and the legacy of the facilities built for major events such as the Olympic Games (Searle, 2002).

After the 1992 Barcelona Olympic Games, which has been widely recognized as a paradigm of contemporary urban regeneration, city leaders started to develop the concept of Barcelona as a 'sport city and tourist attraction' (Coaffee, 2007; Duran, 2005; Smith, 2012) which was part of a much longer-term plan of transformations in the city. Similar to other cities worldwide, one of the elements on which the city of Barcelona has focused is the staging of a wide portfolio of national and international events. Alongside the events, it is also worth remarking that the operation of the tour and museum at Camp Nou stadium, which was officially set up in 1984, has also contributed to bringing more visitors to the city, which is currently one of the main tourist destinations in Europe. As such, in the period 1984–2008, as the FC Barcelona Centre of Documentation confirms, this magnificent stadium has been visited by nearly 18 million people, and in 2008 alone the museum received 1,231,344 visitors (cited in Paramio *et al.*, 2010: 76–77). Therefore, the combination of major sporting events, relevant sport facilities and the contribution of sports heritage strategies may be in certain cities, as Barcelona shows, a major catalyst of the tourism strategy envisaged by city leaders as well as a central part of the regeneration of derelict areas.

One of the recurrent challenges that entrepreneurial cities face is how to achieve a balance between their economic and political support for major sports events and infrastructure, mainly with public funds, and their support for community-level participation in sport. One example to analyse is the city of Valencia. Like Barcelona, Valencia offers another significant example of sports-led urban regeneration that combines the holding of different types of events, including the 2007 America's Cup and the Formula One and massive developments in the city linked to those events, promoting local sports facilities in the city (with around 112 community facilities), but one of the key differences with Barcelona is the tremendous transformation of the banks of the River Turia into a massive area, probably the largest urban park in Spain with an area of 110 hectares and a length of 8 km, for sport and recreation in the centre of the city (Bosch Reig, 2011).

Unlike the European Capitals of Culture branding and concept, which was launched by the European Commission in 1985 to support cultural city regeneration in a variety of industrial and post-industrial cities (Tallon, 2010), the European Commission postponed similar recognition in the area of sport until 2001. Since then, the European Capitals of Sport Association (ACES), under the umbrella of the European Commission, has set up recognition as European Capital of Sport Awards to those cities with a population of over 500,000 inhabitants. At the time of writing, Valencia has been awarded this emblematic recognition as part of their sport policy for the year 2011 (Table 22.4).

The effects and legacy of unsuccessful bids of Madrid to the Olympic Games of 2012 and 2016

Some authors and urban leaders claim that even failed bids for the Olympic Games can be valued as a strategic decision to promote the entrepreneurial city by contributing to a myriad of effects on the city such as the revitalization of the local economy, to enhance the city image and, as in the case of Madrid, to accelerate significant urban transformations in some areas of the city. A considerable number of authors including Alberts (2009), Burbank *et al.*, (2001), Essex and Chalkey (1998), Hiller (2000), Levin (2010) and Lenskyj (1996, 2000) remark that one of the managerial concerns would be to assess the legacy and effects of bidding for and (mainly) failing to get the Olympic Games. Therefore, the current state of sports venues and infrastructure envisaged for the Madrid 2012 and 2016 Olympic project will be analysed in this section.

Table 22.4 European capitals of sport (2001–2013)

2001. Madrid	2007. Stuttgart
2002. Stockholm	2008. Warsaw
2003. Glasgow	2009. Milan
2004. Alicante	2010. Dublin
2005. Rotterdam	2011. Valencia
2006. Copenhagen	2012. Istanbul
	2013. Antwerp

Source: www.aces-europa.eu (accessed 12 March 2011)

Spain has not hosted the Olympics since the 1992 Barcelona Games; therefore the Madrid bid was inspired by the much-acclaimed Barcelona model. As part of this, one of Madrid's key motivations for bidding for the 2012 as well as for the 2016 Games was to accelerate significant transformations in two areas of the city, the east and south parts, which would be difficult to accomplish under normal circumstances, as Nieto and Sobejano (2001) note. As in other candidate cities, the bid was valued by city leaders and all political parties as a new economic strategy to enhance the city's *brand* to attract international business and tourists.

The decision to launch a bid for Madrid to host the Olympics had been a long time coming. Over the years, Madrid has bid to host the Games four times, but failed in the previous three attempts in 1972 (competing against Munich and Detroit), 2012 and 2016, and it is currently bidding for the 2020 Games. As part of what Shoval (2002) defines as a new phase of the Olympics, in the most recent bids for the Games of 2012 and 2016, Madrid has been involved in a major competition, pitching against global cities such as London, New York, Chicago, Tokyo or Paris.

Making bids for the Olympics is very costly, even in the bid phase, requires considerable resources and is also a long-term process (Payne, 2006). The Madrid bid for the 2012 Games was supported by Mayor Álvarez del Manzano in 2002 and thereafter his successor, Mayor Ruiz Gallardón (2003)[6] kept up the momentum supporting the 2012, 2016 and more recently the 2020 bids. As mentioned, the complexity of the Games has substantially increased the cost of bidding for cities. The Madrid bid for the 2012 Games had an estimated cost of €18.6 million with officials of the Madrid bid stating that around 70 per cent of the venues needed for the Games were already in place. Compared to the bid project for 2012, there are substantial differences as the cost of the bid for the 2016 Olympics had increased substantially to an estimated $40.4m (€ 55.8m) where the promoters of the 2016 Madrid bid emphasized that 77 per cent of the venues were already built. If we compare the bid budget for all the cities that were candidates for the 2016 Games as reflected in Table 22.1, the overall cost was $179.4 million, with most cities disbursing similar figures, Madrid having the lowest budget ($40.4m) and Chicago the largest ($49m).

Irrespective of the bid outcome, the Madrid project promised to enhance sporting infrastructure and sport participation in the city as potential benefits to the city and its citizens. Trying to fulfil the demands on candidate cities from the IOC for sports venues and infrastructure, the 2016 bid document mentioned the urban regeneration of the city as one of their key themes after stating that:

> [O]ur concept (of the Games) delivers in two areas of the city: the Core Zone; the heart of the Games and the River Manzanares zone (the lungs of the Games). It will create over 50 hectares of new park land, planted with over 40,000 new trees and will transform a current landscape of 780 derelict hectares into green spaces for sport and recreation.
>
> (Madrid 2016 Bid, 2006)

This project will be described in greater detail later.

From the technical point of view, the Madrid project is very solid as the 2012 and 2016 IOC's evaluation committee clearly pointed out. Years later, the Madrid bid to host the 2016 Games incorporated two new facilities built to support the failed bid for the 2012 Games. The Madrid 2016 bid included 28 venues, with 13 located in the east of the city around the proposed Olympic stadium, the Aquatic Centre and the Olympic village, ten in the west of the city in the River Manzanares Zone and the rest in central areas and in nearby cities.

Though the 2016 Madrid bid emphasized that 77 per cent of the facilities were built, two of the main key facilities, the proposed Olympic Stadium and the Aquatic Centre, still had not been finished and all venues planned for sports such as rowing, canoeing, shooting or archery had yet to be built and are dependent as well as other infrastructure on the bid outcome at the IOC session in Buenos Aires on 7 September 2013 which will select the host city of the 2020 Olympic Games.

While one of the most evident examples of any bid on cities would be most commonly in relation to the building of new or the upgrading of existing sports venues, in the case of Madrid 2012 and Madrid 2016, the main effect may be seen in the building of new infrastructure as the bid documents clearly promise. In essence, the bid has helped to build new Metro stations, the building of Terminal 4 at Barajas airport and especially two connected flagship projects, the transformation of the River Manzanares (Madrid Rio) and the building of six kilometres of underground roadways (Madrid Calle 30). After having a low sporting profile prior to the 2012 bid, the 2012 and 2016 bids themselves have accelerated the hosting of major sporting events as part of the policy response, a stance still active today. In the last decade, Madrid has hosted over 250 events. Among others, a wide array of permanent and 'ad hoc' sporting events such as the European Indoor Athletic Championships and Road Cycling, Taekwondo and Archery World Championships (2005), Women's World Cup Hockey or Badminton World Championships (2006), Men's European Basketball Championship (2007), Euro League Basketball Final Four, Gymnastics World Cup Final (2008), as well as Federation Tennis Final Cup (2008), Master Series Madrid ATP Tennis, popular races to the more recent Champions League Final at Bernabeu Stadium, all in 2010.

But this flagship project (Madrid Rio), officially launched in April 2011, is mainly expected to contribute to the physical regeneration of the eastern part of the city and to both banks of the River Manzanares for sport and recreational uses. Evidence of this dramatic change that has taken place in eastern Madrid includes the opening of a great variety of sports and leisure facilities for traditional and new sports such as 30 km of cycling routes, 17 paddle courts and tennis courts, fitness areas, artificial football pitches, skate park and roller skating, city beaches and children's play areas. In addition to these positive effects, this project (and Madrid Calle 30) has helped to improve the aesthetic aspect of large public spaces and quality of life for those residents living in eastern Madrid and will probably contribute at a later stage to improving the socio-economic conditions of those areas.

However, the construction of new sports venues and especially the infrastructure associated with the bids has also had negative effects on the city and its citizens. In particular, the capital cost allotted for developing two of the main infrastructure projects (Madrid Rio and Madrid Calle 30) estimated at approximately € 5,000 million, has been critical to the increasing debt of the Madrid City Council (€7,008 million at the time of writing) (Bank of Spain, 2011) (see Table 22.5 which shows the evolution of Madrid City Council debt since the city officially started the bidding process in 2003 to the current time). This difficult economic situation at local level affects other public projects in other areas of the city and the running of public services. This is one of the recurrent challenges that any entrepreneurial city, as the case of Madrid represents, needs to face considering the massive investments made by the city in sports, cultural and transport infrastructure over a limited number of years.

Table 22.5 Financial debt of Madrid Town Hall (2003–11) (million €)

2003	1,455
2005	3,337
2007	5,805
2009	6,762
2010	6,453
2011	7,008

Source: Bank of Spain, debt of town halls in Spain, 2011

The combination of local factors (such as the increased financial debt at local level) and global factors (such as the deep economic crisis) has led the Madrid Town Hall to undertake cost-control measures that are also affecting the new Madrid bid for the 2020 Olympic Games. Just after Mayor Ruiz Gallardón announced that Madrid will bid again for a third consecutive time for the 2020 Olympic Games, he called for austerity, saying:

> The city will not spend any additional funds on building new infrastructure and sports venues until the next IOC session in Buenos Aires, Argentina on 7 September 2013 when the host city for the 2020 Summer Olympic Games will be decided.[7]

Conclusions and future direction of sports and urban regeneration research

It has been recognized that there is neither a unique sport strategy linked to urban regeneration nor an accepted model to drive regeneration through sport initiatives worldwide. In fact, there are interesting parallels, and some key differences, between the sport initiatives adopted in North American cities and those adopted in European cities and elsewhere. However, common to all cities is the economic impact which remains the dominant discourse used by political elites to promote all kind of sports strategies linked to urban regeneration.

The sport and urban regeneration relation has generated huge public, political and commercial interest. Another recurrent issue is that sport and urban regeneration have become a global phenomenon as more cities worldwide have valued a whole array of sports events and projects as major opportunities to address some of their urban problems, a trend that is likely to continue in the coming years, though there may be some doubt about the capability of some cities to deliver efficiently on major projects. It is not only cities in developed countries that are involved in competing for bidding and running major events that include building sports venues and infrastructure, but also this global phenomenon opens up more business opportunities for more developed countries that are helping the bids of emerging countries as already mentioned. As such, countries such as Australia, UK or Spain have set up a national structure and staff to manage sporting events bidding.

In terms of making recommendations for future research and studies of sports and urban regeneration, we need to go beyond and investigate unexplored areas such as the relationship between stadia, arenas, museums of sport, halls of sport in what Smith (2006) calls 'Sports-City' zones and their potential as tourism resources for cities. There are other areas of study that have received less attention. These include the legacy and effects of bidding and failing to stage the

Olympics, as the case of the two consecutive failed bids of Madrid for 2012 and 2016 Olympic Games contribute to an extent in this area (Alberts, 2009; Cochrane *et al*, 1996; Essex and Chalkley, 1998; Levin, 2010; Paramio-Salcines and Dobson, 2004, Paramio *et al.*, 2011; Shoval, 2002). This area is still relevant when we analyse the current applicant cities for the forthcoming 2020 Olympic Games bidding process (International Olympic Committee, 2011).[8] There are other areas that need attention such as how mega events are related to urban processes (Burbank *et al.*, 2001; Hiller, 2000; Gold and Gold, 2007; Smith, 2012) or the evaluation of the 'real' costs and benefits of hosting sporting events and projects on cities and their inhabitants (Davies, 2010, 2011; Rosentraub, 1997). Trying to address these and other significant issues, the recent work of Larissa Davies (2011: 1439) highlights that one of the challenges that the study of sport and urban regeneration has still to face is the evaluation of sport–city-led regeneration projects, especially with the current worldwide economic crisis:

> [There is] a need to develop a more comprehensive understanding of the role of sport in the regeneration process to maximize the potential benefits offered by sport related developments and to justify and sustain public expenditure on sport in the future.

23

METHODOLOGIES FOR EVALUATING THE USE OF SPORT FOR DEVELOPMENT IN POST-CONFLICT CONTEXTS

María Rato Barrio and Clemens Ley

Introduction: sport and development in post-conflict societies

Looking back over the years on publications in academic journals or on the International Platform on Sport and Development (www.sportanddev.org), the websites of NGOs, sport federations and also non-sporting organisations we observe an increasing interest taken in sport for development. Unfortunately, the increasing use of sport activities in development projects is not sufficiently represented in scientific research, and rigorous project evaluation is still scarce. In addition, more critical reflection is needed, as at times we forget the ambivalent nature of sport, which is how it can promote, for example, inclusion and peace as well as exclusion and violence (Coakley, 2007, 2011; Coalter, 2007b, 2010; Giulianotti, 2010; Giulianotti and Armstrong, 2011; Hartmann and Kwauk, 2011; Jarvie, 2011; Kay, 2009; Levermore, 2011; Levermore and Beacom, 2012; Ley and Rato Barrio, 2010).

Furthermore, post-conflict contexts have their own particular burden and peculiarities that need to be addressed. Conflicts often destroy in a complex, traumatic and long-lasting way individuals, families, communities, and social, economic, political and cultural resources and networks. Most often, the consequences of conflicts are evident over long periods of time, underlying reasons are unaddressed, and conflicts stay latent or even escalate into violence again. In these situations, the population is more vulnerable to abuse and manipulation. For example, in Guatemala the history of racism and discrimination suffered particularly by the *Mayan* population has been put behind them in its most brutal and overt form (for example, the systematic massacres in the 1980s during the civil war); however, it still exists in more subtle forms. Women, in particular, have been the direct target of violence that aimed to destroy communities at their most intimate point. They still are one of the most affected and targeted groups in the population suffering from continuous incidents of violence and discrimination, enacted with impunity, that create a general atmosphere of fear. Community cohesion and mutual support structures are destroyed as a result of the conflict and ongoing discrimination (Ley, 2009).

Education has suffered not only in quality and in terms of the priority given to it during the conflict, but also from abuses and social–political influences that aim to control the people, to maintain or obtain power, and have the effect of destroying communities, families and lives. As a consequence, youth growing up and educated in conflict or post-conflict contexts are affected by the lived experiences, their thoughts manipulated and oppressed, with little evidence of opportunities to construct a positive future (Ley, 2009; Rato Barrio, 2009).

In a post-conflict context, sport is used in various ways, for example, in community empowerment, education and awareness creation, crime reduction, social inclusion, counselling, promotion of mental health and well-being, conflict transformation, reconciliation and peace building, or socio-economic development. A wide range of different approaches through sport are used according to the objectives in each development project that can be categorised as predominantly professional, recreational, educational, preventive or therapeutic approaches.

Different strategies can be identified, including for example: pedagogical methodologies; personal and community empowerment through capacity building, participatory processes, life skills and leadership training; network building; organising sport events, leagues and regular training; building of teams, spaces and platforms for interaction; and peer education. The trainers and facilitators are considered to play a crucial role in most of the projects. Other key aspects of projects in this context have been the local leadership and ownership of the initiative, context-specificity of the initiative and the provision of accessible, protected and safe environments (Rato Barrio and Ley, 2010b).

As a tool, sport is mostly not used in isolation, rather it is combined with other games, movement and body-centred activities or techniques. According to the focus on 'plus sport' or 'sport plus' (Coalter, 2006), these tools are also combined more or less intensively with other interventions and recreational, educational, preventive and therapeutic tools, for example, group discussions, self-supporting groups, painting, community service, peer education, etc. Sport most often makes use of tools from various disciplines, as physiological and psychosocial processes are determinants for the success of sport. In fact, interdisciplinary and holistic approaches and networking are required to respond to the complex and multidimensional context of conflict and violence. Despite the increasing scientific interest, evidence about the effectiveness and mediating processes in sport for development is missing in this context.

Evaluating the use of sport in post-conflict societies

Evaluation of sport and development initiatives in post-conflict societies aims to analyse the results of the intervention or organisation and the role of different approaches, strategies and tools used in specific contexts. It aspires to contribute with relevant and meaningful knowledge to the improvement of evidence-based sport and development policies. According to the need for multidimensional interventions and development policies in post-conflict contexts, the evaluation must be holistic as well. Thereby, evaluation is using normal research methods and procedures within a specific evaluation framework.

However, evaluation in post-conflict contexts is affected by the specific situation and has to adapt to local personal and social circumstances in order to avoid harm. It is worth underlining key principles which inform our own position and that of others working in the field at this point. This includes adhering to general ethical principles, such as the principle of *nonmaleficence* (obligation not to do harm) and of *beneficence* (obligation to remove harm and to do good); *respect* for persons and communities (respect for individual and community values, reputation, cultural diversity, etc; autonomy; protection for individuals and vulnerable groups); *justice* (fairness; equity); and *integrity* of the person and community. Researchers must be aware and honest about their own capacities, limitations, competence, belief systems, values and interests. Evaluation design should incorporate widely accepted research ethics in all phases (including in the dissemination of results), informed consent; adequate communication in a language the participant fully understands; voluntary participation and the right to withdraw at any time; confidentiality; anonymity; protection of participants and provision of safeguards; and risk-benefit analysis (Diesfeld, 2004; Israel and Hay, 2006; Louw and Delport, 2006; Rato Barrio and Ley, 2010b).

Logic models are widely used to plan and implement development projects (see for example Chapter 4 in this volume). They allow us to structure evaluation, for example according to *inputs, activities, outputs, outcomes* and *impact*. Applied in evaluation, we can distinguish descriptive and analytical approaches (Henry, 2009; Rato Barrio, Ley, and Durán González, 2009). However, there are also challenges in using the logic model approach, and it has been argued that this approach follows occidental (e.g. linear versus cyclic) thinking and structures; it is too rigid and does not capture the complexity of the process (e.g. limiting itself to unrealistic cause–effect relationships); and that it can present difficulties in collaborative approaches (Echart Muñoz, Cabezas Valencia, and Sotillo Lorenzo, 2010; Hill and Thies, 2010).

There is a wide range of experiences in the field of education, health promotion and management that uses approaches similar to the logical model, for example, the CIPP model (Stufflebeam, 2003) referring to *Context, Input, Process* and *Product* (some include also *Transfer*); or models for evaluation and quality management in companies and in rehabilitation (Baldus, Huber, Pfeifer, and Schüle, 2007; Wydra, 2006) distinguishing, for example, structure, process and results evaluation. These models provide multiple phase evaluation frameworks.

Theories of change can be used in the logical model for project planning and evaluation; for example, assuming or describing which *inputs* and *activities* are producing what kind of *outputs, outcomes* or *impact*. From an analytical perspective, they aim to explain how and why an initiative works or fails (Henry, 2009). A theory of change approach in evaluation can be described 'as a systematic and cumulative study of the links between activities, outcomes, and contexts of the initiative' (Connell and Kubisch, 1998, p. 17).

In the field of monitoring and evaluation, a movement away from traditional implementation-based approaches toward new results-based approaches is noted (Kusek and Rist, 2004). The result-based management (RBM) is a mainly donor-driven approach that predominantly focuses on the outcomes and impacts in order to analyse what are we actually achieving. Evaluation in the RBM focuses on the question of *what for?*, arguing that implementation-orientated evaluation is limited to the description of what has happened, without assessing the actual results. However, RBM has its own critics and challenges (Mayne, 2007); for example, it focuses mainly on the outcomes and impact, reducing the significance of insights into processes. This is a significant limitation since it is not only essential to know what has been achieved, but also to understand what have been the factors responsible for such change. This is fundamental as we need to make recommendations for further sport and development policies.

These approaches should not be seen in isolation. Theories of change, logic models and result-based management can be useful and complementary tools in evaluation of programmes, when adequately used and implemented. In all these approaches, key considerations for evaluation are concerned about the development of adequate indicators and links between the multiple steps (e.g. *input, activities, outputs, outcomes* and *impact*). Also, they all necessarily simplify and try to narrow down reality to a measurable scheme. Consequently, they face challenges in the complex reality in post-conflict contexts. Thus it is argued that flexibility and adaptation to the local context is paramount and rigid preconceptualised evaluation models should be avoided.

Furthermore, we must be aware of our own cultural background and theoretical, methodological and ethical references which continuously influence our research endeavours. It may differ importantly from *others*; for example, indigenous people may have a different approach towards knowledge development (Smith, 1999). The participation or leadership of local researchers is crucial not merely for translation, but to initiate, develop, understand and maintain locally meaningful research processes. A self-critical approach is required. In addition, reflection on who and how we include different groups of population is crucial. For example, most evaluation initiatives focus only on active participants, who most likely appreciate the programme as they are taking part in it, and are not analysing drop-outs or excluded people. The latter, however, could give us valuable information to improve sport for development policies. Sport can be quite exclusive. Projects might encounter the risk of including only participants with certain characteristics positively associated with a tendency to volunteer to take part in sport. Thus, it is important that evaluation encompasses people both in and outside of the sport project, comparing them, and analyses reasons for drop-out or exclusion.

Sport and development practitioners are likely to face unexpected results and challenges in their daily work. 'Yet, you rarely see any evaluator who has done field work to uncover possible unintended circumstances' (Patton, 2010). In the mainly positive descriptions and analysis of the field of sport for development, evaluators might tend to anticipate mainly positive results, looking to provide support for the dominant positive and *evangelistic* perspective on sport for development (Coakley, 2011; Kay, 2009). This can have the effect of limiting the perspective for analysing unexpected or negative factors.

According to the project management cycle, the evaluation results should consequently feed into the planning and implementation of further interventions and improvements of the existing project (Patton, 2008). Evaluation should not only inform policy makers and organisers. Information should be discussed with the participants. Despite a general shift from *summative* to *formative* evaluation, results are not always used for learning purposes, fed back to participants or followed by actions. It is essential that evaluation process and results are useful and meaningful for the project and participants. Therefore, the results should not be disseminated *after* having decided about the future actions (Patton, 2008).

Patton (2010) argued that 'much of what evaluation has been doing is simplifying complex reality, rather than engaging with it'. Participatory approaches, such as participatory action research (PAR) or participatory evaluation, offers an alternative and distinctive way to engage directly with the participants, who actually become (co-)evaluators of their own situation, organisation or intervention. They do not limit themselves to the analysis of a situation; they aim to contribute to empowerment, capacity building, self-determination and ownership. In addition, they mostly become more relevant for the participants than external evaluation. For example, 'the key characteristic of PAR – collaboration between participants and researchers – often increases relevance of research and improves its social validity, meanwhile maintaining the standards of scientific rigour' (White, Suchowierska, and Campbell, 2004, p. S3).

The continuous feedback and dialogue among participants and with the broader community is an inherent component to maximise community participation, transparency and wider ownership of the results. Therefore, adapted communication channels (often including visualisation and creative techniques) are used in order to make the information accessible and understandable to the participants and broader audience. The production, discussion and dissemination of the results can be an action by itself, for example, for awareness creation, knowledge transfer or community network building. The process of evaluation can become as important as the results to contribute to a transformation or improvement of the situation (Ander-Egg, 1990; Bradbury and Reason, 2001; Fals-Borda and Anisur Rahman, 1991; Feuerstein, 1990; Khanlou and Peter, 2005).

Meanwhile, general recognition of the importance of participatory approaches has increased considerably during the last three decades; to call a project or evaluation participatory has become somewhat fashionable and 'participation' a buzzword (Cornwall and Brock, 2005; Leal, 2007). In fact, participation can be understood in different ways and we can define a continuum between passive participation, active participation and self-determination (see Figure 23.1). For some people, conducting a survey asking the participants for their opinion is a participatory process. Others argue that active participation must be given in all phases of an evaluation, starting from the establishment of the topic, aims and indicators, and including research design, implementation, data production, analysis, discussion and dissemination. However, many people argue that the essential key of a participatory approach is that participants have the power of decision making. Autonomous evaluation and self-determination would be the final aim of empowerment and capacity building (Ander-Egg, 1990; Berger and Peerson, 2009; Bradbury and Reason, 2001; Fals-Borda and Anisur Rahman, 1991; Feuerstein, 1990; Khanlou and Peter, 2005; Löfman, Pelkonen, and Pietilä, 2004; Villasante, 1999; Villasante, Montañés, and Martí, 2002).

Alvira Martín (1991, 1997) indicates four preconditions that must be fulfilled in order to conduct a participatory evaluation:

- the participants want to evaluate and learn;
- they have the capacity, time and access to be able to do it;
- they are truly interested in the exercise and process;
- their participation will motivate them to apply and fulfil the recommendations they come up with.

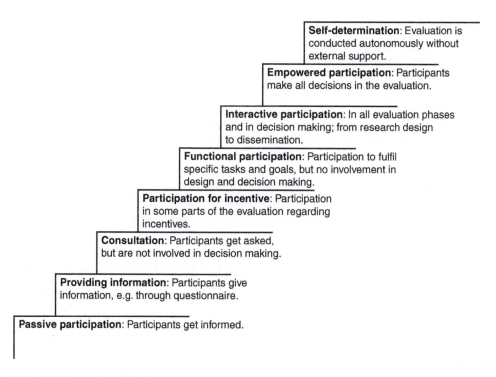

Figure 23.1 Steps of participation.

In the complex and multidimensional context of violence and conflict, the use of participatory approaches presents both opportunities and challenges. A fully participatory approach is not always possible, as access to information, time constraints (participatory processes in general tend to invest more time), capacities (participatory processes might require preparation in advance and capacity building) or power relations can inhibit or limit the process. In some contexts, communitarian meetings have been violently suppressed during the conflict or even in the post-conflict context; thus, an open participatory approach might be accompanied by fear and risks of repression from certain parties or groups (Pérez-Sales, 2006).

In general, the facilitator is taking a primary methodological role in the research process, while the participants are becoming (co-)researchers. As a consequence, some researchers may fear a loss of power with control increasingly out of their hands. Some might not be well prepared and sufficiently capacitated in participatory techniques, as a rigorous preparation as well as flexibility in the process is required. Others may conduct participatory techniques to confirm their own predetermined results by guiding the participants in a certain direction. Manipulation, not only by the facilitator but also by the participants, is a danger in participatory processes. In conflict and post-conflict contexts this has to be taken into account as the population in general may be more vulnerable to manipulation.

Thus, vulnerabilities, conflictive constellations and power relations must be analysed and taken into consideration throughout the participatory process. Some community members might opt not to take part at all owing to fear, oppression or discrimination, especially when certain other individuals, groups or parties take part. Opponents of the participatory process must be identified as well as potential risks. In conflict contexts, a decision to run a participatory evaluation with one group or type of participant excluding others, impacts on the assumed *neutrality* of the external facilitator. However, this decision can be an intentional one in order to facilitate support for the voice of the most vulnerable population. From a research perspective, stating transparently and extensively the characteristics of participants and *intersubjectivity*, and demonstrating *reflexivity* in the research process is paramount.

Not all participants speak up and analyse the situation honestly unless certain conditions are fulfilled. External and internal power inequalities related to gender, presence of authoritarian leaders, social–cultural hierarchies, groups in conflict, expectations about foreigners or external facilitators, etc. might bias expression in forums and assemblies. Several participatory processes in separated groups or special preparations, techniques and capacity building might be required in order to capture all voices and allow inclusive analysis and decision making in participatory evaluation. Other barriers to participation are stigma, transport, time, place and security.

In PAR 'the responsibility for practical action and research is shared with participants' (Löfman *et al.*, 2004, p. 333). This includes discussion, negotiation and guaranteeing of ethical issues, such as informed consent, voluntary participation, confidentiality, protection of participants, risk–benefit analysis, and so on (see Blake, 2007; Khanlou and Peter, 2005; Minkler, 2004; Minkler *et al.*, 2002; Truman, 2003). The initiator of the process is expected to raise ethical considerations from the beginning. However, it is part of the participatory process to negotiate and take responsibility for the actions in the group.

Research methods and instruments are determined in the participatory process of common decision making. Besides *traditional* quantitative (questionnaire, systematic observation, sociometric test, etc.) and qualitative instruments (interview, focus group, participatory observation, etc.), techniques widely used in participatory research and evaluation include:

- participatory techniques for analysis (mapping; graphics; drawings; cross tables; most significant change; photo-interviewing or photo-voice; video; story writing or telling; projective techniques; etc.);
- (bodily active) group techniques (games; role play; sociodrama; etc.);
- triangulation (among methods/instruments, researchers and research participants/source of information);
- techniques for consensus building (voting; ranking, Philips 6–6; etc.);
- techniques for devolution and feedback (forums; assemblies; group discussions; exposi-tions; comment box; etc.);
- visualisation techniques (wall painting; posters; photographs; audiovisual materials; multi-media; comics; role play; theatre; etc.).

Three case studies in Guatemalan post-conflict context

In the post-conflict context of Guatemala, the authors were involved in the conducting and evaluating of various programmes, using a range of different methodologies over a period of 12 months (November 2007 to November 2008). The various programmes addressed different groups of populations (youth, women, children, teachers, communities in conflict) through capacity building and interventions with various partner organisations and community groups.

We present three examples here as a vehicle to discuss evaluation and research methodolo-gies. For further details on intervention methodologies and research results we refer to other publications, since they can only be described here in brief to contextualise the discussion about evaluation and research (Ley, 2009; Ley and Rato Barrio, 2011a; Rato Barrio, 2009; Rato Barrio and Ley, 2010a, 2010c, 2011, 2012).

Case study I: Sport to promote interculturalism (PIDE programme)

This educational community development programme with Guatemalan youth aimed to pro-mote intercultural living together among ethnic groups in conflict. It was built on a theoretical framework with specific goals, phases, strategies and activities. It used different kinds of sports, games, dynamics, creative and participatory activities, dramatisation, popular theatre, etc. com-bined with verbal reflections, discussion groups, group assignments and presentations. Activities were planned according to the specific goals of each session and to the corresponding inter-cultural phase and transversal issues (Rato Barrio, 2009; Rato Barrio and Ley, 2010a, 2010c, 2011, 2012).

The research assessed the goals of the intercultural concept (change in attitudes towards diversity and intercultural *living together*), and the objectives and contents of the three defined phases (*decentring, comprehension* and *negotiation*). This has been successfully approached via multiple case studies, combining quantitative and qualitative techniques and multiple phase evaluation (Rato Barrio, 2009). A logic model was used in the project planning and evaluation, distinguishing *context, inputs, activities, outputs* and *outcomes*.

The research included 100 participants in four intervention groups and a control group was obtained with 557 youths (Rato Barrio, 2009). The majority of the participants were between 15 and 19 years old. Written informed consent was obtained by the participants and their parents or tutor (if the participant was under 18 years old), as well as from the schools and community organisations involved. Participants were taking part in the PIDE programme over a period of six months in ethno-linguistic mixed groups (Ladino/mestizo and three Mayan groups: Kaqchikel, K'iche' and Tz'utujil).

The strengths of the PIDE programme evaluation were the use of the multiple case studies approach, a multiple phase framework and the combination and triangulation of quantitative and qualitative techniques, such as questionnaires, sociometric tests, field diaries of the participants and of the researchers involved, audiovisual material, and projective techniques (e.g. tests of word association).

A questionnaire about attitudes towards cultural diversity in Guatemala was used, which was partially based on Díaz-Aguado (1996), adapted to the local context and piloted before being used in the research. It included four scales related to the affective–cognitive and behavioural components of tolerance. The results of all four scales showed good internal consistency with Cronbach's alpha scores of 0.784 (scale 1), 0.82 (scale 2), 0.922 (scale 3) and 0.927 (scale 4) (Rato Barrio, 2009). We compared the experimental group with the control group and analysed the four experimental subgroups, comparing the final results with the baseline study (pre-post test). The first two scales evaluated the affective and cognitive components of tolerance. Scale 1 of the questionnaire concerns aspects more related to social desirability, being less sensitive to change, and it is included in the questionnaire to mediate the harsher elements of scale 2, which, on the other hand, are necessary as they are more sensitive to the detection of intolerant behaviour (Rato Barrio, 2009). Comparing the results of the initial and final measures, scale 2 is shown to have positively and significantly changed in the experimental group overall ($t = 2.112$; $p = 0.037$), while there were no significant changes in the control group ($t = 0.563$; $p = 0.575$). The questionnaire also measured behavioural disposition towards the indigenous/*Mayan* population (scale 3) and towards the Ladino population (scale 4) and detected changes in a significant and positive way in the experimental group in scale 4 ($t = 2.965$; $p = 0.004$), while the control group showed no significant changes ($t = 0.126$; $p = 0.90$). Although the samples in each subgroup were small ($n = 16–31$), the scales were sensitive to differences among the four experimental groups and among the ethnic groups, and gave useful information on the initial status and changes in each subgroup. The results of the questionnaire were triangulated to the qualitative data as the same variables and categories were analysed.

Various alternative and creative research instruments were used. For example, to evaluate interaction among the participants, we played at the beginning of the programme a touch/chase game where participants could help each other by giving hands in pairs and as such being 'protected' and 'untouchable' for the chaser. Searching for help and offering help were two variables for analysis. The four facilitators were asked to observe and to note in their diaries after the session how they perceived the interaction among the participants from the different ethnic groups; if they helped each other, who helped whom and when; if they sought support, who from whom and when; if some participants were excluded, etc. In addition, the participants were asked to write a one page diary based on guiding questions. At the end of the programme, the same game was played again and the same questions were asked in the diaries. The observation showed how participants at the beginning of the programme sought help only from their friends and interaction among the different ethnic groups was very limited. Some participants even described having felt excluded. At the end of the programme, interaction improved considerably and participants commented on it in the verbal reflection phase.

The field diaries of the participants and facilitators were considered as very valuable in the research process. Observations were triangulated among the facilitators and with the participants, as well as with the other research instruments, such as the sociometric test.

For the sociometric test, a questionnaire asking for preferences with whom participants wished to play, work, etc. was administered in the initial, intermediate and final phase of the programme. Questions such as 'With which three classmates would you like to spend more leisure time?' were asked. Figure 23.2 shows the mapping of the preferences at the beginning (left) and at the end of the programme (right) of one intervention group.

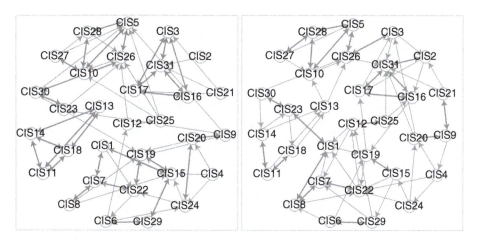

Figure 23.2 Sociogram of choices regarding the question 'With which three classmates would you like to spend more leisure time?' at the beginning of the programme (left) and at the end of the programme (right)

We can observe changes in the groupings (e.g. CIS14, CIS13, CIS18, CIS11 were a closed unit of one ethnolinguistic group at the beginning, but opened up during the programme). In addition, leaders and key players in the network were analysed (e.g. CIS1 or CIS31) and individual scores regarding election and rejection were determined. The data were triangulated with the corresponding diary of each analysed participant and observation from the facilitators. Improved interaction among ethnolinguistic groups was detected (Rato Barrio, 2009).

Meanwhile, in this context each of the research instruments used on its own had its limitation in terms of reliability. The strength of the research design was that several traditional and creative research instruments were measuring the same variables and categories, allowing a critical comparison and contrast of the data produced. Triangulation of the research instruments as well as of the observers was an essential element and contributed to a coherent image and deeper understanding of the processes and outcomes of the programme that permitted concrete recommendations for action.

The evaluation results showed some notable improvement in the affective–cognitive and behavioural components of tolerance towards diversity and in the intercultural phases, especially in developing *decentring* processes and *comprehension*. With regard to the theories of change, there is a directly proportional relationship in the improvement of the following aspects: inter-ethnic interaction, communication, trust, awareness of *others* and their cultures, the appreciation of one's own culture, awareness of convergences, appreciation of cultural diversity, and reduction of prejudice – all important steps in the methodological model used in the PIDE programme (Rato Barrio, 2009). The active and participatory character of the PIDE programme played an important role, as well as the learning by playing, the abilities of the facilitators and the social–cultural appropriateness of the sessions. Regarding the question concerning what participants liked most in the programme, they cited: 'The creation of games. Another way of explaining themes' (AB1); 'Above all I liked the methodology used as it is very interesting and useful as it was like learning by playing' (PA3); 'I found it very interesting to get to know that games are a very effective means to interrelate with the others and to make friendships' (FP4).

In spite of some limitations in research (small sample size of some subgroups) and intervention (limited duration of programme, irregular participation, problems with the facilities) at the end the conclusion was reached that the proposed model of intervention and research could be of considerable use in other studies and intercultural projects (Rato Barrio, 2009).

Case study II: Sport to promote psychosocial health among women

In this programme of Psychosocial Action through Movement, games and sport (APM) in Guatemala with two groups of *Mayan* women (in total 56 participants) who were suffering or had suffered violence, the authors used different kinds of sports, games and relaxation exercises, as well as creative and participatory tools, and verbalisation techniques to promote psychosocial health aspects and self-supporting effects in the group. All activities were contextualised and used according to the specific objectives of the three phases of the programme: (a) interaction and integration of the group (the stabilising phase); (b) expression of experiences of violence (the confrontation phase); and (c) searching for alternatives and solutions (the phase of integration of experiences and alternatives) (Ley and Rato Barrio, 2011a).

Qualitative (participant observation, diaries, interviews and participatory group techniques) and quantitative (questionnaire) methods were used. The qualitative results confirmed, supplemented and deepened the quantitative results. However, both methods showed their strengths and limitations in this study, as well as the need for holistic and multi-method research designs in the context of violence and conflict.

In the piloting of the questionnaire, difficulties were perceived regarding some expressions. The collaboration with the local university, a sociologist, psychologist and community worker was essential to improve social–cultural appropriateness; meanwhile maintaining meanings and concepts of the questionnaire that would allow comparison to other social–cultural contexts. This collaboration was also essential in the translation to Spanish and Kaqchikel, and back translation of the questionnaire.

Some participants had never been to school and showed a limited capacity of concentration. In addition, the women had no previous experience with questionnaires. Moreover, they were not used to questions about their well-being. In fact, in the context of oppression and machismo in the Guatemalan post-conflict context, the women were surprised to be asked for their opinion. Apart from more explanation, it was necessary to establish initial interaction and trust with the women, before administrating the questionnaire. In order to provide trust and confidentiality, for the women, it was also important that the (international and local) facilitators were not from the same community as themselves, as mistrust and fear were widespread in the community as a legacy of the civil conflict.

The administration of the questionnaire took quite a long time, owing to the challenges described above. It was surprising for us that some women actually expressed that they liked filling out the questionnaire as it made them think about themselves and about some aspects of their lives they had never paid attention to before. They said that the questionnaire was relevant and meaningful to them. In that sense, the research was contributing to the intervention process.

Despite the challenges, the questionnaire showed internal consistency in the results of the group of 56 women (Cronbach's alpha of 0.792) and was sensitive to measure changes in self-esteem and 'Sense of coherence'[1] (Ley, 2009).

Flexibility was an advantage in the personal semi-structured interviews that contributed to a better understanding of their experiences in the programme and of the perceived changes. Length of enquiry was adapted to the capacity of each woman, and translation and further explanation of the questions were provided when wished and needed. Possible bias and power-relations were taken into account. In this study, it was essential that the interviewer had a trustworthy relation with the interviewee and that they did not come from the same community (Ley and Rato Barrio, 2011b).

Participatory observation was recorded after each session by three facilitators in field notes and diaries, which were transcribed afterwards and analysed by categories. The recorded data of the three diaries proved to be complementary and very rich in information. It was triangulated with the data from the other research instruments.

In the programme a wide range of creative and participatory group techniques were used, such as dramatisation, role-playing, contextualised games and dynamics. These mostly bodily active and movement-based techniques were combined with phases of reflection about the experiences and feelings, so that non-verbal and verbal expressions were continuously mixed. The search for alternatives and solutions was shown in an active and participatory way. Apart from their therapeutic and educational aims, these contextualised participatory group techniques became a rich source of information for the evaluation of the programme. They allowed the participants to observe themselves, to examine their challenges and to analyse possible solutions, in a protected contextualised situation, inducing resultant feelings and reactions. These situations were perceived as relevant and close to reality, and the women transferred the experiences made in them to other life situations (Ley and Rato Barrio, 2011a, 2011b). The non-verbal and verbal information was captured in the diaries of three facilitators and by audiovisual media, such as audio and video recorders.

The *outcome* evaluation of the APM programme showed improvements of cognitive (knowledge and strategies to handle stressful situations), and psychological (self-esteem and emotional relaxation) resources. The self-esteem and the sense of coherence (SOC) increased significantly in the research group of 33 women who participated in both the initial and final evaluation (t = 3.56, p = 0.001 and t = 2.49, p = 0.018). Analysing the *inputs* and *processes* of intervention, the active, dynamic and participative character of the programme was highlighted as a main factor for these changes and as a distinct feature compared to other programmes in the field of gender-based violence. Other decisive aspects were: the learning process through games and verbal reflection, the confidential atmosphere, the role of the facilitators, the active involvement of the participants, the relaxation exercises, and the participatory group techniques. The high motivation and (mostly) regular participation from the first involvement, despite the daily difficulties and limited opportunities for women, and the high level of importance they assigned to the programme, speaks to a high degree of pertinence and social–cultural appropriateness of the APM programme (Ley, 2009; Ley and Rato Barrio, 2011a).

Case study III: Participatory action research as community intervention around the sport field

A participatory action research (PAR) project was undertaken in the framework of the Sport and Education for Peace programme DePaz,[2] an initiative to promote a culture of peace among three neighbouring villages in the rural area of Guatemala that had been in an unresolved conflict for several decades. We started in one village, being a group of eight interested people from a local organisation, school teachers, a worker at a financial cooperative and ourselves (the authors of this chapter).

In the first workshops, we discussed the aim and objectives of the PAR, introduced the process of PAR and agreed on the roles and responsibilities of each participant. The members of the local organisation were to coordinate the process, we (the authors) offered methodological training and guidance as facilitators, the teachers and other participants were to reach out to their work environment as researchers. Together we formed the core PAR group, being however open to further participants who might join at a later stage. In this first session, we introduced some techniques, such as brainstorming with cards, problem and objective trees, Philips 6–6, SWOT analysis, role-playing, sociodrama and popular theatre, interview and questionnaire, ranking and visualisation procedures.

Thereby, relevance and applicability of the techniques were discussed among the group. Afterwards, the research procedures were negotiated and ethical considerations discussed. The PAR aimed to analyse the situation of the village and to use the popular multipurpose sport field for dissemination of the results. In this regard, it was clearly evident that the topic was sensitive as the conflict is latent and causes were not addressed. Therefore, it was decided to avoid questions and direct confrontation with the violent conflict of the past. The responsibility of each participant to conduct the research in a sensitive manner was accordingly stressed. It was also concluded that the children and youth should have more of a voice and that they should contribute meaningfully to the process as the future leading generation. In order to analyse the situation of the village, the school teachers decided to conduct research in their classrooms by using participatory techniques. A short questionnaire was also elaborated to access other work environments, such as the financial cooperatives in the community. In addition, the local organisation approached other schools, community members and the council of elders of the village to ask for their participation. A mapping of the different stakeholders in the village was undertaken.

In the next workshop, quite rich and extensive information was reported back on small cards, big papers or questionnaire sheets. This was analysed and triangulated by the PAR group and categorised by emergent themes (sport, recreation, culture, environment, health, education, gender and human rights). Then the discussion focused on past, present and future, with input from the village council on changes in the village regarding tradition and modernity. In the field of sport, this was quite obvious, as traditional games and sports, as for example the Mayan Ball Game, were disappearing. On the other side, football, for example, was becoming commercialised in this area through the building of a five-a-side artificial grass facility for profit purposes. Various aspects of the resulting analysis provided reflections on changes in the value systems and in priorities, whereby education; basic living conditions; community spirit; and relationship with the environment were major concerns.

It was decided to paint the results on the walls around the much frequented public multipurpose sports field. The paintings were to focus on a positive spirit of transmitting the history and present situation of the village in relation to building for the future; to focus rather on the (possible) solutions and educational messages than directly on the problems or the delicate sensitivities in relation to the conflict. In order to visualise the results, the group decided to use drawings from the school pupils of the village.

Once the drawings were produced, gathered and analysed by the PAR team, the broader community was invited to discuss and evaluate them and their contents. Few other members from the community took part in this phase of feedback, although various invitations were sent out and people were personally approached. As reasons for the modest community participation, the PAR group indicated a lack of knowledge and experience in this kind of methodology; fear of getting involved in something related to the *past* conflict; lack of community cohesion; time constraints; perceptions of no direct immediate benefits of participation in the PAR; competing priorities, especially the low priority of participation compared to daily needs. However, the school teachers, pupils and youth took leadership in this process. The group voted for the most relevant drawings and asked the corresponding artists to improve some aspects of the drawing according to the results from the PAR discussions and feedback, and to contribute to the overall design of the painting of the walls around the sport fields. As a result, the wall painting was jointly done with the help of a projector that displayed the drawings on the wall. Positive messages were displayed as a result of the PAR process in order to raise awareness about the different themes analysed before.

Although participation of the broader community was limited during the process, feedback regarding the wall paintings was very positive. As a result, the mayor approached the local organisation to implement a similar process at the village hall. Some weeks after the first PAR, a similar process was requested and successfully implemented in the neighbouring village. Wall painting is a very relevant and pertinent visualisation technique in Guatemala and was used in a range of projects throughout the country. The sport ground proved an ideal place for dissemination, as it is a popular place and educational messages are visible for players and spectators.

Conclusions

The post-conflict context is challenging evaluation initiatives, as various structures are destroyed; latent conflicts might persist; fear and inequalities in power relations are widespread, and the population might be more vulnerable to manipulation. Context-specific factors have to be considered in evaluation in order to avoid harm, to sustain research ethics and to detect possible bias. Evaluation initiatives should be relevant, holistic, useful and meaningful for the community. We thus conclude this chapter with a summary of the lessons learned from these three case studies

Evaluation of sport and development initiatives in post-conflict context aims to analyse the results of the intervention as well as the decisive mechanism and conditions that lead to successful intervention policies. A multiple phase evaluation framework is highly recommended to evaluate not only the outcomes and impact but also the processes that lead to the results (and associated theories of change).

In a participatory approach, the evaluation aims to contribute to empowerment, capacity building and learning processes for the broader community. Participatory evaluation is often more relevant to the participants, as they become active (co-)researchers, taking the decisions throughout the entire evaluation process and developing interactive feedback with the community. However, as described in the third example, participatory processes also face challenges in the specific context that might inhibit participation. Therefore, we can describe different forms or steps of participation, as visualised in Figure 23.1. Meanwhile, we strive for achieving self-determination, empowerment and ownership in the evaluation process; context-specific factors must be taken into consideration to make this progressively happen.

The three case studies exemplified different evaluation methodologies, challenges and opportunities in the post-conflict context. They show that a holistic and multi-method evaluation design using both qualitative and quantitative research instruments is needed to address challenges in the specific context and to improve research validity.

A wide range of different research tools were described. Advantages and disadvantages of more *traditional* research tools, such as questionnaires and interviews were discussed in the specific context. Alternative and creative tools were described as well as the opportunity for observation in participatory group activities, such as dramatisation, contextualised games and dynamics.

These research instruments must be selected and adapted to be suitable and appropriate for the research aims and participants. A key component of any evaluation initiative in such a context should be the triangulation of the data from different research instruments, researchers and sources of information (e.g. intervention participants and non-participants; persons from different groups in conflict). Thus, specific attention must be given to inequalities in power relations (e.g. gender, conflict-specific or social–cultural group-specific inequalities) among the community, the participants and the researchers. Experiences of manipulation, abuse, fear and mistrust are frequent in post-conflict contexts. These factors might influence participation, decision making and bias in evaluation. In addition, access to information; conflictive relations, incompatibilities and competing interests; migrations and internally displaced people; community heterogeneity; social–cultural beliefs; influence of politics, media and communication channels; previous experiences with evaluation and research instruments; cognitive capacities; motivation; time, language and logistical constraints; and other context-specific factors should be considered in any evaluation efforts in post-conflict contexts.

Finally, as evaluation should be meaningful and useful, results should be disseminated to the relevant stakeholders at a timely relevant point in order to influence further actions. Adequate dissemination strategies should be used for feedback to the broader community, as for example, painting the research results on the walls around the sport field.

PART V

Social theory and sports policy

24

FEMINIST ANALYSIS OF SPORT POLICY

Sally Shaw

Introduction

Sport has been a major focus of governmental funding since the mid-1960s. Many governments claim that sport is a 'social good' at both the elite and participatory levels. In New Zealand, for example, Sport New Zealand (Sport NZ)[1] spends NZ$70 million per year on 'providing opportunities for New Zealanders to participate in recreation every day and getting more New Zealanders winning on the world stage' (Sport, 2012). Sport NZ (Sport and Recreation New Zealand) perceives this spend to be an 'investment' that will result in more medals at international sporting events and more participation by New Zealanders in sport and recreation.

This expenditure represents considerable investment in sport by New Zealand and other similarly minded governments. Such investment is fuelled by various country and city specific pledges to become the 'most active' (Activcity, 2011; Vuolle, 2010) and the predominance of, and value attributed to, medal tables at high profile sport events such as the Olympic Games. These considerations have led to substantial policy development in order to regulate and target government spending in sport. Sport policies have become the focus for researchers from the UK (e.g. Green and Houlihan, 2005b), New Zealand (Sam and Jackson, 2004), and Canada (Thibault, 2005), who have been interested in the philosophies that have influenced such policies, the complexities of implementing them, and their outcomes.

Despite this interest in national and international sport policy, an area of neglect has been the implications for gender within this research field. This is surprising given that, internationally, women continue to be under-represented as athletes, coaches, administrators, and officials within sport. Much of the rhetoric regarding sport in national government policies refers to the social good that is perceived to exist in the creation of sport through physical activity, confidence building, and community development (Sport and Recreation New Zealand, 2002). However, the language and rhetoric used within sport policy development often does not recognise or question the stereotypes, behaviours, and beliefs that reinforce sport as a gendered institution, which undermines social good potential. In other areas of policy, such as health and immigration, research has been conducted that examines, critiques, and forms a basis for change within gendered policy development (Outshoorn and Kantola, 2007). To date, similar approaches have been lacking within sport.

The purpose of this chapter is threefold. First, to outline the need for a feminist lens in sport policy analysis. Second, to offer a review of how various feminisms might be used to examine sport policy such as the promotion of elite performance or participation, focusing on policy development in the New Zealand context. Finally, to examine some of the potential for a feminist driven focus on sport policy to offer alternatives to policy makers. In conclusion, I argue that feminist approaches to understanding the wider body of sport policy offer fundamentally alternative avenues for sport policy development, which may benefit the sport sector in the long run.

Why feminism in sport policy research?

Most Western governments have been influenced to various degrees by a neoliberal framework over the past 20 years. The neoliberal approach advocates minimal government involvement, opting for 'arms length' governance that 'encourages both institutions and individuals to conform to the norms of the market' (Kantola and Outshoorn, 2007, p. 11). Neoliberalism requires a focus on budgetary constraint, audit, and competition. The market rather than any government influences social mission and therefore dictates the environment in which organisations operate. Commentators have noted how this approach can shift resources away from explicit social missions to those driven by social marketing (Kantola and Outshoorn, 2007). For sport, the shift has been seen as a move from an overt focus on women's inclusion in sport, coaching or administration, which were evident in the 1990s in New Zealand (Hillary Commission, 1989), to 'hot topics' such as exercise and recreation participation, obesity prevention, and winning medals. This means that gender is no longer a focus of sport policy; rather, it has been mainstreamed into policies regarding participation, health, or high performance achievement.

This process is known as gender mainstreaming, which can lead organisational decision makers to think carefully about gender in all of their policies, and not just relegating gender to the machinery of policy development (Outshoorn and Kantola, 2007). Gender becomes everybody's responsibility within the state or organisation, rather than a policy that may be perceived to reflect reverse discrimination, put too much focus on one demographic group, or have little relevance to a wider population. In countries that have embraced gender mainstreaming, for example Sweden, consultancies and other sources of expertise have developed into an industry that advises on gender mainstreaming (Bergqvist, Blandy and Sainsbury, 2007). In this way, gender mainstreaming has become the promotion of the expression of gender within wider policy development.

Despite the potential positive outcomes of gender mainstreaming, it does face critique within research and policy development. With a broad approach to including gender within all policies and decisions, it is very hard to make priorities (Bergqvist et al., 2007). As Shaw and Penney (2003) found, administrators were responsible for following Sport England's gender mainstreamed policy, which they found confusing and unspecific. Consequently, it became very hard to target women's specific needs within organisations or programmes that have historically been dominated by men. For example, in Shaw and Penney's (2003) research, sport administrators were influenced by the funding promises that were attached to a broad awareness of gender within their organisations and spent very little time targeting specific groups, such as low income women, or women from minority racial backgrounds. Such groups miss out when gender mainstreaming is the norm because less powerful minorities need targeted, specific policies to assist their inclusion in society. In contrast, it is often women from privileged backgrounds who benefit from gender mainstreaming, owing to their greater access to information and resources.

In New Zealand, which provides the context for this chapter, gender mainstreaming has been a feature of the political landscape since the late 1990s. SPARC's predecessor, the Hillary Commission, introduced affirmative action policies and/or activities that were about enhancing women to fit the requirements of the organisations, expressed as 'empowering women' or 'supporting women' or 'enhancing leadership skills' (Cameron, 1996, p. 193). Since the demise of the Hillary Commission and the rise of SPARC, explicit reference to gender has been removed from policies and organisational rhetoric. Instead, commitments to gender have been reduced to a general commitment to 'ensuring the interests of our targeted groups are reflected in the core strategies that drive our work' (Sport and Recreation New Zealand, 2009, p. 18). This approach has continued during the change into Sport NZ.

Some commentators may suggest that this reduction in focus on gender as a target area, and women in particular is a measure of success because they no longer need special policies. Indeed, the amount of regular physical activity for women remained constant from 2002/3–2006/7 (Ministry of Health, 2006/7). However, in other areas of sport, women remain under-represented in high performance and participatory levels of governance, coaching, leadership, and administration.

Given New Zealand's experiences, in which despite ten years of gender mainstreaming with sport policy there has been little or no improvement in women's participation in sport administration, management and coaching at a number of different levels, it is arguable that gender should be back on the sport policy agenda. Moreover, gender is not just about women: rather, men's issues are silenced within a gender mainstream policy machine. This is potentially even more the case within sport, where it is assumed that men are the dominant gender and will have little or no problem in their access to sport. However, as Shaw and Cameron (2008) have noted, while men are dominant in sport organisations, there is a predominance of old boys' networks which allows men to mentor and promote other men that are from similar backgrounds. Gender mainstreaming, with its 'one size fits all' approach, is unlikely to meet the needs of specific groups within sport policy development. Gender, it appears, needs to get back on the agenda.

Putting gender back on the agenda: feminisms and sport policy

A number of versions of feminism have developed during its evolution from the late 1960s. In this chapter, I focus on four, showing how these various feminisms examine policy, and how each would put gender on the sport policy agenda. The first three can be loosely categorised under the broader label of 'liberal feminism'. As Bensimon and Marshall (1997) suggest, liberal feminism is 'a gentle, more socially/politically acceptable perspective ... emphasizing women's equal access to domains where men dominate, chipping at the glass ceiling' (p. 3). Finally in this section, I present some ideas regarding the inclusion of radical feminism within sport policy.

Fixing women

This first version of feminism argues that women do not have the skills or backgrounds to achieve or participate as successfully as men in organisations and wider societies, and so they must be trained to have the same skills as men, usually by men. Such programmes are based on an implicit assumption that men are and should be in dominant positions of power, and that women should try to aim for the 'attainment of equality' (Bensimon and Marshall, 1997, p. 4). A good example of the outcome of this approach was reflected in Donna Cullen's commentary after the 2011 Sky Sport debacle regarding commentator Andy Gray's comments about female line judges in football not understanding the offside rule, because they were women. Cullen, a director of Tottenham Hotspur, defended football against allegations of sexism and described how she had achieved her version of equality in football, saying:

in more than 20 years of working in football, I cannot say sexist remarks like that have ever been an issue for me. I believe I am treated as an honorary male in football, and I don't believe being female has anything to do with my work.

(TVNZ, 2011)

The intent of this remark was probably to show that she was treated as 'one of the boys' and did not feel that being a woman had undermined her experiences in football, despite its traditional dominance by men. However, a more critical reading would suggest that being an 'honorary male' is required to be accepted within football administration. Women who are not 'honorary males' are therefore not accepted, and would need to be 'fixed', that is change their behaviour in order to attain equal status with the men in administration.

Value women

In this second version of feminism, which is also known as cultural feminism (Bensimon and Marshall, 1997), women's stereotypical attributes, such as child caring and nurturing are valued. Without doubt, there is room within sport for people who like to work with children. However, it has been argued that women are most often found in these roles, and they are positions that are valued less than those associated with elite or adult sport (Shaw and Allen, 2009). By making space for women as coaches of young children, or participation-level athletes, women are arguably benefitting from social and organisational efforts to present them with equal opportunity to coach. However, they do so within a gendered social context that values men as coaches more highly (Shaw and Allen, 2009).

Policy analysis and development from such perspectives assumes the existing structures of sport to be gender neutral (Hawkesworth, 1994). They do not take into account the argument that often such structures implicitly favour men and men's sports, for example through the dominance that men's sport has within funding and media exposure. Similar norms ensure that high performance sports are valued more greatly and overtly than participation. If women want access to these environments, they are expected to be 'fixed' or 'valued' to fit with these existing structures. There is no room within 'value women' to challenge assumptions and views regarding participation. When policies are put in place that are intended to assist a marginalised group, in this case women, it is imperative that policy makers consider the full interests of that group and the wider assumptions about the policy area. In this example, women are offered the opportunity to engage in coaching but the historical, cultural, and social norms of sport as patriarchal are so strong that without awareness of gender and monitoring of the outcomes of the policy, gender stereotypes and assumptions can be reinforced, rather than challenged.

Equal opportunities

Equal opportunities assumes that if women and men are offered the same opportunities and processes, then they will achieve the same outcomes (Hawkesworth, 1994). For example, in sport, the development of formal application procedures for coaching and administration positions is assumed to reduce the vagueness and unfairness of 'shoulder tapping'. This assumption may, however, be gendered, that is 'certain factors make it more difficult for women than for men to achieve the same outcome by following the same procedures' (Hawkesworth, 1994, p. 105).

In sport, we see the repercussions of equal opportunities policies as well. Managers in sport organisations often speak about recruiting 'the best person for the job', arguing that gender has nothing to do with their choices, and that there are equal opportunities for women and men in their organisations (Shaw, 2006). When pushed, however, there may be an implicit understanding that men are 'better' at sport than women, and have better networks. Men will therefore be more suited to high level administrative, officiating, and coaching positions (Shaw and Allen, 2009). Frequently, such appointments are presented as gender neutral, which means that gender 'doesn't matter'. Researchers in this area have, however shown that gendered assumptions about women and men often play a part in recruitment and career progression (Shaw, 2006).

Comment on liberal feminism and sport policy

As in other fields such as education (Marshall, 1997), the liberal feminist approach has provided openings for women in sport that might not have otherwise existed. For example, the NZ Olympic Commission's Women in Governance programme has moved to encourage women to become involved and upskill to volunteer to stand for executive and board positions in New Zealand sport organisations. The Hillary Commission's various sport development programmes targeted women as an interest group and made gender more visible on the NZ sport platform.

Liberal feminist approaches to policy analysis and development do not, however, critique the state as an institution, rather they work with the state. As Bensimon and Marshall (1997) argue, 'the liberal stance naively accepts token changes, expecting individual women to persevere in male domains' (p. 4). Further, Connell (1990, p. 512) neatly argues:

> Liberal feminism, in effect, treats the state as an arbiter that has been captured by a particular group, men. This analysis leads directly to a strategy for redress: capture it back … If men presently run the governments, armies, and bureaucracies, the solution is more access, packing more and more women into the top levels of the state until balance is achieved.

Using this model, as Sawer (2007) argued, femocrats (liberal feminist public servants) in Australia were able to become influential within the Australian state apparatus and push for programmes for women. In many ways this worked, and Australian government policy was forward thinking in its approach to the inclusion of women in the late 1980s. This success was, however, vulnerable to political whims and when John Howard's Liberal-National (conservative) government came to power in 1996, the influence of femocrats, their institutions and departments was severely reduced. Others have argued that the rise of the femocrats led to the corporatisation of feminism and removed much of its political edge (Hawkesworth, 1997).

There are parallels within sport. When gender relations are recognised in sport, the solution is to add more women until there are reasonably equal numbers of women and men. An example of this is the Women in Governance programme. It has been argued that by increasing numbers of women on boards and at other high levels within organisations, a 'log jam' will occur, which will eventually break, spilling greater numbers of women into these higher levels. The tide of women's progress will, it is argued, be unstoppable and also affect policy from within (Vinnicombe, Singh, Burke, Bilimoria, and Huse, 2008). Critics have dubbed the liberal feminist approach the 'add women and stir' approach (Hall, 2002), which merely serves to increase numbers of women but does nothing to address social, financial, and cultural inequities that are manifest in society and reflected in sport organisations and policy.

Radical approaches to policy and sport

More radical approaches to feminism allow for the consideration of critique of the institutions of state, particularly with regard to power and culture, the development of knowledge, and language (Bensimon and Marshall, 1997). The first stage is radical feminism's acknowledgement and celebration of the differences within the category of 'women'.

Radical feminism explicitly highlights that it is women from minority ethnic, ability, age, and sexuality groups that are under-represented within many social situations, ranging from access to facilities and state assistance to powerful positions in organisations. Brush (2003), for example, notes how state support in the USA is gendered but also easier to access for people with better education and employment. She notes that for ex-soldiers, who are overwhelmingly male, or better educated women, it is relatively easy to access these generous benefits as 'they are administered with minimal intrusion, little stigma, and no means test' (Brush, 2003, p. 84). In contrast, benefits that are available to low income mothers 'are stingy, intrusive, stigmatized, and targeted through means tests' (Brush, 2003, p. 84). As Brush argues, women who are low income mothers are greatly in need of state support and may not have the skills to negotiate the complex welfare system.

The development of sport policy also reflects such pressures. In their study of women on low income and their access to recreation opportunities in Canada, Frisby and Hoeber (2002) discovered that, in order to 'prove poverty', participants had to show facility staff income statements, which were then put on file. The women in Frisby and Hoeber's study found this practice to be embarrassing and demeaning. While feminists from a liberal perspective might have argued that the programme enabled more women to access leisure facilities, Frisby and Hoeber's more radical approach highlighted the problems faced by these low income women. These constraints were arguably a direct result of neoliberal policies that promote market forces and make low-cost, subsidised entry to facilities difficult, regardless of the socio-economic implications for those accessing that funding. As a result of that research Frisby and her team were able to change the recreation centres' policies to be more inclusive of women (Frisby and Millar, 2002). A radical approach that critiqued the basis of the policy was able to lobby for policy change that recognised the sensibilities of the low income women and more women involved in sport.

Radical feminist approaches to policy also encourage a critique of how policy affects the development of societal views and organisational culture. Neoliberal policies have resulted in systematic changes with regard to how organisations are operated, and the cultures that are valued. For example, the Performance Based Research Fund (PBRF) in New Zealand and the Research Excellence Framework (REF) in the UK are both direct consequences of the influence of 20 years of neoliberal policies within the education sector in universities. The concept of performativity is at the core of these frameworks (Roberts, 2006) and has reduced academic inquiry to a stream of measurable outputs. Universities are required to slavishly follow such frameworks in order to receive funding. The culture of universities has undoubtedly changed throughout the PBRF process, with fraught debates over what is 'good research' when measurement tools favour natural science articles and outputs over all others. Moreover, that culture favours men who are more likely to have an unbroken career path (rather than take long periods of parental leave, for example) and conduct research in the natural sciences (Ransley, 2007). Despite the gender neutral portrayal of PBRF, radical feminists would argue that the core values of this measurement process are gendered and work against many women.

In sport, similar outcomes driven policies have had an effect on the culture of organisations. Sport NZ's funding processes are characterised by the pursuit of outputs, particularly in high performance. 'Success' for sport organisations is measured by their ability to achieve gold medals at international competitions and their level of importance to New Zealand (Sport and Recreation New Zealand, 2006a). This 'investment' style of funding undoubtedly creates a perception of clarity and transparency. However, it has had dramatic implications for teams whose performance has fallen below an acceptable standard, with funding being quickly and severely cut. For example, in 2008, SPARC's funding of women's hockey fell from NZ$400,000 to zero in one year (stuff.co.nz, 2008). This cut was due to poor results on the world stage by the women's team. However, it did not take into account the efforts by NZ Hockey to nurture young talent through development programmes, the retirement of experienced players, or the cyclical nature of high performance sport. The cuts undermined development efforts as age group commitments were reduced, thus removing the opportunity for older age group players (e.g. a 20-year-old in a U21 team) to take on leadership roles in those teams. Radical feminism would demand an examination of the policy that led to the undermining of these young women's potential to enter into leadership roles, the implications for future leadership within hockey, and how those women were affected. Radical feminists would not be satisfied with an argument based on an investment model that does not account for external, uncontrollable factors.

Finally, radical feminism is just that: radical. From this perspective, the analysis of policy and its implementation can be challenged. As Bensimon and Marshall (2003) have argued, a radical feminist approach to analysing policy, in their case education policy, encourages fragmentation of the structures and bureaucracies that we take for granted. They state that 'we do not believe that being nice, taking the master's language only, accepting gradual loosening of patriarchal structures, is good enough' (Bensimon and Marshall, 2003, p. 337). They elaborate, describing the 'master's language' and tools as current processes of policy development and analysis that are androcentric, and do not recognise gender within policy. Yet, as the majority of this chapter has shown, gender is a key feature of policy development but many policy makers, and analysts, are 'gender blind' or portray policy as gender neutral. Further, Bensimon and Marshall argue that it is not just 'women's policies' that have gender as a central feature; rather, all policies are in some way gendered, favouring dominant groups of men and masculinities over most women and subordinate masculinities. They argued in 1997 that radical feminist policy analysis enables the examination of 'how patriarchy is manifest in the control of women's identities' (Bensimon and Marshall, 2003, p. 6) within policy development.

It is on this note that Bensimon and Marshall further explain the usefulness of radical departures from the norm in policy analysis. Opening up analysis to radical forms means that challenging questions can be raised in the examination of marginalised groups. In sport the identities of the New Zealand Black Ferns (the NZ women's rugby team) are constructed through policies that take men's sport as the norm and women's sport as a sometimes awkward add-on. Despite winning four consecutive rugby world cups, these women are underfunded and receive little popular attention. The women's domestic provincial competition in New Zealand has been abandoned for 2011, which will lead to a less robust development programme (Scrum Queens, 2010). Radical feminism allows us to question why sport has developed to support and promote such an approach to funding. Without a radical critique, these policies, driven by budget controls and a market oriented framework, allow the constant undermining of women's sport to continue. The public are unaware, or do not care, about the predicament of teams such as the Black Ferns, so there is no public pressure for change. It would be inconceivable for similar cuts to be made to the men's national programme without public outcry. Without radical change to policy development such unjust, gendered restrictions on funding are met with a mere shrug of the shoulders and a 'so what? It's women's sport'.

Radical feminism in a post-feminist world

For many contemporary readers, the above arguments will have little currency. We are, after all, in a world where women's active leisure is promoted by organisations such as Sport England, and exposure of some women's sports, such as golf, is gaining traction. Sponsorship and media attention are available to successful women athletes as they are for their male counterparts. Surely then, these achievements point to the success of liberal feminism, its inclusion within some policy directions and subsequent influence on society, and a lack of need to focus on more radical approaches that disrupt the fabric of our sport organisations? Indeed, for some, the idea of radical feminism is repugnant, as images of radical feminism in contemporary popular press 'cause young women to recoil in horror' (McRobbie, 2009, p. 16). As *The Guardian* newspaper's satirical blog Pass Notes argued, 'by using the term "radical feminist" as an insult, [there is an implication that] the target is philosophically extreme, politically biased against men' (Pass Notes, 2011). In addition, the views of post feminism, which believes that feminism's work is 'done' appear to be a popular standpoint. In popular fiction, for example, characters such as Bridget Jones have been analysed as post feminist: they can enjoy their sexuality, independence and freedom (McRobbie, 2009). In sport, the parallels are clear: in a post-feminist world, women can participate in sport, receive sponsorship and be lauded as world champions, but the key social and cultural norms regarding sport are influenced by male-centred sport policy. What post feminism refuses to address, however, are the key social and cultural norms that are underpinned by male-centred policy development.

In countering the post-feminist perspective and trying to answer the 'so what' question, I recognise and promote the idea that the presentation and development of radical feminist ideas needs to focus on solutions to the problem of gendered policy analysis and development, and not just criticising (Bensimon and Marshall, 2003). I argue that in order to work towards equity, gender needs to be put at the centre of policy development. For example, current thinking allows an organisation such as the Women's Sport and Fitness Foundation to produce a factsheet that encourages increasing numbers of female participants in sport. In this document, *11 Compelling Reasons Why Sports should Work with Women and Girls* (Women's Sport and Fitness Foundation, 2011), five reasons relate to increasing or sustaining funding, and three are for public relations reasons. These values are firmly rooted in neoliberal rhetoric regarding budgetary control. None of the reasons include improving the organisation through making changes for women.

If we place gender, rather than sport, at the centre of policy analysis, we may achieve some sustainable change. As Marshall (1997) argues, this process can be liberating, understanding gender as having complex and multiple meanings, not limited to taken for granted assumptions about women. For example, rather than basing a high performance sport funding model around a seemingly 'gender neutral' understanding of sport, we would look at the constraints around women's high performance sport and how they can be addressed. A way forward is rather than making feminism accountable to policy development with questions such as 'how can feminism or women be incorporated into this policy', radical feminist policy developers invert the question, and ask 'what is it that feminism asks this policy to do?'. Returning to the discussion of PBRF, Bensimon and Marshall, 2003 provide an example from tertiary education, in which it could conventionally be asked 'why are women less productive than men in research outputs?'. This type of question makes men's outputs the norm, which means women are always being compared with men. A radical feminist policy critique might ask 'in what ways does gender impact productivity?'. This question allows for the problematising of gender within the tertiary context, and allows for discussion regarding the ways women are treated; for example, if they go on maternity leave and their 'tenure clock' keeps ticking. Also, it allows for discussions around considerations such as informal networks, which can be gendered to include and exclude specific groups of men based on ethnicity or sexuality, for example.

So how can these questions be applied to sport? Rather than asking how the Black Ferns can fit within the male dominated landscape of high performance sport, questions should be framed by 'how do our assumptions about gender limit funding and the potential for meaningful development for the Black Ferns and women's rugby?' Equally, when sport participation policies are developed, the questions posed should move away from 'how (if at all) do we encourage women to play more sport or recreate actively within current health guidelines?'. Instead, policies developed by radical feminist thought would ask 'how do assumptions about gender impact active recreation participation?'. This approach encourages discussions regarding gender, gendered recreation experiences, and issues around childcare and time out for parents, particularly mothers, to engage in recreation experiences (Spowart, Burrows, and Shaw, 2010). A good example of the need for this sort of reflection is evidenced in SPARC's advertisements to encourage volunteers. These advertisements, on national NZ television, offer vignettes of volunteer activities. While men coach, prepare sports fields, and officiate in these advertisements, SPARC's only vision of a woman volunteer was to hold the coats while the team played. Such advertisements are designed by marketing experts who succeed spectacularly in reinforcing gender stereotypes. They also unwittingly show exactly how those stereotypes work against involvement in meaningful roles in volunteering. The women in such advertisements have passive roles to play in sport. The radical question is 'how do our assumptions about gender affect women's involvement in volunteering?' If we assume that women do nothing except hold coats, then that is how they will continue to be perceived. If we recognise, celebrate, and promote women's huge involvement in volunteer sport, and think about how we might challenge our gendered assumptions about their involvement, we might develop change.

Undoubtedly, putting gender at the centre of policy development and analysis results in hard questions, and does not fit easily within the current funding or government structures. Indeed, they are questions that can create animosity, fear and antagonism from people who are vested in traditional policy development and analysis positions. However, they are questions that could lead to equity, in which our assumptions about gender in sport are examined and challenged with a view to change, rather. As well as working towards this key part of radical feminism, putting gender at the centre of questions allows a departure from women as being the only focus of gender policies, which is a limitation of radical feminism. By focusing on gender, we can also include marginalised men within our discussions, an area of neglect within sport policy.

In this chapter, I have offered an alternative version of sport policy analysis and development, framed by radical feminism. This alternative does not have to be 'recoiled from in horror', rather it simply asks that we put our assumptions about gender at the front of the policy development, reflect on them, and move towards policy development that is underpinned by a commitment to promoting gender as central to our sport policies and organisations.

25

A POSTCOLONIAL APPROACH TO SPORT POLICY

Case study of the Maghreb region in North Africa

Mahfoud Amara

Introduction

In this chapter I seek to develop an explanation of postcolonial approaches to sports policy by focusing in particular on the range of experiences in the Maghreb region of North Africa. A postcolonial approach to sport policy should take into account the colonial history and particularly the legacy of colonialism with regard to the diffusion of modern sport and subsequently the adoption of sport as a form of resistance against colonial hegemony; as a means also, as in the case for instance of the Front Libération Nationale (FLN) football team in Algeria, for the internationalisation of nationalist movements' struggle for independence (Amara and Henry, 2004).[1] In the post-independence stage, sport as other domains in post-colonial societies was shaped by nationalist ideologies, which in the case of North Africa were defined by the centralised state apparatus, represented by the Party states (the case of FLN in Algeria and the Doustourian Socialist Party in Tunisia) and the Monarchic-state (the case of Morocco) founded around historical legitimacy (resistance against French colonialism) and a sense of belonging to Arab–Islamic values. Their ideologies were also influenced by the bipolar world system that characterised international relations in the 1960s and 1980s. Algeria chose to take a socialist and Third Worldist (anti-imperialist) trajectory based on heavy industrialisation, whereas Morocco and Tunisia chose a more liberal economy open to foreign investments, particularly from western Europe. The three countries adopted more or less a secular stance not necessarily in the sense of divides between religious and political spheres but based on the institutionalisation of Islam, which is put in the service of Socialism in Algeria, the political legitimacy of Al-Mekhzen, or the royal institution, in Morocco, and Bourguibism in Tunisia, in reference to Habib Bourguiba's modernisation project which was inspired by that of Mustafa Kemal Atatürk (Kemalism) in Turkey. It is a secular position to statehood based, according to Lamchichi, on 'social transformations from the top which control or even monopolize the religious discourse which stop any political contestation that is theologically formed' (Lamchichi, 1993: 34). One can argue that the secular ideology of the three states partially explains the more active participation of their female athletes in national and international competitions in comparison to other Arab nations (Henry *et al.*, 2003). This is sometimes used by regimes as an argument against Islamist movements that oppose their policies.

The colonial history and post-independence projects for nation-state building explain the early engagement of these three countries in the Maghreb region, in comparison to other countries in North Africa (e.g. Mauritania and Libya) and in the Middle East, with modern sport, both in practice and in policy terms. Of course, when we say the Middle East we are not referring here to Egypt, which is the first Arab country to have joined international sport organisations and to participate in international sport competitions. Egypt was the first African or Arab country to participate in the football World Cup in 1934. The same is true for Sudan, which has been a member of FIFA since 1948, and the IOC since 1956.

To return to the Maghreb region, Tunisia, which was a French protectorate (1881–1956), joined the IOC in 1957, followed by Morocco in 1959. Algeria, which was a French colony from 1830–1962 (divided into six *départements* belonging to France), had to wait until 1964 to join the IOC. An understanding of the political system in these countries helps us to make sense of the rationale for intervention in sporting affairs by regimes. In Morocco we learn from the work of Lyazghi (2006) that even before the independence of Morocco, sport and particularly football was the domain of the palace (*Al Makhzen*). A strong indication of this was the naming, after the independence, of sport federations as 'Royal Federations' rather than 'National Federations'. In Tunisia, the head of the state, Habib Bourguiba (1959–87) followed by Zine El Abidine Ben Ali (1987–2011), was very influential in the party-state's strategy to host the Mediterranean Games. Abbassi contends that:

> The Mediterranean theme, and the plural identity it represents, has imposed its ideological hegemony on other identity themes (Maghrebin, Arab, African and Muslim). A politically neutral horizon – neither oriental nor occidental, or it is both oriental and occidental – the Mediterranean Sea appears to be an ideal symbolic place for Tunisian identity and a basis of union between the Tunisian Diaspora and their land of origin.
>
> (Abbassi, 2007: 129)

The adoption of socialist ideology explains Algeria's late adoption (at least officially) of commercial values in sport in comparison to Tunisia and Morocco where sponsorship, for instance in football matches, by multinationals and local private companies has been the norm. Professional sport was perceived in the aftermath of independence to be incompatible with Algeria's values of socialism and anti-imperialism. This is well illustrated in the following excerpt taken from *El Moudjahid* newspaper (a propaganda organ for the single-party FLN from the 1960s to the late 1980s) in 1965 which associated professionalism with colonial exploitation:

> Those [sports managers] who wanted to develop professionalism, they are not aware of the consequences that this move could have on the sport domain. They are already projecting that the next season [1965–66] they should gain a monopoly hold on valuable players by promising them some financial remuneration. On the other hand, there are players who want to transform football to a full time activity [a financial source] using threatening procedures vis-à-vis their clubs' directors ...
>
> (*El Moudjahid*, September 1965, reported by Chehat, 1993: 53; translated from French)

With regard to internal politics, the party-states in Tunisia and Morocco and the monarchic state in Morocco have used sport to mobilise the populations around the state's ideology and to legitimise their modernisation projects and policies for nation state building. Sport has been at the centre of development strategies in Tunisia and more recently in Morocco, for the promotion of the tourism industry. A number of international events in athletics, tennis and golf have been organised in these two countries to attract more tourists in the region. Tunisia (at least before 2011) and Morocco (having bid four times to host the FIFA World Cup, in 1994, 1998, 2006 and 2010; Ben El-Caïd, 2004) have been new destinations for foreign sport clubs to prepare for their domestic and international competitions, due to their closeness to Europe, weather conditions, the quality of tourism and sports infrastructures.[2] In Algeria the priority today is to negotiate the shift from oil-based economy to service economy and in political terms from conflict to post conflict. This explains the emphasis today in the official discourse in developing sport practice among the youth. The qualification of the Algerian national team for the 2010 FIFA World Cup after 24 years of absence was presented in the Algerian media as the beginning of a new era and the return of Algeria to the international scene.

Elite sport policy

In 2009 I travelled to Algeria, Tunisia and Morocco, to undertake exploratory field work on the elite sport policies of these three countries. Four lengthy interviews were conducted in Morocco (with a former technical director of the national athletics institute in Morocco and currently technical director of the African Confederation of Athletics, as well as with a journalist/researcher) and in Tunisia (with representatives of the Hand Ball Federation and the Bureau of Olympic Preparation and Elite Sport at the Tunisian Ministry of Youth and Sport). In addition, two informal meetings took place in Algeria with the Deputy Director of the Elite Sport Department at the Algerian Ministry of Youth and Sport and the chair of the newly established Commission for Research and Strategy of Elite Sport Development. One of the issues addressed during the interviews was that of the international performance of Maghrebi national teams and athletes in regional and international competitions in general, and in the Olympics in particular.

It could be argued that despite all the measures in place for elite sport development, countries in the Maghreb are still lagging behind when it comes to performance at the highest level of international sport competition – that is, the Olympics. The only chances for medals for Algeria, Tunisia and Morocco are still limited to a few sports disciplines, namely athletics (mainly semi-distance and distance running), judo and boxing (with the exception of the gold medal of Oussama Mellouli for Tunisia in the 1,500 metre freestyle swimming in the 2008 Beijing Olympic Games, which is not necessarily representative of elite sport systems in Tunisia since Mellouli lives and trains in the US).

In response to this a number of interesting themes emerged from the interview with the former director of the Institute of Athletics in Morocco (speaking as an outsider to the current system) and the then (before the fall of Ben Ali's regime in January 2011) director of the Bureau of Olympic Preparation and Elite Sport at the Tunisian Ministry of Youth and Sport (speaking as an insider).

The outsider position

To start with the outsider position, some of the reasons put forward to explain the underperformance of Maghrebi nations in the Olympics, can be summarised as follows.

Non-existence of a model of elite sport

For the interviewee, the success of athletes in the Maghreb at international level was the fruit of individual initiatives and not the result of a well thought out and executed system of elite sport development. Every country in the Maghreb had had its own period of success (Tunisia in the

1960s, Morocco in the 1980s and Algeria in the 1990s) and there was little evidence of policy transfer from one country to another.

> When you meet a policy maker in Algeria or in Tunisia, they give the impression that they are more advanced than Morocco when it comes to elite sport development. When you refer to the results in the field you realise that there is not a big difference. Tunisia was the first country to win Olympic medals in the 1960s. We thought at that time it was a fruit of a well thought out strategy. We wanted to understand the Tunisian model to apply it locally. Then we realised that there was not a model per se. Then Morocco took over the lead in the 1980s with Said Aouita and others. Other Maghreb nations wanted to emulate the Moroccan experience. Followed by Algeria with Morceli and Boulmerka ... then we said maybe Algeria is leading ... In reality there is not a real strategy for elite sport development. It is more the fruits of personal efforts rather than that of a system.

Insufficient national legislation on sport

Most of the laws and decrees that had been adopted were imported from the occident (capitalist or socialist) without considering the existing reality and capacities of each country. The state appears according to the interviewee to have acted in an opportunistic rather than innovative manner. Even those laws that had been adopted had not been applied in an efficient manner or were applied only to reinforce the state's power and influence within national sports organisations, to claim the political capital gained from success in certain sports, such as track and field in Morocco, which had been achieved at the detriment of other sports disciplines.

> For instance the first law of PE in Morocco appeared only in 1989 while modern sport practice had been exercised since the nineteenth century and the period of the French protectorate. Sport associations before 1989 did not have a specific status. Algeria and Tunisia had a plethora of laws before Morocco but they were all inspired by French jurisdictions. Even socialist Algeria in the 1970s ... in fact we have perfect laws that are not applied. Our laws are rather more conceptual projects than the codification of an activity. The 1989 law in Morocco was sporadically applied. Paradoxically the only article that was fully applied was Article 22 concerning the suspension of a federation and its replacement by an administrative commission to supervise the election of a new general assembly ... There is no state policy for elite sport development in Morocco. Usually the state takes advantage of successful individual initiatives. For instance the National Athletic Institute started with five athletes, to be extended to 20 athletes and then, with the help of the Ministry, to one hundred athletes. After that, the state asked public companies to sponsor the Institute, developing thus what started as a successful individual initiative into a system for the development of elite athletics in Morocco. Algeria and Tunisia have adopted a similar system. The willingness of the state to intervene does not mean that there is a system or a policy. This explains the non-existence of sport performance institutes for other disciplines such as boxing, swimming or gymnastics.

The lack of a scientific approach

The state's intervention in the reform of elite sport policy is based on subjective estimation rather than on a scientific foundation that recognises (according to the interviewee) the genetic constraints of the population and the socio-economic conditions of nations in the Maghreb.

Accordingly, track and field despite the high level of competition between nations should remain a priority sport in comparison to swimming, which in terms of infrastructure is one of the most expensive Olympic sports.

> We are we putting our effort in a sport, athletics, where there is the highest level of competition between nations with the highest level of participant countries. Maybe because it is a sport discipline for the poor. It needs less finance and less infrastructure. For less developed countries performing well in athletics, to overcome the shortcomings in other sectors, is a political act. We are in South–South competition which makes it even harder … When it comes to prioritising certain Olympic sport disciplines over others, this is a philosophical question. We can go with the policy of convincing the population not to invest too much for instance in basketball because we cannot do well at international level. The same is true for instance in swimming which is more costly than other sports. The chance of winning a Gold medal in swimming is very low, one of the most expensive Gold medals … I am in favour of limiting the number of sport disciplines … There are sport disciplines where we have a good critical mass to choose from and others not.

Inefficiency of the national sport system

The inefficiency of the national sport system was explained as resulting from the import of existing laws, the lack of scientific approach, the clash of interests between existing departments for elite sport development and the confusion of means (human and material capabilities) with the amount of injected cash.

> In terms of the elite sport system in Morocco, in theory, there is a department within the Ministry of Youth and Sport which is in charge of elite sport. There is also a similar department within the National Olympic Committee. Both are inefficient. They do not have a real impact on the activity. It is only now (after the 2008 Beijing Olympic Games) that we estimated that we had a poor performance (although the basis for this evaluation is unclear). The government started to provide more money to prepare for the next Olympics. Is it starting on a strong foundation? I do not think so, because the fundamentals for elite sport development are not respected. Now that the NOC has been given more power I started hearing about sports such as cycling … If I was involved I would not invest a penny in cycling or swimming in Morocco, particularly for the Olympic Games. It is good at sport for all levels but not at elite level. We should not invest just because Tunisia won a Gold medal in swimming today. This is an example to show that the current policy is not based on scientific criteria … Pseudo-decision makers who do not have scientific knowledge they think that it is a matter of means. For them means are equal to money. Furthermore, giving more power to the NOC over MYS [Ministry of Youth and Support] has created some tensions. There have been some clashes between MYS and the athletic federation which is becoming more powerful again.

The insider position

If we take the insider perspective, a number of themes emerge from the interview with the representative of the Tunisian Ministry to explain some of the reasons for the relative success of Tunisia on the international stage (and to a lesser extent in the Olympics), considering Tunisia's human and financial capabilities in comparison to other nations in the Maghreb.

Evaluation methods

Evaluation methods, according to the interviewee, should consider the factor of time. Tunisia's reform of elite sport dates only from 1996, nine years after president Ben Ali took power. Taking into account Tunisia's capabilities in relation to its population size (10 million inhabitants) and its economy, other performances such as qualification for the Olympics and world championships, qualification for the final in international competitions, medals in world championships should not be underestimated, according to the interviewee.

> The evaluation of the nation's success is relative. If you look at Tunisia, in medal terms with the exception of El Guemmoudi in athletics 40 years ago, we have not won many medals, particularly in recent years. This is despite having a strategy in place. The results may take time to arrive, the time for the structure of elite sport to be rooted in place. For the last 15 years since the Atlanta Olympic Games Tunisia has achieved only a bronze medal in boxing, a strategy for elite sport development was initiated. In the last Olympics Tunisia won a Gold medal in swimming. Success should not be evaluated only in terms of numbers of medals. We have had a number of qualifications for the last Olympics. We had 46 athletes qualified; only 26 were allowed to participate taking into account those athletes with the highest chance of winning a medal and junior athletes in preparation for the 2012 Olympic Games. It was one of the most successful participations with seven athletes qualifying for the final and nine athletes in the top 16 world ranking with an average age of participating athletes being 23. Some may consider this comparison as dogmatic. But Tunisia has only 10 million inhabitants. In political terms, the president is encouraging sport but everything depends on the existing capacities of the country. We are spending a considerable amount of money on sport but compared to other countries it is still low. In developed countries there is a culture of private sponsorship which helps the state. In our country everything is funded by the state. For a country like Tunisia which does not have natural resources and depends exclusively on human resources it is not easy.

Targeting strategy

Although Tunisia does not depend on a few sports, financial means seem to be the primary measure in its targeting strategy for elite sport development followed by the popularity of the sport and the likelihood of performance at the international stage.

> In 1994 there was the first speech of the president around sport policy in Tunisia. In 1995 we had the first laws for the organisation of elite sport. Targeted sports at that time were football, handball, volleyball, boxing, judo, swimming and track and field. It depended on the performance of Tunisian athletes. There is a high participation of Tunisians in handball, volleyball and football. Basketball was not targeted at that time because it was hard to compete with other African nations. Target sports receive more money only when there is a result. For instance in judo, before 2001 we had a budget for judo. After the Gold medal in the 2001 Judo World Championships (staged in Tunisia), the budget had increased. The number of athletes subscribed in the National Judo Federation had increased too. Judo had a senior and junior world champions and a junior vice world champion and fifth position in the Olympics. Now we have increased our targeted sports to karate, taekwondo, weightlifting, wrestling, fencing (we had an athlete aged 17 ranked 7) The other point to consider is our targeting strategy. We do not depend on one or a few sports. Maybe

the results are weak in the Olympics in comparison to other countries which have better means. We know that a medal in the Olympics cost millions.

Organisation

What makes Tunisia unique in the Maghreb region, at least according to the interviewee, is its systematic strategy for the detection of young talented athletes, starting from the organisation of elite sport at local, regional and national levels and finishing with the pyramidal links between the school and elite sport system. Even PE teachers are directly employed by the Ministry of Youth and Sport to serve its agenda of elite sport development. The other condition is the adequate sport infrastructures inherited from the organisation of the Mediterranean Games. Tunisia seems to be upfront in comparison to Algeria and Morocco with regard to the preparation and the welfare of elite athletes.

At primary level, sport clubs and sport associations are attached to the centres of sport promotions (non-specialised). There is a signed convention between the primary school, sport clubs and the federation. The PE teacher is employed by the Ministry of Youth and Sport and not the Ministry of Education which is in the Maghreb unique to Tunisia. At the next level we have the centres of training specialised in one sport and managed by the federations. Furthermore we have sport schools for athletes supervised by the Ministry of Youth and Sport. The next level is regional centres for the preparation of athletes in charge of regional selections which work with sports high schools. Then we have the national teams working with specialised national centres, to arrive at the end at the national elite sports. Most sports respect the same structure. The national elite centres have their own accommodation. There are four in the country. There is a strategy to look after the athletes and to encourage them which is managed by the Direction of Elite Sport which belongs to the General Directorate of sport at the Ministry. We have also the bureau for Olympic preparation and the supervision of elite athletes … As for the categorisation of elite athletes, we have with the federations what we call a contract programme. There are clauses set by the ministry to respect. There are also contract objectives for the targeted athletes. Each athlete has a contract with his/her federation, supervised by the Ministry, based on the objectives set by the athletes in relation to the Olympic Games, World Championships, and African Championships. Every year the performance of the athlete is evaluated. An athlete with a gold medal is placed in the category A. Each category has its own type of advantages e.g. a salary, free accommodation, free access to elite athletes' restaurants, access to the national centre of sport and medical sciences, access to scientific and psychological and social care. An athlete can be classified in a lower category if he/she does not achieve the assigned objectives. There is a category for talented junior athletes who do not receive a salary but have access to all other advantages. If they achieve suitable performance they would integrate to a higher category.

Conclusion

One could argue that knowledge about sport in these three countries cannot be understood outside their internal political dynamics and in relation to policy making, outside the influence of political elites, symbolised by Al-Makhzen in Morocco, and national leaders such as Ben-Bella, Boumedien and Bouteflika in Algeria or Bourguiba and Ben Ali in Tunisia. Similarly, knowledge in sport cannot be understood independently of the economic dynamics, the economic deficits or dysfunction in the three countries. These are influenced according to Santucci (1993) by the following factors:

- external factors: the crisis of capitalist economies, the decline of oil and phosphate prices in the world market, world inflation, instability of the American dollar;
- internal factors: demographic expansion, unemployment, the financial weight of war in Western Sahara for Morocco and the civil war in Algeria, in addition to seasons of exceptional drought and foreign debt.

The use of sport for international relations or for the promotion of nation state ideologies, such as Third-Worldism, the Non-Aligned Movement, Pan-Africanism, and Pan-Arabism, in the international sport arena, explains in a way Bourguiba and Ben Ali's regimes' strategies in Tunisia, to promote the Mediterranean identity and thus to present Tunisia as a tolerant and modern (secular) nation. For Morocco, the ideal of African unity goes against its national interest, at least at the moment, because of the African Union's position towards the question of Western Sahara. This explains Morocco's policy to boycott the Pan-African Games organised by the Association of National Olympic Committees of Africa (ANOCA) under the patronage of the African Union. Algeria on the other hand, because of its foreign policy in the region and its Third-Worldist ideology, has been more active in hosting the Pan-African Games, whereas despite its French cultural influence Algeria chooses not to be a member of l'Organisation Internationale de la Francophonie and thus not to take part in the Francophone Games. Since the 1990s Algeria has shifted its fundamental policy position from socialism to market economy; hence, professional sport which was previously identified with neo-imperialism is accepted today as the norm. The switch to market based logics in sport, however, has not been immediate and although the project of the professionalisation of sport was first discussed in 1998, the official launch of the first professional football league only took place in 2011.

In relation to performance at international level, particularly in the Olympics, countries in the Maghreb are still reliant on a few sports to win medals. These are Athletics, Boxing and Judo. This is attributed by the interviewees to a lack of financial resources, the absence of a rational scientific approach, discrepancies between the existing ('imported') laws and the reality of sporting practice, and the absence of a successful model of elite sport development in the Maghreb; although, one should note that a number of reforms are being put in place to restructure the elite sport system, starting from the development of sport infrastructures, initiation of new sport laws to regulate for instance the remuneration of athletes and coaches, the finance of training camps and participation of national teams in regional and international competitions, and the development of categorisation systems for international sport competitions and national elite athletes in relation to their international level (Amara, 2012). However, the results of these reforms are yet to be seen particularly since the region, as in the rest of the Arab world, has been facing a wave of popular uprising. However, for all the growing evidence of a realisation of the significance of sport and sports policy we should underline that in the broader political scheme the impact of sporting success has its limits. The policy of Ben Ali's regime, for example, was to use sport as a showcase for national development through the staging of international competitions such as the Mediterranean Games in 2001 and the African Cup of Nations in 1994 and 2004, and could point to Tunisian success in major sports competitions in the 2004 African Cup of nations in Football, the qualification of the Tunisian national football team for the the World Cup in 1998, 2002 and 2006, and the Gold medal of Oussama Mellouli in the 2008 Beijing Olympic Games; however, all these sporting successes could contribute little to the prevention of the regime's fall.

26

THE ECONOMICS OF SPORT POLICY

Christoph Breuer and Kirstin Hallmann

Economics is the social science that analyses how people make choices under conditions of scarcity. Scarcity itself is a multidimensional construct that encompasses, among others, scarcity of financial, time, human, material, spatial/infrastructural resources. As almost every individual and organisational decision is made under such constraints, economics can contribute to the understanding and explanation of numerous phenomena (Becker and Murphy, 2001). This includes developing knowledge in order to optimise structures, processes, and welfare distribution. Optimising, in an economic sense, means increasing efficiency. Thus, economics can contribute to the body of knowledge of sport policy in different ways: by explaining why and when governments should intervene in sport systems; by contributing to the understanding of strategic behaviour in the sport policy field; and by providing models, tools and methods for evaluating sport policies. Further, (neo-institutional) economics can help in understanding the impact of legal norms and institutions on actors in the sports system. With the help of the economic perspective, more effective and efficient sport policies with regard to institutional arrangements can be shaped. Finally, the economics of sport policy can help to distinguish and explain various logics of sport systems and their consequences for sport policy issues. Each of these aspects is discussed in turn in the following sections.

Regulatory policy of sport

A first field in which economics can contribute to the body of knowledge of sport policy is the *regulatory policy of sport*. Numerous questions are of importance for sport policy makers, such as the socially desirable level of sport participation; the contribution of sport to public interest objectives such as public health, education, social inclusion, employment; the extent of sport subsidisation; the responsibility for the construction and operation of sport facilities; or whether sport should be partly state run or organised. Therefore, it is necessary to understand the sport market which consists of the buyers and sellers of the sport product. In any given market there is a point of equilibrium between supply and demand: that is, a point at which a balance between demand and supply exists. The private market equilibrium ('pme' in Figure 26.1) indicates where the individual demand curve meets the supply curve. The actual participation rate is smaller than the social demand. Figure 26.1 further points out that the level of supply is insufficient at the equilibrium price.

With regard to sports, it can be said that the demand for sports is a function of the perceived costs by those interested in participating in sports. The costs include the overall costs of the practice of an individual, that is, monetary costs (e.g. membership fees), and other costs such as time costs are taken into consideration. Thereby, a high percentage rate of participant demand can be expected when the costs are considered as low, and vice versa. A peculiarity of sport is that it contributes not only to satisfying individual needs (internal effects) for the direct participants, such as individual fitness, fun, and well-being: thanks to those who are active in the whole population, physically inactive individuals also benefit (external effects). These external effects can be attributed to physical activity in general, and more specifically to physical activity in a sport club that fosters specific external effects. Central aspects that contribute to the welfare product of sport and sport organisations are societal integration, socialisation, democracy, and health (Heinemann, 2005; Rittner and Breuer, 2004). That is why the social demand for sport is higher than the individual demand (see Figure 26.1).

The positive external effects of sport (clubs) lead – supposing a pure market coordination without any political interventions – to a smaller collective demand for sport and sport clubs than is desired society-wide. This is due to the aggregated individual value of sport (expected internal effect) being smaller than the economic value (expected internal plus external effect).

Another drawback within this context is that the sport facility itself, as special infrastructure and special sport product, is very costly and is usually not fully financed via the market. For instance, swimming pools often generate only 20 per cent of their operating costs. A privately operated pool could not provide an adequate supply for swimmers as the fees would need to be prohibitively high, leading first to decline in users, and then to the bankruptcy of the provider! Thus, considered from a pure market coordination perspective, the demand would remain below a societally desired level. However, demand below the societal optimum legitimates regulatory interventions as direct or indirect subsidies for sport actors for welfare-oriented reasons, and is indicated by the difference between the price paid by an individual and the optimal price for society that will be filled by the subsidy (see p_1 and p_2 in Figure 26.1). Consequently, sport and sport organisations can be considered as merit goods and are subsidised.

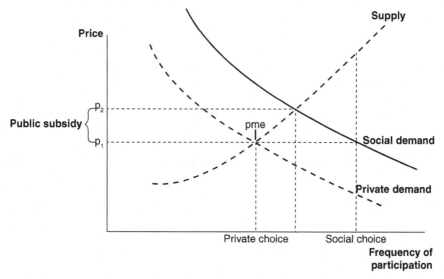

Figure 26.1 The justification for public subsidies to meet the social demand objective
Source: Avice *et al.* (2011, p. 26)

Figure 26.1 clearly shows the external effects demand for subsidising sport and sport clubs. Nevertheless, some sport clubs fail to offer adequate sports for various groups of the population (e.g. the elderly or people working late) and neglect to use their club, for instance, for societal integration. A reason might be that sport clubs are usually dependent on the voluntary engagement of their members to offer, for example, volleyball in the evening. Commercial sport providers in contrast do offer particular programmes in the evening; however, they focus only on high-demand sports (e.g. yoga) and sports that do not require large sport halls (e.g. basketball). A purely commercial sport provision would consequently also be dysfunctional; and that is true as well for sole provision of sports by clubs. Competition fosters the potential for innovation, but at the municipal level a need to balance the diverse sport providers arises, and possible substitution effects need to be taken into consideration.

Understanding strategic behaviour in sport politics

Economic approaches such as the foundation for strategic behaviour in sport politics represent a second area where economics can contribute to sport policy. At the core of economic theory stands the *Homo oeconomicus*: that is, a typical decision maker who acts out of pure self-interest. S/he strives to maximise utility (i.e. his/her personal happiness); his/her choices are completely rational; and s/he has all information available. Yet, other approaches in economics argue that this always-rational *Homo oeconomicus* is purely fictitious and that human rationality is bounded. Following the bounded rationality approach it is assumed that human decision makers may try to be rational, but it is unusual that all alternatives are (or can be) known. As a consequence, decisions are taken on the basis of incomplete information. The behaviour is therefore described as *satisficing*, in contrast to *maximising* (Douma and Schreuder, 2008; Frank, 2003). Satisficing describes an economic concept indicating that an individual is satisfied with the first best solution that is offered. Todd and Gigerenzer (2003) highlight in this context that bounded rationality can also be regarded as a suboptimal outcome of the limited human cognitive system. The bounds can consequently either be external or internal, or consist of an interrelationship of both the external and internal bounds. Yet, the internal and external bounds need to be closely linked when interrelated. The internal bounds can be shaped through evolution while the external bounds are more difficult to influence (Todd and Gigerenzer, 2003). Nonetheless, the foundations of the *Homo oeconomicus* approach are valuable in explaining decision making. For instance, Frank (2003) illustrates the rational choice of the *Homo oeconomicus* where the benefits should exceed the costs. Although monetary values are often used as denominator (Frank, 2003), costs and benefits can also refer to non-monetary constraints such as time, and advantages such as improved health. On this view, policies with a focus on individuals should take the specific costs and benefits into account in order to enhance their effectiveness. For example, a policy aiming at increasing the number of volunteers in sport should reflect the different costs as well as the various benefits of voluntarism for the individual. Then it becomes quickly clear that a single-solution approach (e.g. based on monetary gratification alone) might fail.

People facing limited resources try to maximise their individual utility. This is termed constrained maximisation and reflects three basic economic pillars: (1) individual attempts to maximise happiness; (2) limited resources; and (3) rational choices that people make based on available resources in order to increase happiness (Heinemann, 1995; Leeds and von Allmen, 2005). As all decisions in an organisation are taken by human beings, individual decisions also influence organisational behaviour and how policies are formulated and executed.

Another area in which economics can contribute is that of rational decision making in sport policy and evaluation of sport policy effectiveness. The concept of opportunity costs falls into this category. These costs, often neglected as they are not explicit, should, however, be considered in decision making. Opportunity costs accrue when, for instance, one activity is chosen over another. To put it briefly, opportunity costs arise due to the activities *not chosen* (Mankiw, 2004), meaning that opportunity costs are 'equal to the revenue that could have been generated by the best alternative use' (Douma and Schreuder, 2008, p. 45). The value of the foregone opportunities is often not considered and, as a consequence, suboptimal decisions are taken (Frank, 2003). The concept of opportunity costs is fundamental in economics and is applicable to numerous fields; for example, when the net present value of an investment for a new sport facility is estimated. Pertaining to volunteering, the conclusion of this concept is that the marginal value of volunteering can be considered as the opportunity costs of any other activity not undertaken (Downward, Dawson, and Dejonghe, 2009). Yet, as Downward *et al.* (2009) emphasise, the opportunity costs of time per se are not an appropriate representation of volunteering as human capital also needs to be taken into consideration.

With regard to decision making, both in general and in the sport context, decisions taken can be considered from the perspective of game theory (Douma and Schreuder, 2008). Game theory is applied in decision making under conditions of uncertainty, or with moral hazards, or where problems exist such as asymmetric information and signalling (Mizrahi, Mehrez, and Friedman, 2006). Game theory describes situations in which at least two people, deciding interdependently, are involved. In classical game theory it is assumed that all people involved take rational decisions, and that all players base their decisions on rational choice (Douma and Schreuder, 2008). The application of game theory to sport offers a useful tool in developing sport policies. For example, in the context of doping, the policy to be developed must stress equal chances using, for instance, drug diaries or instruments to decrease the benefits of doping (that is, increase the costs of doping to users, and increase the benefits for athletes who do not dope). In this context, Bette and Schimank (2006) and Daumann (2008) illustrate a sport example based on the well-known 'prisoner's dilemma' in general economics (e.g. Frank, 2003). Using this example, it is assumed that the market (i.e. the competition) consists of two athletes of equal strength and capabilities, each deciding whether or not to take drugs to increase her/his performance. Both athletes have to determine their strategy beforehand (ignoring previous competitions). Say the prize money (including immaterial benefits of the victory) amounts to €10,000, and costs of €2,000 accrue for the athlete who uses doping. Each athlete's chance of winning is interrelated to both his own strategy and to that of the other athlete. This means that athlete A has a better chance to win when he is using doping and his opponent, athlete B, is not using it (and vice versa). The chances of both are equal when both take drugs, or when both do not use doping. However, there are differences with regard to prize money. When no doping is involved, no costs accrue for drugs and the redemption is €5,000 for each athlete. When both use doping, costs of €2,000 accrue to each, and, having equal chances, the prize money amounts to €3,000 each. When only one of the athletes decides to take drugs, he has a 90 per cent chance to win the prize money minus the costs of €2,000 for the drugs – hence €7,000. The opponent has only a 10 per cent chance to win and thus will only receive €1,000. Therefore, the application of game theory to this situation reveals that to use doping (and hope the opponent does not) is the dominant option for each athlete (Daumann, 2008). Hence, anti-doping policies could be developed more effectively by taking such aspects into account.

Table 26.1 Odds of winning and amount of prize money as example of game theory applied to doping choices of two athletes

	ATHLETE B *no doping*	ATHLETE B *doping*
ATHLETE A	Odds for A 50 % / Odds for B 50 %;	Odds for B 90 % / Odds for A 10 %;
no doping	Prize for A €5,000 / Prize B €5,000	Prize for B €7,000 / Prize for A €1,000
ATHLETE A	Odds for A 90 % / Odds for B 10 %;	Odds for B 50 % / Odds for B 50 %;
doping	Prize for A €7,000 / Prize for B €1,000	Prize for B €3,000 / Prize for A €3,000

Source: cf. Daumann (2008, p. 91)

Economic evaluation of sport policies

There are of course numerous sport policies that a government or governing body might formulate, covering a wide range of objectives – such as increasing mass participation; using sport to address poor physical activity levels and ameliorate community health issues; or using sport for urban regeneration and economic development (Houlihan, 2009; Hoye, Nicholson, and Houlihan, 2010). Health care programmes are inaugurated by governments, sporting organisations, or municipalities to achieve such policy objectives. For instance, concerning the evaluation of participation rates, national health surveys such as Active People in the UK, or municipal-led surveys, form the basis for all economic assessment and policy implications that are based on those evaluations. With regard to urban regeneration, sport events are often used as an instrument to develop the city (e.g. in terms of improving infrastructure or creating other such 'legacy' effects). Examples from cities that have hosted major events (Olympic Games or Commonwealth Games) such as Barcelona, Manchester, or Munich are often cited as positive examples. Although cities hosting such events often initially regard them as a positive instrument inaugurating positive effects, research shows that there are also negative effects of event hosting that cannot be neglected (e.g. Coates and Matheson, 2011; Preuss and Solberg, 2006). Mules and Dwyer (2005, p. 339) highlight that every government has a key question surrounding a sport event: 'What degree of support, if any, is required?'. They point out further that the answer varies depending on the expected benefits and costs (Mules and Dwyer, 2005) referring to utility maximisation. Humphreys and Prokopowicz (2007) emphasise that every economic assessment begins with a comparison of the costs and benefits involved. With regard to events, possible indicators could be the number of visitors, the duration of their stay, and their expenditure (Wilson, 2006). However, there is another approach to evaluate the benefits of sport events and facilities apart from the economic assessment, namely the measurement of intangible benefits such as community pride, image enhancements, and further positive externalities (Sidaway and Zimbalist, 2000). In this context, the contingent valuation method (CVM) is used. This method is appropriate when estimating the value of public goods (e.g. Johnson and Whitehead, 2000) or measuring the willingness to pay (WTP) in sport clubs: 'Contingent valuation (CV) is a survey-based method frequently used for placing monetary values on environmental goods and services not bought and sold in the marketplace' (Carson, 2000, p. 1413). Thereby, a hypothetical market is created and respondents are questioned to indicate their WTP for an improvement in, for instance, a public good or better service in a sport club (Humphreys, Johnson, Mason, and Whitehead, 2010). While the procedure and analysis is based on a hypothetical scenario, this approach to rational sport policy making can nonetheless assist policy makers in their decisions as CVM is predictive of the monetary value of an investment. For example, policy problems may arise concerning the implementation of taxes. Here, a question is how high taxes should be in light of residents' WTP to help fund mega-sport events such as the London 2012 Olympics.

With regard to the economic impact of sport and sport policies, there are many different approaches to evaluating these impacts. Common approaches include economic impact studies, cost–benefit analysis, input–output analysis, cost-effectiveness analysis, and social return on investment; and we consider each of these in turn. (1) The term *economic impact study* is used on the one hand as an umbrella term to describe economic evaluation and, on the other hand, it represents an approach for economic evaluation that itself needs to be distinguished from other approaches. The basic difference between an economic impact study and, for instance, a cost–benefit analysis is that the former measures the additional income created by, for example, a sport event. In contrast, the latter focuses on benefits for the local population and which type of money is considered as cost (Késenne, 2005). While the economic impact study is able to indicate a monetary value for the impact, Késenne (2005, p. 134) emphasises that this does not provide policy makers a 'sensible argument' to support a project (since, if the study is undertaken a priori, its outcome is only hypothetical). A cost–benefit analysis, however, does provide this information (e.g. Crompton, 1995; Késenne, 2005; Preuss, 2004a). There are two types of economic impact approaches. The first approach focuses entirely on the incoming money and ignores the money spent by the inhabitants for event tickets, assuming that they would have spent the money elsewhere without the event taking place. The second type takes the additional income created through hosting the event into account (e.g. extra jobs or government tax returns) (Késenne, 2005). A combination of both approaches can also be found in the literature. (2) *Cost–benefit analysis* is one of the most widely known types of economic assessment (Robinson, 1993c). This type of evaluation assessment integrates all possible costs and benefits – whether they are tangible or intangible – and expresses those in monetary terms (Preuss and Weiss, 2003; Robinson, 1993a). The advantage of expressing all costs and benefits in monetary values is the comparability to returns on investment in other areas of the economy (Robinson, 1993a). It is thus considered as a valuable tool for improving the decision-making process, providing precise definitions, quantifiable indicators for both the costs and benefits, and exposition of alternatives that can be formulated to assist the decision-making process (Bootman, Rowland, and Wertheimer, 1979). However, the lack of available information is considered a major shortcoming of the cost–benefit analysis (Rueda-Cantuche and Ramirez-Hurtado, 2007). One study found that people believe that the economic advantages of hosting an event are limited to a few organisations and individuals (Rueda-Cantuche and Ramirez-Hurtado, 2007). A policy implication of this result could be to show the local community the range of potential impacts in order to prevent such assumptions. (3) Conversely, *input–output analysis* takes the interdependencies between economic units into account, its results being thereby restricted to direct economic impact (Heyne, 2006). Input–output analysis has been criticised recently for its rigidness – that is, exclusion of factor constraints, fixed costs and prices, and neglect of interactive industry effects (Dwyer and Forsyth, 2009). (4) *Cost-effectiveness analysis* focuses on comparison of the costs and outcomes, both measured in natural units (Robinson, 1993b). Suitable measures of effectiveness are key in this type of analysis. In a health context, for instance, 'life years gained' is considered a suitable measure. Using this measure it was shown, for instance, that exercise programmes are a cost-effective tool in reducing coronary heart disease (Hatziandreu, Koplan, Weinstein, Caspersen, and Warner, 1988). This result can be used by community policy makers to promote general sport participation or particular sports such as swimming or gymnastics. (5) *Social return on investment* (SROI) is an approach measuring the earnings of social investments. Sport policy decisions (e.g. increasing sport participation) are usually not aimed at creating cash flow but instead at producing health, social cohesion, or public welfare improvements. Consequently, other measures need to be established, such as increase in participation rates, or number of members in local sport clubs. Yet, the indicators of evaluation need to be chosen carefully and should be specific, measurable, attainable, realistic, and timely. Lingane and Olsen (2004) indicate that SROI consists of four steps: collecting social performance data, prioritising the data that needs to be tracked, incorporating the data into decision making, and evaluating the data. Thereby, SROI is a management tool for supporting the policy maker in decision making.

Which type of economic assessment should be used to assist in decision making regarding sport policies depends on the problem to be tackled and the type of available measures to be employed. Yet, it has to be noted that Taks, Késenne, Chalip, and Green (2010) showed that one study (which means one dataset) can produce different results if different types of economic evaluation are applied.

Institutional/legal support for efficient sport systems

Economics can contribute to better understanding of the impact of legal norms and institutions on the actors in sports systems. In particular, neo-institutional economics should be taken into account since this economic perspective serves to form more effective and efficient sport policies regarding institutional arrangements.

Neo-institutional economics have been developed out of neoclassical theory and are characterised by three assumptions: bounded rationality, opportunistic behaviour, and long-term and incomplete contracts with extended risks (Breuer and Hovemann, 2006; Douma and Schreuder, 2008). Overall, neo-institutional economics encompasses three theoretical approaches, which are partly overlapping (Franck, 1995): (1) property rights theory, (2) principal agent theory, and (3) transaction cost theory (Blum, Dudley, Leibbrand, and Weiske, 2005). With regard to sport economic policies, these three directions of neo-institutionalism are important, for example in the analysis of financing options of sport facilities, since stakeholders from the public as well as the private side can be involved (Breuer and Hovemann, 2006).

Within the theory of property rights, neo-institutional economics differentiates between permitted and non-permitted actions in a society or system, and how the behaviour of actors in this system is thereby influenced. Property rights exist with regard to usage (*usus*), change (*abusus*), acquisition of profits through the usage of a good (*usus fructus*), and the right to sell the good. The focus is not on the original goods, but on the rights to use these goods. Moreover, external effects and transactions costs need to be considered (Breuer and Hovemann, 2006; Erlei, Leschke, and Sauerland, 2007). With regard to sports policies, property rights play an important role, particularly concerning sport facilities. Here, the question arises to what extent public institutions, for example municipalities, have to engage in the provision of sport facilities to produce efficient outcomes. A best-practice model in this respect is that sport clubs become the operators of sport facilities, being financially and constructively supported by the municipalities. Thus, the municipality is no longer itself the operator of the facility but guarantees the operation and provision of such facilities through the sport clubs. Thereby, sport clubs are highly interested in finding economically sustainable solutions for the operation of facilities. Such a model is normally backed by contracts between sport clubs and municipalities and leads to both a reduction of public costs (e.g. investment costs, maintenance costs, management costs of the facilities) and a more efficient operation of the facilities. Thus, the property rights of the sport facilities are transferred from the municipality to the sport clubs (Breuer, 2010). This model is closely linked to principal agent theory, which is part of economic contract theory, and encompasses the assumption that the principal gives or lends certain of its rights to an agent. Sticking to the above-mentioned example, the municipality (principal) transfers the rights to use and operate the sport facility to a sport club (agent). It is assumed that the agent aims at maximising his/her utility, which does not necessarily have to be of advantage to the principal. Crucial within this theory is what the principal knows about the behaviour of the agent. If the principal can observe the behaviour of the agent, this scenario is called symmetrical information. In contrast, if the principal does not know the behaviour, or can only get a hint of the effort of the agent by gathering information which raises costs, this scenario is called asymmetrical information (Blum *et al.*, 2005; Breuer and Hovemann, 2006; Douma and Schreuder, 2008).

In contrast to the assumption of a perfect market where no transaction costs arise, the transaction costs theory particularly focuses on these costs and makes them the most important efficiency criterion. This approach was originally developed by Coase (1937) and has led to many different attempts to define transaction costs. Franck (1995) states that transaction costs encompass all damages that arise out of the bounded rationality of economic actors. Among others these can be search, information, monitoring, or assertion costs. Regarding the above-mentioned policy example of sport facilities and the transfer of property rights from municipalities (principal) to sport clubs (agent), transactions costs arise for municipalities since they need to control the technically correct adherence of the contract with the sport club (Breuer, 2010).

Overall, neo-institutional economics builds a basis for sport policies that aim at reaching the highest possible efficiency potentials and should therefore focus on areas where the highest potential lies – in municipalities, for example, on sport infrastructure. Possibilities to decrease public spending can be found in an increasing commercialisation, and thereby a substitution of public through private funds. Moreover, cooperation between sport clubs and municipalities regarding the usage and operation of sport facilities can increase efficiency (Breuer, 2010).

Economic logics of sport systems

Concerning sport systems, the economics of sport policy can help in distinguishing and understanding the different logics behind sport systems and their consequences for sport policy issues. With regard to the economics of sports this is particularly important when taking into account the differences that exist between North America (mainly USA) and Europe (Andreff, 2007) and consequently lead to differences in sport policies.

Generally speaking, sport systems and modern sports can be described as highly formalised, with rules similar to those of liberal democracies since they also have governing bodies that are run by elected officials. The process of formalisation has predominantly taken place in Great Britain and the United States, and what has evolved out of the process is the North-American model of sport, which strongly differs from the European model, particularly regarding commercial considerations (Sloane, 2009). Overall, the North-American model has strong cultural, economic, and political undertones: it is based on self-governing associations of independent clubs; it is independent of the state; and it is highly commercially oriented. To survive economically, cost efficiency is vital (Szymanski, 2009). Compared to that, the European economic viability model is based on private donations and club subscriptions (Sloane, 2009), as well as public subsidies from institutions such as the state or municipalities since sport is regarded as a merit good (Breuer, 2010).

Key differences between the European and the American models are displayed in Table 26.2. A major characteristic of the European model is utility maximisation (e.g. playing success, attendance) compared to the profit maximising objective in the North American model. A further major difference that also impacts on the economic situation of clubs is the promotion and relegation system with open leagues that is common in Europe, whereas in North America closed leagues exist and relocation of sports franchises is possible. What is of extensive usage in North America, but nonexistent or not common in Europe, are player drafts, roster limits, revenue sharing, and salary capping. On the other hand, stock market flotation of clubs has recently been increasing in Europe but restricted in North America. All these different characteristics in the two systems regarding the codes of competition of professional sports leagues consequently engender different sport policies (Sloane, 2009).

Moreover, since the media, and thereby TV broadcasting, have become increasingly important as a source of income, policies regulating how TV rights are sold, that is, in a centralised or decentralised form, have an impact on the (in)equality in sports leagues in terms of income distribution and competitive balance. In most European leagues, with the exception of Spain, Portugal, and Italy, broadcasting rights are sold in a pooled way, that is, centralised. The same applies to North American leagues. There are different viewpoints as to what is the best way in economic terms. Although decentralised, namely, individual selling, seems economically preferable since centralised selling creates a monopoly causing welfare losses, the economics of professional team sports leagues might justify centralised selling due to the characteristic of co-optation in sports leagues (Késenne, 2009).

Table 26.2 Key elements of professional sports leagues

	European model	*North American model*
Objectives	Utility maximisation	Profit maximisation
Structure	Open leagues, promotion and relegation	Closed leagues
Size	Large number of clubs per head of population	Restricted number of clubs
Geographical pattern	Restricted geographical movement of clubs	Exclusive territories but franchise mobility
International competition	Important at club and national level	Absent
Player drafts	None	Extensive
Sale of players	Sale of players for cash common	Restrictions on sales of players for cash
Roster limits	None	Extensive
Revenues sharing	Limited	Extensive
Salary capping	Limited, but increasing	Extensive
Stock market flotation	Recent	Restricted

Source: Sloane (2009, p. 301)

27

SPORT GOVERNANCE

Russell Hoye

The concept of governance in relation to sport has attracted increased attention in recent years from policy makers, researchers and industry stakeholders. This is both a product of the concern to develop appropriate standards of corporate behaviour among sport organisations and recognition that the state cannot be responsible for the delivery of universal forms of provision in areas of policy such as sport and other social domains. To date, these two issues have largely been treated separately within the mainstream media and by researchers. The purpose of this chapter is threefold. First, it provides an overview of the application of the concept of governance in the sport industry before briefly exploring the nuanced nature of governance as it applies in diverse sporting contexts. Second, it provides an analysis of the limitations of formal governance systems in these various sporting contexts focusing on macro-level issues such as regulation and enforcement challenges in federated networks, and micro-level issues such as regulating director behaviour and ensuring ethical standards are upheld in the governance of sport organisations. Third, and finally, the chapter reviews the relationship between sport policy and governance, in particular the increasing influence of the state via sport policy on the governance of sport and the implications this has for the independence of sport.

What is governance?

At the organisational level, governance is the system by which the elements of an organisation are directed, controlled and regulated. Bob Tricker, considered by many to be the founder of corporate governance studies, highlighted the distinction between management and governance when he wrote 'if management is about running a business, governance is about seeing that it is run properly' (Tricker, 1984: 7). Organisational-level governance deals with issues of policy and direction for the enhancement of organisational performance as well as ensuring statutory and fiduciary compliance by organisational members. An effective organisational governance system not only provides a framework in which the business of organisations are directed and controlled but also 'helps to provide a degree of confidence that is necessary for the proper functioning of a market economy' (Organisation for Economic Co-operation and Development, 2004: 11). Having an effective governance system in place, as Hoye and Cuskelly (2007: 1) stated:

assures stakeholders that the organization in which they have invested money, time, effort or their reputations, is subject to adequate internal checks and balances and that the people empowered to make decisions on behalf of the organization (the board) act in the best interests of the organization and its stakeholders.

The concept of governance can also be applied at the macro level for sport, to describe the overall system by which all the actors associated with delivering sport are controlled, coordinated and held accountable. Indeed, Forster (2006: 72) noted the complexity involved in the governance of sport when he stated that 'sport is intermediated, controlled and contested by great numbers of organisations'. This complexity is also evident when comparing the many different organisational types that make up the sport sector, each of which has different governance structures and legal frameworks. These range from international sport federations, international event associations, national and state/provincial governing bodies, professional sport leagues and franchises, and government owned sport stadia.

Forster (2006: 72) used the term global sports organisations (GSOs) to identify those sport governing bodies that are the 'supreme organs of governance in sport whose authority is global'. He cited four major examples: the International Federation of Football Associations (FIFA), the International Olympic Committee (IOC), the International Association of Athletics Federations (IAAF) and the World Anti-Doping Authority (WADA) respectively responsible for football, the Olympic movement, athletics and anti doping regulations. Forster makes the important distinction that these GSOs usually serve one of three main governance functions: governance of a sport, governance of a sporting event, or governance of a specialist function such as anti-doping regulation and enforcement or arbitration. By far the most common are those GSOs that govern a sport, and Forster (2006: 73) provides a useful list of their typical functions:

- the creation and maintenance of the laws and rules of a sport and its competitions;
- the global development of a sport at all levels;
- the development and governance of the athletes within a sport;
- arbitration and/or resolution of disputes within a sport;
- holding of global events, such as world championships, within the sport;
- maintenance of relationships within sporting bodies within a sport, especially affiliated national associations within the sport;
- maintenance of relationships with government, regulatory authorities and those sporting bodies outside the sport; and
- maintenance of relationships with commercial entities such as sponsors.

Limitations of governance systems

There are a number of limitations associated with the governance of sport that can be crudely categorised as macro- or micro-level limitations. At the macro level, scholars such as Amara, Henry, Liang and Uchiumi (2005), and Hamil, Morrow, Idle, Rossi and Faccendini (2010) have explored a number of issues associated with the governance of football (soccer) in a comparative study of five nations and Italy, respectively. These studies highlight the deficiencies in governance that exist within sport leagues, especially in terms of the governance relationships between leagues and clubs.

Amara *et al.* (2005: 190) compared the governance systems for football in five countries (England, France, Algeria, China and Japan) in order to (in part) highlight the 'variety of models of sport-business whose characteristics are the product of local histories, political and sporting cultures, economic conditions, and [other factors]'. In so doing, they outlined fundamental differences between the governance systems of England (neoliberal), China (state-sponsored restrictive capitalism), Algeria (state designed model of non-amateurism), Japan (corporate capitalism–public partnership model) and France (*dirigiste* state model); specifically in the relationships between principal stakeholders, or as they termed it: 'different configurations of power' (Amara *et al.*, 2005: 204). Each of these systems was seen as a battlefield between stakeholders, with each vying for control of scarce resources within their respective governance systems.

Hamil *et al.* (2010) provided an in-depth examination of the many failings in governance that have plagued Italian football in recent years. While they noted that:

> there is a clear and transparent system of regulatory oversight for the Italian football industry [and a licensing system that] suggests a high standard of club governance should exist … there is a very serious gap between theory and practice, a gap which has had significant consequences for the health of the Italian football industry.
>
> (Hamil *et al.*, 2010: 379)

They document a litany of problems that have plagued Italian soccer over the last three decades including betting scandals, doping, false passports, bribery and match fixing, and violence, which they concluded is largely a result of inappropriate ownership and governance structures among football clubs. Aside from the problems of clubs being controlled by familial networks with little separation of ownership and control (one of the central tenets of effective governance), Hamil *et al.* (2010: 388) noted that 'what emerges in football are networks consisting of powerful individuals connected with clubs, governing bodies, political parties and the media, which are in prominent positions to influence decision making within football and the business of football'. Compounding these issues is the lack of competitive balance in the Italian league and the growing disparity of resources between mid-tier clubs and those few large clubs that play in the lucrative UEFA Champions League. Unsurprisingly, they concluded that Italian football should adopt 'modern regulation – including sanctions for misdemeanours – and clear guidelines for strong governance' (Hamil *et al.*, 2010: 404).

At the micro level, the failings of many governance systems used by sport organisations have been well documented (Australian Sports Commission, 2005; Hoye and Cuskelly, 2007; Hoye and Doherty, 2011; Sport and Recreation New Zealand, 2004, 2006; UK Sport, 2004). It should be noted that most sport governance research efforts have focused on the efficacy of GSOs that govern sport, along with investigations of the efficacy of their member associations, usually at the national or state/provincial level, particularly as most government policy affects the operation of national governing bodies. Some of the more common criticisms have been that representative voting systems often do not result in the best people being elected to governance roles; that people are not appointed or selected for board service on the basis of specific skills or competencies; that sport boards are often poor at transparent reporting to stakeholders; there is a lack of accountability for those individuals serving on boards; there are ongoing problems in regulating director behaviour (as they are usually voluntary as opposed to the corporate sector where remuneration for directors is the norm); and there is a lack of robust mechanisms to ensure high ethical standards among board members. In one of the first studies of the governance of football in England, Michie and Oughton (2005: 529) highlighted many of these issues when they concluded that:

> One area of corporate governance where football clubs are particularly weak regards the need to have clear and transparent procedures for the appointment of directors and

non-executive directors, including independent non-executive directors. Clubs are especially weak on the provision of induction and training for new and existing directors. Results from our survey also reveal that clubs need to improve their internal risk control and business planning systems. A set of guidelines – or code of corporate governance – for football that set out clear and manageable standards in these regards would do much to improve the state of the game.

A recent study of national sport federations by Numerato and Baglioni (2011) highlighted many of the problems inherent in the governance of these volunteer controlled organisations. They sought to explore whether the dark dimensions of social capital (i.e. the negative consequences of interacting with others in groups or via networks) were evident in the governance practices of national sport federations for football, handball and sailing in two countries (the Czech Republic and Italy). Their study established that three types of the dark side of social capital were evident in the behaviours of individuals involved in governing sport. First, in some cases, groups of individuals deliberately sought to 'build strategically exclusive coalitions' (Numerato and Baglioni, 2011: 8) within a sports federation so that they could exclude teams from securing access to resources, while others sought to manipulate the composition of others' networks in order to secure resources for their own organisations during official voting or decision-making processes such as the allocation of hosting rights for sport events. Second, Numerato and Baglioni (2011: 9) found evidence that the social ties of some people in governance roles can be misused to the detriment of sport organisations: 'the interconnectedness between the sport and non-sport sectors is sometimes misused for economic or political interests'. They cited the example of politicians using their links to football to get elected to office and the fact that 'social ties between board members and sponsors are sometimes perceived as constraining sports development' (Numerato and Baglioni, 2011: 10). Third, they also found evidence that some 'sports volunteers and officials active in sport governance can construct the appearance of prosperous civic engagement' (Numerato and Baglioni, 2011: 12) and merely portray the appearance of democratic and transparent governance processes.

In sum, these limitations of governance at the micro and macro levels highlight that while standards of behaviour and codes of conduct may be in place to guide the behaviour of individuals in governance roles, supplemented by training and professional development activities, the reality is that the governance of sport organisations (and all other organisational types for that matter) will always be subject to the frailties of human nature and the motives of those who may deliberately seek to abuse their privileged position. Nevertheless, this has not deterred governments from intervening in the governance of sport, as discussed in the next section.

Sport policy and its relationship with governance

The relationship between government action, most notably via policy, and the governance of sport manifests in three ways: (1) how government and associated policy has addressed the legitimacy of sport to be self-governing, (2) the direct impacts that specific policies have had on the nature and efficacy of sport governance within national governing bodies and their members, and (3) the more indirect effects of governments' shift to work via partnerships and the concomitant pressures for sport governing bodies to work with others for the delivery of sport. Each of these is examined in turn.

Maintaining legitimacy

Hoye and Cuskelly (2007) argued that sport governing bodies will be increasingly asked to operate within a sophisticated market that requires them to work within a complex network of professional clubs or franchises, broadcasters, sponsors, passive consumers (i.e. spectators, fans or supporters) and the more active consumers of their sport (volunteers, coaches, participants). The commercialisation of sport, especially increased broadcast rights revenue from the staging of professional leagues and major sport events, presents sport governing bodies with major challenges, especially in terms of maintaining their legitimacy. Morgan (2002), via an analysis of the issues surrounding the structuring of elite competitions in professional sport, highlighted the likely threats to legitimacy confronting sport national governing bodies (NGBs). Morgan argued that the objectives of the major stakeholders for a professional sport including the spectators, the sport NGB, the clubs that provide the playing talent to the competition or league, and the corporations holding the broadcast rights are rarely aligned, leading to disputes about the best way to structure and govern the competition, the composition of teams, scheduling of games, and player contract conditions (Morgan, 2002).

Morgan (2002: 49) stated that sport NGBs have traditionally controlled national competitions via their authority that is 'based on its legitimacy as the elected governing body, its control of key assets such as the national team brand and the national stadium, and its ability to reward members by distributing revenue'. Thus, Morgan argued, if the sport NGB maintains the ability to select teams for international competition and the distribution of associated broadcast and match day revenues, their legitimacy will be largely unchallenged. Other models do exist where the sport NGB is not central to decision-making power: the cartel model of the National Football League (NFL), the promoter-led model in boxing, and the oligarchy, 'an alternative form of non-market bi-lateral governance' (Morgan, 2002: 50) that operates within English football. Morgan noted that challenges to sport NGBs' legitimacy tend to emerge over who controls domestic elite competitions; thus, sport NGBs need to decide whether their role is to be:

> solely regulatory, i.e. concerned with the rules of the game, the welfare of players, standards of refereeing and coaching and the running of the national team [or should they] exert a commercial control over negotiations with sponsors and broadcasters, and the design and marketing of the competition.
>
> (Morgan, 2002: 54)

There is some protection for sport governing bodies' legitimacy. The independence of sport federations and other governing bodies of sport was legitimised in the 1999 Nice Declaration by the European Council when it recognised that 'it is the task of sporting organisations to organise and promote their particular sports, particularly as regards the specifically sporting rules applicable and the make-up of national teams' (Arnaut, 2006: 132). The basis for this 'self-organisation and self-regulation is an important expression and legacy of European civil society from the end of the 19th to the beginning of the 21st century' (Arnaut, 2006: 23). The European Council also noted that governing bodies for sport 'must continue to be the key feature of a form of organisation providing a guarantee of sporting cohesion and participatory democracy' (Arnaut, 2006: 133). However, sport governing bodies should not be complacent as highlighted by the Governance in Sport Working Group (2001: 3) when it stated that governing bodies for sport must earn the right to keep their 'specificity recognized' otherwise 'legislators at both national and international level will come under increasing pressure to legislate and courts will apply laws treating sports bodies like any other commercial organisation'.

The debate over the legitimacy of sport to be self-governing reached a crescendo with the release of the White Paper on Sport in July 2007 by the European Commission. A paper by Hill (2009: 254), the Head of UEFA's EU Office, couched the White Paper as a backward step for sport's specificity – 'the unique characteristics that distinguish it from normal economic activity'. Hill charted the course of a number of substantive decisions by the EU in relation to the specificity of sport and the ability of individuals, clubs and associations affiliated to a sport governing body to be beholden to its own set of sporting rules and to be seen as somewhat outside the application of competition policy and community laws. Hill (2009: 260) highlighted the balancing act the White Paper attempts to walk between reaffirming 'the features that distinguish sport from classic commercial activity [versus] a clear statement that community law must apply to the economic aspects of sport'. He argued that recent court rulings on the ability of sport to self-regulate had 'adopted the following reasoning: there is a commercial component to what sports governing bodies do; therefore, the entirety of their activities, including the regulatory function, must respect all provisions of EU law including competition policy' (Hill, 2009: 262–263). This view, he argued, suggests that the courts have ignored or misunderstood the fact that sport governing bodies create certain rules and regulations to actually increase competition between their member organisations. The implication is that sport governing bodies may not be in total control over such matters as promotion and relegation of teams between divisions, or the number of teams that may compete in a league. Hill concluded that the ambiguity inherent in the White Paper fails to fully address these issues, leaving a question mark over sports' ability to self-govern.

Policy impacts on governance

The second way that government action has impacted the governance of sport has been the direct impacts that specific policies have had on the nature and efficacy of sport governance within national governing bodies and their members. One of the first studies of these effects was conducted by Grix (2009) (and also reported in part in Goodwin and Grix, 2011), who investigated the impact of UK sport policy on the governance of athletics. Grix's examination focused on the impact of the Labour government's modernisation programme on UK Athletics (UKA) whereby UKA modernised its values, techniques and practices in response to UK sport policy and adopted what he termed was a 'narrow, short-term target-centred approach to athletics' (Grix, 2009: 31).

The modernisation programme run by UK Sport essentially required national sport governing bodies to professionalise their management systems; a process previously described by Green and Houlihan (2006) as one of the ways government has sought to directly influence the management and administration of NGBs. In the case of UKA, this influence is clear: (1) the Department for Culture, Media and Sport (DCMS) set targets for UK Sport funding outcomes; (2) in turn, UK Sport set targets for UKA; and (3) UKA, in turn, set targets for national associations such as England Athletics, who then set targets for their Regional Divisions. This, argued Grix, is evidence of the DCMS 'governing' all the way down the system to community level sport. Grix (2009: 46) concluded that the overt intervention in the governance of UKA by the government (mainly via UK Sport) contributed to eight key problems:

- Lines of communication and accountability that are upwards toward UK Sport, Sport England and the DCMS, and not downwards to the grass-roots of the sport (most other NGBs appear more democratic and much closer to the grass-roots of their sport, including, in part, democratically elected boards).

- The 'professionalisation' (that is, introduction of business values and practices) of the management of athletics in the UK has, arguably, been taken too far in the direction of for-profit organisations.
- A lack of actors (in management) with intimate knowledge of the sport discipline who would be in a position to temper the impact of New Managerialism, in particular.
- A focus on short-term targets, as opposed to long-term sport development. There is little evidence of a structured development system for bringing through young talent (most of the successful NGBs have tried and tested talent identification systems).
- A narrow focus on athletes who are already good (i.e. not enough emphasis on upcoming athletes).
- UKA has no time or resources to investigate the wider issues behind the demise of athletics.
- Volunteers, athletes and officials are being bypassed in the process of the governance of athletics in the UK; potential know-how and knowledge is not being drawn upon to assist in the successful governing of the sport.
- This can lead to a lack of trust between the NGB and the grass-roots of the sport.

The example of UKA highlights how government policy can lead to a shift in governance from being accountable to organisational members towards being more accountable to a major government funding agency. This examination of government policy effects was extended across other sports by Green (2009) who argued that the UK Labour government introduced a new level of accountability for sport organisations to adopt good governance practices, along with a promise to redirect funding away from those sports that failed to adopt such measures. This was tagged as a No Compromise approach by UK Sport, aimed at ensuring the sport governing bodies were well placed to deliver elite sport success on the world stage. Green (2009: 140) highlighted the overt interventionist nature of the government's approach to sport governance:

> The shaping and guiding of the conduct of NGBs, and especially the threat of funding reappraisals if NGBs fall short of the high standards now required under the No Compromise approach, draws attention to a key insight from the writings on changing modes of governance. That is, as a government agency, UK Sport's power does not rely 'upon the traditional Hobbesian means of sovereignty plus coercion' (Davies 2006, p. 254), but draws increasingly on a range of disciplinary techniques of manipulation of the ways in which organisations such as NGBs will operate in the future.

UK Sport employed performance-focused strategies such as 'performance management, target-setting, KPIs, evidence-based policy, and sanctions' (Green, 2009: 140) to operationalise their approach to ensuring better standards of governance within sport organisations. Green (2009: 140–141) concluded that:

> all sport organisations in receipt of public money for policy interventions are facing up to working under realigned modes of governance where current rules of the game privilege rationalist processes and scientific ways of knowing, reinforcing the dominance of highly resourced, managerial and technical forms of knowledge.

Green (2009: 141) also concluded that 'under current and emerging governance arrangements in the UK, an illusory screen of plural, autonomous and empowered delivery networks for sport obscures the very close ties to, and regulation from, the centre'. In other words, the key government agencies directly influence the way in which national level sport governing bodies are governed and managed in order to facilitate the delivery of sport policy outcomes.

The impact of government policy on sport governance is not restricted to the UK. Soares, Correia and Rosado (2010) reported similar conclusions in relation to the governance and management of sport organisations in Madeira, Portugal. In their study they found that the decisions made by regional sport associations 'had to take into account the policy of the Regional Government of Maderia, given their dependency on public funding in order to carry out their activities and sporting events' (Soares *et al.*, 2010: 20). Indeed, they concluded that the sport policy of the Madeira government was the 'most significant factor determining the strategies of the associations' (Soares *et al.*, 2010: 5).

These examples illustrate how governments have sought to overtly influence the governance of sport organisations via the imposition of performance targets as part of funding agreements between elite sport agencies and national governing bodies, direct interventions to reshape and professionalise governance systems in sport, and indirectly influencing strategy and governance priorities through funding support. It must be said that, in general, sports seemed to have largely acquiesced to these influences, perhaps in the absence of other funding sources required to maintain their services or to become competitive in an increasingly difficult elite sport performance environment.

Indirect effects via partnerships

One important aspect of government policy effects on the governance of sport in the UK has been the development of County Sport Partnerships. McDonald (2005: 593) argued that 'as with social policy in general, partnerships in sport policy have emerged to become the key mechanism of service delivery'. His argument is based on an analysis of the evolution of UK sport policy since the mid 1990s when the government started taking a more active role in the strategic development of sport. He pointed to two major drivers of this increased role: first, the injection of money into sports infrastructure through sport being identified as one of the good causes to which National Lottery money should be directed; and second, the deterioration of elite performances by UK athletes and teams that forced both major political parties in the UK to adopt a formal policy position about sport. With the formulation of a national policy for sport came attempts to improve the governance of those organisations charged with delivering sport as discussed earlier in this chapter.

McDonald (2005: 594) noted that the development of a national sport policy required the creation of some mechanism to control its delivery in addition to the existing voluntary driven governing bodies of sport. This mechanism was in the form of Regional Sports Boards (RSBs)[1] that were charged with overseeing Sport England policy in regions, 'which in turn set the development framework for the 45 County Sport Partnerships (CSPs)' whose role is to:

> bring together a range of public, statutory and third sector organisations, such as national governing bodies of sport, local educational institutes, coaching bodies, as well as a number of agencies from the health services, the criminal justice system, local authorities and the various regeneration agencies. They occupy a pivotal position, as they are responsible for applying national policy to local conditions.
>
> (McDonald, 2005: 594)

These County Sport Partnerships did not attract a great deal of academic attention until a study reported by Phillpots, Grix and Quarmby (2010) and also in Grix (2010) and in Grix and

Phillpots (2011) that focused (in part) on the governance arrangements and working relationships between CSPs and the lead government agency, Sport England. The part of their analysis that is relevant here was the finding that 'the increasing dominance of a government imposed target driven culture had led in some cases to stultification of the delivery of sport policy at local level' (Phillpots *et al.*, 2010: 9). The partnership approach was also considered problematic in that:

> Several respondents also highlighted how CSPs were in a 'catch-22' situation in which they were required to serve both the needs of their sub-region and partner organizations, whilst also having to achieve nationally defined PSA [Public Service Agreement] targets and KPIs as a condition of their funding by Sport England.
>
> (Phillpots *et al.*, 2010: 9)

The performance based system of funding enacted by Sport England also brought with it penalties for failure to deliver agreed outcomes, an especially problematic situation for CSPs who were virtually totally dependent on Sport England funds:

> Government imposed targets and the power of Sport England to punish sport agencies by withholding funding on the basis of their performance was indicative of the fiscal control exerted over CSPs, whose existence and viability was heavily reliant on their patronage.
>
> (Phillpots *et al.*, 2010: 9)

Phillpots *et al.* (2010: 13) argued that in contrast to other aspects of government activity or policy contexts, where 'the state's ability to determine and deliver policy has been eroded', the example of CSPs represent exactly the opposite. They concluded that CSPs are not autonomous agencies immune to state interference, rather they 'exist in a tightly regulated policy context in which the work of local stakeholders is regulated and indeed appears to be micromanaged by a range of government-imposed funding mechanisms such as KPI and PSA targets' (Phillpots *et al.*, 2010: 13). Further, while CSPs do illustrate how central government, via Sport England, has sought to work through a multitude of voluntary sector partners to improve the delivery of sport, they posited that the 'resource-dependent relationships that exist within the structural arrangements for County Sport Partnerships are indicative of central government's desire to reassert control over local sport delivery systems' (Phillpots *et al.*, 2010: 13). Finally, this shift towards CSPs 'to govern grassroots sport authorized government (through DCMS and the sport quango Sport England) to exercise direct control over a localized, county-based sport delivery system' (Phillpots *et al.*, 2010: 13). In contrast to other areas of government that have emphasised decentralisation, these new governance arrangements for CSPs should be considered hierarchical and a top-down approach, and in some ways a direct challenge to the ability of sport to be self-governed and directed.

Conclusion

This chapter has explored the many roles that sport governing bodies have in facilitating the delivery of sport. It has also analysed the limitations of formal governance systems in sport at both the macro level (such as regulation and enforcement challenges in federated networks) and micro level (such as regulating director behaviour and ensuring ethical standards are upheld in the governance of sport organisations). The majority of the chapter has been devoted to reviewing the relationship between sport policy and governance, in particular the increasing influence the state has over the governance of sport. This influence is apparent in how government policy has addressed (albeit very poorly) the legitimacy of sport to be self-governing, especially in the context of the European Union, the direct impacts of specific policies on the nature and efficacy of sport governance within national governing bodies and their members, and the indirect effects of governments' shift to force sport to work within highly regulated partnership arrangements to deliver sport in the context of a national policy agenda.

The jury seems still to be out on whether this increased influence of government on sport governance is positive for sport. It has certainly had its critics, especially from those within the UK sport system who have had to endure what some have described as eternal flip-flopping by government between the competing policy priorities of mass participation, elite sport and event legacies. This seems to be the great danger in relation to the implications enhanced government intervention has for the independence of sport. While government policy can change with political party ideology, ministerial whims, the need for new policy initiatives or opportunities to secure major events (i.e. London Olympics), sport will be forever subject to having its targets shifted, funding criteria changed, delivery models influenced and micro-managed, and will be required to work in partnership with non-sport organisations to assist in delivering 'non-sport' policy goals. What is clear is that we need to know more about the effects this government intervention has on the sporting experience of individuals and whether sport would still govern itself effectively if government withdrew from its interventionist treatment of sport.

28

SPORTS POLICY
AND SOCIAL CAPITAL

Eivind Å Skille

Introduction

There is a large and increasing interest – among political decision makers as well as among academic scholars – in the relationship between sport and social capital (see for example, Groeneveld, Houlihan and Ohl, 2011; Hoye and Nicholson, 2008). This interest stems mainly from these two points of departure (Houlihan and Groeneveld, 2011): (i) sport's omnipresence in society linked with the fact that sport is the voluntary organization domain with the most participants by far in many countries; and (ii) it 'is also the product of the mythology that surrounds sport and which is evident in the policy outputs of many ... organizations ... which assumes that participation in sport can generate positive outcomes' (p. 1). There has been a parallel growth in the interest in the governance of sport organizations (Houlihan and Groeneveld, 2011). This interest can be strengthened by the theoretical assumption, as the brief sketch of three influential social capital theorists will show below, that the generation of social capital is taking place outside the bounds of the governance of states.

The popularity of the term social capital, its adoption as a policy slogan, and governments' claims about the role of sport in building social capital is the backdrop for this paper. The aim of this paper is to evaluate attempts to implement social capital through sport. In other words, the interactive process between policy making and implementation will be put under scrutiny. The first part will comprise a discussion of the various understandings of social capital, focusing on the three most influential theorists: Coleman, Bourdieu and Putnam. The second part of the chapter will present a review of articles about sport and social capital. The final part of the chapter comprises a discussion of sport policy and social capital, examining critically the possibilities for implementation of social capital through sport.

Theories of social capital

Coleman has a rational actor approach to social capital. He conceptualizes it as 'a variety of different entities with two elements in common: they all consist of some aspect of social structures, and they facilitate certain actions of actors whether persons or corporate actors' (Coleman, 1988, p. 98). Coleman developed the concept of social capital in order to analyse the development of human capital (educational competence generated through the school system). In that respect, social capital can be seen as the use of networks and reciprocity with others that facilitate the achievement of goals that cannot be reached otherwise than through some elements of collective action. It is conceived as a means to an end (the individual's human capital).

In line with the rational actor tradition that is Coleman's point of departure, the individual's benefit of social capital is his emphasis. Nevertheless, Coleman does not deny the societal benefits of social capital. Moreover, he acknowledges that social capital may 'differ for different persons' (1994, p. 300), and that unequal distribution of social capital stems from the interplay between structure and agency. The structural dimension refers to the pattern of connections between individuals that facilitate flow of information and the possibility of establishing nurturing relationships. Sports, and sport organizations, can be examples of such structures (see for example Barros and Barros, 2005).

Bourdieu's concept of social capital developed in order to analyse (re)production of social inequalities. Bourdieu defined social capital as 'the aggregate of the actual or potential resources that are linked to possession of a durable network of more or less institutionalized relationships of mutual acquaintance and recognition' (Bourdieu, 1986, p. 248). It must be seen in relation to his other forms of capital (economic, cultural and symbolic) as an attribute for a social class or group's total stock of resources. Social capital is always connected to an institutionalized network. The potential positive outcome of membership in such a network facilitates the reciprocity that in turn generates the benefits.

A complex element of Bourdieu's theory is how social capital can be exchanged into other forms of capital. The amount of social capital that can be possessed depends on the network of connections that an individual can use for her pursuit, and the composition (the amount of each form) of capital possessed by other members of the network (Bourdieu, 1986). Bourdieu's theory considers the existence of community social networks, but at the same time treats the potential and actual resources possessed by the members of networks. These features make Bourdieu's theory relevant to sport studies, as does the fact that it recognizes the potential dark sides of social capital, for non-members of a network (see for example Tonts, 2005; Coalter, 2007a).

Although Coleman and Bourdieu are both relevant for sport studies (see for example Tonts, 2005), Putnam is the most influential theorist with regard to sport studies of social capital (see section below). Putnam operates with various definitions of social capital. In Putnam (1995b, p. 67) social capital is defined as 'features of social organization, such as networks, norms, and social trust, that facilitate coordination and cooperation for mutual benefit'. In Putnam (1998), he defines it with reference to norms and networks of civil society which in turn facilitate collective action. In Putnam (2000, p. 19) he defines social capital as 'connections among individuals – social networks and the norms of reciprocity and trustworthiness that arise from them'.

In sum, social networks, norms of reciprocity are all constitutive parts of Putnam's understanding of social capital. And the availability of social capital is correlated with the population's engagement in voluntary organizations. This focus has made his perspective much used in studies of civil society (Anheier and Kendall, 2002; Weisinger, 2005). For Putnam, social capital is a collective characteristic that is generated through reciprocity and trust among individual members of society. The level of social capital is conceived to have implications for a number of (positive) outcomes for the community, thus the more social capital there is in a community, the better off the community is.

Coleman, Bourdieu and Putnam differ in their respective theoretical approaches to social capital. Coleman (1994) focuses on the micro level and views social capital as a function of actions pursued by individuals. But he shares with Bourdieu the small-scale networks of social actors that facilitate the generation of social capital. Bourdieu (1986) uses the concept to analyse how the unequal distribution of social capital creates (and constrains) opportunities for people through social networks. Putnam (1995, 1998, 2000) has a macro-level perspective, and sees social capital as an outcome of social organizing that relates closely to the development and sustainability of interdependent trust between people in a society.

Coleman and Bourdieu emphasize individuals' potential utilization of resources in networks, while Putnam emphasizes the reciprocity of social networks, especially through civic engagement. Both Bourdieu and Putnam conceive social capital as immanent in social networks. Putnam focuses more than Bourdieu on the reciprocity as a consequence of social networks, while Coleman focuses on how this reciprocity has mutual benefits for the individual. Coleman, Bourdieu and Putnam all agree that networks are important for the generation of social capital and for its deployment. Local sport clubs are an institutionalized form of networks and of core interest for empirical studies of how social capital is developed (Skille, 2008).

Social capital in sport studies

The articles reviewed in this section were relatively widespread geographically and therefore culturally. Out of the 16 articles found, five were from Australia, three were from the United Kingdom, two were from Norway, one was from the Czech republic, one was from Madeira, two were from Canada, one was from Japan, and one was cross-national (collecting data in Milan and Melbourne). A sketch of the context and methodological approaches for each article is presented in Table 28.1. To various degrees, the articles show that social capital in sport relates to three themes: first, it is more or less obvious that social capital is about participation in sport. Second it is believed that social capital can be developed through volunteering in sport. And third, it could be hypothesized that social capital is generated through engagement in other settings surrounding sport, such as being a spectator or even an active members of a fan club etc.

Barros and Barros (2005) aimed to estimate a model for human capital compared to a model for social capital for sport administrators in their survey among professional sport administrators in sport clubs in Madeira (n = 252). As could be expected by following the theoretical approach of Coleman as sketched above, the analysis of the relative importance of human capital and social capital for sport administrator's earnings, showed that human capital was ranked first: 'sport administrators must first acquire the appropriate education and then establish social ties in order to maximize their earnings' (p. 60).

Sherry, Karg and O'May (2011) wanted to understand the attitude changes of spectators at socially associated events, and to understand how change in spectators' attitude can produce enduring social impacts, when they surveyed spectators at the Homeless World Cup in soccer, in Melbourne (2008, n = 366) and Milan (2009, n = 145). It is suggested that 'spectator attitudinal change can facilitate the behavioral outcomes which lead to the development of social capital'. And it is believed that it can 'deliver social benefits to the host community' (Sherry *et al.*, 2011, p. 122). Just over half of the attendees at the Homeless World Cup events in Melbourne and Milan reported that the particular event had changed their attitude towards homeless people. The changes were categorized into awareness, enhanced opinions and empathy.

The above studies clearly lean on the rational actor way of thinking that Coleman advocates, thus the findings will always be that social capital may be a means to another end (individual interest in general, human capital in particular). In that respect, they somewhat differ from the studies using Bourdieu or Putnam. The latter all show that social capital can be a positive outcome in itself. They also show that there may be some unintended and potentially rather negative consequences related to sport participation and sport organization.

Table 28.1 Description of reviewed articles

Author(s)	Context	Methods	Theory
Barros and Barros (2005)	Madeira	Survey among professional sport administrators in sport clubs (n = 252)	Coleman
Sherry, Karg and O'May (2011)	Melbourne and Milan	Survey among spectators at Homeless World Cup in soccer, in Melbourne 2008 (n = 366), Milan 2009 (n = 145).	Coleman
Okayasu, Kawahara and Nogawa (2010)	Japan	Survey (n = 203) among members in two types of sport clubs (comprehensive and traditional) and different residential areas (metropolitan and district).	Putnam
Spaaij and Westerbeek (2010)	Australia	Secondary analysis.	Putnam
Tonts (2005)	Australia	Interviews (n = 40) with representatives of sport clubs, local voluntary groups and local government.	Coleman, Bourdieu, Putnam
Zakus, Skinner and Edwards (2009)	Australia	Secondary analysis.	WHO's definition (p. 987)
Atherley (2006)	Australia	Case study of 25 sport clubs. Documentary analysis. Survey (n = 169) of sport club office bearers, sportspersons, spectators and service personnel. Interviews (n = 20) with governments, sport organizations.	Putnam
Harvey, Levesque and Donnelly (2007)	Canada	Survey among volunteers in two sport organizations, in two communities (urban and suburban) and two language communities (English and French) (n = 271).	Bourdieu and social network
Perks (2007)	Canada	A representative survey among adult (15 year old and older) Canadians (n = 14,724).	Putnam
Seippel (2006)	Norway	A random sample of adults were surveyed (n = 1695).	Putnam
Walseth (2008)	Norway	Interviews with second generation immigrants, all Muslim women aged 16-25 (n = 15).	Putnam
Kay and Bradbury (2009)	UK	Survey (n = 160) of and interviews (n = 10) with project participants. Interviews (n = 33) with educational and sport professionals.	Putnam
Jarvie (2003)	UK	Secondary analysis.	Coleman, Putnam; communitarian theories.
Coalter (2007a)	UK	Secondary analysis.	Coleman, Bourdieu, Putnam; citizenship theories
Numerato (2008)	Czech republic	Czech republic. Ethnography in federations.	Putnam, Bourdieu, Coleman
Hoye and Nicholson (2009)	Australia	Document analysis.	Putnam

For example, Okayasu, Kawahara and Nogawa (2010) investigated the generation of social capital in sport clubs, on the basis of the type of sport clubs and the location of sport clubs, by a survey (n = 203) among members in two types of sport clubs (comprehensive and traditional) and different residential areas (metropolitan and district) in Japan. Drawing on Putnam, they found differences in the production of social capital, dependent on the type of sport club. Comprehensive sport clubs, which include several sport activities as well as more cultural activities, and have multi-generational members and aim to accommodate everybody, create more social capital than do traditional sport clubs with one sport activity only. Also, the location of a sport club (being in a more community-based residential area instead of a more city-like area) may help explain differences, in terms of an increased level in its ability to create social capital, but the results were more ambivalent on that point.

A number of studies from Australia show positive and potentially negative issues related to sport and social capital. Spaaij and Westerbeek (2010) aimed to establish a link between the activities executed by sport business organizations and the social capital that these activities may generate. It is argued that sport business organizations to varying degrees engage in activities that are related to social responsibilities. Such activities can lead to the generation of different forms of social capital: bonding, bridging and linking. It is further argued that the organizations will, dependent on whether the sport business organization is profit or surplus oriented, exploit opportunities in different markets for social capital in order to advance their business objectives.

Tonts (2005) examined the relationship between sport participation and the creation and expression of social capital, as well as the relationship between volunteering in sport and the creation and expression of social capital, by interviewing representatives of sport clubs, local voluntary groups and local government in rural Australia (n = 40). Sport is an important arena for creation and maintenance of social capital. Participation and volunteering in sport clubs increase social capital, both in terms of bonding local people who knew each other and bridging people who were not known to each other before sport participation. There is also a dark side of the development of social capital in sport clubs: that bridging between Aboriginal and non-Aboriginal people was weak is an example of a number of cases where 'networks and bonds associated with some clubs or particular sports acted to exclude certain citizens on the basis of race, class, gender and status' (Tonts, 2005, p. 147).

Zakus, Skinner and Edwards (2009) explored the relationships between sport participation and social capital, sport volunteerism and social capital, and between sport spectatorship and social capital with data from other Australian empirical studies (secondary analysis). Australian people consider sport as an important part of their lives. Nevertheless, sport stands out as a two-edged sword. It is conceived that sport and sport organizations are playing a leading role in the development of social capital at various levels. Thus, sport and sport organizations take part in the enhancement of life in Australia. By contrast, it is underscored that sport is also an arena for exclusion, on the basis of various elements. These elements can be social, economic, cultural factors, as well as those based on ethnicity, gender, ability and location.

Atherley (2006) aimed to identify elements of social capital at local and regional levels, conducting a case study of 25 sport clubs. The case study utilized a multi methods approach, and found that local sport clubs provide for social capital in a number of ways. At a community scale level, the sport club activities promoted community identity and belonging. At a regional scale level, sport clubs adapted strategies of trust to regional competitors and partners. In sum, sport plays a role in the formation of bonding social capital primarily at a local or community level, while it plays a role in the formation of bridging social capital primarily at the regional level (between local communities represented by sport clubs).

Although pointing to a general positive relationship between sport (being a participant, a volunteer or a spectator) and social capital, several studies underscore some nuances. For example, the following two from Canada question the causal and predictive value of sport in relation to social capital. Harvey, Levesque and Donnelly (2007) explored the relationship between sport volunteerism and social capital, by surveying volunteers in two sport organizations in two communities (urban and suburban) and two language communities (English and French) in Canada (n = 271). Employing Bourdieu and social networks as analytical tools, they found a strong relationship between sport volunteerism and social capital. This relationship was valid also after controlling for gender, language and age. The direction of the relationship, the causality, is more uncertain. Is it volunteerism that leads to social capital, or vice versa?

Perks (2007) tested whether organized sport participation in youth predicts involvement in community activities as adults, using data from a representative survey among adult (15 years old and older) Canadians (n = 14,724). Perks (2007) applied Putnam's theoretical approach, and found that participation in organized sport as youth was positively related to community involvement as adults, but the predictive strength was weak. Moreover, the influence that youth sport participation had on adult community involvement was stable throughout the life cycle.

Seippel (2006) investigated social capital (general trust and political interest) in members of voluntary organizations including sport, using data from the Norwegian part of the John Hopkins Comparative Nonprofit Sector study (a random sample of adults, n = 1695). Employing Putnam, he found that there are significant relationships between both the indicators of social capital, generalized trust and political interest, and membership in a voluntary organization. There are significant relationships between generalized trust and being a member of a sport organization, but the relationship is stronger for members of other voluntary organizations and even stronger for those who are members of both types of voluntary organizations (sport and non-sport). The same pattern is found for political interest, but the relationships are weaker.

Walseth (2008) investigated the relationship between participation in sport clubs and development of social capital among Muslim women in Norway, and interviewed female Muslim immigrants (so-called second generation, children of immigrants themselves born in Norway) aged 16–25 (n = 15). She found that participation in sport clubs develops both bonding and bridging social capital. Through participation in sport clubs, Muslim women in Norway bond with people they know or know of and develop a community of similarity. Participation in sport clubs may also develop bridging relationships. These are weaker but sometimes necessary for information.

Kay and Bradbury (2009) examined whether involvement in a programme for sport volunteering developed skills that would lead to the creation of social capital in young people in the UK. A structured programme for youth volunteers was investigated by survey (n = 160) and interviews (n = 10) with project participants, as well as interviews (n = 33) with educational and sport professionals. Applying Putnam, Kay and Bradbury (2009) found that sport volunteerism can be a mechanism for developing skills and experience for young people that can lead to the creation of social capital. The authors are clear in relation to criticisms about whether sport can help develop socially good outcomes, and hold that it can. At the same time, they acknowledge that there are many factors, personal and structural, that may influence the creation of social capital.

I will end this review by presenting four out of the 16 reviewed articles that most specifically treat sport policy. Jarvie (2003) examined the relationships between sport and sport policy ideals related to communitarianism, social policy and civic society, by discussing cases (examples drawn from other empirical studies) of relationships between community and local sport clubs. Jarvie (2003) found that it is unrealistic to use the concept of social capital without taking into account ownership, obligations and stakeholders of sport organizations (sport clubs). Sport may contribute to the generation of social capital, but at the same time there are examples of how sport does not do so. It is argued 'that it is unrealistic to expect sport to be totally responsible for sustaining a sense of community or citizenship or even reinforce notions of social capital' (Jarvie, 2003, p. 152).

Coalter (2007a) explored the nature of sport's presumed contribution to the development of social capital through secondary analysis and with the UK context as the point of departure. Coalter (2007a) holds that it is unclear what the contribution of sport clubs can be in the creation of social capital. The national level policy makers underestimate the influence of the voluntary sector in relation to the possibility of developing social capital. In that respect, three policy questions are identified: first, it could be questioned what type of social capital is developed in what type of sport club and in what community (cf. Seippel, 2006; Okayasu *et al.*, 2010); second, what is the nature of the process generating social capital? Third, if social capital is generated in sport settings, does it have a wider societal role? In addition to the very conditional contribution of a sport club's contribution to the creation of social capital for its insiders, there is much exclusion and marginalization related to the very existence of an 'isolated' unit such as a sport club.

Numerato (2008) explored civic engagement in three Czech sport federations (football, handball and sailing), through ethnographic work including participant and non-participant observation, interviews and documentary analysis. It was found that civic engagement in sport associations may result in a societal well-being on the basis of democratic governance. On the other hand, it does also 'contribute to the creation of negative "vibrations"' (p. 31) that stem from the interaction between organizational bodies at national and local levels. Barriers (lack of social capital such as trust and reciprocity) in the relationship between national and local levels of sport organizations undermine the efficiency of sport governing bodies. Thus the negative vibrations make it difficult to get the policy made at the top implemented through the grass-roots.

Hoye and Nicholson (2009) analysed how the concept of social capital and similar terms are manifested and transferred in government sport policy in Australia, by scrutinizing political and non-political institutions through qualitative document analysis of policy statements in five states of Australia. With a perspective drawing on Putnam they found that policy makers at a state level tend to make a number of unfounded assumptions about the positive and causal relationship between sport and social capital. The beliefs seeded in government policies are easily transmitted to other institutions because of similarities between institutions of various sectors and at different levels.

Social capital and sport policy – concluding discussion

The findings from the review above can be categorized into three groups. First, a majority of the studies reveal a positive attitude towards the relationship between sport – whether for participants, volunteers or spectators – and the generation of social capital. Although the outcome in terms of social capital forms or definitions differ, it seems that sport's potential as a positive contributor is independent of whether Coleman's individualist, Bourdieu's group oriented, or Putnam's societal perspective is deployed.

Second, and at the same time, most studies find nuances or uncertainties with regard to the relationship between sport and social capital. Some authors question the direction or causal relationship between the correlation between sport involvement and social capital (Harvey *et al.*, 2007; Perks, 2007). Could it be that people with much social capital play sports, rather than it being the sport that gives them this social capital? Others find that social capital is best developed in sport clubs where there are many foci other than sport, for example cultural activities (Okayasu *et al.*, 2010), or that other voluntary organizations are better in creating social capital than sport organizations (Seippel, 2006). Why do decision makers then repeatedly point at sport organizations as a salvation solution?

Others again are more explicit when they hold that there are not only nuances in the relationship between sport and social capital, there is even a clear negative side related to it. For example, Tonts (2005) underscored that the positive outcome related to social capital through sport is conditioned by the very fact that people participate. When certain groups, such as Aboriginals in Australia are excluded from sport participation compared to other Australians, the social capital that could bridge different people becomes – or remains – weak. Or, as Walseth (2008) showed, different forms of social capital (bonding and bridging), both took place primarily within the minority community, and not necessarily between different groups of people. While Tonts (2005) and Walseth (2008) treat ethnicity, Zakus *et al.* (2009) also add elements such as social, economic, cultural, gender, ability and location factors to the list of possible exclusion mechanisms of sport.

Third, all of the reviewed papers comprising more policy oriented analyses (Jarvie, 2003; Coalter, 2007; Numerato, 2008; Hoye and Nicholson, 2009), share a scepticism towards the relationship between sport – or more precisely sport policy – and the generation of social capital. However, they differ with regard to the level of policy making they treat, and to what degree they scrutinize the relationship between policy making and implementation. Numerato's (2008) focus on efficiency of organizations is interesting in a sport management perspective, but it also addresses a more universal sociological and political question in respect of sport. There is a challenge related to the interaction between national sport organizations and local sport clubs as implementers, because people at various levels do not trust each other and have different objectives.

In that respect, Numerato (2008) revealed some limitations of a top-down way of thinking. As Hoye and Nicholson (2009) showed, the concept of social capital is established and interchanged within and across political and non-political institutions. Moreover, policy makers' naïve expectations related to the relationship between sport and social capital that are transmitted between institutions are seldom accompanied by specific aims, plans and resources (an implementation process). It is presumably taken for granted that the generation of social capital is implemented in sport clubs, without taking into account the filtering functions of the organizations between policy makers and grass-roots implementers. In order to visualize an abstract context of which policies of social capital are made and implemented, Figure 28.1 shows the relationship between policy makers at the state level and the sport clubs supposed to implement the social capital policy.

Although there are differences across countries with regard to the structure and numbers of sport organizations on national and regional levels, they all play a role as filtering actors between policy makers and implementers. Moreover, the organizations, including national sport associations, have their own policy goals which only to varying degrees overlap with the goals of the state. Another point that is illustrated in the figure, is that sport clubs may have an effect, independent of whether the work is based on state or other's policies, on the members and potentially on other citizens (if considering only the two lower boxes of Figure 28.1).

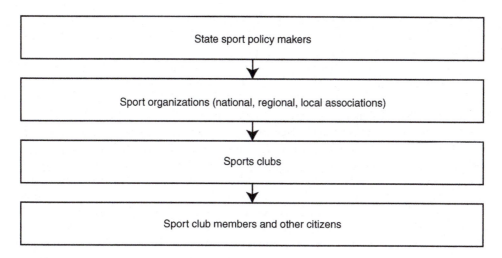

Figure 28.1 An abstraction of the relationship between state policy and grass-roots sport clubs

I have argued elsewhere that an appropriate way to analyse sport policy is to take the implementing actor/body as the point of departure (Skille, 2008). In the study of expectations from sport, for example with regard to generation of social capital, an analytical framework is needed that accounts for internal as well as external institutional elements of grass-roots sports clubs. While institutional theory is traditionally criticized for focusing on reproduction (Skille, 2008), two processes with a potential for change will be addressed. These are *bricolage* and translation (Campbell, 2004). First, 'actors often craft new institutional solutions by recombining elements in their repertoire through an innovative process of *bricolage* whereby new institutions differ from but resemble old ones' (Campbell, 2004, p. 69). Second, 'new ideas are combined with already-existing institutional practices and, therefore, are *translated* into local practice in varying degrees and in ways that involve a process very similar to *bricolage*'.

The difference between *bricolage* and translation is that the latter includes 'the combination of *new* externally given elements received through diffusion as well as old locally given ones' (Campbell, 2004, p. 80, italics in original). During translation new elements are actively imported and treated to fit into the receiving context. Despite some criticism (see Skille, 2008), the strength of translation theory is its accounting for an organization's internal processes of new combinations of internal institutional elements, *and* the import, interpretation and implementation of external institutional elements. 'The point is, for the study of sport clubs and central sport policy that, if ... central sport policy influences the practice of sport clubs, it does so through the sport clubs representatives' interpretation of the phenomenon' (Skille, 2008, p. 193). Whether the import of the idea of social capital leads to any change in the practice of sport clubs, this – according to Campbell (2004) – may depend on whether it is substantive or symbolic (pp. 69–70). While the former refers to practice, the latter is about rhetoric and political correctness; however, substantive *bricolage* and symbolic *bricolage* are not mutually exclusive.

Social capital creation through sport involvement may be – and probably is – symbolic among decision makers and somewhat substantive at the grass-roots level, simultaneously. The rhetoric and the practice are linked by legitimacy. Although, as Jarvie (2003) emphasizes, it is unrealistic to believe that sport clubs will unconditionally generate social capital, decision makers may retain this belief because it fits into a broader belief system. It can be held that the core activities of sport clubs (training and competitions), as well as societal goods such as social capital, are all elements of broader Western myths related to sport (Skille, 2010, 2011). Myths they are because they are commonly held beliefs that contribute to the interpretation of meaning related to a phenomenon – in this case sport. As long as policy makers, sport providers and sport participants all hold the same myths about sport, for example that it generates social capital, they work together (DiMaggio and Powell, 1991; Meyer and Rowan, 1991).

In that respect, the policy questions addressed by Coalter (2007a) are never necessarily taken into consideration by policy makers. National governments do not investigate how social capital is developed differently in different types of sport clubs (e.g. Seippel, 2006; Okayasu et al., 2010) because they usually treat sport as one entity. Moreover, whether social capital has a wider societal role, is not discussed. It is simply taken for granted that it does because it is part of the myth. Following this analysis, decision makers on state level should be cautious with regard to the expectations from voluntary sport organizations as implementers of government sport policy. Policy makers should include policy implementers' perspectives at an earlier stage in order to make policy realistic: substantive rather than rhetorical (Campbell, 2004). Practitioners in sport organizations could emphasize that, although competitiveness is at the core of sport activity, sport has a number of unintended (but still well-known) outcomes. One of these can be denominated social capital, which in turn can be taken into account as one element of many going into the potential wider social role for sport.

NOTES

2 Theorising the analysis of sport policy

1 There are a number of excellent introductions to the ontological and epistemological paradigms relevant to the social scientific study of sport in general and the study of policy in particular. Among the most useful are Grix (2004), Hay (2002), Van Evera (1997), Marsh and Stoker (2010) and Landman (2008).

4 Meta-evaluation, analytic logic models and the assessment of impacts of sport policies

1 There were two waves of survey collected, respectively, in 2011 and 2012. The data reported here were only drawn from the 2012 survey as it collected respondents' participation rate before the Games and after, which we believe was more appropriate to the context and well reflected the London 2012 impact (if there is any).

2 For a detailed data analysis please refer to Chen and Henry (2012).

6 The global governance of sport

1 This mention added in the IOC Code of Ethics refers mostly to section 4 of the BUPs, although responsibility is not a principle defined in the BUPs.

7 The developing role of the European Union

1 *Walrave and Koch v. Association Union Cycliste Internationale*, case C-36/74 [1974] ECR 01405.

2 *Donà v. Mantero*, case C-13/76 [1976] ECR 01333.

3 *Jean Marc Bosman v. Union Royale Belge Sociétés de Football Association*, case C-415/93 [1995] ECR I-4921.

4 The case of the Danish tennis federation and their official ball supplier (European Commission 1998b).

5 The case of the Fédération Internationale de l'Automobile (FIA) and Formula 1 (European Commission 2001a).

6 Free movement of workers, goods, capital and freedom to provide services.

8 Non-governmental organisations in Sport for Development and Peace

1 The way to comparatively refer to countries is extremely contentious in the academic and policy communities. As applied in this chapter, the 'Global South' is not just another name for the 'South' or 'the developing world'. The term denotes a community of people at different geographical locations who experience a common set of problems – problems that emanate, by and large, from deep inequities of power within and between nations (see UNDP, 2004).
2 EduSport (Education through Sport) Foundation is a Zambian registered indigenous SDP NGO founded by the author in 1999.
3 Used here to depict the way of life in an organisation.

10 Multiculturalism and federal sport policy in Canada

1 The study was funded by the Social Sciences and Humanities Research Council of Canada.
2 Capacity refers to 'the essential components of the [sport] system required to achieve the sport participation and excellence goals of this policy – such as coach/instructor education, facilities, sport medicine, sport science, research and the use of technology – to meet the needs of athletes/participants' (Sport Canada, 2002, p. 18).
3 Interaction refers to the 'increase[d] collaboration, communication, and cooperation amongst the partners in the sport community, government and the private sector, which in turn will lead to a more effective Canadian sport system' (Sport Canada, 2002, p. 19).
4 We would like to acknowledge that we agree with Coakley and Donnelly's (2009) criticism of Canada's official use of the term 'visible minority'. They point out that Ukrainian immigrants to Canada are not a visible minority because their skin colour is white, while black Jamaican immigrants fall under this label because of their skin colour. It is this type of language that contributes to racial stereotyping because whiteness becomes the taken-for-granted standard by which everyone else is compared.
5 The Canadian Sport Policy was renewed in 2012 (Sport Canada, 2012). Like the original 2002 policy document, the 2012 policy identifies the importance of inclusion, diversity and the integration of new Canadians through sport participation. The 2012 Canadian Sport Policy even calls for partnerships with non-sport partners including agencies operating in the areas of citizenship and immigration.

11 European models of sport

1 It should be noted that the VOCASPORT Project findings relate to the sports policy systems as they stood in 2004. Nevertheless, this provides an insightful basis for the discussion of policy change.
2 The 98 interviews covered either aspects of the social network analysis exclusively or the relationship between the SNA and the other two interventions.
3 Although the interviews focused on all three interventions employed, commentary is restricted here to the implications of the social network analysis.
4 A Local Area Agreement (LAA) in the UK was a three-year agreement between central government and a local area working through its Local Strategic Partnership. The agreement represented a set of improvement targets which local entities committed themselves to achieving with a delivery plan setting out what each partner is intending to do to achieve those targets. The targets were set to reflect the vision, priorities and challenges set out in the ten-year vision statement, the Sustainable Community Strategy which was required by national government. The Coalition Government abandoned LAAs in 2010.
5 The PESSCL (Physical Education School Sport Club Links) strategy introduced in 2002 set a target for every child to take part in a minimum of two hours PE and School Sport per week by 2010. This was increased to a target of three hours per week with the introduction of the PESSYP strategy (Physical Education and Sport Strategy for Young People) in 2008 to supplant PESSCL. The system involved detailed monitoring of pupil sporting activity and school policy delivery.

12 Globalisation, sport policy and China

1 The 'One Protocol and Two Licences' policy was one approach the Chinese government adopted to attempt to force the Jia A and Jia B clubs to not only put more resources into their reserve teams instead

of recruiting talent from other domestic clubs, but also to give up their leagues' main commercial rights, including broadcasting, advertising and sponsorship.

2 The Games of the New Emerging Forces (GANEFO) were the games set up by Indonesia in late 1962 as a counter to the Olympic Games. The PRC was GANEFO's main supporter. The PRC's objective was to use GANEFO to help develop sport in Asia and Africa and combat the 'forces of imperialism and sports organisations manipulated by imperialist countries' (Fan and Xiong, 2003: 330).

3 China's involvement in the Olympic Movement can be traced back to the 1920s when Mr Wang Zhenting, a high-ranking diplomat and sports leader under the government of the Republic of China (ROC), was selected as the first Chinese IOC member in 1922. China's National Amateur Athletic Federation (CNAAF) was recognised by the IOC as the Chinese Olympic Committee. Before 1949, China under the ROC participated in the 1932 Los Angeles, 1936 Berlin and 1948 London Olympics. In 1949 most of the Chinese Olympic Committee members fled to Taiwan with the ROC government, but maintained contact with the IOC and claimed jurisdiction over Olympic affairs both for the mainland and Taiwan. However, the ROC's claim was challenged by the PRC, since the CNAAF was still based in Nanjing. It was recognised by the PRC government, and renamed in October 1949 as All-China Sports Federation (ACSF) (*Zhonghu quanguo tiyu zonghui*), and claimed jurisdiction over all Chinese Olympic activities. However, both federations were affiliated to the corresponding international federation, and both consequently sought recognition from the IOC (Hwang, 2002: 155; Fan and Xiong, 2003: 320).

14 Sport and media policy

1 'Listed events' are those events that are listed by a government as part of 'anti-siphoning' (or similar) regulations. These events are often considered of such national importance or significance that they should be able to be viewed on free-to-air television, to which the vast majority of the population has access. A government lists events so that pay or cable television providers are unable to have exclusive broadcast rights, which would prevent a significant proportion of the population from viewing the event.

16 Methodologies for identifying and comparing success factors in elite sport policies

1 Flanders is the northern, Dutch-speaking part of Belgium (6.3 million inhabitants), Wallonia the southern, French- and German-speaking part (4.0 million inhabitants). In Belgium the Flemish community (Flanders) and the French/German speaking community (Wallonia) have separate sport policies at each level, from local to national (including three separate ministers of sport). Apart from the Olympic Committee (Belgisch Olympisch en Interfederaal Comité), whose main task is to select athletes for the Olympic Games, there is no national (federal) policy or structure for sport, nor are there expenditures on sport at federal level. Therefore Flanders and Wallonia are seen in this research as if they are two distinct nations. It was an established fact that policy analysis for Belgium as a nation could not be determined by summing both regions.

21 Sport development and community development

1 For capacity building, Eade (1997) offers a respected overview and Verity (2007) provides a fulsome overview of the literature; also, see Adams (2008) in relation to sports development. Plant (1974) and Taylor (2003) give a flavour of the community development literature, while Pedlar (1996) and Perks (2007) provide two examples of application to sport and leisure fields. It is important to note that social capital should not be confused with community development; clearly the former is important for the latter to occur, but they are separate and distinct concepts.

2 Many sophisticated accounts of social capital can be found in the plethora of literature that exists on social capital, including Bartkus and Davis (2009), Lewandowski (2006), Field (2003), Johnston and Percy-Smith (2003), Baron, Field and Schuller (2000). For accounts of social capital that focus on sport and sport development policy, see for example Adams (2011b), Nicholson and Hoye (2008), Coalter (2007a), Blackshaw and Long (2005).

3 Among the organisations that have not been considered are those from the private sector. Although some private sector organisations are involved in sport and community development, such organisations are less common in comparison with those from public and voluntary sectors (Hylton and Totten, 2008).

4 For overviews of modernisation, see Finlayson (2003), Pratchett (2004) and Coates (2005) – each of which is presented within its political context. Modernisation and sport is covered in many contexts, but see Houlihan and Green (2009), who examine two major national sport agencies in the UK, Adams (2011a), who investigates tensions between modernisation and mutual aid at the grass-roots level, and Green (2007a), who examines the governance and operation of sport under modernised conditions.

5 The Coalition Government came about as a result of the 2010 general election. The major partner is the Conservative party, led by Prime Minister David Cameron, together with the Liberal Democrats, led by Deputy Prime Minister Nick Clegg. These two political parties secured between them almost 60 per cent of the vote.

6 Big Society, according to Cabinet Office minister Francis Maude, is a reaction to the failure of the 'big government' of the previous government and involves clear aspects of localism in mobilising the British heritage of civil society and social action (2010). The key drivers for the Coalition Government in achieving a 'Big Society' are consequently volunteering, philanthropy and a desire to, in the words of the current Prime Minister; connect 'private capital to investment in social projects' (Cameron, 2010).

22 Sport and urban regeneration

1 Those five countries (Brazil, Russia, India, China and South Africa) are colloquially known as BRICS and represent a target market for hosting sporting events in the coming decade.

2 Moore offers interesting insights into the evaluation of the impacts of the National Football Museum on the city of Preston, UK. In addition to the economic and social impacts on this area, the Museum has also helped to change the image of this industrial town and to be awarded city status. As Moore notes, the 'the presence of the National Football Museum in Preston was a significant factor in the city being awarded City status, as part of the Golden Jubilee celebrations of Her Majesty the Queen in 2002. Preston was chosen ahead of 25 other major English towns' (2008: 458).

3 Drawing on the North American experience, Chapin (2004) considers three physical indicators to measure whether or not a sport project has contributed to achieving its development goals: if the project has contributed (a) to the reuse of existing building or spaces, (b) to promoting new construction within the surrounding district or nearby areas and (c) to creating a new entertainment or sports district. Without leaving the North American experience, architects such as John et al. (2007) point to the case of Baltimore as a good example of integrating sport and urban regeneration after using the new Oriole Park at Camden Yards to regenerate the south side of the city's waterfront, while others such as Baade's (1996) study of Chicago and Rosentraub et al.'s (1994) study of Indianapolis claim a relatively small impact of using sport as a development strategy.

4 A considerable number of contributions have been published as special issues of journals on urban studies on this topic, such as *Urban Affairs Review* (vol. 18, no. 1, 1996, Urban Policy Forum: Professional Sport and Economic Development), *Urban Studies, Journal of Urban Affairs, International Journal of Urban and Regional Research* or *European Planning Studies* (vol. 10, no. 7, 2002; the whole issue is devoted to Urban Regeneration and Sports Stadia). There is a gradual impetus towards the development of literature in this field by sport management (e.g. the *Journal of Sport Management*, vol. 22, no. 4 and no. 5, 2008 on Special Sport Events) or more recently broader social analysis (*Sport in Society*, vol. 13, 2010, which deals with Sport in the City), cultural studies and policy (e.g. the *International Journal of Culture Policy*, vol. 14, no. 4, 2008) or sociological journals (e.g. *The Sociological Review*, vol. 54, 2006). The growing interest in the connections between sport and cities by academics, practitioners and politicians has also motivated the running of major conferences dedicated to this field. As such, one of the first conferences was *Sport in the City: Culture, economic and political considerations* in Memphis in November 1996, followed by the Second *Sport in the City* conference in 1998 in Sheffield and in 2005 the *First European Capital of Sport Conference Sport and Urban Development* in Rotterdam, or in 2007 the *Sport in the City* symposium in Dunedin, New Zealand in 2007 (Sam and Hughson, 2010, 2011).

5 Japan spent more than $4 billion and South Korea spent $2 billion on an extensive stadium-building programme: 20 for the 2002 World Cup new stadia that were expected to enhance economic activity and significant transformations in the 20 host cities. Four years later, Germany built five new stadia and upgraded another six stadia, including the Olympianstadion of Berlin, to host the 2006 World Cup. In

terms of capital costs, both processes demanded great funds; more than €1,400 million was spent. Likewise, Euro 2004 contributed greatly to stadia development in Portugal after the construction of ten stadia and the upgrading of a further three, with an overall cost of €650 million.

6 In the 2011 Spanish General Elections, the Conservative party gained an absolute majority in the national parliament. Mayor Ruiz Gallardón (who was behind the Madrid 2012, 2016 and 2020 bids) left the Madrid City Council to become the Minister of Justice.

7 Interview at www.rtve.es/deportes/20110713/gallardon-confirma-candidatura-madrid-jjoo-2020/447320.shtml (accessed 12 September 2011).

8 Six cities have been accepted by IOC as applicants for the 2020 Olympic bidding process. It is worth mentioning that the current applicant cities all have in common that they have failed bids in recent years: Doha and Baku (failed bids for the 2016 Games), Istanbul (four failed bids for the 2000, 2004, 2008 and 2012 Games), Tokyo (held the 1964 Olympic Games, but failed bid for the 2016 Games), Madrid (three failed bids for the 1972, 2012, 2016 Games) and Rome (held the 1960 Olympic Games, but failed bid for the 2004 Games). However, owing to the economic climate, Italy's Prime Minister Mario Monti has withdrawn Rome's bid to host the 2020 Olympic Games, saying the country's economic concerns make such a financial commitment 'irresponsible'.

23 Methodologies for evaluating the use of sport for development in post-conflict contexts

1 The sense of coherence (SOC) is a central element in the Salutogenesis model of Antonovsky (1987). It can be considered as a cognitive–affective component of perception and valuation (i.e. of the state of tension and available resources, expressing ones' fundamental position and attitude towards oneself, the happenings, life events and the world).

2 DePaz stands for Deporte y Educación para la Paz, which means Sport and Education for Peace.

24 Feminist analysis of sport policy

1 Sport New Zealand is the government funding body for sport in NZ. From 2002–2012 it was called Sport and Recreation NZ (SPARC).

25 A post-colonial approach to sport policy

1 The Algerian national team was formed during the Algerian revolution, in clandestine circumstances, in 1958 in Tunisia.

2 There is growing competition for such activities coming from the Arabian Peninsula. We can cite for instance the link between Manchester United Academy and Dubai Sport City; the opening, in partnership with Abu Dhabi's Baniyas Holding, of Real Madrid Foundation for Social Sports Academy in the UAE; Real Madrid will even have its own island by 2015 in the Emirate of Ras Al Khaimah in the UAE. There is also the ASPIRE zone in Qatar, which is becoming an attractive destination for European clubs for their pre- and mid-season preparations and branding compaigns. Having understood the importance of attracting major football clubs for the branding of the country and for public relations, Algeria wants also to have its own Real Madrid Academy. To this end an agreement between the Algerian Ministry of Youth and Sport and Real Madrid Foundation was signed in 2011.

27 Sport governance

1 In 2009 regional office staffing of Sport England was greatly reduced and regional boards were disbanded.

REFERENCES

Abbassi, D. (2007). Sport et usages politiques du passé dans la Tunisie des débuts du XXIe siècle. *Politique et sociétés*, *26*(2–3), 125–142.

Abend, G. (2008) The meaning of 'theory'. *Sociological Theory*, *26*(2), 173–199.

Abercrombie, N., Hill, S. and Turner, B. S. (2000) *The Penguin Dictionary of Sociology*. London: Penguin Books.

Activcity (2011) Sport and physical activity in Edinburgh. Available: www.activcity.info/info/1/activcity (accessed 24 January 2011).

Adam, D. (2007) Les langues officielles et la participation des athlètes francophones dans le système sportif canadien. In J. P. Augustin and C. Dallaire (Eds) *Jeux, sports et francophonie: L'exemple du Canada* (pp. 27–50). Talence, France: Maison des Sciences de l'Homme d'Aquitaine.

Adams, A. (2008) Building organisational/management capacity for the delivery of sports development. In V. Girginov (Ed.) *Management of Sports Development* (pp. 203–224). London: Butterworth-Heinemann.

Adams, A. (2011a) Sports development and social capital. In B. Houlihan and M. Green (Eds) *Handbook of Sports Development* (pp. 72–86). London: Routledge.

Adams, A. (2011b) Sport and social capital in England. In M. Groeneveld, B. Houlihan and F. Ohl (Eds) *Social Capital and Sport Governance in Europe* (pp. 85–107). London: Routledge.

Alberts, H. (2009) Berlin's failed bid to host the 2000 Summer Olympic Games: Urban development and the improvements of sports facilities. *International Journal of Urban and Regional Research*, *33*(2), 502–516.

Albrow, M. (1996) *The Global Age*. Cambridge: Polity Press.

Alcock, P. (2010) Building the Big Society: A new policy environment for the third sector in England. *Voluntary Sector Review*, *1*(3), 379–389.

Alexander, T., Thibault, L. and Frisby, W. (2008) Avoiding separation: Sport partner perspectives on a long-term inter-organisational relationship. *International Journal of Sport Management and Marketing*, *3*(3), 263–280.

Al-Tauqi, M. S. (2003) Olympic solidarity: Global order and the diffusion of modern sport between 1961–2003. PhD. Loughborough: Loughborough University.

Alter, C. and Murty, S. (1997) Logic modelling: A tool for teaching practice evaluation. *Journal of Social Work Education*, *33*(1), 103–117.

Alvira Martín, F. (1991) *Metodología de evaluación de programas*. Madrid: Centro de Investigaciones Sociológicas (CIS).

Alvira Martín, F. (1997) *Metodología de evaluación de programas: un enfoque práctico*. Buenos Aires: Lumen/ Humanitas.

Amara, M. (2012) *Sport, Politics and Society in the Arab World*. London: Palgrave Macmillan.

Amara, M. and Henry, I. (2004) Between globalization and local 'modernity': The diffusion and modernization of football in Algeria. *Soccer and Society*, *5*(1), 1–26.

Amara, M., Aquilina, D., Henry, I. and PMP Consultants (2004) *Education of Elite Young Sportspersons in Europe*. European Commission, Brussels: DG Education and Culture.

Amara, M., Henry, I., Liang, J. and Uchiumi, K. (2005) The governance of processional soccer: Five case studies – Algeria, China, England, France and Japan. *European Journal of Sport Science*, *5*, 189–206.

Amendola, G. (2000) *La ciudad postmoderna* [*The postmodern city*]. Madrid: Celeste Ediciones.

Amselle, J. I. (2006) The world inside out: What is at stake in deconstructing the west? *Social Anthropology*, *14*(2), 183–193.

Ander-Egg, E. (1990) *Repensando la investigación-acción participativa*. Vitoria-Gasteiz: Departamento de Trabajo y Seguridad Social del Gobierno Vasco.

Andersen, J. S. (2007) Towards a global coalition for good governance in sport. *Play the Game* Press Release, 26 January. Available: www.playthegame.org/knowledge-bank/articles/towards-a-global-coalition-for-good-governance-in-sport-1096.html (accessed 19 April 2011).

Anderson, B. (1991) *Imagined Communities: Reflections on the origins and spread of nationalism*. London: Verso.

Andreff, W. (2007) New perspectives in sports economics: A European view. In M.-L. Klein and M. Kurscheidt (Eds) *Neue Perspektiven ökonomischer Sportforschung*. Schorndorf: Hofmann.

Anheier, H. and Kendall, J. (2002) Interpersonal trust and voluntary organizations: Examining three approaches. *British Journal of Sociology*, *53*(3), 343–362.

Antonovsky, A. (1987) *Unraveling the Mystery of Health: How people manage stress and stay well*. San Francisco, CA: Jossey-Bass.

Aquilina, D. (2009) Degrees of success: Negotiating dual career paths in elite sport and university education in Finland, France and the UK. PhD. Loughborough: Loughborough University.

Aquilina, D. (2013) A study of the relationship between elite athletes' educational development and sporting performance. *International Journal of the History of Sport*, *30*(4), 374–392.

Aquilina, D. and Henry, I. (2010) Elite athletes and university education in Europe: A review of policy and practice in higher education in the European Union Member States. *International Journal of Sport Policy and Politics*, *2*(1), 25–47.

Arai, S. and Pedlar, A. (2003) Moving beyond individualism in leisure theory: A critical analysis of concepts of community and social engagement. *Leisure Studies*, *22*(3), 1–18.

Archer, M. (1995) *Realist Social Theory: The morphogenetic approach*. Cambridge: Cambridge University Press.

Armstrong, G. (2004) The lords of misrule: Football and the rights of the child in Liberia, West Africa. *Sport in Society*, *7*(3), 473–502.

Arnaut, J. L. (2006) *Independent European Sport Review 2006*. Brussels: UK Presidency of the European Union.

Ashworth, K., Cebulla, A., Greenberg, D. and Walker, R. (2004) Meta-evaluation: Discovering what works best in welfare provision. *Evaluation*, *10*(2), 193–216.

Atherley, K. M. (2006) Sport, localism and social capital in rural Western Australia. *Geographical Research*, *44*(4), 348–360.

Atkinson, R. and Moon, G. (1994) *Urban Policy in Britain: The city, the state and the market*. Basingstoke: Macmillan.

Australian Broadcasting Authority (2001) *Investigation into Events on the Anti-Siphoning List*. Sydney: Australian Broadcasting Authority.

Australian Competition and Consumer Commission (2003) *Emerging Market Structures in the Communications Sector*. Canberra: Commonwealth of Australia.

Australian Productivity Commission (2000) *Broadcasting: Inquiry Report*. Canberra: Commonwealth of Australia.

Australian Sports Commission (2005) *Governing Sport: The role of the board – A good practice guide for sporting organisations*. Canberra, Australia: Australian Sports Commission.

Auweele, Y. vanden (2010) Challenging modern Sport's moral deficit: Towards fair trade, corporate social responsibility and good governance in sport. *Journal of Community and Health Sciences*, *5*(2), 1–9.

Avice, E., Barget, E., Breuer, C., Chavinier, S., Fonteneau, M., Gouget, J. J., et al. (2011) *Analysis of the Internal Market Barriers to the Funding of Grassroot Sports in the EU*. Paris, Brussels, Cologne: Internal Report.

Avineri, S. and de-Shalit, A. (Eds) (1992) *Communitarianism and Individualism*. Oxford: Oxford University Press.

Baade, R. (1996) Professional sports as catalysts for metropolitan economic development. *Journal of Urban Affairs*, *18*(1), 1–18.

Baade, R. and Dye, R. (1988) Sports stadiums and area development: A critical review. *Economic Development Quarterly*, *2*(3), 267–275.

Baade, R. and Matheson, V. (2000) An assessment of the economic impact of the American Football Championship, the Super Bowl, on host communities. *Reflects et Perspectives*, *39*(2–3), 35–46.

Bacchi, C. (2000) Policy as discourse: What does it mean? Where does it get us? *Discourse: Studies in the Cultural Politics of Education*, *21*(1), 45–57.

Bacchus, A. (2009) Current projects, upcoming events and how UK trade and investment sector groups can help companies to promote themselves to overseas venues and tier 1 contract winners.

In *Proceedings of the Global Sports Events: Business Opportunities for UK Companies Conference.* Belfast: Invest Northern Ireland.

Bailey, R. (2005) *Evaluating the Relationship between Physical Education, Sport and Social Inclusion.* London: Routledge.

Baimbridge, M. (1998) Outcome uncertainty in sporting competition: The Olympic Games 1896–1996. *Applied Economics Letters, 5*(3), 161–164.

Baldus, A., Huber, G., Pfeifer, K. and Schüle, K. (2007) Qualitätsmodell für die Medizinische Rehabilitation. *Bewegungstherapie und Gesundheitssport, 23*(1), 6–18.

Baldwin, R. and Cave, M. (1999) *Understanding regulation: Theory, strategy and practice.* Oxford: Oxford University Press.

Bale, J. and Moen, O. (1995) *The Stadium and the City.* Keele: Keele University Press.

Ball, S. J. (1993) What is policy? Texts, trajectories and toolboxes. *Discourses, 13*(2), 10–17.

Banda, D. (2010) Zambia: Government's role in colonial and modern times. *International Journal of Sport Policy, 2*(2), 237–252.

Bank of Spain (2011) *Boletín Estadístico (Statistic Report).* Banco de España, Madrid.

Baron, S., Field, J. and Schuller, T. (Eds) (2000) *Social Capital: Critical perspectives.* Oxford: Oxford University Press.

Barros, C. P. and Barros, C. D. (2005) The role of human and social capital in the earnings of sports administrators: A case study of Madeira island. *European Sport Management Quarterly, 5*(1), 47–62.

Bartkus, V. O. and Davis, J. H. (Eds) (2009) *Social Capital: Reaching out, reaching in.* Cheltenham: Edward Elgar.

Baumgartner, F. R. and Jones, B. D. (1993) *Agendas and Instability in American Politics.* Chicago, IL: University of Chicago Press.

Bayle, E., Durand, C. and Nikonoff, L. (2008) Organisation and evolution of the French elite sport 'model'. In B. Houlihan and M. Green (Eds) *Comparative Elite Sport Development: Systems, structures and public policy* (pp. 145–164). London: Butterworth–Heinemann.

BBC (2009) Legal threat to anti-doping code. 22 January. Available: http://news.bbc.co.uk/sport1/hi/front_page/7844918.stm (accessed 19 June 2012).

BBC (2010) Muslim and Sikh boxers fight to overturn beard ban. BBC News, 13 January. Available: http://news.bbc.co.uk/2/hi/8451615.stm (accessed 13 April 2011).

Beacom, A. and Levermore, R. (2008) International policy and sport-in-development. In V. Girginov (Ed.) *Management of Sports Development* (pp. 109–126). Oxford: Butterworth-Heinemann.

Beamish, R. and Ritchie, I. (2004) From chivalrous 'brothers-in-arms' to the eligible athlete: Changed principles and the IOC's banned substance list. *International Review for the Sociology of Sport, 39*(4), 355–371.

Becker, G. and Murphy, K. M. (2001) *Social Economics: Market behavior in a social environment.* Cambridge, MA: Harvard University Press.

Beckett, A. H. and Cowan, D. A. (1979) Misuse of drugs in sport. *British Journal of Sports Medicine, 12*(4), 185–194.

Ben El-Caïd, S. (2004) La Coupe du Monde de football au secours du Maroc. *Confluences Méditerranée, 50*(summer), 75–78.

Beneworth, P. and Dauncey, H. (2010) International urban festivals as a catalyst for governance capacity building. *Environment and Planning C, 28,* 1083–1100.

Bensimon, E. M. and Marshall, C. (1997) Policy analysis for postsecondary education: Feminist and critical perspectives. In C. Marshall (Ed.) *Feminist Critical Analysis II: A perspective from post-secondary education* (pp. 1–21). London: Falmer Press.

Bensimon, E. M. and Marshall, C. (2003) Like it or not: Feminist critical policy analysis matters. *The Journal of Higher Education, 74*(3), 337–342.

Benson, J. K. (1982) Networks and policy sectors: A framework extending inter-organisational analysis. In D. Rogers and D. Whitton (Eds) *Inter-organisational Coordination* (pp. 137–176). Iowa, IA: Iowa University Press.

Bercovitz, K. (1998) Canada's Active Living policy: A critical analysis. *Health Promotion International, 13*(4), 319–328.

Bercovitz, K. (2000) A critical analysis of Canada's 'Active Living': Science or politics? *Critical Public Health, 10*(1), 19–39.

Berger, G. and Peerson, A. (2009) Giving young Emirati women a voice: Participatory action research on physical activity. *Health and Place, 15*(1), 117–124.

Bergqvist, C., Blandy, T. O. and Sainsbury, D. (2007) Swedish state feminism: Continuity and change. In J. Outshoorn and J. Kantola (Eds) *Changing State Feminism* (pp. 224–245). Basingstoke: Palgrave Macmillan.

Bergsgard, N., Houlihan, B., Mangset, P., Nødland, S. and Rommetvedt, H. (2007) *Sport Policy: A comparative analysis of stability and change*. London: Butterworth-Heinemann.

Bernstein, A. (2008) The social life of regulation in Taipei City Hall: The role of legality in the administrative bureaucracy. *Law and Social Inquiry, 33*(4), 925–954.

Bette, K.-H. and Schimank, U. (2006) *Die Dopingfalle: Soziologische Betrachtungen [The Doping Trap: Sociological Considerations]*. Bielefeld: Transcript Verlag.

Bevir, M. and Rhodes, R. (2003) *Interpreting British Governance*. London: Routledge.

Bevir, M. and Rhodes, R. A. W. (2011) The stateless state. In M. Bevir (Ed.) *The Sage Handbook of Governance* (pp. 203–217). London: Sage.

Bevir, M. and Richards, D. (2009) Decentring policy networks: A theoretical agenda. *Public Administration, 87*(1), 3–14.

Bhaskar, R. (1978) *A Realist Theory of Science*. Hassocks: Harvester Press.

Bhaskar, R. (1986) *Scientific Realism and Human Emancipation*. London: Verso.

Bibby, R. (1990) *Mosaic Madness: The poverty and potential of life in Canada*. Toronto, ON: Stoddart.

Bickenbach, F. and Liu, W. H. (2010) *The Role of Personal Relationships for Doing Business in the GPRD, China: Evidence from Hong Kong Electronics SMEs*. Kiel: Kiel Institute for the World Economy.

Bickman, L. (1989) Barriers to the use of program theory. *Evaluation and Program Planning, 12*(4), 387–390.

Biddle, S. J. H. and Foster, C. (2011) Health behaviour change through physical activity and sport. In B. Houlihan and M. Green (Eds) *Routledge Handbook of Sports Development* (pp. 501–516). London: Routledge.

Biddle, S., Hagger, M., Chatzisarantis, N. and Lippke, S. (2007) Theoretical frameworks in exercise psychology. In G. Tenenbaum and R. Ecklund (Eds) *Handbook of Sport Psychology* (pp. 537–559). Hoboken, NJ: John Wiley & Sons.

Bingham, L. B. (2011) Collaborative governance. In M. Bevir (Ed.) *The Sage Handbook of Governance* (pp. 386–401). London: Sage.

Bissoondath, N. (2002) *Selling Illusions: The cult of multiculturalism in Canada*. Toronto, ON: Penguin Books.

Black, D. R. (2010) The ambiguities of development: Implications for 'development through sport'. *Sport in Society, 13*(1), 121–129.

Blackshaw, T. and Long, J. (2005) What's the big idea? A critical exploration of the concept of social capital and its incorporation into leisure policy discourse. *Leisure Studies, 24*(3), 239–258.

Blaikie, N. (2010) *Designing Social Research* (2nd Edn). Cambridge: Polity Press.

Blake, M. K. (2007) Formality and friendship: Research ethics review and participatory action research. *ACME: International e-Journal for Critical Geographies, 6*(3), 411–421.

Blatter, J. (2007) Sport must retain its autonomy. *FIFA.com*, 18 January. Available: www.fifa.com/aboutfifa/federation/president/news/newsid=109957.html (accessed 5 August 2011).

Bloyce, D. and Smith, A. (2009) *Sport Policy and Development: An introduction*. London: Routledge.

Blum, U., Dudley, L., Leibbrand, F. and Weiske, A. (2005) *Angewandte Institutionenökonomik. Theorien – Modelle – Evidenz [Applied Institutional Economics. Theories – Models – Evidence]*. Wiesbaden: Gabler.

Blunt, A. and McEwan, C. (Eds) (2002) *Postcolonial Geographies*. London: Continuum.

Bogerd, J. (2010) Twee kanten van de medaille. Sleutelfiguren uit de schaatssport over de gevolgen van de ontwikkeling van merkenteams voor het topsportklimaat van het langebaanschaatsen en talentontwikkeling in het bijzonder [Two sides of the medal. Key figures in skating about the consequences of the development of branding teams for the elite sport climate and talent development in particular]. Unpublished masters thesis. Utrecht: University of Utrecht.

Bolles, R. (1996). *What Colour Is Your Parachute? A practical manual for job-hunters and career changers*. Berkeley, CA: Ten Speed Press.

Bolton, N., Fleming, S. and Elias, B. (2008) The experience of community sport development: A case study of Blaenau Gwent. *Managing Leisure, 13*(2), 92–103.

Boo, S. and Kim, M. (2010). The influence of convention center performance on hotel room nights. *Journal of Travel Research, 49*(3), 297–309.

Bootman, J. L., Rowland, C. and Wertheimer, A. I. (1979) Cost–benefit analysis. *Evaluation and the Health Professions, 2*(2), 129–54.

Bosch Reig, I. (2011) El Parque del Turia. Pulmón Verde, Deportivo y Cultural en Valencia. In J. C. Cerezo Gil, V. Mas Llorens and E. Orts López (Eds) *I Congreso Europeo de Infraestructuras Deportivas* (pp. 100–107) *(1st European Conference on Sports Facilities)*. Valencia: Ajuntament de Valencia.

Bourdieu, P. (1986) The forms of capital. In J. Richardson (Ed.) *Handbook of Theory and Research for the Sociology of Education* (pp. 241–258). New York: Greenwood.

Bourg, J.-F. and Gouguet, J.-J. (2006) Sport and globalisation: Sport as a global public good. In W. Andreff and S. Szymanski (Eds) *Handbook on the Economics of Sport* (pp. 744–754). Cheltenham: Edward Elgar.

Bourke, A. (2003) The dream of being a professional soccer player. *Journal of Sport and Social Issues, 27*(4), 399–419.

Brace-Govan, J. (2004) Weighty matters: Control of women's access to physical strength. *The Sociological Review, 52*(4), 503–532.

Bradbury, H. and Reason, P. (2001) *Handbook of Action Research: Participative inquiry and practice*. London: Sage Publications.

Bramwell, B. (1997) Strategic planning before and after a mega-event. *Tourism Management, 18*(3), 167–176.

Brandtstädter, S. (2003) With Elias in China: Civilizing process, local restorations and power in contemporary rural China. *Anthropological Theory, 3*(1), 87–105.

Braybrooke, D. and Lindblom, C. (1963) *A Strategy of Decision*. New York: Free Press.

Brent, R. J. (1996) *Applied Cost–Benefit Analysis*. Brookfield, VT: Edward Elgar.

Breuer, C. (2010) Der Beitrag des Sports zur Kommunal- und Regionalentwicklung [The contribution of sport for urban and regional development]. In W. Tokarski and K. Petry (Eds) *Handbuch Sportpolitik* (pp. 128–140). Schorndorf: Hofmann.

Breuer, C. and Hovemann, G. (2006) *Finanzierung von Sportstätten: Perspektiven der Sportvereine und Kommunen [Financing of Sport Facilities: Perspectives of sport clubs and municipalities]*. Cologne: Institut für Sportökonomie und Sportmanagement.

British Universities and Colleges Sport (2008) News Item – 55% of GB Olympic medallists come through university system. Available: www.bucs.org.uk/news.asp?section=000100010002&itemid=1741&search=55%25+of+GB+Olympic+medallists+come+through+university (accessed 23 September 2008).

British Universities and Colleges Sport (2012) Placing HE in the performance pathway: A performance analysis of the World University Games. Available: http://viewer.zmags.com/publication/9c26ceeb#/9c26ceeb/4 (accessed 13 April 2011).

Brohm, J.-M. (1978) *Sport: A prison of measured time*. London: Ink Links.

Broodryk, J. (2002) *Ubuntu: Life lessons from Africa*. Tshwane: Ubuntu School of Philosophy.

Brooks, R. V., Firth, R. G. and Sumner, N. A. (1975) Detection of anabolic steroids by radioimmunoassay. *British Journal of Sports Medicine, 9*(2), 89– 92.

Brouwers, J. (2012) Comparison of elite sport policies in tennis in Australia and Belgium. PhD working paper. Queensland: Griffith University.

Brown, G., Chalip, L., Jago, L. and Mules, T. (2002) The Sydney Olympics and Brand Australia. In N. Morgan, A. Pritchard and R. Pride (Eds) *Destination Branding: Creating the unique destination proposition* (pp. 163–185). Oxford: Butterworth-Heinemann.

Brunet, F. (1994) *Economy of the 1992 Olympic Games*. Barcelona: Centre d'Estudis Olympics, Universidad Autónoma de Barcelona.

Brush, L. D. (2003) *Gender and Governance*. New York: Altamira Press.

Bubb, S. (2011) Comment: Cuts could be the big society's banana skin. Available: www.politics.co.uk/comment-analysis/2011/02/19/comment-cuts-could-be-the-big-society-s-banan (accessed 21 February 2011).

Buisseret, T. J., Cameron, H. M. and Georghiou, L. (1995) What difference does it make? Additionality in the public support of R&D in large firms. *International Journal of Technology Management, 10*(4–5), 587–600.

Burbank, M., Andranovich, G. D. and Heying, C. H. (2001) *Olympic Dreams: The impact of mega-events on local politics*. Boulder, CO: Lynne Rienner.

Burnett, C. (2010) Sport-for-development approaches in the South African context: A case study analysis. *South African Journal for Research in Sport, Physical Education and Recreation, 32*(1), 29–42.

Bustelo, M. (2002) Meta-evaluation as a tool for the improvement and development of the evaluation function in public administrations. Paper presented at the 2002 EES Conference: *Three movements in contemporary evaluation: learning, theory and evidence*. Available: www.evaluationcanada.ca/distribution/20021010_bustelo_maria.pdf (accessed 13 April 2011).

Cabinet Office (2010) *The Compact: The Coalition Government and civil society organisations working effectively in partnership for the benefit of communities and citizens in England*. London: Cabinet Office.

Cable News Network (CNN) (2011) FIFA defends hijab ban after Iranian team forfeits Olympic qualifier. *CNN*, 7 June. Available: http://edition.cnn.com/2011/SPORT/football/06/07/football.iran.hijab.fifa/index.html (accessed 7 June 2011).

Callicott, R. (2000) The economic importance of major sports events. *Proceedings of the International Conference on the Role of Sport in Economic Regeneration*. Durham.

Cameron, J. (1996) *Trailblazers: Women who manage New Zealand sport*. Christchurch: Sports Inclined.

Cameron, D. (2010) 'Big Society' speech, Liverpool, 19 July 2010. Available: www.number10.gov.uk/news/big-society-speech (accessed 13 April 2011).

Campbell, J. L. (2004) *Institutional Change and Globalization*. Princeton, NJ: Princeton University Press.

Canada Department of Justice (1987) *Canadian Television Broadcasting Regulations*. Ottowa, Canada: Department of Justice.

Canada Department of Justice (1991) Canadian Broadcasting Act, 1991. Ottowa, Canada: Department of Justice. Available: www.laws.justice.gc.ca/en/B-9.01 (accessed 19 February 2011).

Canadian Policy Research Initiative (2005) Social capital as a public policy tool. Available: http://policyresearch.gc.ca/doclib/PR_SC_SocialPolicy_200509_e.pdf (accessed 19 February 2011).

Canadian Television Network (CTV) (2011) Hockey Canada shooting for more immigrant players. *CTV News*, 19 February. Available: www.ctv.ca/CTVNews/TopStories/20110219/hockey-canada-shooting-for-more-immigrant-players-110219 (accessed 19 February 2011).

Carrington, B. and McDonald, I. (Eds) (2009) *Marxism, Cultural Studies and Sport*. London: Routledge.

Carson, R. T. (2000) Contingent valuation: A user's guide. *Environmental Science and Technology*, *34*(8), 1413–1418.

Cashman, R. (2006) *The Bitter-Sweet Awakening: The legacy of the Sydney 2000 Olympic Games*. Petersham, NSW: Walla Walla Press.

Cave, M. and Crandall, R. (2001) Sports rights and the broadcast industry. *The Economic Journal*, *111*(469), F4–F26.

Chaker, A. N. (2004) *Good Governance in Sport: A European survey*. Strasbourg: Council of Europe Publishing.

Chalip, L. (1995) Policy analysis in sport management. *Journal of Sport Management*, *9*(1), 1–13.

Chalip, L. (1996) Critical policy analysis: The illustrative case of New Zealand sport policy development. *Journal of Sport Management*, *10*(3), 310–324.

Chalip, L. (2004) Beyond impact: A general model for sport event leverage. In B.W. Ritchie and D. Adair (Eds) *Sport Tourism: Interrelationships, impacts and issues* (pp. 226–252). Clevedon: Channel View Publications.

Chalip, L. (2005) Marketing, media, and place promotion. In J. Higham (Ed.) *Sport Tourism Destinations: Issues, opportunities and analysis* (pp. 162–176). Oxford: Butterworth-Heinemann.

Chalip, L. (2006) Towards social leverage of sport events. *Journal of Sport and Tourism*, *11*(2), 109–127.

Chalip, L., Johnson, A. and Stachua, L. (Eds) (1996) *National Sports Policies: An international handbook*. London: Greenwood Press.

Chalip, L. and Costa, C. A. (2005) Sport event tourism and the destination brand: Towards a general theory. *Sport in Society*, *8*(2), 218–237.

Chalip, L. and Leyns, A. (2002) Local business leveraging of a sport event: Managing an event for economic benefit. *Journal of Sport Management*, *16*(2), 132–158.

Chalip, L. and McGuirty, J. (2004) Bundling sport events with the host destination. *Journal of Sport Tourism*, *9*(3), 267–282.

Chalip, L., Green, B. C. and Hill, B. (2003) Effects of sport event media on destination image and intention to visit. *Journal of Sport Management*, *17*(3), 214–234.

Chambers, D. (2009) *Race Against Me: My story*. Alicante: Libros International.

Chan, G. (2006) *China's Compliance in Global Affairs: Trade, arms control, environmental protection, human rights*. Singapore: World Scientific.

Chapin, T. (2004) Sports facilities as urban redevelopment catalysts: Baltimore's Camden Yards and Cleveland's Gateway. *Journal of the American Planning Association*, *70*(2), 193–209.

Chapman, S., Byrne, F. and Carter, S. M. (2003) 'Australia is one of the darkest markets in the world': The global importance of Australian tobacco control. *Tobacco Control*, *12*(3), 1–3.

Chappelet, J.-L. (1991) *Le système olympique*. Grenoble: Presses Universitaires.

Chappelet, J.-L. (2002) 'L'Agence mondiale antidopage: un nouveau régulateur des relations internationales sportives'. *Relations Internationales*, *111*, 381–401.

Chappelet, J.-L. (2005) Une commission d'éthique pour la gouvernance du mouvement olympique. *Ethique publique*, *7*(2), 132–143.

Chappelet, J.-L. (2010) *The Autonomy of Sport*. Strasbourg: Council of Europe Publishing.

Chappelet, J.-L. (2011a) Towards better Olympic accountability. *Sport in Society*, *14*(3), 319–331.

Chappelet, J.-L. (2011b) The role of governments in the fight against corruption in sport. *Play The Game*, 18 March. Available: www.playthegame.org/news/detailed/the-role-of-governments-in-the-fight-against-corruption-in-sport-5124.html (accessed 19 April 2011).

Chappelet, J.-L. (2012) From daily management to high politics: The governance of the International Olympic Committee. In L. Robinson, P. Chelladurai, G. Bodet and P. Downward (Eds) *The Handbook of International Sport Management* (pp. 7–25). London: Routledge.

Charlton, T. (2010) 'Grow and sustain': The role of community sports provision in promoting a participation legacy for the 2012 Olympic Games. *International Journal of Sport Policy and Politics*, *2*(3), 347–366.

Chehat, F. (1993) *Le livre d'or du sport Algérien*. Algiers: ANEP.

Chelladurai, P. (2001) *Managing Organizations for Sport and Physical Activity: A system perspective*. Scotsdale, AZ: Holcomb Hathaway.

Chelladurai, P. and Chang, K. (2000) Targets and standards of quality in sport services. *Sport Management Review*, *3*(1), 1–22.

Chema, T. (1996) When professional sports justify the subsidy: A reply to Robert A. Baade. *Journal of Urban Affairs*, *18*(1), 19–22.

Chen, D. S. (2009) Changes in social organizational principles of Taiwan society. *Chang Gung Journal of Humanities and Social Sciences*, *22*(2), 247–274.

Chen, S. and Henry, I. (2012) A realist approach to policy evaluation for London 2012 Olympic legacy in a non-hosting region: A pilot study – an evaluation of the Workplace Challenge Programme. Paper presented at *The 20th EASM Conference: Sport between business and civil society*, 18–21 September, Aalborg, Denmark.

Cheng, P. P. (1988) Political clientelism in Japan: The case of 'S'. *Asian Survey*, *28*(4), 471–483.

Cheng, T. J. (2001) Transforming Taiwan's economic structure in the 20th Century. *The China Quarterly*, *165*(S1), 19–36.

Cheol, H. P. (2008) A comparative institutional analysis of Korean and Japanese clientelism. *Asian Journal of Political Science*, *16*(2), 111–129.

Cheung, A. B. L. (2011) Budgeting and finance. In M. Bevir (Ed.) *The Sage Handbook of Governance* (pp. 270–285). London: Sage.

Chien, H. C. (2008) Deconstructing money politics so as to consolidate democracy. *Taiwan Democracy Quarterly*, *5*(3), 185–192.

Chinese Professional Baseball League (2003) The logo of 14th CPBL championship. Available: www.cpbl. com.tw/news/Newsread1.asp?Nid=1734 (in Chinese) (accessed 1 March 2011).

Chomsky, N. (1999) *The Umbrella of US Power: The Universal Declaration of Human Rights and the contradictions of US policy*. Open Media Pamphlet.

Christiansen, A. V. (2011) 'The fear of getting caught is massive!': On athletes arguments for not doping. Conference paper presented at the annual meeting of the North American Society for Sport History, Austin, TX.

Christie, M., Crabtree, B. and Slee, B. (2001) An economic assessment of informal recreation policy in the Scottish countryside. *Scottish Geography Journal*, *116*(2), 125–142.

Chu, Y. H. and Lin, J. W. (2001) Political development in the twentieth century Taiwan: State-building, regime transformation and the construction of national identity. *The China Quarterly*, *165*(S1), 102–129.

Chung, C. N., Mahmood, P. I. and Mitchell, W. (2009) *Political Connections and Business Strategy: The impact of types and destinations of political ties on business diversification in closed and open political economic contexts*. Available: http://faculty.fuqua.duke.edu/~willm/bio/cv/working_papers/2007_11_PoliticalTies.pdf (accessed 1 March 2011).

Clawson, M. (1966) *Economics of Outdoor Recreation*. Washington, DC: Resources for the Future.

Coaffee, J. (2007) Urban regeneration and renewal. In J. Gold and M. Gold (Eds) *Olympic Cities: City agendas, planning and the world's games, 1896–2012* (pp. 150–164). London: Routledge.

Coakley, J. (2007) *Sports in Society: Issues and controversies*. New York: McGraw-Hill.

Coakley, J. (2011) Youth sports: What counts as 'positive development'? *Journal of Sport and Social Issues*, *35*(3), 306–324.

Coakley, J. and Donnelly, P. (2009) Race and ethnicity: Are they important in sports? In *Sports in Society: Issues and controversies* (2nd Canadian edition) (pp. 259–298). Toronto, ON: McGraw-Hill Ryerson.

Coalter, F. (2006) Sport-in-development: Process evaluation and organisational development. In Y. vanden Auweele, C. Malcolm and B. Meulders (Eds) *Sport and Development* (pp. 149–161). Leuven: Lannoo Campus.

Coalter, F. (2007a) Sports clubs, social capital and social regeneration: 'Ill-defined interventions with hard to follow outcomes'? *Sport in Society*, *10*(4), 537–559.

Coalter, F. (2007b) *A Wider Role for Sport: Who's keeping the score?* London: Routledge.

Coalter, F. (2008) Sport-in-development: Development for and through sport? In M. Nicholson and R. Hoye (Eds) *Sport and Social Capital* (pp. 39–68). Oxford: Butterworth-Heinemann.

Coalter, F. (2010) The politics of sport-for-development: Limited focus programmes and broad gauge problems? *International Review for the Sociology of Sport*, *45*(3), 295–314.

Coase, R. H. (1937) The nature of the firm. *Economia*, *4*(16), 386–405.

Coates, D. (2005) *Prolonged Labour: The slow birth of New Labour Britain.* Basingstoke: Palgrave Macmillan.

Coates, D. and Humphreys, B. R. (1999) The growth effects of sports franchises, stadia and arenas. *Journal of Policy Analysis and Management*, *18*(4), 601–624.

Coates, D. and Matheson, V. (2011) Mega-events and housing costs: Raising the rent while raising the roof? *The Annals of Regional Science*, *46*(1), 119–137.

Cochrane, A., Peck, J. and Tickell, A. (1996) Manchester plays Games: exploring the local politics of globalization. *Urban Studies*, *33*(8), 1319–1336.

COE (2005) *Recommendation Rec(2005)8 of the Committee of Ministers to Member States on the Principles of Good Governance in Sport.* Adopted by the Committee of Ministers on 20 April 2005 at the 924th meeting of the Ministers' Deputies.

Cohen, J. and Cohen. P. (1995) *Applied Multiple Regression/Correlation Analysis for the Behavioral Sciences.* Mahwah. NJ: Erlbaum Associates.

Coleman, J. (1988) Social capital in the creation of human capital. *The American Journal of Sociology*, *94*, 95–120.

Coleman, J. (1994) *Foundations of Social Theory.* Cambridge, MA: Belknap Press.

Collins, M. (1989) The economic impact of sport job generation and economic activity case studies: Bracknell and the Wirral, *Proceedings of the Sports Council's National Seminar and Exhibition*, London, pp. 21–24.

Collins, M. (2010) From 'sport for good' to 'sport for sport's sake' – not a good move for sports development in England? *International Journal of Sport Policy*, *2*(3), 367–379.

Collins, M. and Kay, T. (2003) *Sport and Social Exclusion.* London: Routledge.

Collins, M., Henry, I. and Houlihan, B. (1999) *Sport and Social Inclusion: A report to the Department for Culture, Media and Sport.* Loughborough: Loughborough University, Institute of Sport and Leisure Policy. Available: www.sportdevelopment.org.uk (accessed 11 April 2011).

Colwell, J. (1982) Quantity or quality: Non-linear relationships between extent of involvement and international sporting success. In A. O. Dunleavy, A. W. Miracle and C. R. Rees (Eds) *Studies in the Sociology of Sport* (pp. 101–118). Fort Worth, TX: Christian University Press.

Commonwealth of Australia (1992) *Broadcasting Services Act.* Canberra: Commonwealth of Australia.

Commonwealth of Australia (1999) *Shaping Up: A review of Commonwealth involvement in sport and recreation in Australia.* Canberra: Commonwealth of Australia.

Commonwealth of Australia (2004) *Broadcasting Services (Events) Notice (No. 1).* Canberra: Commonwealth of Australia.

Commonwealth of Australia (2005) *Inquiry into the provisions of the Broadcasting Services Amendment (Anti-Siphoning) Bill 2004.* Canberra: Commonwealth of Australia.

Compass (1999) *Sports Participation in Europe: A project seeking the co-ordinated monitoring of participation in sport in Europe.* London: UK Sport.

Competition Commission (1999) *British Sky Broadcasting Group Plc and Manchester United Plc: A report on the proposed merger.* London: Competition Commission.

Connell, J. P. and Kubisch, A. C. (1998) Applying a theory of change approach to the evaluation of comprehensive community initiatives: Progress, prospects, and problems. In A. Fulbright-Anderson, A. C. Kubisch and J. P. Connell (Eds) *New Approaches to Evaluating Community Initiatives* (Vol. 2, pp. 15–44). Washington, DC: The Aspen Institute.

Connell, R. W. (1990) The state, gender, and sexual politics. *Theory and Society*, *19*(5), 507–544.

Conrad, K. J. and Randolph, F. L. (1999) Creating and using logic models: Four perspectives. *Alcoholism Treatment Quarterly*, *17*(1–2), 17–32.

Conzelmann, A. and Nagel, S. (2003) Professional careers of the German Olympic athletes. *International Review for the Sociology of Sport*, *38*(3), 259–280.

Cooksy, L. J. (1999) The Meta-Evaluand: The evaluation of project TEAMS. *American Journal of Evaluation*, *20*(1), 123–136.

Cooksy, L. J., Gill, P. and Kelly, P. A. (2001) The program logic model as an integrative framework for a multimethod evaluation. *Evaluation and Program Planning*, *24*(2), 119–128.

Copper, J. F. (2009) The devolution of Taiwan's democracy during the Chen Shui-bian era. *Journal of Contemporary China*, *18*(60), 463–478.

Corbella, L. (2011) Time to change the tune on multiculturalism. *The Vancouver Sun*, 14 February, A9.

Cornwall, A. and Brock, K. (2005) What do buzzwords do for development policy? A critical look at 'participation', 'empowerment' and 'poverty reduction'. *Third World Quarterly*, *26*(7), 1043–1060.

Corry, D. and Stoker, G. (2002) *New Localism: Refashioning the centre–local relationship*. London: New Local Government Network

Council of the European Union (2008) Summary: Presidency conclusions on the Brussels European Council, Presidency, 11 and 12 December. Available: www.eu-un.europa.eu/articles/en/article_8365_en.htm (accessed 20 March 2011).

Cowie, C. and Williams, M. (1997) The economics of sports rights. *Telecommunications Policy*, *21*(7), 619–634.

Crabbe, T. and Slaughter, P. (2007) Reaching the 'hard to reach': Engagement, relationship building and social control in sport based social inclusion work. *International Journal for Sport Management and Marketing*, *2*(1–2), 27–40.

Creswell, J. W. (2009) Editorial: Mapping the field of mixed methods research. *Journal of Mixed Methods Research*, *3*(2), 95–108.

Creswell, J. W. and Plano Clark, V. L. (2007) *Designing and Conducting Mixed Methods Research*. London: Sage.

Crompton, J. L. (1995) Economic impact analysis of sports facilities and events: Eleven sources of misapplication. *Journal of Sport Management*, *9*(1), 14–35.

Crompton, J. L. (2004) Beyond economic impact: An alternative rationale for the public subsidy of the major leagues sports facilities. *Journal of Sport Management*, *18*(1), 40–58.

Crotty, M. (2003) *The Foundations of Social Research: Meaning and perspective in the research process*. London: SAGE.

Cutler, A. C. (2003) *Private Power and Global Authority: Transnational merchant law in the global political economy*. Cambridge: Cambridge University Press.

Cutler, A. C., Haufler, V. and Porter, T. (Eds) (1999) *Private Authority and International Affairs*. Albany, NY: SUNY Press.

Czarniawska-Joerges, B. (2004) Narratives of individual and organizational identities. In M. J. Hatch and M. Schultz (Eds) *Organizational Identity: A Reader* (pp. 407–435). Oxford: Oxford University Press.

DaCosta, L. and Miragaya, A. (2002) *Worldwide Experiences and Trends in Sport for all*. Oxford: Meyer & Meyer Sport.

Danermark, B., Ekstrom, M., Jakobsen, L. and Karlsson, J. (2002) *Explaining Society: Critical realism in the social sciences*. London: Routledge.

Danziger, M. (1995) Policy analysis postmodernized. *Policy Studies Journal*, *23*(3), 435–450.

Darnell, S. C. (2007) Playing with race: *Right to Play* and the production of whiteness in 'development through sport'. *Sport in Society*, *10*(4), 560–579.

Darnell, S. C. (2010) Power, politics and sport for development and peace: Investigating the utility of sport for international development. *Sociology of Sport Journal*, *27*(1), 54–75.

Daumann, F. (2008) *Die Ökonomie des Dopings* [*The Economics of Doping*]. Hamburg: Merus Verlag.

Davies, L. (2005) Not in my back yard: sport stadia location and the property market. *Area*, *37*(3), 268–276.

Davies, L. (2010) Sport and regeneration: A winning combination? *Sport in Society*, 13(10), 1438–1457.

Davies, L. (2011) Sport and regeneration: A winning combination? In M. Sam and J. Hughson (Eds) *Sport in the City: Cultural connections* (pp. 22–43). London: Routledge.

Davies, W. (2006) The governmentality of New Labour. *Institute for Public Policy Research*, *13*(4), 249–256.

De Bosscher, V. (2007) *Sports Policy Factors Leading to International Sporting Success*. Published doctoral thesis. Brussels: VUBPRESS.

De Bosscher, V., Bingham, J., Shibli, S., van Bottenburg, M. and de Knop, P. (2007) *Sports Policy Factors Leading to International Sporting Success*. Oxford: Meyer & Meyer Sport.

De Bosscher, V., Bingham, J., Shibli, S., van Bottenburg, M. and de Knop, P. (2008) A *Global Sporting Arms Race: An international comparative study on sports policy factors leading to international sporting success*. Aachen: Meyer & Meyer.

De Bosscher, V., de Knop, P. and Heyndels, B. (2003) Comparing relative sporting success among countries: Create equal opportunities in sport. *Journal of Comparative Physical Education and Sport, 3*(3), 109–120.

De Bosscher, V., de Knop, P. and van Bottenburg, M. (2009) An analysis of homogeneity and heterogeneity of elite sports systems in six nations. *International Journal of Sports Marketing and Sponsorship, 10*(2), 111–131.

De Bosscher, V., de Knop, P., van Bottenburg, M. and Shibli, S. (2006) A conceptual framework for analysing sports policy factors leading to international sporting success. *European Sport Management Quarterly, 6*(2),185–216.

De Bosscher, V., de Knop, P., van Bottenburg, M., Shibli, S. and Bingham, J. (2009). Explaining international sporting success: An International comparison of elite sport systems and policies in six nations. *Sport Management Review, 12*(3), 113–136.

De Bosscher, V., Shibli, S., van Bottenburg, M., de Knop, P. and Truyens, J. (2010) Developing a methodology for comparing the elite sport systems and policies of nations: A mixed research methods approach. *Journal of Sport Management, 24*(5), 567–600.

De Pelsmacker, P. and van Kenhove, P. (1999) *Marktonderzoek: Methoden en toepassingen [Market Research: Methods and Applications]* (3rd Edn). Leuven–Apeldoorn: Garant.

Deem, R. (1988) Feminism and leisure studies: Opening up new directions. In E. Wimbush and M. Talbot (Eds) *Relative Freedoms: Women and leisure* (pp. 5–17). Milton Keynes: Open University Press.

DeLeon, P. (1998) Models of policy discourse: Insights versus prediction. *Policy Studies Journal, 26*(1), 147–162.

Denlinger, K. (1980) Warfare on drugs increases. *Washington Post*, 12 February.

Department for Culture, Media and Sport (2008a) *London 2012 Olympic and Paralympic Games Impacts and Legacy Evaluation Framework*. London: DCMS.

Department for Culture, Media and Sport (2008b) *Playing to Win: A new era for sport*. London: DCMS.

Department for Culture, Media and Sport (2009) *List of Protected Events*. London: DCMS.

Department of Canadian Heritage (2010) *Environmental Scan 2010: Trends and issues in Canada and in sport*. Ottawa, ON: Department of Canadian Heritage.

Department of Canadian Heritage (2011) Welcome! Available: www.pch.gc.ca/eng/1266037002102/1265993639778 (accessed 19 February 2011).

Depperu, D. and Cerrato, D. (2008) *Analysing International Competitiveness at the Firm Level: Concepts and measures*. Available: www3.unicatt.it/unicattolica/dipartimenti/DISES/allegati/wpdepperucerrato32.pdf (accessed 15 August 2008).

Dery, D. (1999) Policy by the way: When policy is incidental to making other policies. *Journal of Public Policy, 18*(2), 163–176.

Descoeudres, G. (1979) Six Questions to the President of the IOC: Lord Killanin analyses the problems of Olympism. *Olympic Review, 137*, 139–141.

Díaz-Aguado Jalón, M. J., Royo García, M. P., Segura García, M. P. and Andrés Zuñeda, M. T. (1996). *Programas de educación para la tolerancia y prevención de la violencia en los jóvenes. Instrumentos de evaluación e investigación*. Madrid: Instituto de la Juventud, Ministerio de Trabajo y Asuntos Sociales.

Dictionary of Human Geography (2007) *Dictionary of Human Geography*. London: Blackwell Publishing.

Diesfeld, H. J. (2004) Ethics of international health research and the north south dilemma. *Medical Mission Dialogue* (28 February), 11–23.

Digel, H., Burk, V. and Fahrner, M. (2006) High-performance sport: An international comparison. *Edition Sports International, 9*.

DiMaggio, P. and Powell, W. W. (1991) The iron cage revisited: Institutional isomorphism and collective rationality. In W. W. Powell and P. DiMaggio (Eds) *The New Institutionalism in Organizational Analysis* (pp. 63–82). Chicago, IL: University of Chicago Press.

Dimeo, P. (2007) *A History of Drug Use in Sport, 1876–1976: Beyond good and evil*. London and New York: Routledge.

Dimeo, P. and Hunt, T. (2011) Saint or Sinner? A reconsideration of the career of Prince Alexandre de Merode, Chair of the International Olympic Committee's Medical Commission, 1967–2002. *International Journal for the History of Sport, 28*(6), 925–940.

Directorate-General of Budget, Accounting and Statistics (2011) *National Accounts Yearbook 2010*. Taipei: Executive Yuan.

Dodd-Butera, T. and Broderick, M. (2011) Health policy and poison control centers: Providing analysis utilizing a logic model. *Clinical Toxicology, 49*(6), 603–603.

Doherty, A. and Taylor, T. (2007) Sport and physical recreation in the settlement of immigrant youth. *Leisure/Loisir*, *31*(1), 27–55.

Donnelly, P. and Kidd, B. (2003) Realising the expectations: Youth, character, and community in Canadian sport. In *The Sport We Want: Essays on current issues in community sport* (pp. 25–44). Ottawa: Canadian Centre for Ethics in Sport.

Donnelly, P. and Nakamura, Y. (2006) *Sport and Multiculturalism: A dialogue.* Report for Canadian Heritage. Toronto, ON: University of Toronto Centre for Sport and Policy Studies.

Douma, S. and Schreuder, H. (2008) *Economic Approaches to Organizations.* Harlow: Prentice Hall.

Downward, P., Dawson, A. and Dejonghe, T. (2009) *Sport Economics: Theory, evidence and policy.* Oxford: Butterworth-Heinemann.

Dryzek, J. S. and Dunleavy, P. (2009) *Theories of the Democratic State.* Basingstoke: Palgrave Macmillan.

Duan, Q. (2005) China's IT leadership. Unpublished doctoral dissertation. University of College Park, Maryland.

Duke University Libraries (n.d.) Non-governmental organizations (NGO) guide. Available: http://guides.library.duke.edu/ngo_guide (accessed 20 November 2011).

Dunning, J. H. and Kim, C. (2007) The cultural roots of guanxi: An exploratory study. *The World Economy*, *30*(2), 329–341.

Duran, P. (2005) The impact of the Olympic Games on tourism. Barcelona: The legacy of the Games 1992–2002. In I. Urdangarín and D. Torres (Eds) *New Views on Sport Tourism* (pp. 77–91). Mallorca: Calliope Publishing.

Dwyer, L. and Forsyth, P. (2009) Public sector support for special events. *Eastern Economic Journal*, *35*(4), 481–499.

Eade, D. (1997) *Capacity Building.* Oxford: Oxfam.

Eade, D. and Sayer, J. (2006) *Development and the Private Sector: Consuming interests.* Bloomfield, NJ: Kumarian Press.

Eakin, J., Robertson, A., Poland, B., Coburn, D. and Edwards, R. (1996) Toward a critical social science perspective on health promotion research. *Health Promotion International*, *11*(2), 157–165.

East, L. (2002) Regenerating health communities: Voices from the inner City. *Critical Social policy*, *22*(2), 273–299.

Echart Muñoz, E., Cabezas Valencia, R. and Sotillo Lorenzo, J. A. (Eds) (2010) *Metodología de Investigación en Cooperación para el Desarrollo.* Madrid: IUDC–La Catarata.

EduSport Foundation (2011) Welcome to EduSport. Available: www.edusport.org.zm (accessed 18 March 2011).

Eisenhardt, K. (1989) Building theories from case study research. *Academy of Management Review*, *14*(4), 532–550.

Elkin, S. (1987) *City and Regime in the American Republic.* Chicago, IL: Chicago University Press.

Elliott, J. L. and Fleras, A. (1990) Immigration and the Canadian ethnic mosaic. In P. S. Li (Ed.) *Race and Ethnic Relations in Canada* (pp. 51–76). Toronto, ON: Oxford University Press.

Emery, P. R. (2001) Bidding to host a major sport event: Strategic Investment or Complete Lottery. In C. Gratton and I. Henry (Eds) *Sport in the City: The role of sport in economic and social regeneration* (pp. 90–108). London: Routledge.

Emery, P. R. (2002) Bidding to host a major sports event: The local organising committee perspective. *International Journal of Public Sector Management*, *15*(4), 316–335.

Emler, N. (2001) *Self-esteem: The Costs and Causes of Low Self-Worth.* York: Joseph Rowntree Foundation.

English Partnerships (2008) *Additionality Guide: A standard approach to assessing the additional impact of interventions.* London: English Partnerships.

Ericsson, K. A. (2003) Development of elite performance and deliberate practice: An update from the perspective of the expert performance approach. In K. Starkes and K. A. Ericsson (Eds) *Expert Performance in Sports: Advances in research on sport expertise* (pp. 49–85). Champaign IL: Human Kinetics.

Erlei, M., Leschke, M. and Sauerland, D. (2007) *Neue Institutionenökonomik* [*Neo-institutional economics*]. Stuttgart: Schäffer-Poeschel.

Escobar, A. (1995) *Encountering Development: The making and unmaking of the Third World.* Princeton, NJ: Princeton University Press.

Essex, S. and Chalkley, B. (1998) Olympic Games: Catalyst of urban change. *Leisure Studies*, *17*(3), 187–206.

Etzioni, A. (1993) *The Spirit of Community: Rights, responsibilities and the communitarian agenda.* London: HarperCollins.

Euchner, C. C. (1993) *Playing the Field: Why sports teams move and cities fight to keep them.* Baltimore, MD: Johns Hopkins University Press.

European Commission (1984) *A People's Europe.* Report from the ad-hoc committee. Brussels: COM (84) 446.

European Commission (1998a) *The European Model of Sport: Consultation Document of Dg X.* Brussels: European Commission.

European Commission (1998b) *The Commission Conditionally Approves Sponsorship Contracts between the Danish Tennis Federation and Its Tennis Ball Suppliers.* IP/98/355, 15 April. Brussels: European Commission.

European Commission (1999a) *The Helsinki Report on Sport.* Report from the European Commission to the European Council with a view to safeguarding current sports structures and maintaining the social function of sport within the Community framework. Brussels: COM (1999) 644 final, 10 December.

European Commission (1999b) *Principles and Guidelines for the Community's Audiovisual Policy in the Digital Age.* Brussels: COM (99) 657 final, 14 December.

European Commission (1999c) *Commission Debates Application of Its Competition Rules to Sports.* European Commission Press Release. Brussels: IP/99/133, 24 February.

European Commission (2001a) *Commission Closes Its Investigation into Formula One and Other Four-Wheel Motor Sports.* European Commission Press Release. Brussels: IP/01/1523, 30 October.

European Commission (2001b) *Outcome of Discussions between the Commission and FIFA/UEFA on FIFA Regulations on International Football Transfers.* European Commission Press Release. Brussels: IP/01/314, 5 March.

European Commission (2002) *Commission Closes Investigations into FIFA Regulations on International Football Transfers.* European Commission Press Release. Brussels: IP/02/824, 5 June.

European Commission (2003) *Commission Clears Uefa's New Policy Regarding the Sale of the Media Rights to the Champions League.* European Commission Press Release. Brussels: IP/03/1105, 24 July.

European Commission (2005) *Commission Decision Pursuant to Article 81 of the EC Treaty and Article 53(1) of the EEA Agreement (Case Comp/C.2/37.214 – Joint Selling of the Media Rights to the German Bundesliga).* Brussels: OJ L 134/2005, p. 46, 19 January.

European Commission (2006) *Commission Decision Relating to a Proceeding Pursuant Article 81 of the EC Treaty (Case Comp/C-2/38.173 – Joint Selling Media Rights to the Fa Premier League).* Brussels: C(2006) 868 final.

European Commission (2007a) *Action Plan Pierre de Coubertin.* Accompanying document to the White Paper on Sport. Brussels: SEC 934, 11 July.

European Commission (2007b) *White Paper on Sport.* Brussels: EC. Available: http://ec.europa.eu/sport/white-paper/whitepaper8_en.htm (accessed 11 April 2011).

European Commission (2008). *Guide to Cost–Benefit Analysis of Investment Projects.* Available: www.rws.nl/images/Cost-Benefit%20Analysis%20for%20Investments_tcm174-275338.pdf (accessed May 2008).

European Commission (2009) *Portfolio of Indicators for the Monitoring of the European Strategy for Social Protection and Social Inclusion: 2009 update.* Brussels, EC. Available: http://ec.europa.eu/social/main.jsp?catId=756&langId=en (accessed 11 April 2011).

European Commission (2011) *Developing the European Dimension in Sport Communication from the Commission to the European Parliament, the Council, the European Economic and Social Committee and the Committee of the Regions.* COM(2011) 12 final. Brussels: European Commission.

European Council (2000) *Declaration on the Specific Characteristics of Sport and Its Social Function in Europe, of Which Account Should Be Taken in Implementing Common Policies.* Presidency Conclusions. Nice: European Council, 7–9 December 2000.

European Parliament (2007) *Resolution of the European Parliament on the Future of Professional Football in Europe.* Rapporteur: Ivo Belet (A6-0036/2007, 29 March).

Eze, C. (Ed.) (1998) *African Philosophy: An anthology.* London: Blackwell Publishers.

Fainstein, S. and Fainstein, N. (1986) Regime strategies, communal resistance, and economic forces. In S. Fainstein, R. Hill, D. Judd and M. Smith (Eds) *Restructuring the City: The political economy of urban development* (pp. 245–282). New York: Longman.

Fairclough, N. (1989) *Language and Power.* New York: Longman.

Fairclough, N. (1995) *Critical Discourse Analysis: The critical study of language.* London: Longman.

Fairclough, N. (2003) *Analysing Discourse: Textual analysis for social research.* London: Routledge.

Fals-Borda, O. and Anisur Rahman, M. (Eds) (1991) *Action and Knowledge: Breaking the monopoly with participatory action research.* New York: Apex Press.

Fan, H. and Xiong, X. (2003) Communist China: Sport, politics and diplomacy. In J. A. Mangan and H. Fan (Eds) *Sport in Asian Society*. London: Frank Cass.

Faulkner, B., Chalip, L., Brown, G., Jago, L., March, R. and Woodside, A. (2000) Monitoring the tourism impacts of the Sydney 2000 Olympics. *Event Management, 6*(4), 231–246.

Feinstein, L., Bynner, J. and Duckworth, K. (2005) *Leisure Contexts in Adolescence and Their Effects on Adult Outcomes*. London: Centre for Research on the Wider Benefits of Learning.

Ferstl, C. (2010) The Olympic Movement: A critique on the dissemination of sport in the Taiwanese culture. Unpublished master's dissertation. Zhangua: Da Yeh University.

Feuerstein, M. T. (1990) *Partners in Evaluation: Evaluating development and community programs with participants*. London: Macmillan.

Field, J. (2003) *Social Capital*. London: Routledge.

FIFA (2006) *FIFA and UEFA Stress the Vital Importance of Football Autonomy*. Media Release, 26 October. Available: www.fifa.com/aboutfifa/federation/releases/newsid=106979.html (accessed 20 March 2011).

Filo, K., Funk, D. C. and O'Brien, D. (2009) The meaning behind attachment: Exploring camaraderie, cause, and competency at a charity sport event. *Journal of Sport Management, 23*(3), 361–387.

Fine, B. (2010) *Theories of Social Capital: Researchers behaving badly*. London: Pluto Press.

Finlayson, A. (2003) *Making Sense of New Labour*. London: Lawrence and Wishart.

Fleming, J. and Rhodes, R. A. W. (2005) Bureaucracy, contracts and networks: The unholy trinity and the police. *Australian and New Zealand Journal of Criminology, 38*(2), 192–205.

Flyvbjerg, B. (2001) *Making Social Science Matter*. Cambridge: Cambridge University Press.

Forester, D. A. (2010) African relational ontology, individual identity, and Christian theology: An African theological contribution towards an integrated relational ontological identity. *Theology, CxIII*(874), 243–253.

Forester, J. (1993) *Critical Theory, Public Policy and Planning Practice: Towards a critical pragmatism*. Albany, NJ: State University of New York Press.

Forster, J. (2006) Global sports organisations and their governance. *Corporate Governance, 6*(1), 72–83.

Foster, K. (2000) Can sport be regulated by Europe? An analysis of alternative models. In A. Caiger and S. Gardiner (Eds) *Professional Sport in the European Union: Regulation and re-regulation* (pp. 43–64). The Hague: TMC Asser Press.

Foucault, M. (1972) *The Archaeology of Knowledge*. London: Routledge.

Foucault, M. (1978) *The History of Sexuality. Volume 1: An introduction* (trans. R. Hurley). New York: Pantheon.

Foucault, M. (1980a) Two lectures. In C. Gordon (Ed.) *Power/Knowledge: Selected interviews and other writings 1972–1977* (pp. 78–108). Harlow: Harvester Press.

Foucault, M. (1980b) Power and strategies. In C. Gordon (Ed.) *Power/Knowledge: Selected interviews and other writings 1972–1977* (pp. 134–145). Harlow: Harvester Press.

Foucault, M. (1981) *The History of Sexuality: An introduction*. London: Penguin Books.

Foucault, M. (1991) Governmentality. In G. Burchell, C. Gordon and P. Miller (Eds) *The Foucault Effect: Studies in governmentality* (pp. 87–104). Hemel Hempstead: Harvester Wheatsheaf.

Foucault, M. (1994a) Truth and power. In J. Faubion (Ed.) *Michel Foucault: Power: Essential works of Foucault 1954–1984, Vol. 3* (pp. 111–133). London: Penguin Books.

Foucault, M. (1994b) The subject and power. In J. Faubion (Ed.) *Michel Foucault: Power: Essential works of Foucault 1954–1984, Vol. 3* (pp. 326–348). London: Penguin Books.

Foucault, M. (1994c) Governmentality. In J. Faubion (Ed.) *Michel Foucault: Power: Essential works of Foucault 1954–1984, Vol. 3* (pp. 201–222). London: Penguin.

Franck, E. (1995) *Die ökonomischen Institutionen der Teamsportindustrie [The Economic Institutions of the Team Sports Industry]*. Wiesbaden: Gabler.

Frank, R. (2003) *Microeconomics and Behavior*. New York, NY: McGraw-Hill.

Franke, W. and Berendonk, B. (1997) Hormonal doping and androgenization of athletes: A secret program of the German Democratic Republic. *Clinical Chemistry, 43*(7), 1262–1279.

Frazer, E. (2002) Local social relations: Public, club and common goods. In V. Nash (Ed.) *Claiming Community*. London: IPPR.

Friedman, M. and Friedman, R. (1962) *Capitalism and Freedom*. Chicago, IL: University of Chicago Press.

Frisby, W. (2011) Learning from the local: Promising physical activity inclusion practices for Chinese immigrant women in Vancouver, Canada. *Quest, 63*(1), 135–147.

Frisby, W. and Hoeber, L. (2002) Factors affecting the uptake of community recreation as health promotion for women on low incomes. *Canadian Journal of Public Health*, March/April, 129–133.

Frisby, W. and Millar, S. (2002) The actualities of doing community development to promote the inclusion of low income populations in local sport and recreation. *European Sport Management Quarterly*, 2(3), 209–233.

Frisby, W. and Ponic, P. (forthcoming) Sport and social inclusion. In L. Thibault and J. Harvey (Eds) *Sport Policy in Canada*. Ottawa, ON: University of Ottawa Press.

Frisby, W., Thibault, L. and Kikulis, L. (2004) The organizational dynamics of under-managed partnerships in leisure service departments. *Leisure Studies*, 23(2), 109–126.

Fuguitt, S. and Wilcox, S. J. (1999) *Cost–Benefit Analysis for Public Sector Decision Makers*. Westport, CT: Quorum Books.

Furlong, R. (1994) Tobacco advertising legislation and the sponsorship of sport. *Australian Business Law Review*, 22(3), 159–189.

Futterman, M. (2010) The Vancouver forecast. Weighing politics, risk and the home-ice advantage: which countries will rack up the most medals. Available: http://online.wsj.com/article/SB100014240 52748704820904575055602223303266.html (accessed 19 February 2011).

García, B. (2001) Enhancing sport marketing through cultural and arts programs: Lessons from the Sydney 2000 Olympic Arts Festivals. *Sport Management Review*, 4(2), 193–219.

García, B. (2009a) Sport governance after the White Paper: The demise of the European model? *International Journal of Sport Policy*, 1(3), 267–284.

García, B. (2009b) The new governance of sport: What role for the EU? In R. Parrish, S. Gardiner and R. Siekmann (Eds) *EU, Sport, Law and Policy: Regulation, re-regulation and representation* (pp. 115–136). The Hague: TMC Asser Press.

García, B. (2010) The governance of European sport. In P. Dine and S. Crosson (Eds) *Sport, Representation, and Evolving Identities in Europe* (pp. 22–38). Oxford: Peter Lang.

García, B. (2011) The EU and sport governance: Between economic and social values. In M. Groeneveld, B. Houlihan and F. Ohl (Eds) *Social Capital and Sport Governance in Europe* (pp. 21–40). London: Routledge.

Garelli, S. (2008) *Competitiveness of Nations: The fundamentals*. International Institute for Management Development, *World Competitiveness Yearbook*. Available: www02.imd.ch/wcc/yearbook (accessed 2 August 2008).

Garrett, G. (1998) *Partisan Politics in Global Economy*. Cambridge: Cambridge University Press.

Garrett, R. (2004) The response of voluntary sports clubs to Sport England's lottery funding: Cases of compliance, change and resistance. *Managing Leisure*, 9(1), 13–29.

GB Editor (2010) *Initial Olympic bid campaign budgets critical to success – Or so it seems*. Available: www.gamesbids.com/eng/winter_olympic_bids/annecy_2018/1216135109.html (accessed 21 August 2010).

Gearing, B. (1999) Narratives of identity among former professional footballers in the United Kingdom. *Journal of Aging Studies*, 13(1), 43–58.

Gee, J. P. (2001) *An Introduction to Discourse Analysis: Theory and method*. London: Routledge.

Georghiou, L. (1998) Issues in the evaluation of innovation and technology policy. *Evaluation*, 4(1), 37–51.

Giddens, A. (1976) *New Rules of Sociological Method: A positive critique of interpretive sociologies*. New York: Basic Books.

Giddens, A. (1984) *The Constitution of Society: Outline of the theory of structuration*. Cambridge: Polity Press.

Giddens, A. (1990) *The Consequences of Modernity*. Cambridge: Polity Press.

Giddens, A. (1991) *Modernity and Self-Identity: Self and society in the late modern age*. Cambridge: Polity Press.

Giddens, A. (1994) *Beyond Left and Right: The future of radical politics*. Stanford, CA: Stanford University Press.

Giddens, A. (1998) *The Third Way: The renewal of social democracy*. Cambridge: Polity Press.

Gilbert, H. and Tompkins J. (1996) *Post-colonial Drama: Theory, practice, politics*. New York: Routledge.

Gilpin, R. (2001) *Global Political Economy*. Princeton, NJ: Princeton University Press.

Girginov, V. and Hills, L. (2009) The political process of constructing a sustainable London Olympics sports development legacy. *International Journal of Sport Policy*, 1(2), 161–181.

Girginov, V. and Sandanski, I. (2011) Bulgaria. In M. Nicholson, R. Hoye and B. Houlihan (Eds) *Participation in sport: International policy perspectives* (pp. 91–108). London: Routledge.

Gitman, L. J. and Zutter, C. J. (2012) *Principles of Managerial Finance* (13th Edn). Upper Saddle River, NJ: Prentice Hall.

Giulianotti, R. (2004) *Sport and Modern Social Theorists*. Basingstoke: Palgrave Macmillan.

Giulianotti, R. (2010) The sport, development and peace sector: A model of four social policy domains. *Journal of Social Policy*, 40(4), 757–776.

Giulianotti, R. (2011) Sport, transnational peacemaking, and global civil society: Exploring the reflective discourses of 'sport, development, and peace' project officials. *Journal of Sport and Social Issues*, *35*(1), 50–71.

Giulianotti, R. and Armstrong, G. (2011) Sport, the military and peacemaking: History and possibilities. *Third World Quarterly*, *32*(3), 379–394.

Giulianotti, R. and Robertson, R. (2007) Sport and globalization: Transnational dimensions. *Global Networks*, *7*(2), 107–112.

Glaser, B. and Strauss, A. (1967) *The Discovery of Grounded Theory*. Chicago, IL: Aldine.

Gliner, J. A. and Morgan, G. A. (2000) *Research Methods in Applied Settings: An integrated approach to design and analysis*. Mahwah, NJ: Lawrence Erlbaum Associates.

GOI (2010) Dossier to the IOC on the Government of India guidelines on good governance in Sports Bodies. Delhi, 16 June. Available: http://yas.nic.in/index1.asp?langid=1&linkid=180 (accessed 19 April 2011).

Gold, J. and Gold, M. (2007) *Olympic Cities: City agendas, planning and the world's games, 1896–2012*. London: Routledge.

Gold, T. B. (2010) Taiwan in 2009: Eroding landslide. *Asian Survey*, *50*(1), 65–75.

Gold, T., Guthrie, D. and Wank, D. (2002) *Social Connections in China: Institutions, culture, and the changing nature of guanxi*. Cambridge: Cambridge University Press.

Goldman, B., Klatz, R. and Bush, P. (1984) *Death in the Locker Room*. South Bend, IN: Icarus Press.

Goodman, R. and Peng, I. (1996) The East-Asian welfare states: Peripatetic learning, adaptive change, and nation building. In G. Esping-Andersen (Ed.) *Welfare States in Transition: National adaptations in global economies* (pp. 192–221). London: Sage.

Goodwin, M. and Grix, J. (2011) Bringing structures back in: The 'governance narrative', the 'decentered approach' and 'asymetrical network governance' in the education and sport policy communities. *Public Administration*, *89*(2), 537–556.

Governance in Sport Working Group (2001) *The Rules of the Game: Conference report and conclusions*. Brussels: Governance in Sport Working Group.

Government of Canada (2011) *Canadian Multiculturalism Act, Assented to 21st July 1988, Current to July 11, 2011*. Ottawa, ON: Minister of Justice. Avalable: http://laws-lois.justice.gc.ca/PDF/C-18.7.pdf (accessed 19 February 2011).

Government Social Research Unit (2007) *The Magenta Book: Guidance notes for policy evaluation and analysis*. London: HM Treasury.

Graefe, P. (2006) State restructuring, social assistance, and Canadian intergovernmental relations: Same scales, new tune. *Studies in Political Economy*, *78*, 93–117.

Graefe, P. (2008) The spending power and federal social policy leadership: A prospective view. *IRPP Policy Matters*, *9*(3), 53–106.

Grant Thornton, ECORYS, and Centre for Olympic Studies and Research Loughborough University (2011a) *Meta-evaluation of the Impacts and Legacy of the London 2012 Olympic Games and Paralympic Games Summary of Reports 1 and 2: 'Scope, research questions and strategy' and 'Methods'*. London: Department of Culture Media and Sport.

Grant Thornton, ECORYS, and Centre for Olympic Studies and Research Loughborough University (2011b) *Report 1: Scope, Research Questions and Strategy: Meta-evaluation of the impacts and legacy of the London 2012 Olympic Games and Paralympic Games*. London: Department of Culture Media and Sport.

Grant Thornton, ECORYS, and Centre for Olympic Studies and Research Loughborough University (2011c) *Report 2: Methods: Meta-evaluation of the impacts and legacy of the London 2012 Olympic Games and Paralympic Games*. London: Department of Culture Media and Sport.

Grant Thornton, ECORYS, and Centre for Olympic Studies and Research Loughborough University (2012) *Report 3: Baseline and Counterfactual: Meta-evaluation of the impacts and legacy of the London 2012 Olympic Games and Paralympic Games*. London: Department of Culture Media and Sport.

Gratton, C. and Preuss, H. (2008) Maximizing Olympic impacts by building up legacies. *International Journal of Sport History*, *25*(14), 1922–1938.

Gratton, C., Shibli, S. and Coleman, R. J. (2005) Sport and economic regeneration in cities. *Urban Studies*, *42*(5–6), 1–15.

Green, B. C. and Chalip, L. (1998) Sport tourism as the celebration of subculture. *Annals of Tourism Research*, *25*(2), 275–291.

Green, B. C., Lim, S. Y., Seo, W. J. and Sung, Y. (2010) Effects of cultural exposure through pre-event media. *Journal of Sport and Tourism*, *15*(1), 89–102.

Green, M. (2004a) Changing policy priorities for sport in England: The emergence of elite sport development as a key policy concern. *Leisure Studies, 23*(4), 365–385.

Green, M. (2004b) Power, policy, and political priorities: Elite sport development in Canada and the United Kingdom. *Sociology of Sport Journal, 21*(4), 376–396.

Green, M. (2005) Integrating macro- and meso-level approaches: A comparative analysis of elite sport development in Australia, Canada and the United Kingdom. *European Sport Management Quarterly, 5*(2), 143–166.

Green, M. (2006) From 'sport for all' to not about 'sport' at all? Interrogating sport policy interventions in the United Kingdom. *European Sport Management Quarterly, 6*(3), 217–239.

Green, M. (2007a) Governing under advanced liberalism: Sport policy and the social investment state. *Policy Sciences, 40*(1), 55–71.

Green, M. (2007b) Olympic glory or grassroots development? Sport policy priorities in Australia, Canada and the United Kingdom, 1960–2006. *International Journal of the History of Sport, 24*(7), 921–954.

Green, M. (2008) Non-governmental organisations in sports development. In V. Girginov (Ed.) *Management of Sports Development* (pp. 89–107). Oxford: Butterworth-Heinemann.

Green, M. (2009) Podium or participation? Analysing policy priorities under changing modes of sport governance in the United Kingdom. *International Journal of Sport Policy, 1*(2), 121–144.

Green, M. and Houlihan, B. (2004) Advocacy coalitions and elite sport policy change in Canada and the UK. *International Review for the Sociology of Sport, 39*(4), 387–403.

Green, M. and Houlihan, B. (2005a) Integrating macro- and meso-level approaches: A comparative analysis of elite sport development in Australia, Canada and the United Kingdom. *European Sport Management Quarterly, 5*(2), 143–166.

Green, M. and Houlihan, B. (2005b) *Elite Sport Development: Policy learning and political priorities*. London: Routledge.

Green, M. and Houlihan, B. (2006) Governmentality, modernisation and the 'disciplining' of national sporting organisations: Athletics in Australia and the United Kingdom. *Sociology of Sport Journal, 23*(1), 47–71.

Grillo, R. D. (1997) Discourses of development: The view from anthropology. In R. D. Grillo and R. L. Stirrat (Eds) *Discourses of Development: Anthropological perspectives* (pp. 1–33). Oxford: Berg Publishers.

Grix, J. (2004) *The Foundations of Research*. Basingstoke: Palgrave Macmillan.

Grix, J. (2009) The impact of UK sport policy on the governance of athletics. *International Journal of Sport Policy, 1*(1), 31–49.

Grix, J. (2010) The 'governance debate' and the study of sport policy. *International Journal of Sport Policy, 2*(2), 159–171.

Grix, J. and Phillpots, L. (2011) Revisiting the 'governance narrative': 'Asymmetrical network governance' and the deviant case of the sports policy sector. *Public Policy and Administration, 26*(1), 3–19.

Groeneveld, M., Houlihan, B. and Ohl, F. (Eds) (2011) *Social Capital and Sport Governance in Europe*. London: Routledge.

Gu, F. F., Hung, K. and Tse, D. K. (2008) When does guanxi matter? Issues of capitalization and its dark sides. *Journal of Marketing, 72*(4), 12–28.

Guba, E. (1990) *The Paradigm Dialogue*. Newbury Park, CA: Sage Publications.

Guba, Y. and Lincoln, E. (1989) *Fourth Generation Evaluation*. London: Sage.

Gullickson, A., Wingate, L., Lawrenz, F. and Coryn, C. L. S. (2006) *The NSF Advanced Technology Education Program: Final evaluation report*. Kalamazoo: Western Michigan University, The Evaluation Center.

Guo, S. and DeVoretz, D. J. (2006) *Chinese Immigrants in Vancouver: Quo Vadis?* Working paper series, Research on Immigration and Integration in the Metropolis. Vancouver, BC: Vancouver Centre of Excellence.

Haas, E. (1968) *The Uniting of Europe: Political, social and economic forces 1950–1957* (2nd Edn). Stanford, CA: Stanford University Press.

Hall, M. A. (2002) The discourse of gender and sport: From femininity to feminism. In S. Scraton and A. Flintoff (Eds) *Gender and Sport: A reader* (pp. 6–17). New York: Routledge.

Hall, P. and Soskice, D. (2001) Introduction. In P. Hall and D. Soskice (Eds) *Varieties of Capitalism: The institutional foundations of comparative advantage* (pp. 1–68). Oxford: Oxford University Press.

Hall, T. and Hubbard, P. (1998) *The Entrepreneurial City: Geographies of politics, regime and representation*. Chichester: John Wiley & Sons.

Halpern, D. (2005) *Social Capital*. Cambridge: Polity Press.

Ham, C. and Hill, M. (1993) *The Policy Process in the Modern Capitalist State* (2nd Edn). Hemel Hempstead: Harvester Wheatsheaf.

Hamil, S., Morrow, S., Idle, C., Rossi, G. and Faccendini, S. (2010) The governance and regulation of Italian football. *Soccer and Society*, *11*(4), 373–413.

Handelman, D. (1990) *Models and Mirrors: Towards an anthropology of public events*. New York: Cambridge University Press.

Hanley, N. and Spash, C. L. (1993) *Cost–Benefit Analysis and the Environment*. Aldershot: Edward Elgar.

Hannerz, U. (1991) Scenarios for Peripheral Cultures. In A. D. King (Ed.) *Culture, Globalization and the World-System* (pp.107–128). London: Macmillan.

Hanstad, D. V. and Loland, S. (2009) Elite athletes' duty to provide information on their whereabouts: Justifiable anti-doping work or an indefensible surveillance regime? *European Journal of Sport Science*, *9*(1), 3–10.

Harding, A. and Le Galès, P. (2000) Globalization, Urban change and urban policies in Britain and France. In A. Scott (Ed.) *The Limits of Globalisation: Cases and arguments* (pp. 181–201). London: Routledge.

Hardy, B. and Rhodes, R. (2003) Beliefs and institutional change: The UK national health service. In J. Fleming and I. Holland (Eds) *Government Reformed: Values, institutions and the state* (pp. 65–87). Aldershot: Ashgate.

Hargreaves, J. (1986) *Sport, Power and Culture*. Cambridge: Polity Press.

Harris, S., Mori, K. and Collins, M. (2009) Great expectations: Voluntary sports clubs and their role in delivering national policy for English sport. *Voluntas*, *20*(4), 405–423.

Hartmann, D. and Kwauk, C. (2011) Sport and development: An overview, critique, and reconstruction. *Journal of Sport and Social Issues*, *35*(3), 284–305.

Harvey, D. (1990) *The Urban Experience*. Oxford: Blackwell.

Harvey, J., Levesque, M. and Donnelly, P. (2007) Sport volunteerism and social capital. *Sociology of Sport Journal*, *24*(2), 206–223.

Harvey, J., Thibault, L. and Rail, G. (1995) Neo-corporatism: The political management system in Canadian amateur sport and fitness. *Journal of Sport and Social Issues*, *19*(3), 249–265.

Hastings, A., McArthur, A. and McGregor, A. (1996) *Less than Equal: Community organisations and estate regeneration partnerships*. Bristol: Policy Press.

Hatziandreu, E. I., Koplan, J. P., Weinstein, M. C., Caspersen, C. J. and Warner, K. E. (1988) A Cost-effectiveness analysis of exercise as a health promotion activity. *American Journal of Public Health*, *78*(11), 1417–1421.

Hawkesworth, M. (1994) Policy studies within a feminist frame. *Policy Sciences*, *27*(2–3), 97–118.

Hay, C. (2002) *Political Analysis: A critical introduction*. Basingstoke: Palgrave Macmillan.

Hay, C. and Marsh, D. (2000) *Demystifying Globalization*. London: Palgrave.

Hayhurst, L. M. C., Wilson, B. and Frisby W. (2010) Navigating neoliberal networks: Transnational internet platforms in sport for development and peace. *International Review for the Sociology of Sport*, 46, 1–15.

Head, B. (2009) Evidence-based policy: Principles and requirements. In Productivity Commission (Ed.) *Strengthening Evidence-based Policy in the Australian Federation* (Roundtable Proceedings Volume 1) (pp. 13–26). Canberra: Productivity Commission.

Health Canada (2010, December) Migration health: Emerging perspectives. *Health Policy Research Bulletin*, 17, 3–6. Available: www.hc-sc.gc.ca/sr-sr/alt_formats/pdf/pubs/hpr-rpms/bull/2010-health-sante-migr-eng.pdf (accessed 19 February 2011).

Heclo, H. and Wildavsky, A. (1974) *The Private Government of Public Money*. London: Macmillan.

Heinemann, K. (1995) *Einführung in die Ökonomie des Sports* [*Introduction into the Economics of Sport*]. Schorndorf: Verlag Hofmann.

Heinemann, K. (2005) Sport and the welfare state in Europe. *European Journal of Sport Science*, *5*(4), 181–188.

Heinrich, C. J. (2011) Public management. In M. Bevir (Ed.) *The Sage Handbook of Governance* (pp. 252–269). London: Sage.

Held, D. and McGrew, A. (2002) *The Global Transformations Reader: An introduction to the globalisation debate*. Cambridge: Polity Press.

Held, D. and McGrew, A. (2007) *Globalisation/Anti-Globalisation*. Cambridge: Polity Press.

Held, D., McGrew, A., Goldblatt, D. and Perraton, J. (1999) *Global Transformations: Politics, economics and culture*. Cambridge: Polity Press.

Henry, I. (2005) *Sport and multiculturalism: A European perspective*. Barcelona: Centre d'Estudis Olympics UAB. Available: http://olympicstudies.uab.es/pdf/wp102_eng.pdf (accessed 11 April 2011).

Henry, I. (2009) Estrategias de deporte e integración social: el uso del deporte para la integración social de refugiados y solicitantes de asilo. In J. Durán González (Ed.) *Actividad Física, Deporte e Inmigración. El reto de la Interculturalidad* (pp. 63–79). Madrid: Consejería de Deportes de la Comunidad de Madrid.

Henry, I. and Gratton, C. (Eds) (2001) *Sport in the City: The role of sport in economic and social regeneration.* London: Routledge.

Henry, I. and Ko, L. (2009) European models of sport: Governance, organisational change and sports policy in the EU. In K. Petry and W. Tokarski (Eds) *Handbuch Sportpolitik* (pp. 63–78). Berlin: Hofmann-Verlag.

Henry, I. and Lee, P. C. (2004) Governance and ethics. In J. Beech and S. Chadwick (Eds) *The Business of Sport* Management (pp. 25–42). London: Pearson.

Henry, I. and Nassis, P. (1999) Political clientelism and sports policy in Greece. *International Review for the Sociology of Sport, 34*(1), 43–58.

Henry, I. and Paramio-Salcines, J. L. (1999) Sport and the analysis of symbolic regimes: A case study of the city of Sheffield. *Urban Affairs Review, 34*(5), 641–66.

Henry, I., Al-Tauqi, M., Amara, M. and Lee, P. C. (2007) Methodologies in comparative and transnational policy research. In I. Henry (Ed.) *Transnational and Comparative Research in Sport: Globalisation, governance and sport policy.* London: Routledge.

Henry, I. P., Amara, M. and Al-Tauqi, M. (2003) Sport, Arab nationalism and the Pan-Arab Games. *International Review for the Sociology of Sport, 38*(3), 295–310.

Henry, I., Amara, M., Al-Tauqi, M. and Lee, P. (2005) A typology of approaches to comparative analysis of sports policy. *Journal of Sport Management, 19*(4), 480–496.

Henry, I., Downward, P., Harwood, C. and Robinson, L. (2008) *Sports Partnerships Promoting Inclusive Communities: Lincolnshire, Leicester-Shire and Rutland Sports Partnerships.* Invest to Save Project number 430/7: Monitoring and Evaluation Report. Loughborough: Institute of Sport and Leisure Policy/Centre for Olympic Studies and Research.

Hettne, B. (1995) *Development Theory and the Three Worlds* (2nd Edn). Harlow: Longman Scientific and Technical.

Hewitt, S. (2009) *Discourse Analysis and Public Policy Research.* Newcastle University.

Heyne, M. (2006) *Die ökonomischen Effekte von Fußballweltmeisterschaften: Das Beispiel 'Fußball-WM 2006'* [*The Economic Effects of the World Cup: The case of 'Football World Cup 2006'*]. Marburg: Tectum Verlag.

Hi, S. B. (2006) Does corporate social responsibility need social capital? *Journal of Corporate Citizenship, 23*, 81–91.

Hill, C. J. and Lynn, L. E. (2005) Is hierarchical governance in decline? Evidence from empirical research. *Journal of Public Administration Research and Theory, 15*(2), 173–195.

Hill, J. (2009) The European Commission's White Paper on Sport: A step backwards for specificity? *International Journal of Sport Policy, 1*(3), 253–266.

Hill, J. R. and Thies, J. (2010) Program theory and logic model to address the co-occurrence of domestic violence and child maltreatment. *Evaluation and Program Planning, 33*(4), 356–364.

Hill, M. (2009) *The Policy Process* (5th Edn). London: Pearson Education.

Hillary Commission (1989) *National Policy for Women and Sport.* Wellington: Hillary Commission.

Hiller, H. (2000) Mega-events, urban boosterism and growth strategies: An analysis of the objectives and legitimations of the Cape Town 2004 Olympic bid. *International Journal of Urban and Regional Research, 24*(2), 439–458.

Hindley, D. (2002) An examination of the utility of the concept of governance in relation to the sports of swimming, football and cricket. PhD. Loughborough: Loughborough University.

Hirst, P. and Thompson, G. (1998) *Globalisation in Question: The International economy and the possibilities of governance.* Cambridge: Polity Press.

HM Treasury (2003) *The Green Book: Appraisal and evaluation in Central Government Treasury Guidance.* Available: www.hm-treasury.gov.uk/d/green_book_complete.pdf (accessed 19 February 2011).

Hoberman, J. (1992) *Mortal Engines: The science of performance and the dehumanization of sport.* New York: Free Press.

Hoberman, J. (2005) *Testosterone Dreams: Rejuvenation, aphrodisia, doping.* Berkeley, CA: University of California Press.

Hodge, R. and Kress, G. (1993) *Language as Ideology* (2nd Edn). London: Routledge.

Hoehn, T. and Lancefield, D. (2003) Broadcasting and sport. *Oxford Review of Economic Policy, 19*(4), 552–568.

Hognestad, H. and Tollisen, A. (2004) Playing against deprivation: Football and development in Nairobi, Kenya. In G. Armstrong and R. Giulianotti (Eds) *Football in Africa: Conflict, conciliation and community* (pp. 210–228). London: Palgrave Macmillan.

Holton, R. J. (2005) *Making Globalization.* Basingstoke: Palgrave Macmillan.

Home Office (1998) *Compact: Getting it right together Cm4100.* London: The Stationery Office.

Hong Kong Broadcasting Authority (2007) *Generic Code of Practice on Television Programme Standards.* Hong Kong: Hong Kong Broadcasting Authority.

Hong, F., Ping, W. and Xiong, H. (2005) Beijing ambitions: An analysis of the Chinese elite sports system and its Olympic strategy for the 2008 Olympic Games. *The International Journal of the History of Sport, 22*(4), 510–529.

Hood, C. (1991) A public management for all seasons? *Public Administration, 69*(1), 3–19.

Hood, S. J. (1996) Political change in Taiwan: The rise of Kuomintang factions. *Asian Survey, 36*(5), 468–482.

Horch, H. D. (1998) Self-destroying processes of sports clubs in Germany. *European Journal for Sport Management, 5*(1), 46–58.

Horkheimer, M. (1982) *Critical Theory.* New York: Seabury Press.

Horton, K. (2011) Aid agencies: The epistemic question. *Journal of Applied Philosophy, 28*(1), 29–43.

Houlihan, B. (1994) Homogenization, Americanization, and Creolization of sport: Varieties of globalisation. *Sociology of Sport Journal, 11*(4), 356–375.

Houlihan, B. (1997) *Sport, Policy and Politics: A comparative analysis.* London: Routledge.

Houlihan, B. (1999) Anti-doping policy in sport: The politics of international policy co-ordination. *Public Administration, 77*(2), 311–334.

Houlihan, B. (2003) Sport and globalisation. In B. Houlihan (Ed.) *Sport and Society: A student introduction* (pp. 553–573). London: Sage Publications.

Houlihan, B. (2004) Civil rights, doping control and the world anti-doping code. *Sport in Society: Cultures, Commerce, Media, Politics, 7*(3), 420–437.

Houlihan, B. (2005a) Public sector sport policy: Developing a framework for analysis. *International Review for the Sociology of Sport, 40*(2), 163–185.

Houlihan, B. (2005b) Sports globalisation, the state and the problem of governance. In T. Slack (Ed.) *The Commercialisation of Sport* (pp. 52–71). London: Sage Publications.

Houlihan, B. (2008a) Politics, power, policy and sport. In B. Houlihan (Ed.) *Sport and Society: A student introduction* (pp. 33–55). London: Sage.

Houlihan, B. (2008b) Sport and globalisation. In B. Houlihan (Ed.) *Sport and Society: A student introduction.* London: Sage.

Houlihan, B. (2009) Government objectives and sport. In W. Andreff and S. Szymanski (Eds) *Handbook on the Economics of Sport* (pp. 254–259). Cheltenham: Edward Elgar Publishing.

Houlihan, B. and Green, M. (2006) The changing status of school sport and physical education: Explaining policy change. *Sport Education and Society, 11*(1), 73–92.

Houlihan, B. and Green, M. (2008) *Comparative Elite Sport Development.* London: Butterworth-Heineman.

Houlihan, B. and Green, M. (2009) Modernization and sport: The reform of Sport England and UK Sport. *Public Administration, 87*(3), 678–698.

Houlihan, B. and Groeneveld, M. (2011) Social capital, governance and sport. In M. Groeneveld, B. Houlihan and F. Ohl (Eds) *Social Capital and Sport Governance in Europe* (pp. 1–20). London: Routledge.

Houlihan, B. and Lindsey, I. (2008) Networks and partnerships in sport development. In V. Girginov (Ed.) *Management of Sport Development* (pp. 225–242). Oxford: Butterworth-Heinemann.

Houlihan, B. and Lindsey, I. (2013) *British Sport Policy in Britain.* London: Routledge.

Houlihan, B. and White, A. (2002) *The Politics of Sports Development: Development of sport or development through sport.* London: Routledge.

Houlihan, B., Bloyce, D. and Smith, A. (2009) Developing the research agenda in sport policy. *International Journal of Sport Policy, 1*(1), 1–12.

House, E. R. (1991) Realism in research. *Educational Researcher, 20*(6), 2–9.

Howman, D. (2011) Time for a World Sports Integrity Agency. Statement from WADA Director General David Howman following the European Union Sports Forum, Budapest, 21–22 February.

Hoye, R. and Cuskelly, G. (2007) *Sport Governance.* London: Butterworth-Heinemann.

Hoye, R. and Doherty, A. (2011) Nonprofit sport board performance: A review and directions for future research. *Journal of Sport Management, 25*(3), 272–285.

Hoye, R. and Nicholson, M. (Eds) (2008) *Sport and Social Capital.* London: Butterworth-Heinemann.

Hoye, R. and Nicholson, M. (2009) Social capital and sport policies in Australia. *Public Management Review, 11*(4), 441–460.

Hoye, R., Nicholson, M. and Houlihan, B. (2010) *Sport and Policy: Issues and analysis.* Oxford: Elsevier.

Hsu, J. Y. (2009) The spatial encounter between neoliberalism and populism in Taiwan: Regional restructuring under the DPP regime in the new millennium. *Political Geography, 28*(5), 296–308.

Hsu, J. Y. (2010) State transformation and regional development in Taiwan: From developmentalist strategy to populist subsidy. *International Journal of Urban and Regional Research, 35*(3), 600–619.

Hulme, M. and Lee, A. (2009) *New Opportunities for PE and Sport: Evaluation summary.* London: Big Lottery Fund.

Humphreys, B. R. and Prokopowicz, S. (2007) Assessing the impact of sport mega-events in transition economies: EURO 2012 in Poland and Ukraine. *International Journal of Sport Management and Marketing, 2*(5/6), 496–509.

Humphreys, B. R., Johnson, B. K., Mason, D. S. and Whitehead, J. C. (2010) *Estimating the Value of Medal Success at the 2010 Winter Olympic Games* (Working Paper). Edmonton: University of Alberta.

Hunt, T. M. (2011) *Drug Games: The International Olympic Committee and the politics of doping, 1960–2008.* Austin, TX: University of Texas Press.

Hwang, D. B., Golemon, P. L., Chen, Y., Wang, T. S. and Hung, W. S. (2009) Guanxi and business ethics in Confucian society today: An empirical case study in Taiwan. *Journal of Business Ethics, 89*(2), 235–250.

Hwang, D. J. (2002) Sport, imperialism and postcolonialism: A critical sport in China 1860–1993. Unpublished doctoral thesis. Stirling: University of Stirling.

Hylton, K. and Totten, M. (2008) Community sport development. In K. Hylton and P. Bramham (Eds) *Sports Development: Policy, process and practice* (pp. 77–117). London: Routledge.

Imrie, R. and Raco, M. (2003) Community and the changing nature of urban policy. In R. Imrie and M. Raco (Eds) *Urban Renaissance? New Labour, community and urban policy* (pp. 3–36). Bristol, Policy Press.

INEUM Consulting and TAJ (2007) *Study on the Training of Young Sportsmen and Sportswomen in Europe.* Brussels: European Commission.

Ingerson, L. and Westerbeek, H. (2000) Determining key success criteria for attracting hallmark sporting events. *Pacific Tourism Review, 3*(4), 239–253.

International Olympic Committee (1974) The 74th session: Resumé of the work. *Olympic Review, 74–75* (January/February).

International Olympic Committee (1981) IOC circular to IFs. *Olympic Review, 165.*

International Olympic Committee (1993) Olympic Solidarity: The last 10 years. *Olympic Review.* Lausanne: IOC.

International Olympic Committee (1999) 2000 Olympic reforms. *Olympic Review, XXVI*(17).

International Olympic Committee (2002) *Olympic Games Study Commission: Interim Report to the 114th IOC Session.* November. Mexico: IOC.

International Olympic Committee (2008) *Educating Sports Persons for Life Post Competition.* Paper presented at the World Forum: Sport and Education for the New Generation, Busan, Korea.

International Olympic Committee (2010a) *XIII Olympic Congress: Proceedings.* Lausanne: IOC.

International Olympic Committee (2010b) *Sports Betting: A challenge to be faced.* Recommendations for the IOC Seminar held in Lausanne, 24 June 2010.

International Olympic Committee (2011) *2020 Candidature Acceptance Procedure.* Lausanne: IOC.

International Olympic Committee (2011) *The Olympic Charter.* Available: www.olympic.org/Documents/ olympic_charter_en.pdf.

Investopedia (2012) Dictionary. Available: www.investopedia.com/terms/n/npv.asp#ixzz1cR8N4WyA (accessed 1 February 2011).

Israel, M. and Hay, I. (2006) *Research Ethics in the Social Sciences.* London: Sage Publications.

Jackson, S. J., Grainger, A. and Batty, R. (2005) Media sport, globalisation and the challenges to commercilisation: Sport advertising and cultural resistance in Aotearoa, New Zealand. In T. Slack (Ed.) *The Commercialisation of Sport* (pp. 207–225). London: Frank Cass.

Jago, L., Chalip, L., Brown, G., Mules, T. and Ali, S. (2003) Building events into destination branding: Insights from experts. *Event Management, 8*(1), 3–14.

Jammulamadaka, N. and Varman, R. (2010) Is NGO development assistance mistargeted? An epistemological approach. *Critical Review, 22*(2–3), 117–128.

Jarvie, G. (2003) Communitarianism, sport and social capital: 'Neighbourly insights into Scottish sport'. *International Review for the Sociology of Sport, 38*(2), 139–153.

Jarvie, G. (2006) *Sport, Culture and Society: An introduction*. London: Routledge.

Jarvie, G. (2011) Sport, development and aid: can sport make a difference? *Sport in Society*, *14*(2), 241–252.

Jarvie, G. and Maguire, J. (1994) *Sport and Leisure in Social Thought*. London: Routledge.

Jeffery, N. (2008) We're beating drug cheats: Rogge. Available: www.theaustralian.com.au/news/were-beating-drug-cheats-rogge/story-e6frg7mo-1111117289173 (accessed 29 March 2011).

Jessop, B. (1990) *State Theory: Putting the capitalist state in its place*. Cambridge: Cambridge University Press.

John, G., Sheard, R. and Vickery, B. (2007) *Stadia: A design and development guide*. Oxford: Architectural Press.

John, P. (1998) *Analysing Public Policy*. London: Pinter.

John, P. (2003) Is there life after policy streams, advocacy coalitions, punctuations? Using evolutionary theory to explain policy change. *The Policy Studies Journal*, *31*(4), 481–498.

Johnson, A. T. (1982) Government, opposition and sport: The role of domestic sports policy in generating political support. *Journal of Sport and Social Issues*, *6*(2) (Fall/Winter), 22–34.

Johnson, B. K. and Whitehead, J. C. (2000) Value of public goods from sports stadiums: The CVM approach. *Contemporary Economic Policy*, *18*(1), 48–58.

Johnson, K. N. and Ali, A. (2002) A tale of two seasons: participation and medal counts at the summer and winter Olympic Games. Available: www.wellesley.edu/economics/wkpapers/wellwp_0010.pdf (accessed 15 February 2011).

Johnston, G. and Percy-Smith, J. (2003) In search of social capital. *Policy and Politics*, *31*(3), 321–334.

Jokl, E. (1964) Health, wealth, and athletics. In E. Simin (Ed.) *International Research in Sport and Physical Education* (pp. 218–222). Springfield, IL: Thomas.

Jokl, E., Karvonen, M., Kihlberg, J., Koskela, A. and Noro, L. (1956) *Sports in the Cultural Pattern of the World*. Helsinki: Institute of Occupational Health.

Jones, C. (2001) A level playing field? Sports stadium infrastructure and urban development in the United Kingdom. *Environment and Planning A*, *33*(5), 845–861.

Jones, P. and Evans, J. (2008) *Urban Regeneration in the UK*. London: Sage.

Jordan, B. (2006) *Social Policy for the Twenty-First Century: New perspectives, big issues*. Cambridge: Polity Press.

Jordan, G. B. (2010) A theory-based logic model for innovation policy and evaluation. *Research Evaluation*, *19*(4), 263–273.

Kanerva, J. (2004) The Finnish university system and support for athletes. Paper presented at the Elite Sportspersons, Education and Vocational Preparation, UK Sport, London.

Kantola, J. and Outshoorn, J. (2007) Changing state feminism. In J. Outshoorn and J. Kantola (Eds) *Changing State Feminism* (pp. 1–20). Basingstoke: Palgrave Macmillan.

Kaplanidou, K. and Karadakis, K. (2010) Understanding the legacies of a host Olympic city: The case of the 2010 Vancouver Olympic Games. *Sport Marketing Quarterly*, *19*(2), 110–117.

Kau, M. Y. M. (1996) The power structure in Taiwan's political economy. *Asian Survey*, *36*(3), 287–305.

Kay, A. (2005) A critique of the use of path dependency in policy studies. *Public Administration*, *83*(3), 553–571.

Kay, T. (2009) Developing through sport: Evidencing sport impacts on young people. *Sport in Society*, *12*(9), 1177–1191.

Kay, T. and Bradbury, S. (2009) Youth sport volunteering: Developing social capital? *Sport, Education and Society*, *14*(1), 121–140.

Kellett, P., Hede, A.-M. and Chalip, L. (2008) Social policy for sport events: Leveraging (relationships with) teams from other nations for community benefit. *European Sport Management Quarterly*, *8*(2), 101–121.

Kelly, C. (2010) England 2018 World Cup bid cost. Available: www.bbc.co.uk/news/uk-england-11908445 (accessed 10 December 2010).

Kelso, P. (2011) Inside Qatar's bid – from Abuja to Buenos Aires. *The Daily Telegraph*, 15 January, 2-3.

Kendall, J. (2005) The third sector and the policy process in the UK: Ingredients in a hyperactive horizontal policy environment. *Third Sector European Policy Working Paper No.5*. Centre for Civil society. London: London Scholl of Economics and Political Science.

Kennett, C. (2002) Leisure, poverty and social exclusion: An analysis of leisure card schemes in Great Britain. PhD thesis. Loughborough: Loughborough University.

Kennett, C., Cerezuela, B., Sagarazazu, I. and Correa, R. (2008) El paper de l'esport en la integració de la població adulta estrangera immigrada a Catalunya. In *Recerca i immigració* (pp. 83–101). Barcelona: Generalitat de Catalunya: Secretaria per a la Immigració.

Keohane, R. (2002) Global governance and democratic accountability. Unpublished lecture. London: LSE.

Késenne, S. (2005) Do we need an economic impact study or a cost–benefit analysis of a sports event? *European Sport Management Quarterly*, 5(2), 133–142.

Késenne, S. (2009) The impact of pooling and sharing broadcast rights in professional team sports. *International Journal of Sport Finance*, 4(3), 211–218.

Khanlou, N. and Peter, E. (2005) Participatory action research: Considerations for ethical review. *Social Science and Medicine*, 60(10), 2333–2340.

Kicking AIDS Out Network (2010) History. Available: www.kickingaidsout.net/WhatisKickingAIDSOut/Pages/History.aspx (accessed 30 December 2010).

Kidd, B. (2008) A new social movement: Sport for development and peace. *Sport in Society*, 11(4), 370–380.

Kidd, B. and Donnelly, P. (2000) Human rights in sports. *International Review for the Sociology of Sport*, 35(2), 131–148.

Kidd, B., Edelman, R. and Brownell, S. (2001) Comparative analysis of doping scandals: Canada, Russia, and China. In W. Wilson and E. Derse (Eds) *Doping in Elite Sport: The politics of drugs in the Olympic Movement* (pp. 153–188). Champaign, IL: Human Kinetics.

Kim, N.-S. and Chalip, L. (2004) Why travel to the FIFA World Cup? Effects of motives, background, interest, and constraints. *Tourism Management*, 25(6), 695–707.

Kimmage, P. (1998) *Rough Ride: Behind the wheel with a pro cyclist.* London: Yellow Jersey.

Kingdon, J. W. (1984) *Agendas, Alternatives, and Public Policy.* Glenview, IL: HarperCollins.

Kissoudi, P. (2008) The Athens Olympics: Optimistic legacies – post-Olympic assets and the struggle for their realization. *International Journal of the History of Sport*, 25(14), 1972–1990.

Kiviaho, P. and Mäkelä, P. (1978) Olympic success: A sum of non-material and material factors. *International Review of Sport Sociology*, 13(2), 5–17.

Knights, D. (2004) Michel Foucault. In S. Linstead (Ed.) *Organization Theory and Postmodern Thought* (pp. 14–33). London: Sage.

Kolev, B. (2008) Lex sportiva and Lex Mercatoria. *International Sports Law Journal*, January–April.

Koller, D. (2008) How the United States Government sacrifices athletes' constitutional rights in pursuit of national prestige. *Brigham Young University Law Review*, 5, 1465–1544.

Kooiman, J. (2003) *Governing as Governance.* London: Sage.

Kopp, R. J., Krupnick, A. J. and Toman, M. (1997) *Cost–Benefit Analysis and Regulatory Reform: An assessment of the science and the art.* Washington, DC: Resources for the Future. Available: www.rff.org/documents/rff-dp-97-19.pdf (accessed November 2010).

Krich, J. (2002) A shy 24-year-old slugger holds the pride of his diplomatically isolated island in his strong hands. *The Asian Wall Street Journal*, March, 8–10.

Krznaric, R. (2006) The limits of pro-poor agricultural trade in Guatemala: Land, labor and political power. *Journal of Human Development*, 7(1), 120–23.

Ku, Y. W. (2010) Social cohesion in a divided society: Lessons from Taiwan's welfare politics. In K. H. Mok, K. K. Leung and Y. W. Ku (Eds) *Social Cohesion in Greater China: Challenges for social policy and governance* (pp. 95–120). Singapore: World Scientific Publishing.

Kuhn, T. (1996) *The Structure of Scientific Revolutions*, (3rd edn). Chicago, IL: Chicago University Press.

Kuo, C. T. (2000) Taiwan's distorted democracy in comparative perspective. *African and Asia Studies*, 35(1), 85–111.

Kuper, G. and Sterken, E. (2008) Evaluation of Beijing 2008 Olympic medal tally forecasts: Who has won? Unpublished paper acquired via personal correspondence with the authors.

Kuper G. and Sterken, E. (2010) Evaluation of Vancouver 2010 Olympic medal tally forecasts: Who has won? Unpublished paper acquired via personal correspondence with the authors.

Kurer, O. (1996) The political foundations of economic development policies. *The Journal of Development Studies*, 32(5), 645–668.

Kusek, J. Z. and Rist, R. C. (2004) *Ten Steps to a Results-based Monitoring and Evaluation System: A handbook for development practitioners.* Washington DC: The International Bank for Reconstruction and Development/The World Bank.

Lamchichi, A. (1993) Malaise social, islamisme et replis identitaires dans le monde arabe. *Confluences Méditerranés*, 6(Spring), 33–45.

Landman, T. (2008) *Issues and Methods in Comparative Politics* (3rd edn). London: Routledge.

Latty, F. (2007) *La lex sportiva: Recherche sur le droit transnational.* Leiden: Martinus Nijhoff Publishers.

Law, C. (1994) Manchester's bid for the Millennium Olympic Games. *Geography*, 79(3), 222–231.

Lawson, H. A. (2005) Empowering people, facilitating community development, and contributing to sustainable development: The social work of sport, exercise, and physical education programs. *Sport, Education and Society*, *10*(1), 135–160.

Leach, R. and Percy-Smith, J. (2001) *Local Governance in Britain*. Basingstoke: Palgrave Macmillan.

Leal, P. A. (2007) Participation: The ascendancy of a buzzword in the neo-liberal era. *Development in Practice*, *17*(4/5), 539–548.

Ledeneva, A. (2008) Blat and guanxi: Informal practices in Russia and China. *Comparative Studies in Society and History*, *50*(1), 118–144.

Lee, R. (2009) Social capital and business and management: Setting a research agenda. *International Journal of Management Reviews*, *11*(3), 247–273.

Leeds, M. and von Allmen, P. (2005) *The Economics of Sports*. Boston, MA: Pearson.

Leeuw, F. and Vaessen, J. (2009) *Impact Evaluations and Development: NONIE Guidance on Impact Evaluation*. Washington, DC: World Bank.

Lefebvre, H. (1968) *Le droit à la ville* [*The Right to the City*]. Paris: Editions Anthropos.

Le Galès, P. (2011) Policy instruments and governance. In M. Bevir (Ed.) *The Sage Handbook of Governance* (pp. 142–159). London: Sage.

Lemarchand, R. and Legg, K. (1972) Political clientelism and development. In R. C. Macridis and B. E. Brown (Eds) *Comparative politics* (pp.149–178). Chicago, IL: Dorsey Press.

Lenihan, H. (2011) Enterprise policy evaluation: Is there a 'new' way of doing it? *Evaluation and Program Planning*, *34*(4), 323–332.

Lenskyj, H. (1996) When winners are losers: Toronto and Sydney bids for the summer Olympics. *Journal of Sport and Social Issues*, *20*(4), 392–410.

Lenskyj, H. (2000) *Inside the Olympic Industry: Power, politics and activism*. New York: State University of New York Press.

Leow, A. C. S. (2011) Policy-as-discourse and schools in the role of health promotion: The application of Bernstein's transmission context in policy analysis. *Discourse: Studies in the Cultural Politics of Education*, *32*(3), 309–328.

Levermore, R. (2008) Sport: A new engine of development? *Progress in Development Studies*, 8(2), 183–190.

Levermore, R. (2011) Evaluating sport-for-development: Approaches and critical issues. *Progress in Development Studies*, *11*(4), 339–353.

Levermore, R. and Beacom A. (2009) *Sport and International Development*. Basingstoke: Palgrave.

Levermore, R. and Beacom, A. (2012) Reassessing sport-for-development: Moving beyond 'mapping the territory'. *International Journal of Sport Policy and Politics*, *4*(1), 125–137.

Levin, P. T. (2010) Failed mega-events as urban development engines? The Planned Village for Stockholm 2004. *Proceedings of the Shanghai Forum, Shanghai, China*. Available: http://www.academia.edu/250652/Failed_Mega-Events_as_Urban_Development_Engines (accesssed 22 May 2013).

Levine, N. (1974) Why do countries win Olympic medals: Some structural correlates of Olympic Games success. *Sociology and Social Research*, *58*(4), 353–360.

Levitas, R. (2000) Community, utopia and New Labour. *Local Economy*, *15*(3), 188–197.

Levitas, R. (2005) *The Inclusive Society? Social exclusion and New Labour* (2nd edn). Basingstoke: Palgrave Macmillan.

Lewandowski, J. D. (2006) Capitalizing sociability: Rethinking the theory of social capital. In R. Edwards, J. Franklin and J. Holland (Eds) *Assessing Social Capital: Concepts, policy and practice* (pp. 14–28). Newcastle: Cambridge Scholars Publishing.

Lewin, K. (1951) *Field Theory in Social Science: Selected theoretical papers*. New York: Harper & Row.

Lewis, D. (2007) *The Management of Non-Governmental Development Organizations* (2nd edn). London: Routledge.

Lewis, J. (2005) New Labour's approach to the voluntary sector: Independence and the meaning of partnership. *Social Policy and Society*, *4*(2), 121–131.

Lewis, P. A. (2000) Realism, causality and the problem of social structure. *Journal for the Theory of Social Behaviour*, *30*(3), 249–268.

Ley, C. (2009) *Acción psicosocial a través de movimiento, juegos y deporte en contextos de violencia y de conflicto. Investigación sobre la adecuación sociocultural de la 'terapia a través del deporte' y evaluación de un programa con mujeres en Guatemala*. Doctoral thesis. Madrid: Universidad Politécnica de Madrid (UPM).

Ley, C. and Rato Barrio, M. (2010) Movement, games and sport in psychosocial intervention: A critical discussion of its potential and limitations within cooperation for development. *Intervention*, *8*(2), 106–120.

Ley, C. and Rato Barrio, M. (2011a) Movement and sport therapy with women in Guatemalan context of violence and conflict. *Body, Movement and Dance in Psychotherapy: An International Journal for Theory, Research and Practice*, 6(2), 145–160.

Ley, C. and Rato Barrio, M. (2011b) Evaluierung der psychosozialen Intervention APM in Guatemala. In K. Petry, M. Groll and W. Tokarski (Eds) *Sport und internationale Entwicklungszusammenarbeit* (pp. 159–182). Cologne: Sportverlag Strauss.

Li, T.Y. (1996) *The Selected Compilation of Chinese Reform Document of Sport (1992–1995) (internal document)*. The Lecture of State Councilor Li Tieying for 1993 All States Sports Minister Conference. Beijing: NSC.

Liang, S. L. (1993) Social development, power and the formation of sports culture: An analysis of Taiwanese baseball society, history, and culture, 1895–1990. Unpublished master dissertation (in Chinese). Taipei: National Chengchi University.

Lin, C. Y. (2003) Taiwan sport: The interrelationship between sport and politics through three successive political regimes using baseball as an example. Unpublished doctoral dissertation. Brighton: Brighton University.

Lindblom, C. (1959) The science of muddling through. *Public Administration Review*, 19(2), 78–88.

Lindblom, C. E. (1977) *Politics and Markets: The world's political–economic systems*. New York: Basic Books.

Lindsey, I. (2009) Collaboration in local sport services in England: Issues emerging from case studies of two local authority areas. *International Journal of Sport Policy*, 1(1), 71–88.

Lindsey, I. (2010a) Improving partnership, increasing participation? A decentred study of a local sport and physical activity alliance. *Sport Policy Conference, University of Birmingham, 19 July 2010*.

Lindsey, I. (2010b) Governance of lottery sport programmes: National direction of local partnerships in the new opportunities for PE and sport programme. *Managing Leisure*, 15(3), 198–213.

Lindsey, I. and Banda, D. (2010) Sport and the fight against HIV/AIDS in Zambia: A 'partnership approach'? *International Review for the Sociology of Sport*, 46(1), 90–107.

Lingane, A. and Olsen, S. (2004) Guidelines for social return on investment. *California Management Review*, 46(3), 116–135.

Lister, R. (2004) The Third Way's social investment state. In J. Lewis and R. Surrender (Eds) *Welfare State Change: Towards a third way?* (pp. 157–181). Oxford: Oxford University Press.

Liu, Y., Taylor, P. and Shibli, S. (2009) Sport equity: Benchmarking the performance of English public sport facilities. *European Sport Management Quarterly*, 9(1), 3–21.

Livingston, L. A., Tirone, S. C., Miller, A. J. and Smith, E. L. (2008) Participation in coaching by Canadian immigrants: Individuals accommodations and sport system receptivity. *International Journal of Sports Science and Coaching*, 3, 403–415.

Lock, D., Taylor, T. and Darcy, S. (2008) Soccer and social capital in Australia: Social networks in transition. In M. Nicholson and R. Hoye (Eds) *Sport and Social Capital* (pp. 317–338). Oxford: Butterworth-Heinemann.

Lock Kunz, J. and Sykes, S. (2007) *From Mosaic to Harmony: Multicultural Canada in the 21st century: Results of regional roundtables*. Ottawa, ON: Policy Research Initiative.

Löfman, P., Pelkonen, M. and Pietilä, A.-M. (2004) Ethical issues in participatory action research. *Scandinavian Journal of Caring Sciences*, 18(3), 333–340.

Logan, J. and Molotch, H. (1987) *Urban Fortunes: The political economy of place*. Berkeley, CA: University of California Press.

Long, J., Welch, M., Bramham, P., Butterfield, J., Hylton, K. and Lloyd, E. (2002) *Count Me In: The dimensions of social inclusion through culture and sport*. London: DCMS.

Louw, B. and Delport, R. (2006) Contextual challenges in South Africa: The role of a research ethics committee. *Journal of Academic Ethics*, 4(1), 39–60.

Lukes, S. (1974) *Power: A radical view*. London: Macmillan.

Lukes, S. (1993) Three distinctive views of power compared. In: M. Hill (Ed.) *The Policy Process: A Reader* (pp. 51–58). Hemel Hempstead: Harvester Wheatsheaf.

Lukes, S. (2005) *Power: A Radical View* (2nd Edn). Basingstoke: Palgrave Macmillan.

Luukkonen, T. (2000) Additionality of EU framework programmes. *Research Policy*, 29(6), 711–724.

Lyazghi, M. (2006) *La Makhzénisation du Sport*. Dat El Baida: Matbaat el Nadjah.

Lynn, L. E. (2011) The persistence of hierarchy. In M. Bevir (Ed.) *The Sage Handbook of Governance* (pp. 218–236). London: Sage.

MacAloon, J. J. (2008) 'Legacy' as a managerial/magical discourse in contemporary Olympic affairs. *International Journal of the History of Sport*, 25(14), 2060–2071.

McCree, R. (2009) Sport Policy and the New Public Management in the Caribbean. *Public Management Review, 11*(4), 461–476.

McCurry, J. (2011) China overtakes Japan as world's second-largest economy. *The Guardian*. Available: www.guardian.co.uk/business/2011/feb/14/china-second-largest-economy (accessed 14 February 2011).

McDonald, I. (2005) Theorising partnerships: Governance, communicative action and sport policy. *Journal of Social Policy, 34*(4), 579–600.

McEldowney, J. J. (1997) Policy evaluation and the concepts of deadweight and additionality. *Evaluation, 3*(2), 175–188.

MacFarquhar, R. (1997) *The Politics of China: The eras of Mao and Deng*. Cambridge: Cambridge University Press.

McGillvray, D. and McIntosh, A. (2006) 'Football is my life': Theorizing social practice in the Scottish professional football field. *Sport In Society, 9*(3), 371–387.

McHugh, D. (2006) Cost–benefit analysis of an Olympic Games. Master's thesis. Kingston, ON: Queen's University.

McKay, J. (2004) Reassessing development theory: Modernisation and beyond. In D. Kingsbury, J. Remenyi, J McKay and J. Hunt (Eds) *Key Issues in Development* (pp. 53–58). Basingstoke: Palgrave Macmillan.

McKenna, J. and Dunstan-Lewis, N. (2004) An action research approach to supporting elite student-athletes in higher education. *European Physical Education Review, 10*(2), 179–198.

MacKenzie, R., Collin, J. and Sriwongcharoen, K. (2007) Thailand – lighting up a dark market: British American Tobacco, sports sponsorship and the circumvention of legislation. *Journal of Epidemiology and Community Health, 61*(1), 28–33.

McRobbie, A. (2009) *The Aftermath of Feminism: Gender, culture, and social change*. London: Sage.

Madrid 2016 Bid (2006) *Madrid 2016 Applicant City. Replies to the Questionnaire for Cities Applying to become Candidates Cities to host the Games of the XXXI Olympiad in 2016*. Madrid: Madrid 2016 Bid.

Madzivhandila, T. P., Griffith, G. R., Fleming, E. and Nesamvuni, A. E. (2010) Meta-evaluations in government and government institutions: A case study example from the Australian Centre for International Agricultural Research. Paper presented at the *Annual Conference of the Australian Agricultural and Resource Economics Society*. Available: http://agecnsearch.umn.edu/bitstream/59098/2/Madzivhandila%2c Percy.pdf (accessed 13 April 2011).

Maening, W. and du Plessis, S. (2009) Sport stadia, sporting events and urban development: International experience and the ambitious of Durban. *Urban Forum, 20*(1), 61–76.

Maening, W. and Schwarthoff, F. (2006) Stadium architecture and regional economic development: International experience and the plans of Durban, South Africa. In D. Torres (Ed.) *Major Sport Events as Opportunity for Development: The international promotion of the city* (pp. 120–129). Valencia: MMVI.

Maguire, J. (1999) *Global Sport: Identities, societies, and civilizations*. Cambridge: Polity Press.

Majone, G. (1994) The rise of the regulatory state in Europe. *West European Politics, 17*(3), 77–101.

Maloney, W. (1999) Contracting out the participation function: Social capital and chequebook participation. In J. W. van Deth, M. Maraffis, K. Newton and P. F. Whiteley (Eds) *Social Capital and European Democracy* (pp. 100–110). London: Routledge.

Maloney, W., Smith, G. and Stoker, G. (2000) Social capital and urban governance: Adding a more contextualised 'top-down' perspective. *Political Studies, 48*(4), 802–820.

Mankiw, N. G. (2004) *Principles of Macroeconomics*. Boston, MA: South Western College Publishing.

Mann, M. (1993) Nation-state in Europe and other continents: Diversifying, developing, not dying. *Daedulus, 3*(Summer), 115–140.

Mark, M. and Weiss, C. H. (2006) The oral history of evaluation, part 4: The professional evolution of Carol H. Weiss. *American Journal of Evaluation, 27*(4), 475–484.

Markula, P. and Pringle, R. (2006) *Foucault, Sport and Exercise: Power, knowledge and transforming the self*. London: Routledge.

Marsh, D. and Rhodes, R. A. W. (1992) *Policy Networks in British Government*. Oxford: Clarendon Press.

Marsh, D. and Stoker, G. (2010) *Theory and Methods in Political Science* (3rd edn). Basingstoke: Palgrave Macmillan.

Marsh, D., Smith, M. J. and Hothi, N. (2006) Globalization and the state. In C. Hay, M. Lister and D. Marsh (Eds) *The State: Theories and Issues* (pp. 172–189). New York: Palgrave Macmillan.

Marshall, C. (1997) *Feminist Critical Policy Analysis*. Washington, DC: Falmer Press.

Marshall, C. (1999) Researching the margins: Feminist critical policy analysis. *Educational Policy, 13*(1), 59–76.

Matsumoto, M. (2002) Political democratization and KMT party-owned enterprises in Taiwan. *The Developing Economies, XL*(3), 359–380.

Maude, F. (2010) Big society is better society. *New Statesman, 139*(5021).

Maxwell, J. A. (1996). *Qualitative Research Design: An Interactive Approach.* Thousand Oaks, CA: Sage.

Maxwell, J. A. (2010) Using numbers in qualitative research. *Qualitative Inquiry,* 475–482.

Mayne, J. (2007) Challenges and lessons in implementing results-based management. *Evaluation, 13*(1), 87–109.

Mayocchi, L. and Hanrahan, S. (2000) Transferable skills for career change. In D. Lavallee and P. Wylleman (Eds) *Career Transitions in Sport: International perspectives* (pp. 95–110). London: Fitness Information Technology.

Mennell, S. and Goudsblom, J. (1998) *On Civilization, Power and Knowledge: Heritage of sociology.* Chicago, IL: Chicago University Press.

Merikoski-Silius, T. (2006) *Critical Evaluation of Aspects of the Athletes' Study and Career Support Service in Finland.* Lausanne: Université Claude Bernard.

Meyer, J. W. and Rowan, B. (1991) Institutionalized organisations: Formal structure as myth and ceremony. In W. W. Powell and P. DiMaggio (Eds) *The New Institutionalism in Organizational Analysis* (pp. 41–62). Chicago, IL: University of Chicago Press.

Miah, A. (2004) *Genetically Modified Athletes: Biomedical ethics, gene doping and sport.* London and New York: Routledge.

Michael, E. (2006) *Public Policy: The competitive framework.* South Melbourne: Oxford University Press.

Michels, R. (1911/1962) *Political Parties: A sociological study of oligarchical tendencies in modern democracy.* New York: Collier Books.

Michie, J. and Oughton, C. (2005) The corporate governance of professional football clubs in England. *Corporate Governance, 13*(4), 517–531.

Miller, G. (1979) *Behind the Olympic Rings.* Lynn, MA: H. O. Zimman.

Miller, P. and Kerr, G. (2002) Conceptualizing excellence: Past, present, and future. *Journal of Applied Sport Psychology, 14*(3), 140–153.

Miller, P. and Kerr, G. (2003) The role experimentation of intercollegiate student athletes. *Sport Psychologist, 17*(2), 196–219.

Miller, R. (1999) *Researching Life Stories and Family Histories.* London: Sage.

Ministry of Health (2006/7) *New Zealand Health Survey.* Wellington: Ministry of Health.

Minkler, M. (2004) Ethical challenges for the 'outside' researcher in community-based participatory research. *Health Education and Behavior, 31*(6), 684–697.

Minkler, M., Fadem, P., Perry, M., Blum, K., Moore, L. and Rogers, J. (2002) Ethical dilemmas in participatory action research: A case study from the disability community. *Health Education and Behavior, 29*(1), 14–29.

Misener, L. and Mason, D. (2008) Urban regimes and the sporting events agenda: A cross-national comparison of civic development strategies. *Journal of Sport Management, 22*(5), 603–627.

Misener, L. and Mason, D. (2009) Fostering community development through sporting events strategies: An examination of urban regime perceptions. *Journal of Sport Management, 23*(6), 770–794.

Mizrahi, S., Mehrez, A. and Friedman, L. (2006) Game theory and the sport sciences: Setting an optimal threshold level in sport competitions. *International Journal of Sport Management and Marketing, 1*(3), 255–262.

Møller, V. (2005) Knud Enemark Jensen's death during the 1960 Rome Olympics: A search for truth? *Sport in History, 25*(3), 452–471.

Møller, V. (2010) *The Ethics of Doping and Anti-Doping.* London and New York: Routledge.

Moore, K. (2008) Sports heritage and the re-imaged city: the National Football Museum, Preston. *International Journal of Culture Policy,* 14(4), 445–461.

Moore, M. and Hartley, J. (2008) Innovations in governance. *Public Management Review, 10*(1), 3–20.

Morgan, D. (2007) Paradigms lost and pragmatism regained: Methodological implications of combining qualitative and quantitative methods. *Journal of Mixed Methods Research, 1*(1), 48–76.

Morgan, M. (2002) Optimizing the structure of elite competitions in professional sport: Lessons from rugby union. *Managing Leisure, 7*(1), 41–60.

Morgan, W. J. (1994) *Leftist Theories of Sport: A critique and reconstruction.* Urbana, IL: University of Illinois Press.

Morrison, Z. (2003) Cultural justice and addressing 'social exclusion': A case study of a single regeneration budget project in Blackbird Leys, Oxford. In R. Imrie and M. Raco (Eds) *Urban Renaissance: New Labour and urban policy* (pp. 139–162). Bristol: Policy Press.

Morton, R. H. (2002) Who won the Sydney 2000 Olympics? An allometric approach. *The Statistician, 51*(2), 147–155.

Mules, T. and Dwyer, L. (2005) Public sector support for sport tourism events: The role of cost–benefit analysis. *Sport in Society, 8*(2), 338–355.

Mulroy, E. A. and Lauber, H. (2004) A user-friendly approach to program evaluation and effective community interventions for families at risk of homelessness. *Social Work, 49*(4), 573–586.

Mwaanga, O. (2001) *Kicking AIDS Out Through Movement Games*. Oslo: Norwegian Development Agency.

Nash, V. (Ed.) (2002) *Reclaiming Community*. London: IPPR.

National Audit Office (2005) *UK Sport: Supporting elite athletes*. Report by the Comptroller and Auditor General. London: The Stationery Office.

Neuman, M., Bitton, A. and Glantz, S. (2002) Tobacco industry strategies for influencing European Community tobacco advertising legislation. *Lancet, 359*(9314), 1323–1330.

New, B. and LeGrand, J. (1999) Monopoly in sports broadcasting. *Policy Studies, 20*(1), 23–36.

Newman, J. (2001) *Modernising Governance: New Labour, policy and society*. London: Sage.

Newton, K. (1999) Social capital and democracy in modern Europe. In J. W. van Deth, M. Maraffis, K. Newton and P. F. Whiteley (Eds) *Social Capital and European Democracy* (pp. 3–22). London: Routledge.

Nicholls, S. (2009) On the backs of peer educators: Using theory to interrogate the role of young people in the field of sport-in-development. In R. Levermore and A. Beacom (Eds) *Sport and International Development* (pp. 156–175). New York: Palgrave Macmillian.

Nicholls, S., Giles, A. and Sethna, C. (2011) Perpetuating the 'lack of evidence' discourse in sport for development: Privileged voices, unheard stories and subjugated knowledge. *International Review for the Sociology of Sport, 46*(3), 249–264.

Nichols, G. (2007) *Sport and Crime Reduction*. London: Routledge.

Nichols, G. and Crow, I. (2004) Measuring the impact of crime reduction interventions involving sports activities for young people. *The Howard Journal of Criminal Justice, 43*(3), 267–283.

Nicholson, M. (2007) *Sport and the Media: Managing the nexus*. Oxford: Elsevier, Butterworth-Heinemann.

Nicholson, M. and Hoye, R. (Eds) (2008) *Sport and Social Capital*. Oxford: Butterworth-Heinemann.

Nicholson, M., Hoye, R. and Houlihan, B. (2011) Conclusion. In M. Nicholson, R. Hoye and B. Houlihan (Eds) *Participation in Sport: International perspectives* (pp. 294–308). London: Routledge.

Nieto, F. and Sobejano, E. (2001) Madrid Games. In Ministerio de Fomento (Ed.) *Madrid Games: Madrid en Juegos* (p. 7). Dirección General de la Vivienda, la Arquitectura y el Urbanismo, Ministerio de Fomento.

Nilsson, N. and Hogben, D. (1983) Metaevaluation. *New Directions for Program Evaluation, 1983*(19), 83–97.

Niskanen, W. A. (1971) *Bureaucracy and Representative Government*. Chicago, IL: Aldine-Atherton.

Noll, R. G. (2007) Broadcasting and team sports. *Scottish Journal of Political Economy, 54*(3), 400–421.

Noll, R. and Zimbalist, A. (2000) Sports, jobs and taxes: Are new stadiums worth the cost? In R. Wassmer (Ed.) *Readings in Urban Economics* (pp. 169–175). London: Blackwell.

Novikov, A. D. and Maximenko, A. M. (1972) The influence of selected socio-economic factors on the level of sports achievements in the various countries. *International Review of Sport Sociology, 7*, 22–44.

Nowlin, M. (2011) Theories of the policy process: State of the research and emerging trends. *The Policy Studies Journal, 39*(S1), 39–60.

Numerato, D. (2008) Czech sport governing bodies and social capital. *International Review for the Sociology of Sport, 43*(1), 21–34.

Numerato, D. and Baglioni, S. (2011) The dark side of social capital: An ethnography of sport governance. *International Review for the Sociology of Sport, 47*(5), 594–611.

Oakley, B. and Green, M. (2001) The production of Olympic champions: International perspectives on elite sport development system. *European Journal for Sport Management, 8*(1), 83–105.

O'Brien, D. (2006) Event business leveraging: The Sydney 2000 Olympic Games. *Annals of Tourism Research, 33*(1), 240–261.

O'Brien, D. (2007) Points of leverage: Maximizing host community benefit from a regional surfing festival. *European Sport Management Quarterly, 7*(2), 141–165.

O'Brien, D. and Chalip, L. (2008) Sport events and strategic leveraging: Pushing towards the triple bottom line. In A. G. Woodside and D. Martin (Eds) *Tourism Management: Analysis, behaviour and strategy* (pp. 318–338). Oxford: CAB International.

O'Brien, D. and Gardiner, S. (2006) Creating sustainable mega event impacts: Networking and relationship development through pre-event training. *Sport Management Review, 9*(1), 25–47.

OCASI (Ontario Council of Agencies Serving Immigrants) (2005) *OCASI Research on Inclusive Recreation Model for Immigrants and Refugee Youth, Provisional Model.* Toronto, ON: OCASI. Available: www.google.ca/search?sourceid=navclient&ie=UTF-8&rlz=1T4SKPB_enCA385CA386&q=Ontario+Council+of+Agencies+Serving+Immigrants+Provisional+Model (accessed 18 February 2011).

Ochel, W. and Röhn, O. (2006) Ranking of countries: The WEF, IMD, Fraser and Heritage indices. CESito DICE Report, *2*, 48–60.

Offe, C. (1984) *Contradictions of the Welfare State.* Cambridge, MA: MIT Press.

Office of the Commission of Official Languages (2000) *Official Languages in the Canadian Sports System, Volumes 1 and 2.* Ottawa, ON: Minister of Public Works and Government Services.

Oh, C. and Hammitt, W. E. (2010) Determining economic benefits of park trails: Management implications. *Journal of Park and Recreation Administration, 28*(2), 94–107.

Ohmae, K. (1990) *The Borderless World.* London: Collins.

Ohmae, K. (1995) *The End of the Nation State.* New York: Free Press.

Okayasu, I., Kawahara, Y. and Nogawa, H. (2010) The relationship between community sport clubs and social capital in Japan: A comparative study between the comprehensive community sport clubs and the traditional community sports clubs. *International Review for the Sociology of Sport, 45*(2), 163–186.

Okner, B. (1974) Subsidies of stadiums and arenas. In R. Noll (Ed.) *Government and the Sports Business* (pp. 325–348). Washington, DC: Brookings Institution.

Olssen, M. (1999) *Michel Foucault: Materialism and education.* Westport, CT: Bergin & Garvey.

Olympic Solidarity (1975) *Activity Report, as to May 10 1975.* Lausanne: International Olympic Committee.

Olympic Solidarity (1986) *Report 1986.* Lausanne: International Olympic Committee.

Olympic Solidarity (2001) *Under way! 2001 Report.* Lausanne: International Olympic Committee.

Olympic Solidarity (2005) *Aligning Strength: 2005 Report.* Lausanne: International Olympic Committee.

Omidvar, R. and Richmond, T. (2005) Immigrant settlement and social inclusion in Canada. In T. Richmond and A. Saloojee (Eds) *Social Inclusion: Canadian perspectives* (pp. 155–177). Toronto, ON: Laidlaw Foundation.

Önsel, S., Ülengin, F., Ulusoy, G., Aktas, E., Kabak, Ö. and Topcu, I. (2008) A new perspective on the competitiveness of nations. *Socio-Economic Planning Sciences, 42*(4), 221–246.

Ooijen, B. (2010) *Education and sport: Dual careers – perspective of the European Commission.* Paper presented on behalf of DG Education and Culture – Sport Unit Maribor, Slovenia.

Organisation for Economic Co-operation and Development (2004) *OECD Principles of Corporate Governance.* Paris: OECD.

Orloff, A. S. and Palier, B. (2009) The power of gender perspectives: Feminist influences on policy paradigms, social science and social politics. *Social Politics, 16*(4), 405–412.

Osborne, D. and Gaebler, T. (1992) *Reinventing Government.* Reading, MA: Addison-Wesley.

Outshoorn, J. and Kantola, J. (Eds) (2007) *Changing State Feminism.* Basingstoke: Palgrave Macmillan.

Oviatt, D. (2011) Hockey Canada looks to new source to fill rinks. *The Vancouver Sun*, 15 February, p. C9.

Pack, C. and Glyptis, S. (1989) *Developing Sport and Leisure: Good practice in urban regeneration.* London: DOE.

Pap, E. (2011) Pacific coast association shooting for 20,000 skaters: National initiative targets recent immigrants and First Nations families while enrolment on the West Coast continues to climb. *The Vancouver Sun*, 17 March, p. F5.

Papadimitriou, D. and Taylor, P. (2000) Organisational effectiveness of Hellenic national sports organisations: A multiple constituency approach. *Sport Management Review, 3*(1), 23–46.

Paradiso, E. (2010) Corruption and politics in Argentine soccer. Unpublished doctoral dissertation. Nova Scotia: Dalhousie University.

Paramio, J. L., Buraimo, B. and Campos, C. (2008) From modern to postmodern: The development of football stadia in Europe. *Sport in Society, 11*(5), 517–534.

Paramio-Salcines, J. L. (2000) Public–private partnerships, sport and urban regeneration in Britain and Spain. Unpublished PhD thesis. Loughborough: Loughborough University.

Paramio-Salcines, J. L. and Dobson, N. (2004) The role of major sports events as a new strategy in Western urban policies: The case of Madrid and London bids to the 2012 Olympic Games. *Proceedings of the 12th European Sport Management Congress, Ghent, Flanders/Belgium*, pp. 235–236.

Paramio-Salcines, J. L., Beotas, E. and Dobson, N. (2011) The two unsuccessful bids of the city of Madrid to the 2012 and 2016 Olympic Games and its effects on sports venues and infrastructure in the city. *Proceedings of the 19th European Sport Management Congress, Madrid*, pp. 369–370.

Paraschak, V. (1989) Native sports history: Pitfalls and promises. *Canadian Journal of History of Sport*, *20*(1), 57–68.

Parrish, R. (2003a) *Sports Law and Policy in the European Union*. Manchester: Manchester University Press.

Parrish, R. (2003b) The birth of European Union sports law. *Entertainment Law*, *2*(2), 20–39.

Parrish, R. (2003c) The politics of sports regulation in the EU. *Journal of European Public Policy*, *10*(2), 246–262.

Parrish, R. (2003d) The politics of sports regulation in the European Union. *Journal of European Public Policy*, *10*(2), 246–262.

Parrish, R. (2008) Access to major events on television under European Law. *Journal of Consumer Policy*, *31*(1), 79–98.

Parrish, R. and Miettinen, S. (2008) *The Sporting Exception in European Union Law*. The Hague: TMC Asser Press.

Parsons, D. W. (1995) *Public Policy: An introduction to the theory and practice of policy analysis*. Aldershot and Brookfield, VT: Edward Elgar.

Parsons, W. (1996) *Public Policy: An introduction to the theory and practice of policy analysis*. Cheltenham: Edward Elgar.

Pass Notes (2011) Radical Feminists. *The Guardian*, 9 February. Available: www.guardian.co.uk/world/2011/feb/08/pass-notes-radical-feminist?INTCMP=SRCH 24 (accessed 10 February2011).

Patton, M. (1978) *Utilisation-Focused Evaluation*. Beverly Hills, CA: Sage Publications.

Patton, M. Q. (1997) *Utilization-Focused Evaluation: The new century text* (3rd edn). Thousand Oaks, CA: Sage Publications.

Patton, T. (2008) *Utilization-Focused Evaluation* (4th edn). Saint Paul, MN: Sage Publications.

Patton, T. (2010) Panel discussion at Carleton University hosted by the International Development Research Centre, the World Bank and the International Program for Development Evaluation Training, June (recorded by T. Brown). Available: www.idrc.ca/EN/Programs/Evaluation/Pages/ArticleDetails (accessed 15 February 2011).

Pawson, R. (2006) *Evidence-Based Policy: A realist perspective*. London: Sage Publications.

Pawson, R. and Tilley, N. (1997) *Realistic Evaluation*. London: Sage Publications.

Payne, M. (2006) *Olympic Turnaround*. London: Praeger.

Pedlar, A. (1996) Community development: What does it mean for recreation and leisure? *Journal of Applied Recreation Research*, *21*(1), 5–23.

Peffley, M. A. and Hurwitz, J. (1985) A hierarchical model of attitude constraint. *American Journal of Political Science*, *29*(4), 871–890.

Pérez-Sales, P. (2006) *Repensar experiencias. Evaluación (y diseño) de programas psicosociales. Metodologías y técnicas*. Grupo de Acción Comunitaria. Available: www.psicosocial.net (accessed 10 July 2006).

Perks, T. (2007) Does sport foster social capital? The contribution of sport to a lifestyle of community participation. *Sociology of Sport Journal*, *24*(4), 378–401.

Persson, C. (2002) The Olympic Games site decision. *Tourism Management*, *23*(1), 27–36.

Peters, G. (2008) *The Two Futures of Governing: Decentering and recentering process in governing*. Working Paper 144, Political Science Series. Vienna: Institution of Advanced Studies.

Phillips, N. and Hardy, C. (2002) *Discourse Analysis: Investigating processes of social construction*. Thousand Oaks, CA: Sage Publications.

Phillpots, L., Grix, J. and Quarmby, T. (2010) Centralized grassroots sport policy and 'new governance': A case study of County Sports Partnerships in the UK – unpacking the paradox. *International Review for the Sociology of Sport*, *43*(3), 265–281.

Piattoni, S. (2001) Clientelism in historical and comparative perspective. In S. Piattoni (Ed.) *Clientelism Interests and Democratic Representation: The European experience in historical and comparative perspective* (pp. 1–30). Cambridge: Cambridge University Press.

Pierre, J. and Peters, B. G. (2000) *Governance and the State*. Basingstoke: Palgrave Macmillan.

Pierre, J. and Stoker, G. (2000) *Towards Multi-Level Governance: Developments in British politics*, 6. London: Macmillan.

Pieth, M. (2011) *Governing FIFA: Concept Paper and Report*. 19 September. Available: http://fr.fifa.com/mm/document/affederation/footballgovernance/01/54/99/69/fifagutachten-en.pdf (accessed 20 March 2011).

Piggin, J. (2010) Resistance is not futile: Effects of challenging public sport and recreation policy. *International Journal of Sport Policy*, *2*(1), 85–99.

Piggin, J., Jackson, S. and Lewis, M. (2009a) Telling the truth in public policy: An analysis of New Zealand sport policy discourse. *Sociology of Sport Journal*, *26*(3), 462–482.

Piggin, J., Jackson, S. and Lewis, M. (2009b) Knowledge, power and politics: Contesting 'evidence-based' national sport policy. *International Review for the Sociology of Sport*, *44*(1), 87–101.

Piven, F. F. (2008) Can power from below change the world? *American Sociological Review*, *73*(1), 1–14.

Plant, R. (1974) *Community and Ideology*. London: Routledge & Kegan Paul.

Porter, M. E. (1990) *The Competitive Advantage of Nations*. London: Macmillan Press.

Pratchett, L. (2004) Local autonomy, local democracy and the 'New Localism'. *Political Studies*, *52*(2), 358–375.

Preuss, H. (2004a) Calculating the regional economic impact of the Olympic Games. *European Sport Management Quarterly*, *4*(4), 234–253.

Preuss, H. (2004b) *The Economics of Staging the Olympic Games*. Northampton, MA: Edward Elgar Publishing.

Preuss, H. and Solberg, H. A. (2006) Sport-Mega-Events – Langfristige Tourismuseffekte [Sport mega events – long-term tourism effects]. *PlanerIn – Fachzeitschrift für Stadt-, Regional- und Landesplanung*, *1*, 12–15.

Preuss, H. and Weiß, H.-J. (2003) *Torchholder value added: Der ökonomische Nutzen der Olympischen Spiele 2012 in Frankfurt Rhein/Main*. Eschborn: AWV-Verlag.

Prideaux, S. (2005) *Not so New Labour: A sociological critique of New Labour's policy and practice*. Bristol: Policy Press.

Prime Minister's Office (2000) Joint Statement by the Prime Minister the Right Honourable Tony Blair MP and Chancellor Gerhard Schroeder. September 2000. Available: www.pm.gov.uk/output/Page2855.asp (accessed 2 May 2012).

Prime Minister's Office (2001) Joint Statement by the Prime Minister and Chancellor Gerhard Schroeder. 30 January 2001. Available: www.pm.gov.uk/output/Page2653.asp (accessed 2 May 2012).

Pringle, R. (2005) Masculinities, sport and power: A critical comparison of Gramscian and Foucauldian inspired theoretical tools. *Journal of Sport and Social*, *29*(3), 256–278.

Putnam, R. (1993) *Making Democracy Work: Civic traditions in modern Italy*. Princeton, NJ: Princeton University Press.

Putnam, R. (1995a) Tuning in, tuning out: The strange disappearance of social capital in America. *PS: Political Science and Politics*, *28*(4), 664–683.

Putnam, R. (1995b) Bowling alone: America's declining social capital. *Journal of Democracy*, *6*(1), 65–78.

Putnam, R. (1998) Foreword. *Housing Policy Debate*, *9*(1), v–viii.

Putnam, R. (2000) *Bowling Alone: The collapse and revival of American community*. New York: Simon & Schuster.

Putsis, W. P. (1998) Winners and losers: Redistribution and the use of economic impact analysis in marketing. *Journal of Macromarketing*, *18*(1), 24–33.

Rabinow, P. (Ed.) (1984) *The Foucault Reader*. New York: Pantheon Books.

Raeymaekers, T. (2007) The power of protection: Governance and transborder trade on the Congo–Ugandan Frontier. Unpublished doctoral dissertation. Ghent: Ghent University.

Rahmatian, M. (2005) *Contingency Valuation Methods*. Available: http://iwlearn.net/publications/misc/caspianev_rahmatian_cvm.pdf (accessed 13 April 2011).

Rail, G. (2002) Postmodernism and sport studies. In J. Maguire and K. Young (Eds) *Theory, Sport and Society* (pp. 179–207). Oxford: JAI.

Ramose, M. B. (1999) *African Philosophy through Ubuntu*. Harare: Mond Press.

Ransley, J. (2007) Patriarchy dominates PBRF system. *Salient* (July). Available: www.salient.org.nz/news/patriarchy-dominates-pbrf-system (accessed 28 March, 2011).

Raphael, D. (2000) The question of evidence in health. *Health Promotion International*, *15*(4), 355–367.

Rasmussen, K. (2010) Platini wants a European sports police to fight corruption. *Play The Game*, 18 May. Available: www.playthegame.org/news/detailed/platini-wants-a-european-sports-police-to-fight-corruption-4754.html (accessed 19 April 2010).

Rato Barrio, M. (2009) La Actividad Física y el Deporte como herramientas para fomentar el Interculturalismo en contextos postbélicos, en el marco de la Cooperación para el Desarrollo. Un proyecto en Guatemala (Centroamérica). Doctoral thesis. Madrid: Universidad Politécnica de Madrid.

Rato Barrio, M. and Ley, C. (2010a) Interculturalism through physical activity and sports in cooperation for development. *The International Journal of Sport and Society*, *1*(1), 271–283.

Rato Barrio, M. and Ley, C. (2010b) Principios de intervención en proyectos físico-deportivos de Cooperación Internacional para el Desarrollo Humano. In E. Mata Gómez de Ávila, P. Burillo Naranjo and A. Dorado Suárez (Eds) *¿Cómo hacer del Deporte Herramienta para el Desarrollo?* (pp. 544–568). Toledo: Asociación Española de Investigación Social Aplicada al Deporte (AEISAD).

Rato Barrio, M. and Ley, C. (2010c) An intervention model to promote intercultural living together in and through physical education and sport. In S. Cazzoli and B. Antala (Eds) *Integration and Inclusion in Physical Education* (pp. 134–144). Bratislava: International Federation of Physical Education (FIEP).

Rato Barrio, M. and Ley, C. (2011) Interkulturalität und Sport in der Entwicklungszusammenarbeit. In K. Petry, M. Groll and W. Tokarski (Eds) *Sport und internationale Entwicklungszusammenarbeit* (pp. 57–74). Köln: Sportverlag Strauss.

Rato Barrio, M. and Ley, C. (2012). La promoción intercultural a través del deporte en contextos postbélicos. *Anduli. Revista de Ciencias Sociales, 11*, 101–116.

Rato Barrio, M., Ley, C. and Durán González, J. (2009) Derechos Humanos y Cooperación para el Desarrollo en y a través del Deporte. In J. A. Moreno and D. González-Cutre (Eds) *Deporte, intervención y transformación social* (pp. 13–58). Río de Janeiro: Shape.

Ray, A. (1984) *Cost–Benefit Analysis: Issues and methodologies.* Baltimore, MD: Johns Hopkins University Press.

Reaves, J. A. (2002) *Taking in a Game: A history of baseball in Asia.* Lincoln, NE: University of Nebraska Press.

Reich, R. B. (1991) *The Work of Nations: Preparing ourselves for 21st-century capitalism.* New York: Knopf.

Rhodes, R. A. W. (1994) The Hollowing out of the State: The Changing Nature of the Public Service in Britain. *The Political Quarterly, 65*(2), 138–151.

Rhodes, R. A. W. (1997) *Understanding Governance: Policy networks, governance, reflexivity and accountability.* Buckingham: Open University Press.

Rhodes, R. A. W. (2007) Understanding governance: Ten years on. *Organization Studies, 28*(8), 1243–1264.

Right to Play (2011) History: The history of right to play. Available: www.righttoplay.com/International/about-us/Pages/History.aspx (accessed 18 March 2011).

Rittner, V. and Breuer, C. (2004) *Soziale Bedeutung und Gemeinwohlorientierung des Sports.* Cologne: Sport and Buch Strauß.

Roberts, K. (2004) *The Leisure Industries.* Basingstoke: Palgrave Macmillan.

Roberts, P. (2006) Neoliberalism, performativity, and research. Paper presented at the Philosophy of Education Society of Australasia, University of Sydney, Sydney, Australia, 23–26 November.

Robidoux, M. (2006) The nonsense of Native American sport imagery: Reclaiming a past that never was. *International Review for the Sociology of Sport, 41*(2), 201–219.

Robinson, R. (1993a) Cost–benefit analysis. *British Medical Journal, 307*(6909), 924–926.

Robinson, R. (1993b) Cost-effectiveness analysis. *British Medical Journal, 307*(6907), 793–795.

Robinson, R. (1993c) Economic evaluation and health care. What does it mean? *British Medical Journal, 307*(6905), 670–673.

Roche, M. (1994) Mega-events and urban policy. *Annals of Tourism Research, 21*(1), 1–19.

Roche, M. (2000) *Mega Events.* London: Routledge.

Roche, M. (2008) Putting the London Olympics into perspective: The challenge of understanding mega-events in '21st century society'. *Journal of the Academy of Social Sciences, 3*(3), 285–290.

Roderick, M. (2006) A very precarious profession: uncertainty in the working lives of professional footballers. *Work Employment and Society, 20*(2), 245–265.

Rogge, J. (1995) The Olympic Movement and the European Union. *Olympic Review, XXV*(5) (October–November), 44–45.

Rogge, J. (1997) The recognition of sport by the European Union. *Olympic Review, XXVI*(14) (April–May), 15–16.

Rogge, J. (2002) The challenges of the third Millennium. Opening speech made at the International Conference on Sports Events and Economic Impact, Copenhagen, 18 April 2002.

Rogge, J. (2010) Speech from the IOC President, First World Olympic Sport Convention, Acapulco, 23 October. Available: www.olympic.org/Documents/Conferences_Forums_and_Events/2010-ACNO-Acapulco/ANOC2010-First-World-Olympic-Sport-Convention-Acapulco-eng-final-2010.pdf (accessed 19 April 2010).

Rogulski, A. and Miettinen, S. (2009) The EU and sport: The implementation of the White Paper on Sport and future prospects. *International Journal of Sport Policy, 1*(3), 245–251.

Roniger, L. and Gunes-Ayata, A. (1994) *Democracy, Clientelism, and Civil Society.* Boulder, CO: Lynne Rienner.

Room, G. (1995) *Beyond the Threshold: The measurement and analysis of social exclusion.* Bristol, Policy Press.

Rose, A. K. and Spiegel, M. M. (2009) *The Olympic Effect*. Working paper. Berkeley, CA: Department of Economics, University of California.

Rose, N. (1990) *Governing the Soul: The shaping of the private self*. London: Routledge.

Rose, N. (1999) *Powers of Freedom: Reframing political thought*. Cambridge: Cambridge University Press.

Rosentraub, M. (1997) *Major League Losers: The Real Cost of Sports and Who's Paying for it*. New York: Basic Books.

Rosentraub, M., Swindell, D., Przybylski, M. and Mullins, D. (1994) Sport and downtown development strategy: If you build it, will jobs come? *Journal of Urban Affairs*, 16(3), 221–239.

Rosselet, S. (2008) *Methodology and Principles of Analysis*. International Institute for Management Development World Competitiveness Yearbook. Available: www02.imd.ch/wcc/yearbook (accessed 2 August 2008).

Rossi, B. (2004) Revisiting Focauldian approaches: Power dynamic in development projects. *Journal of Development Studies*, 40(6), 1–29.

Roy, D. (2003) *Taiwan: A political history*. New York: Cornell University Press.

Rudd, A. and Johnson, R. B. (2010) A call for more mixed methods in sport management research. *Sport Management Review*, 13(1), 14–24.

Rueda-Cantuche, J. M. and Ramirez-Hurtado, J. M. (2007) A simple-to-use procedure to evaluate the social and economic impacts of sporting events on local communities. *International Journal of Sport Management and Marketing*, 2(5/6), 510–525.

Rumphorst, W. (2001) *Sports Broadcasting Rights and EC Competition Law*. Geneva: European Broadcasting Union.

Russ-Eft, D. and Preskill, H. (2008) Improving the quality of evaluation participation: A meta-evaluation. *Human Resource Development International*, 11(1), 35–50.

Russo, F. and Williamson, J. (2007) Interpreting causality in the health sciences. *International Studies in the Philosophy of Science*, 21(2), 157–170.

Ryan, P. (2010) *Multicultiphobia*. Toronto, ON: University of Toronto Press.

Sabatier, P. and Jenkins-Smith, H. (1993) *Policy Change and Learning: An advocacy coalition process*. Boulder, CO: Westview Press.

Sabatier, P. (1999) The need for better theories. In P. Sabatier (Ed.) *Theories of the Policy Process* (pp. 3–19). Boulder, CO: Westview Press.

Sabatier, P. A. (2006) Fostering the development of policy theory. In P. A. Sabatier (Ed.) *Theories of the Policy Process* (pp. 321–336). London: Westview Press.

Sabatier, P. and Jenkins-Smith, H. (1993) *Policy Change and Learning: An advocacy coalition approach*. Boulder, CO: Westview Press.

Sabatier, P. and Weible, C. M. (2007) The advocacy coalition framework: Innovations and clarifications. In P. Sabatier (Ed.) *Theories of the Policy Process* (2nd Edn). Boulder, CO: Westview Press.

Sack, A. and Johnson, A. (1996) Politics, economic development, and the Volvo International Tennis Tournament. *Journal of Sport Management*, 10(1), 1–14.

Sage, G. (1990) *Power and Ideology in American Sport*. Champaign, IL: Human Kinetics.

Said, E. W. (2006) Resistance, opposition and representation. In B. Ashcroft, G. Griffiths, and H. Tiffin (Eds) *The Post-Colonial Studies Reader* (2nd Edn) (pp. 95–98). Oxford: Routledge.

Sam, M. P. and Hughson, J. (2010) Sport in the city: cultural and political connections. *Sport in Society*, 13(10), 1417–1422.

Sam, M. P. and Hughson, J. (Eds) (2011) *Sport in the City: Cultural connections* (pp. 22–43). London: Routledge.

Sam, M. P. and Jackson, S. J. (2004) Sport policy development in New Zealand: Paradoxes of an integrative paradigm. *International Review for the Sociology of Sport*, 39(2), 205–222.

Sam, M. P. and Jackson, S. J. (2006) Developing national sport policy through consultation: The rules of engagement. *Journal of Sport Management*, 20(3), 365–384.

Sandelowski, M., Voils, C. and Knafl, G. (2009) On quantitizing. *Journal of Mixed Method Research*, 3(3), 208–222.

Sandercock, L. (2004) Sustaining Canada's multicultural cities. In C. Andrew (Ed.) *Our Diverse Cities* (Vol. 1, pp. 153–157). Ottawa, ON: Metropolis.

Sanderson, I. (2002) Making sense of 'what works': Evidence based policy making as instrumental rationality. *Public Policy and Administration*, 17(3), 61–75.

Sandy, R., Sloane, P. and Rosentraub, M. (2004) *The Economics of Sport: An international perspective*. New York: Palgrave Macmillan.

Santucci, J. (1993) Etat, légitimité et identité au Maghreb: Les dilemmes de la modernité. *Confluences Méditerranée*, 6(Spring), 65–78.

Sassone, P. G. and Schaffer, W. A. (1978) *Cost–Benefit Analysis: A handbook*. New York: Academic Press.

Sawer, M. (2007) Australia: The fall of the femocrat. In J. Outshoorn and J. Kantola (Eds) *Changing State Feminism* (pp. 20–41). Basingstoke: Palgrave MacMillan.

Scharpf, F. W. (2000) *Governing in Europe*. Oxford: Oxford University Press.

Scheurich, J. (1997) *Research Method in the Postmodern*. London: Falmer Press.

Schimmel, K. S. (1995) Growth politics, urban development and sports stadium construction in the US: A case study. In J. Bale and O. Moen (Eds) *The Stadium and the City* (pp. 111–156). Keele: Keele University Press.

Schimmel, K. S. (2001) Sport matters: Urban regime theory and urban regeneration in the late capitalist era. In I. Henry and C. Gratton (Eds) *Sport in the City: The role of sport in economic and social regeneration* (pp. 259–277). London: Routledge.

Schlager, D. (2006) A comparison of frameworks, theories, and models of policy processes. In P. A. Sabatier (Eds) *Theories of the Policy Process* (pp. 293–320). London: Westview Press.

Schram, S. F. (1993) Postmodern policy analysis: Discourse and identity in welfare policy. *Policy Sciences*, 26(3), 249–270.

Scott-Little, C., Hamann, M. S. and Jurs, S. G. (2002) Evaluations of after-school programs: A meta-evaluation of methodologies and narrative synthesis of findings. *The American Journal of Evaluation*, 23(4), 387–419.

Scriven, M. (1969) An introduction to meta-evaluation. *Educational Products Report*, 2(1), 36–38.

Scriven, M. (1991) *Evaluation Thesaurus*. Newbury Park: SAGE.

Scrum Queens (2010) Black Ferns plans suffer major setback. Available: www.scrumqueens.com/news/black-ferns-plans-suffer-major-setback (accessed 4 February 2011).

Searle, G. (2002) Uncertain legacy: Sydney's Olympic stadiums. *European Planning Studies*, 10(7), 845–860.

Seippel, Ø. (2006) Sport and social capital. *Acta Sociologica*, 49(2), 169–183.

Sellers, J. M. (2011) State–society relations. In M. Bevir (Ed.) *The Sage Handbook of Governance* (pp. 124–141). London: Sage.

Shadish, W. R., Cook, T. and Campbell, D. (2002) *Experimental and quasi-experimental designs for generalized causal inference*. Boston, MA: Houghton Mifflin.

Shaomin, L. (2004) Why is property rights protection lacking in China? An Institutional Explanation. *California Management Review*, 46(3), 100–115.

Sharp, J. (2008) *Geographies of Post-colonialism*. London: Sage Publications.

Sharpe, E. (2006) Resources at the grassroots of recreation: Organisational capacity and quality of experience in a community sport organisation. *Leisure Sciences*, 28(4), 385–401.

Shaw, J. (2010) *Revisiting the Politics–Administration Dichotomy: The political intrusion in the democratic governance in Taiwan (2000–2009)*. Available: www.psa.ac.uk/journals/pdf/5/2010/786_765.pdf (accessed 16 March 2011).

Shaw, S. (2001) Conceptualizing resistance: Women's leisure as political practice. *Journal of Leisure Research*, 33(2), 186–201.

Shaw, S. (2006) Gender suppression in New Zealand regional sports trusts. *Women in Management Review*, 21(7), 554–566

Shaw, S. and Allen, J. B. (2009) The experience of high performance women coaches: A case study of two regional sport organisations. *Sport Management Review*, 12(4), 217–228.

Shaw, S. and Cameron, J. (2008) The best person for the job: Gender suppression and homologous reproduction in senior sport management. In C. Obel, T. Bruce and S. Thompson (Eds) *Outstanding: Research about women and sport in New Zealand* (pp. 211–226). Hamilton: Wilf Malcolm Institute of Educational Research.

Shaw, S. and Penney, D. (2003) Gender equity policies in national governing bodies: An oxymoron or a vehicle for change? *European Sport Management Quarterly*, 3(2), 78–102.

Shaw, S. and Pooley, J. (1976) National success at the Olympics: An explanation. In C. Lessard, J. P. Massicotte, and E. Leduc (Eds) *Proceedings of the 6th International Seminar: History of Physical Education and Sport* (pp. 1–27). Quebec: Trois Rivières.

Shehu, J. and Mokgwathi, M. (2007) A discourse analysis of the national sport and recreation policy for Botswana. *Sport, Education and Society*, 12(2), 193–210.

Sherry, E., Karg, A. and O'May, F. (2011) Social capital and sport events: Spectator attitudinal change and the Homeless World Cup. *Sport in Society*, 14(1), 111–125.

Shibli, S. and Bingham, J. (2008) A forecast of the performance of China in the Beijing Olympic Games 2008 and the underlying performance management issues. *Managing Leisure: An International Journal*, *13*(3/4), 272–292.

Shilbury, D. and Moore, K. A. (2006) A study of organizational effectiveness for national Olympic sporting organizations. *Nonprofit and Voluntary Sector Quarterly*, *35*(1), 5–38.

Shivji, I. S. (2007) *Silences in NGO Discourse: The role and future of NGOs in Africa*. Oxford: Fahamu.

Shoval, N. (2002) A new phase in the competition for the Olympic Gold: The London and New York bids for the 2012 Games. *Journal of Urban Affairs*, *24*(5), 583–599.

Shutte, A. (1993) *Philosophy for Africa*. Rondebosch, South Africa: UCT Press.

Sidaway, J. (2008) Post-development. In V. Desai and R. B. Potter (Eds) *The Companion to Development Studies* (2nd Edn) (pp. 16–19). London: Hodder Education.

Sidaway, J. Siegfried, J. and Zimbalist, A. (2000) The economics of sports facilities and their communities. *Journal of Economic Perspectives*, *14*(3), 95–114.

Sihlongonyane, M. F. (2009) 'Community development' as a buzz-word. *Development in Practice*, *19*(2), 136–147.

SIRC (2002) *European Sporting Success: A study of the development of medal winning elites in five European countries*. Final Report. Sheffield: Sport Industry Research Centre.

Sixsmith, J. and Boneham, M. (2003) Volunteering and the concept of social capital. *Voluntary Action*, *5*(3), 47–60.

Skelcher, C. (2000) Changing images of the state: Overloaded, hollowed out, congested. *Public Policy and Administration*, *15*(3), 3–19.

Skille, E. Å. (2008) Understanding sport clubs as sport policy implementers. *International Review for the Sociology of Sport*, *43*(2), 181–200.

Skille, E. Å. (2010) Competitiveness and health: The work of sport clubs seen from the perspectives of Norwegian sport club representatives. *International Review for the Sociology of Sport*, *45*(1), 73–85.

Skille, E. Å. (2011) The conventions of sport clubs: Enabling and constraining the implementation of social goods through sport. *Sport, Education and Society*, *16*(2), 253–265.

Skocpol, T. (2003) *Diminished Democracy*. Norman, OK: University of Oklahoma Press.

Sloane, P. J. (2009) The European model of sport. In W. Andreff and S. Szymanski (Eds) *Handbook on the Economics of Sport* (pp. 299–303). Cheltenham: Edward Elgar Publishing.

Smith, A. (2006) The development of 'Sports-City' zones: An assessment of their potential value as tourism resources for urban areas. In D. Torres (Ed.) *Illes Balears Forum 2006: Sport and Tourism Global Destinations network for development of regions*. Rio de Janeiro: Noos Institute.

Smith, A. (2010) Leveraging benefits from major events: Maximising opportunities for peripheral urban areas. *Managing Leisure*, *15*(3), 161–180.

Smith, A. (2012) *Events and Urban Regeneration: The strategic use of events to revitalise cities*. London: Routledge.

Smith, A. and Leech, R. (2010) 'Evidence? What evidence?': Evidence-based policy making and school sport partnerships in north west England. *International Journal of Sport Policy*, *2*(3), 327–345.

Smith, A. and Waddington, I. (2004) Using 'sport in the community schemes' to tackle crime and drug use among young people: Some policy issues and problems. *European Physical Education Review*, *10*(3), 279–298.

Smith, B. and Sparkes, A. C. (2009) Narrative analysis and sport and exercise psychology: Understanding lives in diverse ways. *Psychology of Sport and Exercise*, *10*(2), 279–288.

Smith, L. T. (1999) *Decolonizing Methodologies: Research and indigenous peoples*. London: Zed Books.

Smith, M. J. (2010) From big government to Big Society: Changing the state–society balance. *Parliamentary Affairs*, *63*(4), 818–833.

Snelgrove, R. and Wood, L. (2010) Attracting and leveraging visitors at a charity cycling event. *Journal of Sport and Tourism*, *15*(4), 269–285.

Snelgrove, R., Taks, M., Chalip, L. and Green, B. C. (2008) How visitors and locals at a sport event differ in motives and identity. *Journal of Sport and Tourism*, *13*(3), 165–180.

Soares, J. Correia, A. and Rosado, A. (2010) Political factors in the decision-making process in voluntary sports associations. *European Sports Management Quarterly*, *10*(1), 5–29.

Solesbury, W. (2001) *Evidence Based Policy: Whence it came and where it's going*. ESRC UK Centre for Evidence-Based Policy and Practice: Working Paper 1. London: University of London.

Solinger, D. (2006) The nexus of democratization: Guanxi and governance in Taiwan and the PRC. Available: http://repositories.cdlib.org/csd/06-13 (accessed 16 March 2011).

Sørensen, E. and Torfing, J. (2008) Introduction: Governance network research: Towards a second generation. In E. Sørensen and J. Torfing (Eds) *Theories of Democratic Network Governance* (pp. 1–24). Basingstoke: Palgrave Macmillan.

Spaaij, R. (2009) The social impact of sport: Diversities, complexities and contexts. *Sport in Society, 12*(9), 1109–1117.

Spaaij, R. and Westerbeek, H. (2010) Sport business and social capital: A contradiction in terms? *Sport in Society, 13*(9), 1356–1373.

Sport and Recreation New Zealand (2002) *Our Vision, Our Direction.* Wellington: SPARC.

Sport and Recreation New Zealand (2004) *Nine Steps to Effective Governance: Building high performing organisations.* Wellington, New Zealand: SPARC.

Sport and Recreation New Zealand (2006) *Nine Steps to Effective Governance: Building high performing organisations* (2nd Edn). Wellington, New Zealand: SPARC.

Sport and Recreation New Zealand (2009) *Sport and Recreation – Everyone: Every Day: Sport and Recreation New Zealand's strategic plan 2009–2015.* Wellington, New Zealand: Sport and Recreation New Zealand.

Sport Canada (2002) *The Canadian Sport Policy.* Ottawa, ON: Canadian Heritage.

Sport Canada (2007) *Proposal Sport Canada 2008–12 Action Plan for Official Languages in Response to the Recommendations of the Report: Linguistic barriers to access to high performance sport – study 2005.* Ottawa, ON: Canadian Heritage.

Sport Canada (2010) Welcome to Sport Canada. Available: www.pch.gc.ca/sportcanada/index-eng.cfm (accessed 19 February 2011).

Sport Canada (2011) Canadian Sport Policy renewal consultations 2011: Discussion paper on diversity (targeted populations). Ottawa, ON: Sport Canada. Available: http://sirc.ca/CSPRenewal/documents/Eng/Q4_Diversity_EN.pdf (accessed 19 February 2011).

Sport Canada (2012) Canadian Sport Policy 2012. Ottawa, ON: Canadian Heritage. Available: http://sirc.ca/CSPRenewal/documents/CSP2012_EN.pdf (accessed 19 February 2011).

Sport England (2007) *Sport England Policy Statement: The delivery system for sport in England.* London: Sport England.

Sport England (2009) *Active England: Final report.* London: Sport England.

Sport for Development and Peace International Working Group (SDP IWG) (2008) *Harnessing the Power of Sport for Development and Peace: Recommendations for governments.* Toronto, ON: Right to Play.

Sport New Zealand (2012) About Sport NZ. Available: http://sportnz.org.nz/en-nz/About-SportNZ/24 (accessed 12 June 2012).

Sports Council (1988) *Sport in the Community: Into the 90s.* London: Sports Council.

Spowart, L., Burrows, L. and Shaw, S. (2010) I just eat, sleep and dream of surfing: When surfing meets motherhood. *Sport in Society, 13*(7/8), 1185–1202.

Stake, R. E. (1967) Countenance of educational evaluation. *Teachers College Record, 68*(7), 523–540.

Statistics Canada (2008a) *Aboriginal Peoples in Canada in 2006: Inuit, Métis, and First Nations, 2006 census.* Ottawa, ON: Minister of Industry.

Statistics Canada (2008b) *Canada's Ethnocultural Mosaic: 2006 census.* Ottawa, ON: Minister of Industry.

Statistics Canada (2010) *Projections of the Diversity of the Canadian population.* Ottawa, ON: Ministry of Industry.

Stewart, B., Nicholson, M., Smith, A. and Westerbeek, H. (2004) *Australian Sport: Better by design? The evolution of Australian sport policy.* London: Routledge.

Stodolska, M. and Alexandris, K. (2004) The role of recreational sport in the adaptation of first generation immigrants in the US. *Journal of Leisure Research, 36*(3), 379–413.

Stoker, G. and Marsh, D. (1995) Introduction. In D. Marsh and G. Stoker (Eds) *Theory and Methods in Political Science* (pp. 1–12). Basingstoke: Palgrave Macmillan.

Stoker, G. (1998) Governance as theory: Five propositions. *International Social Science Journal, 50*(155), 17–28.

Stoker, G. (2000) Introduction. In G. Stoker (Ed.) *The Politics of British Local Governance.* Basingstoke: Macmillan.

Stoker, G. (2004) *Transforming Local Governance.* Basingstoke: Palgrave Macmillan.

Stoker, G. (2006) *Why Politics Matters: Making democracy work.* Basingstoke: Palgrave Macmillan.

Stone, C. (1989) *Regime Politics: Governing Atlanta, 1946–1988.* Lawrence, KS: University Press of Kansas.

Stone, C. (1993) Urban regimes and the capacity to govern: A political economy approach. *Journal of Urban Affairs, 15*(1), 1–28.

Strange, S. (1994) *States and Markets.* London: Continuum.

Strange, S. (1996) *The Retreat of the State: The diffusion of power in the world economy.* Cambridge: Cambridge University Press.

Strategy Unit (2002) *Game Plan: A strategy for delivering Government's sport and physical activity objectives.* London: DCMS.

Stuff.co.nz (2008) Hockey, basketball, badminton cop funding cuts Available: www.stuff.co.nz/sport/762250 (accessed 4 February 2011).

Stufflebeam, D. L. (1971) The relevance of the CIPP evaluation model for educational accountability. *Journal of Research and Development in Education, 5*(1), 19–25.

Stufflebeam, D. L. (1974) *Meta-evaluation.* Kalamazoo, MI: Western Michigan University Evaluation Center.

Stufflebeam, D. L. (2001) The metaevaluation imperative. *American Journal of Evaluation, 22*(2), 183–209.

Stufflebeam, D. L. (2003) The CIPP model for evaluation. In T. Kellaghan and D. L. Stufflebeam (Eds) *International Handbook of Educational Evaluation* (pp. 31–62). Dordrecht: Kluwer Academic Publishers.

Stufflebeam, D. L. and Welch, W. L. (1986) Review of research on program-evaluation in United States school districts. *Educational Administration Quarterly, 22*(3), 150–170.

Suen, W. (1992) Men, money and medals: An econometric analysis of the Olympic Games. Discussion paper from the University of Hong Kong.

Sugden, J. and Tomlinson, A. (1998) *FIFA and the Contest for World Football: Who rules the peoples' game?* Cambridge: Polity Press.

Sullivan, J. (2010) Legislators' blogs in Taiwan. *Parliamentary Affairs, 63*(3), 471–485.

Svoboda, M. and Donnelly, P. (2006) *Linguistic Barriers to Access to High Performance Sport Study – 2005.* Ottawa, ON: Canadian Heritage. Available: http://dsp-psd.pwgsc.gc.ca/Collection/CH24-12-2005E.pdf (accessed 19 February 2011).

Szwarcberg, M. (2009) Making local democracy: Political machines, clientelism, and social networks in Latin America. Unpublished manuscript. Notre Dame: Kellogg Institute for International Studies.

Szymanski, S. (2009) The Anglo-American model of sport. In W. Andreff and S. Szymanski (Eds) *Handbook on the Economics of Sport* (pp. 304–307). Cheltenham: Edward Elgar Publishing.

Tacon, R. (2007) Football and social inclusion: Evaluating social policy. *Managing Leisure, 12*(1), 1–23.

Taks, M., Chalip, L., Green, B. C., Késenne, S. and Martyn, S. (2009) Factors affecting repeat visitation and flow-on tourism as sources of event strategy sustainability. *Journal of Sport and Tourism, 14*(2/3), 121–142.

Taks, M., Késenne, S., Chalip, L. and Green, B. C. (2010) The (non-)sense of including residents' expenditures in economic impact studies of sport events. In ECSE (Ed.) *Book of Abstracts of the 2nd European Conference in Sport Economics* (pp. 30–32). Cologne: ECSE.

Tallon, R. (2010) *Urban Regeneration in the UK.* London: Routledge.

Tan, T. C., Cheng, C. F., Lee, P. C. and Ko, L. M. (2009) Sport policy in Taiwan, 1949–2008. *International Journal of Sport Policy,* 1(1), 99–111.

Tang, C. P. (2003) Democratizing urban politics and civic environmentalism in Taiwan. *The China Quarterly, 176,* 1029–1051.

Tashakkori, A. and Teddlie, C. (1998) *Mixed Methodology: Combining qualitative and quantitative approaches.* Thousand Oaks, CA: Sage Publications.

Tashakkori, A. and Teddlie, C. (2003) *Handbook of Mixed Methods in Social and Behavioural Research.* Thousand Oaks, CA: Sage Publications.

Taylor, M. (2003) *Public Policy in the Community.* Basingstoke: Palgrave Macmillan.

Taylor, P., Crow, I., Irvine, D. and Nichols, G. (2000) Methodological considerations in evaluating physical activity programmes for young offenders. *World Leisure and Recreation, 42*(1), 10–17.

Taylor, P., Nichols, G., Holmes, K., James, M., Gratton, C., Garret, R., Kokolakadikis, T., Mulder, C. and King, L. (2003) *Sports Volunteering in England 2002.* London: Sport England.

Taylor, S. (1997) Critical policy analysis: Exploring contexts, texts and consequences. *Discourse, 18*(1), 23–35.

Taylor-Powell, E. (1999) Logic model notes. Paper presented at the University of Wisconsin's Providing Leadership for Program Evaluation.

Terret, T. (2008) The Albertville Winter Olympics: Unexpected legacies – failed expectations for regional economic development. *International Journal of the History of Sport, 25*(14), 1903–1921.

Tesh, S. (1990) *Hidden Arguments: Political ideology and disease prevention policy.* New Brunswick, NJ: Rutger University Press.

Thibault, L. and Babiak, K. (2005) Organizational changes in Canada's sport system: Toward an athlete-centred approach. *European Sport Management Quarterly, 5*(2), 105–132.

Thibault, L., Frisby, W. and Kikulis, L. M. (1999) Interorganizational linkages in the delivery of local leisure services in Canada: Responding to economic, political and social pressures. *Managing Leisure*, 4(3), 125–141.

Thompson, C. (2008) *The Tour de France: A cultural history*. Berkeley, CA: University of California Press.

Thornley, A. (2002) Urban Regeneration and Sports Stadia. *European Planning Studies*, 10(7), 813–818.

Tien, C., Lo, H. and Lin, H. (2011) The economic benefits of mega events: A myth or a reality? A longitudinal study of the Olympic Games. *Journal of Sport Management*, 25(1), 11–23.

Tirone, S. (2000) Racism, indifference and the leisure experiences of South Asian Canadian teens. *Leisure/ Loisir*, 24(1), 89–114.

Tirone, S. (2010) Multiculturalism and leisure policy: Enhancing the delivery of leisure services and supports for immigrants and minority Canadians. In H. Mair, S. M. Arai and D. G. Reid (Eds) *Decentring Work: Critical perspectives on leisure, social policy, and human development* (pp. 149–174). Calgary, AB: University of Calgary Press.

Todd, J. and Todd, T. (2001) Significant events in the history of drug testing and the Olympic Movement: 1960–1999. In W. Wilson and E. Derse (Eds) *Doping in Elite Sport: The politics of drugs in the Olympic Movement* (pp. 65–128). Champaign, IL: Human Kinetics.

Todd, P. M. and Gigerenzer, G. (2003) Bounding rationality to the world. *Journal of Economic Psychology*, 24(2), 143–165.

Todd, T. (1987) Anabolic steroids: The gremlins of sport. *Journal of Sport History*, 14(1), 87–107.

Toft, T. (2003) Football: Joint selling of media rights. *European Commission Competition Policy Newsletter*, 3(Autumn), 47–52.

Tokarski, W., Steinbach, D., Petry, K. and Jesse, B. (Eds) (2004) *Two Players One Goal? Sport in the European Union*. Oxford: Meyer & Meyer Sport.

Tolbert, P. S. and Hiatt, S. R. (2009) On organisational oligarchies: Michels in the twenty-first century. In P. S. Adler (Ed.) *The Oxford Handbook of Sociology and Organisation Studies*. Oxford: Oxford University Press.

Tomlinson, J. (2007) Globalization and cultural analysis. In D. Held and A. McGrew (Eds) *Globalisation Theory* (pp. 148–170). London: Polity Press.

Tonazzi, A. (2003) Competition policy and the commercialization of sport broadcasting rights: The decision of the Italian Competition Authority. *International Journal of the Economics of Business*, 10(1), 17–34.

Tonts, M. (2005) Competitive sport and social capital in rural Australia. *Journal of Rural Studies*, 21(2), 137–149.

Toohey, K. and Veal, A. J. (2007) *The Olympic Games: A social perspective* (2nd Edn). Wallingford: CAB International.

Torgerson, D. (1986) Between knowledge and politics: Three faces of policy analysis. *Policy Sciences*, 19(1), 33–60.

Torkildsen, G. (2005) *Leisure and Recreation Management*. London: Routledge.

Townsend, P. (1979) *Poverty in the United Kingdom: A survey of household resources and standards of living*. Harmondsworth: Penguin Books.

Transparency International (2008) *Why Sport Is not Immune to Corruption*. Study prepared by Transparency International – Czech Republic, compiled by Radim Bureš. Available: www.coe.int/t/dg4/epas/ Source/Ressources/EPAS_INFO_Bures_en.pdf (accessed 19 April 2011).

Treasury Board of Canada Secretariat (1998) *Benefit–Cost Analysis Guide*. Available: http://classwebs.spea. indiana.edu/krutilla/v541/Benfit-Cost%20Guide.pdf (accessed 19 February 2011).

Tremblay, M. S., Bryan, S. N., Perex, C. E., Ardem, C. I. and Katzmarzyk, P. T. (2006) Physical activity and immigrant status: Evidence from the Canadian Community Health Survey. *Canadian Journal of Public Health*, 97(4), 277–282.

Tricker, R. I. (1984) *Corporate Governance*. London: Gower.

Truman, C. (2003) Ethics and the ruling relations of research production. *Sociological Research Online*, 8(1). Available: http://www.socresonline.org.uk/8/1/truman.html (accessed 7 March 2011).

Truyens, J., de Bosscher, V., de Knop, P. and Heyndels, B. (2011) Het topsportbeleid atletiek in Vlaanderen en Nederland: een vergelijkende studie [Elite sport policy athletics in Flanders and the Netherlands: a comparative study]. Steunpunt Cultuur, Sport en Media. Paper accepted for Publication.

Tsai, J. H. (2009) Political structure, legislative process, and corruption: Comparing Taiwan and South Korea. *Crime Law Social Change*, 52(4), 365–383.

Tseng, W. C. (2002) President urged merger of two leagues. Available: http://tw.news.yahoo. com/2002/12/18/sports/ctnews/37103394.html (in Chinese) (accessed 16 March 2011).

Tseng, W. C. (2003) President will attend merger ceremony. Available: http://tw.news.yahoo.com/2003/01/11/sports/infotimes/3753137.html (in Chinese) (accessed 16 March 2011).

TVNZ (2011) Sky sacks Andy Gray. Available: http://tvnz.co.nz/football-news/sky-sacks-sexist-gray-4007442 (accessed 27 January 2011).

UCI (2004) Rules of good governance. Available: www.uci.ch/Modu les/BUILTIN/getObject.asp?MenuId=&ObjTypeCode=FILE&type=FILE&id=MzQxMDk&LangId=1 (accessed 19 April 2011).

UK Sport (2003) *European Sporting Success: A study of the development of medal winning elites in five European countries.* London: UK Sport.

UK Sport (2004) *Good Governance Guide for National Governing Bodies.* London: UK Sport.

UK Sport (2005) *Staging Major Sports Events: The Guide.* London: UK Sport.

UK Sport (2008) *Home Advantage: The performance benefits of hosting major sporting events.* London: UK Sport.

UK Sport (2011) Investments in sport, London 2012. Available: www.uksport.gov.uk/pages/london-2012 (accessed 7 March 2011).

UNDP (2004) *Forging a Global South: UN Day for South-South Cooperation.* New York: UNDP.

Ungerleider, S. (2001) *Faust's Gold: Inside the East German doping machine.* New York: St Martin's Press.

United Nations (2003) *Sport for Development and Peace: Towards achieving the Millennium Development Goals.* Geneva: United Nations.

United Nations (2008) *Sport as a Means to Promote Education, Health, Development and Peace.* Available: www.un.org/themes/sport (accessed 28 May 2010).

United Nations General Assembly (2006) *Sport for Development and Peace: The way forward.* Report of the Secretary-General, A/61/73. New York: UNGA.

Uppal, V. (2009) The impact of the Commonwealth Games 2010 on Urban Development of Delhi. *Theoretical and Empirical Research in Urban Management, 1*(10), 7–29.

Vail, S. E. (2007) Community development and sport participation. *Journal of Sport Management, 21,* 571–596.

Van Bottenburg, M. (2000) *Het topsportklimaat in Nederland* [*The Elite Sports Climate in the Netherlands*]. 's Hertogenbosch, the Netherlands: Diopter-Janssens and van Bottenburg bv.

Van den Berg, A. and Janoski, T. (2005) Conflict theories in political sociology. In T. Janoski, R. R. Alford, A. M. Hicks and M. A. Schwartz (Eds) *The Handbook of Political Sociology* (pp. 72–95). Cambridge: Cambridge University Press.

Van Evera, S. (1997) *Guide to Methods for Students of Political Science.* Ithaca, NY: Cornell University Press.

Van Harberden, P. and Raymakers, T. (1986) Self-help groups and governmental policy in the Netherlands. *Journal of Voluntary Action Research, 15*(2), 24–32.

Van Rossum, F. and de Meyer, S. (2012) SPLISS cities: stedelijke topsportondersteuning in Vlaanderen en Nederland: Validering van het SPLISS model op stedelijk niveau. [SPLISS cities: elite sport support by cities in Flanders and the Netherlands: Validating SPLISS at the local level]. Unpublished masters thesis. Brussels: Vrije Universiteit Brussel.

Venerando, A. (1964) Italian experiments on the pathology of doping and ways to control it. Attached as Appendix VIII to Council of Europe, Council for Cultural Cooperation, Committee for Out-of-School Education. *Doping of Athletes: A European Study,* 47–53.

Venkatachalam, L. (2004) The contingent valuation method: a review. *Environmental Impact Assessment Review, 24*(1), 89–124.

Verity, F. (2007) *Community Capacity Building: A review of the literature.* Adelaide: South Australian Department of Health.

Villasante, T. R. (1999) De los movimientos sociales a las metodologías participativas. In J. M. Delgado and J. Gutiérrez (Eds) *Métodos y técnicas cualitativas de investigación en ciencias sociales* (Vol. 3, pp. 399–424). Madrid: Síntesis.

Villasante, T. R., Montañés, M. and Martí, J. (2002) *La investigación social participativa. Construyendo ciudadanía.* Barcelona: El viejo topo.

Vinnicombe, S., Singh, V., Burke, R. J., Bilimoria, D. and Huse, M. (2008) *Women on Corporate Boards of Directors: International research and practice.* Cheltenham: Edward Elgar.

VOCASPORT Research Group (2004) *Vocational Education and Training in the Field of Sport in the European Union: situation, trends and outlook.* Lyon: Européan Observatoire of Sport and Employment. Available: www.eose.org/ktmlpro/files/uploads/Final%20Report%20English%20Version.pdf (accessed 13 April 2011).

Voet, W. (2002) *Breaking the Chain: Drugs and cycling the true story*. London, Yellow Jersey Press.

Vogel, S. K. (1996) *Freer Markets, More Rules: Regulatory reform in advanced industrial countries*. New York: Cornell University Press.

Voy, R. (1991) *Drugs, Sport and Politics*. Champaign, IL: Leisure Press.

Vrkljan, B. (2009) Constructing a mixed methods design to explore the older driver–copilot relationship. *Journal of Mixed Methods Research*, 3(4), 371–388.

Vuolle, J. (2010) A demanding vision: The world's most active sports nation by 2020. *Motion: Sport in Finland*. Available: www.lts.fi/filearc/1077_Motion110_16-20_lowres.pdf (accessed 7 March 2011).

Waddington, I. (2000) *Sport, Health and Drugs: A critical sociological perspective*. London: Spon.

Waddington, I. (2010) Surveillance and control in sport: A sociologist looks at the WADA whereabouts system. *International Journal of Sport Policy and Politics*, 2(3), 255–274.

Wai, Z. (2007) Whither African development? A preparatory for an African alternative reformulation of the concept of development. *African Development*, XXXII(4), 71–98.

Walker, A. (1995) The dynamics of poverty and social exclusion. In G. Room (Ed.) *Beyond the Threshold: The measurement and analysis of social exclusion* (pp. 102–128). Bristol: Polity Press.

Walker, R. (2001) Great expectations: Can social science evaluate New Labour's policies? *Evaluation*, 7(3), 305–330.

Walseth, K. (2008) Bridging and bonding social capital in sport: Experiences of young women with an immigrant background. *Sport, Education and Society*, 13(1), 1–17.

Wang, C. S. and Kurzman, C. (2007) Dilemmas of electoral clientelism: Taiwan, 1993. *International Political Science Review*, 28(2), 225–245.

Wang, G., Macera, C. A., Scrudder-Soucies, B., Pratt, M. and Buchner, D. (2005) A cost–benefit analysis of physical activity using bike/pedestrian trails. *Health Promotion Practice*, 6(2), 174–179.

Wang, L. (2007) Ma Chengquan said: the premier mission of the 2007 CSL season is to fully support the 2008 Beijing Games and the second is to stabilize the development of the CSL. Available: http://sports.sina.com.cn/j/2007-02-26/00532767670.shtml (accessed 26 February 2007).

Ward, R. J., Shackleton, C. H. and Lawson, A. M. (1975) Gas chromatographic-mass spectrometric methods for the detection and identification of anabolic steroid drugs. *British Journal of Sports Medicine*, 9(2), 93–97.

Waring, A. and Mason, C. (2010) Opening doors: Promoting sport inclusion through increased sports opportunities. *Sport in Society*, 13(April), 517–529.

Watkins, T. (2008) Introduction to cost benefit analysis. Available: www.applet-magic.com/cbapod.htm (accessed 3 March 2011).

Weatherill, S. (2009) The White Paper on Sport as an exercise of better regulation. In S. Gardiner, R. Parrish and R. Siekmann (Eds) *EU. Sport, Law and Policy: Regulation, re-regulation and representation* (pp. 101–114). The Hague: TMC Asser Press.

Weed, M. (2003) Why the two won't tango! Explaining the lack of integrated policies for sport and tourism in the UK. *Journal of Sport Management*, 17(3), 258–283.

Weisinger, J. Y. (2005) A grounded theory for building ethnically bridging social capital in voluntary organizations. *Nonprofit and Voluntary Sector Quarterly*, 34(1), 29–55.

Weiss, C. H. (1997) How can theory-based evaluation make greater headway? *Evaluation Review*, 21(4), 501–524.

Weiss, L. (1997) Globalization and the myth of the powerless state. *New Left Review*, 225, 3–27.

Weiss, L. (2003) *State in the Global Economy: Bringing domestic institutions back in*. Cambridge: Cambridge University Press.

White, G. W., Suchowierska, M. and Campbell, M. (2004) Developing and systematically implementing participatory action research. *Archives of Physical Medicine and Rehabilitation*, 85(4 Suppl 2), S3–12.

Whitelegg, D. (2000) Going for gold: Atlanta's bid for fame. *International Journal of Urban and Regional Research*, 24(4), 801–808.

Whiteley, P. (1999) The origins of social capital. In J. W. van Deth, M. Maraffis, K. Newton and P. F. Whiteley (Eds) *Social Capital and European Democracy*. London: Routledge.

Whitson, D. and Macintosh, D. (1996) The global circus: International sport, tourism, and the marketing of cities. *Journal of Sport and Social Issues*, 20(3), 278–297.

Wholey, J. (1994) Assessing the feasibility and likely usefulness of evaluation. In J. Wholey, H. P. Hatry and K. E. Newcomer (Eds) *Handbook of Practical Program Evaluation* (pp. 15–39). San Francisco, CA: Jossey-Bass.

Wieczorek, E. (1976) Olympic solidarity. *Olympic Review 107/108*, 531–533.

Willets, P. (2006) *UNESCO Encyclopaedia of Life Support Systems*. Section 1, Institutional and Infrastructure Resources Issues; Article 1.44.3.7, NGOs. Paris: UNESCO.

Williams, O. (2010) Why GB should expect their best ever Winter Olympics. *BBC Sport*. Available: www.bbc.co.uk/blogs/olliewilliams/2010/02/team_gb_facts_figures.shtml (accessed 6 April 2013).

Wilson, R. (2006) The economic impact of local sport events: Significant, limited or otherwise? A case study of four swimming events. *Managing Leisure, 11*(January), 57–70.

Wodak, R. and Meyer, M. (2001) *Methods of Critical Discourse Analysis*. London: Sage Publications.

Wolf, F. (2010) Enlightened eclecticism or hazardous hotchpotch? Mixed methods and triangulation in comparative public policy research. *Journal of Mixed Methods Research, 4*(2), 144–167.

Women's Sport and Fitness Foundation (2011) *11 Compelling Reasons Why Sports should Work with Women and Girls*. Available: http://wsff.org.uk/publications/fact-sheets/11-compelling-reasons-why-sports-should-work-women-and-girls (accessed 16 March 2011).

Wong, M. (2010) Guanxi management as complex adaptive systems: A case study of Taiwanese ODI in China. *Journal of Business Ethics, 91*(3), 419–432.

Wong, P. N. (2008) Towards a more comprehensive analysis of warlord politics: Constitutive agency, patron–client networks and robust action. *Asian Journal of Political Science, 16*(2), 173–195.

Wood, G. and Gough, I. (2006) A comparative welfare regime approach to global social policy. *World Development, 34*(10), 1696–1712.

Wood, P. and Landry, C. (2008) *The Intercultural City: Planning for diversity advantage*. London: Earthscan.

Woolcock, M. (1998) Social capital and economic development: Towards a theoretical synthesis and policy framework. *Theory and Society, 27*(2), 151–208.

World Economic Forum (2007) *The Global Competitiveness Report 2007*. New York: Palgrave Macmillan.

Wu, C. L. (2003) Local factions and the Kuomintang in Taiwan's electoral politics. *International Relations of the Asia Pacific, 3*(1), 89–111.

Wydra, G. (2006) Assessmentverfahren in der Bewegungstherapie. *Krankengymnastik – Zeitschrift für Physiotherapeuten, 57*, 943–951.

Xing, X. and Chalip, L. (2006) Effects of hosting a sport event on destination brand: A test of co-branding and match-up models. *Sport Management Review, 9*(1), 49–78.

Yeates, N. (2009) Social politics and policy in an era of globalization: Critical reflections. In N. Yeates and C. Holden (Eds) *The Global Social Policy Reader* (pp. 35–56). Bristol: Polity Press .

Yin, R. (2003) *Case Study Research: Design and methods*. London: Sage.

Yin, R. K. (1998) The abridged version of case study research: Design and method. In L. B. D. J. Rog (Ed.) *Handbook of Applied Social Research Methods* (pp. 229–259). Thousand Oaks, CA: Sage Publications.

Yin, R. K. (2009) *Case Study Research: Design and methods* (4th Edn, Vol. 5). Thousand Oaks, CA: Sage Publications.

Young, R. J. C. (2003) *Post-colonialism: A very short introduction*. New York: Oxford University Press.

Yu, J. W. (2007) *Playing in Isolation: A history of baseball in Taiwan*. Lincoln, NE: University of Nebraska Press.

Yuen, B. (2008) Sport and urban development in Singapore. *Cities, 25*(1), 29–36.

Zagnoli, P. and Radicchi, E. (2009) Do major sports events enhance tourism destinations? *Physical Culture and Sport Studies and Research*, XLVII, 44–63.

Zahariadis, N. (2007) The multiple streams framework: Structure, limitations prospects. In P. A. Sabatier (Ed.) *Theories of the Policy Process* (2nd Edn) (pp. 65–92). Cambridge, MA: Westview Press.

Zakus, D., Skinner, J. and Edwards, A. (2009) Social capital in Australian sport. *Sport in Society, 12*(7), 986–998.

Zhang, X. (2006) China in the global economy. In D. A. Kelly, R. A. Rajan and G. H. L. Goh (Eds) *Managing Globalization: Lessons from China and India* (pp. 25–54). London: World Scientific Publishing.

Zhanga, X., Ding, P. and Baoa, J. (2009) Patron–client ties in tourism: The case study of Xidi, China. *Tourism Geographies, 11*(3), 390–407.

Zhu, H. and Chung, C. N. (2010) The portfolio of political ties and market entries of business groups in emerging economies. Available at http://opensiuc.lib.siu.edu/pnconfs 2010/34 (accessed 20 March 2011).

Zhuang, G., Xi, Y. and Tsang, S. L. (2010) Power, conflict, and cooperation: The impact of guanxi in Chinese marketing channels. *Industrial Marketing Management, 39*(1), 137–149.

Ziakas, V. and Costa, C. A. (2010) Between theatre and sport in a rural event: Evolving unity and community development from the inside-out. *Journal of Sport and Tourism, 15*(1), 7–26.

INDEX